scott, foresman and company

3145 Piedmont Road, N.E.

Atlanta, Georgia 30305

college division

# THE DEVELOPMENT OF THE AMERICAN ECONOMY

*The European backgrounds,*
*the dynamic growth,*
*the present status,*
*and some urgent problems of*
*the American economy.*

# the DEVELOPMENT of the AMERICAN ECONOMY

**Robert D. Patton** • **Clinton Warne**
*The Ohio State University*

SCOTT, FORESMAN AND COMPANY

Library of Congress Catalog Card #63-17121

# TABLE OF CONTENTS

*Part III: The American Economy in*

*Today's World*

# LIST OF ILLUSTRATIONS

All illustrations in the text are numbered with a Roman numeral to indicate the chapter and an Arabic numeral to indicate order in the chapter.

# PREFACE

A decade has passed since the first edition of this text appeared. As the life of educational books goes, this is a long span. Not that the economic life of America has stood still during those years—far from it. These years have been as filled with growth and change as any in our history. Problems of both domestic and international kinds have accompanied—as they always do—growth and change. But history doesn't change, although our interpretation of it does. The story must be brought up to date from time to time, of course, but the meaning of history for wise contemporary action—a theme to which *The Development of the American Economy* is devoted—does not emerge easily, nor does it change rapidly.

Possibly the most startling change of the past ten years has been the enormous growth of space technology and of corresponding attention to the physical sciences on which this technology is based. By contrast, the arts and humanities have seemed to be cast into the shade. Even the social sciences, including economics, have not had the enthusiastic attention which they formerly received, as for example, during the troubled decade of the 1930's. Yet economic concerns cannot be put aside, and our international economic problems are becoming more acute, although they are being dealt with more and more frequently by the quantitative methods of physical science and engineering. College courses in the historical aspects of economics are not the courses which are increasing in number or enrollment. Mathematical statistics and econometrics are now the growing fields. Quantitative methods and materials have also made heavy inroads into all other fields of inquiry. Even economic history has become, to an extent, fair ground for the creation and testing of mathematical growth methods.

All this, of course, represents a great forward surge in human knowledge and understanding. Clearly, there has been a new industrial revolution as striking in many ways as that associated with the invention of power-driven machinery. The new industrial revolution has applied nonhuman power to the process of computation by the use of new electronic devices. Machines can now perform many analytical operations better and incomparably faster than the human mind. But in our recognition of a great achievement, we need to remember that our new computing machines are only able to make—much faster and without tiring—quantitative comparisons which are individually quite simple to the human mind. Our amazement at their accomplishment is simply that the bulk of their analytical product is so far beyond any reasonable possibility for unaided man that it seems to be qualitatively different. It isn't. Quantitative methods, and their servants, the electronic computers, can only do what a human mind instructs them to do. They can aid man, not replace him.

Here is where historical study is irreplaceable. Man, the evolving animal who has gambled his survival on a quality we name reflective intelligence, can only decide his future actions by learning from his experiences of the past. Quantitative methods are a great help in such learning but the creative elements in the evolutionary processes of the past can never be put in quantitative form as they are recognized. With its faltering light, perceptive intelligence seeks clarity by search for factors of possible qualitative significance. If communication with other individuals enables them also to recognize a quality and to acquiesce in a collective estimate of its importance, criteria for measuring it can soon thereafter be agreed to. When that has occurred, the basis for quantitative treatment has arrived. It is clear, however, that the initial act of creation or discovery is qualitative in nature, and derives from the perception of an individual reflecting upon the meaning of experience. Whoever this individual may be, he is a student of history.

Fortunately, students of history can scarcely avoid becoming philosophical, and they are well aware that the course of history is amply marked by the ebb and flow of enthusiasms. The opening of a new possibility for action very often results in excesses in that direction, necessitating subsequent retraction. It is to be hoped that the rush of social scientists to make their work quantitative will soon temper itself to the point that there will be no danger of neglect of inquiries into the meaning of historical experience. Students of all ages need to be introduced to reflective consideration of the human past, its values and its problems. The authors of *The Development of the American Economy* are particularly grateful to their publishers for support in presenting to the present college generation their own modest attempt to find wisdom for the economic decisions of today and tomorrow in knowledge of and reflection upon the experience of the past. Events do shape ideas, but ideas equally shape events. It has been said that peoples who ignore their history are condemned to relive it. The freedom of any generation to be master of its own fate lies not in escape from existing society and its contradictions, but in understanding and using with skill the complex structure of social life as it is.

Thoughtful users of the first edition of this text, originally titled *The American Economy*, have suggested some rearrangement of materials and, especially, greater integration of economic ideas within the narrative of economic development. These changes have been made to the extent possible. But a virtue of a smallish book in a large field is the opportunity it offers teachers to enlarge upon an area of their own particular interest or competence. Teaching, we believe, is essentially permitting younger scholars the opportunity to observe more mature scholars at work. The availability in paperback form of many commentaries, special studies, and reprints of source materials now gives the teacher latitude to put course materials together to parallel the lines of his own thought. This should increase the sincerity and thus the effectiveness of his own teaching. The revised bibliographies have been designed to aid this process.

Most importantly of all, Clinton L. Warne has become a coauthor of the second edition. He is primarily responsible for revision and extension of the chapters covering the period after the Second World War. Both authors have contributed to the Flow Charts, which should give at least a modicum of information about persons, ideas, and theories related to the central theme of the text.

# the DEVELOPMENT of the MODERN ECONOMY

DEVELOPMENT of the MODERN ECONOMY

**PRODUCTION**

AGRICULTURE

INDUSTRY

MANAGEMENT

TECHNOLOGY

**EXCHANGE**
(GOODS AND SERVICES)

COMMERCE

TRANSPORTATION

MONEY AND CREDIT

*F*rom the early Middle Ages
to the mid-twentieth century,
this special flow chart insert presents
an overall view in summary of the
background, development, and principal features
of the American economy:

Early Middle Ages, 600 A.D.-900 A.D.

Later Middle Ages, 1000 A.D.-1500 A.D.

Transition from medieval to modern economy

Era of growing commerce and nationalism in Europe

Europe: world markets and industrial revolution, 1600-1850

America: from colony to nation, 1607-1850

America: fulfillment of national economy, 1860-1910

America: a matured world economic power

Manorial system established on all good farming lands in populous areas.

Three field system of planting and crop rotation:
     One field plowed and planted in fall to wheat or rye,
     One field plowed and planted in spring to barley or oats,
     One field left fallow (unplanted) for rough pasture.

Meadows beside streams kept in common for winter hay and pasture.

Most industry on very small scale in rural homes and villages:
     Some specialization even in villages, e.g., smiths, and millers.
     Weaving of cloth in almost every home; also shoemaking.

In towns of larger size, specialization of skilled craftsmen was leading to growth of guilds and disposal of product by barter, or sale for cash.

On the manorial estates, the supervision of work was carried out by officers appointed by the lord, e.g., steward, bailiff, and reeve. Duties were assigned and performance checked.

Industrial production depended upon personal skills and little supervision was needed.

Guilds laid down rules to be followed by members of the craft.

Farming methods based on the wooden plow pulled by ox teams.

Much hand work with rakes, hoes, and flails for beating the grain from the straw.

Water power used to grind grain into flour.

Household and farming skills passed down from generation to generation.

Handicraft skills taught by the guilds' apprenticeship system.

Informal trade in goods and services always took place within village communities. Formal trade at market said to have arisen from periodic exchange of goods at the boundary between manors.

Larger and more accessible markets became commercial towns, trading extensively with surrounding areas. Professional traders formed merchant guilds to supervise the trade of the town.

Ox-carts or wagons used where suitable roads existed. Animals driven to market; light goods carried.

For heavier shipments and for longer distances, boats were used in coastal waters and on rivers.

Lack of adequate and cheap transportation forced the economic system to remain locally self-sufficient.

Because of high degree of economic self-sufficiency, little money or credit used. Coins remaining from ancient days of Roman occupation were hoarded as treasures rather than used in business.

Credit infrequently used except as aid to person or family in temporary need due to misfortune.

Not an important economic institution in this period because of the high degree of economic self-sufficiency.

Lords, as owners of land, the most important factor of production in this period, were in a strategic position to demand a substantial share of the farm produce. This they received from the required labor of serfs and villeins on the lord's portion (demesne) of the farming land, all of which went to the lord for his family and servants. Serfs and villeins worked a half or more of their time on demesne lands.

Villeins and serfs received income as produce of their own work on 30 acres, more or less, of land which was their legal "holding." This provided subsistence for a family, but little more.

Some "freemen" had larger holdings with no labor required on the demesne.

Craftsmen and merchants, though not numerous in this period, had the chance to enjoy the full fruits of their labor, since they were free. Income might be large enough to make the recipients wealthy men.

Businessmen, as we know them, were almost non-existent in this period except on small scale mentioned above.

In a very few places, larger scale operations such as shipbuilding, mining, distant trade or money lending occasionally created a type of forerunner to the modern businessman.

The type of economy described above produced a society with sharply divided classes of lords, or aristocracy, and peasants. The latter were "bound" to the soil, both legally and by economic necessity.

Lords, in turn, owed feudal obligations of service, usually military, to the king or superior lord.

Freemen on manors and merchants or craftsmen in towns became the "middle class."

Political authority rested upon the system of feudal obligation between social classes. The king or emperor had nominally supreme power, but the inadequacy of transportation gave lords great power locally.

Villeins and serfs had some voice in enforcing customary rights on the manor, but could not appeal beyond the rulings of the lord.

Freemen and townsmen were more independent under the king or emperor.

Economic thinking followed traditional lines and centered upon the self-sufficient, agricultural, non-trading economic system with well-marked social classes. Within this system, anyone who did his work properly was considered to be worthy of an income to preserve his status. The beginnings of specialization and trade raised such problems as the justice of interest charges, the just price, and the just wage.

Manorial system continued, but with increasing changes in the later centuries of the period:
> More land held by freemen by grant of lords or kings.
> Near commercial towns where farm produce could be sold for cash, some serfs bought freedom from labor service (commutation) and became merchants or true farmers by leasing land from lords to be operated with hired farm laborers.
> Lords fenced land for pasturing sheep if it was unused or after ejecting serfs.

Home industry for home use continued, but declined relatively as more was bought.

Guilds of merchants and craftsmen became the rule in all populous towns.

> In later centuries, some merchants became capitalists by hiring workers to work in shops, or by "putting-out" raw material to be manufactured by workers in their own homes in the villages. Thus work was provided for serfs put off the land.

Where land was leased by operators, they became true managers.

Craft guilds developed no management system, considering quality of work to be personal.

> Where the "putting-out" system arose, the craft idea that quality of work was personal continued, and home workers were not supervised. However, poor work could be refused payment.

Basic farming methods remained the same, but more land being farmed by free owners or large-scale tenant operators permitted the beginning of experimentation.

Manufacturing methods remained basically the same, except that more experimentation with machines was beginning to take place where demand was keen, and larger scale of operation permitted greater division of labor.

Better ships and sailing rigs permitted sailing of open oceans which brought discovery of new lands and greater trade by the end of the period.

Commerce grew rapidly in this period, providing an increasing proportion of goods used, and employment for an increasing proportion of people.

Local trade was dominated by town guilds, but periodic fairs and weekly markets to which outsiders might come prevailed very widely.

Distant trade also attracted merchants, and came to be organized by the Hanseatic League, among German merchants; and the companies of Merchant Staplers and Merchant Adventurers in England.

Ships were used and foreign trading posts were established.

Growth of trade required better transportation facilities. Roads and wagons used but were never very satisfactory. Decline of manors made road conditions even worse.

Rivers and coastal waters were used more extensively. Large cities arose on rivers and at good ports along the sea coasts.

Better ships, sails, and navigation instruments permitted the development of ocean navigation.

The use of money and credit came into their own during this period as local and distant trade expanded. Being new, they were not understood. Rulers manipulated the coinage, debasing its value for their own benefit. As more money was needed, it became increasingly scarce. Precious metals were sought by all explorers.

Loans were made by individual money-lenders. At first, borrowers were thought to be in personal need and lending was a charitable act for which interest should not be charged. Toward 1500, borrowing to make more money was better understood.

Became the key institution of the newly developing segments of agriculture and manufacturing. More producers were producing for the market rather than for themselves or on order from a customer; more consumers were looking to the market for goods to supply their needs.

With growth, market processes began to be better organized. Merchant guilds maintained free markets for their members, excluding others. Fairs and weekly markets had their controlling customs. Middlemen of various kinds arose between buyers and sellers.

Lords continued to enjoy a favorable income position, but freemen and large-scale tenant operators increased in number and improved their income status. The latter sold their agricultural produce to yield themselves an income in cash.

Many serfs and villeins continued living in manorial villages, but as commutation and enclosure took place, their work was at least partially off the land.

The "Black Death," in this period, made a shortage of common labor, and tended to improve the position of those at the bottom of the income scale.

In addition to the serfs and villeins mentioned above who cannot be classified easily because of variations in their status, probably most agriculture workers remained as they had been for centuries.

Craftsmen and merchants did increase sharply in numbers and in income. Their improved status attracted recruits from agriculture to establish a basis for a new middle class in late medieval society. In this respect, they overlap the classification of businessmen listed immediately below.

A class of businessmen, in the modern sense, first made its appearance in European society in this period. The membership was neither absolutely nor relatively large from a contemporary viewpoint. But they were genuine businessmen in the sense that they sought their incomes by using capital and hiring labor to make a profit in manufacturing or commerce. Some of them were money-lenders also. The most successful members of this new social class acquired incomes to rival or exceed those of the lords.

The middle class increased in numbers and influence. Its income came from trade, manufacture, and money lending, not from land ownership. It was an urban class, whereas the lords were rural in residence and outlook. The towns in which the middle class carried on its business demanded and received freedom from feudal obligation. They gained charters to govern themselves directly under the king.

No real urban working class appeared in this period, although its beginnings were evident in the changes taking place on the manor and in the villages.

Revolutionary changes in government did not take place during this period. Towns obtained more power to elect their own officials and to have their own courts.

Absolute political power as a hereditary right of families of the landed aristocracy was not seriously challenged, largely because the monarch gained support and revenue from the middle class, while the merchants and townsmen gained rights to carry on their business from the king.

New types of economic activity caused great concern during this period. As a result, the foundations of modern economic thought were laid in the late centuries of the middle ages. Selling at a profit, i.e., at a price higher than cost, was at first thought to be sinful as a sign of avarice, but later was recognized to be payment for a service rendered to the buyer. Charging interest on loans was viewed in the same way, since money was thought to be barren, but was later accepted as proper when loans made a productive business possible.

| 1300 | 1400 | 1500 | 1600 |

A real break-up of the manorial system was underway during this period.

Enclosure of the open fields which had been spotty in earlier centuries, now occurred in entire areas where sheep could be pastured to produce wool for the growing cloth industry.

Growing urban markets for agricultural produce encouraged consolidation of holdings to increase output and permit experiments in methods.

Production at home for family use continued to diminish.

Guilds continued to control the trade of many towns, but did not expand output to meet needs of regional and overseas markets.

Journeymen refused admission to guilds organized in opposition to masters.

Putting-out system expanded in clothmaking and other industries using domestic workers.

The tradition of good quality work depending on the personal knowledge and skill of the worker continued, but where either farming or manufacturing operations attained large scale, the need for managerial supervision became apparent.

The beginnings of technical development mentioned in earlier centuries continued, but there was no revolutionary change until later. The improvement in ships and sailing had great effects upon life in general and foreign trade in particular. The invention of the printing press had great ultimate effects on society.

The discovery of new trade routes and the building up of commercial empires by European countries, especially just before and after 1500, was the striking development of the period.

The Hanseatic League began to lose out. In England, the Company of Merchant Staplers was increasingly superseded by the more aggressive Merchant Adventurers. The latter played an important part in financing the colonization of North America.

Local transportation continued to be slow and costly.

Better shipping led to a great increase in coastal and overseas commerce.

The monetary and credit system came to be used more widely as trade and commerce spread. Medieval attitudes toward money lending tended progressively to die out.

Goldsmiths began to issue deposit receipts which could be passed from buyer to seller like paper money. Also to make loans.

Scriveners, as professional drafters of contracts, also arranged loans.

# TO MODERN ECONOMY

Virtually all of the economic developments in these centuries had the effect of putting the market more and more into the center of the economic system.

Local markets handled a larger proportion of the daily needs of the people; more and more producers received their income from sales on the market.

Foreign trade created regional and world markets.

The increase of trade at all levels and the growth of a new middle class, receiving its income from trade, tended to lower the status of landowners. Still, their position was a strongly entrenched one and they held on for many years longer.

The ordinary worker either in agriculture or manufacturing did not benefit noticeably by the economic developments of this period. Often, as by enclosure of manorial fields, unemployment was not balanced by new jobs in industry or commerce.

Medieval agencies which might have aided such people were themselves weakened and unable to help. In England, the national government had to take over by passing Poor Laws in the reign of Elizabeth I.

Businessmen, and the kings whom their taxes could support, were the greatest beneficiaries of virtually all of the economic developments of the period. While they did not have the social prestige of aristocratic landowners, many of them began to have larger incomes and to accumulate greater wealth than most lords had ever had.

Especially in the later centuries of this period, businessmen of great wealth either purchased or were given titles by monarchs to signal the social prestige which they had achieved.

No marked changes in other classes.

A period of dynastic wars among nobles for the prize of the absolute sovereign power of developing national states such as England, France, and Spain.

Favored nobles gained power through the king; others lost power in a relative sense. Serfs and villeins often gained freedom but no real political power.

Businessmen thrived on strong government but had little power themselves.

The breaking up of feudalism and the manor strengthend the feeling of individuals that it was proper to rise above your class, to make a profit in manufacture or trade, or to engage in money lending.

The growth of the market aided these developments and turned thought to such issues as how prices are established and how interest rates are determined. Old ideas persisted, however, and the political sovereign still retained power to regulate economic practices.

Agricultural changes begun in earlier centuries were accentuated in this period as the growth of a market economy changed old ways of making a living.

Enclosures of large tracts were authorized by acts of Parliament. Rural people moved to towns or engaged in manufacturing work in the villages.

Need for food in cities and towns led to systematic experiments with farming methods to increase food supply.

Guilds continued to lose control in all major industries as national government assumed control of wages, prices and working conditions. The mercantile policy sought to increase high quality manufacture at low prices for export, and industrial diversification for self-sufficiency at home.

Industrial production grew, and the domestic system dominated all important industries as more and more rural people turned from agriculture to manufacturing at home.

Inventions of machines became more and more common, especially after 1700.

Industrial management undeveloped because production still depended on personal skill.

Foreign trade was the big business of the period, and in it the joint-stock company was the dominant form of business organization, with centralized, professional management of the commercial and financial activities of the company.

Only a few merchant-manufacturers in the domestic system gathered their workers together in large shops to make cloth or other manufactured goods. Where this occurred, management problems began to arise in industry as well.

The technology of ocean navigation was now well established. On land, need for better transportation had no major effect other than the beginning of canal building by the 18th century.

Division of labor, as the technology of using human effort, greatly increased with the growth of trade.

Demand for goods created interest in improved technology by the end of this period. Invention of machines began to be viewed as a way of increasing income, rather than as a destroyer of jobs for workers. By 1700 and after, important inventions were developed.

Domestic commerce increased in volume, with wholesalers of various kinds developing to supply the well-established retail trade.

Foreign markets were developed all over the world by European merchants, and foreign products greatly changed the diet, dress, and home furnishings of Europeans.

Individual foreign traders associated in such companies as the Merchant Adventurers lost out more and more to joint-stock companies, such as the Netherlands or English East India Companies.

Capitalistic forms of business organization becoming more dominant.

Growth of trade of all kinds meant more and more transportation of goods and people. Regional and world-wide economic specialization depended upon this growth of transport.

No revolutionary changes in methods of transport in this period except as cited above under *Technology*. Urgent need for better transport forecast developments for later centuries.

Money and credit became the foundation of the largest and most advanced businesses. The coinage became more dependable, drafts were used for payments over long distances, bills of exchange became standard for foreign payments, as well as credit bills and drafts for delayed payments.

Joint-stock banks were first established in this period, although many individual money lenders, dealers in bills, financial brokers, and bankers continued. Financial exchanges or "bourses" also arose, dealing in all kinds of bills and in the stocks of new companies.

# AND NATIONALISM IN EUROPE

The market became the dominant economic institution in the more advanced countries and in the newly developing segments of the economies of virtually all countries all over the world.

Markets were not necessarily "free," because many traditional attitudes and controls modified their operation. But since they were new, they could usually escape the more severe kinds of traditional control.

Capitalism and free enterprise became more thoroughly established as a corollary of the growth of markets.

Landowners became increasingly the conservative and nondynamic element in society. Traditional rents and shares continued to be received, but other sources of income received by other classes grew far more rapidly.

Some more progressive landowners tried to improve their position by experimenting with new farming methods, and by exploiting the resources found on their holdings.

Agricultural and manufacturing workers benefitted less than proportionally in the general economic development occurring in this period. New methods improved productive efficiency, but often brought unemployment to some workers and less than proportionate demand for more workers.

Many of these people sought opportunity in America when settlement was opened up.

Businessmen continued to be the principal direct beneficiaries of the expansion of commerce and manufacturing.

Outstanding merchants, bankers, and manufacturers became the wealthy men of the day. Capital rather than land was the source of their income.

The business classes, or bourgeoisie, continued to gain in wealth, social prestige and power. They were not yet a dominant or ruling class, but they were moving in that direction.

The new workers in commerce and industry were not yet sharply differentiated from agricultural workers, and had not achieved a distinct identity.

Landowners continued to hold their position as possessors of the highest social prestige, but, in other respects, their position was deteriorating.

The centuries of absolute monarchy in Europe. National power was now sufficiently consolidated internally so that, by the end of the period, no real threat to the monarch remained.

Further, national sovereignty also demonstrated its outward thrust by conquest of new territories throughout the world, accompanied by the establishment of trading rights and colonies where they were thought to be desirable to strengthen the hold of the mother country.

The wealth of successful businessmen brought them the goodwill and favor of the monarch, but no great increase in their political power.

The age of Mercantilism. The moral aspects of economic activity declined in importance, and the dominant interest became to develop an economic policy by which the power of the sovereign and his nation could be increased. Within the country, this involved a large population of skilled people, use of all natural resources economically, and husbanding of financial resources. Externally, it involved export of manufactured goods primarily, import of raw materials only if not available at home or in colonies, and use of military power to back up merchants.

The manorial system disappeared in western Europe during this period.
> Nearly all land was enclosed, wool production was confined to hilly areas, and food production was increased on suitable land.

Experiments with farming methods produced an Agricultural Revolution in the effort to meet the needs for food of growing cities: crops were rotated and clovers for winter feed were introduced; fertilizer and selective animal breeding were also introduced.

The century 1750-1850 marked the Industrial Revolution. Power machines were introduced, production was stepped up enormously, and man, for the first time, was freed from the drudgery of repetitive hand labor.

Machines required large capital investments, moved industry to cities, and created new classes of capitalist owners and wage-earning workers.

Mass production made many kinds of goods widely available.

Industrial management significant in this period. At first, older attitudes continued, but soon the need for new concepts began to be recognized. Division of labor was extended; incentive wage systems were introduced; closer supervision and planning of work were found to be necessary; safety and sanitation, neglected at first, were studied and improved; and a movement was started toward shortening of working hours.

The Industrial Revolution was, in fact a technological revolution.

For the first time in human history, need for greater production to supply already developed markets led to systematic efforts to develop machines and processes to supply those markets. These efforts opened an era of invention and the application of science to the practical needs of life such as had never before existed.

Natural resources assumed a new importance in the life of nations.

The growth of commerce was the basic reason for changes outlined above in the techniques of production. This growth continued to develop a continuously greater volume and new practices in the distribution of goods: Machine production of standardized goods opened the way for advertising, and salesmanship; new types of functional middlemen were needed; and new channels of distribution were developed.

The need for better transport became more intense with greater volumes of goods moving in commerce and with industrial fuel and raw materials now requiring movement also.

Improved MacAdam roads were built as turnpikes near industrial cities. Canals connected mines and quarries with consuming industries.

By 1800, the steam engine was experimentally applied to transport, and, by 1825, the steam locomotive and railway became practical.

After early troubles with speculative excesses, joint-stock banks became dominant in meeting business needs for money and credit in this period. All types of financial instruments used in business today were in use to some degree in this period.

As property used in business grew, so did insurance to provide protection against loss by fire or at sea.

Stock exchanges made a fluid market for corporate capital issues.

The first period in which a true market economy can be said to have come into existence. The destruction of the final elements of feudal society, and the outgrowing of town dominance brought a national economy in which markets could flourish if left free to do so. Finished goods were allocated to users by the mechanism of market price, while land, labor and capital were allocated to producers by the same market mechanism.

Owners of agricultural land continued to be laggards as receivers of the growing national income.

Speculative interest arose in lands supplying fuel or raw materials for industry, but this benefited only a relatively few owners.

Improvements in farming methods produced larger incomes but they went to capital and management rather than to the land as such.

Workers of all types were in oversupply during this period due to rapidly rising population and increasing productive efficiency in agriculture and industry which temporarily replaced some labor.

Incomes and living conditions of workers were very bad and only began to improve slightly by the end of the period in the mid-nineteenth century.

All of the factors favoring the income of businessmen cited in the previous period continued to have even greater effect in this period.

In industry, this was a period of individual businessmen and partnerships, rather than of joint-stock companies.

Opportunity for expansion was everywhere, and businessmen flourished.

The bourgeoisie came into its own during this period. Businessmen now had the greatest incomes, and they began to have some of the social prestige and political power which the landed aristocracy had formerly enjoyed exclusively.

Workers in industry and agriculture had neither income nor prestige. Toward the end of the period, workers began to have greater political power due to the relaxation of property requirements in voting.

Political power became more and more popular.

Lords lost a portion of their political prestige and power.

Businessmen gained power by causing government to relax many of its controls over business (laissez faire). Also, many businessmen got into Parliament in England by literally buying seats.

Workers were politically weak but gaining in influence due to better education and revised requirements for voting.

The age of the classical economics and laissez faire.

Business tactics were often ruthless, but it was widely felt that every man had a natural right to do that which was advantageous to himself. The harsh consequences of this policy led to various forms of socialism in the nineteenth century and, on the eve of midcentury, to the socialist theories of Karl Marx.

A few theoretical criticisms of classical economies also appeared.

| 1607 | 1700 | 1800 | 1860 |
|---|---|---|---|
| Farming was primarily for subsistence. Lumbering, hunting and fishing provided raw materials for use at home and for export. Land use was largely exploitative. It was believed that all the land might never be needed. | After a century of settlement, commercial farming was beginning in older sections. Exploitative subsistence farming continued on the frontier. Around 85% of the people lived on the land. | This was the period of the "westward movement." Grain and livestock went from west to cities. New machines developed to farm new lands. | |
| Home manufacture for home use at first. Shipbuilding and other industries using native materials soon grew, some for export to England. Mercantile policy forbade American competition with English industry. | Meatpacking, mining, sawmills, and flour mills grew rapidly to use raw products. Manufacture largely handicraft. Clash of American merchants and manufacturers with Mercantilism helped bring on Revolutionary War. | U.S. industry freed from British control began rapid growth. Some types checked by foreign competition. Factory-type production begun. | |
| No true managerial function existed in this early period. | Some small shops arose, nominally to train apprentices, but supervision was required. Putting-out system developed in cloth, shoes and hardware industries in New England, but little real management required. | Use of power machines in factories created the need for management. | |
| Techniques needed were those of the frontiersman and self-sufficient farmer. Skills brought from Europe could not be used very often under primitive conditions in America. | Higher skills brought into use as conditions became more settled. Specialization and division of labor grew. Power machinery introduced by 1800. | The modern technological revolution began in the U.S. Power machines brought from Europe and new ones invented here, especially for farming. | |
| Little purely local commerce at first. Goods were bought from Europe and produced for export. Regional and craft specialization brought more domestic commerce as conditions became more settled. | Colonies became a vital part of English mercantile trade, importing fine goods and exporting raw products. Foodstuffs and rougher manufactures supplied to agricultural areas, especially the South. | Domestic commerce between industrial and farming areas grew in importance with the westward movement. U.S. ships important in carrying trade. | |
| Use of river and coastal navigation and forest trails for pack horses. Great distances and varied resources made transport a key to economic growth. Sailing ships maintained contact with Europe. | Rivers and coastal waters continued to be used, and better roads were built. Urgent need for better transport led to many projects for improvement. | Many improved roads were built; also many canals. Steamboats and railways developed and used in U.S. as early as any other part of the world. | |
| Money and credit always hard to get. Indian wampum and tobacco used to some degree. Need for European goods kept colonies drained of cash. Barter of goods. | With growth of colonies, shortage of media of exchange became critical and a cause of war with England. Some paper money used. Banking and money lending developed only in larger towns. Banks operated by individuals or partners. | New money system created and banks chartered. Use of credit grew. Big city banks became strong, but "wildcat banks" often failed. | |

# TO NATION, 1607-1860

Markets, except overseas, undeveloped before 1700.

Growth of specialized production among colonies and overseas gave the market a place of greater importance in the American economy.

Seaport cities led backwoods areas in this respect, and, of course, Europe led America.

Better transport and the great expansion of manufacturing brought a market-centered economy to the United States, paralleling that of Europe.

Landowners, as a favored income class, have never occupied as important a position in America as in older countries of Europe. At a very early stage, Americans became great speculators in the future value of land and natural resources. Many individual fortunes were made by successful land speculators. Individual ownership of farm lands prevailed from the earliest years and became the basis of our agriculture, but income from land was never distinguished from labor income or investment in stock and machinery.

Anyone could and did speculate in land, and land incomes did not go to a special class.

Throughout this period, as stated above, the actual tillers of the soil were also owners, and labor income was not distinguished from land income. Farm tenants were typically young families saving to buy a farm.

Slavery in the South was a special situation which prevailed until the Civil War. Until 1800, manufacturing was usually done by independent craftsmen and there was no distinct class of industrial workers.

As factories rose after 1800, an industrial class of workers with moderate incomes appeared.

Search for markets and raw materials by businessmen in this period.

Frontier conditions and Mercantilism in England forced a large measure of self-sufficiency.

Until the Revolution, business was largely foreign trade and the extractive industries which supplied it. Largest incomes to foreign trading merchants in the North, and tobacco planters in the South.

After 1800, shipping and foreign trade continued, but industry grew most rapidly.

Aristocratic attitudes derived from European feudalism persisted in America in spite of the fact that colonization here was a kind of protest against European society. Nevertheless, America was, and has always been, as free of class rigidities as any society anywhere.

The Revolutionary War revealed some class feelings, yet had the probable effect of minimizing them.

The westward movement, as a symbol of the abundant opportunity in America, was a great leveler of class distinctions.

The absence of privileged classes nominally made political power in America completely democratic.

In the colonial period, proprietors, members of founding companies, planters, wealthy merchants and the professional classes enjoyed disproportionate political influence.

Those living in remote sections were almost self-governing and had only intermittent influence on the central colonial government.

After 1800, planters in the South and merchants or bankers in the North retained special influence.

Mercantilist thinking was quite generally accepted at first, but its restriction of economic development led to its rejection by 1770.

Yet, the hardships and risks of life under primitive conditions bred a strong sense of individualism, self-reliance, and, in consequence, opposition to government regulation.

The resulting typically American amalgam combined a strong nationalism with strong individualism, but retained suspicion of government power.

After 1800, *laissez faire* reigned supreme, except for the belief that government should protect, and if necessary, subsidize individuals.

America, in this period, offered the first known example in human history of a great country troubled with food surpluses. The plains were opened to settlement, railroads were built, and grain and live-stock poured out to the cities of the East and to Europe.

Machinery, fertilizers, and selective breeding of livestock and grains made this astounding result possible. Farm prices fell and various political protest movements arose in consequence.

Within this period, American industry had its Industrial Revolution.

Markets had become nation-wide, transportation was available for raw materials and finished prod-ucts, machinery was adapted from Europe and invented here, and capital, although in insufficient supply, was available to bring the greatest industrial expansion in our history.

Home manufacture declined and factory industry spread from New England and the Atlantic coast to the upper Mississippi Valley.

The rise of large-scale industry with heavy capital investment made necessary the greatest care in the use of personnel and equipment.

"Scientific management" was developed by F. W. Taylor and others in the latter decades of the period.

Business management was too new, however, to get full attention. Executives of large corporations were likely to be lawyers or financiers rather than trained managers.

The improved technology in industry, transportation, communication and other fields which was put to use in this period showed, beyond question, the value of systematic study of industrial problems.

Standardized parts, semi-automatic machines, and conveyor-line assemblies were all developed and proved.

New industries resulted from scientific advances, e.g., electricity, chemicals, and rubber.

Growth of commerce had induced the growth of industry and now mass production necessitated mass distribution.

Department stores, mail-order houses, and chain stores in various lines got their start in this period.

In general, distributive functions were highly elaborate, and new types of functional middlemen were developed for particular conditions. Various types of credit arrangements were also used.

Improved transportation made the expansion of commerce and industry possible. The economic potential of America could not be realized until the railroad tied distant areas together with cheap transport.

Steamboats on the Mississippi and its tributaries continued, but the use of canals declined. Steam-ships completely took over ocean navigation and lowered ocean freight costs.

The automobile and motor truck began to come into use after 1890.

Monetary troubles before 1860 resulted in the National Bank Acts after 1860. New national banks were chartered under national supervision. They provided a sound banking system. New National Bank Notes were issued and state bank notes were taxed out of existence. A system of reserves was set up for national banks, both for notes and for demand deposits on which checks could be drawn. Checks were used more and more by business, as were other kinds of credit.

# NATIONAL ECONOMY, 1860-1910

| 1860 | 1870 | 1880 | 1890 | 1900 | 1910 |
|------|------|------|------|------|------|

The growth of industry, the growth of specialized farming, and the general growth of cities indicated a greater division of labor and increase of skill, and, in consequence, a far greater dependence upon buying and selling products and labor in the market.

There was now in America the modern type of highly productive, interdependent, market-oriented economy. It had many advantages, but it was sensitive and vulnerable to conditions which upset market equilibrium.

Conditions affecting the economic status of landowners remained much as they had been earlier. Speculation in urban land was added to our traditional speculation in farm land.

Acres of land in cultivated farms increased until the end of this period, although the actual number of farm landowners had been declining relatively since 1790 and reached an absolute peak at the end of this period. Farm surpluses reduced farm incomes and caused complaint.

Farmers relatively worse off in income position, but retained hope for the future through cost-cutting and greater production.

The foundations for an industrial wage-earning class were established in this period as industries expanded their scale of operations.

Immigration from southeastern Europe swelled the ranks of industrial workers and prevented labor shortages which might have increased wages.

Unions began to grow, but were usually opposed by employers.

The businessman came into his own in this period, as daring speculators and operators built railroads and industries, opened resources and developed markets for their product. This was the age of the "tycoon," the "captain of industry," or the "robber baron," as one might choose.

Fortunes were made and lost within one generation, often several times. The names of Harriman, Hill, Morgan, Rockefeller, and Carnegie became legendary, but lesser businessmen also shared great increases in wealth.

Businessmen constituted the new class in American society, and they made strenuous efforts to achieve social prestige to match their new wealth. They were not instantly successful in equaling the status of established professional people or successful politicians. Yet, their influence in formulating governmental policy was growing.

Farmers continued to be politically powerful. Industrial workers were at the bottom of the scale, both politically and socially.

Political power shifted westward during this period following the progress of land settlement and the admission of new western states.

The Republican Party held the loyalty of older farm sections and gained the support of business to give it control of the federal and most northern state governments throughout most of this period.

Movements reflecting farm discontent in both the North and South constantly challenged Republican policies, but gained no solid control.

Laissez-faire policies continued to prevail but tariff protection for new industries grew also.

Farm discontent focussed on the railroads and heavy industries and led to railroad rate regulation and anti-trust laws by 1890.

Americans thought of their country as offering ample opportunity to anyone willing to work and save to get ahead. All economic problems did not disappear, however, and further government action was sought.

American agricultural production provided food for the United States and surplus for export to our allies during World Wars I and II, and to needy nations at other times.

Animal power declined sharply while farm tractors and gas-engine-powered machines took over completely on American farms. Extension of animal and plant breeding, of the use of fertilizers, and of insecticides caused production to soar.

Food surpluses led to abandonment of poorer farm lands throughout the period, as more food was produced by fewer acres. The American farm problem continued to be one of surplus.

Industrial expansion continued, but not at as rapid a rate as agricultural production. Still, new production records continued to be set throughout the period except during depressions.

Newer industries grew faster than some of the basic industries of earlier years, e.g., electrical machinery, chemicals of many new kinds including plastics and synthetic fabrics, electronic equipment including radio and television as well as automatic computers and controls, automobiles and trucks, and light metals, especially aluminum.

Industry made possible the high rate of farm production by supplying machinery, fertilizers, etc.

Management became the key to business success in this period. Foresight and willingness to take long chances continued to be important, but they were not sufficient for solid growth without skilled management.

Personnel investigations were made and their results applied to bring both high production and more agreeable conditions of work.

Management concepts began also to be applied to other aspects of business such as marketing, credit and collections, accounting, etc.

American and world experience in the twentieth century demonstrated the value—in fact, the necessity—of effort directed toward technical improvement of industrial processes. There was a significant correlation between the growth rates of various industries and the money spent on research and development.

Many industries found their business in types of production which did not exist a few years previously. The prosperity of the entire economy was recognized as depending upon the success of the continuous search for better products and better ways of making them.

Mass distribution grew to dominate the entire field of commerce at the sacrifice of older and smaller units. Standardized and often branded products, advertised by the mass media of radio, television, and mass-circulation periodicals, and distributed by a system of nationwide dealers or through agents or chains of producer-owned stores, became characteristic.

After World War II, with a marked trend away from farms and from the centers of older cities to larger metropolitan areas depending upon the automobile for transportation, there arose a trend for distributive units to cluster together in suburban shopping centers.

The major transportation development of the twentieth century brought the passenger automobile, the motor truck and the aeroplane into dominant positions.

Passenger miles travelled rose sharply, but the passengers were carried by private automobiles over a network of public highways and turnpikes, and by common carrier airlines and buses.

Private and common carrier motor transports sharply increased their proportion of freight carried, mostly of lighter and more valuable type. Railroads retained heavy bulk freight but lost out relatively.

Credit of various types more and more replaced cash payment in business during the period. The Federal Reserve System established in 1913, extended its degree of control over lending by banks and other financial institutions. It was also increasingly given the public responsibility of managing the issuance of currency and credit in a way that would maintain stable prices and yet stimulate economic growth. The devices which would accomplish this objective remained uncertain. The new governmental responsibility also brought tax and revenue policy into close relationship with money and credit management.

# WORLD ECONOMIC POWER, 1910-1950

1910        1920        1930        1940        1950

The dependence of both producers and consumers upon the market which had been growing for centuries in Europe and America, continued to grow during this period. It is not yet clear at what point the intense specialization of the modern world will reach a limit. The "do-it-yourself" movement of the 1950s may indicate that a turning point is near when it becomes fun to develop varied skills, even if a better product or service could be purchased.

Further extension of the market economy may be further checked if government and business cannot learn how to maintain growth with stability. Central management may replace the market.

Growth of population and shifts of industry to new areas with population following industry have led to increased landowner incomes in some sections and stable or declining incomes in older rural and urban areas from which people are moving.

Movements of residences, light industries, and shopping centers to the outer fringes of urban areas have also led to higher land incomes in some sections and lower in others.

Highly productive farm land remained high in price, but poorer land not suitable for residential or industrial use declined sharply, often reverting to local government ownership.

Farming income generally lagged due to excess production but farmers in the best locations fared reasonably well. Farms continued to be abandoned for agricultural purposes.

Increasing automation led to more output with a stable manufacturing population. Union membership stabilized, although labor income kept pace with expanding production.

Employment in trade and service occupations increased more than proportionally as national output of goods and services increased.

Negro employment began to grow in trade and industry.

The maturing of a business economy meant that the internal problems of many kinds of businesses became more and more alike. A skilled and experienced manager in one industry or business could frequently shift to a relatively similar type of work elsewhere. Thus, in this period, the businessman tended to become a member of a class of professional business managers. Successful practitioners of professional business management might receive very large incomes, by one device or another, from their firms. Second- and lower-level executives became a kind of upper working class. The nineteenth-century captain of industry was gone.

The professional business class became the new social elite of America. They were the members of the best clubs, lived in the finest homes in exclusive residential suburbs, vacationed in the most expensive winter hotels in Florida or elsewhere, and traveled to Europe or around the world at other seasons, often on their firm's expense account.

Nearly everyone else in the U.S. did as well as their incomes would permit to duplicate the living pattern of the new elite.

The new business elite financed political campaigns and heavily influenced governmental policy.

Farm and labor discontent with the laissez-faire policies favored by business and the Republican Party led to Democratic control of the federal government for 26 of the 40 years of this period. Farmers demanded federal price supports in one form or another and industrial workers demanded federal aid in improving wages and working conditions.

Periods of great prosperity demonstrated the productive potential of the free enterprise system and prevented the growth of radical ideas. Business attitudes dominated political thought in this period, party differences being only matters of degree and personality.

Largely because of the great depression of the 1930's, a large and growing school of thought accepted the necessity of governmental guidance and planning to maintain full employment and high levels of productivity and growth. The form and degree of this intervention by government became the touchstone of both political and economic difference of opinion. Recurring lags in economic growth brought renewed demands for new and more effective government guides and stimuli to business. There was opposition to these demands, of course, but support for them spread into both major political parties, and, in effect, changed their older platforms.

THE MARKET

DISTRIBUTION (INCOME)

LANDOWNERS

FARMERS AND WORKERS

BUSINESSMEN

SOCIETY AND GOVERNMENT

SOCIAL CLASSES

POLITICAL POWER

ECONOMIC THOUGHT

# Introduction:

# A historical view of economic life

Our ancestors not many generations back were little aware that there would soon be a social science called economics. They would have well understood the idea of economy, for that has been an element of human activity from the very beginning. Even many animals and plants store up food or water to prepare for the time when such necessities of life might be lacking. But although they practiced economy every day of their lives, our ancestors would have been alarmed to discover that there was a broader significance to economy than merely making ends meet.

Obviously something has happened between their day and ours. Does the growth in the emphasis given to economics mean that something new has been added to the civilization of our day as compared to theirs? Or is the apparent growth in the emphasis on economics merely the result of more accurate and more complete expression of an ever present human interest in economy? Probably something of both is involved.

## Economy, economics, economic systems

All that we know about primitive human societies indicates that a very great deal of attention was given to providing food, clothing and shelter. This was true for many centuries before anyone could have talked or written about "economic problems." The processes of getting food, or making clothes, and of providing shelter came to be established by habits of action that seemed reasonable under the circumstances. Not much attention seemed to be required to the general plan of what we would now call working. These economic habits were scarcely worth writing about even after written language forms had been developed, and were in use for other apparently more important human interests. In fact, since economic matters were largely traditional, they came to be included with what we today call morals. The first recorded ideas that we would now classify as economic thought were very often incorporated in works devoted to an analysis and exposition of the principles of justice and morality in human affairs.[1] We are probably safe in concluding therefore, that the natural human interest in staying alive guaranteed that, even in the earliest cultures, attention to economic problems was always present, even if to us this attention seems to be buried either inconspicuously within customs of living and working or, more evidently, within the moral codes of the day.[2]

But beyond this observation—to turn to the first question posed above—it is evident that civilizations do go through a process of development and elaboration. Certainly, our European-American civilization is no exception to this rule. If we would look to the law or science or music or art of almost any period of the near or distant past, we would be almost sure to find great changes. Elements that were very weak and perhaps barely getting a start, might have become far larger and stronger. The development of economics seems to be an illustration of this point. When such developments do occur, one can be sure that the beginning development seemed to feed itself to provide sustenance for further growth. In the case of economics, attention to the problems of producing and distributing food, clothing, and other necessities of life brought the reward of greater efficiency, or of getting more of these necessities with less effort. Such a desirable reward obviously invited still more intensive effort to carry the process further. The success of these efforts not only brought increases in the standard of living which we in the contemporary world are privileged to enjoy, but also brought the greatly increased attention to and detailed analysis of economic matters noted above.

As a consequence of both of these elements which we have just discussed, the present age of the world has indeed become an economic one. Economic elements are involved in the relations between the nations of the world as well as between the various classes and groups within any one nation. To each one of us as individuals, it becomes very important to understand and thus to be able to promote effectively the economic interests which will make our lives as happy and secure as possible. From narrow personal to broader social and political points of view, we feel the need for deeper understanding of the economic elements of contemporary life. Perhaps the need for economic understanding has grown upon us faster than we as individual citizens have been able to keep up with. In any case, we have come to know that an understanding of our economic life is a contemporary necessity for intelligent living and a test of our mettle as individuals.

## The historical view of economic systems

The personal question that confronts each of us, then, is: In what way can I best and most accurately come to an understanding of the complex pattern of personal and group relationships of which a modern economic system—or economy—is composed? There conceivably might be as many ways of looking at our economic system as there are persons to look at it. But doubtless many of these ways would be similar. Indeed, one of the strange aspects of the problem—and a very confusing one if we don't understand it thoroughly—is that every economic system contains, as one of its elements, a way of looking at itself and its own problems. Until one has studied economic systems from different points of view, it may not be realized that seemingly conflicting points of view are possible and may have a good bit of logic and experience to justify them. After one realizes that there are varied possible and perhaps logical ways of looking at our economic system, he will then become aware that in his own personal situation there is a point of view toward the economy which

[1] In this connection it should be remembered that the modern word *moral* has its root in the Latin word *mos* —plural, *mores*—which means custom.

[2] See Glossary, *Economy*.

is likely to be shared by most of those who see economic problems from an essentially similar position in society. In America today, for example, there are many, many people talking and writing about economic questions who do not seem to realize that there could be any possible justification for a point of view different from their own. Many, if not indeed most books on economic issues exhibit this characteristic. Such a state of affairs occurs most probably when the point of view which is adopted is the most common or dominant one. That is because there is then no one of great importance to question the prevailing viewpoint. Nevertheless, as we consider this situation, we can see that it embodies a point of view which can only be described as narrow. To take a point of view without displaying awareness that one really has, in fact, adopted but one viewpoint out of a possible variety of others can, indeed, only be called narrow-minded.

But is there any way of escaping this situation? Are we not inevitably the creatures of our own time and place? Must not you and I think as twentieth-century Americans because that is what we are? Indeed we must be twentieth-century Americans, but we need not be narrow-minded ones. The objective of education is to develop our mental outlook toward broader intellectual horizons. What we call "liberal" courses in a college program are courses designed to achieve this objective. For the purpose of this book—the providing of foundations for a broad analysis and evaluation of the American economy—we, too, have to be restricted to a point of view. One cannot ride on two different roads simultaneously. But the point of view we have chosen—while it obviously is far from the only possible one—is the best one we can discover to enable us to escape intellectual imprisonment within our own historic age and place. We are going to try to see the American economy as a living, growing thing. It has not always been as it is now; nor will it remain unchanged in the future.

The American economy is a historic development. The economic experience of each day, month, and year adds to that history. How better prepare ourselves to be broad-minded judges of the wisest economic policies of the future than to be informed and critically analytical of the policies that have grown up and been tested by the experience of the past?

The use of an understanding of history as a way of gaining a better understanding of one's own present and future is by no manner of means generally accepted now nor has it been so in the past. A liking for historical study has commonly been a matter of personal taste. One might either like it or dislike it as he might like or dislike a book, or as a student might like or dislike certain courses of study in school. The use of history which we intend to make, however, has a deeper importance. We propose to use a historical approach to the study of our contemporary economic system, not just because we find it interesting, but because it offers both a broader and a deeper understanding of our present and future problems than we know how to obtain in any other way. Since this is not a widely used approach, perhaps we had better explore the basis for it still further.

### The physical sciences and the social sciences

In respect to their historical backgrounds, the physical sciences and the social sciences are quite different. As man sees them, the stars, the chemical elements, the rocks and minerals of the earth's crust—objects of study by physical scientists—seem practically to be unaffected as to the basic laws of their behavior by the particular history through which they may have passed. They have a history, of course, as is clearly evident in the case of rocks or soils, but the pattern of reactions of these physical objects is not altered by their history. In the social sciences, which are concerned with the behavior of human beings in social groups, the situation is quite different. The ways in which men react is fundamentally changed by their history. A child from a family in which he has been loved and well cared for will most likely become a quite distinct kind of human being from one who has been cuffed about and neglected at home. It is true that both children may have the same chemical processes of digesting food, but their social behavior will probably be different. One may become an able and constructive member of society; the other a criminal and a burden to both society and himself. They are two different people from a social point of view. Yet how can a third person, as observer, understand the behavior of either child except through a knowledge of his background and personal history? The social sciences do not study the relatively unchanging physical and physiological aspects of man, but his actions in company with other men. It is these social actions which depend upon the historical background of the individual and the group far more than they depend upon more fixed biological roots of human life.

One further observation may be made about the use of the historical method in the social sciences. The oldest sciences are astronomy, mathematics, and related physical sciences. They were the first to develop that very special type of reasoning which we now call the scientific method. Using this method, scientists achieved great success in adding to human knowledge, some of which could be put to use for economic purposes. In the western European nations where the scientific method developed, it carried considerable prestige. History, as the record of events that happen through time, had very little importance in this new method of reasoning that developed in the physical sciences. Rather, the fruits of the scientific method seemed to be truths or laws which were timeless, in the sense that they were true regardless of variations taking place through time. When economic and other social thinkers sought to extend our knowledge of man in his social relations, it was both natural and perhaps inevitable that they applied methods of reasoning which seemed to have the stamp of approval upon them for their success in other fields. In this way, the social sciences were founded by the use of a method of reasoning developed in and appropriate to the physical sciences. Since the successes of the physical sciences have grown cumulatively since their establishment several centuries ago, it has been true that thinkers in the social sciences have never, until recently, felt the need to pay very much attention to the particular characteristics of their own field of study. It is our effort to look impartially at the inherent characteristics of man's actions in social situations that has led us to recognize the indispensability of historical background for social understanding. Even if this approach is not widely followed as yet, as a scientific method, its logical basis seems to be well established.

## Economic systems and economic thought before 1500

What kinds of things do we see as we undertake to apply a historical point of view to the investigation of the modern economic system as simply the current phase of an age-long process of change and growth? Since this question is broad enough to cover not only the investigations which we shall be able to make in this book but also to provide a general framework for an entire lifetime of inquiry into economic problems, perhaps it would be wise to make a preliminary survey of the ground which we shall be able to cover as an introduction to our more detailed studies.

As we begin this introductory survey of economic development into the ways various human societies have managed their economic affairs and the ways they have thought about economic problems, let us remind ourselves, as we have previously noted, that each plan of economic life that we may find is very likely to carry along with it a way of looking at and thinking about itself. From our often distant vantage point, this combination of a way of life, coupled with a way of thinking about life, appears to be almost a case of a people and an age sealing themselves up in a sterile bottle as protection against outside contamination. This closing off process never works completely, but it usually slows down social adjustments and makes them more difficult when they do come. To see and understand this tendency of historic systems of economic action and economic thinking to go together and jointly to resist or reject any alternatives, is one of the most valuable results of the use of the historical approach.

### The earliest beginnings

The beginnings of the human story rest in such a distant past that we can know next to nothing from direct evidence of any of its economic elements. Continuing exploration and research add new elements to the story, but do not do much to relieve our ignorance of economic life in the very earliest times. Excavations at sites of human residence sometimes uncover bones or shells that must have represented the use of animal foods but these tell us practically nothing about the system of human relations that accompanied the securing and consuming of suitable animal forms for food. Our knowledge of these remotest beginnings has to be indirect—by inference—from the simpler economic societies that exist today or have existed within historic times. From this indirect point of view, we are perhaps justified in classifying the earliest economic societies as traditional, i.e., as societies which secured their livelihood by methods which came to be followed by habit and which were not thought of in any specific or conscious way. Such economic thought as there was would be limited to the solution of immediate problems of economy. These have always existed, for every living thing—plant, animal, or man—either by intelligent choice or by built-in automatic mechanism, must, if life is to continue, make the right responses at times when the requisites of life are scarce. But in such simpler societies we find no economic thought nor any evident intellectual awareness of such a general notion as that of an economic system; only the routine following by habit of particular ways of getting and using the needs of life.

### The ancient world

In the ancient world, when man's intellectual life had been developed very much further, at least by some individuals in the society, we find that economic matters were treated primarily as moral questions. The word *moral,* we have seen, is derived from the idea of custom, but, in the ancient world, it had acquired that additional element of meaning which is today dominant, namely that a *moral* act is also a *right* act. To Aristotle in ancient Greece, for example, the work of tending the herds of sheep or the vineyards was clearly right, good, and economical. On the other hand, money-lending simply for gain was neither right nor economical because he did not see that it would contribute to the overall livelihood of the society, as the work of the husbandman clearly would. Throughout the ancient world, and up to the beginning of the modern age, we find this point of view prevailing. What we would call directly productive work on the farm or in manufacturing was good. Activities which seemed to involve nothing more than the trading of goods for profit or were purely financial were disapproved. We cannot now accept this distinction between productive and unproductive activities, and, indeed, it is now possible for us to see that the distinction could exist simply because it was not searchingly analyzed.

Nevertheless, we must recognize that the ancient world had developed the idea that economic matters are primarily matters of human relationships. Economic actions had to be viewed as having either good or bad effects upon society and judged accordingly. They may have been wrong in their specific judgments, in our view, but they made economics a social science, insofar as they systematically thought about it at all. In this respect, economics was to be distinguished from such physical sciences as astronomy and also from the technical details of productive work such as sheepherding or the tending of a vineyard.

The Middle Ages brought no striking changes in economic outlook. It was a period in which the ancient civilizations of Greece and Rome went through a great upheaval with the eventual reassembly of the fragments into characteristic subgroups which were to become the nations of Europe in modern times. Of course, there were also modifications in the economic life of Europe in the medieval era to bring about adaptation to the conditions of life that had to be faced in a practical way. Chapter 2 will be devoted to a consideration of the particular aspects of medieval economic life. But typically, economic problems continued to be treated as moral ones in the Middle Ages as they had very largely been treated in the ancient world. Stresses and strains became increasingly severe as time passed, eventually disrupting the pattern which was at the core of medieval life. Yet the period itself made no great contribution to economic life or economic understanding beyond the development and extension of practices and points of view which had originated within ancient civilizations.

## Economic systems and economic thought since 1500

### *Mercantilism*

The centuries after 1500 A.D. deserve to be called modern because they revealed distinctly new and different elements. From the point of view of social structure, the most important new phenomenon was the emergence of the national state to a dominant position. This does not require much explanation today, for nationalism is still with us and national loyalties and points of view are understood by everyone. At the beginning of the modern era, however, it was a new phenomenon. A common devotion to the common good of the inhabitants of a geographic area brought in sequence common moral standards as to what

was right or wrong economically or politically. The predominance of moral concerns in the ancient and medieval worlds could drop out of sight in the modern nation states, although surviving intact beneath the surface, because standards of morality were common to all citizens of such states.[1] Economic problems that were of concern did not appear as moral but only as technical matters of detail as to how the national well-being might be promoted. In economic thought, this technical viewpoint gave rise to a body of assorted doctrines known as *Mercantilism,* so called because they all related to the activities of merchants.[2]

Our earlier discussions have suggested that when a change in economic thought occurs, we should look for a corresponding change in the pattern of economic activities associated with securing a livelihood. The early modern centuries clearly brought such a change, as we shall see later (Chapters 2 and 3). Whether the changed ways of providing a livelihood brought new points of view, or vice versa, is an issue which we need not try to decide. In any case, the systems of agriculture and local handicraft industry which prevailed throughout both the ancient and medieval worlds to a predominant degree, began to give way extensively before an expansion of trade at all levels—local, national, and world-wide.

Nationalism has remained as a characteristic phenomenon of the political structure of the modern world, but mercantilist economic ideas have largely passed away or been adapted to changing conditions. In part, Mercantilism in its earlier forms was so narrowly nationalistic that it defeated its own goals. In part also, its success in promoting trade and the national wealth brought about such changed conditions that the ideas and policies of earlier Mercantilism were no longer useful.

---

[1] A corollary of the rise of a national economic and political morality which goes beyond our present discussion may be noted in passing. The dominance of national morality virtually suppressed any kind of international morality. The absence of codes of international right and wrong has been a source of trouble throughout the modern era.

[2] See pp. 78-80 for a fuller discussion of Mercantilism.

The merchant class had become more wealthy than very many human beings had ever been before. The growth of their trade required that more people turn to the production of goods for sale. Great changes in industry occurred, resulting in the Industrial Revolution. The industrial system took on the characteristics which we know so well today in an economically well-developed country like the United States. Because these changes created the economic world in which we live today, we will need to look at them as closely as possible, both as they were started in Europe, especially England (Chapters 4 and 5), and as they were carried forward in the United States (Chapters 6 and following). Also, and for the same reason, we will need to examine with care the economic ideas and viewpoints which came into general acceptance with the Industrial Revolution. Since this is a period closer to our own, and since the thought of the period represented an elaboration of economic concepts more complete than ever before—many of the ideas being accepted today—a general review of the newly developing ideas about the structure and functioning of the economic system can well be presented here as an introduction to the more detailed presentation that will occupy our attention at a later stage of our treatment.

### The free market economics of
### Adam Smith and Jean Baptiste Say

If we undertake to reduce all of the economic changes in the early modern centuries in Europe to their simplest underlying element, we would have to name economic specialization as that element. Adam Smith, who wrote the first comprehensive economic treatise[1] analyzing and explaining the new economic system that was beginning to arise, called this specialization "division of labor." As Smith very clearly pointed out, division of labor means that every individual who can limit his efforts to one special part of a total

[1] *The Wealth of Nations,* published in 1776.

job to be done, can thereby become much more efficient. He also pointed out that there can be specialization within a single shop making one product as well as between different shops. Any type of production, whether agricultural or industrial, can profit from this kind of specialization.

Some degree of specialization has taken place as far back as we know anything about economic life. However, by modern standards, it was at a very low level during many parts of the centuries of ancient and medieval times. During the latter part of the Middle Ages, we shall see, specialization began to increase both in handicraft industrial production and to some degree in agriculture. Where there is specialization, the specialized producers must have opportunity to trade their products with other specialists. In this way trade and commerce arise. Adam Smith pointed out that in early times rivers and seacoasts offered the best opportunity for specialized producers to get together for trade. Thus, he said, towns arose on rivers and at points on seacoasts providing good port facilities. From small beginnings in ancient times, specialized production and trade have grown as conditions permitted through the centuries. The economic life of the period in Europe after about 1500 A.D. showed probably the most rapid growth of trade in human history. This growth resulted in the kind of economic system which Smith explained and which, to a considerable degree, remains with us today. Let us look at the essentials of this system, as they were seen by Smith, and as they are seen today, nearly two centuries later.

Smith repeatedly refers to the new system which was developing as the system of "natural liberty." *Liberty* implies freedom of action for individuals and *natural* implies, as Smith seemed to believe, that this freedom for individuals was a part of the order of nature. If governments did not interfere with the natural liberty of individuals, Smith believed, all economic problems of production, exchange of goods, and income would be worked out to the best advantage of everyone. This system, from our twentieth-century perspective, is what we call the system of free markets and free competition. If individual freedom of economic action is not restricted, except to prevent violence and to require individuals to keep their business contracts, the entire economic system will develop in an efficient, just, and orderly manner. But the system cannot work well where political or social institutions limit the economic freedom of action which individuals may have.

Outside of England, Smith's ideas were accepted as essentially correct at an earlier time in France than in any other country. A disciple of Smith's—Jean Baptiste Say—in undertaking to present Smith's ideas more clearly and systematically wrote a book which became the first college textbook in economics and provided a generally approved picture of the structure and functioning of the economic system. Because it was so widely accepted, a presentation of the elements of the economic system derived primarily from Say's book[1] will give us a clear picture of the economic system as it was viewed at that time. In many parts of the world, this view has only been modified and extended—not superseded—since early in the nineteenth century.

### Basic economic processes: production

The basic process of economic life is producing the materials and services by which life is sustained. This process is called *production*. The performance of any operation or function which aids in supplying either the necessities or the enjoyments of life is a productive activity. Anything which contributes to a productive activity is a *factor of production*. Human labor, for example, is perhaps the most fundamental factor of production. To realize this, one has only to ask himself: How many of the human beings now alive would be alive or could remain alive without human effort devoted to supplying the needs of living? In spite of this fundamental truth, however, there are necessities and enjoyments which do

[1]*Traité d'Économie Politique* (Paris, 1803). Translated into English from the fourth French edition by C. R. Prinsep (Boston, 1821).

not require effort. Air is always available when we need it if we are in good enough physical condition to use it. A nice day can be enjoyed as we go about our usual activities without the effort of anyone. Air is called a *free good* because it is available without being produced by human labor. Goods or services which have to be produced by work before we can enjoy them are called *economic goods*. Free goods are abundant—sufficient for any possible use—without productive effort, whereas economic goods are scarce, not available without producing them.

Labor alone is not sufficient for production. It must have something on which to work. Agriculture was for so many centuries the principal type of work of most human beings, that economic thinkers used the general word *land* for all of the materials furnished by the environment upon which labor exerted its efforts. Perhaps the terms *natural resources* or *natural materials* might now be better, since either would include the raw materials upon which labor is expended in industrial production, as well as the land used in agriculture.

Even the performance of productive services like those of professional men—doctors, lawyers or engineers—requires buildings for office space and some small quantities of materials as a minimum. Thus, all productive labor must depend on natural materials, not created by labor but essential as a second and independent factor of production.

These two factors of production were noted not only by Adam Smith and J. B. Say but had been almost standard as far back in history as economic matters had attracted any attention at all. To the Mercantilist writers of the sixteenth and seventeenth centuries, these factors were the solid platform on which all economic policies of the nation should be based. But the growth of commerce and industry in the three centuries following the beginning of the modern era expanded and elaborated the economic system and brought into importance a new factor of production—*capital*. The productive function of capital was little understood in the ancient world and throughout the Middle Ages as we have seen. Mercantilist writers dealt to some degree with the functions of capital but were not very clear about it and did not incorporate the concept of capital in a definite way into their economic policies. Adam Smith's *Wealth of Nations* was the first important economic work to incorporate the idea of capital into the basic structure of the economic system as it was presented. Even Smith did not call it capital but rather "stock." Yet the idea is clear and fundamental to Smith's thought. J. B. Say and other thinkers who followed Smith's lead developed the idea more fully.

As Smith viewed the productive process, workers couldn't simply work. They had to have something on which to work. Such materials came from nature originally and thus could be described, as a productive factor, simply as natural materials. However, as raw materials were worked upon by productive workers, their value would increase as they became partly finished products. During the productive process, and as they gradually changed from raw materials to finished products, they belonged to persons who owned them not for any direct value they might have had in their unfinished state, but only as goods that would some day be finished and could then either be enjoyed, if produced for one's own use, or sold for the use of others. Even after such goods were finished, if they were to be sold but had not yet been sold, their value was not direct but existed only in the anticipation of future sale. It was these goods—from raw materials to semi-finished goods to finished goods—which Smith referred to as stock. They were a stock of goods in process.

Goods of this kind were not all of stock. Workmen had to be fed, clothed, and housed while they were engaged in productive work. From the point of view of a whole society, it takes a stock of food, clothing and housing, as a minimum, to support productive workers. These items too were, therefore, a part of stock. Besides, workmen required tools, machinery, and suitable buildings in which to work. These also become a part of stock in Smith's view. The common element in all of these components of stock is that all of them are used not to meet the needs or enjoyments of life directly, but to contribute in some way to the producing of goods that will have value in that they will be capable of contributing directly to a livelihood.

In the course of time, through the efforts of J. B. Say and other writers, Smith's concept of stock eventually was refined and expanded into the concept of capital. Capital may be defined as anything produced for the purpose of aiding further production. Even this seems like a primitive definition in today's advanced economic system. We think of capital as a sum of money because we can overlook the raw materials, machinery, etc., which lie behind it and for which a monetary sum is merely expressing the value. We also can overlook the fact that capital is goods which aid production because all we need to think of is that the use of capital brings an increase of value or income. Thus, our more comprehensive contemporary definition is that capital is virtually any economic value which yields an income. We don't place a capital value on human beings whose efforts yield income because we believe that individuals are free and not tied to a machine, and because we live to enjoy life, not only to create more income. The older view was too limited to a physical' concept of the productive process. Yet, there is much loose thinking about the idea of capital today, so that it is useful for us to remember the views of the productive process through which the concept of capital as a third factor of production emerged.

*Basic economic processes: exchange*

If goods are produced by specialists and not for personal use, they must be traded to other persons who wish to use them. This necessity gives rise to trade as has been noted and practiced to some degree since the earliest times. All of the activities related to exchanging have been called parts of the basic economic process of *exchange* by economists of the past century. The activities have been perfectly well known for centuries but they were not given the collective name *exchange* until after the time of J. B. Say. Exchange includes the direct act of exchanging goods between specialized producers—more specifically called barter. It also includes transporting goods to advantageous places of sale or trade, which we call markets. In addition, since barter has become rather infrequent, exchange includes all of the problems of monetary payment and financing which have become very important aspects of our contemporary economic system. The contemporary word *marketing* covers many of the parts of both selling and buying which are included in exchange as a basic economic process. The exchange process is not complete until the produced goods are in the hands of those who wish to use them. The expansion of trade and the development of commercial institutions which marked the first great stage in the development of the modern economic system can be thought of as an expansion of the economic process of exchange.[1]

### Basic economic processes: consumption

When goods have been produced and exchanged so that they are at last in the hands of a person who wishes to use them, the basic economic process of *consumption* can begin as the user desires. This process was noted by J. B. Say as the final round in the flow of goods from raw material through manufacturing and transportation to eventual users. In recent years, a number of economists have specialized in the various aspects of consumption. There are now acknowledged to be serious economic problems relating to the kinds of goods available to consumers, to the suitability of these goods to consumer needs, and to the judgment of consumers in selecting goods from the market. But until recently, the process of consumption has not been extensively studied by economists. Since the days of J. B. Say, consumption has been recognized as the logical final step in the flow of goods within the economic system, but not much further analysis was devoted to it. No precise

[1]See Glossary, *Commercial revolution.*

reason can be given for this fact, but it can be inferred that prior to the twentieth century with its mass production, the biggest economic problem had always seemed to be to get enough to satisfy human needs. The increased attention being currently given to problems relating to consumption may, in this light, be taken as a by-product of the success of the efforts of the past century to increase production. When we are able to produce so many things in such great abundance, we become more concerned with getting the proper things produced from the ultimate consumer's point of view.

### Basic economic processes: distribution

The three processes which we have described fully comprehend the flow of goods but they tell us nothing of the flow of income as raw materials are increased in value by processing to become finished goods in the hands of consumers. The chief problem involved may be stated as follows: since a number of specialists have contributed to the creation of a serviceable product in the hands of a consumer, how shall the final value of the product to the consumer be divided up among the long series of persons who have helped in the processes of production and exchange? This is a question of dividing up a final consumer value, and the process of accomplishing the task was named *distribution* by J. B. Say. There is a still older use of the word *distribution* which means the spreading out of economic goods from a center, where they are produced, to all of the places in which consumers may wish to have them. The term is used in the same way at the present time by businessmen and students of the marketing process. Economists, however, have followed the lead of J. B. Say and always use the word *distribution* to mean a dividing up of an economic value. Great care must be taken to be sure which meaning is intended when the word is encountered in an economic or business discussion. The essential distinction to be kept in mind is that the economist's use of the word *distribution* always means a dividing up of a *value,* whereas the business or marketing man's use always refers to the spreading out of *physical goods* from the point of production to the point of consumption.

The economist's concept of distribution, as a basic economic process, is on a different footing from the other basic processes. The other processes are concerned with the flow of goods from the first stages of production through to consumption, whereas distribution is concerned with the flow of economic value which arises from this flow of goods. Although J. B. Say was the first economist to give the process a name, it was recognized more or less clearly long before his time. Distribution being concerned with an abstract value, the shares of value going to the different persons who contribute to production and exchange can only be measured in money. As we shall see, the use of money has almost invariably been a necessity as soon as there began to be specialized production and exchange of goods. Economic thinkers, at least as early as the Mercantilists, observed that the flow of goods was paralleled by the flow of monetary value. They referred to this as the "veil of money." They thought of it as a veil because their principal interest was in the creation of useful goods. But since the veil of money was always paralleled by goods, they were as willing to achieve their nationalistic objectives by manipulating the monetary system as they were willing to achieve the same results by direct controls over production and trade.

Adam Smith, followed by J. B. Say, saw even more clearly the parallel between the creation of economic goods and the creation of value expressed in monetary terms. Smith and Say opposed any interference by government for they saw all of the basic economic processes, including the intangible one of distribution, as taken care of by the free actions of individuals in the market place. That is, everyone would know his own economic interests and would seek to promote them if he were given a chance. If the economic system were really free, any person could sell his services to any employer who would hire him or could go into business for himself to produce any product or service he felt that he was qualified to undertake. In the latter case, the product or service could be sold for the best price he could get. From this market process, laborers would go to employers who could use their services in production or exchange most efficiently. The pay received by these workers would reflect the value which their employer could get by the sale of the product or service to which they had added value by their work. Self-employed persons would also be able to sell their product or service in the market for a price which would reflect the judgment of consumers as to its value. In all of these activities, laborers and independent businessmen would be competing with each other. Only the successful, which means the efficient, producers could stay in business. Others would have to seek better luck in some other type of activity. Through all of these actions, labor, capital, and raw materials would be put to use, economic goods would be created and directed toward consumers, values would be created by the prices which goods could command in the market, and these values would be distributed to all contributors to the productive process by the value which these contributors themselves could command in the market. Also, there would be a close parallel between the flow of goods and the flow of money income. All would be adjusted to secure both efficiency and justice through the competition of all who found it to their interest to enter into the competition.

### Critics of free market economics

If this picture of the economic system seems complicated, it must be remembered that it is still highly simplified when compared to the real complexities of that time and much more simplified when compared to the economic system of the twentieth century. It was very soon discovered that many things prevented the system from working as smoothly as it had been pictured. Lord Lauderdale, in 1804, published a book which criticized Smith, his Scottish fellow countryman, for asserting that "private wealth" and "public wealth" were the same.[1] Private wealth, said Lauderdale, is increased when a desired good is made more scarce, but the public wealth suffers if goods are scarce instead of abundant. In effect, Lauderdale was questioning the competitive system, because if it is possible for an individual to keep goods scarce, he then has a monopoly to at least some degree. The criticism was not accepted widely enough to weaken in a serious way the general belief in the free market as a self-stabilizing mechanism.

Yet, it showed that the views of Smith, Say, and their followers were really highly simplified. As we look back at their theoretical views —now called "classical economics" because it was so simplified and became rather narrowly formalized—we can see that even their description of the basic economic processes is rather arbitrarily simplified. For example, if production is the creation of useful values to consumers, why are not the merchants and financiers and transportation agencies who perform exchange services also to be regarded as producers? Even in Smith's day, was a workman who took a small piece of iron and hammered it into a nail any more productive than other people who took the nail to a place where a consumer wished to use it and handled the financial aspects of selling it to him? The nail was of no value until the consumer had it for use.

Or to take another kind of illustration of the oversimplification of classical theory from a later period: If workers object to the speed and tension of certain industrial operations and insist upon a slower pace because it is more comfortable, are they not accepting lower production and lower pay in order to enjoy their work? Is not this action similar to consumption? Consumption is the destroying of useful values for the support and pleasure of life. Pleasant but less efficient work methods amount to a mixing of production and consumption.

To sum up, the classical economic view seems to contemporary economic thinkers to have achieved a convincing simplicity only by

making rather arbitrary definitions and assumptions. The economic processes are not now necessarily viewed only as the early theoretical systems pictured them. Lord Lauderdale had much to be said on his behalf. There are many persistent impediments to free competition. Some individuals and business firms are able to control the supply of goods and services to the market in ways which amount to at least partial monopoly. The market is not always self-stabilizing, as Smith and Say assumed that it was. It is not always sufficiently free to produce both efficiency and justice for the economic system. Yet the development of the classical theory was the greatest forward step in the history of economic thought. In spite of weaknesses which later came to light, it was the first successful attempt to provide a unified explanation of the operation of the economic system. It seemed to the people of the time as the best possible explanation of the new kind of economic system which was developing before their eyes. It met a need of its age and moved into later ages carrying with it a very high prestige. In reality, it has provided the basic economic thinking of the nations of western Europe ever since, as well as of the other parts of the world in which the influence of the Western nations has been predominant.

### Socialism and communism

Yet, the classical view of the economic system did not please everyone. Lord Lauderdale was merely the first of the critics. Interestingly, the critical points of view which gained the widest support related very little to the logical foundations of the theoretical system, but rested upon dissatisfaction with the results which the free market system was supposed to yield. Most of these dissatisfactions led to what we today know as socialism. In one form or another, socialist movements gained substantial followings during the nineteenth century in Germany, France, and other European countries as well as—to a lesser degree—in Great Britain. In the United States, socialism aroused only slight interest. Many

[1]*An Inquiry into the Nature and Origin of Public Wealth* (Edinburgh, 1804).

religious groups of European origin came to America to set up more or less socialistic communities in the new country, but they never came close to the heart of American economic and political thinking. When classical economics was criticized in America, as it was in the voluminous writings of the Philadelphia publisher and author Henry C. Carey, it was only because of some of its pessimistic theories relative to excessive population growth due to scarcity of good land. This seemed simply preposterous in a country with unbounded areas of good farm land begging for settlers to populate it.

In Europe, however, socialism retained its hold and grew whenever the workings of the free market system seemed to be particularly ineffective. The most famous socialist writer was Karl Marx, a German who was driven out of his own country and did most of his writing in England where belief in personal liberty gave him more opportunity. Marx' most famous works were the *Communist Manifesto* (1848), a pamphlet in which he appealed to the workers of all countries to arise and unite against their employers, and the ponderous, three-volume *Capital,* published from 1867 to 1894, elaborating his theories in the greatest detail. These works have become the bibles of the most extreme socialists. Socialist movements, wherever they exist, owe at least some allegiance to Marxist ideas. The twentieth-century communist movement, which began to acquire a wide following after the successful overthrow of the czarist government in Russia in 1917, considers Marx to be its patron saint. Other communist scholars such as Lenin and Stalin regarded their work principally as the interpretation, elaboration, and application of Marx' theories. Communist theorists accept the most basic of the logical postulates of the classical economics, but direct the development of their theory to prove that working people are exploited unjustly by their capitalist employers. Communism has become the most powerful opponent of the free market system. It arose, as a theoretical system, from the failures of the free market system, but has grown and spread, not where the free market system has been in existence and where its defects in practice might show up, but rather in agrarian countries in which the free economic and political system has never existed and where the people do not understand it. Marx gave the free market system the name *capitalism,* the term by which it is now most commonly known.

### Keynesian economics

Within the western European nations and in the other parts of the world originally colonized by those nations, the free market, capitalistic system thrived and grew throughout the nineteenth and twentieth centuries. The system had its defects, which had been noted for more than a century, and were not solved, but capitalism pushed them aside in the great waves of economic prosperity which it brought. Nonetheless, these sometimes hidden and ignored defects remained, and when any circumstances interrupted or stopped the progress of the free market economic system, critics were sure to be heard again, emphasizing and developing in new ways the critical points which had been made by the system itself in the early stages of growth. Yet none of these critical viewpoints made any real dent in the general acceptance of the essential classical economic explanations. It was not until the Western nations had experienced a long series of economic depressions extending throughout the nineteenth and twentieth centuries that the tremendously destructive impact of the world-wide depression beginning in the United States in 1929 seemed to be the "straw that broke the camel's back." It developed critical economic thought to the point where it was integrated into a new kind of view of the functioning of the system.

The Cambridge University economist—John Maynard Keynes (pronounced Kānz)—who in 1936 published his *General Theory of Employment, Interest and Money*, became the principal spokesman for this first sympathetic but fundamental revision of the classical view of the economic system in more than one hundred and fifty years. Keynes gave credit to

Lord Lauderdale, T. R. Malthus[1] and other critics who had appeared from time to time through the years, but developed his own thought more completely than theirs.

The essential ingredient of the new Keynesian view was Keynes' unwillingness, based on amply demonstrated historical experience in depressions, to accept the inference of the classical position that if individuals were left to themselves, all workers who wished to work would find jobs somewhere, all capitalists who had capital available for business would find some satisfactory place to put it to use, and all owners of natural resources would find satisfactory ways to put them to productive employment. Keynes would not accept the idea that the free market would automatically result in full levels of employment for all of the factors of production. Rather, he said, conditions might exist—and obviously did exist at certain times—in which a perfectly free market might stabilize itself with substantial unemployment of labor, capital, and resources. A great deal of debate among economists and businessmen immediately arose over the justification for Keynes' views. He was both criticized and defended very widely. Regardless of the points that might be made or lost in debate, the Keynesian theories seemed to many persons to explain the conditions that actually existed in the system. Keynes' ideas were the basis for the most sweeping revolution in economic thinking in the capitalist nations since Adam Smith.

Keynes' thought can be said to be a functional rather than a structural criticism of classical views. That is, he did not quarrel with the classification of basic productive factors and processes, but only with the way in which a free market would bring about the use of these factors. Throughout the nineteenth century, economists had developed explanations of the employment and wages of labor, of the employment and profit to capital, and of the use and rent of land and natural resources. Keynes did not attack these explanations; he simply thought other things were more important. To him the big question was why the market could become stabilized and quiescent while the factors of production were partially unemployed. This condition, Keynes concluded, was due to attitudes which might be perfectly reasonable and economical to the persons concerned yet might result in withholding factors of production from use, particularly capital, or lead consumers to defer purchases. To detect whether or not such attitudes were having a bad effect on the system, the factors to watch were the levels of production and employment and the *income flows* which resulted from production. These income flows would not automatically remain at their highest possible level, but needed to be watched to see if some action should be taken, either by private agencies or governmental ones, to stimulate or discourage either investment or consumption. Normally, discouragement would not be required unless further investment and consumption would not stimulate production but merely bring about an inflation of prices.

If we reduce both the older and the Keynesian explanations of the economic system to most abbreviated form, we might say that the classical view stated that levels of employment and income will take care of themselves if the market is kept entirely free of either private or public restraining factors. In the Keynesian view, even without public or private restraint in the market, income flows through the market mechanism must be watched so that if they sag below a satisfactory level, steps may be taken by private action— or public, if necessary—to restore them to a proper point. Most of the means of achieving this result, in Keynes' view, would be by control of monetary and credit policies.

Keynes' influence was very great throughout the decade of the 1930's in America and western Europe. His theories seemed to explain the cause of the great depression which all nations were suffering. He also seemed to provide a guide to private businesses as to what they should do to avoid depressions. But if

[1]*Principles of Political Economy* (London, 1820). Malthus built upon the work of Lord Lauderdale but extended Lauderdale's ideas considerably.

they failed to act as they should or if their actions proved to be insufficient, there was always the dagger of governmental action hanging over their heads. To some critics of Keynes, this threat of governmental action seemed to make his system of thought socialistic. While the depression was at its worst, even many businessmen accepted the Keynesian analysis as the best system there was to explain the existing conditions, even if it was not very palatable to them. Labor leaders accepted Keynes with open arms. His emphasis on the necessity of maintaining income flows if there was to be a general prosperity seemed to provide a ready-made argument for high wages, not only for the benefit of labor but for everyone else.

## Summary

The need for economy is an ever-present fact of human life. This condition may be due either to the limited means of livelihood which nature freely supplies us, or to the human tendency to want more, regardless of the amount nature gives us. In either case, scarcity is a basic fact and economy is required of us to meet it. This need gives rise to patterns of action which we call economic systems or economies. We have observed briefly how these economic systems have changed within the periods of time of which we have knowledge. At any point of time, there are both ways of acting to meet economic needs and ways of thinking about the system of action. Action and thought tend to be correlated but not perfectly. Each is partly cause and partly effect of the other. This is a unique situation of the social sciences. It applies much less directly to the physical sciences. Economic understanding depends upon a parallel understanding of the dependence of ideas upon conditions and, to a degree, of conditions upon ideas.

Every human being looks at the active social system about him from a point of view which is uniquely his own. Everyone's understanding of the society of his day reflects the patterns of action and the patterns of thought which he has acquired, probably unknowingly, from his environment. These individual understandings differ in relation to social or economic phenomena, as they do not differ in relation to our understanding of weather conditions or how to boil water. Yet, a true social science only becomes possible when there can be a common understanding of social processes among all of those who are informed. In the search for a base for a scientific understanding of society, we are driven to study the historical development of systems of economic action and economic thought. No other course seems to have such a solid logical foundation. Every individual necessarily lives in a situation which is personal to himself. If we cannot fully escape it, as we cannot, we can come nearer to escaping it to a broader more scientific view of society by knowing the elements of the situation into which we have grown.

In the present introduction, we have sketched some major elements in the development of the modern economic system which originated in western Europe and spread out all over the world. We have paralleled this narrative with some account of the economic ideas which prevailed during the same developmental process. The remainder of this book will examine in somewhat greater detail these same developmental processes leading to the economic conditions and problems of understanding which confront us in our daily lives. Final solutions of problems are possible only to those who close their minds to continuing developments. For purposes of daily action in business, government, and elsewhere, a halt must be called, inquiry must stop, and action must be decided upon. This is necessary and proper. But for scientific understanding and as preparation for the next round of problems to come up without end, continuing inquiry is indispensable. It is to this endless inquiry which constitutes the intellectual life of mankind that we give unqualified devotion. It is hoped that our inquiry into our economic condition will make some small contribution thereto.

# Part I: The European Backgrounds

Part I: The European Backgrounds

# Chapter 1: Economic life at the dawn of modern times

Life in the twentieth century is based upon many institutions which began to take form in the long span of time known to historians as the medieval period, or the Middle Ages. These centuries following the disintegration of Roman power and unity extend from around 500 A.D. onward for a thousand years. Within them, basic ideas of law, government, religion, and economic life which had failed to provide sufficient cohesive power to hold Roman civilization together were diffused throughout western Europe and given a re-evaluation under conditions markedly different from those that had prevailed at Rome. Because of different conditions, the institutions of medieval life developed a distinct pattern, uniquely their own, yet usually carrying within it something of the heritage from the civilization of the Mediterranean area in ancient times. Like all civilizations, that of the Middle Ages was not totally satisfying to those who lived within it. Elements of value in the ancient civilizations were lost or submerged because the politically chaotic conditions of the earlier Middle Ages did not permit them to be retained.

But denial and frustration under proper circumstances become a challenge to action. Lawlessness usually invites a more powerfully backed law. Ruinous and incessant local warring brought support for stronger and more broadly based government to maintain the peace. The poverty and hard work of a locally self-sufficient economic organization made the advantages of economic specialization and trade more attractive. From such urges, the basic elements of a new outlook upon life became more frequently evident in the late centuries of the Middle Ages. As the forces of change achieved effect, they were in turn nourished and strengthened by the effect they had achieved.

In time, the accumulation of changes became so great that, historians agree, a break had occurred between medieval and modern times. No historic break is ever complete and final in an absolute sense. Remnants of old ways persist; new ways are never completely dominant. But by 1500 in Europe it was evident that the clock of time had swept forward into a new era, an era which witnessed the higher development of many of the institutions begun in the Middle Ages.

## Rural life in the Middle Ages

### Reasons for the predominance
### of agriculture

One of the most striking differences between medieval and modern economic life is the much larger proportion of people in the earlier period who derived their livelihood from work on the land. The principal reasons for this state of affairs were the low yield from agriculture and the relative unimportance of trade. It has been estimated that the average yield of wheat in the Middle Ages was six bushels per acre. Two of these bushels had to be saved for the next year's seed, leaving only four bushels which could be used for food. Today a farmer on good land, with less laborious planting and harvesting, also sows two bushels of seed per acre, but gets a harvest of thirty to forty or more bushels per acre. Under medieval conditions, it is not surprising that at least nine-tenths of the people were tillers of the soil. Only a little of their production could be spared to feed the nonagricultural portion of the population.

Nor was the keeping and feeding of livestock on a better basis. Corn was not known until the discovery of America; it is now our principal livestock feed. Lacking corn, medieval farmers could support their cattle, sheep, and hogs only by allowing them to forage in the woods and wasteland. For winter feed they had only the small amount of hay they could cut from the summer grass of the low lying meadows. Very little grain could be spared from human use to feed animals. Thus, meat and milk were scarce and of poor quality. It is no wonder that the meat-hungry, medieval lords zealously preserved hunting rights in the

woodland for themselves, since the deer, boar, or pheasant which the hunt might yield would make a very substantial addition to the meat supply available to them. As for the peasants, their supply of meat consisted of very little beyond a fowl or a ham for holidays and an occasional grouse or animal shot or snared illegally on the lord's hunting domain. The daily diet consisted of dark bread baked from coarsely ground wheat or rye, supplemented by a bit of cheese made from the milk of goats or cattle, and washed down either by wine or by beer or ale made from barley and hops.

Another factor contributing to the predominance of agriculture in the Middle Ages was the lack of any political authority to maintain law and order over large areas. The medieval period, coming as it does between the fall of the Roman Empire and the emergence of strong national states at the beginning of the modern era, was characterized by the absence of effective central government. Highways built by the Roman emperors were not kept in good condition and robbers were not suppressed. Merchants could not safely carry on their business except in limited areas. These conditions did not prevail everywhere, but they were so widespread that there was little opportunity for the great majority of the people (especially in central and northern Europe) to supplement their own resources with goods obtained outside the local community. Self-sufficiency was the order of the day.

### The manorial system

The core of medieval economic life is found in the manor. In so far as one can generalize about an institution possessing so many different forms, the manor was a small rural village of a few hundred people. It was an economic, social, and political unit pretty largely sufficient unto itself. It would usually be located on or near a stream, which would constitute the village water supply and might also provide water power for the lord's mill and means of transportation. The agricultural land of the manor would spread out across the valley from the marshy meadows near the stream to the wooded hills on either side. A manor of fifty families might have several thousand acres of land, so that the villagers might have to travel as far as two or three miles to reach the most distant part of the manorial fields (see Fig. 1-1, p. 39).

The farming system used on the manors is often called the open-field system, or, more specifically, the three-field system. Either name is satisfactory, because the fields were open (that is, the individual holdings were not fenced off from one another), and in western Europe there were usually three distinct open fields. One of these fields would be plowed in early fall and planted to wheat or rye; another would be plowed in the spring and sowed to oats, barley, peas, or beans, or some of each; the third field would be fallow, that is, unplowed and growing up in grass and weeds, crops having been harvested from it the two preceding years. Since good pasture was scarce, the fallow field would be used to permit the livestock of the manor to get from it such forage as they could.

A unique feature of the manorial system was the internal arrangement of the fields. They were not farmed as whole fields but were subdivided into long strips of one acre each, of which there might be from several hundred to several thousand in each field. An acre was a convenient unit for plowing and other farm work, and, since everyone had to return to the village in the evening anyway, there was no inconvenience in starting work on another strip in the morning. Perhaps to insure an even distribution of good and bad ground, or perhaps because of the methods of cultivation used, the strips of each peasant were scattered throughout the fields and were not concentrated in one place. Similarly, the farm land of the lord was usually scattered in strips throughout the open fields, but he often had about half of the total arable land.

The tools and equipment used on the manor were, by modern standards, very poor and crude. The principal implement was the plow. In parts of Europe it was no more than a heavy forked piece of wood, one end of which

was dragged through the ground by one or more teams of oxen. Elsewhere, it might be a somewhat better implement, with a piece of iron attached to the point, so fashioned as to turn the soil over on its edge as the plow was pulled through it. A plow of this type was the forerunner of the modern moldboard plow, which contains a curved iron plate to lift, turn, and pulverize the soil. There were also hand tools such as hoes, rakes, and shovels, mostly or entirely made of wood. Harvesting of the grain crops was done by a hand sickle, and the cut grain and straw were tied into bundles to await threshing. Threshing was done by beating the heads of the grain with a flail on a smooth piece of ground or on a floor. The straw could then be raked off, the chaff blown or fanned away, and the grain gathered up.

Plowing and harvesting were the biggest blocks of work to be done on the manor. The farming system neatly divided the work of plowing between spring and fall. Harvesting and threshing could usually be completed during the summer before time for fall plowing. To own both a plow and the necessary ox teams to pull it was beyond the fondest dreams of the average villager. Usually, one could not hope to own more than a plow, or an ox or two, so that the complete plowing outfit had to be made up by the coöperation of the group. The other tools and implements were less costly, so that the average diligent and hardworking villager might accumulate all he would need of them.

From the social point of view, the manor was very different from a modern rural village which might be no larger. It was commonly under the control of a lord who was as frequently a church dignitary as a lay noble, although even the lord would not own the land in the modern sense. He usually received only the use of the manorial land and people from a higher lord or the king, in return for rendering military service by supplying and paying a specified number of men. Medieval society was organized on the basis of mutual obligation, and everyone received rights and privileges at the cost of assuming obligations. Just a few people on the manor were "free men," in

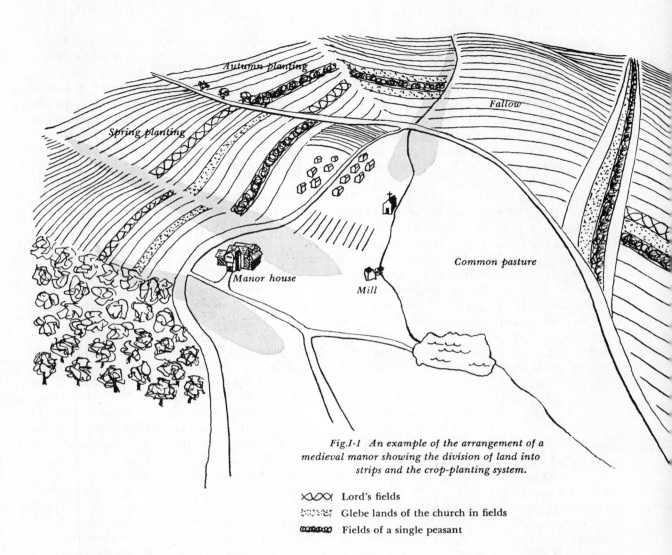

Fig.I-1 *An example of the arrangement of a medieval manor showing the division of land into strips and the crop-planting system.*

✕⟨⟨✕  Lord's fields

░░░░  Glebe lands of the church in fields

⬤⬤⬤⬤⬤⬤  Fields of a single peasant

the sense that they could leave if they wished to and could appeal to the king's court over the lord's head if he did not satisfactorily settle any dispute. Everyone else was "bound" to the manor in some way or other. Most were commonly villeins, virgaters, or serfs, in the speech of different areas, but might occupy almost the same position in the manor. They had no rights of importance except those received from the lord. They had to settle their disputes in his manorial court and grind their grain for a fee at his mill, and they could not leave without his permission. They were not true slaves, however, because they could make it very hard for the lord to violate the "custom of the manor," and in remembering and interpreting that custom the people had as much voice as the lord. The lord owed his serfs protection in time of war and justice in his court. In the early medieval period, there were a few true slaves, but not very many slaves were needed, and most of them seem to have been able to acquire ten- to thirty-acre holdings of land and to become serfs or villeins as the years passed.

Almost everyone living on the manor was engaged in one way or another in agricultural operations. The only exceptions, on the typical manor, were the miller and possibly one or two craftsmen to assist in making and repairing the tools and in building and repairing houses. The freemen worked on the land too, but since they were not bound to the lord, they could devote their time to their own land. Everyone else not only had to take care of his own holding but also was forced to devote two or three days a week to work on the lord's land. This was called "week work," and it was the most burdensome obligation which medieval people had to bear. There were, in addition, numerous smaller obligations which rested upon the people of the manor. In the spring and fall, special gifts of food had to be given to the lord. Also, when a son inherited his father's holding with the lord's consent, he had to give his best animal to the lord; when a son or daughter married, the villein had to present a gift to the lord. There were many other similar small obligations which the people disliked very much because many of them were irregular; but, in total, the burden of these "boon gifts" was much less than that of week work.

### The decline of the manor

The manor was never a perfectly self-sufficient agricultural village and political and social unit. Although transportation was poor and there was not sufficient security on the highways far from home to permit merchants to flourish, trade and the merchant class never entirely disappeared during the darkest part of the Middle Ages. There was also barter and trade between the residents of nearby manors, and some goods—salt and millstones, for example—always had to be brought in from a distance. There were always a few venturesome souls who would willingly assume the risks of smuggling valuable and scarce items through surrounding hostile territory to command high prices from the kings and nobility.

As political security increased over ever wider areas during the late centuries of the Middle Ages, merchants were always ready to take advantage of the newly found security to ply their trade. Money and the precious metals, which had been chiefly items of value to hoard, began to find use as media of exchange.

Where conditions were favorable, local market towns began to appear and grow in size. These towns were distinct from manorial villages in more than size, because they were primarily trading and not agricultural centers. As the townsmen prospered, the villeins of surrounding manors looked upon their economic success enviously. Security of livelihood on the manor seemed less attractive when freedom might offer the opportunity for real prosperity in the town. Thus, as the conditions appeared under which trade could thrive and grow, dissatisfaction with the conditions of manorial life also grew.

While the basic cause of the growth of commercial towns lay in the political stability which made obvious and practicable the advantages of manufacture and trade, their rate of growth was stimulated for a time by the disruptive effects of the Black Death, which swept western Europe in its most severe form in the years 1349 to 1351. The disease was the bubonic plague carried by parasites on rodents, and it swept over Europe like a great killing wave, leaving from a third to a half of the people in some areas dead as it moved on. The effect on normal living can scarcely be imagined. Fields were not tended, and domestic animals were not fed and ran wild; often it was hardly possible for the living to bury the dead. In the aftermath, the economic pulls that were developing before the Black Death had freer opportunity to become effective. Villeins who had been envying the prosperity of their cousins and former neighbors in the towns might now be able to leave the manors because old rules could not be enforced against them. Others who were content to remain on the manor found a powerful bargaining advantage over their lords in the scarcity of labor and could negotiate more lenient and more profitable terms for themselves. As markets for farm produce developed in the towns, such lightly obligated villeins could produce food in excess of their family needs to sell in the markets for cash. The services to the lord could often be converted into cash payments by a process called commutation, and the villein could become master of his own time.

By these and similar processes of change, the manor at the end of the Middle Ages was ceasing to be what it had long been. Those who remained on the land tended more and more to become specialized food producers, feeding not only themselves but the distant townsmen as well. The inhabitants of the thriving towns, in turn, were becoming specialized traders, as well as craftsmen, to make and sell the manufactured goods needed both by other townsmen and by rural people. Peace and security permitted specialization of work both in the country and in the towns, and created a place for the merchant who would buy, sell, and transport goods between specialized producers and consumers, wherever the latter might be found.

## Medieval towns: their business and businessmen

### The towns and feudalism

As traders clustered in suitable locations, eventually to form commercial towns, many problems arose regarding the relationship of the townsmen to the feudal system. Feudalism, with its economic basis in the manorial system of farming, anchored most people to the soil as a guarantee of a labor supply to the lords and as an assurance of a secure livelihood to the people themselves. To be able to trade, merchants had to move about the country, and to do that they had to be free of any feudal obligations that would tie them down to one place. Thus, there was a kind of inherent hostility between the merchants and the nobles who were the principal beneficiaries of most feudal obligations.

The earliest merchants were men who had escaped from their lord or who may never have been bound to a lord. The Black Death made it easier for many others to escape from serfdom and become free. Nevertheless, every lord could assert his traditional right to levy such taxes as he pleased on any merchant entering his estates. There were taxes for using the roads, for crossing the bridge, and for putting up a stall to display the merchant's wares. Such taxes might be very numerous and unpredictable in amount. Obviously, the merchants could not thrive until such obligations were reduced to manageable proportions.

In the course of time, the establishment of free towns and the gaining of rights by those towns for their citizens went a long way toward freeing tradesmen from the restrictions of feudalism. The merchants had one very powerful weapon with which to oppose the ancient rights of the nobles—they had money, that marvelous substance for which men have both literally and figuratively lost their heads. The merchants could pay the nobles for the surrender of old rights, and the lords or kings were often willing to sell out. In this way, many towns secured "charters of freedom" for themselves and their citizens. They became "isles of freedom in a sea of serfdom." But since freedom had its price, it was necessary for the townsmen to organize themselves, both for their own internal government and for the securing of funds to make a single payment to the lord in place of the many smaller taxes he had previously collected. The free, self-governing town became characteristic of the later Middle Ages.

### Trade and handicraft in the towns

Since the towns arose as commercial and industrial centers, it is hard to distinguish the organizations which townsmen created to foster and direct business from those which controlled town government. For either purpose, the guilds were the key organizations. A few of the very oldest European towns had guilds of merchants, or merchant guilds, as far back as there are records available. Apparently, the hostility and suspicion which attached to merchants because they did not "belong" in feudal society where everyone else had his own place led them to band together for mutual defense and advancement from the very earliest times. Then too, the Catholic Church developed economic doctrines which regarded selling for a profit and lending money at interest as indications of the sin of avarice in the heart. To prove that this was not necessarily a correct view of these essential commercial practices was a task which had to be undertaken collectively rather than individually. As more towns arose in the later Middle Ages, merchant guilds sprang up nearly everywhere.

The guild could negotiate with the lord or king for the relaxation of some of his feudal prerogatives which restricted the operations of merchants, and could raise the money from members to make payments to him for their new privileges. Later, as manufacture—literally making by hand—became more important, separate guilds of artisans or craftsmen arose. In the larger and more important commercial and industrial centers, these craft guilds superseded the merchant guilds in the latter part of the medieval period. A large town might have dozens of craft guilds, including those of workers in food, textiles, leather, and metals. A striking survey of their extent is this one by Professor H. S. Lucas:

Almost every large town had its barbers, surgeons, bowyers, fletchers, wainwrights, wheelwrights, saddlers, lorimers, pewterers, potters, coopers, chandlers, masons, carpenters, plasterers, thatchers, sawyers, turners, basketmakers, glaziers, leadsmiths, locksmiths, farriers, cutlers, brassbeaters, coppersmiths, goldsmiths, silversmiths, ironmongers, weavers of all kinds of cloth, fullers, dyers, spinners, carders, bleachers, croppers, tanners, furriers, cordwainers, hosiers, beltmakers, cobblers, glovers, tailors, hatters, butchers, fruiterers, grocers, tapsters, millers, oil pressers, fishmongers, brewers, bakers, soapmakers, broommakers, innkeepers, etc. The larger the town, the greater the array of crafts.[1]

### Security and social standing
### through the guilds

From a modern point of view, a guild was a rather closely knit association of small, independent businessmen. One could not get into

[1] H. S. Lucas, *Renaissance and Reformation* (New York: Harper and Row, 2nd ed., 1960) p. 15.

the guild until he had assured its members that he was well qualified as a skilled workman in the trade. Normally, entrance was secured by a boy's serving a five- to seven-year apprenticeship with a member of the guild, during which time he was supposed to learn the skills and processes of the trade. At the end of his apprenticeship, the boy, now grown to young manhood, could move to other shops in his own or nearby towns to work for masters as a trained journeyman worker. After a year or so as a journeyman, he could present a masterpiece of his own making to prove his worthiness of guild membership. If accepted, he must pay the entrance fee which would entitle him to full membership and authorize him to set up shop as a qualified merchant or craftsman in his own business.

Guild members were subjected to many regulations restricting their freedom. Hours of work and of buying and selling were established by the guild. Inspectors, or wardens as they were called, might come around at any time during business hours to examine the articles being made or sold to see that they measured up to guild standards. Inferior articles, or "false wares," might be confiscated, and if there were repeated offenses the member might be fined or put up to public ridicule in the marketplace. All such regulations seem to have been prompted by the desire of townsmen to establish themselves as honorable citizens. Trade, it must be remembered, arose in an economic system which had been almost exclusively agricultural with largely self-sufficient communities. The trader was an outsider and everyone expected him to trick and cheat them if he could. Therefore, it was essential that merchants and craftsmen prove to their fellowmen by their conduct that they were indeed honorable and trustworthy men. Since the traders were the ones who had created the towns and secured their freedom, they also controlled the town government through their guilds. Guild members chose the mayor and aldermen, and thus had complete control both of the government and the business of the town. In this way, they had all necessary power to establish the conduct of townsmen on a high plane. Some of them, such as the members of the "liveried" companies of London, became very wealthy and constituted an aristocracy of wealth, dominating the towns as completely as the traditional aristocracy dominated the rural areas.[1]

When one takes into consideration the social attitudes of the Middle Ages, the guilds were successful organizations. They did facilitate the growth of specialization of work by providing economic machinery for getting goods from the specialists who made them to the consumers who wished to use them. In this way they increased economic efficiency and made a higher standard of living possible. They made manufacture and trade honorable and prosperous callings. They gave their members security of livelihood, particularly through the mutual aid functions which they also performed, such as giving aid to a member in trouble in a strange town, and assisting the widow of a deceased member to carry on the business. They eventually overcame the moral suspicions of the Church toward selling for a profit by demonstrating that merchants and craftsmen were personally charitable men, duly faithful to the Church, who merely were seeking a proper livelihood for themselves and their families. While we have no need of guilds with all their detailed regulations in modern life, they played a valuable rôle in the development of business in the medieval era.

### Inter-regional trade in the Middle Ages

THE ITALIAN MERCHANTS. The manufacture and trade carried on in the typical town by members of the guilds were essentially local. That is, they supplied only the residents of the town itself and the surrounding countryside. The picture of medieval business, however, would not be complete without sketching in the inter-regional manufacturing and trade which also took place. Italian and German

[1] Lucas, *op. cit.*, pp. 16-17.

merchants were active in this trade over larger areas long before the English. The Italians were strategically situated between northwestern Europe and the East, which by common repute was fabulously rich. Merchants from Venice, Genoa, and Pisa carried the rich fabrics, jewelry, leather goods, spices, and perfumes of the Orient from eastern Mediterranean ports to their home towns, and thence to the fairs of northern France and Belgium. The merchants of northern Europe, as well as the kings and nobles, came to these fairs to buy their luxuries and finely manufactured goods. The Italians also became the most highly skilled craftsmen of medieval Europe— the artisans of Florence, in particular, becoming famous for their fine dyed wool cloth for ecclesiastical robes, their leather work, and their stained glass. These goods, as well as the articles obtained from the Orient by way of Arab traders, were taken by sea, river, and overland to the fairs and markets of the rest of Europe (see Fig. I-2, p. 45). The Italian merchants were the first large-scale traders of Europe, and many modern methods of business organization, finance, accounting, and commercial law originated with them.

THE HANSEATIC LEAGUE. Compared to southern Europe, Germany, England, and northern Europe represented a backward area. This region had no fine manufactures in the earlier Middle Ages and was essentially a food- and raw-material-producing area. Nevertheless, German merchants pushed trade vigorously, mostly by sea. They secured lumber from Norway; furs and beeswax from the forests of Russia; and fish, for which they developed a secret salting process, from the Baltic Sea. In England they secured wool, and sheep skins with the wool attached, which were used for warm winter clothing. Every important German town had its "hanse," very much like the merchant guild except that the merchants were overseas rather than local traders. These local hanses were organized about 1358 into the Hanseatic League, which for more than two centuries was one of the most powerful bodies in northern Europe economically, politically, and even militarily, as it undertook to protect its members. The products of northern Europe were taken to markets in western and southern Europe, where the Germans could buy in exchange the fine wares available there. The Hanseatic League had a monopoly on most phases of English foreign trade until the latter part of Queen Elizabeth's reign (1597). Internal dissension among the cities of the League as well as the rise of strong national monarchies in western Europe finally led to its decline and disappearance.

THE ENGLISH TRADING COMPANIES. While the Italian and German merchants were developing markets all over Europe, the English remained pretty largely a home-loving island people. The most important commodities which England had for export in the Middle Ages were wool, wool fells (sheep skins with the wool still attached), hides, and tin. These were called the staples, and they were the only commodities in which trading privileges were reserved to English merchants. Even in the case of the staples, the English did not take their products abroad seeking markets, but merely collected them at designated "staple" ports where foreign merchants might buy them. The first organized group of English merchants engaged in foreign trade was the Merchants of the Staple or Merchant Staplers, who bought the staple products from producers and assembled them at the staple ports for export. The Staplers were organized in guild-like fashion, although the individual merchants were men of greater wealth and of larger-scale operations than the average member of a local guild. They were essentially a conservative group who seemed to adopt the attitude, "We have the goods; if you want them, come and get them."

For some time, the Staplers remained the only English group of foreign traders with specially defined rights granted by royal charter. With the development of both general foreign trade in Europe and English manufacture, there arose the possibility of foreign trade in commodities other than the staples. Merchants who were not members of the Staplers, and thus did not have the right to trade in the monopolized staples, began to im-port and export any other goods of which they could obtain a supply and for which they could find a market. At first, these merchants were merely gathering up the neglected crumbs of foreign trade, but as time went on these crumbs became more important than the staple trade. Eventually these merchants organized themselves as the Company of Merchant Adventurers and boldly challenged the exclusive privileges of both the Merchant Staplers and the Hanseatic League. As English weavers began to turn out at least the commoner grades of woolen cloth in volume, the Adventurers sought markets for it in Germany and the Scandinavian countries where the cold climate created a demand for wool. They also began to secure wines and other luxury products in the eastern Mediterranean area and in Spain and Portugal in direct competition with the Italian merchants.

In the course of time the Adventurers were also able to secure a royal charter to legalize their position. Every important English port city had some merchants who were members of the Adventurers. They pushed trade vigorously and eventually secured such a strong position in English foreign trade that they replaced the Staplers and were able to persuade Queen Elizabeth to revoke the special privileges granted to the Hanseatic League more than two hundred years earlier. It was the Adventurers who put up much of the capital for the establishment of English colonies in America and elsewhere throughout the world. They laid the foundations for England's later leadership in world trade.

*The rise of a new business class*

All of these developments both in England and throughout Europe were of the greatest economic significance. They really represented the birth of a new kind of economic system, the system which today we call the capitalistic or free-enterprise system. Perhaps the most conspicuous of these new developments was the appearance of a class of people who made their living not by producing food or making goods for their own direct use, but by produc-

Fig.I·2 The chief centers of medieval trade in Europe. Fairs were held at those marked ■

ing or buying and selling goods to meet the needs of others. These people were economic specialists, either as food producers, craftsmen and manufacturers, or as merchants. In their new capacity, the extent of their operations came to depend on the wealth at their command to acquire a stock of goods. Particularly was this true of the foreign-trading merchants. The purpose in acquiring a stock of goods was to make a profit by selling the goods to others who desired them for use. Wealth used for such a purpose is what we define today as capital. The foreign traders, and to a lesser degree the craftsmen, small merchants, and farmers who were selling their surpluses, were becoming capitalists. Economic success came to depend less on personal skill than on the size of the capital fund available for use in the business. The degree of comfort and luxury which one might enjoy did not depend on the skill and efficiency he had in producing goods for his own use, but on the extent of the profit he could make with which to buy the goods and services of others. Of course, skill was required to direct the use of capital and the hired labor of others, but it was a new kind of skill—the skill of capitalistic business management.

The growth of a new class of capitalistic businessmen also introduced a new economic attitude into medieval thinking. The specialized producer or the merchant was more likely to regard his wares in terms of salability than in terms of usefulness to himself. Of course, salability depended pretty largely on the prospective buyer's estimate of the usefulness of the article to himself, but the relationship between salability and usefulness was not simple and direct. So far as the seller was concerned, his success in business depended wholly on the salability of his goods. This new importance of making a profit through the sale of an article made business what our modern businessmen sometimes call it—a game, in which salable goods are the counters. As in all games, it became possible, at times, to fool your opponent, in this case the customer.

Then, too, both sellers and buyers came to depend on disposing of their goods to others, or acquiring the goods they desired from others, by exchanges taking place in the market. The market, the means of bringing together buyer and seller, was started on the way to becoming what it is today, the core or center of our economic system through which nearly all modern economic processes are carried through to completion. Money (see p. 55, Chapter 2) came into its own as the indispensable medium of exchange in the marketing process. A skillful merchant who had accumulated a large capital for use in his business could purchase the products of many other persons with his profits and could enjoy the use of those goods far beyond his own personal capacity to produce goods for himself. The use of capital paved the way for the capitalists to displace the old medieval nobility in a privileged social position, a position which they could gain through the free competition of the market place and could hold only so long as they continued to be successful in business. The emphasis came to be on individual initiative and achievement rather than on hereditary social status.

As capital made possible an increased scale of business operations and introduced new economic attitudes, it also created a need for new business practices and methods. Both the Italian and the German merchants found that the granting of credit was often necessary to facilitate sales. At the great commercial fairs of France and Belgium, money changers who did a thriving business in exchanging the currencies of different countries also became money lenders by buying up promissory notes (i.e., promises to pay given by the merchants) for later collection. Some Italian merchants became practically exclusively bankers and operated branches in the leading ports of the Mediterranean and Atlantic coasts of Europe. They not only handled monetary exchanges between countries in settlement for shipments of goods, but also provided short-term loans to aid other merchants in their business.

New bookkeeping and accounting methods were also needed when business success depended upon making a satisfactory return on the capital invested in the business. The earliest beginnings of accounting go back to the Arab traders of the Mediterranean basin in the early centuries of the Christian era, and even further back into antiquity. The Italians adopted the methods handed down to them by the Phoenicians, Romans, and Arabs and developed them for their own use. All the basic concepts of modern accounting, such as double entry, assets and liabilities, and profit and loss, made their appearance and eventually spread throughout European trading nations. It is important to reëmphasize that the use of accounting in business reflected a new attitude. When production came to be for sale in the market, and when the extent of business operations came to be limited by the capital available, it was necessary to have accurate and complete financial statements by which to measure the success of the business enterprise. Financial records had been unnecessary when production was for the use of the producer only.

Although all of these business developments occurred within the medieval period, they were really nonmedieval in the sense that they did not fit readily into a society in which nearly everyone had his own supposedly permanent position in a system of classes established by law and tradition. The fact that these developments in business did take place forecast the end of the medieval social and economic system. None the less, we must always remember that these developments appear as important ones to us today because our knowledge of later history enables us to see that they were just the beginnings of the later flowering of a capitalistic, free-enterprise economy. No one at the time could have foreseen how far the development of capitalism would go. Even in the later centuries of the medieval era (the fourteenth and fifteenth centuries), the old, self-sufficient, agricultural economy still reigned supreme for the great majority of the people. There were commercial and industrial cities and towns, but they were relatively few, and only a small percentage of the people lived in them. There were merchants, bankers, and specialized craftsmen producing for sale, but they represented only a small part of the total population. For most of the people, economic and social life went on pretty much as it had for centuries. There were cracks in the dike, however, and in the course of time widespread forces became operative to overthrow the medieval pattern of social and economic life, and to extend that manner of living and making a living which we call modern.

## The medieval era becomes outmoded

### *The missionary spirit of Christianity*

Perhaps the most difficult questions in the history of mankind are those relating to the causes for the rise and decline of the great world civilizations. Why should not medieval civilization have continued? The civilizations of China and India, for example, did not undergo particularly great changes from the late centuries of our Middle Ages onward into modern times. What were the forces which disrupted medieval life in Europe and started the building of modern western civilization?

No one can give a fully satisfactory answer to that question, but an important part of the answer lies in the missionary spirit of Christianity. Jesus had taught that every human being had a soul which was of as much value in the sight of God as that of any other human being. He had also commanded his followers to go throughout the world preaching the Gospel. These ideas were basically hostile both to the isolationism and to the class distinctions of medieval life. They created a new interest in the peoples of distant lands and a desire to bring them within the Christian fold. The Crusades, which occurred intermittently from the eleventh to the thirteenth centuries, were an early and rather crude manifestation of the Christian missionary impulse. The Crusaders brought fire and the sword rather than brotherly love, to the Holy Land, but the crusading impulse, none the less, reflected a concern on the part of European people over the condition of a distant land. In later centuries, Christian missionaries followed close on the heels of explorers throughout the world, and at times even preceded them into unexplored lands.

Both the Crusades and the later missionary activity served to widen the intellectual horizons of Europeans. They discovered that other people had many kinds of goods and many arts and crafts completely unknown in Europe. The Arabs had beautiful rugs and tapestries, fine steel for blades, superb horses, and many foods which Europeans came to like and desire for themselves. The knowledge of and desire for all of these things paved the way for inter-regional trade, and increased European dissatisfaction with the old way of life.

### Growing intellectual curiosity

Accompanying the increase of Christian missionary zeal, there was also a growth of general intellectual curiosity about many of the aspects of life. Roger Bacon in the thirteenth century, and others like him in later centuries, applied the careful inquiring point of view to studies of physical phenomena which later gave rise to modern science. Writers and artists were beginning to show a concern for the life and experiences of the common people and to depict them in their works. The spoken languages of the common people came to be used far more frequently in written works than the Latin which had been almost universally used in medieval writings. It has been said that the prevailing attitude of the Middle Ages was otherworldly; that is, one was expected to accept all the troubles and toil of the earthly life with resignation as preparation for a happier life in the next world. In contrast to this older view, the newer one, which has been called "Humanism," was not necessarily less concerned with the future life, but it was more concerned with the environment, the experiences, and the conditions of the present life. Voices began to be raised against the political and religious institutions of medieval life. The followers of John Ball, who was a promoter of the Peasant's Revolt in England in the fourteenth century, quoted the searching lines:

> When Adam delved and Eve span,
> Who was then the gentleman?

All of these evidences of a new spirit in the life of the later Middle Ages, when taken together, can be interpreted as a phenomenon which helped to pave the way for the Renaissance, the Reformation, and the growth of popular control over government marking the beginning of the modern era.

### The growth of trade and travel

The later centuries of the Middle Ages were marked by an increase of trade and travel both locally and inter-regionally. The Crusades were, without doubt, the greatest single factor in getting the people in western Europe out of the simple routine of daily life in their home communities and showing them something of the ways of strange and distant peoples. Those who returned from the Crusades brought stories which aroused the interest and curiosity of their neighbors and prepared them to accept eagerly the accounts of the individual travelers who came later. With knowledge of other peoples came a desire for the kinds of goods they had and used. Medieval life, before it had undergone significant change, was the product of isolation. It was largely self-sufficient economically, politically, and socially because people could not have lived any other way. Both local and distant travel tended to break down this isolationism. Trade, following in the wake of travel, brought about the development of new and larger-scale business enterprises, in which capital became an important factor. These developments provided powerful and growing forces to disrupt medieval life.

### The centralization of political power

The Middle Ages followed upon a period of several centuries before and after the time of Christ in which there had been widespread shifting and migration of Europe's people. Historians and geographers offer various explanations of these movements; their result, which is of more concern to us, was the overthrow of previously existing social and political systems and something pretty close to general chaos. The early centuries of the medieval period (the sixth to tenth centuries) can be considered centuries of transition, for they were occupied with the working out of a new political and social alignment to meet the existing conditions. The product of that new alignment was medieval civilization. It was not achieved easily. The period was marked by a number of futile attempts to recreate a centralized political authority, such as the Roman Empire had provided, and by incessant warring among nobles, each seeking to establish and extend his own domain.

As the realigning process tapered off to a conclusion, the sources of political power became more certain and stable. Also, by expeditious marriages and by successful wars, some of the kings and nobles were able to extend the areas under their political control to considerable size by medieval standards. The lesser nobles lost out, but the existence of wider areas with uniform laws and administration made it possible for merchants and travelers to move about with greater safety. It was a gradual process whereby the number of rulers was constantly declining. At first the lesser nobles were replaced by the greater, who in turn gave place to strong kings. In England, the Wars of the Roses ending in 1485 resulted in the establishment of the Tudor line of monarchs, who had more complete political control over the nobles than had ever been held by English kings before them. Similar results were achieved at about the same time or soon after in France, Spain, and Russia. Out of wider political unity came a new awareness of national identity. The people of Europe came to think of themselves for the first time as belonging to nations. This new political feeling and the new centralization of political power in the hands of national monarchs caused and marked the end of the Middle Ages.

## The medieval view of its own economic life

### The economic system

There is little evidence that medieval people were either aware of the special characteristics of their economic system or much concerned about it. At least this is true of the older agricultural aspects of their life. The privileges and duties of both lords and their servile dependents were so well worked out in the experience of centuries that the system seemed almost to operate itself. There was no evident concern about the efficiency of the system because no one knew how it could be improved. Equally, there was little concern about the justice of the social and economic positions of the classes in medieval society, for again these positions seemed to be dictated by the necessity of making a living for all.

The growth of trade began to bring an end to such self-satisfaction, as we have seen. As guilds and other trading organizations arose, it was of course necessary for them to adapt themselves to the dominant social and economic views appropriate to the agrarian mode of life. But the adaptation could not, in the nature of the case, be a perfect one, and problems arose. We have already noted that the ultimate reaction to these problem situations was the development of a new kind of economic system. But it should also be noted that awareness of such problems began to bring a broader awareness of the economic system as a whole. In other words, concern over immediate problems opened the door to the development of a theory about how the economic system should work.

### Medieval economic thought

This development of a general theory, however, did not go very far by modern standards. The fact that the Christian church was the most powerful social institution to carry over from Roman to medieval times had resulted in making theological and moral questions those which gave tone to the intellectual life of the age. The stable agrarian life had not presented problems to blend into the other preoccupations of the mind of the time. So it is not surprising that the economic problems appearing with a trading economy should be viewed primarily as moral and ethical ones.

The principal problem was that of a "just price." Concern over price policy could be traced back to ancient Greek thinkers, but, among medieval thinkers, the theory was brought to its fullest development by Thomas Aquinas in the thirteenth century.[1] In his view, the "just price" could not be a precise one but should take account of various factors affecting buyers and sellers. It should take account of cost, apparently to such sellers as guild members. But it might be adjusted somewhat to reflect the need of the buyer and the value he would derive from making the purchase. Guild policies on prices were evidently based on such ethical doctrines of justice in the exchange of goods.

The medieval economic doctrine which has probably attracted more attention than any other was the prohibition of usury or interest on a loan of a sum of money. Certain exceptions to this prohibition were allowed, but the basic thought was that money was not productive. Therefore, to charge usury for a loan which produced nothing was to charge something for nothing. This was an obvious violation of justice. As a modern reader examines what Aquinas and other medieval writers say on this subject, it is clear that they had no understanding that money could be used as capital in business and thus be a factor of production.

These doctrines of just price and usury scarcely add up to a general theory of the operation of an economic system. But they do bring economic problems within the scope of general ideas—justice, in this case—of the kind which a general economic theory would require. Whether or not we would agree with

*what* medieval thinkers concluded about their problems, we can at least see that changing conditions coming with the growth of trade led them to lift economic problems from the level of routine habit and to place them within the framework of broad ideas of social welfare. Very few persons except the great philosophers of ancient Greece had taken this step before.

Acknowledging the great contribution to economic thought made by medieval scholars, we still find ourselves forced to make inferences in order to get even partial answers to the kinds of questions we would like to have answered. The plain fact of the matter seems to be that medieval people had little notion that economic societies, including their own, were constantly undergoing processes of development and growth. They knew of change, but they seem not to have realized that change is continuous and due to discoverable causes and not haphazard. This lack of awareness of change has existed almost down to our own time. Thus we can only do our best to draw our own conclusions as to the nature of the processes of economic development in the periods which we shall examine.

Within these limitations, we can say that the medieval economic system was, in origin, a response to the need for personal security. Production of food, clothing, and shelter had to be on a local basis because security on a broader scale was not possible at first. In later centuries, greater security permitted the rise of trade and economic specialization.

The way medieval people thought about their system, as we have already seen, seems to have been determined by the slowness of change and thus the dominance of custom, and by the great influence of the church. But since they seem to have had little notion of a continuing process of economic development, it is obvious that they could have had little idea of directing their efforts toward achieving the growth of the economic system, particularly in directions which might be chosen in advance as desirable. This is one of the most noticeable differences between the medieval and modern economic systems.

[1] Aquinas' principal economic writings are contained in his *Summa Theologica*.

## A modern view
## of medieval economic life

### A land and labor system

From the standpoint of the way in which the people of the Middle Ages produced the things they needed to live, theirs was a system of economy based upon land and labor. Capital as we know it today, in the form of inventories, machinery, buildings, fixtures, and the necessary cash to carry on large-scale operations, did not enter into medieval production to an important degree. The factors which determined the limits of production were land and labor. Since the average person, then as now, had only his own efforts and abilities with which to make a living, it was the limits of what one person could achieve which held down the standard of living. Those who fared better than the average were the favored few who could either enjoy the entire fruits of their own productive efforts without having to share them with someone higher up (freemen), or those still more favored who were in a position to command the labor of others on land which they controlled (the nobility).

### Distribution
### of wealth by social classes

In the medieval economic system, the ordinary people constituted the labor supply and the lords controlled the land. Production would not have been possible without some sort of working arrangement between these groups to divide up the product to which both had contributed. This distribution was achieved by the social and political system in which the people came to be divided into classes with quite rigid rights and duties. The ordinary villein or serf was obligated to spend part of his time each week working on the lord's land in return for the use of a specified amount of land to which he could devote the remainder of his time, producing for his own use. The social position of the villein became rigidly crystallized by custom, and from his social position his share in the distribution of wealth was determined.

The nobles, as landlords, had rights to the land equally fixed by custom. The amount of land a lord might retain for his own use was usually many times greater than that available to a villein. He would not have been able to farm it and to derive the produce from it without the labor of many other people. But the lord was not merely a landlord in the modern sense. The villeins were bound to the soil, and were required to spend two or three days a week working on their lord's land. Thus, the farm produce available to the lord was far greater in quantity than that which the villeins could produce for themselves, for his class status enabled him to control both the land and a labor supply. It is evident that the economic basis of wealth in the Middle Ages was in sharp contrast to that of the modern world, where wealth and a large income are primarily derived from the ownership or control of capital used in business.

### The low level of technical efficiency

No society can have wealth to enjoy unless it both knows how and has the means to produce it. Medieval people had land and labor, but they did not know how to use them effectively, by modern standards. Nor did they know how to build the power machines which have made modern industry so highly productive. Even the gain in the productive efficiency of hand manufacture which comes from specialization and trade was not possible until the later Middle Ages because of the dangers of travel. In the overall view, the level of productive or technical efficiency in the Middle Ages was low. This low level was partly due to a lack of knowledge of processes, materials, and tools which were not developed until later centuries; partly, it was due to political and social conditions. Only after they had been corrected would the proper environment exist for rapid technical development.

## Strengths and weaknesses of the medieval economy

The medieval economy had great strengths and eventually developed great weaknesses. On the credit side must be placed the fact that in an era of turmoil, when the peoples of Europe were shifting about in search of a more secure livelihood, and when, in consequence, centralized government broke down and could not be replaced, the pattern of economic and social life which we now call medieval brought a gradually increasing order out of chaos. Religion, government, social life, and making a living were woven together into a pattern that gave a measure of unity and integration to human existence which has been the envy of many persons since. Life was hard and not always safe, hours of work were long, pleasures were few, and luxuries were almost nonexistent, but medieval people enjoyed economic and emotional security. With his spiritual and intellectual life entrusted to the parish priest, his political functions managed by his lord except for the small matters coming before the manorial court, and his work laid out before him by the custom of the manor and the supervision of the lord's steward, there was little to worry or concern medieval man.

The entries on the other side of the ledger made up a longer list as the centuries rolled by. Most of them centered around one prevailing theme, the inflexibility and unprogressiveness of medieval life. The very virtue of the Middle Ages—the feeling of security which was extended to all of life's interests and to all classes of society—became in time the source of undermining influences. Like many valuable things long possessed, security began to lose its charm. Security was preserved by the retention of traditional ways, but initiative and imagination were thereby restricted. Political security of life and economic security of livelihood began to permit travel and the gaining of new ideas. More and more people could indulge in the luxury of exploring the possibilities latent in these ideas, of finding out about distant places and unaccustomed ways of living and thinking. New ways of governing and making a living appeared to be both possible and desirable. New thoughts in relation to religion, philosophy, science, and life in general became appealing. The old ways with their security seemed to be barriers to a brighter, more lively, and more interesting future. After ten centuries, the imagination of western Europe was captured by the lure of new ways of thinking and living, despite the risks involved, and people turned away from the old to embark on a search for the new.

## FOR FURTHER READING

Boissonade, P. *Life and Work in Medieval Europe.* New York: Alfred A. Knopf, Inc., 1927.

Clapham, J. H., and others (eds.). *The Cambridge Economic History.* Cambridge, England: The Cambridge University Press, 1952. Best historical background.

Clough, Shepard B., and Cole, Charles W. *Economic History of Europe.* 3rd ed. Boston: D. C. Heath & Co., 1952. Part I.

Day, Clive. *Economic Development in Europe.* New York: The Macmillan Co., 1942. Chapters 1—5.

Dietz, Frederick C. *An Economic History of England.* New York: Henry Holt & Co., 1942.

Heaton, Herbert. *Economic History of Europe.* Rev. ed. New York: Harper & Brothers, 1948. Chapters 4—10.

Knight, Melvin K. *Economic History of Europe to the End of the Middle Ages.* Boston: Houghton Mifflin Co., 1926. Chapters 4, 5, and 6.

Lipson, Ephraim. *Economic History of England.* London: Black (A. & C.) Ltd., 1959.

Roberts, David W. *Outline of the Economic History of England.* New York: Longmans, Green & Co., Inc., 1931. Part I, Chapters 1—3.

Sellery, G. C., and Krey, A. C. *Medieval Foundations of Western Civilization.* New York: Harper & Brothers, 1929.

Soltau, Roger H. *An Outline of European Economic Development.* New York: Longmans, Green & Co., Inc., 1935. Chapter 3.

Stephenson, Carl. *Medieval History.* Rev. ed. New York: Harper & Brothers, 1943.

Thompson, James W. *Economic and Social History of the Middle Ages, 300-1300.* New York: Century Co., 1928.

Tickner, Frederick W. *Social and Industrial History of England.* New York: Longmans, Green & Co., Inc., 1929. Chapters 1—12.

Usher, Abbott Payson. *Introduction to the Industrial History of England.* Boston: Houghton Mifflin Co., 1920. Chapters 3—7.

# Chapter 2:

# Widening the economic horizon

The events of the past do not come in packages carrying convenient labels. If they did, the period around the year 1500 would mark as convenient a point as any to wrap up the events of the preceding thousand years and put on them the label "The Middle Ages." From that time on, the forces which had already begun the undermining of the medieval way of life made the conditions of living so different in the countries of western Europe that the modern age had arrived.

### The Commercial Revolution

*The end of an old era and*

*the beginning of a new*

Many elements entered into the new mode of life. The Nordic and Germanic migrations from northern toward southern Europe had ceased during the course of the Middle Ages

and the quarrels over boundaries and other matters among medieval nobles had also gradually subsided. Peace and order were restored to western Europe, where they had been difficult to find for quite a long time after the fall of the Roman Empire. It became safe to travel outside of one's home territory, and merchants and peddlers were not long in taking advantage of the opportunity. The Crusades gave incentive to the growth of trade through knowledge of other commodities and other peoples which they brought to many thousands of medieval people. When it became possible to travel, medieval people did travel, and when they traveled they began to carry merchandise from place to place.

Once trade and travel had really begun, the intense localism or provincialism of the Middle Ages began to break down. People began to know about their more distant neighbors. Increased knowledge of the way other peoples lived made many discontented with their own lives. In particular, resentment increased toward feudalism, that peculiar mixture of partial freedom and slavery which was characteristic of the Middle Ages. The great merchants, and the smaller ones who followed their lead, found it desirable to throw their support behind the rising national monarchs. The king was able to provide more certain conditions within his realm, and the merchants had found that stability of law and government was an important prerequisite to their own profit. Along with the weakening of feudalism and its detailed regimentation of the daily affairs of life there came a strengthening of the ideal of personal freedom. This new ideal was a rather weak growth in most respects until the seventeenth and eighteenth centuries, but the very increase of the national sovereign's absolute power left more of life's more personal concerns to the control of the individual. In time, political absolutism and individual liberty became opponents to the death, but, for the sixteenth century and immediately after, the rise of absolute political power in the hands of the king created a sense of greater personal freedom among the people through the overthrow of feudalism's intimate regimentation of personal life.

Accompanying these political and social changes were similar changes in religion, philosophy, literature, and art. The selfish ambition of monarchs served as a principal battering ram to breach the ramparts of feudal society and government, but once the breach was made, many other elements of a new way of life could enter and widen it. The Catholic Church had been an integral part of the regimented life of the Middle Ages. As national monarchs grew toward absolute power, the Church was able to retain, for a time, much of its traditional function and prestige. But eventually a clash came. The ambitious monarch could not accept without challenge the traditional authority of the Church. The Protestant Reformation was a great turning point in world history because increasingly powerful political and economic interests came to the support of the religious reformers. From the point of view of economic and social history, the Reformation was part of the attack on the Middle Ages. Where it was successful,

the results were greater power for the political monarch and greater freedom for the growth of business.

The Reformation upset not only the power of the Church over medieval life but the very foundations of that life as well. Many areas experienced a drastic redistribution of land as Church property was confiscated and taken over by nobles or by the towns. Nearly a third of England is estimated to have changed hands during the Reformation period, the sixteenth century. The change in ownership often provided new stimulus to the expansion of commercial activities and strengthened the power of the towns. Of equal importance was the more favorable attitude of Protestantism toward commercial activities. Whereas the Catholic Church had frowned upon most business activity and had taught that the service of God was the only really acceptable occupation, the new religions actually extolled commercial activity and thereby provided substantial moral impetus for its active pursuit. Calvinism in particular regarded industrious devotion to one's business and the achievement of worldly success as outward signs of inner goodness.

The use of money and credit had grown during the later Middle Ages. The Romans had brought coined money into western Europe in the first centuries of the Christian era. The Norsemen also had their own coined money, for they too were traders as well as raiders. Medieval people had a small amount of this money, but, since trade was practically impossible, there was nothing to do but hoard it. However, as buying and selling began to increase, the money was brought out into circulation and put to use. The Italian and German Hanseatic merchants depended heavily on money as a measure of value and as a medium of exchange. They also tried to increase the money supply through mining operations in central Europe and through exchange with Arab merchants. The desire for additional supplies of money was one of the important causes of the search for a direct route to the Orient. If no money had been available, trade would have been hampered very seriously. As it was, an acute shortage of money soon developed as trade expanded. In the leading centers of trade, money changers, who made exchanges among the many different kinds of currencies, and money lenders became essential parts of the developing market economy.

A further mark of the arrival of a new era in human history was the new outlook on life at least partially prepared for by these political, economic, and religious developments. It is entirely understandable that the predominant position of the Church in medieval society should have given first ranking to those acts and duties which were regarded as creating an assurance of heavenly rewards in the life after death. The new political and economic developments carried with them the possibility of substantial achievements on earth. The new outlook did not ignore the duty of every individual to keep his feet on the path that would lead to salvation, but it found a new enthusiasm for those acts and interests which offered rewards in power, prestige, and pleasure in the present life. This new outlook has been called "humanism" or the "humanist movement." It was as much cause as consequence of the Reformation and the rise of political nationalism. It was by nature a rather diffuse movement, for the only core it possessed was the wide range of human interests and concerns. For a time, humanism found its inspiration in the literary and philosophic writings of ancient Greece and Rome, where strictly religious ideas were less dominant than they had been in medieval Europe. Eventually, the new humanist spirit outgrew the ancient classics and found an outlet in a concern for the ordinary man in his ordinary daily affairs. Books and plays were written in the language of everyday speech. Pictures were painted of ordinary people engaged in their regular activities. Eventually, too, that interest in the world, its forces, materials, and life to which we now give the name science was powerfully stimulated by the earthly orientation of the humanist movement. All in all, a new spirit was growing. There was more concern to discover and en-

large the best in life, not only for the great and learned, but also for the humble.

### Nature of the Commercial Revolution

Commerce rather than agriculture or manufacturing experienced the primary stimulus from the changes of this new era. Political stability at home and political expansion abroad created unparalleled opportunities for the rising commercial classes of the western European nations. Commerce did in fact expand enormously, particularly in the sixteenth and early seventeenth centuries. New forms of organization were required to carry on business on the new scale. New attitudes toward profit-making became appropriate and were needed to make business expansion possible. All of these economic developments which followed upon political unification and expansion constituted a real Commercial Revolution, and in time agriculture and industry were brought within the orbit of expanding economic change.

From the economic point of view, the Commercial Revolution represented an expansion of specialization and a decline of economic self-sufficiency. More people were satisfying more of their wants by buying what they needed rather than by going to work to produce the needed goods. To realize the full effect of that simple statement, each of us would have to imagine how our own lives would be if we suddenly had to get everything we wanted for our own use by our own direct, productive effort. Specialization had begun with local trade, but with the discoveries of new trade routes it reached worldwide proportions. People in Europe were producing goods which they were not to use themselves, but which were sent to America or Asia for the use of the natives of those continents. In return, however, European traders brought back to Europe goods produced in America or the Orient which European people were able to use without having to perform the work of producing them. Europeans developed a way of living in which they depended upon Americans and Asians to produce part of what they needed, and, of course, the opposite was also true. Because they used their own special skills or the advantages of their own special climate and resources, each side gained through such trade. The result was an *extension of geographic specialization and an intercontinental division of labor.*

A number of other characteristics of the Commercial Revolution are closely related to the growth of specialization. Because there was less dependence upon one's self, there was more dependence upon the market through which the products of other people were secured. In fact, where family and community self-sufficiency characterized the Middle Ages, *dependence upon the market* became characteristic of the new era. Through the market, groups of producers not only in one's own country but throughout the world were brought together. The market became, like the hub of a wheel, the center at which all the criss-crossing lines of trade met and the modern economy became an interdependent market economy in contrast to the self-sufficient medieval economy. Now, the actions of the Chinese and Javanese and American Indians came to have a vital effect on the lives of Europeans. Producers wished to receive a high price for the products of their work; buyers wished to get the product as cheaply as possible. Thus the two parties had opposing interests so far as price was concerned, but a common interest in the gain in productive efficiency which specialization made possible. The pull of economic interest, after the Commercial Revolution, went beyond the limits of the family, as in the self-sufficient economy, to far larger and more scattered groups. Members of these groups did not know each other or speak the same language. Yet through trade and the market they discovered common economic interests.

### Results of the Commercial Revolution

There can be no doubt that the Commercial Revolution did more to bring a free and happy life to people in western Europe than anything that had happened up to that time.

Life offered more material goods, a wider range of ideas and experiences to add interest and stimulate thinking, and a feeling that the best was yet to be. Individuals were under less restraint in their personal conduct than they had been in the Middle Ages, and they also experienced pride in the power and prestige of their respective nations. Many limitations of life in the Middle Ages, which must have seemed irremovable, had been removed. The barriers were down, horizons were widened, and the people responded with enthusiasm.

Expanding trade and increased economic specialization brought with them a higher level of productivity. When more goods were produced, there were more goods to be enjoyed by someone. Many people, in fact the majority, remained at a poverty level, but many who participated in the growing trade were much better off than they had ever been before. The Commercial Revolution created a class of "new rich" merchants who eventually became wealthier than the medieval landlords. The higher standard of living for more people showed itself in a demand for better food, better clothing, better houses, and better home furnishings. A long list of new foods from America and the East gradually came into use, including sugar, citrus fruits, coffee, tea, chocolate, potatoes, and maize (American corn). Cotton and the older textile fibers became more abundant, and made possible more and better clothing. Glass windows, wood floors, and tile roofs became more common in houses. As houses were made drier and more weather-tight, wall paper, carpets, and finely made furniture began to come into use. Even those who did not share directly in these new comforts for living could at least know that they existed and could hope that some day they might be secured.

From the political point of view, the Commercial Revolution contributed to the consolidation of the strong centralized governments which through discovery and conquest became also the seats of world empire. Of course the tendency toward centralization of political power in the later Middle Ages had originally contributed to the development of trade, but it is equally true that trade, once started, became a powerful factor in the further development of the strong centralized governments. In England, for example, the Tudors were supported by the growing merchant class. The king imposed his own financial burdens on the merchants, but these were much preferred to the many taxes and regulations imposed on them by the lords or by the towns. At least throughout the sixteenth century, the merchants contributed to the strengthening of royal power by their relatively willing acceptance of the obligation of providing financial aid to the crown. Later, they changed their minds.

The commercial changes which we have been describing could not occur without disturbing the relationship between the various parts of the economy as they had existed in the Middle Ages. Medieval agriculture had not been designed to meet the needs of a market economy, but some food supplies were available for sale or barter to others not living on the land. Thus a trading class could get started, and as goods were brought in from elsewhere, the time saved in buying goods instead of producing them for one's self permitted more land to be farmed and larger supplies of food to be produced. The growth of a market and a trading class tended to convert agriculture from a self-sufficient to a commercial basis. Economic specialization, beginning in trade and commerce, thus soon included agriculture within its scope.

The methods of manufacturing goods were similarly changed by the Commercial Revolution. In the strictly self-sufficient economy, goods needed by the family were produced by the members of the family for their own use. This condition was never universal, for the members of any one family never had all the skills necessary to make all the things they needed. The making of such things as cloth, shoes, candles, and soap was done at home, but the making of knives and hardware, and the grinding of grain and other operations were done by specialists even in the earlier portion of the Middle Ages. The growth of trade very soon created the problem of a source of supply of goods to be traded, and led to the development of a great deal more specialized manufacture. The methods of making goods, from the technical point of view, did not change, since the work was still done by hand and depended on personal skill. It was noted in Chapter 1 that in medieval towns craft guilds often replaced the earlier merchant guilds as specialized manufacture increased. The Commercial Revolution carried the process further. Many more craft guilds were organized, but, more important, in those types of production in which the growth of demand was greatest, there was a tendency for a new method of industrial organization to spring up. This was the domestic or putting-out system, in which the work was again done in the home as in the earlier Middle Ages, except that now it was done for merchant-capitalists who expected to sell the product in distant markets (see p. 66 ff., Chapter 3, for a full discussion of this).

The growth and expansion of commerce also created new business problems which required the adaptation of business organization to meet the new conditions and new needs. No activity that could properly be called business took place in a self-sufficient economy. The local trade and handicraft manufacture of the later Middle Ages existed with individual businessmen operating their own businesses as proprietors, except that they had to belong to and abide by the rules of their guild. This proprietorship form of business organization, however, could not meet the needs of the world trade which the Commercial Revolution brought. Foreign trade had to be conducted as a big business if it was to be carried on at all. Capital in large quantities became a necessity to provide ships, cargoes, and warehouse facilities. Various forms of partnership and finally the joint stock company (see below p. 70 ff.) were developed to provide both the necessary capital for large-scale ventures and also skilled management. In addition, new forms of business were needed. Banks assumed a new importance, and insurance companies and stock exchanges were created to provide special services to other businesses. All of these business developments had as a common characteristic the greater importance of capital. In fact, they indicate that the capitalistic economic system had arrived.

## The new commercial empires

A new geographic basis of European life was brought about by the Commercial Revolution as the result of a long series of discoveries beginning in the last half of the fifteenth century. These discoveries were made possible by the perfecting of the magnetic compass, the astrolabe for determining latitude from the stars, the lateen or triangular sail with which it was possible to sail against the wind by tacking from side to side, and larger and stronger hulls capable of withstanding the winds and waves of the oceans. The ultimate cause of these discoveries was an attitude of mind not unrelated to those discussed in a preceding section, that is, an interest in man and the world in which he found himself. The discoveries themselves, however, and their effects, were so definite, so concrete, and so dramatic that hardly anyone could miss knowing about them. Thus, in a very real sense, the discoveries became the hallmark or badge of the new era.

The effects of the discoveries were many and varied. One of the most general was the shifting of the trade routes of the world from the land, rivers, and shores of inland seas to the trackless open oceans. New channels of trade brought new bases of wealth and power. The Germans and Italians, who had been the great traders of Europe in the later centuries of the Middle Ages, found themselves left behind. In their places, merchants from the Atlantic seaboard countries rose to prominence.

### Portugal

The honor of beginning the important series of geographical discoveries belongs to Portugal. Prince Henry the Navigator became interested in exploration while governor of a southern province of Portugal and after fighting in Morocco. Repeated explorations were made upon his initiative beginning with the year 1418. The Cape Verde Islands were discovered in the Atlantic Ocean, and the coast of Africa was gradually explored. After Henry's death in 1460, explorations were continued, and in 1486 Bartholomew Diaz reached and rounded the Cape of Good Hope at the southern tip of Africa.

The motives of these explorations are not clear. Curiosity and love of the sea may have influenced Prince Henry in addition to his zeal to spread Christianity to the East. However, after the Spanish had made new discoveries from the voyages of Columbus, national rivalry and desire for new trade routes to the east began to provide more powerful incentives for still further exploration. The Portuguese outfitted a small fleet under Vasco da Gama which set out for the Far East around the Cape of Good Hope in 1497. After many delays and discouragements he reached Calicut on the western coast of India more than a year after leaving Portugal. Da Gama became a national hero, and many fleets were soon following the route that he had opened up. Portugal's early beginning in exploration had finally yielded results which, though less spectacular than those of Spain, were of far greater commercial importance.

In the decades following da Gama's discovery, the Portuguese were obliged to fight to protect the gains they had made. The Venetians stirred up Moslem traders to attack the merchants from Portugal, who were cutting them out of their established trade. First under Francisco d'Almeida and then under Affonso d'Albuquerque, the Portuguese fought back and were in general successful in establishing themselves in possession of the rich spice trade. They established fortified posts down the west coast of Africa, and from the Red Sea to India, in the East Indies islands, and eventually up to China and Japan. Spices were secured from the posts at Java, Sumatra, Amboina, and Malacca. Other goods were obtained from the posts in India and at Macao in China. Meanwhile, in 1500 Pedro Alvárez Cabral, sailing in a southwesterly direction from Portugal for the Indies, sighted land and claimed it for his country. This was Brazil, whose discovery also placed Portugal in a very strong position in the trade that was to develop with the new world.

It seems strange at first thought that with such a favorable start Portugal did not become one of the great and wealthy nations of the modern world. It has been said that the Portuguese were indifferent merchants, that, having secured the Oriental products so much in demand in Europe, they adopted a "come and get it" attitude. On the other hand, they have been defended as diligent workers and businessmen. The truth probably is that the demands of a great maritime empire which Portuguese explorations created were too great for such a small country to meet. Portugal did not have the commercial organization needed to distribute throughout Europe the goods secured in the East. She also lacked capital to finance properly and to expand the trade which practically fell into her lap. Her population was insufficient to provide crews for her merchant fleets and administrators and settlers for her overseas empire, while she maintained and even expanded her operations at home. Then, too, political domination by Spain at a very inopportune time (1580-1640) permitted this commercial rival to gain advantages in world trade which Portugal could never overcome and also gave to the Dutch an opportunity to seize parts of Portugal's empire.

## Spain

Spain was unified in 1479 under Ferdinand and Isabella. The Mohammedan Moors, who had invaded and occupied large parts of Spain from their north African stronghold, were driven out, and wealth began to flow in from the New World after the discoveries of Columbus. Until these events occurred, Spain had been largely an agricultural country and was not prepared to be placed in the forefront of the new developments which were to make Europe the center of world empire.

Because of Portugal's priority in explorations southward along the African coast, the

Spanish were induced to try out the proposal of Christopher Columbus that he sail directly westward to reach the Indies. Although the suggestion had the backing of eminent geographers, it was still a highly uncertain venture. When Columbus did sight land in October 1492, following a month's voyage, it was long thought that this land mass might be some remote part of India and it was not realized that a new hemisphere had been discovered. This uncertainty persisted despite the successful demonstration that the world was round, when in 1522 the crew which had set sail in 1519 with Ferdinand Magellan in the ship *Victoria* returned to Europe. As a result of the original claims made by Columbus and Magellan, which were expanded and developed by a number of other explorers in the sixteenth century, Spain became the proud possessor of the American continents from what is now the southern part of the United States southward, with the exception only of Brazil, recognized as Portuguese from Cabral's discovery.

Although Portugal was more successful than any other power in achieving a satisfactory route for trade to the East, Spain was most successful in securing the precious metals which all the explorers also hoped to find. In Mexico, Central America, and Peru, the Spaniards found that the natives had silver and gold, which the Spaniards acquired from them by trickery and bloodshed if necessary. These precious metals and other valuable loot from America began to flow back to Spain in great quantities. The yearly addition to the supply of gold increased substantially in the later sixteenth century and the supply of silver was multiplied seven or eight times.

In time, these precious metals proved to have a deceptive value to the Spanish. The earliest effect of exploration upon the Spanish economic system was stimulating. Providing crews and equipping expeditions made employment active. Supplying goods for trade with native populations in the newly discovered areas gave a boost to both production and distribution. Soon, however, the inflow of silver and gold from America into a Spanish economy that was not capable of any very

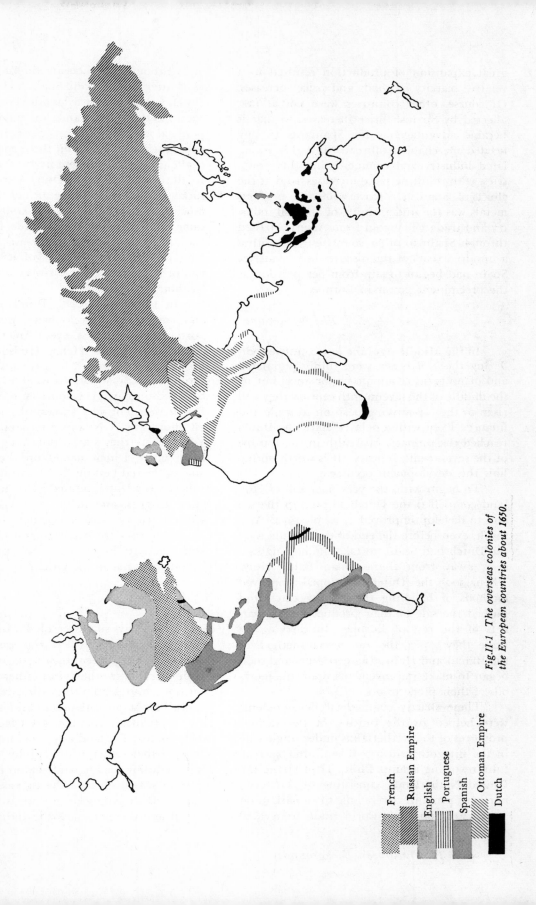

Fig.II-1  The overseas colonies of
the European countries about 1650.

French

Russian Empire

English

Portuguese

Spanish

Ottoman Empire

Dutch

great expansion of production resulted in a relative scarcity of goods and price increases. Of course, other countries were not at first affected by Spanish price increases, so that it became advantageous for Spaniards to buy needed merchandise abroad. But this stimulated industry and commerce in other countries, with resulting price increases, so that the effect of Spanish discovery of the precious metals was the undermining of Spanish industry and trade. The gold from America passed through Spain to other countries, and within a hundred years of the discoveries in America Spain had begun to slip from her position as the preëminent power in Europe.

### The Netherlands

In the Middle Ages the low countries bordering the North Sea were thinly populated and of no great economic importance, but by the middle of the seventeenth century they had risen to the top-ranking position in trade and finance. Even with a delayed start, the Dutch reached the pinnacle of wealth in the Europe of the seventeenth century. It is worth noting how this development occurred.

To begin with, the very poor soil of Holland compelled the Dutch to take to the sea and to develop improved types of ships. As a result, even before the end of the Middle Ages the Dutch had begun to take the herring fisheries away from the German Baltic cities. Then, too, the Dutch developed improved methods of handling the herring catch and pushed the sale of their product in the markets of the rest of Europe. In carrying on trade, they copied the commercial methods of the Italian and Hanseatic merchants and soon began to make improvements upon the methods of their predecessors.

These strictly commercial developments were helped by the uniting of the various provinces of the Netherlands under single rule in the fifteenth century. Then, after successfully revolting against Philip II of Spain, the United Netherlands, consisting of the seven northern provinces, were able to embark upon a policy of building world trade from 1580 on. Although they began almost a hundred years after Portugal and Spain had started, the Dutch boldly set out to use the Portuguese sea routes to the Spice Islands, to establish trading posts along the African coast in order to strengthen their grasp on those routes, and to challenge the Portuguese in the Spice Islands. In all these ventures the Dutch were in general successful, and soon the wealth of the East was flowing to Amsterdam. The island of Java became the center of Dutch trade in the East Indies. It contributed to the wealth of Holland for centuries, because of its spices and two other commodities discovered much later —rubber and oil.

In the New World, Dutch exploration and commercial development were less important. Nevertheless, every American school child knows about Henry Hudson's voyages up the river to which he gave his name and through Arctic waters to what is now called the Hudson Bay. As colonizers in America the Dutch were not very successful. Their greatest effort was at New Amsterdam, later New York, where they stayed only long enough to leave many Dutch names on the map and among the old families. In Central and South America the Dutch pirated Spanish and Portuguese cargoes, and made several attempts to seize territory and to establish colonies. These efforts were partly successful, although Dutch activity in America never compared in extent with that in the Orient.

### England

The early successes of Portuguese and Spanish explorations left the English with only two alternatives if they were going to gain trade or colonies—they must either seek different trade routes from those already discovered or else fight it out with other nations, especially the Portuguese, for the privilege of using their routes. England at first adopted the former of these alternatives. John Cabot, an Italian sailing for England, set out in 1497 and 1498 in search of a northwest passage to the Indies. He was blocked by ice in the Arctic Ocean and did not reach the Indies. He did discover Labrador, however, and the valuable fisheries off the Newfoundland coast, and gave England a claim to the north Atlantic coast of North America. Attempts to reach the Indies by a northeast passage around the northern tip of Norway were likewise fruitless.

After these failures, it was apparent that trade with the East was going to have to be carried on by way of the routes used by the Portuguese and Spanish. John Hawkins and later Francis Drake led expeditions which attacked and robbed Spanish and Portuguese ships and brought their treasure to England. These "sea dogs," as they came to be called, also entered Spanish and Portuguese trading areas and secured products there which were transported back to Europe and sold at tremendous profit. Their bold depredations gave the English such a start in the oriental trade that the sub-continent of India eventually became English territory. In 1600 Queen Elizabeth granted a charter to the English East India Company which continued for more than 250 years the rich trade made possible originally by such men as Hawkins and Drake.

In the New World the English seemed to be edged out of the most promising territories. There was no wealth which could be easily picked up and carted off from the coastal areas of eastern North America. There were soil and climate suitable for farming, but little from which traders could derive immediate advantage. In this respect, the apparent misfortune of the English turned out to be their ultimate good fortune. Since there was little wealth to be quickly and easily gathered, the English had to come to America as settlers and developers rather than as conquerors and exploiters. In later centuries, when conflict between the imperial powers began, the English nearly always had the advantage of greater numbers. English territory in America was solidly held by farmers who had cleared the land and would not give it up easily. Thus, in conflicts with the Dutch, Spanish, and French, the English were almost always able to hold their own and expand at the expense of others. In the long run, the less romantic occupations of farming, fishing, lumbering, and mining produced greater wealth than that which came from the gold, jewels, and spices of the Orient.

*France*

At the beginning of the period of exploration, France would probably have been rated as the wealthiest and most powerful nation of Europe. It is probable that her wealth and power at home kept her from experiencing the enthusiasm for exploration felt by the other countries. She did support exploration of the coasts of America from early in the sixteenth century, and claimed territory ranging from South America and the West Indies islands to the St. Lawrence Valley in Canada. She also laid claim to certain Pacific islands and to territory in Asia. None of her explorations were followed up with vigor, and none contributed greatly to her wealth or power at home. Some settlements were made, particularly in the Canadian province of Quebec, where the continuation of the French language and French customs are about all that remain today of a once sizable French territory.

## The impact of new forces upon agriculture

*Instability of the manorial system*

The medieval manor, although it had never been the absolutely unchanging institution that some former historians pictured, none the less changed relatively little and slowly until the end of the Middle Ages approached. As a system of field cultivation it did not fit special conditions such as those in hilly regions suitable only for pasturing animals. The manor had never existed in pure form in areas where, for one reason or another, field cultivation was impossible. In addition, many if not most manors had some land which, because of its character as swamp, or forest, or rocky hillside, had never been included in the regular manorial lands. Such lands, as well as occasional pieces of tillable field, might be enclosed for the sole use of the lord or perhaps of a freeman residing in the manor. At its best, the real manor never corresponded perfectly with the theoretical manor.

As the decades and centuries passed, the changes that had gradually crept into manorial life tended to accumulate. Lords or freemen who had separated their lands from the common open fields and enclosed them with hedges started a trend which continued on by inheritance, generation after generation. By the year 1500 hardly a manor in western Europe failed to have some land enclosed. The system of personal obligations of villeins to their lords had undergone even greater changes. Through the years, it was the lack of personal freedom which irked medieval people more than the open-field farming system. The Black Death, the Crusades, and other great social upheavals of the Middle Ages nearly always resulted in greater freedom for more people. The growth of a market for farm products gave many villeins a cash income which they could use to substitute for personal service duties. By 1500, serfdom as a half-free legal status was practically nonexistent in England and some other parts of western Europe.

### Commercial farming and enclosure

Human beings have never seemed to be very contented with restrictions upon their personal freedom, such as those included in some aspects of serfdom, but reaction against the open-field farming system which was associated with serfdom came only when an economic change occurred which made another system more advantageous. The change which reacted against the manorial farming system was the coming of economic specialization and trade. This change had begun to reach significant proportions in the late centuries of the Middle Ages. During these centuries, the farm system had begun to change in response to the pressure of a developing commerce. The Commercial Revolution, with its rapid development of trade, inevitably had even more sweeping effects upon agriculture. In fact, the agricultural developments of the sixteenth and seventeenth centuries were so rapid and so far reaching that they began a movement which by the eighteenth century had become an Agricultural Revolution. In agriculture as in commerce, many ideas and methods of the present day stem from these early modern centuries.

Agricultural developments went through several phases under the pressure of expanding commerce. In the later Middle Ages, in the vicinity of growing commercial towns, farming also became commercial in the sense that it was carried on for a cash market away from the agricultural village. With the change to commercial production of farm crops went a change to free labor. Serfs and villeins commuted their service obligation to cash rents, which they paid by the sale of surplus produce from their lands. Lords were less closely tied to their lands when commutation had taken place extensively, and at the same time they found more need of cash to buy the new goods available. Many of them leased out their own larger acreage to freemen, stewards, or anyone capable of undertaking such large projects. Speaking literally, a farmer is one who makes a periodic payment for the use of the land. In this sense, the lessees of former manorial estates became the first true farmers of modern times. They were large-scale commercial farm operators who depended on the hiring of former serfs for wages to get their work done.

Enclosure was usually the external symbol that something was happening to the old manorial system, although change did not invariably show up in this way. Large-scale lessees would usually consolidate the scattered strips of a lord for greater efficiency, if the lord had not done so before making the lease. Villeins who had escaped personal service by commutation usually consolidated their holdings also, but did not always withdraw them from the open fields and enclose them. So long as better farming was the purpose, consolidated tracts might either be enclosed or left in the open fields as the free tenants preferred. Enclosure of this type had been going on at a gradually increasing rate for several centuries before 1500. It created no social disturbance of note, but did bring about more intensive and efficient production of food stuffs. Because of growing supplies of farm produce, more and more people could shift to commercial and industrial work in the towns.

## Enclosure for greater wool production

When the full impact of the Commercial Revolution began to be felt toward the middle of the sixteenth century, the demand for wool for the growing cloth trade was intensified, especially in England. In the Middle Ages, England had exported raw wool to Flanders, where Flemish weavers had become the most skilled clothmakers of northern Europe. Gradually the English cloth industry had been improved and expanded so that England was becoming an exporter of wool cloth. The Commercial Revolution increased the market for English cloth in Europe, in the Orient, and eventually in the New World. From an exporter of raw wool, England became an importer of wool from Spain. The price of wool was high, and adequate and steady supplies were not available.

This condition in the wool market made it advantageous to produce wool wherever that was possible. Landowners, especially those with larger holdings, began to enclose their lands to convert them into pasture. Holders of smaller plots in manorial villages were edged out. Nor was paid employment on the same land possible, because one or two men with dogs could take care of many acres of land devoted to pasturing sheep. In England great

social unrest and suffering resulted. Popular writings and Parliamentary records during the sixteenth century were full of protests that the humble and peaceful sheep had become a ferocious beast eating up men, women, and children. Parliament did make efforts to check enclosure, for it was often illegal, carried out in disregard of the rights of small holders. Landlords profited by it, however, and the supply of wool was increased.

There is no evidence that this sixteenth-century enclosure for wool production was extensive enough to cut food supplies available to the towns. Productive efficiency in agriculture was increasing during the sixteenth century primarily because of more careful and more intensive cultivation. By the latter half of the seventeenth century, however, the growth of towns, trade, and industry had reached such a point that larger and more dependable food supplies became necessary. The attention of farmers began to be turned to the problem of improving agriculture and increasing output. New crops, new methods, and new devices were tried. The ultimate results of these efforts were not felt until the eighteenth century. Enclosure continued quietly and unobtrusively after the furor over it in the mid-sixteenth century died down. In the seventeenth and later centuries, enclosure was almost always to improve farming methods, and did not result in displacing so many people as the sixteenth-century enclosure for keeping sheep. The coming of a new way of living and making a living in the towns had the effect of completely revolutionizing rural life as well.

## FOR FURTHER READING

Cave, R. C., and Coulson, H. H. *A Source Book for Medieval Economic History*. New York: Bruce Publishing Co., 1936.

Day, Clive. *Economic Development in Europe*. New York: The Macmillan Co., 1942. Chapters 1—4.

Hammond, John L., and Hammond, Barbara. *The Rise of Modern Industry*. 5th rev. ed. New York: Harcourt, Brace & Co., 1937. Chapters 1—4.

Roberts, David W. *Outline of the Economic History of England*. New York: Longmans, Green & Co., Inc., 1931. Part II, Chapters 1—3.

Salzman, Louis F. *English Industries in the Middle Ages*. Oxford: Clarendon Press, 1923.

———— *English Trade in the Middle Ages*. Oxford: Clarendon Press, 1931.

Soltau, Roger H. *An Outline of European Economic Development*. New York: Longmans, Green & Co., Inc., 1935. Chapters 4 and 5.

Tickner, Frederick W. *Social and Industrial History of England*. New York: Longmans, Green & Co., Inc., 1929. Chapters 16—27 and 32.

Tawney, R. H. *Religion and the Rise of Capitalism*. Mentor (NAL). Paperback.

Weber, Max. *The Protestant Ethic and the Spirit of Capitalism*. Scribner, 1958. Paperback.

# Chapter 3: The birth of capitalism

**T**he ultimate effect of commercial expansion was the Industrial Revolution, which began in the eighteenth century and which is still going ahead vigorously in the twentieth. The earliest local trade could take place between persons who had by some good fortune produced more wheat, or wool, or cloth than they immediately needed. Trade was an exchange of surplus production. Obviously such a haphazard condition could not last long, and specialized producers of various kinds soon appeared. The additional changes in methods of manufacturing which were brought on by the Commercial Revolution were the result of further specialization of industry to meet the demands of a market which had now grown to national and worldwide proportions.

### The putting-out system

From about 1300 onward, the manufacture of many kinds of goods came to be concentrated more and more in the hands of specialized craftsmen organized in craft guilds in the towns. In a few places in England, but more particularly in Flanders, where commerce was more highly developed, there was a tendency for enterprising manufacturers to expand the scale of their operations beyond that customary for members of the guilds. One such person was Thomas Blanket of Bristol, who in 1339 is recorded as having employed weavers and other workers in his house to manufacture a type of soft woolen cloth which still bears his name. In the previous century Jehan Boinebroke of Douai in Flanders was accused of supplying material to small masters to be worked up for him in their own houses. History might not have recorded the deeds of Blanket and Boinebroke except that, because of these activities, they were regarded as violators of guild rules, for which they were called to account.

The rapid expansion of trade which culminated in the Commercial Revolution gave a strong incentive to enterprising producers to expand operations either by bringing more workers together in their own shops or by supplying material to be worked up at home. Both methods of increasing output were used. The latter became much more common and gave its name to the system of industrial organization which superseded the guilds in those branches of industry most affected by the expansion of trade. The new system came to be called the "putting-out" system, or the "domestic" system, because its most distinctive feature was the putting-out of raw material by entrepreneurs to be worked on in the worker's home. The domestic system must not be confused with the older and more primitive system of household industry which existed in the self-sufficient economy. Although in each case the work was done in the home, under the domestic or putting-out system the product was not for the worker's family use but for sale to someone else.

The putting-out system developed in a number of industries and in various countries and regions, and came to have quite widely different characteristics. It is difficult to outline a set of characteristics of the putting-out system which would have been true of every industry in every country. There were underlying common causes for the development of the system, such as the growth of market demand, but the response to these causal forces was distinctive in each industry and area (compare Fig. III-1, p. 69, with Fig. III-2, p. 71). Perhaps we can get the most complete picture of it, and at the same time remain true to fact, by describing a specific industry in a specific country where it was fully developed. For this purpose the woolen cloth industry as it developed in the western counties of England will serve very well. In most ways, this industry represents about as advanced a development of the putting-out system as could be found.

### The cloth industry of
### western England: a case study

The king-pin of the woolen industry in western England was the *clothier*. He was not a manufacturer in the medieval sense of a hand worker, nor was he a manufacturer in our present-day sense as the owner or manager of a factory or industrial plant. He was an employer and the director of industrial operations, but he left to the workers the carrying out of the work in detail. How and when they did their work was largely a matter of their own discretion. The clothier was interested only in the quality and quantity of the finished work. Basically, he was a trader or merchant who purchased raw material and provided it to successive craftsmen until the finished product was ready for sale. Then he sold it, usually to a wholesale merchant of some type, through whom it ultimately reached the final consumer.

The essentially commercial character of the clothier's operations becomes even clearer as we examine them in detail. The raw wool was secured either from the large wool growers direct, or from wool merchants or staplers who had purchased it from the growers. Larger clothiers probably more often made direct purchases, whereas the ones with less capital, who were forced to operate on a smaller scale, would patronize the stapler. The sorting, carding, and spinning of the wool into yarn ready for weaving were most commonly done in the clothier's shop by hired labor, since the operations were rather simple. That was not always true of spinning, however, and it was often performed as extra labor by housewives or single women who thereby acquired the name of spinsters. Where the work was done at home, the spinners would come to the clothier's shop in the village and secure the wool, which they would bring back later in the form of yarn. Weavers were almost always home workers under the putting-out system, and they too would come to the clothier's shop for yarn which they would weave into cloth and return for payment. If there were additional operations to be performed to get the cloth ready for sale, they were done by men variously called "cloth dressers," "shearmen," or other localized names. Finishing was usually shop rather than home work and might be done by the cloth dressers in their own shops as work put out to them by the clothiers, or it might be done by hired labor in the clothier's own establishment. At the end of the long series of operations, the finished cloth was sold by the clothier to agents or factors who were centered in special cloth markets in the larger seaport towns. Of these markets, Blackwell Hall in London was most famous. The factors in turn sold the cloth to exporting merchants such as the Merchant Adventurers or to wholesale dealers in the larger cities.

### The putting-out system and the craft guilds

The putting-out system arose primarily as a response to a growing demand for goods to supply new and expanding markets. It is interesting to speculate whether or not the guilds might have met this growing demand had they been willing to relax some of their rules to permit members to hire more apprentices and journeymen and to engage in business on a larger scale. Some clothiers and other merchant-capitalists who put out work to be done at home had been guild members. In general, though, the guilds did not understand the full meaning of the great flood of demand that faced them. Instead of adjusting to and profiting by this flood, they permitted themselves to be drowned by it. Because the guilds controlled the town governments, they forced the expanded production of goods to come from outside the jurisdiction of the towns. The rural villages were the only other places available. The putting-out system was an adaptation to expanding demand, on the one hand, and guild monopoly in the towns, on the other hand. In both cases, it was taken for granted that the work would be done by skilled workers, for no machines to replace hand workers had yet been invented. The putting-out system was a realistic adjustment to existing conditions and served as a very important step in the development of the modern industrial system.

### How the putting-out system changed the economy

The most important economic aspect of the putting-out system was that it represented the first large-scale application of capital to manufacturing as a means of securing increased production. The clothiers and corresponding individuals in other industries were the first industrial capitalists of the modern era in the sense that they assumed the risks attendant upon supplying capital for large-scale business enterprise.

Other aspects of the putting-out system were closely related to the fact that it was a system for larger-scale production which was achieved by putting more people to work by using more capital to finance them. *Production now was for wholesale selling.* In the self-sufficient economy, the producer and consumer would be either the same person or members of the same family. In the guild system, the producer was specialized, but he sold at retail to consumers who were his neighbors or at least lived in the same community. Under the putting-out system, additional middlemen, as wholesale merchants, or brokers, or merchant-capitalists (clothiers, for example), came between the producer and the final consumer. None of these middlemen changed the product or added to its physical properties in any way, but because they were available to handle raw material, partially processed goods, and the finished product, the entire manufacturing process could be carried out on a larger scale and with greater efficiency. The coming of the use of capital and a more elaborate marketing organization increased the specialization of work, added to overall efficiency, and set the stage for the development of the elaborate marketing and distribution institutions of today.

*In the putting-out system, the worker became more or less dependent upon his capitalist employer.* If trade was brisk, the worker might make a pretty good living; if it was poor, he was in a bad way because he might have no other resources to earn a livelihood. The un-

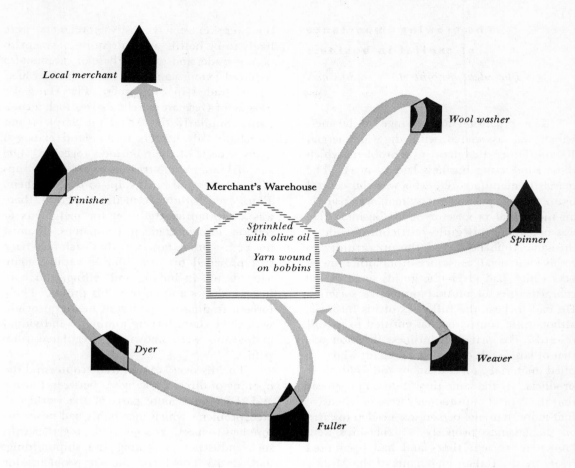

**Fig. III-1** *The operation of the putting-out system in the Florentine wool industry about 1400. The processes start at top right where the wool is sent to be washed.*

employed could be stranded badly, and create a serious social and economic problem. The problem was less serious than it might have been, simply because the workers under the putting-out system often remained part-time farmers. Where the system was most fully developed, the worker was completely dependent upon the capitalist employer, but commonly, the home workers had at least a little land.

*A class of people was created who secured their living from the investment of their capital.* The great majority of mankind always has lived and still lives from labor or personal service of some kind, physical or mental. In the Middle Ages, the lords and kings lived from the income of their lands. Many people in all but communistic countries still derive income from land or real property. Only when capital became important in economically productive activity was the opportunity created for the appearance of a class of people who obtained their principal income from capital investment. It was the Commercial Revolution which created this opportunity. The putting-out system brought into existence a class of merchant-capitalists in manufacturing while the growth of large-scale commerce, which was the driving force behind the development of the putting-out system, itself created a larger and more conspicuous class of commercial capitalists.

## The growing importance
## of capital in business

### The idea of joint stock in business

The expansion and change in business which was associated with the Commercial Revolution created many new problems which those conducting business had to meet. The merchant-manufacturer, who was the central figure of the putting-out system, was usually an individual proprietor of his business. He was not under any guild restrictions, while at the same time he lacked the opportunity to receive financial assistance from other members which had given the guilds some of the characteristics of mutual protective societies. He had to bear the full risks of his business, although, of course, he was entitled to its full rewards. His principal business function was that of large-scale capitalist merchant who supplied materials to craftsmen and sold their products. At the same time it does not appear that the capital requirements were so extensive that more than one person was needed to carry on the business properly. Partnerships were known in ancient times and had been used freely by the Italian merchants of the Middle Ages. They do not seem to have been used commonly by the merchant manufacturers. Rather, the putting-out system was characteristically based upon a fuller development of the legal rights and duties as well as the economic functions of the merchant manufacturer as a sole proprietor.

While sole proprietorship was the best kind of arrangement for the merchant manufacturer, men engaged solely in commerce and trade found that their requirements for capital were so great as to make some other form of business organization more desirable. The earliest modifications of the guild system came in those types of business in which the capital requirements began to exceed what individual businessmen could meet. Well back in the medieval period, foreign trade provided conditions that were too severe for very many individual merchants. Ships and warehouse facili-

ties were extremely costly, foreigners were likely to be hostile and to require payment to permit trade, and the purchase of cargoes also required extensive means. In such cases merchants traded in companies. The Hanseatic League of German merchants was such a company. Similarly the Merchant Staplers and Merchant Adventurers in England managed many aspects of their business together. The city of Venice made treaties to aid her groups of merchants and built ships to lease to them. Thus, even within the medieval period, there was a substantial tradition for merchants to conduct foreign trade in companies. It must not be forgotten, however, that each merchant still provided his own trading capital, managed its use in buying and selling, and bore his own losses and enjoyed his profits. These foreign trading companies of medieval origin with their characteristic joining of individual and group were known as "regulated companies."

The discovery of new trade routes and the opening of direct trade by sea between Europe and the most remote parts of the world created problems which merchants had never before had to meet. Foreign trade, together with such industries as mining and shipbuilding, had always posed the biggest problems for businessmen. The opening of all-water trade routes brought the European merchant into direct contact with markets and sources of supply all over the world. Arabian and Italian middlemen were eliminated, at least in part, by the north European trader. The geographical discoveries created enormous trading opportunities, but there were relatively few merchants who were able single-handedly to profit from them.

These new needs of business, especially in foreign trade, led to the development of the joint-stock company. There had been some ancient and medieval precedent for the idea of joint-stock in business, but it had not been direct. In most respects, the joint-stock company (see Fig. III-3, p. 73) and its later development, the corporation, are entirely modern business institutions which have arisen to meet modern business needs.

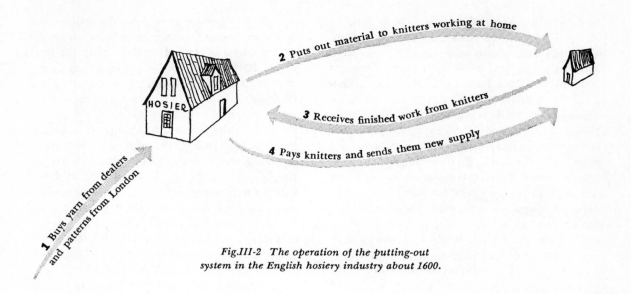

*Fig.III-2  The operation of the putting-out
system in the English hosiery industry about 1600.*

In the figure: **1** Buys yarn from dealers and patterns from London · **2** Puts out material to knitters working at home · **3** Receives finished work from knitters · **4** Pays knitters and sends them new supply · HOSIER

### The advantages of joint-stock organization

There were three primary needs of large-scale business enterprises which could be met better by a joint-stock arrangement than by any other. In the first place, *the new trading opportunities involved more risk of loss than had commonly existed before in business.* There were, to be sure, promises of greater profits too, but the hazard of being wiped out financially by loss of ships at sea, by piracy, or by any one of a number of other dangers, was always present. Few merchants who could raise the necessary capital to outfit a ship for a long ocean voyage could stand the danger of losing all they had. The older regulated companies had provided certain facilities to members and had made treaties to protect them from piracy or unjust seizure of their goods, but had not provided any way to protect them from the great inherent dangers of their trade. The dangers of the new overseas trade were greater than ever before and there had to be some way to reduce the risk to the merchants or they could not afford to undertake it in spite of the promise of large profits.

The joint-stock company met the need in large part by splitting up the capital invested in a trading venture. No one merchant needed to buy any larger part of the stock than he wished. The total risk of a venture could be shared by a large number of stock-holders. The owner of shares of stock in a present-day corporation is ordinarily not responsible for the debts of the corporation except to the full amount of the par value of his stock. This is called "limited liability." The early joint-stock company did not have the added advantage of limited liability of stockholders, but, even without it, the risk to shareholders could be divided up in a way not possible in any other form of business organization existing then.

Another need of the new foreign trade was *capital in far larger amounts than any previous type of business had required.* There were some individual merchants, of course, who by themselves had enough capital to undertake distant trading ventures. They might even be willing to risk it in the fabulously rich trade to the Indies. But there were not enough such individuals to meet the needs of the new trade adequately. In this respect, also, joint-stock met the need. When a person did not have to finance an expedition himself but merely had a chance to buy as large a share in one as he wished and could afford, there were thousands of Europeans who were anxious to participate in the new business opportunities. The joint-stock company, like a small meshed fish net, caught the financial minnows as well as the whales. By selling shares of stock, one could gather together the savings of persons of moderate means into sums large enough to finance the greatest business ventures. In fact, the joint-stock idea had not been developed very far until some businesses became so large that they could not have grown up or survived except on the joint-stock basis. Of course, banks and other financial institutions which arose and expanded as part of the Commercial Revolution, also played a part in gathering together the capital sums needed for large-scale business. There can be little doubt, however, that the joint-stock idea was of greater importance from the very beginning of modern business in raising the amounts of capital needed for the successive steps in the expansion of business.

When the ownership of business had become scattered among numerous stockholders, there arose the *problem of providing adequate and unified management*. This problem was partly a result of the rise of joint stock, but it was promptly solved by the further development of the same idea. Management policies of the joint-stock company quickly came to be determined by the majority vote of the shares. By this method, a unity and centralization of policy was achieved which was entirely impossible, for example, in the regulated company. As soon as the machinery was developed to provide for a single policy for a large group of stockholders, it became possible to seek out and employ the most skilled managers available. These managers did not have to be owners; they did have to have ability, and perhaps experience, in meeting the problems of the kind of business which they were to manage. On the other hand, the owners did not themselves have to know how to run the business, so long as they were capable of selecting competent managers. The joint-stock company did two things so far as management is

concerned: it made management a professional function, and it separated ownership from the performance of the job of managing the business. Both were very important, and this characteristic of the joint-stock company aided in drawing in capital from all sources to meet the growing needs of business.

The oldest joint-stock company was chartered in 1555 in England to trade with Russia. It was given a trade monopoly by both the English king and the Russian czar and was called the Muscovy Company. It struggled for more than a century to build up trade against the competition of the Dutch, and in the face of the uncertain conditions within Russia. It did not have great success and finally gave up its charter and reverted to a regulated company. The greatest and most successful joint-stock companies were the East India Companies chartered in England in 1600 and in Holland in 1602. Both companies had been preceded by looser organizations of merchants. The Dutch company was a permanent joint-stock from the beginning, whereas the English company was organized for single voyages, or short periods of years, until 1657 when the stock was made permanent. Both companies prospered and became the wealthiest of their day. The English East India Company continued until 1858 to rule and until 1833 to have exclusive trading rights in India. The Hudson's Bay Company, chartered in 1670, is still in existence and doing business in Canada, although it surrendered its exclusive trading rights in 1869. It is the only chartered company which has continued from the period of the Commercial Revolution until the present.

*The growth of*

*banking and credit institutions*

As the Italians were the first merchants of Europe in early modern times, so also were they the first bankers. Banking has always been closely associated with commerce, for only in the exchange economy is there any very important need of money, credit, and the

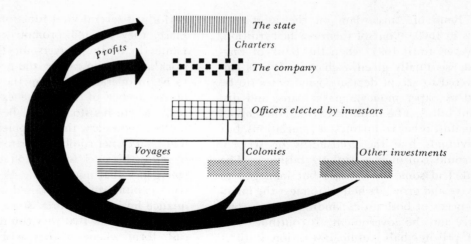

Fig.III-3 *The organization of a joint-stock company.*

services of banking. In the later Middle Ages Italians had set up branch banking facilities in all the major commercial centers of Europe. The center of the London financial district today is Lombard Street, named for the Italians from Lombardy who used to frequent it. When the Commercial Revolution created greater needs for money, credit, and exchange, the foundation had already been laid by the Italians.

The first development of banking in England seems to have been by scriveners, who were public clerks available to write out contracts or any documents required to be in writing. Persons with excess funds available for lending apparently paid a commission to the scriveners for arranging a loan. In the first half of the seventeenth century, foreign commerce was expanding under the leadership of the new joint-stock companies, and the medieval prohibition of usury, or lending at interest, was weakening in its effect, due to the recognition that a loan of money could be productive. With these favoring circumstances, money-lending by scriveners grew greatly and often became their principal business.

After the middle of the sixteenth century, the scriveners had keen and successful competition in money-lending from goldsmiths. As the name suggests, the goldsmiths were origi-

nally craftsmen in gold and the precious metals. Their business required that they have strong rooms to protect their precious metals from thieves. As money came into wider use with the growth of trade and the increase in European money supplies from American discoveries, the goldsmiths were often asked to keep sums of money in their strong rooms for a fee. As they began increasingly to perform this deposit function, they found that their deposits were never called for all at the same time. They could make loans and receive interest on the deposit balances left with them. This was especially possible as they also began to issue "Goldsmith's Notes" as receipts for money left with them, which began to circulate as paper money without the gold or silver ever being drawn out. They also began to honor drafts drawn against deposits left with them. Thus, the goldsmiths were carrying on the banking functions of accepting deposits, making loans, honoring checks, and issuing notes.

The successes of the goldsmiths in turn invited further competition. Since the joint-stock idea was being used widely during the seventeenth century, especially in the latter half, it was perhaps natural that a number of projects for a joint-stock bank should be proposed in England, following the founding of the Bank of Amsterdam on the joint-stock basis in 1609. None of them reached fruition, however, until 1694, when the Bank of England was finally given a charter. It was empowered to accept deposits, issue notes (to be used as paper money), make loans, and discount bills.[1] The Bank was given a monopoly as against other companies or associations, but individuals like the goldsmiths or scriveners could continue a banking business. The Bank had some hard times but managed to survive and grow. It helped to meet the financial needs of both an expanding foreign commerce and the government. It continued as a half private, half public institution until it was taken over as an entirely governmental agency in 1946.

### Stock exchanges, insurance, and speculation

The earliest exchanges in Europe were bourses, or financial markets, rather than stock exchanges strictly speaking. The first was founded at Antwerp in 1531. It was a "continuous fair" at which dealings took place in commodities, bills of exchange, and insurance. Other bourses sprang up later in the chief cities of western Europe. As joint-stock companies increased in number, especially after 1600, dealings in their shares began to take place at the bourses. Finally, true stock exchanges were founded, beginning with the London Stock Exchange chartered in 1698.

By providing a single central market place where buyers and sellers of shares of stock could come together, these stock exchanges

performed several vital functions. In the first place, they assisted promoters of new companies in finding buyers for their shares of stock and thus in raising the necessary capital to begin operations. From the point of view of the owner of stock, the exchange was a place where his stock could be sold on short notice if necessary, though sometimes at a loss. Thus, an owner could liquidate his investment by selling his stock for cash to meet any sudden emergency that might arise. Because this was true, capital could be raised more easily to finance business ventures, since the owners of the capital knew that they could get it back in cash form whenever they wished by selling their shares of stock on the exchange. The prices prevailing on the stock exchanges very quickly came to be regarded as barometers of the business outlook, just as they are today. When conditions seemed to be favorable for large earnings on shares of stock, potential investors would be willing to pay good prices for them. When the outlook was not good, selling slowed down and prices dropped. Speculative judgment of buyers and sellers could come into play on the early stock exchanges as it does today.

Accompanying the Commercial Revolution and its many new types of commercial activity were increased dangers to life and property. In the Middle Ages movable property had little place in the economic system. As soon as it became possible to make a living by buying and selling goods of various kinds, property other than land assumed a new importance and its ownership was subject to new risks. Methods of insuring the safety of ships and their cargoes were among the first to develop. Some of these early insurance methods were closely tied up with money lending. Often, insurers of either property or lives were little more than systematic or scientific gamblers. These insurance activities were usually located in the great commercial centers, often at the bourses. Fire insurance is said to have received its greatest initial impetus from the disastrous effects of the great London fire which occurred in 1666. The growth of all types of insurance played an important part

[1] To discount a bill means to buy a promissory note at less than its full ultimate value. The discount is due to the fact that the buyer of the note has to put up cash now, and then has to wait until the note comes due before he is reimbursed. The amount of the discount depends upon the rate of interest. To discount a bill is the same thing as lending money at interest. The only difference is that in discounting the interest is deducted in advance from the face value of the note as a discount. Like lending, discounting is a banking function.

in the development of capitalistic business in the modern world.

It is not surprising that the occasional enormous profits of commercial ventures together with the numerous new financial institutions developed during the sixteenth and seventeenth centuries should result in an orgy of speculative excesses which eventually brought loss to almost everyone involved. Holland, France, and England each had a mania of its own particular kind. The Dutch lost their heads (and sometimes their shirts) over the supposed value of tulip bulbs, single bulbs of rare varieties selling for the equivalent of thousands of present-day dollars. The crash came in 1637. France's boom and "bust" came over John Law's promotion of the shares of the Mississippi Company which was organized to develop Louisiana. Even the government trembled when the speculative "Mississippi Bubble" collapsed in 1720. England's speculative fever embraced a great number of joint-stock promotions, but centered in the South Sea Company, which was chartered in 1711. The boom in the shares of the English company closely paralleled that of the French company, and it also collapsed in 1720. The result of these speculations was to put a heavy damper on the use of the joint-stock idea in business for more than a century. In England Parliament in 1720 passed the "Bubble Act," which severely restricted the issuance of company charters.

### The new rôle of capital

In its simplest aspect as a factor of production, capital is anything whose value comes not from any direct ability to satisfy a want, but from its usefulness in helping to produce something which is capable of satisfying a want. Capital is a tool. The use of capital can take place only when the technical knowledge of how to use tools to help with work has been developed. The increased use of capital brought about by the Commercial Revolution may not seem to rest on a knowledge of how to make increased use of tools and equipment in producing. Yet it really did. Technical knowl-

edge relates not only to tools, machines, and equipment but also to ways of doing work. Specialization by crafts and specialization by regions or areas made trade between the specialists possible and necessary. It increased productive efficiency. The knowledge of the economic advantage of specialization and trade is as genuinely technical knowledge as the knowledge of the way to produce more cloth by using a power-driven loom. It is, therefore, also correct to say that the wealth represented by stocks of goods for sale, by warehouses and shops, by banks with money to lend to help merchants with their business, and by carts or ships for hauling merchandise is capital, for each of these things is useful for carrying on a more productive type of economic activity. The particular forms of capital needed for commercial activity are often called "mercantile" or "commercial" capital. Capital in the form of money, or capital used in facilitating monetary transactions, is called "financial" capital. These forms of capital are to be contrasted with "industrial" capital, used to assist in the direct production of goods, which did not increase in amount to any important degree until the effects of the Industrial Revolution were felt in the eighteenth and nineteenth centuries.

A larger scale of operation invariably accompanies the increased use of capital. Each of these factors is part cause and part effect of the other. If one has the knowledge of ways to use tools to help him in his work, he can produce more. Thus, historically capital has always increased the scale of operations whenever it has come into use. On the other hand, there are some jobs so big and so hard to do, that if you do not know how to use tools or equipment of some kind to help you they simply cannot be done. Commercial voyages to the Far East were jobs of this kind. Direct trade with the Orient involved as large and strong ships as could be built; it involved large cargoes of merchandise; and it involved great risks of loss. Unless one had the capital to meet these requirements, and knew the trade routes, direct trade with the East was simply impossible. History does not record that any small-scale trader ever started from Europe for India in a row boat with a sack of beans to sell. Both as cause and result, the expanded trade by way of more distant overseas routes brought about a greatly increased quantity of capital and augmented its importance as a factor of production in the economic system.

All of the combined factors which brought about increased use of capital were, at the same time, bringing new importance to the concept of property. From his primitive days man had always recognized the importance of land or the natural environment, and had known that he could get his living from that environment only by work. Some kind of property right in land has existed in all societies that we know anything about, even if it was only a tribal right to hunting grounds. In many societies land has been owned or controlled by certain individuals who could collect an income from others for the right to use it. In such cases a few of the people might live, or even become wealthy, as was often true in medieval society, from the income they received as landlords. Never before modern times could anyone derive an income from any source other than labor or land without oppression, except, in the infrequent cases scattered through history from ancient times, where industry or trade was on a large enough scale to involve the use of capital.

The great change in this respect brought about by the Commercial Revolution was that for all practical purposes it introduced into economic life a new source of income, income from the capital of merchants and bankers. The new kinds of property serving as capital consisted of merchants' stocks of goods, warehouses, ships, storerooms, and anything other than land which was useful in business. Also, of course, the documents representing legal ownership of such tangible property became themselves a new kind of intangible property, and thus were also a kind of capital. Such intangibles were shares of stock, bonds, and promissory notes. In time, the total value of these new kinds of property often came to exceed that of the older real property, or land, as it is called today.

Capital used as a productive factor not only became a new source of income; it soon became the most important source in overseas commerce, in banking, in the putting-out system of manufacture, and in a few other scattered places. This was true because, to take advantage of the new opportunities offered by the Commercial Revolution, property in the form of commercial or financial capital was the productive factor which was hardest to obtain in sufficient amount. Labor and land or its products were available in sufficient quantity. The scarcest factor always brings the highest price. In the newer type of business, capital was the scarcest factor and it brought the highest price. Business earnings were calculated as a percentage of invested capital rather than as a certain amount per day's labor hired or per acre of land rented. The motive which spurred businessmen on was the profit motive. Business records were kept in terms of assets and liabilities, and success was measured by profit or loss on capital.

Capital, as a new form of income-yielding property, was dealt with rationally rather than according to tradition. Systems of land ownership have usually been of such ancient origin that historians have been able to do no more than make shrewd guesses as to how they originated. Historically we find land used in tradition-bound ways which also determine very largely the nature and amount of the income to landlords. This was not true of capital as a new form of property. There were no set traditions to be followed, and the businessmen who entered capitalistic businesses had to use their reasoning faculties as to how their capital should be employed. They had to calculate carefully the prospects of success in new and untried fields. The use of capital in business, therefore, came to be associated with a rational, analytical attitude toward business problems.

Furthermore, because there was no uniformity in the exact kinds of property which might be used as capital, the concept of capital itself has always been rather general, abstract, and hard to define in concrete terms. The easiest way to get around the problem of the diverse kinds of property that might constitute capital has been to deal with all of them in terms of value, which is a quality that all kinds of capital have in common. The businessman is not concerned with the various qualities of the property he uses as capital, except as those qualities either result in costs or yield incomes, i.e., affect value. In fact, the business system of modern times, in which capital has played such an important part as a factor of production, has tended to reduce all of life's many problems and considerations to the material values in which the market place deals. From this point of view, the more general value aspect of capital is perhaps more often referred to than the physical aspect of tools, buildings, and equipment used to aid production. One who has always lived in a capitalistic society must be careful not to use the term capital so loosely as to mean almost anything that has value, rather than in its correct sense as something which contributes to the creation of new values.

### The coming of capitalism attended by rising prices

As a consequence of sharply increased prices in western Europe caused by the spread of silver and gold from Spain in the sixteenth century, the tradition-bound land and labor economy of the Middle Ages was weakened seriously and the newer capitalistic businesses were helped.[1] Why was this so?

It is hard for people living today, whose total economic experience has probably been within a money economy, to appreciate the lack of understanding of prices by people who had never lived in a money economy. The medieval economy was based on mutual service obligations in which cash prices played no part. The beginning of trade brought the

use of money and prices, but not a full understanding of their meaning at once. Villeins who had commuted their services for a cash payment were benefited by rising prices if they could sell their own produce for higher prices or could get a higher wage for their labor. Generally, laborers were injured by higher prices because they could not get their customary wage raised as fast as prices rose. The lords were harmed so severely that only a relatively few English noble families came through the price revolution of the sixteenth century without loss of their estates. When pressed to make ends meet in the face of higher prices, the lords mortgaged their estates to money lenders or merchants in the hope that in a few years prices would go down again. When prices stayed up and went higher, the lords were foreclosed and the middle-class capitalists became the new landholders.

In fact, in transactions of every type in which money and prices were involved, the medieval classes—lords and villeins—tended to approach the business at hand with a traditional and static viewpoint. The new merchant classes were not following any tradition, since their activity was new and they had to work out new rules for it. This fresh approach of the merchants led to a rational calculation before entering into any transactions, and thus to the ability to use the transaction for profit. If the merchant could make no profit from a transaction, he declined to do business. Rising prices offered enormous chances for profit to anyone who could foresee the trend. Perhaps the capitalists of the sixteenth and seventeenth centuries were not as well versed in price behavior as some present-day experts, but at least they were far ahead of the general public of that day. Thus, the continuously rising prices for over a century due to the importation of American precious metals had the effect of enabling the capitalist classes to expand their wealth and capital faster than would otherwise have been possible. Because of their rapidly increasing wealth, they could both expand business operations faster and acquire more quickly the prestige which wealth brings.

[1] The economic effects of American precious metals have been most thoroughly explored by Earl J. Hamilton, especially in his *American Treasure and the Price Revolution in Spain, 1501-1650* (Cambridge: Harvard University Press, 1934).

## Mercantilism

The most important political development of the sixteenth and seventeenth centuries was the emergence of strong, centralized national states. Neither the Middle Ages nor the ancient world had known anything quite like the modern nation-state. There had been empires and there had been powerful cities which had built up virtual states around them. The nation was not like either of these. It was based on a common language and mode of living, which gave its members a feeling of unity. Political and economic power could be built upon social unity in a favorable environment.

The growth of trade, beginning in the later Middle Ages and reaching its peak in the Commercial Revolution, created problems which the older forms of government could not meet. Guild regulation of trade resulted in hopeless confusion when merchants began to trade outside of their own towns on a considerable scale. The new overseas trade presented problems which had never existed before, and with which no older agency of government could cope. Ambitious monarchs could and did take advantage of the situation to enhance their own power and prestige. Local government functions were taken over by the national governments. Control of overseas trade and the right to levy taxes upon it were assumed also. A new agency of government, the national state, took upon itself the task of meeting new governmental needs by adopting many attitudes and practices of older governing units, such as the towns and the lords, and fusing them with newly devised policies and practices. The result was a blend, characteristic of the period from the end of the sixteenth to the late eighteenth century, commonly known as Mercantilism.

Perhaps the core of the varied elements making up the mercantile policy was the desire of the new national governments to use their power over the economic life of the country, and most especially over its commerce, to promote the wealth, power, and prestige of the national state. Economic life had traditionally been controlled by government, either that of the lord in the manorial village or that of the free, self-governing town. There was no essential change in the general policy of control, except that it was now a control exercised by the nation instead of by the lord or the town. Being a national policy, and emerging in an era when geographic discovery had brought the nations of Europe face to face on a world-wide front, Mercantilism adopted many devices which do not on the surface appear to be similar to town or manorial policies.

Closer study, however, makes the similarities apparent. Both the local governments and the nation-states wished to promote their own wealth, power, and prestige. Both sought to attain these objectives by close regulation and control of economic life. Since Mercantilism was a national policy, it gave the individual business or businessman greater apparent freedom because there were no new controls to be encountered as merchants moved about within the national territories. Mercantilism also seems to be different in that it had a great deal to do with issuing charters to foreign trading companies and with the way in which their business was conducted. That difference, too, was not basic, since the towns had similarly controlled the guilds.

### Basic propositions of Mercantilism

In any event, the legislative enactments of the national governments of the western European countries in the sixteenth and seventeenth centuries shape up into a pattern and reveal a set of underlying ideas which we know as Mercantilism. At the risk of oversimplification, it may be worth while to list a series of propositions which a good mercantilist of the seventeenth century might have made up to express his ideas. It should be emphasized that these propositions are inferences which we draw today from actions which national governments took in the mercantile era. No flesh-and-blood mercantilist ever made up any such clear, and perhaps too logical, list of ideas.

(1) Make your country self-sufficient, in so far as that is possible. To achieve this result, develop the land and natural resources

fully. Stimulate industriousness on the part of the people and train them to perform all the crafts and occupations essential to the full use of land and resources. This objective is basic, and if it is achieved in substantial degree, it will make the nation sound and strong. To add luster and prestige to the national name, further steps are necessary.

(2) Build up a large national treasure of the precious metals. You can always find someone who will supply you with anything you need, even in emergencies such as war, if you have gold and silver to give him in exchange. You can get needed raw material or food, or you can hire needed troops or charter needed ships. Therefore, the amount of precious metals which a country has stored up is a measure of its power, and thus of its prestige.

(3) Encourage industries whose products can be exported. (This would cover luxury industries particularly, since every country in the sixteenth and seventeenth centuries would produce its own necessities as a first objective of policy. Encouragement of export industries might take many forms, such as giving a monopoly by law to an individual or company so that the industry would be expanded rapidly without fear of competition. This was called a patent. Or the industry might have a partially guaranteed market for its product through a royal guarantee to purchase a certain amount of the output. Very commonly, encouragement would be given by granting a government bounty on export of the product of the industry, i.e., the government would give a certain amount per unit of product to the producer in addition to the price he was able to get from the foreign buyer.)

(4) Import as little as possible. Certainly do not let your country be forced to import the necessaries of life from any other country. That would indicate a fatal weakness in case of war. Also do not import luxuries, because if your people are frugal and hard-working they can get along without them. A substantial but plain standard of living for your people will keep foolish ideas out of their heads, and keep costs of production low for export

industries. Import raw materials only, to be manufactured and resold abroad.

(5) Maintain a favorable balance of trade, i.e., export more than you import as in (3) and (4), so that other countries will have to pay for the excess of their purchases from you in the form of silver or gold. (This is the crux of nearly all of the practical policies of Mercantilism. Other principles might be more important in theory, but in practice this point measured the success or failure of mercantilist policy.)

(6) Build up the number of ships and seamen in your country's merchant marine. Do this by requiring your foreign trade to be carried in your own country's ships manned by native seamen. If this goal is achieved, it will save paying out money to foreigners for freight and insurance, which would have the same effect on the balance of trade as cutting down on imports. Also, in case of war, you will have your own ships to bring in needed supplies or to be converted into fighting ships.

(7) If natural limitations of your country's resources make it impossible to be entirely self-sufficient, then acquire colonies to make up for the deficiencies. Needed raw materials can then be secured from the colonies, and they can buy back manufactured goods from the mother country. If this is done, the need for raw materials which would have contributed to an unfavorable balance of trade can, through trade with the colonies, be turned into a contribution to a favorable balance of trade.

This list of the important elements of Mercantilism does not cover everything that might be mentioned. Practically all other points that might be named, however, are to be inferred from or are related to those included in the list. The mercantilists desired a country with fully developed resources, and with a large population of frugal, hard-working, and well-trained people. They were not afraid of getting too much money, but they were afraid that goods in too great quantities would lead people to become soft and luxury loving. If that should happen, the productive power of the nation would decline, because

*The birth of capitalism* 79

people would not work so hard. The remedy was to export goods for cash and not let their own people get lazy by enjoying the fruits of their own labors.

It is not hard to find holes in mercantilist logic. Is not the hope of getting a higher standard of living a more powerful drive to productive effort than grinding poverty? Is not the pursuit of gold an empty dream in the long run, since gold is only valuable when in use? How are other countries, or colonies, going to send the precious metals to a country year in and year out? All countries cannot export more than they import in order to gain treasure, for one country's exports are another's imports. Unfortunately, however, under the conditions of the sixteenth and seventeenth centuries, colonies were exploited unmercifully, and it was possible to carry out mercantilist policies for a period of years.

The errors of Mercantilism are not especially important to us today. It is important to know that such ideas were widely held and that, in fact, they characterized the age. Their acceptance shows us that the period was strongly nationalistic, and that it was isolationist, in the sense that people were not able to carry their thinking far enough to figure out clearly how colonies or other countries were going to get along on the opposite end of mercantilist policies. Many mercantilist ideas, e.g., belief in a favorable balance of trade, tariff barriers, economic self-sufficiency, have persisted but contain the same weaknesses as they did in the seventeenth century, except that they are more serious because of the greater interdependence of modern economic life.

Capitalism as an economic system had its first great development in modern times under a policy of government control. It is true that Mercantilism seemed to give businessmen greater freedom since, especially in England, it eliminated many local restrictions. Yet the national government retained absolute power to grant or withhold charters to business, and to specify the conditions under which it must operate. There is no evidence that businessmen resented this policy of national govern-ment control, either, as their successors came to do in later times. Apparently, in the early stages of the development of capitalistic foreign trade, businessmen felt that national sponsorship was at least partial protection for the capital invested in it. The national government could and did help to protect its merchants from piracy by other nations, and also helped gain for them favorable trading concessions throughout the world. Businessmen accepted the taxes they had to pay, and the controls they had to obey, as a proper counterbalance for the benefits they received. Not until the very end of the seventeenth century and after did any considerable opposition to government controls develop among businessmen.

## The economic thought of the era of the commercial revolution

It is very clear to students in the twentieth century that the Commercial Revolution brought a different kind of economic system into being. It is not so clear that the people of the sixteenth and seventeenth centuries understood the different characteristics of the new kind of system which had been created. We have seen that the principal goal of Mercantilism as a type of economic thought was to increase the wealth and power of the national state. Since these states were almost uniformly ruled by monarchs with very considerable personal power, it was thought that it was both the privilege and the responsibility of the monarch to establish economic policies which would promote the wealth and power of the nation. Thus we may say that the monarch for himself and his people could establish whatever policies he felt to be desirable. The economic system was viewed as a creation of human beings and was subject to modification to serve human purposes. Yet, there is little evidence of awareness that the system is always developing, and that it is the duty of the sovereign, or someone else, to guide it in desirable directions.

For ourselves, however, in the twentieth century, the observed developments of the era of the Commercial Revolution give us considerable help in learning to analyze an economic system. We can understand the condition which aided the development of economic specialization and trade. We can see how the increased productivity of specialization, as made evident by higher incomes to landowners, workers, and capitalists, promoted further development of that same specialization. Thus, it is understandable to us that new ideas such as specialization produce their own driving force to bring out their own full potential. We can see, too, that such changes in the economic system itself also bring changes in the way people think about their own system. The change in the understanding of and attitude toward money lending is a good example of such a change in thinking.

From our own contemporary understanding of economic processes, it is also possible to detect advancement in this respect in the sixteenth and seventeenth centuries. Without doubt, land and labor continued to be viewed as the basic productive factors as they had been in the Middle Ages and probably for long centuries prior to that period. We have seen that the increase in the use of capital as a factor of production was, to us, almost the distinctive economic phenomenon of the Commercial Revolution. Yet, it appears to have been so new that the economic thinkers of the time could not—or at least did not—get the productive role of capital deeply woven into their economic thinking. On the other hand, there clearly was the beginning of recognition that income received by each of the factors of production through the processes of income distribution had major effects back upon the nature of the productive processes from which the incomes derived.

This is really to say that there was developing a conception of the unity and interrelatedness of all parts of the economic system. This notion was often indicated by the phrase "the great wheel of commerce" which appears in the economic writings of the time. It is also indicated by the fact that the term *political economy,* i.e., the economy of a political unit such as the nation-state, came into use during the period. Our present term *economics* is a further development from the term *political economy*. Mercantilist thinkers still thought of political economy as subject to the policies of the sovereign, rather than as the natural result of the exercise of economic judgment by individual producers. This latter individualistic point of view awaited the period of the Industrial Revolution to which we shall next come.

## European economic life by 1700

The economic, social, and political changes which occurred in western Europe between 1500 and 1700 were sweeping ones. The foundations of medieval life had given way and a new basis for life was being laid. Two of the great pillars of modern society were being hewn out. They were, first, the conception of a society of free men, and, secondly, the conception of increasing efficiency in the production of wealth through specialization and capitalism. It would be hard to say that one of these pillars was of greater importance than the other. If a priority had to be assigned, it probably should go to the idea of a free society. Without at least some freedom, it would have been virtually impossible to develop the increased economic efficiency which came with specialization and trade.

The combination of increased personal freedom and increased economic specialization and trade began to produce a type of social life in the sixteenth and seventeenth centuries which was crisscrossed by currents of dynamic change. Population, which had probably been about stationary during the Middle Ages, took a sharp upturn. Although there was a trend from farming to manufacturing and trade, the food supply remained adequate because of more intensive land use. Increased production of goods of all kinds meant a higher standard of living because there was more to be divided up. This higher standard of living was not, however, enjoyed by all, since farm and industrial workers were not in a position to benefit by it because of high prices. The greatest share of the economic gains went to the merchant class, but even so they represented a larger proportion of the population than had ever before enjoyed what could be called a fairly high living standard.

Commercial towns and cities gained in size, not only through the natural growth of population but also through migration from rural areas. In the towns, specialization of economic functions was taking place in both trade and manufacturing. This meant that larger quantities of goods could be produced and handled to supply wider markets. Markets, in fact, were becoming world-wide and great joint-stock trading companies had grown up to carry on trade wherever opportunities existed.

In connection with the great trading companies, and the banks and financial institutions which supplied them with capital, there arose a new class of merchants and bankers who had in common the one new and unique characteristic that they received their livelihood from the investment of capital. It was these capitalists who benefited most from the economic developments of the period. Because of their wealth they were able to influence national governments and, in general, to impress upon contemporary society something of the spirit of rational calculation which was in no small part responsible for their own gain in prominence and power. At first the capitalist class had supported the monarchy to achieve uniformity of the rules under which business must be operated, and for other advantages. The mercantile policy of the national monarchs gave businessmen more freedom. Later, when business had become stronger, businessmen began to feel that their freedom required a different governmental policy. That, too, they were able to have put into effect. Through all changes of the early modern period there was an increase in the responsiveness of government policies to the expressed needs of at least the more powerful groups of the people. This was a movement toward democracy as we know it in the twentieth century. The capitalist class of the sixteenth and seventeenth centuries has to its credit that it fought some of the early battles for free, democratic government.

## FOR FURTHER READING

Bowden, Witt, Karpovich, Michael, and Usher, A. P. *Economic History of Europe since 1750.* New York: American Book Company, 1937. Chapters 2 and 4.

Heaton, Herbert. *Economic History of Europe.* Rev. ed. New York: Harper & Brothers, 1948. Chapter 16.

Knight, M. M., Barnes, H. E., and Flügel, F. *Economic History of Europe in Modern Times.* Boston: Houghton Mifflin Co., 1928. Chapter 2.

Mantoux, Paul. *The Industrial Revolution in the Eighteenth Century.* 2nd rev. ed. Translated by M. Vernon. New York: The Macmillan Co., 1961. Part I, Chapters 1–3.

Unwin, G. *Industrial Organization in the Sixteenth and Seventeenth Centuries.* Oxford: Clarendon Press, 1904.

Usher, Abbott Payson. *Introduction to the Industrial History of England.* Boston: Houghton Mifflin Co., 1920. Chapters 8 and 9.

# Chapter 4: The coming of the Industrial Revolution

The great economic developments of the eighteenth century culminated in the change in industrial methods and the expansion of output now known as the Industrial Revolution. The name suggests a sudden and perhaps forceful transformation. In some industries, the changes were great and they did come rather swiftly, but in general the Industrial Revolution is more correctly viewed as a phase—striking, to be sure—of the economic and intellectual history of the eighteenth, nineteenth, and twentieth centuries. Like other important historical occurrences, the Industrial Revolution was both the result of many developments that had preceded it and the cause of many that were to follow. We can use the name Industrial Revolution for the changes we shall be discussing in this chapter if we remember that it was not a "bolt from the blue" but simply a striking outgrowth of forces which had been at work for a long time, and which were to continue.

The eighteenth century has frequently been called the "Age of Reason." Preceding centuries had been marked by a slow growth of individual, personal freedom. There had been widespread rebellion against what had come to be regarded as arbitrary authority. If outside authority was relaxed, it was assumed that the individual, when thrown on his own responsibility, would act on the basis of reason. By the eighteenth century, such progress had been made in removing restraints upon individuals that many thinkers felt the time had arrived when reason could become the great guide of human conduct. Science in preceding centuries, especially the seventeenth, had opened up so many new fields and found answers to so many baffling questions that now in the eighteenth century, with reason given greater scope, it seemed as if all the problems facing mankind could be solved. All that was needed was the careful and persistent application of human intelligence. This attitude could not help but have its effects upon economic and business life. Invention or technical development in industry was one important effect.

### The dawn of a new day

The Industrial Revolution took place when a rational approach based on the accumulated knowledge of the past was made to the problems of industry. The heart of the development was the discovery of how to use power from a source other than man and animals to drive machines. That may seem to be a simple thing, but it introduced an era in human affairs of which people of former generations could not even dream. When a man or woman had to operate a machine, such as a spinning wheel or a loom or a bellows or an iron forge, it could not be too big or go at a speed faster than one person could maintain. When nonhuman power was harnessed to machines, these machines could be as big and go as fast as the source of power would permit. Size and speed of machinery was no longer limited by the strength of the men employed.

Power-driven machines had to be located where power was available. Workers had to go to the machines, for the machines could not be brought to their homes as had been done formerly. Factories replaced home workshops and industrial towns arose in areas where water or other power was available. Workers who moved from rural villages to great cities became machine attendants instead of skilled hand workers and the effort required of them was different. They worked in large groups for single employers. By all of these changes, products were turned out in quantities never before thought possible. Real wealth was increased enormously, and for the first time in history it seemed possible that man might live without the grinding toil that had been his lot for thousands of years.

In view of the sweeping effects of the Industrial Revolution, we cannot fail to regard it as a true revolution, but to avoid error in our thinking, we must recognize that it was the result of needs and knowledge that had been growing for a long time. It seems that in all forms of growth a stage is reached at which processes that have been going on slowly and perhaps unnoticed suddenly produce situations that superficially seem to be entirely new and different. At the same time, we must avoid the error of concluding that the Industrial Revolution happened and was over with. As we have seen, the basic cause of the Industrial Revolution was an increasingly rational approach to problems of production. The Industrial Revolution itself was simply the first startling result of a method of dealing with problems which has continued to be used ever more extensively to the present time. The analytical or scientific method has continued to yield great and even revolutionary results. Thus, the true view of the Industrial Revolution is as a continuing phenomenon, characterized by regularly occurring production miracles, the ultimate end of which no man can foresee. Almost every economic problem of the past two centuries is an outgrowth of the continuously evolving Industrial Revolution.

### The forces leading to the Industrial Revolution

*The growth of markets*

An increasingly important problem in the eighteenth century was how to supply goods for the great markets which the Commercial Revolution had opened up. By the eighteenth century North and South America had been settled, and extensive trade had been established by Europeans with both the Near and Far East. The sale and transportation away from the area of production of both raw and finished products had become an established practice which had recognized advantages for all concerned. The people of Europe and the rest of the world had gradually acquired the habit of selling their own products and buying other things which they needed from the market. The demand for goods increased, and industry had trouble supplying it. The fear, formerly held, that any improved method of production would cause unemployment among craftsmen was replaced by an eager search and experimentation to find new methods. The Commercial Revolution with its greatly expanded market thus became one of the basic causes of the Industrial Revolution.

## The application of the scientific method

The second factor of a general nature which contributed to the coming of the Industrial Revolution was the gradual development of the scientific method. It is not to be inferred that the people of the eighteenth century had greater intelligence than those of any previous period, but only that conditions had become more favorable for the application of a method of careful, logical investigation of a problem. The Renaissance, the cultural epoch between the thirteenth and seventeenth centuries marking the transition of Europe from medieval to modern life, had broken many traditional barriers and had led to curiosity about many new aspects of life. The attitudes toward knowledge built up during the Renaissance had the effect of making scientific investigations intellectually respectable and of lessening the likelihood of persecution. The general spirit of freedom which increasingly pervaded the early centuries of the modern era and the rather widespread reaction against the authoritarian controls of medieval society also helped to give reason wider scope.

As a result of many elements working together, science had made unparalleled advances by the eighteenth century. Copernicus, Galileo, and finally Sir Isaac Newton had arrived at the fundamental laws of motion to explain the movements of the heavenly bodies. Trigonometry, analytical geometry, and calculus were developed as tools to aid in the investigation of problems of astronomy and physics. Robert Boyle arrived at the present conception of the elements of which the earth is composed, and stated the very important law which bears his name, that, the temperature remaining constant, the volume of a gas varies inversely with the pressure to which it is subjected. Many others also contributed to these and other fields of science. The result was a

new view of the world based on fact, observation, and analysis, not on imagination or fantasy.

It is hard for those living in a world whose intellectual outlook has been determined by the scientific developments of the past two centuries to appreciate the full impact of Newton's work. Everyone has heard the story of the apple falling on him as he lay under the tree, but, more seriously, the work of Newton gave a precise mathematical statement of the attraction of heavenly bodies for one another. He also demonstrated that the same laws which operated in the astronomical sphere would explain just as precisely the action and reaction of smaller bodies on the earth. The result of his demonstration seemed to be conclusive proof of the existence of order in nature. It was harder, after Newton's time, to adhere to older ideas which today we regard as mere superstitions. It was harder to defend logically explanations of phenomena which did not stand up to the test of experience or which were inconsistent with factually proved explanations of related phenomena. Where unanswered questions remained, the work of Newton and others challenging traditional beliefs created the faith that logical answers were there to be found in the same way that Newton had found answers for age-old questions about the heavenly bodies. They seemed to prove satisfactorily that order ruled among the apparently diverse phenomena of the universe and that natural laws relating to these phenomena, even to complex political and economic phenomena, were in existence and could be found by systematic rational analysis. Thus, Newton really created the intellectual world of today in which the tool of rational scientific inquiry is regarded as the most powerful one in the search for knowledge.

The new scientific knowledge was not at first of much direct use in solving industrial problems. The understanding of the full effect of Newton's laws of motion imparted an order to nature which had never existed before, but the discovery did not help to produce more cloth or iron. It is true that James Watt, who perfected the steam engine, understood the Newtonian mechanics, which was involved in the operation of his engine. There were other inventions, too, which were rather closely related to the new theoretical knowledge of science, but in general the greatest effect of science upon industrial processes was in providing proof that physical problems could be solved by careful investigation and analysis. In other words, it was the scientific method which had the greatest effect in starting the Industrial Revolution, rather than the actual scientific knowledge acquired by applying that method. Later, the constantly growing body of scientific knowledge gave rise to an engineering technology concerned with applying science and the scientific method to the practical problems of life.

### The availability of capital

If large-scale industrial organization were to take place, there had to be available large enough quantities of capital to build and put into operation the new machines which inventors were devising. The demands of the market and the knowledge of science could work together to bring about important developments in industry only in those countries and in those areas within countries where the further step could be taken of paying to have machines built and put to work. This step could not be taken everywhere to translate needs and ideas into an actual operating industry. The most favorable areas were those in which industry and commerce were already thriving, and where, therefore, the advantage of large-scale machine methods of production was so evident as to provide a strong inducement to those with capital to invest. Thus, so far as capital supply is concerned, the Commercial Revolution contributed to the Industrial Revolution just as it did in developing markets. Merchants who were already using their capital in trade could quickly see the desirability of the new machines that were invented, and were often willing to invest in them.

Capital arises from the process of saving which can take place only in an economy so productive that its members have a surplus of goods above the minimum needs of life from which they can choose to save. The Commercial Revolution increased production by bringing an increase in geographic specialization, a more intensive use of labor with increased specialization, and a more intensive use of land and natural resources. Thus, by increasing the general wealth of the countries of western Europe where it occurred, the Commercial Revolution increased the capacity of those countries to create capital for the use of business. This effect was amplified by the uneven distribution of the new wealth. A large part of the population even in the wealthiest countries remained near the subsistence level. A minority enjoyed most of the gains coming from the growth of trade, but by that very fact were able to save a larger proportion of these gains to create capital for still further expansion.

In addition, the new financial institutions which rose as part of the Commercial Revolution to furnish a capital supply for commercial ventures were now available to assist in raising and providing capital for industrial use. The banks were just as willing to make loans to manufacturers with good prospects for profitable operation as they were to advance money to merchants. Insurance companies were equally willing to insure industrial and commercial business property. Unfortunately, the joint-stock company, because of the excessive speculation in shares early in the eighteenth century, was in disrepute and was not often used to help in raising capital for new industrial ventures, but other means were found.

### The availability of natural resources

Wherever the new machines were located and industry got a start, new and heavier demands were made upon natural resources. These demands had to be met if industrial reorganization was to grow into a real Industrial Revolution. England achieved an important place in textile manufacture in the early modern period because of the large areas she had which were being profitably used for keeping sheep. Her wool supply acted as a stimulus to the cloth industry, although the industry soon expanded so greatly that wool had to be imported from Spain. In the late eighteenth and early nineteenth centuries, a large section of the English cloth industry switched to cotton, which in its raw state was of course entirely imported. The iron and steel industry provides an even better illustration of the dependence of new processes upon adequate resources. The manufacture of iron was an ancient industry carried on in small forges scattered widely over the earth, since some iron deposits are found almost everywhere. As new methods were developed in the eighteenth and nineteenth centuries, the industry came to be more and more concentrated in strategic areas where the necessary raw materials were conveniently located. Of these raw materials, coal outbalanced the others as a determinant of where the industry could produce cheaply and expand. England had adequate resources of both coal and iron, and became the world's first large-scale producer. Belgium, Germany, and the United States became large producers in later decades, but Holland, whose power and wealth were surpassed by no country in the seventeenth century, did not have the resources to achieve power and greatness in industry as she had in commerce.

### An adequate labor supply

Obviously labor was necessary to expanding industry. Therefore, labor supply should properly be included in any list of factors contributing to the Industrial Revolution. However, it is on a different level from some of the other factors. In the case of natural resources, for example, you either have them or you do not. It really is not quite that simple, but it tends to be that way. In the case of human beings, the matter is somewhat different, since more persons can be secured one way or another if they are needed, at least within certain limits. In a sense, the Industrial Revolution provided its own work force by bringing about an increase in the rate of population growth. This was effected in large measure by a decrease in the death rate made possible by advances in medicine. However, there was a lag of a number of years before this effect began to be felt, and that is why it is valid to include an adequate *initial* labor force as a factor contributing to the Industrial Revolution.

There are other and rather subtle aspects of the labor-supply problem. The first introduction of power-driven machine processes has almost always resulted in a smaller demand for labor because of the increased output per worker when machines are used, despite an increased demand for labor by machine-producing firms. The Industrial Revolution in the English textile industry brought unemployment to many hand weavers. Over a longer period, the lowered costs of production resulting from the use of machines widens the market for the product and necessitates the employment of more workers. In the long run, a growing population and a growing labor supply are necessary for continued expansion of industry.

On the other hand, although the countries which experienced the Industrial Revolution met their own labor requirements for a time by the rapid increase of their populations, the longer-range effect of a higher standard of living achieved by greater industrial efficiency was a restriction of the birth rate by families in order to preserve and extend the advantage of their higher level of income. By the latter part of the nineteenth century, the United States and the countries of western Europe began to experience a declining rate of population growth especially among their industrial workers. Until the end of World War I, the United States could maintain its industrial labor force because of immigration from southern Europe. After 1920, the movement of young people from farms into industry, and increasing employment of women brought continued growth to our labor force. Still later—after 1940—the American birth rate began to rise. It is impossible to say, as yet, what the long-range effects of industrialization may be. Whether forces leading to rising or declining population will win out, we cannot now tell.

It would hardly have been possible for very great industrial development to take place where there was not sufficiently good transportation to permit the growth of commerce. Some light industries, like the manufacture of textiles, could grow where there were only good wagon roads. Others, in which new methods were developed, such as coal mining, iron and steel manufacture, and pottery making, required the cheap movement of heavy materials. Water transportation by river or sea could be used, but only if the materials to be moved were available near water. As a matter of fact, it was the unfulfilled need for better and cheaper transportation which turned inventors toward improving it, as a part of the Industrial Revolution itself. The building of better roads, canals, railroads, and steamships was the ultimate result of their work. At the outset of the period of rapid industrial expansion, however, adequate transportation was a factor in determining whether a start could be made in establishing industry on a large-scale basis, using power-driven machinery and a bulky fuel, coal, as well as bulky raw materials.

## New machines and the factory system

The making of cloth is one of the oldest of industries. Before the full effects of the Industrial Revolution were felt, it was the largest after food production. Now, in industrialized countries, the manufacture of iron and steel and products made from them probably provides employment for more people than any other industry, again excluding agriculture. But a large number of people are still employed making cloth or clothing. On a world basis, it is still possible that the textile and clothing industries occupy first place.

Within historic times, cloth has been made and used almost everywhere, as it was a product in almost universal demand. Since it is light in relation to its value and since it is not perishable, it was one of the first and most important articles of trade, being easily moved and stored. The development of trade and trading towns in the Middle Ages centered about cloth. After the period of discovery, both textile fibers and manufactured cloth played a large part in the trade between Europe and the rest of the world. As a by-product of the Commercial Revolution, when the guilds refused to increase production to meet the needs of wider markets, the putting-out system developed. By this new organization of industry, output was increased greatly so that the trade in cloth could also grow. More and more people were drawn into the various operations of cloth making. The merchant-capitalist clothiers, by the eighteenth century, were even forced to go so far as to furnish homes, shops, and machines for workers in order to get increased output to keep up with the growing demands of the markets.

It was against this background of rising demand being met as well as possible by a rural cloth industry that the Industrial Revolution was projected. Ingenious workmen devised ways of improving and speeding up work. Only the lucky or the persistent had their efforts recognized and remembered. One of the earliest of these was John Kay, who received a patent for his flying shuttle in 1733. Kay had at first worked for a clothier at Colchester in Lancashire, England, but later became a maker of parts for looms. The specifications attached to the patent application described the device as, "A new invented shuttle, for the better and more exact weaving of broad cloths, broad bays, sail cloths, or any other broad goods . . ."[1] It was a device by which the shuttle was equipped with small wheels so that, when struck by wooden hammers at either side of the loom, it would fly

[1] Quoted from Paul Mantoux, *The Industrial Revolution in the Eighteenth Century* (New York: Harcourt, Brace and Co., 1928), p. 211, footnote. This is the best single source for further reading on the Industrial Revolution.

across even an unusually wide loom drawing the cross thread (weft) behind it. It enabled the weaver to make greater speed, to do without an assistant, and to weave much wider cloths than had before been possible. It was not mechanized, but required only hand power for its operation.

Kay's invention was received with hostility. The weavers around Colchester said that Kay was trying to deprive them of their daily bread. He made several moves to other textile centers in the decades following 1733, but his device was either refused or used without payment of royalty. It is said that he escaped from the city of Manchester in the 1750's hidden in a sack of wool. He finally found safety outside of his native country in France. In spite of such rough and unappreciative treatment of the inventor, the flying shuttle gradually came into use. By 1760 its influence was felt throughout the textile industry. With its help, weavers could handle more yarn than the spinners could produce. The price of thread rose, but even so, weavers were often delayed in their work by inability to get their raw material.

Quite logically, the next steps in the textile industry were a series of inventions improving spinning devices to make up the shortage of yarn. A machine called the water frame was patented by Richard Arkwright in 1769, and another called the spinning jenny by James Hargreaves in 1770. Both machines were actually invented and used several years before the patents were granted. Hargreaves' jenny was a simple hand-operated machine which provided a number of spindles instead of the single one on the spinning wheel. The extra spindles, of course, resulted in faster spinning, although pulling out the fiber into a continuous loose bundle, called the roving, still had to be done by hand. Arkwright's water frame used an entirely new principle and prepared the roving as well as spun it into a thread. It was later proved that Arkwright was not the real inventor of this machine. He did see its possibilities, however, made some improvements on it, and was enough of a promoter to raise the capital to get it built and put to work. In its final form it had a series of pairs of rollers, each pair turning together like the rollers on some modern washing machines. The successive pairs of rollers were made to rotate faster than their predecessors. Thus the fiber which was made to pass between them was drawn out to the desired degree of thinness before it was spun.

Arkwright's machine was called a water frame because it required water power to operate it. In his early experiments Arkwright had tried to use horses to work his machines, but they were not satisfactory. His frame was not successful until he turned to water for power. Kay's flying shuttle and Hargreaves' jenny were both hand-operated devices. They speeded up weaving and spinning, but alone they would not have brought about great enough changes to revolutionize the industry. When the water frame came into use, spinning was taken out of the home to a source of water power. This was a fundamental change and has been regarded as the start of the modern factory system. Arkwright's machine might be given credit for bringing the Industrial Revolution to the textile industry were it not for the fact that it was not entirely successful. It did make yarn and make it rapidly, but it could not make the fine, hard-twisted thread which English weavers needed to enable them to compete with fine Indian cotton cloth being imported by the East India Company. Still Arkwright's machine was fairly successful, and he eventually set up his water frames in several factories of his own. He is as deserving as anyone of the title "Father of the Factory System."

The honor of achieving both quality and quantity production of fine yarn for weaving by a power-driven machine goes to Samuel Crompton, who perfected his spinning mule in 1779. The mule used the principle of preparing the roving by rollers, as in the water frame, combined with mounting of the spindles on a carriage which moved back and forth, as in the jenny. Since Crompton used other people's ideas, he could not patent his machine, and he never benefited from it financially. The mule was a big machine requiring power for its operation. It was promptly and widely used, because with it English manufacturers were able to capture the market for delicate cotton fabrics from Indian clothmakers. The water frame continued to be used for coarser yarns, and, together with the mule, within a few years transformed spinning into a factory operation.

By the 1790's yarn had become a drug on the market and weavers' wages had risen, in order to induce more workers to learn the trade, since there were not enough of them to use up the surplus yarn being turned out by the spinning mills. That situation had, of course, been developing for some years. To do something about it, Edmund Cartwright, a rural minister, had had a power loom built to his designs by a carpenter and a blacksmith. He was issued a patent on the loom in 1785. In the next few years he made a number of improvements on it and attempted to operate a small factory using twenty looms to make different types of cottons. That and later projects were dogged by failure. Cartwright was not a good business manager, and the loom still needed further improvements to increase the speed and smoothness of its operation. The hand weavers rose in opposition to the power loom, burning down a large Manchester factory in which four hundred looms were to have been operated by steam power. Cartwright lived to see his loom perfected and widely used, but he did not profit from it himself. The later improvements were made by firms engaged in the manufacture of the looms. The use of the loom spread slowly, and weaving did not become a true factory industry until almost 1840. After that year the number of remaining hand weavers declined sharply, and the spinning of yarn and the weaving of cloth were again back in balance.

While basic changes were occurring in spinning and weaving, other no less important changes were taking place in related industrial processes. The early textile machines were intended for use with wool or linen, which had been known and used in Europe for centuries. The greatest spur to new processes, however, came from the growing popularity of cotton chintzes, calicoes, and ginghams being imported by the East India Company. Everyone connected with the older branches of textile manufacture felt that these new fabrics were stealing away the market. The importation of finished cloth was also a violation of the principle of Mercantilism. There was a keen desire to try out the new machines on cotton, and, in fact, after 1760 all of the inventors designed their machines for cotton. Eventually, as has been noted, new machine processes for cotton were perfected, but the practical success of English and European manufacture depended on several further inventions. It is curious that these other inventions were the only important ones related to the cloth industry made outside of England.

In 1783, Thomas Bell, a Scotchman, perfected a process of pattern or figure printing of cotton by cylindrical copper rollers. His machine would do the work of a hundred men using flat plates, and English manufacturers could now equal the beautiful Indian prints which were so popular. The second vital invention made outside of England was the cotton gin, invented in 1793 by Eli Whitney, an American schoolteacher. It greatly cut the cost of removing the seeds from the cotton fiber, and made American cotton cheaper than Indian cotton which had been imported previously. The gin stimulated not only English cotton manufacturing but cotton growing in America as well. Besides these inventions, a number of other scientific advances had a bearing on the textile industry. The French chemist, Berthollet, had discovered the bleaching power of chlorine about 1785. Within a few years, chlorine bleaching was applied in the cloth industry. At about the same time improved dyes were discovered, and special purpose looms were devised for making lace and figured cloth of various kinds. All together, the inventions and improvements made in the textile industry in Europe, and especially England, turned it into a large-scale factory industry with a commanding position in world markets. Productive capacity had, for a time at least, caught up with consuming capacity.

## New methods
## in the iron and steel industry

The discovery of how to produce iron and how to make useful articles from it was an important dividing point in the development of civilization. Just when the discovery was made is not known, but the art of iron working was developed by the tenth century B.C. in ancient Mesopotamia and the Near East. The small Catalan forge seems to have been in use there when historical records begin, and the sword with a Damascus blade had an enviable reputation throughout the Middle Ages. Until early modern times, a small forge similar to the ancient one from Catalonia continued in use, and European steelmakers probably only rarely equalled the steel of Damascus.

The first stirrings of inventive minds in more recent times seem to have been prompted by difficulties that were encountered in continuing the traditional methods. This was particularly true in relation to an expanding demand for articles made of iron and steel that accompanied the Commercial Revolution and its general quickening of economic life. A patent was granted to Dud Dudley in 1619 in England for a process of making iron with coal instead of the usual charcoal, because, as Dudley wrote, of "charcoal growing very scanty."[1] He encountered difficulties in putting his new furnace into use, and its exact specifications were lost when its inventor died. Others continued experimental work, especially in Germany and England. Final success in developing a process that would produce iron in large quantities with the use of coke for fuel was achieved in the eighteenth century by three generations of Abraham Darbys at the family ironworks in Coalbrookdale, England.

The work of the Darbys established two important new principles for the iron industry: (1) coke could be used successfully for fuel, but (2) to use coke successfully the natural draft of the iron furnace would have

[1] Mantoux, *op. cit.*, p. 292.

to be supplemented by a forced air blast to make the coke burn well enough to increase the heat of the furnace to the proper point. The successes of the Darbys, like most successes, created new problems. There was no satisfactory method for supplying the forced air blast that had now become a necessity of iron manufacture. Large bellows had been used; also an arrangement by which water was made to carry air with it as it fell down a long tube. Later, James Watt's improved steam engine had one of its largest markets at iron works, where it was used to produce air blast. This problem of producing air under pressure was not really solved satisfactorily until the nineteenth century.

The work of the Darby family created another problem in the iron industry. The old Catalan type forge using charcoal had very slowly and with great labor produced soft iron which could be made into nails, hinges, and other needed articles. No one knew the specifications of this iron; it was just iron. After the Darbys had successfully learned to use coke by forcing air into the furnace, they got the iron hot enough so that it became liquid and could be cast in sand molds as cast iron. This speeded up production and cut costs, but it was discovered that the iron was hard and brittle. Some people said the Darbys were frauds and quacks. We now know that the mystery centered about the element carbon. The old-fashioned method of making iron was so slow that by the time the process was finished the carbon content of the iron was very low. The use of charcoal as fuel made a great difference too. The Darby process was fast and the carbon content of their iron was high. This fact was not known at the time, but it was quickly discovered that their iron was not satisfactory for a great many uses. Something more had to be done to it.

The next steps in the improvement of processes in iron manufacture were widely scattered in Germany, France, America, and England. Because England had become the greatest commercial country in the world by the last half of the eighteenth century, the inventions made there were the ones that were put to use. There were at least two sets of duplicate inventions in this period, however.

Eventually the remaining technical problems of large-scale manufacture of iron and steel were worked out, although it took until 1870, a century and a half after the pioneer work of the Darbys, before a satisfactory furnace was developed to produce steel of controlled quality from iron made from ores of varying chemical composition. This was an enclosed saucer-shaped furnace with the burning fuel separated from the molten metal. The modern version of this furnace is called an "open hearth" because the steel can be worked with and alloyed during the period of a "heat." Shaped rollers have also been used since about 1800 to shape heated iron or steel into sheets, bars, beams, rails, or other desired forms. With these developments of the nineteenth century, the iron industry to a very considerable degree was transformed into the steel industry. When steel could be made cheaply, it displaced iron in a great many uses. Furthermore, a multitude of new uses was opened up when inexpensive steel was developed and made available. New machines, as in the textile industry, were made of iron and steel, and the availability of inexpensive steel brought cheaper and faster transportation. More than any other one industry, the iron and steel industry was the heart of the Industrial Revolution.

### New power for transportation and machine tools

In the early stages of the Industrial Revolution the development of large-scale methods was entirely dependent upon water power. In its next stages, extending from the late eighteenth century for over a hundred years, steam provided the power for the improvement and the geographical dispersion of machine methods of production. The transition is almost entirely a result of the work of James Watt, a man whose inventions were achieved by careful application of scientific knowledge.

The early modern experiments in the use of steam power were almost entirely devoted to the problem of pumping water, because the accumulation of water in mines limited the extent of operations. Hand pumping or carrying of water was impractical. Here was a real problem for inventors. Just before 1700, Denys Papin and Thomas Savery had each devised a method of using steam for pumping, but the greatest success was achieved by Thomas Newcomen a few years after 1700 with his "fire engine." This engine of Newcomen's was very slow and required great quantities of fuel for the work done, but it did work. For more than half a century it had no competitor. Watt's engine, which was first patented in 1769, was the result of the fact that he was called upon by his employer, the University of Glasgow, to repair a Newcomen engine. That was in 1765, but a year or two previously he had been occupied with a series of experiments on steam pressure. Watt's first basic improvement on the Newcomen engine was to provide a separate condensing chamber which was constantly kept cool. The cylinder of the engine could then be kept hot and steam applied alternately on either side of the piston. The engine thus delivered more power for its size and used much less fuel because the cylinder was not alternately heated and cooled as in the Newcomen engine. Watt and his partner, Matthew Boulton, sold their first engines, usually to replace the Newcomen engines, at the cost of building them plus a royalty of one-third of the fuel which the customer saved compared with the Newcomen engine.

In 1781 Watt was issued a second patent for adapting his engine to rotary motion. Prior to that time, Watt engines were used only as pumps to replace Newcomen's fire engines. Also, by the early 1780's many of the "kinks" had been worked out of the early models. Watt and Boulton had been assisted in developing the construction of the steam engine by William Murdock, a skilled and faithful foreman of Boulton's firm, and by John Wilkinson, an iron manufacturer who had perfected a method of boring the cylinders accurately. Very quickly after 1781 orders were received from a variety of industries for Watt's engines, which were now not just an improvement on the Newcomen engine, but a real source of motive power. They were used in the iron industry to provide blast for the furnaces and to turn the rolls to shape the metal; flour mills used them to increase the scale of operation and to escape dependence upon falling water; and, of course, the inventors of the new textile machinery turned to Watt's engine eagerly to solve their problems of power supply. By 1800 many were in use not only in England but in other countries. Industrial development could now be carried on freely, unrestricted by the limited amount of water power available.

The history of the steam engine provides another example of the fact that cause and effect seem to intertwine themselves as time moves forward. The development of satisfactory steam power made it possible for the Industrial Revolution to spread. But, if industry were to spread, raw materials must move freely to industrial areas, and finished goods must move off to world markets with equal freedom. The growth of the market had been a powerful initial impulse toward the Industrial Revolution, and that growing market had in turn rested on improved transportation. After the steam engine had been invented, perfected, and put to use, industrial production could expand so rapidly and in so many new places that new demands were placed upon transportation which existing facilities could not properly meet. Increasingly in the last half of the eighteenth century and on into the nineteenth, transportation was a limiting factor in further industrial expansion.

In the Middle Ages, road building had been a local responsibility which had been well enough met to satisfy the limited needs of the time. After the decline of medieval institutions, the roads had fallen into disrepair and no lasting improvement was made, if travelers are to be believed, until after 1750. By that time, the needs of commerce and an expanding industry made it absolutely essential that something be done. Parliament in England had passed the Turnpike Act in

the seventeenth century, permitting private "trusts" to build roads and collect tolls. A number of turnpikes had been built to serve large towns, but not enough to make an adequate road system. In the 1760's, under the leadership of John Metcalfe, a blind engineer, and Thomas Telford and John McAdam, a beginning was made through the turnpike trusts in building a really adequate road system. Iron beams began to be used for bridges, and graded stone was placed on the roads and rolled to provide a smooth durable surface.

The close relationship between industrial development and the need for transportation is also shown in the fact that during the decade following 1760 canal as well as road construction got under way on a large scale. Canals, like roads, had been built many years before 1760, but the new need for them now led to a burst of activity. In England James Brindley completed a seven-mile canal into the city of Manchester for the Duke of Bridgewater in 1761. It cut the cost of coal in the city to a half of its former price. Other canals were built immediately, and by 1777 England had a canal system which crossed the country from north to south and east to west. The coal, iron, and pottery industries could not have grown as rapidly as they did without the cheap transportation of their bulky products which the canals provided for them.

While road and canal systems were being extended, other developments were taking place which were eventually to lead to the steam railroad. From 1763 on, the steam engine was steadily being improved. At about the same time, cast-iron rails and cast-iron wheels began to be used for hauling mine cars. Long before that, mines had used plankways, or iron strips nailed to logs, for rails to provide improved roadways. It was natural that the steam engine and the rail roadbed should be brought together at mines where both had long been used. Richard Trevithick was one of the first to construct a steam-powered locomotive. In 1803 he put one into use in South Wales, but it broke so many cast-iron rails because of its weight that it was used only as a stationary engine. From that time on, a number of experimenters were at work building locomotives. The greatest measure of success went to Timothy Hackworth and George Stephenson, who worked partly together and partly independently. Hackworth in 1827 built the *Royal George*, which was a very heavy engine but for the first time proved more economical in use than horses. It was placed in service on the first English railroad, the Stockton and Darlington, opened in 1825, to haul coal. Stephenson next built a lighter and faster locomotive—the *Rocket*—which won for him the Rainhill Trials, set up in 1829 by the Liverpool and Manchester Railroad for locomotive builders.

Stephenson, who was civil engineer for the Stockton and Darlington and later for the Liverpool and Manchester, made a truly remarkable contribution to the development of both the locomotive and the railway. In 1816 he secured a patent on an improved rail, and in 1818 he made a series of studies on the relationship of grade to the power required to move a load. These studies showed that the same pulling power would move a load only one-sixth as great if the grade were increased from level to a rise of two feet in every hundred. As a result, he recommended that grades should be held down to nearly level, even if considerable expense were encountered in construction. Particularly with the rather weak locomotives which were the best that could be built in the 1820's, this recommendation was crucial. Stephenson, by developing ideas of his own and adapting the ideas of others, made the *Rocket* the most successful locomotive that had been built up to that time. He used a multi-tubular boiler, which increased the rate at which steam could be produced. Of course, such a boiler could not have been constructed until after the work of other inventors had made it possible to roll iron sheets of uniform strength. Having a stronger boiler of larger capacity, Stephenson gave up Watt's idea of condensing steam in his engines and instead directed the exhaust steam up the chimney to produce a forced draft for the fire. These ideas were incorporated in the *Rocket* and later locomotives.

On Stephenson's recommendation, and because of the success of the *Rocket* in the Rainhill Trials, the Liverpool and Manchester Railroad was built with a nearly level grade and with steam locomotives as the source of power. Until the Rainhill Trials the steam locomotive had never been proved clearly to be more speedy and less costly than horses or stationary engines with cables to haul cars uphill so that they might coast down to the next hill. The L. and M. was opened in 1830 and its success led to widespread railroad building in both Europe and America. However, it was realized only slowly in later decades that the railroad could be extended to make great transcontinental systems. Nearly a half-century was required to bring out the full potentialities of the new means of transportation. The immediate benefits were great enough, though, to permit the continued unfolding of new technical developments in industry without undue check because of inadequate transportation. The men of the Industrial Revolution had used current technical advances to solve problems which, if unsolved, would have checked further progress.

It is necessary to consider also the development of methods of building the machines themselves. In the first place, it is clear that wood, from which spinning wheels, hand looms, and water wheels had traditionally been built, was not a satisfactory material. Developments in the iron industry had made cast and wrought iron available in large quantities for machines, but no adequate methods were available to make machine parts accurately. In a number of cases, the theoretical work of inventors was ahead of the practical possibility of translating their ideas into real working machines. That was certainly true of Watt and his steam engine, and of Cartwright and his power loom. On the other hand, the success of Stephenson in building the *Rocket* was partly due to the better metal and more accurately machined parts which he was able to obtain.

Today, the machines which make machine parts are called machine tools. They have become the key to successful industry. The detailed development of machine tools is too technical for most of us to grasp. Suffice it to say that the lathe is a very important machine tool. It is a machine to turn the work, and in a simple nonmechanical form had been used in furniture making and other work for several centuries. A number of inventors made improvements on it, but none more extensively than Henry Maudsley in England. From 1794, when he perfected the slide rest, until his death in 1835, Maudsley continued to make improvements on the lathe. The slide rest held cutting tools firmly against the work which was being turned in the lathe, thus making accurate circular cuts. Maudsley also perfected the screw feed by which the rate of cut could be set accurately and by which accurate screw threads could be cut. Other machine tools for drilling, boring, planing, shaping, and milling were developed in the course of time after the work on the lathe had demonstrated the possibilities of machining metal. With these developments, it was possible for the machine tool builders to keep up with the inventors whose ideas were progressively revolutionizing one industry after another.

### Introducing science into agriculture

The eighteenth and nineteenth centuries brought a continuation of the Agricultural Revolution which had begun in the sixteenth and seventeenth centuries. Throughout the modern period, the stimulus to change in agriculture has come not from within farming itself but from outside, from developments in commerce and later in industry. England became the leader in agricultural advance because her success in commerce and industry provided a more powerful incentive to seek better farming methods than existed in France, Germany, or any other European countries. The first phase of agrarian change had come with the growth of commerce which had led to a breakdown of serfdom, to the sale of farm produce for cash in urban markets, and to enclosure of the open fields for pasturing sheep. By the latter part of the seventeenth century, the increase in the proportion of the total population occupied in commerce or handicraft manufacturing had led to an intensification of agricultural methods and the beginning of enclosure of open fields for better food production, rather than for the keeping of sheep.

Along with the growth of commerce and handicraft manufacture there had come an increase in total population, as well as the shift of a part of the population from agriculture to other occupations. The Industrial Revolution later extended this population increase to an even greater degree, but before that effect was observable, population had increased sufficiently to bring a rise in food prices, and to make more efficient farming desirable. Major improvements in farming methods resulted.

The agricultural improvements of the eighteenth century were made by country gentlemen who had the time, the interest, and the capital to undertake new methods experimentally. The first in the group was Jethro Tull, an Englishman who was trained for the law but returned to his family estate because of ill health. The methods developed by Tull between 1701 and his death forty years later were as follows: (1) Prepare the soil thoroughly by deep plowing to incorporate marl from the subsoil with the topsoil. (2) Space the seeds properly by sowing them in rows. (3) Hoe or cultivate between the rows as long as possible to keep down the weeds. To perform the second operation, Tull invented a grain drill in 1701, and for the third operation he invented in 1714 a cultivator which he called a "horse hoe." He achieved crop yields better than his neighbors with only one-third the seed they were using. He was opposed and ridiculed for his ideas, and died an embittered man, although he never lost hope that his methods of husbandry would spread, as they eventually did.

The next of the agricultural pioneers was Charles Townshend, who, after an active life in important government posts culminating in the prime ministership, returned to his ancestral estate in 1730 when the wheel of political fortune took an adverse turn. Much of his land was barren and poorly drained, and he set out to improve it by intensive methods that he had seen successfully applied in Holland. He was responsible not so much for any single new idea as for gathering together the best available knowledge and experience and applying them vigorously. He marled the thin sandy stretches, he applied Tull's method of sowing and cultivating, and he included turnips and clover with wheat and barley in a four-year rotation which greatly increased the supplies of animal feed for the winter. Townshend's system came to be called the Norfolk system, and it not only made farming profitable on poorer soils but laid the basis for a great increase in the numbers of livestock that could be kept. Without Charles Townshend, John Bull could not have become a beef eater.

The work begun by Tull and Townshend was in a sense rounded out by Robert Bakewell, an independent yeoman farmer, after 1760 when he inherited the family farm from his father. He became interested in the poor, scrawny sheep and cattle which seemed to be the best that could be produced. He discarded crossbreeding and by carefully selecting his parent stock he inbred for desired characteristics in his animals. He kept records of the ancestry of his animals also. In addition, he followed general farm practices that were of the best and saw to it that he had ample supplies of clover, hay, and turnips for winter feeding. He had his own greatest success with sheep, but other farmers who came to understand his methods began breeding work which has resulted in all the livestock breeds of the present day. Farm animals became heavier and more vigorous as a result of careful breeding programs. Dairy and beef types of cattle were developed and the desirable qualities of each increased by selective breeding. Similarly, better breeds of sheep resulted in better mutton and more wool.

Two other men deserve to be added to the list of pioneers of better farming—Arthur Young, a traveler, writer, and lecturer on improved farming methods, and Thomas Coke, a farmer who practiced the new methods and spread knowledge of them by annual "open weeks" at his farm near Holkham in Norfolk. Young was the most tireless advocate of better agriculture. He had failed at managing a farm himself, but by extensive travels into every part of England, and into other countries as well, he popularized the best methods he found in use and criticized the poor ones. Almost alone, Young was responsible for making farming popular among leaders in government and business. George III of England is said to have liked to be called the "Farmer King." Coke, unlike Young, made a great success of farming and met the challenge of critics and skeptics by inviting them to his farm that they might see for themselves. Visitors to his open weeks came from the continent of Europe and from America as well as England. It is said that seven thousand persons attended his open week in 1817, certainly a record for the time. Neither Coke nor Young added to the knowledge of farming, but they deserve major credit for the rapid spread of improved methods.

In the nineteenth century, agricultural improvements continued. Sir Humphrey Davy in England and Justus Liebig in Germany applied their scientific knowledge of chemistry to the problem of crop fertilization. The principles of selective breeding were applied to plants as well as to animals. Valuable improvements in plant yields, disease resistance, and the like have continued to be achieved. Tull's beginning with farm machinery was also continued, but mainly in America, where large areas and sparse population made mechanization of farming highly desirable. By all of these improvements the Agricultural Revolution was continued. Food supplies increased and dietary standards became more adequate in spite of the continued shift of population from rural to urban occupations. The agricultural sector of the economy maintained at least an even pace of improvement with the industrial sector.

By approximately 1825 in England and to a lesser degree on the continent of Europe and in the United States, the Industrial Revolution had become an established fact. Wherever the requisite conditions existed, the application of power production methods in manufacturing and transportation had resulted in more output with less human labor and in moving heavier loads farther and faster than ever before. Agricultural improvement had kept pace to permit man to feed himself with enough time and energy left over to devote to industrial improvement and other interests. Looking backward at these developments from the higher levels achieved in the twentieth century makes them seem rather tame and insignificant. But in the longer perspective of history, they represent an unparalleled achievement with sweeping effects upon ideas, modes of living, and government.

## FOR FURTHER READING

Bogardus, James F. *Europe: A Geographical Survey*. New York: Harper & Brothers, 1934. Especially Chapters 7 and 8.

Bogart, Ernest L. *Economic History of Europe: 1760-1939*. New York: Longmans, Green & Co., Inc., 1942. Chapters 1 and 2.

Bowden, Witt. *Industrial Society in England Towards the End of the Eighteenth Century*. New York: The Macmillan Co., 1925. Chapters 1—3.

Bowden, Witt, Karpovich, Michael, and Usher, Abbott Payson. *Economic History of Europe since 1750*. New York: American Book Company, 1937. Chapters 6—8.

Day, Clive. *Economic Development in Europe*. New York: The Macmillan Co., 1942. Chapter 8.

Hammond, John L., and Hammond, Barbara. *The Rise of Modern Industry*. New York: Harcourt, Brace & Co., 1926. Chapters 5—11.

Hatfield, H. S. *The Inventor and His World*. New York: E. P. Dutton & Co., 1933.

Heaton, Herbert. *Economic History of Europe*. Rev. ed. New York: Harper & Brothers, 1948. Chapters 18—22.

Knight, M. M., Barnes, H. E., and Flügel, F. *Economic History of Europe in Modern Times*. Boston: Houghton Mifflin Co., 1928. Chapter 3.

Mantoux, Paul. *The Industrial Revolution in the Eighteenth Century*. 2nd rev. ed. Translated by M. Vernon. New York: The Macmillan Co., 1961. Part II, Chapters 1—4.

Seligman, Edwin B. A., and Johnson, Alvin (eds.) *Encyclopedia of the Social Sciences*. New York: The Macmillan Co., 1931-1935. Especially article on the Industrial Revolution.

Tickner, Frederick W. *Social and Industrial History of England*. New York: Longmans, Green & Co., Inc., 1929. Chapters 35—38.

Usher, Abbott Payson. *Introduction to the Industrial History of England*. Boston: Houghton Mifflin Co., 1920. Chapters 10—14 and 17.

# Chapter 5: The impact of the

# Industrial Revolution

From practically any point of view, the eighteenth century was truly revolutionary. Although there were no conspicuous changes in methods of carrying on commerce, it continued to expand on the new basis established in the previous centuries. After 1750 the volume of trade swelled to an amount of which no one would previously have dreamed. The Industrial Revolution was definitely under way before 1800, although its greatest results did not show themselves until later. Equally great changes marked the continuation of the Agricultural Revolution in the eighteenth century. Farming became more intensive and more efficient, so that fewer agricultural workers were able to provide a better diet for more city workers. In the sciences, developments of the late seventeenth century were thoroughly tested and extended in the eighteenth. Physics, astronomy, mathematics, chemistry, physiology, and general biology shared in revolutionary advances in scientific knowledge and in the methods of scientific investigation. To cap a revolutionary century, the American and French Revolutions occurred toward its end. Each became an important victory in the never-ending struggle for human freedom from arbitrary authority.

### New economic ideas

With major changes occurring in almost every phase of life, it is not surprising that there were also revolutionary changes in the intellectual outlook of the people of the eighteenth century. Complacency of mind had been disturbed by the Commercial Revolution, and the increase of travel, communication, and economic interdependence that had come in the sixteenth and seventeenth centuries had induced a ferment of new ideas. Eventually, the successes of the scientists seemed to provide a lead to a line of thought which was both broad enough and penetrating enough to become a new guide for the eighteenth century.

It seemed that the human mind had rational powers adequate to bring order out of chaos if applied diligently and systematically. No problems of human life were beyond its reach, because science had shown that the universe was ruled by systematic natural laws which the human mind could discern. It was felt, too, that the mind was possessed not by the state, or the church, or society in general, but by the individual human. The new scheme of thought became hostile to established authority, except as that authority operated in conformity with the ideas of the majority of individuals. Relying upon the rationality of individuals, men of the eighteenth century were optimistic and believed that rational analysis of any problems confronting mankind would make it possible to resolve them. The future appeared to be bright for mankind.

It is often said that the new economic ideas that developed in the eighteenth century were the result of the Industrial Revolution. There is no evidence that that is true, in spite of the fact that new ways of viewing the economic system became important at the same time as new views of the mechanization of manufacturing processes. Rather, there is both historic evidence and logic to support the conclusion that these developments were the different products of a common causal situation. We have seen that a number of causes of, or contributing factors to, the Industrial Revolution can be pointed out. The broader and more general aspects of these same causes were also the causes of the new economic ideas of the eighteenth century. For example, the growth of the market which contributed to the Industrial Revolution also involved travel and contact with new ideas which contributed to the new scheme of thinking. The rise of successful science which helped along the Industrial Revolution also contributed to the new rational view of nature of which the new economic ideas were a part. The Industrial Revolution and the revolutionary new economic ideas were the products of the same causes.

### Opposition to Mercantilism

For a long time—in fact, until around the year 1750—the merchant class in general was more in favor of than against Mercantilism. The merchants welcomed royal authority because it meant at least uniformity in the taxes and rules to which they were subject. Also, they were finding it difficult to obtain adequate capital to finance trade with the remote parts of the world. After royal backing was secured, a hazardous trading venture became somewhat more solid. The prospects for profits were often tremendous, but the merchants needed and welcomed royal aid to help them raise capital, to protect them from the competition of both their own countrymen and foreign merchants, and to help protect them against the hazards of piracy and shipwreck. In brief, the merchants favored the king and were willing to increase his strength by their tax payments in order that they might have a stronger arm on which to lean in developing their businesses along large-scale capitalist lines. They needed the strong, supporting arm of government even if leaning on that arm restricted their freedom of action.

The honeymoon period of the merchant class and the absolute monarchy eventually came upon days when the continuance of mutual understanding and sympathy was more and more difficult. The union had been prompted by the weakness of both sides, and as they respectively acquired strength and stability in their own right, they wished to follow diverging paths. The merchants of the great commercial companies were willing enough to accept the help that the government might give to them, but they came to resent more and more the taxation to which they were subject and the continuation of regulations over the production and sale of goods that harked back to the guild days. Actually, they had become so strong and the trade was so well established that they could get along adequately without government help if its withdrawal was to be the price of freedom from government regulation. The great and successful trading companies had little trouble in obtaining needed capital privately by 1700. The risks had become less because of the stabilization of trade routes and trading areas both in the Orient and in the Americas. The development of banking and the joint-stock company had helped in raising capital and distributing the risk involved in using it in business. The increase of general wealth which the Commercial Revolution had brought made it easier for more people to save part of their income to be loaned to the merchants as capital.

Outside of the relatively few great trading companies which had been granted monopolies by royal charter to particular areas of the world, there arose an increasing number of merchants who were able and willing to carry on trade independently if they could have the freedom to do so. The same factors (more available capital, less risk in business, and more ways of distributing the risks) which had made even the favored chartered companies less zealous for Mercantilism and its policies made this outside group of merchants vigorous opponents of the restrictive aspects of the policy. As early as 1625 the East India Company had begun to have trouble with these outside merchants who were not members of the company. They were called "Interlopers" and in the course of time they became so strong that they were able to force the company to reorganize and take them in. By 1700 there were writers from the merchant class using the argument that trade ought to be free from government regulation. They said that if the trade was not profitable the merchants would quit it anyway, and if it was profitable, they did not need the government to tell them how to run their business. This point of view gradually became so popular that Mercantilism was doomed.

### A new view of government and business

The mere fact that Mercantilism came to be disliked was not of itself enough to displace it as the official policy of the national states. To get rid of something that is disliked, something else that can do the job more acceptably must be developed. If Mercantilism and its philosophy of controlling the economic system to promote the national wealth and well-being were to be replaced, it would

have to be by a new philosophy of the relationship of government and business which would give assurance of even greater wealth and prosperity. The ingredients of such a philosophy were developing in the sixteenth and seventeenth centuries from the effects of the Commercial Revolution, the Renaissance, and the growth of science. The eighteenth century saw the various strands of this new economic philosophy woven together to form a new pattern of economic thinking which remained dominant for nearly two centuries.

The elements of the new pattern of economic thought came from several sources. The incentive for a change from Mercantilism came, of course, from economic development itself. It was the stabilization of markets and the availability of capital which were at the bottom of the desire of merchants to get away from Mercantilism and go it alone. That desire was reinforced by the belief that a rational order was the essential characteristic of the universe, and, since it was individual man who possessed the power of reason, the individual became supremely important in his own right. This belief had been developed by Greek philosophers before the time of Christ, was revived at the time of the Renaissance, and grew continuously in importance after that in western European thought.

The result of these economic and philosophic forces was a new scheme of economic thinking according to which it was believed that individual man ought to be free to seek his own welfare as his reason might direct, and that the government ought not to interfere with him in this activity. In practical terms, this meant an economic system of free enterprise or free competition, or, as it is more commonly called by economic writers, the system of *laissez faire*. This term was coined by a French economist of the eighteenth century and has come to symbolize the idea that government should allow business to be carried on without interference or control.

The new synthesis was not achieved and accepted easily. Many merchants, of course, were ready to go ahead on their own as soon as mercantilist laws were repealed or were allowed to lapse through nonenforcement. They were not philosophers, and they felt no compulsion to ask whether the exercise of economic freedom was right or wrong so long as they found it to their advantage. But philosophers could not dismiss the problem so easily. It had always been recognized that there are some evil human tendencies, among them avarice and selfishness. No one had ever doubted that self-interest or selfishness was a very powerful element among man's motives, but until the eighteenth century it had always been felt that the church, the government, or some other social institution must hold individual selfishness in check or control it so that it might not harm the public. Otherwise, men would constantly be trying to cut each other's throats.

The solution of this philosophical difficulty came in the evolution of the proposition that since man is a product of nature all his traits are inherently good. Also, since the essence of nature is rational harmony, the seemingly bad traits of human behavior are really good traits that are misunderstood. When the problem of self-interest was approached from this angle, as it was by Adam Smith in his *Wealth of Nations* (1776), a new economic theory emerged to the effect that while each individual is acting to promote his own interests, all other individuals are doing the same, so that they come into competition with each other and each is thereby limited in what he can do. Each person acts in his own interest if permitted by the government to do so, but is so limited by competitors in what he *can* do that the final effect of a system relying upon individual self-interest for motivation is that the public welfare is promoted more effectively than by any other system. The well-understood self-interest of each, when combined, makes for the well-being of all. That was the conclusion of Smith's reasoning. It made the new economic ideas appear to be morally right, practically advantageous, and an expression of the unchanging natural laws by which the universe operates and to which human laws and practices should conform for the greatest happiness and welfare of mankind.

Without wishing to shed a tear over the broken and battered body of mercantilist thought, a few further observations should be made about the newer ideas. In the first place, the case for *laissez faire* rested upon the assumption that the existence of free competition was both morally valid and practically possible. That assumption has not been questioned in the nineteenth and twentieth centuries by those who became the defenders of a policy of government noninterference in business. The defenders of *laissez faire* found more comfort in regarding their ideas as part of the immutable natural law by which the world operates. Those who take a more realistic point of view question the assumption that the continued existence of absolutely free competition indefinitely is even possible and recognize that the case for *laissez faire* as a policy of government is weakened in the same proportion as monopolistic elements creep into a business system.

The relatively prompt and widespread acceptance of the new *laissez-faire* system of economic thought is itself something of a miracle. We have said that changes in ideas are likely to be the slowest of all, and so they are—usually. In this case, some special circumstances contributed to a rather sudden shift. Perhaps most important of all was the fact that the economic class which had become the envy of all others because of the rapid increase of its wealth (the merchant class), was the class which had the most powerful incentive to adopt and preach the new ideas. Then, too, the doctrines of the rationality of individual man and of natural law upon which the new economic theory was built, were presented as ancient ideas which through error had been lost. They did not have to be dealt with cautiously and experimentally like most new and perhaps heretical ideas. They could be seized quickly and surely, so that by incorporating them into current thought the errors of the past could be brought to an end at the earliest possible moment. The converts to the new economic ideas did not feel that they had to be ashamed of their convictions. Rather, they were possessed of the self-righteous assurance of the wandering sinner who finally sees the light and returns to the ancestral fold confident of his reception.

Other economists, including Jeremy Bentham, David Ricardo, and J. R. McCulloch in England and J. B. Say in France, supported and extended the economic analysis of Smith's *Wealth of Nations*. The new economic ideas were translated into official government policy in England as rapidly as Parliament could get around to it. Shortly after 1800 the ribbon weavers of London filed a complaint with Parliament that their wages were not being set by the method provided by the labor law which had been enacted originally in the reign of Queen Elizabeth. Parliament replied to the complaint, not by enforcing the law but by repealing it and leaving wage determination to supply and demand. Workers were generally opposed to the *laissez-faire* principle, because the new machine processes were temporarily reducing the demand for labor. The labor market was glutted, wages were depressed and, lacking legal protection of wage levels, the workers suffered; but they were not organized to make their influence felt. They were not eligible to vote in England, and Parliament proceeded to repeal mercantilist laws in spite of them. By 1850, the last important restrictive law dating from the era of Mercantilism had been repealed, and England was firmly embarked on a new policy of economic liberalism, so called because it permitted individuals freedom to manage their own affairs as they pleased. England became the leader among the nations of the world in removing controls from businessmen, including tariffs and all other restrictions on imported goods.

France, somewhat hesitantly, followed England's example. After the French Revolution, the individualistic character of the French people expressed itself in the growth of a very large class of small landowning farmers. France did not have as large a class of big businessmen as England, and therefore pursued the liberal policy with somewhat less enthusiasm. Germany had neither the big business nor many small landowners, and so

was not enthusiastic about economic liberalism. America, on the other hand, possessed a spirit of fierce individualism stemming from the pioneering by which the continent had been settled, but was fearful of free competition between her industries and the older industries of Europe. Thus in the United States economic liberalism was the official policy from the very beginning of its national history, but the government found it convenient to forget that the removal of all tariffs on imported goods was indicated if one believed fully in *laissez faire*, just as much as the removal of government controls over the business activities of private individuals. A dual policy was actually followed.

As we look at the transition to *laissez faire* from the vantage point which history gives us, it cannot be denied that the new policy contributed to world economic development. Perhaps it was not quite the universal panacea for all economic ills of all countries which some of its enthusiastic supporters took it to be because it served their own economic interests so well. Its effect was very bad for a time on some classes of people. But, as economists concerned with the public good as a whole, we should have to admit that *laissez faire* gave better opportunities for development and expansion to merchants and manufacturers than they would have had otherwise. A stage of development had been reached at which individual businessmen were capable of going ahead without government help, and at which the market was opening up opportunities almost everywhere one might turn. The transition from government control to *laissez faire* did hurt some people, but on the whole it gave the class of people who could do most to promote the public good a freer chance to do just that (whether or not this was their conscious objective). The commercial and industrial capitalists were definitely in the saddle as soon as *laissez faire* became effective. They may have started the rest of society upon a rather rough ride, but at least more rapid and substantial progress began to be made toward the life of material abundance than had ever before been achieved.

## Social and economic changes

### Increased production and distribution of goods

A direct and immediate effect of the Industrial Revolution was a sharp acceleration of the rate of output in those industries for which new methods had been developed. More goods meant that wealth was being created at a faster rate, and that a higher standard of living was becoming possible. The goods themselves were turned out by power-driven machines whose great virtue was that they could perform the same productive operation over and over again with unbelievable speed. This process has since come to be called *mass production*. The product is characterized by quantity and absolute uniformity. To move goods from the factory door to the consumer required fast and cheap transportation, and new marketing agencies. Wholesalers and brokers of many types appeared to meet the need. Since the product was uniform, selling could be by sample, and orders could be given for goods to be delivered according to specifications of the buyer. Under such circumstances the traveling salesman put in his appearance. In fact, the whole elaborate marketing and distributing system with which we are familiar today is a by-product of the Industrial Revolution with its great output of standardized goods.

### Capitalistic organization introduced in industry

The achievement of greater output was possible because inventions and technical development put machines in the place of men. To buy these new machines, to provide power to drive them, and to procure raw materials on which they might work required far larger concentrations of capital than had ever before been used in the production of goods. The Commercial Revolution had required capital invested in trade. Until the effects of the Industrial Revolution began to be felt, the biggest businesses were the commercial companies like the East India Company. When the new inventions had been improved to the point of being practical for industrial use, capital began to be required in industry as well as in trade. At first, the industrial capitalists were either individual proprietors of their businesses or members of a partnership. The joint-stock company or corporation was not widely used in industry until the latter half of the nineteenth century. In spite of the larger amounts of capital required as a result of the new inventions, there were still individuals who could raise the necessary amounts. Industries could be established, at least, by the capital which individual promoters might own or borrow. Eventually, the continuous progress of invention and the development of ever more involved but efficient industrial processes led to the great industrial corporations of the present day in the leading industrial countries.

The increased need for capital on the part of industry kept the demand for capital at a high level, as it had been since the effects of the Commercial Revolution began to be felt in the sixteenth century. Since that time the western European countries had greatly increased their wealth and hence their ability to supply capital to business. For two centuries or more, commercial undertakings had been able to absorb all the capital that was raised by the aid of banks, joint-stock companies, and individual savings. The coming of industrial inventions and their continued occurrence through the nineteenth and twentieth centuries added new demand for capital. With this demand added, the total demand for capital continued into the twentieth century to tax the ability of an increasingly wealthy population to supply it.

In view of this generally high demand for capital during the last three and a half centuries, it is not surprising that Western legal and moral, as well as economic, thinking has traditionally taken a scarcity of capital for granted, as though it were some kind of universal truth. It is a sound economic axiom

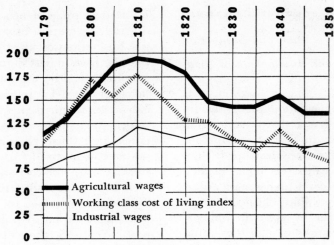

Fig. V-1 *A study of the trends taken by wages and prices in England between 1790 and 1850. Notice the contrast between agricultural and industrial wages and the leveling off of industrial wages after an early spurt. Note too the position of the cost of living line in relation to wages.*

that the greatest care is taken in using the scarcest factor of production. For three or four centuries, capital has been the scarcest factor, strategic in the sense of being the factor about which the most careful planning of strategy has had to be done.

As a result of this strategic position of capital, society has permitted the capitalist, or owner of productive property, a great deal of power in laying down the conditions under which he will permit his capital to be used. If anyone had not liked those conditions, there was little that could be done about it, for capital was relatively scarce and any additional quantities that could be obtained were highly productive for everyone's ultimate benefit. The strategic position and power of capital and the capitalist class thus became one of the characteristics of modern society and the capitalist class has been able to influence the social mores to an extent far greater than its numbers alone would indicate. The sanctity of property when compared, for example, with the legal and moral rights of consumers or workers shows that a capitalist point of view has extended itself into many phases of life wherever Western civilization has spread.

*Industry removed from the home*

*to the factory*

Because of the shift of work from the home to the factory, a great many aspects of the worker's life were changed. One change which workers bitterly resented at first was the discipline of the factory. They could not work early or late as they pleased, nor could they do the work in the way they thought best. They had to be at the factory at a set hour, and must work as long as the employer required. Also, the work in the factory was done under the employer's direction and there were fines for any violation of the rules. The machines were large and costly and belonged to the employer. The Industrial Revolution separated the worker from any ownership either in the machines or in the materials upon which he worked. The worker's financial interest in the work was solely in the wage he expected to be paid. As operators of power machines, workers had greater safety hazards in the factory than in work at home on hand machines. This was generally not appreciated by early factory owners, who took few or no safety precautions. Also, the grouping of many workers together in one room for long work hours brought new large-scale problems of industrial hygiene which were not understood. Light and ventilation were usually bad, contributing to both accident and disease, and sanitary facilities were often almost totally lacking. Production, of course, was on a much larger scale, and the factories drew together larger groups of workers facing common problems than had ever happened before. Out of common situations and problems came common opinions and attitudes. Workers were not organized at first, but the mass psychology which developed among them in the factories was the basis upon which labor organizations eventually grew.

### Unemployment, oppression of workers, and antimachine riots

An early effect of the Industrial Revolution was to create unemployment among hand workers. The aim of the search for new methods in industry was to increase efficiency, which meant to save labor. The successful development of new methods naturally resulted in the displacement of hand workers. This effect was particularly evident in England in the first decades of the Industrial Revolution, but to a degree it has continued ever since and it has appeared in other countries as new methods have been developed and introduced. The unemployment caused by the introduction of labor-saving machines and processes came to be called "technological unemployment."

The first large-scale factory operations were those making use of Arkwright's water frame (p. 90) in the spinning of yarn. The application of power machines in the textile industry caused unemployment in the early years, both because fewer workers could accomplish a larger volume of output and because a whole new labor supply was tapped by the factories in the employment of children and women. Perhaps because the work in the spinning mills was mostly rather light, and be-

cause spinning had been a traditional job for women with some help from the children in the family, the early factories employed a very large proportion of children and women. Wages paid to them were lower than those that would have to be paid to men. The eventual development of a practical power loom forced the hand-loom weavers also to go to the factories for work or remain unemployed. The new weaving mills, like the spinning mills, could employ many women and children as well as men. Protest against these factories and their "engines" arose quite early, even before the employment of men had been seriously affected. In 1779 in Lancashire, England, rioting mobs roamed the countryside breaking machines (water frames), burning factories, and killing anyone who opposed them. Such outbreaks continued sporadically for many years, especially at times when the shortage of employment was aggravated by wars or other conditions which restricted the normal volume of trade.

These employment conditions, existing as they did at a time when the English Poor Law in effect dated back to the sixteenth century, produced terrible abuses of children and the unemployed. The old Poor Law regarded anyone who was not working as being unemployed through his own fault. Those who applied to parish officials for poor relief were called vagrants, and the law specified that the Poor Law authorities might apprentice their children if work could be found for them. Because the new mills were looking for cheap labor and could use children, parish officials were able to lighten the financial burden of providing poor relief by selling the labor of the children whose parents had had to apply for relief. Mantoux gives a vivid description of the situation:

Spinning was quickly learned and needed little strength, while for certain processes the small size of the children and their delicacy of touch made them the best aids to the machines. They were preferred, too, for other and more conclusive reasons. Their weakness made them docile, and they were more easily reduced to a state of passive obedience than grown men. They were also very cheap. Sometimes they were given a trifling wage, which varied between a third and a sixth of an adult wage; and sometimes their only payment was food and lodging. Lastly they were bound to the factory by indentures of apprenticeship, for at least seven years, and usually until they were twenty-one. It was obviously to the spinners' interest to employ as many as possible and thus to reduce the number of workmen. The first Lancashire factories were full of children. Sir Robert Peel had over a thousand in his workshops at once.

The majority of these wretched children were paupers, supplied (one might almost say sold) by the parishes where they belonged. Especially during the first period of machine industry, when factories were built outside, and often far from, the towns, manufacturers would have found it impossible to recruit the labor they needed from the immediate neighborhood. And the parishes on their side were only too anxious to get rid of their paupers. Regular bargains, beneficial to both parties, if not to the children, who were dealt with as mere merchandise, were entered into between the spinners on the one hand and the Poor Law authorities on the other. Lots of fifty, eighty or a hundred children were supplied and sent like cattle to the factory, where they remained imprisoned for many years. Certain parishes drove even better bargains and stipulated that the buyer should take idiots in the proportion of one to every twenty children sent. At the beginning, these "parish apprentices" were the only children employed in the factories. The workmen, very justifiably, refused to send their own. But unfortunately this resistance did not last long, as they were soon driven by want to a step which at first had so much horrified them.[1]

The employment conditions of the pauper apprentices were made still worse by a contract labor system which frequently prevailed. A husband and his wife would contract with the parish authorities for the labor of a group of the children on poor relief, and would then contract with a factory owner to supply the labor of the children to him. The factory owner was thus not the direct employer of the children, and the contractor who had hired them from the parish was respon-

[1] Paul Mantoux, *The Industrial Revolution in the Eighteenth Century* (New York: Harcourt, Brace and Co., 1928), pp. 420-421.

sible only for seeing that they did their work. Often the contractor became the equivalent of a foreman or superintendent in the factory, while his wife managed a large house or dormitory in which the children were lodged and fed. This system was particularly vicious in that no one felt any responsibility for the welfare of the children. The only concern was to get the maximum amount of work out of them. They were roused early in the morning, fed before daylight, and sent off to the factory by the time the light was strong enough for them to see their work. Lunch periods were short and work continued until light failed in the evening. The food was inadequate, and the mills were dark and damp. Tuberculosis was rampant, loss of fingers and arms in the machines was not uncommon, and very few pauper apprentices grew up to be normal, healthy, undeformed adults. In fact, the conditions in the early factories and mines were so bad that when we read of them today we are likely to believe that the account is exaggerated and untrue. Unfortunately, the testimony before English Royal Commissions appointed on several occasions to investigate factory conditions proves beyond a doubt that, horrible as they were, they did exist more widely than we like to think.

With machines taking the place of hand workers, and with children and women taking the place of men as machine attendants, it is not surprising that the supply of labor was so much greater than the demand, and that wages were forced to very low levels. To make matters worse for the workers, Parliament was fast moving toward complete *laissez faire*, so that the protective arm of the government was not available to save workers even from grave abuses. Twelve hours a day was standard working time for the early factories and fourteen hours was common during busy periods. All in all, the factory system left the working class in a dreary state. Hand workers found themselves thrown out of employment or the price of their work heavily cut. If they sought poor relief, their children would be taken away from them and herded off to the factories. If they obtained work in the factories, the hours were long and the wages low. Neither was a very pleasant prospect.

The workers were not content with the conditions in which they found themselves, but, being humble and uneducated folk, they simply had to submit to the beating which unfavorable economic conditions administered. Many of them sank down into an unlovely, sodden mass of humanity—ignorant, dirty, and slovenly in their manner of living and dressing, dishonest and shiftless. A few among those fortunate enough to enjoy a better living standard became ardent reformers determined to bring an end to such conditions. Laws to regulate the work of pauper apprentices date back to 1798 in England and in the 1830's the first English Factory Acts were passed. Others who saw the conditions of workers in an industrial capitalist economic system became critics of the system as a whole. The prospects for the continuation of the capitalist system in the twentieth century would be much better than they are had not the industrial capitalists of the early nineteenth century given so much for the critics of capitalism to feed on. The extremely bad conditions contributed significantly to the reaction against capitalism.

### The growth of industrial cities and slums

The Industrial Revolution led to an entirely new evaluation of the forces affecting the location of industry, because it introduced several highly important factors that had not been involved previously. Before the steam engine was developed, the availability of water power led to the location of industries along swift streams. After the steam engine had been made practical, industry tended to locate in coal-producing areas, since coal was the fuel most commonly used to produce steam. The steam engine first permitted the free growth of industrial towns wherever other factors favored the development of large-scale manufacturing. After canals and railroads had been developed, the dependence of light industry

like textiles on coal was less direct, since coal could easily be moved to them. Industries such as iron and steel that used large quantities of coal were, and still are, pretty much limited as to location by the availability of coal, as well as of iron ore and limestone. Compared with the older hand industry, the new fuel and raw material requirements of machine industry led to the concentration of manufacturing in certain restricted areas where it might not have been carried on extensively before.

There had been large cities since ancient times, so that it is not correct to say that cities as such are a product of the Industrial Revolution. It is true, however, that before the Industrial Revolution industry had not been the cause for the growth of cities. Once a source of power was available which could be set up where it was needed and once machines were available to apply that power to the making of cloth and other products, a completely new basis was laid for the rise of large centers of population. The old hand industry had not required a great concentration of population; in fact, it would have been hampered had living become congested. The new factory industry, on the other hand, required that many workers be employed at the same place, and convenience required that these workers should live near enough to their work to reach it easily.

The progress of the Industrial Revolution, therefore, was marked by the springing up of industrial towns and cities. Since *laissez faire* had become the rule in government, there were no building or sanitary regulations to be followed. Workers whose wages were low could afford little for housing. The idea of public transportation had not been developed, so that workers had to live within walking distance of their source of employment. All of these conditions worked together to produce a type of housing for industrial workers which very quickly became slums of the worst sort. Families were crowded together in one or two rooms which often had no windows for light or ventilation. Water for cooking and bathing had to be carried in buckets from pumps that might be some distance away, and might have to be carried up several flights of steps at that. Construction was not fireproof, and the loss of life in tenement-house fires was often serious. These conditions prevailed because when *laissez faire* was in effect and labor to attend machines was more abundant than capital to build them, there was no purely economic reason to make better provision for a factor of production that was overabundant anyway. Supply and demand will always work under full *laissez faire*, but they may be ruthless in their effect upon those in an economically weak position.

These shifts in the industrial population brought other results. In England, some areas where hand manufacture of textiles had been carried on extensively were left entirely stranded. The unemployed had to be taken care of by parish officials from taxes placed on property. The parishes were so afraid of newcomers that relief would be given only to those who had lived in the parish for a stated number of years. As a result, the unemployed were afraid to go to a new community to get a job because if they failed they would not be eligible for relief. The result was that the inhabitants of stranded communities stayed at home on relief rather than go elsewhere in search of work. In some authenticated cases, the burden of poor relief taxes on property became so heavy that property owners abandoned their property and fled from the parish themselves. Such conditions were too bad to last long, and the ultimate effect of industrial shifts was the moving of population to those places where work was available. The population of industrial countries became very unevenly distributed, with concentrations in industrial areas. On a world-wide basis, migrations to and from industrial countries developed also in the nineteenth century, especially from Europe to America. Population movements of this kind were brought under the control of immigration laws, but within countries migration continued from agricultural to industrial areas or from declining industries to expanding ones. The Industrial Revolution greatly increased the mobility of population.

| INCREASE BETWEEN | | |
|---|---|---|
| 1821 and 1831 | 1,100,000 |
| 1831 and 1841 | 1,270,000 |
| 1841 and 1851 | 1,800,000 |

A. Increase of population living in towns of 20,000 or more in Great Britain between 1821 and 1851.

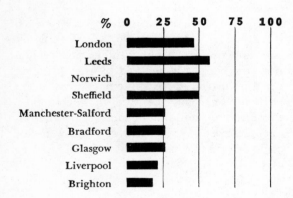

B. % of native-born inhabitants living in big cities (1851).

*Fig. V-2  The shift in England's population from rural to urban areas, brought about by the Industrial Revolution.*

### The rapid increase in population

The conditions described in the two preceding sections would not seem to be favorable to a rapid increase in population, and indeed they were not. They do not tell the whole story of the Industrial Revolution, however. The study of population has shown that a low standard of living does not necessarily mean a low birth rate, in fact, more nearly the opposite. A rapid increase in population occurs not so much from a change in the birth rate as from an improvement in the survival rate of the babies that are born. The Industrial Revolution did bring about an increase in the production of wealth, and, in spite of the immediate worsening of the condition of industrial workers, it eventually brought about an improvement in their standard of living, as well

as that of everyone else. With a higher standard of living came a higher survival rate for
babies, or, as it is more commonly stated, a
reduction in the death rate. In England, which
was the first country to feel the effects of the
Industrial Revolution, the population surged
upward as rarely before. Wherever the Industrial Revolution has spread, the story has been
the same. After a still longer time—a half-century or more—the urban civilization brought
about by industrialization seems to have had
the effect of stopping the rapid increase of
population by a reduction of the birth rate.
For an intermediate period following the introduction of power-machine industry, a rapid
increase in population was one of its important effects.

### The creation of new economic classes

It may seem unnecessary to list specifically
the creation of an industrial capitalist and an
industrial wage-earning class as results of the
Industrial Revolution, but to insure complete-
ness they should be included. The special importance of these new classes is that they have
provided the points of view which have become the basis of controversy and conflict in
contemporary industrial societies. In a society
in which agriculture is predominant, controversy might be between landowners and farm
laborers or between large holders and small
holders. Where modern capitalistic industry
has developed, the economic problems that
arise to be debated are those in which capital,
or management, and labor are likely to have
points of view that cannot be reconciled without discussion and a good bit of give and take.
The owners and managers of industry are
likely to be satisfied with a *laissez-faire* policy,
and to wish to have the government exercise a
minimum of control. Traditionally, labor has
been in a weaker economic position and has
been inclined to look to government for enough
help to compensate for this weakness. The
importance of public issues in which these
traditionally antagonistic points of view are
involved reflects the extent to which the Industrial Revolution has affected political life.

### A new basis for understanding the economic system

Since the period of the Industrial Revolution is so close to our own time—at least from
the long-range view of the historian—the developments and the ways of thinking of that
era are peculiarly important to us in the twentieth century. In fact, no period is probably of
as great importance in establishing the economic practices and thinking which we still
follow. Future generations will certainly have
different estimates of importance, but as of
now, it seems to us that our governmental and
business systems became established in the
period we have just examined.

From this long-range point of view, and
trying to dissect the economic system as a lab-
oratory technician might do with a specimen
under his microscope, we can see that the new
economic system relied upon individual freedom as the older systems had relied upon control and guidance of the individual by some
higher agency of church or state. We have
already seen that this new idea of individual
independence had been fostered by the success
of the growing commercial class. Members of
this class, at least, were willing and eager to
trust to the initiative of individuals who were
seeking their own personal profit as the driving force which would carry the whole society
to the highest possible levels of prosperity.
This would occur through the action of self-
seeking individuals in the market place, where
all would meet—figuratively if not literally—to
drive the best bargains they could. But since
this system did not depend upon government,
or any other social agency, but rested upon the
natural, inborn traits of human beings everywhere and at all times, the system was thought
to be universal both in time and space. This
is to say that it would work anytime and anywhere that society gave it a chance to work.
This system of economic action and thought—
the *laissez-faire* system as we call it—aroused
passionate support by successful merchants
and others who had or could profit by it.
Their leadership succeeded in establishing the

new system throughout the world wherever conditions were such that individuals could see opportunities for their own profit and could convince a controlling group of their fellow men that *laissez faire* should be given a chance to show in practice what it could do.

The English North American colonies—most of which became independent as the United States of America after the Revolutionary War—were among the parts of the world in which the new way of thinking became strongly established. Elsewhere, the *laissez-faire* system spread throughout western Europe and wherever the western European nations carried it to their empires in Asia, Africa, South America and Australia. World trade was not freed of government controls, however, and European countries held their colonies in an economic condition throughout the nineteenth century and into the twentieth, which would have pleased any good Mercantilist of the sixteenth or seventeenth centuries. But the ideas of personal freedom were carried throughout the world—even if in subdued form for colonial peoples.

Germany—a country which had remained divided and economically weak until the nineteenth century—did not respond favorably to the new ways of thinking about the economic system. *Laissez faire* never made a deep impression on German economic thought. Thus it is natural that Germany should be the source of much of the economic thinking which was critical of *laissez faire* and the notion of the automatic regulation of the economic system by the free, competitive market. This critical phase of economic thinking began in the nineteenth century, as an important movement, but has carried over into the twentieth century.

But in England particularly, and throughout the English speaking parts of the world, and to a lesser degree in France, Spain, Italy, the low countries and Scandinavia, the new ideas took deep root. A succession of English thinkers, as we have seen, elaborated a theoretical structure to support the new system of economic action. We have also seen (Introduction, p. 26) that the French economist J. B.

Say provided a framework for viewing the free, competitive, market system which became almost standard. Other economists operating within this essential framework, have continued to the present time to elaborate and extend the economic analysis inherited from Adam Smith, J. B. Say, David Ricardo, and others of their time.

## An interpretation of the new theory of the economic system

It is easy to see that the new view of the economic system as centered upon the actions of free individuals in the marketplace was by far the most adequate explanation of an economic system which had ever been developed. It is now also easy to see—as measured by results—that the system itself was perhaps the best ever developed by mankind. In terms of our own analysis of economic systems, we can understand many of the factors which tended to produce the new kind of market-centered system. We can see it as a natural, evolutionary development of the business system in an increasingly democratic political and social environment. We can understand the strong appeal of personal freedom. We can recognize that many of those to whom economic freedom appealed most strongly would be those who would use it to avail themselves of the opportunities of the new areas of the world. Thus, we can understand why the new *laissez faire* system should become strongly rooted in the colonies of the nations of western Europe and, particularly, in those of England.

But, we can also understand that there would be a wide difference between our own understanding of this development and that of those who brought it about in the eighteenth and early nineteenth centuries. For one thing, the idea of evolution is now commonplace. Charles Darwin published his *Origin of Species* in 1859, more than a century ago. He presented the idea as largely biological, but it is now recognized as having far broader applications. Darwin was stimulated by the facts about population presented by T. R. Malthus (Introduction, p. 33). It is now known, too, that there were advance evidences of the evolutionary point of view long before Darwin, as is nearly always true of major advances in thought. Yet, there is little evidence that the idea of continuous evolution and development affected the generations of thinkers and businessmen who, themselves, developed the free market theory.

On the contrary, all of the evidence is that another, and at least partially contradictory idea, had a far more powerful hold upon their minds and actions—the idea of a rational order in the universe. It was believed that this rational order of nature prescribed certain rights of man, including the right to seek personal gain in the open competition of the market. Insofar as the new system was viewed in this way, it was thought to be beyond the need for any further change. This position can be described as absolute rather than evolutionary. From a point of view which recognizes the evolution of human society and human institutions to be continuous, this is a strange state of affairs, for the concept of rational order is itself one of the great landmarks of human achievement. In the further development of economic thought, as business and social conditions changed, any new ideas which were critical of the *laissez-faire* system had to face the objection that they were contrary to the economic laws of the natural order of the universe.

## Europe's place in the world economy of the nineteenth century

The economic power which Europe had gained as a result of the Commercial Revolution of the sixteenth and seventeenth centuries was extended and made more secure by the Industrial Revolution of the eighteenth century and after. England, in particular, which had been the leader in developing and exploiting the new industrial processes, enjoyed great wealth and extensive influence. Other countries, noting England's prosperity, set out to develop new industries also. Spain, Portugal, and Holland were not very successful because they lacked raw materials. Germany was held back in her industrial development because she was divided into a number of independent states. After the unification of Germany in 1870 her industrialization moved very rapidly, and by 1900 Germany was leading Europe in her production in several basic industries. France continued to have an economy balanced between industry and agriculture. Her industries were mostly light and required artistic quality and hand skill. She did develop the iron and steel industry to some degree, but both England and Germany surpassed her.

While Europe led in industry, the rest of the world supplied her with raw materials and bought her products. As a result of the Commercial Revolution, European nations had established empires in Asia, Africa, and the Americas. After the Industrial Revolution, these empires acquired a new significance, for mass-production industries had an insatiable appetite for raw materials, and finished products must move to market quickly lest the flow of production become clogged. England in particular was fortunate in that she had the wherewithal to support industry at home, and had in her empire a tremendous market. Some countries, like China, were able to remain free of attachment to any one European country, but were included in the European economic orbit nonetheless. The United States and other countries in the Americas were able to gain freedom from Europe in a political sense, but continued to be linked economically.

It may be noted in passing that the industrial demand for raw materials and markets established a new basis for imperialism by the dominant industrial powers. Industrially undeveloped areas came to be regarded as "backward," which made them fair game for the exploitation of the more "advanced" countries. Rivalries developed among the great powers for control of the consuming markets of such populous countries as India and

China and for the raw materials of Malaya, the East Indies, Africa, and South America. It has often been said that World War I occurred because of the hostility that developed particularly between England and Germany as a result of their rivalry in gaining control of world markets and world raw materials. In all of these activities, the nations of Europe were the leaders in the last half of the nineteenth century and the first decades of the twentieth. The United States was also developing rapidly, but home markets and home resources more fully absorbed her energies.

Thus, the nineteenth century found Europe at the pinnacle of her supremacy. It was a supremacy based primarily on economic power, on the ability to produce and distribute goods more cheaply than anyone else in the world and thus to create wealth more rapidly and extensively than ever before. The wealth of Europe gave her prestige. It also gave her military power. For one reason or the other, the ideas and the way of life of Europeans made a deep impression upon all the peoples of the earth. In the Americas, Australia, and New Zealand, a pattern of living and thinking which was originally European has become almost completely dominant. Elsewhere the impression made by European civilization varied, but affected the lives of many peoples.

## FOR FURTHER READING

Bogart, Ernest L. *Economic History of Europe: 1760-1939*. New York: Longmans, Green & Co., Inc., 1942. Chapter 3.

Bowden, Witt. *Industrial Society in England Towards the End of the Eighteenth Century*. New York: The Macmillan Co., 1925. Chapters 3—4.

Hammond, John L., and Hammond, Barbara. *The Rise of Modern Industry*. New York: Harcourt, Brace & Co., 1926. Chapters 12—15.

Knight, Melvin M., Barnes, Harry Elmer, and Flügel, Felix. *Economic History of Europe in Modern Times*. Boston: Houghton Mifflin Co., 1928. Chapter 4.

Mantoux, Paul. *The Industrial Revolution in the Eighteenth Century*. 2nd rev. ed. Translated by M. Vernon. New York: The Macmillan Co., 1961. Part III, Chapters 1—4.

Roberts, David W. *Outline of the Economic History of England*. New York: Longmans, Green & Co., Inc., 1931. Part III, Chapters 7—8.

Soltau, Roger H. *An Outline of European Economic Development*. New York: Longmans, Green & Co., Inc., 1935. Chapter 6.

Tickner, Frederick W. *Social and Industrial History of England*. New York: Longmans, Green & Co., Inc., 1929. Chapters 39 and 40.

Usher, Abbott Payson. *Introduction to the Industrial History of England*. Boston: Houghton Mifflin Co., 1920. Chapters 15 and 16.

# Part II: America's Evolving Economy

Part II: America's Evolving Economy

# *Chapter 6:* *Economic beginnings*

# *in North America*

To understand the attitude of Europeans toward the American continents in the first century or two after their discovery by Columbus, it is necessary to keep in mind the characteristic points of view of the Commercial Revolution and Mercantilism. In the first instance, the portion of America encountered by Columbus was regarded as an outlying and essentially useless part of the Indies which kept Columbus from reaching his real goal, the centers of Oriental trade. Within a few decades, when it was definitely established that the Americas constituted a great land mass lying between Europe and the Orient, a keen competition sprang up among European nations to discover a passage around or through this great land barrier. Only when they failed to find easy ways of getting around America did the explorers begin to search the land and study its native inhabitants for anything of value which they could carry back to Europe. Europeans then began to think of it as a vast and mysterious, but intriguing, new world where anything might be found.

Europeans continued to maintain an exploitative attitude toward the Americas long after permanent settlements had been established on the new continents. Just as the period of discovery made later colonization possible in America, so it also provided the basis for the development of the economic policy of Mercantilism. In fact, the establishment of colonies for the purpose of providing reinforcement of any weak spots in the economy of the mother country became a cardinal part of the mercantilist doctrine. One of the very important aspects of Mercantilism was that policy was formulated by and for one nation as though no other nations had a right to exist. Mercantilism was thus an isolationist and self-centered national policy. This same narrow attitude was applied to colonies. Colonies had no rights or interests of their own which should be supported, except as the interests of the colonies and the mother country could be served by the same policies. Both the land and the people of the colonies were to serve the homeland. At first this policy meant exploring new territories for any natural wealth which could be picked up at once. After such direct and immediate exploitation had been exhausted or had been shown to be fruitless, settlements were established which would permit exploitation on a much larger scale. The colony thus established did not exist for itself or its own people, but for the benefit of the mother country. Any ideas to the contrary which might occur to the colonists could only be a source of friction and trouble.

## The growth of settlements

### The course of exploration

Although the honor of making the first officially verified discovery of America belonged to Spain, expeditions sent out by other countries were soon exploring the coasts of the Americas and establishing claims. In 1500 Cabral, sailing from Portugal for India by the route around Africa, was blown westward off his course in the south Atlantic and reached land, which he called Brazil. Ponce de Leon, sailing north in 1513 from the West Indies islands which Columbus had discovered, explored a land to which he gave the name Florida. A Portuguese sea captain named Ferdinand Magellan, sailing south from Spain in 1519, skirted the Atlantic coast line of South America and rounded it to reach the Pacific Ocean. He sailed his ships across the Pacific to the Philippine Islands, where he was killed. One of Magellan's ships, the *Victoria*, returned to Spain by crossing the Indian Ocean and rounding Africa. This first positive proof that the world was round was the most important of Magellan's discoveries. In addition, his exploration of the South American coast strengthened and defined more accurately the Spanish claim to part of that territory. As a result of the voyages of explorers, and of agreements between the countries and with the pope, American territory south of the Gulf of Mexico was divided between the Spanish and the Portuguese, with the latter established in Brazil and the Spanish everywhere else.

The English were preoccupied with other matters during the early portion of the era of exploration. Nevertheless, the merchants and fishermen of Bristol sent the Italian John Cabot with his three sons on a westerly voyage of exploration in 1497 and 1498. In their several voyages, the Cabots explored the coast of eastern North America from Newfoundland to Florida, and laid claim to land where English settlements were eventually made. Newfoundland became very important because of the excellent fishing on the Newfoundland banks. In fact, there is good reason to believe that they had been visited by European fishermen long before the time of Christopher Columbus. As word of the explorations in this area spread through Europe, fishermen from a number of countries began to go there during the fishing season. The Portuguese established temporary stations, and in 1508 a French expedition landed on what became the Cape Breton peninsula. This beginning of French interest in America was followed by other explorations later in the sixteenth century in what has become Canada.

By 1600 the American claims of Spain, Portugal, England, and France embraced both the northern and southern continents. Of the important European nations, only the Netherlands lacked claims in America, and this lack it was soon to make up. In 1609, the Englishman Henry Hudson, sailing for the Netherlands, established Dutch claims in the area that became New York and the Hudson Valley. No settlements were made until 1624 and 1626, and within forty years thereafter the Dutch surrendered to the more numerous British. North America was left to be divided up by the English, French, and Spanish. The Netherlands remained content with its rich territories in the Orient, while Portugal found herself adequately occupied with her claims in Brazil and islands in the East Indies. The Spanish were strongly entrenched from the Gulf of Mexico southward, while the French were extending their hold from Newfoundland into the interior by way of the St. Lawrence Valley and the Great Lakes. The territory along the eastern Atlantic seaboard from

Florida to the mouth of the St. Lawrence River was that to which English claims remained unchallenged. Probably more by luck than by foresight, the rich agricultural lands in this area established British supremacy in North America.

### The first settlements

The first attempts at settlement in that part of North America which later became the United States were made by commercial companies. The founding of the East India Company in 1600 stimulated the formation of other joint-stock companies. The London Company and the Plymouth Company were chartered in 1606 with rights of trade and settlement on the north Atlantic coast of America. Both companies sent out groups for the purpose of settlement in 1607. The first attempt of the Plymouth Company in what is now Maine was unsuccessful; the London Company's colonizing effort at Jamestown, Virginia, became an eventual success from the point of view of survival, after repeated reinforcements from England, but at great financial loss to the company.

These companies were interested in profit and sent over the kind of settlers who might be appealed to by a chance to make a fortune. There were the genteel but disinherited younger sons of the landed gentry, there were assorted ne'er-do-wells, and a few craftsmen to work up the minerals and precious metals which it was hoped would be found. The little group at Jamestown suffered terribly for the first few years. Disease, starvation, and attacks of the Indians, who had been needlessly antagonized, brought death to from 75 to 90 per cent of those who came over before 1610. These colonists were, on the whole, not the type of people who could adapt themselves easily to the rugged conditions of life in America, nor did they know enough about the new country to have prepared for it in advance.

While the London Company's settlers were still struggling to establish themselves securely on the new continent, a new group in 1619 began making plans and preparations for settlement in America. In 1608 a group of Separatists, a sect which had withdrawn entirely from the Church of England, had left England and had gone to Holland to gain greater religious freedom than they found at home. They found religious freedom as they had hoped, but other circumstances in Holland were not to their liking, and they began to consider a move elsewhere. Stories of the settlement in Virginia reached them and they began negotiations to secure for themselves a grant of land in America. They were successful in getting permission to settle within the territories allotted to the London Company, and in September 1620 they set out for America. Their ship, the *Mayflower*, arrived off Cape Cod in November. The Pilgrims had hoped to go farther south, but, finding it difficult to sail in that direction, they decided to remain where they were and to establish a settlement.

A great difference between the settlements in Virginia and those in Massachusetts was that the Pilgrims intended to make their homes in the New World and were not especially concerned with quick exploitation. It is true that they had agreed to send back to England such commodities as they could produce for export to repay the merchants who had financed the expedition, but the emphasis at the Plymouth colony was always on agriculture and the production of crops for subsistence. The toll of disease during the first winter was severe, but the Plymouth colony never made the great mistakes of antagonizing the Indians and misjudging the requirements of life on the new continent which brought the Jamestown colony so close to extinction on several occasions. Within a few years, as a result of perseverance and more efficient management, Plymouth was increasing in population and spreading out from the point of original settlement.

Conditions in England were not very happy for other dissenting groups in the first half of the seventeenth century. It was an era of bitter contention leading to the Civil War and the beheading of Charles I in 1649. The success of the Separatists in making a settlement at Plymouth led other religious groups to think of migrating to America. Of these, the largest and most influential group was that of the Puritans. Under the leadership of John Winthrop, who later became governor, the Massachusetts Bay Company was formed and established settlements to the north of Plymouth beginning in 1629. Following this start, a heavy Puritan migration set in and made Massachusetts by far the most populous American colony. It has been estimated that between 1630 and 1643 more than twenty thousand people left England for Massachusetts. The conditions to be met and overcome in America became widely known. The way was prepared for many other groups, under varied auspices, to establish settlements in the New World.

A good proportion of the later colonizing came as a branching out process from Virginia and Massachusetts. The fertile valley of the Connecticut River attracted settlers from both Plymouth and Massachusetts Bay and resulted in the establishment of Connecticut as a colony in 1635. Rhode Island was founded by the religious dissenters from Massachusetts Bay, Roger Williams and Anne Hutchinson, in 1637. To the north of Massachusetts, successful settlements were made by people from the older colony, and the area by the late 1630's became New Hampshire.

Virginia also stimulated settlement in territory adjacent to her. The Calvert family received from Charles I a grant of land which lay along the north bank of the Potomac River. The Calverts were Catholics, and they undertook in 1634 to found a settlement where Catholics who were subject to persecution in Europe might take refuge. They named their colony Maryland. Eventually they welcomed all Christians on the basis of mutual tolerance. South of Virginia, migrants from the older colony established permanent settlements in 1653. Other settlers came later, and Charles II granted a charter to create the new colony of Carolina. By 1700, North and South Carolina were distinct.

English settlement along the middle Atlantic coast was delayed by the Dutch occupancy of the Hudson Valley, but in 1664, a show of substantial naval force under command of the Duke of York caused the Dutch to surrender the area almost without bloodshed. The English terms to the Dutch were liberal. They were individually allowed to retain their property, and were denied only the political control of the home government. Almost immediately after New Amsterdam became New York, Dutch settlements to the south were taken over to make another new English colony—New Jersey. In 1681, William Penn received a charter to extensive lands west of the Delaware River. Penn was a Quaker, and he established a colony—Pennsylvania—where full religious tolerance was to be practiced, where taxes were to be equitable, and where other reforms were to be put into effect. English Quakers came to the new colony and there were also groups of Dutch, Welsh, and Swedes, in addition to the Germans who became one of the largest population groups in eastern Pennsylvania.

Beside the colonies which have been mentioned, there were two others which were numbered among the original thirteen. Delaware was granted to Penn by the Duke of York, in spite of Maryland's claims to the area. It remained attached to Pennsylvania until the Revolutionary War. Georgia was not chartered until 1732. It was recognized as being in an area which Spain also claimed. South Carolina favored the grant of Georgia to James Oglethorpe because she wanted a buffer between herself and the Spanish. Oglethorpe was a soldier and was willing to assume the risk of Spanish raids to establish a place where debtors might be given a new chance. The further story of the settlement of North America belongs to the period after the separation of the colonies from England.

### Economic problems faced by the English colonies

Regardless of the motives which prompted settlers to come to American shores, the necessities of living in the new and rugged environment, as well as the opportunities which that environment offered, became conditioning factors in the economic development of the New World. With shipping across the north Atlantic rather uncertain, colonists found themselves very soon unable to depend on supplies from Europe. If there were to be ample reserves of food, they had to be built up from hunting, fishing, and farming carried on in America. Fortunately, the American Indians found along the Atlantic seaboard were reasonably peaceable, and had developed agriculture extensively. The colonists emulated both their methods and their crops, both of which were new to Europeans. As soon as they could, the colonists began trying out the staple European farm crops and farm animals, and areas were found in the varied American climate and soil suitable for nearly all of the imported animals and plants. Thus, agriculture became quickly established in the American colonies as the foundation of economic life. It developed its own characteristics as a blend of European and Indian farming which seemed suitable for American conditions.

Along with farming, there developed other types of productive activity for which America offered good opportunities. Fisheries off the New England coast and northward were productive. The trapping of fur-bearing animals or trading for furs with the Indians could be carried on everywhere. Shipbuilding arose especially in New England to take advantage of the oak which was available for timbers and the pine for spars and masts. In the southern colonies, longleaf and slash pine produced tar, turpentine, and pitch used in building and maintaining ships. And in all the colonies iron forges were constructed using local rock or bog ores, and charcoal for their fuel. These industries arose either because of the need for their products by the colonists or because an advantageous trade could be developed with England or some other country. Most of them were industries depending upon the development of the rich natural resources of the new continent. Seldom did colonial industry turn out finely made products, for life required a larger measure of rugged strength than of skill

and gentility. Many times, colonial industries developed to meet household needs, and later expanded to find markets in other colonies or in Europe.

In general terms, it may be said that settlers in America were forced to give up any preconceived ideas they may have had upon arrival, and to adapt their economic activities to provide the elementary requirements of life. After food, clothing, and shelter were assured, the colonists could devote their energy to those kinds of production which American soil and resources made possible. Gold miners were not needed for many generations, but the equivalent to gold in value was soon found in the furs and ship timbers of the North; in the grain, meat, and hides of the middle colonies; and in the tobacco, rice, meat, and indigo of the South.

## Agriculture and related industries

### In New England

There were two factors which worked together to assure the success of the first white settlements in New England. First, the colonists came with the intention of making permanent homes. As a consequence they were interested in learning how to live in the new country. The second factor was that the Indians living in the Massachusetts area were peaceable farmers who were willing to teach the white men how to grow their staple crops. As a result, agriculture developed quickly and became the mainstay of life in New England.

Besides the meat obtained from hunting, and some fish and berries, the first foods produced by the New England colonists were the corn, pumpkins, squash, and beans which they learned how to grow from the Indians. The corn was planted in hills spaced about four feet apart each way with beans planted in each hill to vine on the corn stalks. Pumpkins and squash were planted to grow over the ground among the hills of corn. Wheat, rye, oats, barley, and buckwheat were introduced from England. They eventually became successful crops but did not displace those which were native to America. The white men found wild cherries and plums growing in New England as well as cranberries, huckleberries, raspberries, and blackberries. These fruits made a valuable addition to the diet and were soon supplemented by apples, pears, quinces, and peaches which were brought from Europe.

Although the Massachusetts Indians were successful farmers, their methods, which were copied by the immigrants from Europe, would have to be rated as quite crude even by European standards of that day. The ground was prepared for crops by cutting or killing the trees of the forested areas, and then digging up the loose soil with some kind of wooden or bone tool the equivalent of a hoe. For more than the first ten years there was not a single plow in Massachusetts. Crops were grown on a field until yields began to decline, when a new field would be cleared. This has been described as a system of rotating fields, rather than rotating crops. The Indians are said to have put a fish in each hill of corn, but this practice was not sufficient to prevent a depletion of soil fertility. The Indians had none of the common farm animals of today, but the colonists soon brought them from Europe. They were badly cared for because, until the productivity of agriculture was greatly increased, there was no adequate supply of livestock feed.

For the first few decades, farming was the basis of the colonial economy wherever settlements were made in New England. By the middle of the seventeenth century, however, yields had declined and farming was more successful on the better lands of the Connecticut River Valley and in the middle colonies. The people of the populous Atlantic coastal area of New England began to look more and more to the sea and to the great forests of pine, oak, and maple as sources of livelihood. Both fishing and shipbuilding had been started very early in New England's history. The north Atlantic fisheries from New England north to the banks of Newfoundland proved to be among the richest in the world. Mackerel, cod, and other varieties of fish were secured to supply not only local need but a growing trade. Whaling vessels pursued the sperm whale for its valuable oil and other products, first in nearby waters and later in both the Arctic and Antarctic oceans.

Along with the growth in fishing and the trade in fish, there very naturally went a growth of shipbuilding, for which New England timber was ideally suited. Timber had to be cut to clear land for farming, and wherever it was near enough to the coast or large streams, it could easily be moved to shipyards or used in the manufacture of barrel staves or ship timbers to be sold elsewhere. Down to the time of the Revolutionary War, fish and fish products remained the largest extractive industry of New England depending on the special natural resources of the region, while shipbuilding and lumber products constituted the second largest industry.

### In the middle colonies

Although the middle colonies—New York, New Jersey, and Pennsylvania—were not settled until a half century or more after Massachusetts and Virginia, their good agricultural lands soon gave them the position of food basket of colonial America. The Atlantic coastal plain is wider at this point than in New England, and the broad river valleys as well as the rolling foothills of the Appalachian Mountains provided a far more fertile soil than the settlers in New England had found. The rainfall of this area is adequate and well distributed and the winters are not too severe. Wheat proved to be well adapted to these conditions and became the staple crop of the area. In addition, beans, peas, corn, and other grains were grown. Livestock feed was more abundant than elsewhere in the colonies, and beef and pork became important agricultural products of the area. All of these food products were produced in such abundance that the middle colonies supplied them to both the northern and southern colonies, and at the same time exported substantial quantities to the West Indies and to Europe.

Because farming could be carried on successfully, there was less incentive in the middle colonies to turn to industrial occupations. Nevertheless, as in New England, there were ample supplies of hardwood lumber which became available from the clearing of new land for farms. From this lumber some ships were built, and planks, boards, barrel staves, and shingles were produced for export. All of the colonies from north to south carried on a trade in furs and skins, which were a by-product of the ever-present forests. Furs, especially beaver, were more important in the North, and deerskins abundant in the middle and southern colonies. New York became a leader in the fur trade because of the excellent opening to the West provided by the Hudson and Mohawk rivers. Fur traders from Pennsylvania pushed over the Alleghenies into the Ohio country, but compared to the New York traders they were handicapped by the long distances which they had to transport the goods to exchange with the Indians. Small quantities of iron were produced in all of the colonies in the early part of the colonial period, but by 1750 the middle colonies were taking the lead. The ore was secured either from bogs or from rock ore deposits which were found in the upland regions of each of the middle colonies. The fuel for smelting the ore was charcoal, which was available everywhere.

### In the southern colonies

After the early failure of attempts to find an easy source of wealth, the colonies from Maryland southward turned to agriculture as their mainstay, just as their northern neighbors had done. Good soil was available nearly everywhere, and because of the long, hot summers the colonists tried to grow palm trees and other tropical plants. The climate was not suitable for wheat, and the Virginia settlers were hard put to it for a few years until they discovered that the tobacco plant would grow well and that there was a ready market for leaf in Europe at very profitable prices. From 1617 onward, tobacco exports from Virginia and later from Maryland increased almost yearly. A profitable form of agriculture had been found. Because of the large amount of hand labor required to plant, weed, pick, and cure tobacco, Negro slaves from Africa were used in its cultivation from the very beginning. The use of slave labor also had the effect of encouraging the growth of large plantations

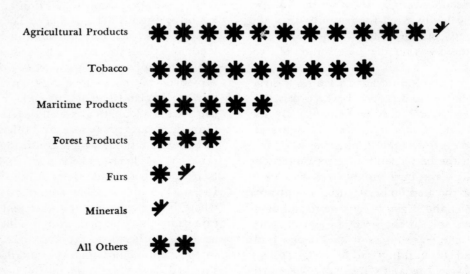

*Fig. VI-1 The chief exports from the British colonies in 1770. Each symbol represents £100,000 worth of visible exports.*

where the slaves could be housed and supervised economically.

South of Virginia, in the Carolinas, there developed for a time a range-cattle industry in the foothills of the Appalachians, such as exists at the present time in the eastern foothills of the Rocky Mountains. The low-lying coastal lands of South Carolina proved capable of growing rice, which had been tried unsuccessfully in Virginia earlier. After 1725, indigo also became an important export of South Carolina, as a result of successful experimental work carried out by Miss Eliza Lucas. Sugar cane was tried with no success until after 1751, when it was introduced into French Louisiana. Oranges, olives, pineapples, ginger, figs, almonds, and other tropical and semitropical plants were tried without commercial success. Perhaps most effort was devoted to building up a silk industry and to the cultivation of the mulberry tree. Mulberry trees would grow, it was found, but the labor costs of silk production proved prohibitive. Cotton did not become an important crop of the southern colonies before 1800.

Aside from agriculture, the extractive industries were probably relatively less important in the southern than in the middle or New England colonies. The coastal waters of the middle South did not especially abound in fish and the forests had no especial advantage for lumber. The southern pine was rich in resin, and the production of naval stores—pitch, rosin, tar, and turpentine—was probably the most important southern extractive industry. Trapping for furs was not as important as farther north, and only in deerskins or buckskins did the South surpass its northern neighbors.

### Manufacture and trade

The same rugged conditions which forced the early colonists to make agriculture the basic part of their economic life also made it essential that they manufacture many of the simple necessities of life for themselves. The universal need for shoes and clothing and the availability of skins, wool, and flax led to the making of at least the rougher types of shoes and clothes in almost every household. In addition, there were candles to be made from tallow, meat to be cured or dried, and other foods to be preserved by drying or pickling in salt brine. The making of flour and meal was sometimes done at home, but this was a sizable undertaking and nearly every community in colonial times had its gristmill for the purpose. Very often, too, there would be a community sawmill to assist in the ever-present job of working up timber into beams and boards for better building construction than was possible with logs alone. Most farm tools and implements were made largely of wood, probably by the men of the household with the aid of the neighborhood blacksmith to make and fit the metal parts.

The general need for the products of handicraft industry, as well as the wide distribution of essential raw materials, early led to some degree of specialization. A skilled craftsman, for example, might spend his entire time going from family to family to make shoes, to split shingles, or to do any one of a hundred other jobs which the family lacked either the skill, the tools, or the time to do. Many craftsmen set up shops to make furniture, harness, and the like, using raw materials furnished by either the customer or themselves. Whether the craftsman was migratory or had his own shop, such work could be either a seasonal and part-time occupation or a full-time one. All degrees of specialization could be found in almost every kind of craft work, ranging from none at all in the most remote self-sufficient frontier families to a fairly extensive refinement of craft skills by full-time workers in the larger and more stabilized communities.

Where conditions were less favorable to agriculture than to industry and trade, as in New England, or where there were special circumstances favoring large-scale manufacture and commerce, specialization at the local market level was accompanied by large-scale production and distribution of the product through wholesale channels before it reached the retail level. Shoemaking, tanning of hides, and iron manufacture were among the industries which developed a type of organization suited to doing business on a larger scale. Many New England farmers built shops in which they engaged in the manufacture of shoes, especially in the winter. The industry developed as a putting-out industry in which merchant manufacturers supplied raw materials to be worked upon by the individual farmers. The unfinished shoes were carried from farmhouse to farmhouse until all necessary operations were completed. They were then sold by the merchant manufacturer, who owned them, to other merchants, who distributed them throughout the colonies.

Iron was manufactured in the colonies at "bloomeries," or forges, and at larger and more extensive works known as "furnaces." The bloomeries might be but little more than blacksmith's forges, where iron ore from bogs was heated in a charcoal fire until a sticky mass of iron was secured which could be hammered out into horseshoes and other necessities for the farm and household. The bloomeries were small-scale operations, mostly supplying their own neighborhood only. In Massachusetts and Virginia, and later in Pennsylvania and other colonies, larger furnaces were erected which were capable of producing from three or four up to ten or twenty tons of iron per week. Such large-scale production required a considerable number of workers to dig the ore and limestone which were required, and to fell trees and make charcoal. Other workers, of course, were required to operate the furnace itself. Molten iron could be secured in the larger furnaces, and kitchen utensils and stove parts could be cast in sand. Bars were also produced for export and for many uses in the hardware and cutlery trades. In "slitting mills" these bars were reduced to thin strips from which nails were made by hand.

It is rather difficult to gauge the extent of industry in colonial America. Iron production was encouraged by England because of her own difficulties in getting raw materials. Most other types of production, except the making of products for household use, were discour-

aged because they would be in competition with English industry. Yet we know that the colonists had an urgent and seemingly insatiable need for all kinds of manufactured products. It is very probable that, wherever circumstances were favorable, industrial production was carried on, even if not much was said about it in official reports.

Strong evidence that specialized manufacture had become important was the amount of trade in colonial America (see Fig. VI-1, p. 122). The earliest trade had been by barter among the settlers and with the Indians. It was soon discovered that a good market for American furs existed in Europe, and colonists began exchanging with the Indians firearms, traps, gunpowder, knives, and trinkets, mostly from Europe, and "firewater" of their own manufacture for furs. They also traded extensively among themselves by direct exchange of goods, using flour, meal, or tobacco as a measure of value and sometimes as a medium of exchange. For example, the local cabinetmaker might be paid for a chest of drawers or a table by some sacks of flour and cured hams.

Only a few decades after the first settlement, each of the colonies from north to south had begun to develop its own special agricultural and industrial advantages. New Englanders became the manufacturers, merchants, and shipbuilders. New York, New Jersey, and Pennsylvania became the chief source of supply for flour, meal, beef, and pork. The southern colonies became producers of agricultural products for export—tobacco, indigo, and later rice and cotton. Trade in these products grew up not only among the colonies themselves, but also with the West Indies and with Europe. The West Indies trade became particularly important to the North American colonies because coined money could be secured from them. In spite of large exports to Europe, most of the colonies were always in debt to Europe because of the many manufactured goods which had to be purchased on the Continent. The adverse trade balance of the colonies could be settled only by cash, and hence they were kept almost continuously short of coin for the normal handling of trade.

The West Indian settlements could use the exports of the northern colonies in large amounts and pay for them partially in precious metals secured from Mexico and South America. Especially as the slave trade became important, with the great majority of the slaves coming to the islands before being transshipped to the mainland, the New England and middle colonies could sell flour, meal, the poorer grades of salted meat and fish, barrel staves, and horses to the West Indies. In return they obtained slaves for southern plantations, sugar, molasses, and coin. Much of the molasses was made into rum in New England distilleries for use in the colonies, for trade with the Indians, and for exchange in Africa for more slaves. The West Indies also could sell their sugar, molasses, and fruit in England to pay, in a roundabout way, for their imports from the mainland colonies by helping to balance the trade deficit incurred by these colonies for the purchase of manufactured goods from England. The West Indies were thus involved in what came to be called the "triangle trade" between the mainland colonies and England. This trade was vital to New England and the middle colonies, because it helped provide a market for their exports and provided them with coin for the conduct of their internal trade. The South was less concerned with the triangular trade, because the big market for southern exports was in northern Europe, and the South was content to buy manufactured goods from the same source. Slave labor for southern plantations was secured through the West Indies, of course.

Even a brief survey of colonial manufacture and trade reveals an increasingly complex economy by the latter half of the eighteenth century. The coastal settlements had become populous and had achieved a substantial degree of specialization in industry and commerce. On the frontier, of course, a more primitive, self-sufficient form of economic life was enforced by the circumstances. In fact, the attractions of the frontier for its possibilities in fur trading, the discovery of rich mineral deposits, and land speculation had a tendency to retard some forms of economic development in

the older settlements by diverting attention elsewhere. None the less, in the decades before the outbreak of the Revolutionary War, the colonial economy was bursting at the seams in several respects. It was pressing against the Allegheny Mountains to enter the Mississippi Valley. Also, the commerce and industry of the East had reached a scale of operation in which capital was becoming important as a prerequisite of business success. Some New England merchants had become very substantial individuals indeed. A very few large-scale indus-

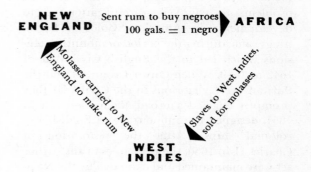

Fig. VI-2 The "triangle trade" about 1740.

tries had been started, but without notable success as yet. All of these developments seemed perfectly proper to the colonists, since they had evolved naturally from existing conditions. England viewed the matter differently, however, and a rift developed between the mother country and the colonies.

### The growing conflict with English Mercantilism

From the beginning of English settlement in North America, there had been differences of opinion between the home government and the colonists. In fact, the largest numerical group among the colonists was composed of those who wished to come to the New World because they disapproved of the policies of the government at home. As the decades rolled by, and as a substantial part of the colonial population came to be made up of native-born Americans who knew of the mother country only by hearsay, it was almost inevitable that the colonies should grow away from England. As a result of short-sighted administrative policies on the part of the English government, this rift came to a head in the Revolution.

During most of the century and a half between the establishment of the English colonies and their revolt against the mother country, the English people and English governments were too preoccupied with their own problems to pay very careful attention to developments in America. Colonial beginnings came during the period of mounting tensions which led to the English Civil War of 1642 to 1649. When Oliver Cromwell and the Puritans were victorious in the Civil War they promptly enacted a broad Navigation Act in 1651, designed to confine trade to English and colonial ships. After the restoration of Charles II in 1660, the principles of the earlier act were maintained and extended by the Navigation Act of that year. This second act prohibited direct trade between foreign countries and the colonies except in English or colonial ships, and for certain "enumerated commodities" such trade was forbidden altogether. These acts would have prevented the lucrative trade between the northern colonies and the West Indies, but, fortunately, for long periods their enforcement was either neglected entirely or was inadequate. This policy of "salutary neglect" permitted the growth of colonial trade with the West Indies, Africa, and southern Europe, a trade which became a vital part of the colonial economy.

The period following the Civil War in England was marked by a growth of parliamentary government. After the war economic conditions were generally good, and the effects of the Commercial Revolution were to bring wealth and the desire for a voice in government to larger and larger segments of the English population. Many colonists had sought greater religious and political freedom in America, and it is only natural that Americans in a frontier environment should resent unreasonable governmental authority even more strongly than did their British cousins. The colonists did not feel that they were surrendering any of the rights of English citizenship when they came to America. As the colonial economy developed and opportunities arose for carrying on various types of commerce and industry, the colonists saw no reason why they should not take advantage of these opportunities. But the English government in power at the time did not agree to that proposition. Through several changes of government, during which the will of the home population was given fuller expression, England stood fast by the policy of Mercantilism, according to which the economy of a colony should be adapted to serve the needs of the mother country, not those of the colony itself. If a more inclusive theory of democracy had been applied by England, it might have been realized that the colonists were entitled to a voice in determining the economic policies which they should follow.

The fundamental hostility between the economic interests of England and those of the colonies would doubtless have led to a showdown before the time when the Revolutionary War actually occurred had it not been for the policy of "salutary neglect." For many decades after 1660, the second Navigation Act was not fully enforced by inspectors in American ports. Colonial traders almost openly flouted the act and developed trade wherever they found it profitable. Under such conditions of nonenforcement, the restrictions and taxes placed by Britain made very little difference.

In 1763 after the end of the Seven Years' War (called the French and Indian War in America), the "old colonial policy," was ended. Whether this was due to a rebirth of British imperialism after the successful conclusion of the war; to a maturing of the mercantile policy as Britain grew in wealth and power from the development of her commerce throughout the world; or merely to a new ministry under George Grenville, an able administrator who believed that a policy is of no value unless it is put into effect, is a question of secondary importance. The significant fact is that these and perhaps other factors did produce a new and vigorously enforced colonial policy. The full details of the "new colonial policy" also need not concern us, beyond the central fact that it indicated a firm determination on England's part to regulate and tax the colonies as she felt wise. At an earlier time, the colonies might not have objected to such a policy, but after a considerable period of almost unrestricted growth, they now felt that certain key aspects of the new policy might destroy some of the principal features of colonial economic life.

In particular, the following elements of the "new colonial policy" stirred up opposition in the colonies:

(1) An order issued by George III in 1763 prohibited settlement beyond the crest of the Allegheny Mountains. Some bands of settlers had already moved into the trans-Allegheny area, and land speculators were anticipating great profits to be made there. In the South especially this order aroused hostility, because new lands for tobacco cultivation were already being sought.

(2) The Sugar Act of 1764 laid a moderate duty on imported molasses, but a duty which was collected. The burden of the tax was actually not heavy, but the colonial traders resented it, because the tax levied by the Molasses Act of 1733 had not been effectively collected. The trade in molasses was vital because from it was made rum not only for use in the colonies but for the crews of the fishing fleets and for the very profitable West Indian and African trade.

(3) An act of 1764 prohibited the issue of bills of credit or paper money by the colonies.

(4) The Stamp Act of 1765 levied taxes on all kinds of contracts, wills, deeds, and papers in legal proceedings. This tax was not only a nuisance but a heavy burden especially on merchants and lawyers. It was a constant thorn in the flesh of the colonists.

Obnoxious as these and other measures were to the colonies, they might have had less far-reaching effects if the colonists had not been experiencing an economic depression at the time. The readjustments following the end of the Seven Years' War had, as in many other postwar periods, brought about a letdown in business activity and a concomitant decline in prices. The depression, like others in history, produced general discontent with existing conditions and left the people highly sensitive to measures that might further affect their fortunes adversely. Unfortunately from the British point of view, many of their acts during this period did have, or seemed to have, exactly this effect. The prohibition of paper-note circulation, coming at a time when prices were already depressed, tended to lower prices still more because of the ensuing decline in the money supply. The war debt, which had been contracted with paper money, was slowly being retired, and there could be no compensatory increase in paper circulation. At the same time, the requirements that the duties levied by the Stamp Act and by other acts be paid in specie (or coin) led to a further drain on the money supply and hence to a further downward pressure on prices.

The Stamp Act and the duties imposed on molasses and on other imported products incurred the wrath of much of the small but highly influential minority at the top of colonial society, the merchants, lawyers, and publishers. The effect of these levies was undoubtedly not even felt by the great majority of the colonists, nor did the levies appear to be very large, but widespread resentment against English rule resulted from their imposition. Ironically, some of the acts which met with the greatest opposition from the colonists were to their own best interests. Thus, the prohibition of paper money was designed to prevent further abuses of this privilege by the colonies, and the limitation on settlement beyond the Alleghenies was designed to provide a breathing spell to negotiate a treaty with the Indians in that territory and prevent further outbreaks.

In the years between 1765 and the outbreak of the Revolution, Britain changed ministries several times, and modified some of the objectionable features of her new policy. The colonists, or rather the vocal and influential minority of them, were thoroughly aroused, however, and were beyond being pacified. In her turn, Britain regarded the words and acts of some of the colonists as treasonable. In December 1773 a band of Massachusetts citizens disguised as Indians threw into Boston harbor a cargo of tea as an act of violent protest against a new tax on tea. This incident—the "Boston Tea Party"—angered Parliament and provoked a series of acts in reprisal which the colonists immediately dubbed the "Intolerable Acts." The colonies were drawn together by a new bond of hostility to British policy, and war became inevitable. It is possible that wiser and more moderate individuals in responsible positions in both Britain and the colonies might have avoided war, but it is clear that the commercial policies of the two parties were basically in opposition, and that one side or the other would have to give in or they would have to put their differences to the test of war.

## Economic effects of the Revolutionary War

### Changes brought by the war

When the hostility between the colonies and Britain broke into open warfare, the colonists were by no means united in the war effort. Although there were perhaps more active revolutionists among the merchant classes of New England than anywhere else in the colonies, even in New England there were many nonsmuggling merchants who would not go to the length of breaking with the Crown. There were also colonial administrators, the clergy of the Church of England, and many members of that church who remained loyal to England. Lawyers, doctors, and other professional people often did not feel keenly the injustices of the Navigation Acts and therefore did not support the Revolution. In the South, although many plantation owners opposed the British land policy which prohibited westward migration, there were many among them who nevertheless remained loyal to the Crown. All in

all, it is probable that a majority of the colonists were not in sympathy with the revolutionists up to the time of the breaking out of actual hostilities; after that, as the sentiments of the country crystallized, and as many Royalists fled, the revolutionary party achieved effective control of colonial governments and policies. Often the wealthiest and best-educated members of colonial society were those who remained loyal to England. The burden of carrying on the Revolution fell upon the humble—men of small property and little education—led by a minority of substantial business and professional men and landholders.

The period of the war marked a sharp gain in the democratic character of American society, largely because of the driving out of many wealthy, conservative, and influential Royalists. A number of the states, as we may now call them, confiscated the lands of Royalists, put them up for sale in small plots, and applied the proceeds to the Continental loans. This action placed persons of moderate wealth in a much more favorable condition. Land tenure in America was made more democratic by laws providing for equality of inheritance and for the elimination of quitrents, entail, and primogeniture.[1] These were legal relics from the days of feudalism by which land holdings could be kept concentrated in the hands of one family generation after generation. Further, the departure of Royalists often left open positions in government which were promptly filled by representatives of the common people. In some respects, the Revolutionary War was also a civil war in which the poorer but more numerous groups rose up to drive out those who occupied positions of wealth and power, giving strong support to popular, democratic government.

[1] Quitrents were annual payments to the lord or king for protection which he was supposed to afford. In America, the payments were made to the colonial proprietor or to the king and were generally small, although bitterly disliked. Entail was a legal privilege of designating the class of persons to inherit lands for generations in advance. Primogeniture was a system by which the eldest son inherited the whole of an estate, with other possible heirs completely excluded.

Even before the war came, eager speculators and hardy frontiersmen had been pushing into the western territory over the mountains in violation of the Order of 1763. The war removed any taint of illegality from such actions, and there remained only the question of coming to terms with the Indians and dislodging the British from the garrisons which they had established. The pace of settlement was stepped up during the war years in Tennessee and Kentucky, as well as in western Pennsylvania and western Virginia. The way was also cleared for settlement in the Ohio Valley and the upper Mississippi Valley, in what has since been called the "Old Northwest."

The conduct of the war itself did not seriously impair the contemporary economic life of the country. Agriculture, in fact, was hardly affected at all. The armies involved in the war were not large, by later standards, and most of the soldiers were near enough to their homes to return for the planting and harvesting of crops. Some American farmers were not above selling their products to enemy commanders. The interruption of the import trade from Europe brought higher prices for American wool and cotton. On the other hand, the southern products—tobacco and rice —seemed to be able to get through the British blockade easily enough to prevent their prices from being lowered to the serious harm of the growers. In general, agriculture probably benefited more from the war than it was harmed by it.

Manufacturing, too, gained by the dislocations caused by the war, and by the termination of British power to restrict the production of finished goods. During the colonial period, England had encouraged the production of bar iron, lumber, and other raw and semi-finished products. The making of finished goods, however, was in most cases forbidden except for use within the home. The war and the blockade against American shipping compelled the home market to depend very largely upon home production for many kinds of goods. Consumers might not be able to get the fine quality wares they had been in the habit of buying from England, but domestic manufacturers felt the powerful stimulus of a strong demand at high prices. Fine wool and linen cloth were especially scarce, and the wearing of "homespun" clothing, even if of inferior quality, became a symbol of patriotism. All kinds of hardware became scarce, both because it could not be imported, and because American artisans turned their efforts to the making of arms and ammunition. New iron and steel furnaces were built in an effort to meet the need. Skilled labor was extremely scarce, and wages rose sharply, which provided an incentive to new workers to acquire the needed skills.

American commerce shared with agriculture and manufacturing the stimulus of enlarged wartime demand, but also had to share with them the burden of severe dislocation. English warships and privateers frequently lay in wait off American shores to seize any ships which tried to run the blockade. On the other hand, Spanish, French, and Dutch ships, which had been banned from American ports by the Navigation Acts, were now welcomed if they could run the blockade. Further, privateering was a game at which two could play, and American shipowners undertook it enthusiastically and with considerable success, especially in the West Indies. Several hundred British ships were seized by American privateers during the course of the war and were either returned to American ports or sold abroad for cash. The outbreak of the war cut off trade with the outside world for a time, but within a year or two luxury goods were again obtainable in the states and American exports were getting through to their accustomed markets abroad, even—by devious paths—to England herself.

### The inflation during the war

One economic effect that was experienced universally in the states was the inflation caused by the methods of financing the war effort. War always gives rise to serious monetary problems, because of the strain on a government of financing military campaigns, and with few exceptions governments have traditionally tended to get themselves into serious difficulties over it. The experience of the Revolutionary War provides us with a valuable object lesson in this respect, and it therefore behooves us to devote special attention to a review of the circumstances.

Financially, the Americans were in trouble from the very beginning of the war, because the Continental Congress was not given any

because of the departure of wealthy Royalists, severely restricted private loans.

Attempts were made to requisition money from the states, but the reluctance of the states to use their taxing power and jealousies between states meant that relatively little aid was procured in this manner. Of a total of $95,000,000 in paper money requisitioned by Congress in the early part of the war, less than half was received, and, because this sum was

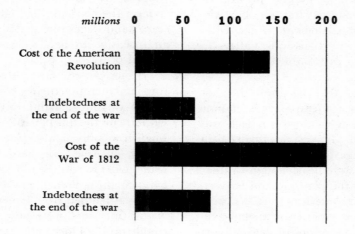

Fig.VI-3 *A comparison between the cost of America's first two wars and the debts which remained following them.*

authority to levy taxes. This is not surprising in view of the fact that taxation was one of the major sources of disagreement between England and the colonies, but at the same time it meant that the Continental Congress could obtain funds only through borrowing or issuance of paper money. Borrowing met with limited success. About $8,000,000 was obtained abroad, mostly from France, but even with other gifts and subsidies from France totalling an additional $2,000,000, this amount came nowhere near covering the cost of the war. Borrowing from domestic sources yielded considerably more, but became increasingly difficult as the war progressed. The increasingly low credit standing of the Congress, deriving in part from its inability to tax and in part from uncertainty regarding the outcome of the war, as well as the decrease in the supply of capital

in paper money issued by the states in ever-increasing volume, it is estimated that its actual value at the time of receipt was less than $2,000,000. Later attempts by Congress to obtain aid in terms of specie and supplies from the states met with a similar lack of success.

Desperately in need of funds with which to obtain supplies and pay the troops, the Continental Congress turned to the time-honored practice of printing its own money. The fact that the states were already pursuing this policy, Massachusetts taking the lead in 1775, provided the Congress with an additional incentive to fall back on this expedient. Initial issues were relatively moderate, $5,000,000 in 1775, $19,000,000 in 1776, and $13,000,000 in 1777. Once begun, however, there was no stop. The rapid increase in the issue of paper money by the states and the precarious position of the

Congress led to a precipitous decline in the value of all paper money, or, in other words, to skyrocketing prices. Faced with the greatly increased costs for the supplies it needed, Congress attempted to offset these higher prices by raising its note issues to $63,000,000 in 1778 and over $140,000,000 in 1779. The result was catastrophic: the roof fell in. By the end of 1779 the currency of the Continental Congress was valueless, forcing the infant nation close to a barter economy, causing suffering and chaos, and leaving in its wake the cynical phrase "not worth a continental."

It is worth noting that during this period Congress made a number of attempts to legislate an end to the price spiral, but, as any economist could have predicted, to no avail. Laws providing stiff penalties for refusal to accept paper money and for valuing paper money below specie only had the effect of driving specie out of circulation and caused many merchants to close their doors altogether. Price and wage agreements between the states were also sought, but the halfhearted coöperation obtained and the consistent tendency of the agreements to lag behind actual prices doomed them to immediate failure. Thus, in November 1779, when Congress recommended new price agreements at levels twenty times higher than prices in 1774, action was already useless because current prices were far above that level.

The final, and inevitable, result occurred in 1780—repudiation of the currency. A considerable sum of this currency was called back by Congress from the states and was destroyed; about $120,000,000, nearly half the total, was disposed of in this manner. The remainder was made convertible into silver at the ratio of 40 to 1, and, in 1790, into government bonds at the ratio of 100 to 1, which is tantamount to repudiation. Fortunately for the war effort, Congress was able to surmount this crisis with the aid of a new issue of money rigidly restricted in amount, issuance of bills of credit, some requisitions from the states, and, later, a sizable loan from Holland. But it was not until 1790, when the first secretary of the treasury, Alexander Hamilton, refunded all the foreign and domestic debts, that the credit of the government was established on a firm footing.

Now, what were the consequences of this inflation? Could it not be argued that, from the government's point of view, the inflation actually reduced the cost of the war because the government bought many of its supplies with the paper money which it later exchanged for a fraction of its value? To an extent, yes, except that these savings were probably more than offset by the increased costs of the bills of credit (or loans) to the government. These bills were issued when prices were greatly inflated and then redeemed at par value after the war, when prices were considerably lower. And when we consider that the inflation caused more havoc and ruin on the American side than all the efforts of the British, it is not so difficult to understand why this event was so serious. It made supplies very difficult to obtain. Not only did Congress and the states have to pay very high prices for goods, but they were frequently unable to obtain them at all. It provided many merchants with a stimulus either to hoard the goods or to sell them to the British.

The morale of the army was also badly shaken. Not only were supplies inadequate, but the rate of pay, which at $7 per month was not startling to begin with, dropped to practically nothing in terms of what it would buy by the end of 1779. It was surprising, not that there were so many desertions from the Continental army and refusals to enlist in it, but that there was an army at all.

The effect of the inflation on civilian life was to disorganize industry and trade, and, as in all such periods, to give to debtors a distinct advantage. In fact, there was one period when creditors actually avoided their debtors, for fear that they might get paid in the nearly worthless currency. They preferred to lend during the inflation and get paid later when money was worth more. Commercial transactions were eventually reduced to a state of barter, with all of the attendant limitations. Wage earners and others receiving fixed incomes also suffered, as such forms of payment traditionally lag behind prices in periods of inflation. For a time, manufacturing and trade were actually benefited by the inflation, because of the possibilities of purchasing goods or raw materials at one price and selling later when prices had risen. This was only a temporary stimulus to business activity, however, and the ensuing failure of the currency led to severe losses and depression. There is little doubt that the inflation almost wrecked the new nation before it could get on its feet. Inadequate taxing power and reliance on the printing press for money inevitably lead to serious problems.

### The forming of a national union

The elements of weakness and disunity which had been revealed during the war period remained as a legacy for the era of peace that followed. In addition, the successful conclusion of the revolutionary effort brought not only great new opportunities but also a host of problems created by the war effort. The new country suddenly found itself standing alone in the world, and it could not be quite sure of either itself or the world. At home there had developed sharp differences of opinion between the agrarian frontiersmen of the country's western borders and the solid propertied interests of the eastern seaboard; abroad American merchants found themselves outside the British trade system, although they were welcomed by and free to trade with Holland and France. Prosperity, as it related both to domestic business and to foreign trade, was spotty and irregular in the first few years after the war. The price inflation which had resulted from the currency issue and credit expansion of wartime caused uncertainty and hardship. The country had a real scare in 1786 when a band of former Revolutionary soldiers got out their muskets again and marched under Captain Daniel Shays in Massachusetts to close the courts and stop the collection of debts by foreclosure sales. This event occurred the year before the meeting of the Constitutional Convention in Philadelphia, and there can be little doubt that Shays' Rebellion served to speed the delegates of the states on their way to Philadelphia to set up a government which could provide law and order, and settle some of the urgent problems of the new country.

The members of the Constitutional Convention, who assembled in Philadelphia in 1787 to replace the Articles of Confederation, under which the government had been operating, perhaps reflected the loyalties, the hopes, and the fears of the American people as well as was possible considering the inevitable fact that they were chosen from the educated classes. If the delegates understood the farmers and artisans of the backwoods communities, it was primarily to fear them. They readily agreed that the new government should have all necessary powers to enforce contracts and protect life and property. They favored assumption of the debt incurred in fighting the Revolution, and restriction of the power of currency issue to the new national government. It was also nearly unanimously agreed that the judiciary should be protected from the people by appointment rather than election of judges, and by life terms for many of the most important judgeships. On these matters there was agreement. Disagreement arose over the powers of the small states as compared to the larger ones, and, indirectly, over the powers of the national government to levy taxes or establish regulations of trade which might adversely affect the interests of individual states or regions. Even in the Constitutional Convention there were advance rumblings of the sectional controversies that have had an important part in American history and that at last led to civil war.

The campaign for the adoption of the Constitution was finally carried to a successful conclusion. George Washington was installed as the first president of the United States on April 30, 1789, and the new government was officially set up and ready to operate. But Congress and the government were not sure of the direction in which they should set out. To help solve that problem, Congress asked Alexander Hamilton, the Secretary of the Treasury, for his recommendations. In

1790 and 1791 Hamilton sent to Congress four reports, on the public debt, an excise tax, a national bank, and manufactures.

Congress followed the recommendations made in each of Hamilton's reports. It was finally voted, after rather bitter debate, to have the new government take over the bonds both of the individual states and of the Continental Congress, and to pay these debts off by new issues of federal bonds. Hamilton argued that this was necessary, even though speculators had acquired many of the bonds, in order that the credit of the new government be established on sound foundations. Congress also voted an excise tax on distilled spirits, although this was repealed about ten years later because of widespread resentment against it. The recommendation for a national bank, patterned somewhat after the Bank of England, like the issue of the public debt, aroused bitter controversy. Thomas Jefferson and his party opposed the recommendation, fearing the building up of a great centralized financial power. However, the bank finally won out in Congress and received a charter for twenty years. Hamilton's last report has become the most famous, since in it he analyzed the probable economic development of the new country, and urged the enactment of a protective tariff to aid in building up industrial power. Congress had enacted a tariff for revenue purposes even before Hamilton's report reached it. To be protective, the tariff should have been higher than it was for the first decade or two of our national history, and on products competing directly with domestic producers. The reasoning of Hamilton's report appealed to powerful elements in the country, and, while it was not done at once, within a few years American tariffs began to be made protective in character.

## The economy of
## the United States by 1800

By the turn of the century the new country had shown itself capable of surmounting many difficulties and getting itself firmly embarked upon what were to be the main paths of its future national development. The political and economic chaos of the first "critical" years after the war was beginning to clear up. In fact, it was not very long after the ending of the American Revolution until the outbreak of revolution in France produced greater economic disorganization in Europe than still existed on this side of the Atlantic. The disruption of normal economic life in Europe permitted Yankee traders to carry their goods to ports from which the still prevalent mercantilist philosophy might otherwise have barred them. In the 1780's, British vessels were carrying the bulk of goods in the American trade, but by a decade later more than 90 per cent of both American imports and exports were being carried in American ships. Furthermore, American merchants who at times found themselves faced with restrictions in Europe discovered a new market in Asia, especially China, which they proceeded to develop vigorously.

The expansion of foreign trade, which began to be evident by 1800, was matched by growth and change at home. American shipbuilders had attained preëminence during the colonial era, and they retained it for a half century or more thereafter. The large proportion of the population which supported itself by subsistence agriculture began to decline even before the beginning of the nineteenth century as commercial and industrial centers began to grow. Not only shipbuilding but many other industries grew and attracted workers. Local trade grew to supply expanding urban centers. Farming began to shift toward commercial production of crops and livestock for domestic and foreign markets. Change and growth were in the air, and the commercial classes of the new country were enjoying a substantial prosperity.

Manufacturing of many kinds also made considerable progress in the years just preceding 1800, to keep pace with the expansion of local and distant markets. In his Report on Manufactures of 1791, Alexander Hamilton referred specifically to a number of industries as being in a thriving condition. His list included leather and leather goods, iron manufacturing, shipbuilding, flax and hemp manufacturing, brick and tile, spirits and liquors, paper, hats, sugar, oil, copper and brass, tinware, carriages, tobacco products, starch and hair powder, lampblack and painters' colors, and gunpowder. Presumably, these were industries which had developed beyond the household or local-market stage and had achieved regional or even wider distribution of their products.

Besides these industries there were others that were carried on in almost every household, and for whose products there was a universal demand. The making of woolen cloth is perhaps the best illustration of an industry of this type. Because the demand for cloth was universal, we have already seen that efforts to produce cloth by machinery were being made in England just at the time when relations between America and England were at their worst, i.e., before, during, and immediately after the Revolutionary War. When more settled conditions came in America, following the adoption of the Constitution, numerous efforts were made, especially in New England, to develop factory methods of cloth making. The most successful of these were the efforts of Almy, Brown, and Slater to build and operate Arkwright water frames and other textile machinery, the plans for which were reproduced in America from memory by Samuel Slater, a young man formerly employed on similar machinery in England. The Almy, Brown, and Slater factory at Pawtucket, Rhode Island, produced cotton rather than woolen cloth because of the more keenly felt need to improve the manufacture of cotton. The factory began operation in 1791, and continued to expand for a number of years.

By 1800 other factories were achieving success in textile manufacture also, using not only cotton, whose production began to increase sharply after Whitney's invention of the cotton gin in 1793, but wool and flax as well. Household production of such universal necessities as textiles began to decline wherever the products of the eastern industries could be transported. In the original thirteen states, specialization and trade replaced self-sufficiency almost everywhere; in the expanding West, living remained more rugged, and those who assumed its hazards still had to do for themselves, or do without.

Besides trade and manufacture, the third great aspect of economic life in America which was in a state of rapid development by 1800 was the opening of the West. The closing of the West had been one of the important sources of friction between the colonists and the mother country. Before the outbreak of war, it has been estimated that there were no more than two or three hundred white residents living beyond the eastern mountains. War broke the log jam, and by its end the number of white settlers had jumped to probably 25,000. Daniel Boone and his associates had cut through the "Wilderness Road" from Virginia into the Kentucky country during the war, and over it immigrants by the hundreds and thousands poured into the fertile lands south of the Ohio River. By 1790 the white population living beyond the mountains had reached 200,000.

This restless and irrepressible westward surge of immigrants forced Congress under the Articles of Confederation to formulate a land policy for the settlement of western lands. This it did in a series of land ordinances in 1784, 1785, and 1787. The Ordinance of 1785 provided for the system of counties, townships, sections, and quarter-sections of land which have become almost standard throughout the United States. Government land, according to this Ordinance, was to be sold at auctions at prices of not less than a dollar an acre and in blocks of not less than 640 acres. The Ordinance of 1787 provided a basis for the government of the new territory and established a bill of rights, including religious freedom, prohibition of slavery, and public support of education. This latter goal was to be achieved by reserving certain sections of land in each township for the support of schools. The Ordinance of 1787, commonly known as the Northwest Ordinance, is unquestionably one of the great documents in American history. Under its provisions a region could achieve territorial self-government when it contained 5,000 free, adult, male citizens and could be admitted to full statehood as soon as it had 60,000 free inhabitants.

Even before 1787, both speculators and prospective settlers had been making preparations to move into the Ohio country. In the spring of 1788, Reverend Manasseh Cutler and General Rufus Putnam led a group of war veterans to a large tract they had acquired at the mouth of the Muskingum River in the name of the Ohio Company. There they established the town of Marietta. Other companies obtained tracts in the Scioto and Miami valleys and began settlement in the same year. In addition, many individual settlers purchased land and moved into the new territory. Kentucky was admitted to the Union as a state in 1792. Tennessee followed in 1796. In the latter year, Moses Cleaveland began settlement of northern Ohio by leading a band of settlers under the auspices of the Connecticut Land Company to a spot on the south shore of Lake Erie where the city named in his honor now stands. By 1803, the Ohio Territory had the necessary 60,000 inhabitants to qualify for admission as a state.

The spreading out of the population over a vastly larger area than the original thirteen colonies had created an acute transportation problem by 1800. Roads over which wheeled vehicles could be drawn were almost nonexistent in the West. Most of the settlers came by way of flatboats on the rivers or with a few of their most valued possessions strapped on horseback. The completion of the Philadelphia to Lancaster turnpike in 1794 seemed to indicate the answer to the urgent need for good roads. Many other privately built roads were authorized throughout the country in the years that followed. Immigrants were willing to put up with the expense of toll gates, if the road was good enough to permit them to haul their goods in wagons and to make speed on their way. For several decades both before and after 1800, private turnpikes furnished the best road transportation available. They introduced the "covered-wagon" era which survived in the Far West until the last quarter of the nineteenth century.

The United States of 1800 was not lacking in economic frustrations, but it had had nearly two decades of independence, and more than one decade of responsible and increasingly respected federal government. Its problems of trade and industry were not solved, but they did not appear insoluble. The march to the West had begun in real earnest. That was a movement which was to give much to the spiritual quality of the American people. The defiance of physical obstacles, the feeling that anyone with energy and willingness to work can achieve personal success, yet withal a great generosity toward the unfortunate—these and other similar qualities which our ancestors perhaps had before they sought these western Atlantic shores were also qualities which the continuing conquest of the West impressed deeply upon them as a people.

## Economic thought and attitudes in the early days of America

Conditions in North America from the beginning of settlement until the establishment of the new government of the United States were more conducive to action than to thought. Early in this period, the colonists were so few and so economically weak that it was natural enough for them to accept willingly the role assigned to colonies in the mercantile theory. Without deep thought about the matter, they could easily perceive that it was their allotted task to develop the resources of the new continent both for their own benefit and that of the mother country. They not only accepted but relied upon the strength of the home government to determine the proper direction of economic development and to stand behind them with its organized power as they proceeded to carry out their portion of the tasks of economic empire building.

By the time of the years of ferment immediately preceding the Revolutionary War, conditions had become different. The colonies were now more populous and more self-reliant due to the success they had achieved in developing the resources of America for their own direct support and for trade overseas. The ideas of certain French economists called "Physiocrats" had begun to circulate in America. Thomas Jefferson and other Americans had encountered members of this group in their travels in France. Physiocratic ideas of the dominance of physical nature in the affairs of men and, particularly, of the basic importance of agriculture in creating a wealthy nation, had great appeal. Many of the policies which Jefferson advocated had evident roots in Physiocratic thought. Alexander Hamilton, another leader of economic thinking in the revolutionary period, remained essentially faithful to mercantilist policies in his belief in the need for a strong government to establish and carry out suitable economic policies. He was loyal to the revolutionary movement, however, in his insistence that the new government of the United States should take over the task of formulating economic policies, but including a policy of full economic freedom for individuals.

But most important of all in determining the economic thinking of the new country were simply the conditions in the country itself. Very few Americans were in a position in 1776, when *The Wealth of Nations* of Adam Smith was published, to devote time to a careful reflection upon the meaning of the work. The free conditions of the frontier, however, were sufficient to create a generally favorable reception for Smith's advocacy of a policy of governmental *laissez faire*. Within a few decades, American thinkers were to raise objections to some aspects of the economic theories built upon the foundation of Smith's work by later English economic theorists, but his concept of a free self-directing system

struck deeper root in the soil of America than it did even in the country of its origin.

In this age of action in America, there was an explicit awareness that a new kind of nation was being built. There was pride in the effort of building and there was confidence that the task could be done. We may say that there was consciousness of national purpose and belief that a new and better kind of society for all could be achieved. In the process of building the new society, the physical barriers of a continent had to be conquered. Its rich resources were there to be used too, both for the sustenance and the enrichment of the strong and the energetic. The new society had to adapt itself to the physical environment, but to an equal or greater degree, this was a privilege. Nature was viewed, not as limiting, but as aiding man. This idea was incorporated into specific economic doctrines in America, as we shall see in the next chapter.

From the exploitation of its developmental possibilities, America became the most technologically oriented nation in the world. That is, we felt that when we learned how to perform a task, it could be done, and we *could* learn. Even at this early stage of our history, this point of view—so dominant at later times — became evident. Systematic investigation — now called research—if pursued long enough and hard enough, we believe, will solve our problems. This research and technical orientation became established first in the applied fields of physical and biological science. We proved to ourselves that we could solve our problems of transportation, agricultural and industrial production, and others. In these fields, we developed a definitely evolutionary conception of our society. It was not so obvious —nor at first so necessary—to realize that this same viewpoint was applicable to other phases of our social structure as well.

## FOR FURTHER READING

Barnes, James A. *Wealth of the American People*. New York: Prentice-Hall, Inc., 1949. Chapters 1–8.

Bidwell, Percy W., and Falconer, John J. *History of Agriculture in the Northern United States, 1620-*

*1865.* Washington: Carnegie Institution of Washington, 1925. Parts I and II.

Bogart, Ernest L., and Kemmerer, Donald L. *Economic History of the American People*. 2nd ed. New York:

Longmans, Green & Co., Inc., 1947. Chapters 1—8.

Brown, Robert E. *Middle-Class Democracy and the Revolution in Massachusetts, 1691-1780.* Ithaca: Cornell University Press, 1955. Chapters 1 and 2.

Bruce, Philip A. *Economic History of Virginia in the Seventeenth Century.* New York: The Macmillan Co., 1895. Chapter 1.

Carrier, Lyman. *The Beginnings of Agriculture in America.* New York: McGraw-Hill Book Co., 1923.

Faulkner, Harold Underwood. *American Economic History.* 8th ed. New York: Harper & Brothers, 1960. Chapters 1—8.

Gray, Lewis C. *History of Agriculture in the Southern United States to 1860.* Washington: Carnegie Institu-

tion of Washington, 1933. Volume I.

Mitchell, Broadus, and Mitchell, Louise Pearson. *American Economic History.* Boston: Houghton Mifflin Co., 1947. Chapters 1—13.

Shannon, F. A. *America's Economic Growth.* 3rd ed. New York: The Macmillan Co., 1951. Chapters 1—6.

Shultz, William J., and Caine, M. R. *Financial Development of the United States.* New York: Prentice-Hall, Inc., 1937. Chapter 2.

Williamson, Harold F. (ed.). *The Growth of the American Economy.* 2nd ed. New York: Prentice-Hall, Inc., 1958. Chapters 1—5.

Wright, Chester W. *Economic History of the United States.* 2nd ed. New York: McGraw-Hill Book Co., 1949. Chapters 1—15.

# Chapter 7: The westward movement and American agriculture to 1860

**B**y 1800, the settlement and exploitation of the West had become almost a national passion. Ever since the end of the Seven Years' War, when French claims to the upper Mississippi Valley were surrendered, there had been an increasing urge to move across the mountains into the rich valleys beyond. The accounts of the first settlements in this area fanned the flames of interest in western lands to a still whiter heat among easterners. To clear away all remaining obstacles to further settlement, whatever might be the nature of those obstacles, became a cardinal point in the economic and political thinking of most Americans.

Without going so far as to attribute all the features of American character to the existence of a western frontier through many formative decades in American national life, one may still recognize that the opportunity for westward expansion did have profound influences. In the early decades following independence, the common desire to acquire and develop the West gave unity to a people who

had previously been united only in opposition to Great Britain. The struggle over the Constitution and the confusion attendant upon the organization of the new government tended to emphasize the differences among the states. But these differences began to seem small in the face of the enormous opportunities of the West. Nor was America plagued by the fears of overpopulation and low wages which beset England and the older European countries. Wages were higher than in Europe both because many immigrants moved on to the West without producing congestion in eastern industrial centers and because the growing population in the West provided a constantly expanding market for eastern industry.

Perhaps the American trait most often attributed to pioneering on the frontier is the spirit of sturdy self-reliance. That trait was essential for those Europeans who first came to America, and the continuance of frontier conditions in the West could not help but reinforce it. In the early years of the settlement of any area, life simply was not possible except for the hardy and self-reliant. Furthermore, the opportunities of the frontier were such that, for those who could face up to the difficulties, the rewards were great. This applied to those wealthy persons from the East or from Europe who had capital to invest in the West, as well as to those of more humble status who had only their labor to invest. For more than a hundred years of American development, capital and labor were the scarce factors of production as compared to land. Always there was more and better land in the West. The abundance of western land made the West the symbol of opportunity, and provided the economic base on which personal self-reliance could rest.[1] American farming methods became traditionally exploitative, and farmers were not concerned to prevent erosion or to maintain the fertility which could make the soil a source of livelihood into the indefinite future. The perspective of time makes these elements of the westward movement understandable; nothing seemed to matter then but opening up, occupying, and profiting from the new lands of the western frontier.

## Gaining title to a continent

### The "Old Northwest"

By the treaty of peace of 1783 ending the Revolutionary War, the United States acquired title to all of the lands east of the Mississippi River and north to the Great Lakes. This provision of the peace treaty with England made necessary the land ordinances passed by the Congress in 1784, 1785, and 1787. Settlement of the area west of the Appalachians, which had begun during the war, now proceeded apace. The only legal hindrances remaining were the negotiation of treaties

[1] Emphasis upon the importance of the frontier in shaping American life, sometimes referred to as the "frontier thesis," is especially the work of Professor Frederick Jackson Turner of the University of Wisconsin, who developed and defended the various aspects of the idea in his work *The Frontier in American History* (New York: Holt, Rinehart & Winston, 1959).

with the Indians and the settling of disputed territorial claims between the states. The first hindrance was eliminated by the victories of General Anthony Wayne and the subsequent Treaty of Greenville, signed with the Indians in 1795. Seven of the original thirteen states claimed western extensions of their lands, several of which conflicted with one another. Maryland refused to ratify the Constitution until these claims should be surrendered to the national government. New York state took the lead by surrendering its claims to western lands in 1780. The same course was soon followed by Virginia, which had the most extensive claims of all. These cessions opened the way for settlement, although the last claims were not ceded by Georgia until 1802. Very shortly after the war, the Northwest Territory was opened up and the tide of immigration swung west across Pennsylvania to the Ohio River. By the early decades of the nineteenth century, Ohio had outstripped several of the older seaboard states in population, and Cincinnati became the leading metropolis of the West by about 1830. Indiana became a state in 1816 and Illinois two years later; most of their population was concentrated in the southern parts. Michigan and Wisconsin were not settled densely enough to become states until 1837 and 1848 respectively. The occupation of the northern part of the Northwest Territory waited upon the making of additional peace treaties with the Indians, and the completion of the Erie Canal. Chicago, which was a mere trading post with very few permanent inhabitants in 1830, had become a city of 100,000 by 1860. Cleveland, with only 6,000 in 1840, had passed 40,000 by 1860.

### The "Old Southwest"

As settlers poured into the new territories over the mountains, they found that their best transportation was provided by the Ohio and Mississippi river systems. This raised the question of the control of the Mississippi, which was of especial importance because of the port of New Orleans at its mouth. France had surrendered control of the area to Spain after the

Seven Years' War, and in 1802 the Spanish governor of Louisiana put into effect regulations which crippled American trade. At about the same time, President Thomas Jefferson heard that France had re-acquired Louisiana, and he dispatched James Monroe to France as a special envoy to purchase port facilities at New Orleans. Monroe and Robert Livingston, American minister in Paris, were astounded when Talleyrand, the French foreign minister, offered to sell them the whole of Louisiana. France needed funds, and other circumstances made former French dreams of American empire fade away. Monroe and Livingston had been authorized to pay up to $10,000,000 to purchase both port rights at New Orleans and the territory of West Florida, which was thought to belong to France. Confronted with this new offer, they did not hesitate to exceed their authority, and the purchase of Louisiana was arranged for the sum of $15,000,000 in American money. The President and the Senate approved the treaty, and the first and largest addition to the territory of the United States became an official fact in 1803. The boundaries of the Louisiana Purchase were not accurately defined, but ultimately all of the present states between the Mississippi River and the Rocky Mountains and north of Texas were carved out of it. Florida was acquired by a treaty with Spain in 1819, marking the end of another set of dreams of empire in North America by a European power.

The territory south of the Ohio River and east of the Mississippi was also being populated. This area came to be called the Old Southwest, although it had no special land ordinance by Congress to determine its exact limits, or its manner of settlement and government, as did the Northwest Territory. The motives for settlement in the Southwest were also somewhat different from those in the North. Tobacco culture, which had been carried on for a century or more in some of the south Atlantic states, had exhausted the soil. Further, the invention of the cotton gin in 1793 had greatly increased the demand for cotton and led to a desire to expand cotton growing. Both tobacco and cotton farmers were

therefore in need of new land. Some of the earliest white settlement in the area on the Gulf of Mexico and east of the Mississippi had been made by small farmers who resembled the characteristic migrants to the Northwest Territory. The heaviest wave of migration to the Southwest, however, came when large planters from the eastern seaboard states moved west with their families, their slaves, and their entire plantation establishments. Such planters either bought out the small earlier settlers, or outbid them at government land auctions. The plantation system became established on all the good farm lands of the Gulf Coast and lower Mississippi Valley area. Louisiana was admitted to statehood in 1812, Mississippi in 1817, and Alabama in 1819. The same migration of planters continued into Arkansas and Missouri, which became states in 1836 and 1821, respectively. Cotton production skyrocketed as the new lands of these states were occupied.

*California and Oregon*

Meriwether Lewis, William Clark, and Zebulon Pike began their explorations of the upper Mississippi and Missouri Valleys within a few years after the Louisiana Purchase in 1803, before settlement had gone very far beyond the Mississippi River. The path of immigration went either through or around the Great Plains area to the Pacific coast. American interest in California was slow to develop. Before 1840, only fur traders penetrated to California and whaling ships stopped for supplies occasionally. In the early 1840's, some farmers began to move into the Pacific Coast valleys, but when war with Mexico broke out in 1846, there were only about seven hundred non-Mexican Americans in California. The discovery of gold at Sutter's Mill near Sacramento in 1848 started the "gold rush," which brought the total population of the area to ninety thousand when California became a state in 1850. The gold seekers came by sea around Cape Horn, or partly by sea after crossing the Isthmus of Panama or other parts of Central America and Mexico on foot,

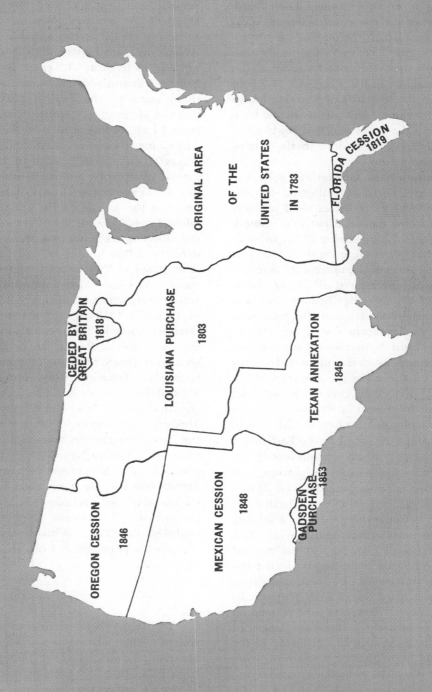

Fig. VII-1 Rounding out the boundaries of
the United States, 1800 to 1860.

or by various routes overland across the North American continent. The latter route was chosen by most immigrants, an estimated 40,000 using it in 1849 alone. Their hardships and trials on the covered-wagon trails constitute a saga which the moving-picture industry of twentieth-century California has burned deeply into the consciousness of the American nation. California gold did contribute greatly to the wealth of America, but in the longer run the other minerals in the California soil and the crops which it could grow were to contribute even more to the wealth of the state and nation.

The migration to Oregon territory, the Pacific coast area north of California, became substantial several years before gold brought California into the national spotlight. American fur traders had competed with English and Russian traders for trading rights in the area since the early years of the nineteenth century. In 1824, Russia surrendered all of her claims south of 54° 40', leaving Britain and the United States as rival claimants for possession of Oregon. No Americans moved into the territory to live until John Bidwell led the first group of immigrants overland in 1841. Still larger numbers overcame the obstacles of the long trek and arrived in Oregon in 1842 and 1843. Marcus Whitman, a Presbyterian missionary who had gone to Oregon with one of the earlier groups, returned to the East to stir up enthusiasm in Washington and among the public generally for greater emigration, and for the building of forts along the way. "Fifty-four forty or fight," referring to the latitude of the northern boundary desired, was a leading slogan in the presidential campaign of 1844. After the election, a compromise was reached by which the United States received all territory to the 49th parallel. By 1846, when England and the United States agreed upon this boundary between American and Canadian territory, Oregon had ten thousand American residents. The gold rush to California in the year 1849 and after distracted attention from Oregon, but after the gold fever had cooled, many immigrants again turned to the north. Oregon became a state in 1859.

The final rounding out of the area of the present continental United States came as a result of the war with Mexico. In the years following 1821, a considerable number of Americans gained concessions from Mexico to settle in its territory of Texas. By 1830, Mexicans of Spanish origin were outnumbered many times by the English-speaking settlers, and the Mexican government imposed restrictions in an endeavor to halt the flood. The American settlers revolted and proclaimed Texas an independent state in 1836. A prolonged controversy followed over the admission of Texas to the United States, but those favoring the action finally won out in 1845, when Texas was annexed. Very soon after that date the United States and Mexico quarrelled over the Texas boundary, and in 1846 President James K. Polk asked Congress to declare war on Mexico, which it promptly did. The peace treaty which Mexico accepted at the end of the war in 1848 gave to the United States all territory north of the present southern boundary west to the Pacific Ocean and north to Oregon territory, with one exception. For this cession of Texas territory, Mexico received $15,000,000 in cash and the cancellation of certain claims of American citizens against the Mexican government. The one exception to the Texas acquisition was a strip of land in what later became New Mexico and Arizona, which was purchased from Mexico in 1853 for $10,000,000, because it was thought to provide the best route for a railroad to California. This transaction is commonly referred to as the Gadsden Purchase. With it the American "empire" was complete from the Atlantic to the Pacific.

### The midcontinental area

By 1859, there were two frontiers in America, one moving westward beyond the Mississippi and the other moving eastward from California and Oregon into the Rocky Mountain area. The first large settlement to fill this gap was made by the Mormons, who moved to Utah in 1847. This religious group had been founded by Joseph Smith in New York state in 1827. They had moved to Ohio in 1831 and to Illinois in 1839 to escape persecution, and then, for the same reason, decided to move to a desert valley in Utah where they hoped at last to find peace. They had some misfortunes and near disasters in the first few years, but eventually became prosperous. There were forty thousand persons in Utah by 1860, but it was not admitted as a state until 1896, because the Mormon church did not renounce the practice of polygamy until 1890. For a few years after 1849, the Mormons profited substantially from the sale of supplies to gold seekers on the way to California.

Beyond the states adjoining the Mississippi River on the west, the only territory which was settled to any considerable extent before the Civil War was that of Kansas and Nebraska. Settlement in these areas was opened up by the Kansas-Nebraska Act of 1854. Kansas began to fill up first, and unfortunately it became a battleground for the sharpening differences between the North and the South over the slavery issue (see p. 186). It did not become a state until 1861, after the first of the southern states had seceded from the Union, leaving the balance of power in Congress with the free states. Nebraska filled up more slowly than Kansas and did not have sufficient population for statehood until 1867.

### Life on the frontier

A mere recital of the statistics and dates of the settlement of the American West misses altogether the human aspects of one of the great migrations in the history of mankind. The first white men in any area in America were the explorers, the fur trappers, the traders, the missionaries, or the seekers for adventure. None of these came as settlers. But they carried back to civilization accounts of the areas through which they had traveled, and thus stimulated the next wave of migrants, who became real settlers. These settlers were nearly always farmers, young, energetic, and ambitious, but poor. They came into an area, bought land that suited them, or just "squatted" on the public domain if they hadn't enough money to buy, and proceeded to build crude log houses, to clear the land, and to get farming operations under way. The work was long and hard, the facilities for living very poor, but with the aid of a wife to cook, weave, sew, churn, and do innumerable other household chores the pioneer farmer could survive, and even, after the first few years, enjoy a kind of rough abundance. Many such farmers had to borrow to pay for land, livestock, and implements and so became sympathetic to a government policy of easy credit and freely issued paper money.

As a new area began to fill up, roads and bridges would be built, a blacksmith and a carpenter would move into the community, and a storekeeper would open up a shop. Schools and churches would spring up. Life would become less primitive and more civilized. Land prices would rise substantially in developed communities. Often, many of the earliest pioneers would become restless and sell out at a substantial profit to move on west to purchase land on the new frontier. Newly arrived immigrants from Europe might spend their accumulated savings to buy such farms from the first settlers, or local land speculators might make such purchases. In any case, better houses made from sawed lumber or brick or stone would likely be built as well as better barns and farm buildings. The whole community would become more stable and would begin to resemble the many prosperous farm communities which can be seen today.

The last stage of frontier development would come when the little crossroads village with its store and blacksmith shop, representing the second stage of development, grew into a substantial commercial or industrial town. The city of Cincinnati well illustrates this evolution. Until after the War of 1812, Cincinnati was not much more than a village at a convenient landing point on the Ohio River. The rapid settlement of Kentucky, Ohio, Indiana, and Illinois in the

1820's made Cincinnati grow into a great meat-packing center ("Porkopolis") serving the surrounding area, as well as a commercial and financial center. Only a relatively few communities were so situated as to be capable of developing into great cities, but when such centers began to appear at strategic places, it was a sign that the frontier had passed and economic maturity had arrived.

The American frontier continued to advance westward and the unsettled area continued to diminish until 1890, when a frontier of settlement officially ceased to exist. The long years when the frontier did exist tended to impress upon Americans the idea that speculation in the future would always be successful. The fact that impoverished but ambitious persons could take a chance on future development and usually come out successfully made Americans profound believers in individual self-reliance and optimists about the existence of opportunity in their country.

One of the best results of the frontier was the development of this individualism and self-reliance among Americans. One of the most unfortunate was the tendency toward wasteful use of natural resources. When new resources could be obtained by moving farther westward, there was little incentive to conserve those on hand, and as a result forests and farming lands were recklessly exploited.

### Transportation to the West

#### *Rivers and canals*

From the beginning of human life on the earth, man has lived in close association with rivers and streams. Even as a hunter, he usually had to live near a stream of water; when he had learned how to farm, stream valleys furnished the most fertile soil. It was only natural that rivers should have become one of the very oldest means of transportation as soon as rafts and boats were developed to carry men and their goods. It was not by accident that the first civilizations sprang up along rivers—Egypt along the Nile, the Mesopotamian civilizations along the Tigris and Euphrates, Indian civilizations along the Indus and Ganges. Water transportation was the natural way for men to travel, for rivers cut through wildernesses men could not penetrate. The settlers in the American colonies were forced to return to the most primitive conditions of living, and rivers naturally became their first important means of inland transportation.

One of the great drawbacks to river transportation is that the river does not always go where the traffic needs to go. That became true in the United States as soon as the territory west of the Appalachian mountains was opened for settlement. Roads were commonly thought of either for local use or as connectors between navigable streams. The greatest enthusiasm for the national pike (see below, p. 147) was occasioned by the fact that it was to connect the Potomac and Ohio Rivers. The heaviest traffic was over that section of the road. Beyond the mountains, the Ohio and the Mississippi became the principal arteries for immigrants and for the delivery of their products once they had settled. Actually, settlers in the Ohio Valley would have preferred to send their surplus products directly to the eastern seaboard had it not been prohibitively expensive. Bulky farm products were floated down the Ohio and Mississippi on barges to New Orleans, where they were sold, but that was not as good a market as the eastern seaboard cities. Furthermore, the return trip up the rivers from New Orleans was too difficult and expensive except for light and very valuable merchandise. The rivers were thus not entirely satisfactory to the inhabitants of their valleys as highways of commerce. Yet, until something better was available, the Ohio and Mississippi continued to be used, at least for certain types of freight.

Experimenting with the application of steam power to water transportation began even earlier than attempts to apply it on land. This was particularly true in America, where relatively sparse populations and rugged terrain made the provision of good means of transportation both essential and difficult. Beginning with Oliver Evans in 1783, a series of inventors worked on the problem of driving a boat by steam. All encountered difficulties which prevented practical success until Robert Fulton built the *Clermont*, which he sailed up the Hudson River from New York to Albany and back entirely by steam power, in August 1807. The *Clermont* had a Watt engine built by the partners Boulton and Watt in England. In the next few years steamboats were put into service on several eastern rivers, and in 1811 the *New Orleans* was built in Pittsburgh and made the trip down the Ohio and Mississippi Rivers to the city for which it was named. It was unable to get all the way back up river, however, so it was placed in service between New Orleans and Natchez. In 1815, the *Enterprise*, built from an improved design, made the trip from New Orleans to Louisville in twenty-five days.

After 1824, when a United States Supreme Court decision indicated that a monopoly on the navigation of the lower Mississippi granted by Louisiana to Fulton and Livingston would not be held valid in the courts, the use of steamboats on the Mississippi and Ohio increased greatly. By 1829, there were 200 steamboats in operation, and by 1842 the number had reached 450. A decade later there were considerably over 1,000, and regular packet service was offered on the important tributaries of the Mississippi by a number of established lines. This rapid expansion in the use of the steamboat on the Mississippi River system was far beyond its use anywhere else, partly because early steamboats were too fragile for ocean use. The first steamboat on the Great Lakes was built in 1816, and ships for the trans-Atlantic service were powered partly by steam as early as the 1830's. Until after the middle of the century, however, more steamboats were in service on the interior rivers of the United States than anywhere else in the world.

While river transport was being improved, the possibilities of canals were not ignored. The English success in canal building in the 1760's and 1770's was well known. Albert Gallatin, the secretary of the treasury, recommended coastal canals in his report to Congress in 1808, and several shorter ones had been built even before that. The agitation for more ambitious trunk canals connecting large bodies of water first achieved success in New York state, where Elkanah Watson had argued for the practicability of a canal connecting the Hudson River and the Great Lakes a decade or more before 1800. Governor DeWitt Clinton took up the battle for the canal, and finally was able to get an appropriation for it from the New York legislature in 1817. Construction was begun at once, and the canal was completed in 1825.

The Erie Canal (as it was named) was an instant success and the tolls collected on it repaid the entire construction cost within ten years. Thereafter, it was a source of net income to New York state. It furnished an outlet to world markets for grain and other products from the Great Lakes area. Freight charges from Buffalo to New York City were cut from $100 to $10 a ton. The time of the trip was cut from twenty days to six. Migrants began to use the canal to gain access to the West, and Buffalo, Cleveland, Detroit, and other cities on the Great Lakes began to grow rapidly. The basin of the Great Lakes began to fill up with settlers as the Ohio Valley had done earlier. By 1850, New York City had passed Philadelphia, Boston, and Baltimore in population and wealth, and became the greatest port on the Atlantic seaboard. The Erie Canal served to join together the great natural waterways of the North American continent, bringing the people of different areas into closer contact.

Other cities of the Atlantic coast—Boston, Philadelphia, and Baltimore—seeing the prosperity brought to New York by the Erie Canal, promoted projects of their own for canals to the interior. All of these projects were ill-fated, partly because the terrain necessitated many locks, and the prospective volume of traffic would not justify the heavy costs which were encountered. Construction dragged on with many delays until the potential and actual competition of the railroads made the projects seem even less wise. By the 1830's, Ohio and Indiana, among the states of the

Northwest Territory, had acquired substantial populations, and great enthusiasm developed to link the Ohio River and Lake Erie by canals across their territory. Ohio built the Ohio and Erie canal between Portsmouth and Cleveland, starting work in 1825 and completing it in 1832. At about the same time, the Miami and Erie canal was built by the state from Cincinnati to Toledo. Indiana also was carried away by the canal mania and undertook the longest canal in the world—the Wabash and Erie—from Evansville on the Ohio River in western Indiana to Toledo, Ohio, on Lake Erie. Construction was begun in 1832, but before the canal was completed the Panic of 1837 struck the country, and Indiana sank hopelessly into debt. Also, the practicability of the steam railroad had by this time been demonstrated, and the enthusiasm for canal building was spent. The canal was completed after a fashion by 1843, but neither the Wabash and Erie nor any other canal in the western states was ever a financial success. By 1840, it was clear that the railroad offered the best solution of the transportation problem for the expanding nation.

Internal transportation by river and canal played a vital part in the economic development of that part of the United States east of the Mississippi River. Pittsburgh, Cincinnati, and Louisville had their start as river towns. Buffalo, Cleveland, Detroit, and Chicago grew only as the Great Lakes were connected with New York by the Erie Canal. Other cities were aided by lesser rivers and canals. The products of industry were carried to markets in the rural regions and farmers were able to ship their grain and livestock to the cities for use there, for processing, and for export overseas. Yet the shortcomings of river and canal transportation led to the eager welcoming of the steam railroad. Neither rivers nor canals could be used throughout the winter in the northern states. Neither could be located exactly where they were needed. Rivers followed their own course and canals could not be built in rough or hilly territory. Railroads could overcome both of these limitations. None the less, it must be acknowledged that water trans-portation played a large part in developing the eastern United States. Centers of population and industry that had risen in the pre-railroad era did much to determine the pattern of the railroad network that developed in later years.

### Roads and turnpikes

In addition to water routes there were in colonial times only local and good-weather roads, which were inadequate for the growing commerce of the states, and especially for the carrying of settlers and their goods to the new lands of the West. The feasibility of privately built turnpikes supported by a toll from users was demonstrated by the Lancaster-Philadelphia turnpike, which went into use in 1794. Lancaster became the largest city in the country not located on a navigable stream or body of water. Other turnpikes by the hundreds were built in New England, New York, Pennsylvania, and, as settlement proceeded, throughout the South and West. Many of them duplicated the principal routes of today.

In spite of the successes of the turnpikes, they did not fully meet the transportation needs of the country. The costs of travel and freight hauling were often prohibitively high. According to the historian James B. McMaster, the average freight cost was about ten cents per ton mile. The price of a bushel of wheat at sixty cents would be doubled if it were hauled as much as two hundred miles. The haul from Philadelphia to Pittsburgh over the mountains cost $125 per ton, several times as high as the average level-country rate. Because of these high freight costs there was much discussion throughout the country of the desirability of federal aid for roads. In 1808, Secretary of the Treasury Albert Gallatin made a report to Congress on roads as well as canals, harbors, and rivers. In his report, Gallatin argued that conditions in America were different from those in Europe, that capital was scarce and certainly not sufficient to build the needed roads without public assistance. He proposed both short canals across the peninsulas projecting into the Atlantic Ocean, to make a kind of inner passage along the coast, and also a great road connecting every coastal state from north to south. He also suggested that roads might be built between the headwaters of navigable streams flowing into the Atlantic Ocean and the tributaries of the Ohio River.

The whole question of public aid in road building came to a focus for the time being in the project for a national road from the Potomac River at Cumberland, Maryland, on through to the West. The project was authorized by Congress in 1806, but no contracts were let until 1811. By 1818, the Cumberland Road, as it was then called, was completed through to the Ohio River at Wheeling, Virginia (now West Virginia). For most of the distance the Cumberland Road followed the trail cut by General Braddock fifty years earlier during the Seven Years' War. Almost at once the new road with its stone surface and solid stone bridges was flooded with wagons and coaches. It was said to resemble more the main street of a great city than a path into the wilderness. The emigrants to the West put their belongings on flatboats at Wheeling and floated on down the Ohio to their destinations. Until 1844, Congress continued to appropriate money for the extension of the road, now called the National Highway, by which time it had reached Vandalia, Illinois. After that, other means of transportation reduced the importance of continuing the road farther to the west. The same shift of interest to canals and railroads contributed to the bankruptcy of most of the private turnpike companies, which left the roads to the care, or lack of it, of local governments. State and federal support of highways as we know it at the present time is the product of the automobile era of the twentieth century.

### The beginning of the rails

In America, as in England, the earliest railways were short tramlines to move heavy material from mines, quarries, or brick yards. Small cars were either pushed by workmen or pulled by horses; in a few cases they were moved by cables operated by stationary steam engines. The possibility of a locomotive powered by a steam engine was visualized in both England and America almost as soon as the steam engine had become a practical success. As early as 1813, George Stephenson was using an improvised locomotive to pull coal cars at a mine in England. Before 1820, John Stevens in Hoboken, New Jersey, set up a model narrow-gauge railroad on which he operated a steam locomotive. Other experimenters were working with locomotives in both England and America. George Stephenson's *Rocket*, winner of the Rainhill trials in England in 1829, finally demonstrated the fact that the steam locomotive was not merely the plaything of inventors but a practical and economical source of power for a railway.

One of the projects by which another seaboard city hoped to equal the success of New York with the Erie Canal was the Baltimore and Ohio Railroad, chartered in 1828, to connect Baltimore with the Ohio River. The railroad was not chartered until a canal project to connect Chesapeake Bay with the Ohio River had been demonstrated to be very costly and of doubtful success. It was at first expected that horses would pull the railway cars, but the Rainhill trials in England persuaded the promotors of the project to turn to steam locomotives. In 1830 the *Tom Thumb*, built by Peter Cooper, went into service on the first few miles of the line. The Baltimore and Ohio thus earned the title of the first real railroad in the United States. The road reached Wheeling, Virginia, in 1853.

Another early railroad project was the Charleston and Hamburg Railroad in South Carolina. The *Best Friend of Charleston*, built for service on this road, was the first American locomotive designed for regular service. It went into operation in 1830. In 1833, when the line was completed to Hamburg, this railroad achieved the honor of being, for a short time, the longest in the world. Meanwhile, other cities were promoting railroads into the territory they served. The first link in the present New York Central system was a line from Albany to Schenectady begun in 1830. The beginning of the Pennsylvania system was a short line from Philadelphia to the Susquehanna River, completed in 1834. Many other short lines were built elsewhere in the country in the early thirties. By 1840, it was clear that railroads could successfully haul freight and passengers long distances, and most of our present systems in the eastern half of the country had been started. By 1860, railroad mileage had reached 30,000 (see Fig. VII-2), and the railroad network east of the Mississippi had been laid out. Extensions beyond St. Louis and Chicago had been made into Missouri, Iowa, and Wisconsin.

The economic effects of the railroads were tremendous. Towns located on railroad lines grew and prospered; those that did not get railroads languished. Freight movement became independent of the seasons, since ice and snow did not stop the railroads as they did the canals. Railroads could also be built to elevations above sea level at which canals became impractical if not impossible. Thus centers of industry and population might develop wherever there was economic justification for them and where adequate transportation could be assured. Railroad freight rates were not necessarily lower than canal rates, but the service was far more speedy. Beyond the immediate economic effects of the railroad, it had the broader social effect of giving some unity to the country, particularly between sections having common economic interests.

The building of the railroads was itself a great national task and a stimulus to other types of employment. The new railroads, especially after 1860, brought in immigrants whose productive efforts in turn increased, or even created, traffic for the railroads. American railroad building had in it a much larger speculative element than was commonly true in Europe. Often, perhaps usually, the speculation brought returns, for the interior of North America was being developed rapidly. But at times it did not, and many railroads found themselves permanently overbuilt and unable to avoid bankruptcy. Whatever the fate of the roads themselves, they contributed greatly to the economic development of the country, making possible a national market to which the various sections and regions could contribute in their own best way.

### The revolution in agriculture between 1800 and 1860

During the period of settlement of the West, between the beginning of the nineteenth century and the outbreak of the Civil War, a true agricultural revolution took place in the United States. In 1800, agriculture in America was very largely what it had been during

*Thousands of miles*

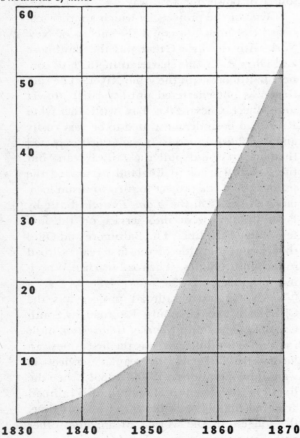

Fig. VII-2 Railroad mileage in the United States, showing miles of road in operation from 1830 to 1870.

the late decades of the colonial era. There was some commercial production of meat and wheat in the North and of tobacco in the South, but, by and large, farming was still subsistence farming. Methods were bound up with tradition and superstition in many sections, and relatively little systematic thought was given to the problem of agriculture, although a few outstanding gentlemen farmers, like George Washington and Thomas Jefferson, were doing considerable experimenting with improved methods of farming and with improved breeds of livestock. Washington turned from tobacco growing on his Virginia plantation to the cultivation of other crops. He was the founder of mule breeding in the United States and was one of the first importers of Spanish merino sheep. Such thoughtful farming methods were exceptional, however, and most rural people followed old methods and consumed nearly all of their product themselves. Improvement was retarded by the availability of new land at the frontier, which even during the colonial period had begun to move slowly westward into the Appalachians.

After 1800 and until the prairie land of the Middle West was reached, frontiersmen continued to farm very much as their colonial predecessors had done. Until settlement reached the Mississippi River, land had to be cleared of its timber by girdling the trees until they died, then cutting them down or pushing them over, and moving them to a great bonfire by a "log rolling." Back in the eastern states, the land had been cleared since 1700 or even earlier and the first few bounteous crops from virgin soil had long since been gathered. Eastern farmers either had to abandon farming due to the unequal competition with the new virgin soils of the West, or had to develop new methods which would increase the output per man hour of labor. Furthermore, as we shall see more fully in the next chapter, commerce and industry expanded in the eastern states, once they were freed from the mercantilist restrictions of Great Britain. Naturally, the commercial and industrial cities of the country developed in the older areas. The existence of nearby urban markets made increasing demands upon and helped maintain the opportunities for eastern agriculture. But the steady improvement of transportation throughout the period made it possible to move foodstuffs from the West to the growing cities or to other areas where any particular product could not be produced to the best advantage.

The response of agriculture to these changing conditions was a series of adaptations which in the total were revolutionary in extent. And not all of the agricultural innovations of the period before the Civil War produced their full effects within that period. Rather, they showed what the new possibilities were, but the benefits continued to be felt in later years and are still being enjoyed. Everywhere there was an effort to design new machines and to find new crops and improved breeds of livestock. Specialization and sale of products away from the farm became the rule rather than the exception. Railroads were available in more and more sections of the country to transport farm produce to the growing markets in the industrial cities. For the most up-to-date and successful farmers, at least, farming was becoming a capitalistic business. The investment in land was becoming a more substantial item, and to this the cost of improved stock, machinery, and buildings had to be added. The family farm unit remained predominant, although a few large-scale farms began to be established, especially west of the Mississippi River. In either case, the successful farmer had to pay careful heed to his markets and to his costs, just as any other businessman had to do.

### Cotton becomes king in the South

Probably the most striking agricultural change in the early history of the American nation was the shift to cotton culture in the South. It will be recalled from our discussion of the coming of the Industrial Revolution, and especially of the developing English textile industry (p. 67), that one of the most powerful incentives for an improvement in methods in the industry was the deep inroad being made in the cloth market by finished cotton fabrics imported from India. The new machines that were developed were used on the traditional wool and on flax (to make linen) at first. But as they were improved and showed that they could be adapted to cotton, that change was made, and raw cotton was imported into England. English manufacturers set out to meet the Indian competition directly. In the twenty years following 1775, the cotton cloth industry in England grew from a low position to the largest of all British industries. The new machines permitted England to underbid Indian handmade cotton cloth, and the new problem was that of obtaining adequate supplies of raw cotton.

The first attempt in America to meet England's new need for cotton came with the introduction of long-staple sea island cotton to the seaboard lowlands and offshore islands of Georgia and South Carolina in 1786. Because the fiber of this type of cotton is longer, it could be handled better in the early and crude English machines. In addition, its seeds were more loosely attached to the fiber, so that the two could be separated by hand much more readily than ordinary or upland cotton. It is estimated that American cotton production, mostly of the sea island type, had reached 1,500,000 pounds by 1790.

This increase in production, gratifying as it was to southern farmers, did not meet the English demand, nor did it suit all farmers of the South because of the very limited areas on which the long-staple cotton could be grown. The solution was attained by growing short-staple upland cotton, which could be raised on any fertile ground in the South and Southwest. With the change to this crop the average annual production for the years 1796 to 1800 was over 18,000,000 pounds—twelve times that of 1790. Almost continuously from that time until 1860 cotton production increased (see Fig. VII-3) until it reached the total of about 1¾ *billion* pounds annually just before the Civil War.[1]

The fruits of increased production could not be enjoyed until some efficient method could be found of separating the seeds from the cotton fiber. This situation came to the attention of a young Connecticut Yankee, Eli Whitney, a Yale graduate of the class of 1792, traveling to Carolina to take a teaching position. On the trip he met the widow and children of General Nathaniel Greene, who had served in the American army during the Revolution. He was invited to spend a few days at their home in Georgia before going on to his position and while there he learned from the manager of Mrs. Greene's plantation about the need for a device to separate the seeds from the cotton fiber. He turned the matter over in his mind and after a few days proposed the plan of a machine to Mr. Miller, the agent of the executors of General Greene.

| years | average annual production in the U. S., in pounds | average New York price of middling upland cotton, in cents | % of crop exported |
|---|---|---|---|
| **1791–95** | 5,200,000 | 33.43 | 31.7 |
| **1796–1800** | 18,200,000 | 49.41 | 36.3 |
| **1801–05** | 59,600,000 | 56.38 | 25.0 |
| **1806–10** | 80,400,000 | 65.38 | 18.9 |
| **1811–15** | 80,000,000 | 52.83 | 14.8 |
| **1816–20** | 141,200,000 | 67.38 | 26.2 |
| **1821–25** | 209,000,000 | 72.93 | 16.2 |
| **1826–30** | 307,244,400 | 82.84 | 10.9 |
| **1831–35** | 398,521,600 | 82.57 | 11.9 |
| **1836–40** | 617,306,200 | 83.15 | 13.0 |
| **1841–45** | 822,953,800 | 84.03 | 7.7 |
| **1846–50** | 979,690,400 | 74.46 | 8.7 |
| **1851–55** | 1,294,422,800 | 76.51 | 9.6 |
| **1856–60** | 1,749,496,500 | 79.51 | 11.5 |
| **1861–65** | no data | no data | 58.9 |

*Fig.VII-3 The striking growth in American cotton production from 1791 to 1865 should be compared with the per cent exported and the changing prices.*

[1] *The South in the Building of the Nation*, 13 vols. (Richmond: Southern Historical Publication Society, 1909–1913), Vol. V, p. 211.

Miller volunteered to pay the expense of making a model and proposed that if it worked successfully, he and Whitney form a partnership to produce the machines. The model was successful, and soon many cotton gins, much larger than the original, were put into use throughout the South. Miller and Whitney made the mistake of trying to restrict the use of their gins by leasing them to users on a royalty basis. It was such a simple device, however, so easily reproduced, and so badly needed, that the patent monopoly broke down. The combination of the cotton gin and the change to short-staple cotton resulted in the great increase in production mentioned above.

The skyrocketing of southern cotton production was not dependent solely upon the growth of demand for the product, or on increased ability to handle it mechanically. The result that was achieved would probably not have been possible had not several other conditions also existed. For one thing, slavery had already become established in the South for the production of tobacco and lesser crops. Much of the good land was already in the hands of large plantation owners before the upsurge of demand for cotton. Cotton proved to be adapted to the slave economy, which in fact developed a new and stronger lease on life than it had ever had before. Cotton does not drain the soil of its fertility as rapidly as tobacco. It bolstered up the existing plantation economy and great planters took it as their main crop. Cotton production increased also because the demand for some of the older crops of the South, such as indigo, rice, and sugar, was either not increasing or was actually declining. Some farmers were badly in need of a new money crop. Finally, the great record of cotton production could not have been achieved had not the new lands of the Gulf states, Arkansas and Texas, been available. The new lands westward from Georgia and the Carolinas were needed for the huge total of cotton production that was achieved. Well before 1860, cotton was king in this great belt of states across the southern United States and dominated the economic, social, and political life of the area.

## The rise of commercial farming in the Northeast

The agriculture of New England and the Middle Atlantic states did not remain unchanged in the face of the economic transformation taking place throughout the country. After a rather gradual but steady early growth, American commerce and industry began to experience a rapid growth shortly before and after 1800, when European merchants and manufacturers were being interfered with by the French Revolution and the Napoleonic Wars. Although the steam engine had been developed in England and had been put to use in the United States, many of the new factories still depended on water power, and found the swift rivers of New England to be their best location. Industrial cities began to rise in favorable areas, especially in New England. Workers were drawn to the factories from surrounding farms. Shipbuilding, fishing, and a worldwide carrying trade also had their center in the seaport towns of New England and the Middle Atlantic states. They, too, drew their workers from the farms of the hinterland.

If these economic developments were not enough to upset eastern agriculture, the opening of the Cumberland Road to Wheeling in 1818, the completion of the Erie Canal in 1825, and the building of railroads to the West in the 1830's and 1840's brought the farm produce of the fertile western lands to the eastern states to compete directly with eastern farm products. Some of the eastern farmlands never had been as fertile as the valley lands of the West, although they had furnished a livelihood and a refuge for several generations of the descendants of the original immigrants from Europe. Now, they could not survive the economic attack on both flanks from local industry and western farm lands, and many thousands of New England farms were abandoned.

Of course, not all eastern farms were on inferior soil. Many valley farms had soil as good as any in the country, although even they could not meet the competition of the exploitative methods that were used on the virgin soils of the West. Grain growing declined in New England, and, in the decade or two before 1860, in the Middle Atlantic states also. Sheep were kept and wool was produced on the rolling and hilly lands to supply the textile mills in the valley towns. Dairying, fruit growing, and truck gardening arose near industrial cities to supply the needs of their growing army of workers. After the opening of the Erie Canal, butter and cheese making moved from southeastern to central and western New York state, where they have remained important ever since. The growth of cigar smoking led to the production of high-grade leaf tobacco for wrappers in the Connecticut Valley. The basic change in eastern agriculture was from the old self-sufficient farming to the production of cash crops for sale in nearby commercial markets. Although some farms had to be abandoned, many other farmers found that the new type of commercial farming brought them a previously unknown prosperity.

### Breaking the prairie sod

As settlement reached and passed the Mississippi, the pioneers met a condition with which they did not at first know how to cope. That condition was the open, treeless prairie covered with a dense grass sod, with tightly matted roots, in the sharpest contrast to the loose, leaf-mold soil of a cleared forest floor. At first, it was supposed that the absence of trees on the prairie indicated poor soil. Not until it had been demonstrated that the prairie soil was really very fertile and would grow excellent crops if only the sod could be "broken" did settlers move eagerly to begin farming on the plains. The problem was to get the sod cut and turned over so that it would rot away, leaving the soil loose and workable. Sometimes this could be done by axes and shovels, but the real tool came to be the "breaking plow." This was a great plow, strong enough to cut through the sod, and

requiring a team of several yoke of oxen to pull it. Even with the breaking plow, it was slow and costly work to turn the sod. And once the job was done, only a rather poor crop of "sod corn" could be obtained the first year, while the sod was rotting away. Thereafter, the usual crop rotation could be followed, or, as was often the case, corn was planted year after year.

The prairie offered new problems and new opportunities. Although breaking the sod seemed slow and costly, it was actually accomplished more cheaply, quickly, and finally than the clearing of a forest. On the other hand, prairie farmers found that building material for houses and barns was scarce. At first, there were no good means of transportation to bring in lumber from the East, and the prairie pioneers had to live in sod houses, with walls built of stacked up blocks of sod. Attempts were even made to use sod similarly stacked for fences to enclose pastures and feed lots. One can imagine that the stock would frequently break through such poor enclosures and cause the prairie farmers a great deal of trouble to recover them. Boards and rails were sometimes brought from the East for fences, but the expense was usually prohibitive. In some parts of the prairie, osage orange hedge made better and cheaper fence than anything else before cheap barbed wire became available. Wire was used for fencing to some degree beginning about 1850, but large-scale and low-cost methods of steel-making were not developed for a number of years after the mid-century. Really satisfactory wire fence did not come until after the Civil War. The prairies brought advantages too, as well as problems, for the flat land encouraged and lent itself well to large-scale, mechanized farming. Many improved types of farm machines had their origin in the East, but they usually found their greatest market and had their widest use at first on the prairie, where their initial awkwardness in turning, or the danger of their upsetting on hillsides, or the difficulty of pulling them uphill did not matter, for there were no hills and the drivers seldom had to make sharp turns.

## New machines for the farm

In spite of the improvements in farm machines and methods which were begun in England by Tull and others shortly after 1700 (p. 78f.), practically nothing was done in America to make further improvements until nearly 1800. Land was too abundant and transportation for farm products was too poor to provide incentive for improving farming methods. Even as late as the early nineteenth century, practically all farm operations except plowing, harrowing, and hauling were done by hand. That is to say, the sowing of seed, the cutting of the grain, and the threshing of the grain were done by hand, with tools no better in principle than those used by the ancient Egyptians hundreds of years before Christ. Eventually, highly developed farming machines and methods came from American inventors, but the start was very slow.

One of the first Americans to achieve public notice for the improvement of a farm tool was Charles Newbold, who patented an iron plow in 1797. Newbold's plow encountered the superstitious belief that iron poisoned the soil, and many farmers refused to use it. In 1814, Jethro Wood patented an improved iron plow made of several iron castings bolted together so that if one part broke or wore out it could be replaced. Within fifteen or twenty years, plows of this type were being widely used. The next major improvement in the plow was made by John Deere, a Vermont-born blacksmith who had migrated to Illinois. He made the plow of steel, which was smoother than cast iron and much more efficient in cutting the prairie sod. Deere established a factory to build his plows at Moline in 1858, and this became the first unit of the great agricultural implement firm which bears his name today. Another famous name found on present-day farm machines is that of James Oliver, who invented a chilled steel plow in 1869. As a result of the work of these men and others, the iron or steel plow became an efficient instrument for working the soil. Farmers could then handle a larger amount of land more efficiently. The new plows could be pulled fast

and they were less cumbersome than the old wooden plow. Thus, the iron plow also contributed to the greater use of horses for farm power and the decreased use of oxen.

While the plow was being improved, other inventors were working on other farm machines. The cradle for cutting grain had come into use after 1800; it was an improvement on the old sickle, although it was still a hand tool which required a great deal of strength and endurance of the cradler. Patents for horse-drawn reapers were issued very close together in 1833 and 1834 to Obed Hussey and Cyrus McCormick. McCormick had begun working on his reaper as early as Hussey, although his patent came later. Both machines were practical and would cut up to fifteen acres a day— as much as half a dozen cradlers could cut. Hussey lacked strong financial backing, and stayed in the East where the market for his reapers was limited. McCormick moved from his home in Virginia to Brockport in western New York and later to Chicago. By 1860, his Chicago factory was turning out 4,000 reapers a year. The McCormick firm was the nucleus of the present International Harvester Company, the largest agricultural implement manufacturer in America. The early reapers merely bunched the grain and pushed it off on the ground so that men following it could pick up the bunches and bind them. Mechanical binders did not come until after the Civil War with other great improvements.

Grain growing was greatly aided by the reaper, but a mechanical thresher was needed to keep the processes in balance. Until the 1830's, grain was threshed by hand flails or was tramped out by animals on earthen threshing floors. Fanning mills were developed to separate the grain from the chaff after the flailing or tramping had been done, but there was great need for a machine to do the entire threshing job. Hiram and John Pitt invented a thresher in 1836 which became the leader among mechanical threshers in both Europe and America. It would both thresh, or beat the grain out of the husk in which it is enclosed, and winnow, or separate the grain from the chaff. It represented a tremendous saving of labor time, and by 1860 had come into use all over the United States wherever grain was grown in considerable quantities.

While the plow, the reaper, and the thresher were probably the outstanding new farm tools or machines, there were others which should not be overlooked. For a time, the reaper was also used to cut grass for hay. The treatment of hay is so different from that of grain, however, that a separate and rapid mower is needed. Such a mowing machine was developed by 1860. Horse-drawn rakes

displaced hand raking of hay also. Jethro Tull in England in the 1730's had developed a grain drill to sow seeds in straight rows at the proper depth. A century later, despite Tull's work, grain was still being sown broadcast by hand in America. However, in the 1840's, a drill to sow wheat and other small grains was developed. The corn planter offered special problems, and it took longer to develop a successful mechanical planter. But before 1860, it was in common use. Along with these machines, harrows to break up plowed ground were greatly improved and cultivators for corn and similar crops were developed.

It is probable that the development of new machines for the farm, in the years between 1830 and 1860, was the most striking agricultural development of the period. It is hard for those living in the twentieth century to appreciate the degree to which farm labor was eased by the new machinery (see Fig. VII-4). The result was that in a time of great westward expansion the average American farmer did not take life easier, but simply undertook the cultivation of more and more acres as machines increased his efficiency. There can be little doubt that it was possible to meet the manpower demands of Civil War armies largely because of the increased agricultural productivity of the men who remained at home. Alert contemporaries realized that they were living in the midst of a revolution. A good summary of the situation appeared in the report of the U.S. Census of 1860:

> By the improved plow, labor equivalent to that of one horse in three is saved. By means of drills two bushels of seed will go as far as three bushels scattered broadcast, while the yield is increased six to eight bushels per acre; the plants come up in rows and may be tended by horse-hoes (cultivators) . . . The reaping machine is a saving of more than one-third the labor when it cuts and rakes . . . The threshing machine is a saving of two-thirds on the old hand flail mode . . . The saving in the labor of handling hay in the field and barn by means of horserakes and horsehayforks is equal to one half.[1]

[1]H. U. Faulkner, *American Economic History* (New York: Harper and Brothers, 7th ed., 1954, p. 213).

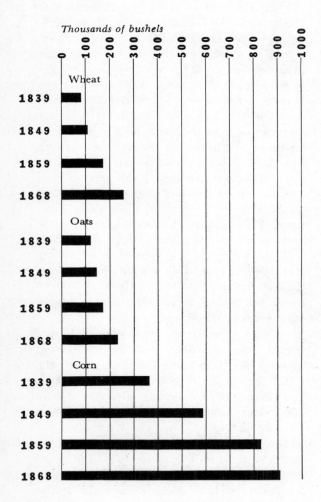

Fig.VII-4 *The development of efficient farming machinery in the United States was accompanied by a substantial expansion in production of the basic crops.*

## Scientific farming and livestock breeding

The attention which was being devoted to scientific farming and stock breeding in Europe in the first half of the nineteenth century was not fully matched in America because of the abundance of fertile land. In Europe, improved farming efficiency *on the same land* was becoming a necessity; in America, when greater production was needed, the first thought was likely to be how and where to get more land. Still, that distinction was not a hard and fast one, for some American farmers were concerning themselves with developing proper crop rotations, higher crop yields, and better livestock. The "Norfolk system," developed by Townshend in England, was modified in America to provide a four-year crop rotation of corn, oats (or barley), wheat, and clover. This rotation became traditional in areas suited to it, although it gradually came to be recognized as a soil-depleting rotation, when continuously followed. In Europe, Sir Humphrey Davy and Gustus Liebig had demonstrated the possibility and desirability of chemical fertilizers to stimulate plant growth, but in America it seemed much easier to get larger crops by moving to new land. However, animal manure had a recognized value for dressing the soil, and in some cases marl or lime was applied.

In the problem of securing better types of livestock, American farmers showed a great deal more enthusiasm. The development of farm machines which could roll easily and swiftly over the land led to an increased demand for horses as farm draft animals. Added to this "on the farm" demand for horses was the "off the farm" demand for them to pull loads on the roads to and from the increasing number of railway freight stations. Also, as roads were opened into unoccupied areas ahead of the railways, "Conestoga horses" were in demand, i.e., horses which were heavy enough to pull loaded wagons, but light enough to cover a considerable daily mileage on the road. Breeding stock was imported from Europe, and special, improved types of horses were developed both for farm and road uses. In Kentucky, and later in Missouri, the breeding of mules to supply southern plantations became a major farm enterprise.

The rearing of sheep on American farms goes back to the earliest colonial days. Sheep, although they are delicate animals in appearance, are capable of surviving more neglect and living under a wider range of physical conditions than any other farm animal. Sheep can stay alive in winter by pawing away the snow to get down to the grass beneath, and if necessary, they can maintain an existence on rocky hillsides where cattle or horses would starve. Besides, sheep produce both wool for clothing and meat for food. It is small wonder, therefore, that colonial farmers brought with them sheep from Europe, and depended on them heavily. In spite of the importance of sheep, little was done to improve them until the breeding work of Robert Bakewell in England produced better mutton types, and until the Napoleonic wars resulted in breaking down the monopoly maintained by the Spanish crown in the fine wool merinos. It is estimated that by 1810, 20,000 merino sheep had been imported from Spain and distributed to farms in every state. From the selective breeding begun early in the nineteenth century all of the present types of both wool and mutton sheep have been derived.

American farmers were also interested in cattle because of their varied uses. Oxen, of course, were the ancient work animals of the farm, although the trend was away from them by the nineteenth century. Hides were always needed for shoes, harness and saddles, and other articles. Milk was appreciated too, although there was little effort to produce milk and dairy products apart from the production of beef. Henry Clay imported Hereford cattle, a beef type, from England in 1817, but the breed did not become numerous until after 1870, when it was found to be suitable for grazing on the western ranges. Other English breeds of cattle were brought to America at about the same period, and helped to bring about a gradual improvement of both beef and dairy types. As settlement pushed west, beef cattle were taken along as a convenient way to market the corn and other feed grains to be produced on the new lands. If no other transportation was available, cattle could be driven to market when they were fattened and ready. Back in the East, declining fertility of the soil and growing urban population turned farmers from the fattening of beef cattle to the keeping of dairy types. By 1860, New York state was the leading dairy area, producing nearly half the cheese in the entire country and more butter than any other state.

The new ideas of stock improvement by selective breeding were applied to swine even more vigorously and with greater success than to the other farm animals. Swine generations are shorter than those of sheep or cattle, and an experiment in breeding can be tested and proved more quickly. The hogs of colonial days were, like sheep, pretty self-reliant animals. If there was a poor feed crop, the colonial farmer might have to let his hogs wander in the woods to shift for themselves. As farming gained a more secure base, the "razorback" of earlier days no longer proved to be a satisfactory animal for feeding up on corn. Selection of breeding stock showed results promptly, eventually leading to the heavy, slow-moving, small-boned hog of today.

The hog followed the westward movement of the frontier as closely as any other farm animal. The meat could be cured and smoked to last through the hot months of summer, and the fat could be rendered into lard for frying and baking. Hogs were thus indispensable to the frontier family. Besides, if the distances were not too great, they could be driven to market.

It is interesting to note how heavily present-day Americans depend upon corn to furnish their meat. Although no important domesticated animal or fowl of today, except the turkey, is of native American origin, most of them depend on American corn for their basic food. We get our meat, milk, and eggs by way of corn. Of the plant foods which are suited for direct human consumption, two

which produce a heavy yield of energy food on a per acre basis—corn and white potatoes—are native to America. The American continents have contributed very greatly to the ability of the human race to feed itself. The results of the uniting of European animals and American food plants were apparent in the expansion of agricultural output during the period to 1860.

## Spreading the new ideas

Conditions in most parts of America were something less than ideal from the point of view of disseminating knowledge of new farming methods. In communities on or near the frontier, it was a hard enough task to get along at all, let alone to worry about how farm work could be done better. In such communities, there was also the extra work of building churches, schools, roads, and bridges besides the regular work of farming. Many frontiersmen could not read, their schools were primitive, and mail service to bring in printed material from the East was not very regular or dependable. Even under such unfavorable conditions, however, the agricultural fair was developed to serve the purposes of both entertainment and education.

The credit for first popularizing the agricultural fair in America is usually given to Elkanah Watson of Pittsfield, Massachusetts. In 1807, Watson is said to have exhibited two merino sheep on the public square at Pittsfield and to have persuaded several neighbors to join him in making exhibits a few years later. He was the same man who had advocated a canal to the Great Lakes from the Hudson and Mohawk Rivers soon after 1790, and was a man of vision and energy indeed. From Watson's early efforts, the Berkshire Agricultural Society arose, to become the oldest fair association in the United States. Similar societies sprang up all over the country in the following decades, most of them sponsoring local agricultural fairs in the summer or fall of the year. By 1860, almost a thousand agricultural societies holding fairs were in existence. The educational value of these fairs cannot be measured, but their cumulative effect in acquainting farm people with the latest improvements in machines, crops, and livestock was and continues to be enormous.

Formal agricultural education had its start in America when the state of Michigan provided in its constitution, adopted in 1850, for the setting up of a college of agriculture. The Michigan State College of Agriculture was opened in 1857. Within a few years Pennsylvania and Maryland also provided for state-supported agricultural colleges. The nation-wide spread of state and federally supported agricultural colleges did not come until after 1862 when the Morrill (Land Grant) Act was passed. Under this act each state was given 30,000 acres of public land for each senator and representative that it had in Congress. This land was to be sold for funds to establish colleges which would furnish instruction in agriculture and the mechanic arts. In the same year, Congress also provided for the setting up of a Bureau of Agriculture in the federal government to collect statistics and publish reports of value to farmers. From 1839 to 1862, the Commissioner of Patents had been allotted small sums by Congress for similar purposes. By 1860, there were also estimated to be nearly a hundred farm journals in existence. How widely read and how influential these papers may have been it is hard to tell. Only one—*The Prairie Farmer*—founded in 1840, still survives.

## FOR FURTHER READING

Barnes, James A. *Wealth of the American People*. New York: Prentice-Hall, Inc., 1949. Chapters 9—11.

Billington, R. A. *Westward Movement in the United States*. Anvil, 1959. Paperback.

Faulkner, Harold U. *American Economic History*. 8th ed. New York: Harper & Brothers, 1960. Chapters 10 and 11.

Shannon, Fred Albert. *America's Economic Growth*. 3rd ed. New York: The Macmillan Co., 1951. Chapters 7, 8, 14, and 15.

Turner, Frederick J. *The Frontier in American History*. New York: Holt, Rinehart & Winston, 1959. Classic work in which Turner develops the "frontier thesis." Also paperback edition, 1962.

Webb, Walter P. *The Great Plains*. Boston: Houghton Mifflin Co., 1931. Paperback edition in Universal Library, 1957. Excellent reading.

Williamson, Harold F. (ed.) *The Growth of the American Economy*. 2nd ed. New York: Prentice-Hall, Inc., 1958. Chapters 6—9.

Wright, Chester W. *Economic History of the United States*. 2nd ed. New York: McGraw-Hill Book Co., 1949. Chapters 16—21.

# Chapter 8: The growth of commerce and industry before 1860

Anatural first reaction of the American people after the successful conclusion of the Revolutionary War was a great sense of relief that the hated orders and taxes imposed by the British government could now be ignored and forgotten. Restrictions on manufacturing, commerce, and western settlement were things of the past. Economic life in America could now follow those lines of development which in the circumstances seemed to be most necessary and potentially profitable.

But the solution of one set of problems almost always leaves in its wake a new set, sometimes less urgent and unpleasant, but none the less problems that cannot be ignored. The American break with Britain gave the newly born state the thrill of realizing that it possessed the powers of a sovereign people, but at the same time took away the comforts and security which it had enjoyed as a privileged member of the British colonial system. American freedom was attained on the eve of the French Revolution and the ensuing Napoleonic Wars, which occurred during two

decades in which the economic and political affairs of Europe were in as thoroughly disordered a condition as in any period of similar length in history. America was on its own, to be sure, but so were the nations of Europe, and they were no longer mindful of American interests as they made moves and countermoves designed to gain advantage for themselves. The United States was young and weak; they were old and strong. At times, almost the whole of the foreign trade of Europe would have fallen into America's lap had she been able to handle it; at other times, the great powers placed such sweeping embargoes on seaborne trade that American ships could hardly leave their ports except in the coastal or Oriental trade. Despite this rough treatment, American foreign trade survived and even grew.

The domestic trade of the United States at first reflected in part the state of foreign trade, since America continued to depend upon Europe for many fine manufactured products; but increasingly, as the magnificent resources of the North American continent were revealed in the westward course of settlement, purely internal considerations became dominant in the domestic trade. When the clearing of the fertile soils of the Mississippi Valley showed that it was no longer possible for the eastern seaboard states to compete in agriculture, the eastern seaboard turned more fully to trade, manufacturing, and banking. Commerce arose within the national market area, reflecting the special advantages of the climate, resources, and people of the various sections. Even before the Civil War, the United States had made measurable progress toward an economy with a high degree of productivity which was at the same time very largely dependent upon its own resources of soil and skill.

## The ups and downs of foreign trade

At the beginning of the nineteenth century the nations of Europe were so preoccupied by war that they came to depend more and more on the United States for food and supplies. This foreign demand brought high prices to American farmers and prosperity to her merchants and shipbuilders. Such a happy condition continued, by and large, until 1807. At that time, the warfare between Britain and France had reached something of a stalemate, and each side came to the conclusion that economic strangulation would have to be added to military and naval action if victory were to be achieved. England placed blockades on all continental ports accessible to France and also on all French colonies and possessions by her Orders in Council of 1806 and 1807. Napoleon retaliated by his Berlin and Milan decrees of the same years, placing a counter-blockade on all English ports and declaring all ships entering or leaving them subject to seizure. These actions utterly ruined American foreign trade, and seemed to overlook entirely the rights of neutrals. Soon there were warlike acts, such as the firing on an American vessel

and the seizure of American seamen by the English, which brought the nation close to war.

President Jefferson was anxious to avoid war, and recommended to Congress the passage of an embargo on all foreign trade. This was done by the Embargo Act of 1807. So far as the merchants and shippers of New England were concerned, this act merely meant that their own government rather than foreign governments prevented them from trading. Their protest against it was bitter, and in 1809 they were able to get the embargo relaxed somewhat by the passage of the Non-Intercourse Act. This Act reinstated foreign trade with all countries except England and France and promised that as soon as either of them should give up its embargo measures, trade would be resumed with it. In 1810 Macon's Bill No. 2 revived trade with both countries but provided that as soon as either should withdraw its restrictions American trade with the other would be stopped. France took advantage of this to trick the United States into controversy with England, and war was declared on England in 1812.

New England was opposed to the war, and before its end was sullenly threatening secession. The West favored it because of intense national pride and desire to acquire additional territory in Florida and Canada. Agriculture suffered somewhat from the cutting off of foreign markets, but not as seriously as the mercantile interests of New England.

After the end of the War of 1812, American foreign trade, which in 1814 fell to its lowest level since independence, rose to its highest level in 1815. English manufactured goods, which had been held up by the war, poured into the American market. This was excellent for ship captains and merchants but ruinous for the manufacturers, who had expanded operations during the years of war and embargo to meet the demands of the home market. Within a few years the abnormal American demand for goods was met, and the volume of foreign trade declined. Until 1830, American import trade did not increase, because of tariff restrictions placed upon many imports and the retaliatory regulations imposed by customers abroad. After 1830, the growth of foreign trade proceeded with fair steadiness except for setbacks suffered in the prolonged depression beginning in 1837 and the short one in 1857. Especially from 1843 to 1860, the growth of American trade was consistent and substantial. Imports included manufactured goods; metal products; and tropical or semitropical foods, such as coffee, tea, sugar, and spices. Cotton was the principal export, amounting to about two-thirds of the total. The United States also exported foodstuffs and some finished and partly finished manufactured goods. By 1860, our total annual exports and imports amounted to more than two-thirds of a billion dollars.

## American shipping and shipbuilding

The ups and downs of foreign trade had a close relation to the prosperity of the American merchant marine, and affected both the building of ships and the extent of their operation in foreign commerce. The correlation is not perfect, however, because, on the one hand, American shipbuilders sold a substantial number of their ships to foreign buyers, and, on the other, a part of the foreign trade was carried in foreign vessels. Until the passage of the Embargo Act in 1807, American trade was growing and the proportion of it carried in American ships was also growing until it reached about 90 per cent. During the next decade, until the end of the War of 1812, America's international relations were in turmoil, and the relative position of its merchant shipping suffered. While, as has been shown above, American trade overseas did not grow in total volume during the 1820's, the proportion of it carried in our own ships again increased, passing 90 per cent in 1826.

American and world foreign trade experienced an enormous growth between 1830 and 1860. Ocean shipping, which had been on an irregular or tramp basis, was supplemented by regular packet service on schedule between principal ports. American ships, which had been the best in the world for many decades, found a new use in this fast service. American shipbuilders not only supplied their own merchants but also sold a substantial tonnage abroad every year. Their ships were better and faster than those of their European competitors and were also cheaper—thanks both to the abundance of good shipbuilding timber in America and to the skill of native shipbuilders. A further advance was made in 1845, when the first clipper ship was built—a model with rakish lines and a great amount of sail—which was soon breaking speed records for wind-driven commercial vessels. Naval designers were carried away with enthusiasm for the clipper, which was without doubt the best sailing ship ever built, and a large number of clippers were put into use up to 1860. The reason they were not used longer did not relate to any defect of the clipper design but to the fact that the steam engine and the iron ship were by then able to surpass the performance of wind and wood.

While Americans were concentrating their attention upon the wooden sailing ship and achieving supremacy in its construction and operation, the British, who lacked timber resources, were experimenting with resources which they did have in greater abundance than anyone else, namely, iron, steel, and a metal-working industry. In spite of the fact that it was Robert Fulton, an American, who made the first successful demonstration of a steam boat (on the Hudson River in 1807), it was the British who pressed the work of adapting the steamboat for ocean navigation. In 1838 the *Great Western* made the transatlantic voyage in $13\frac{1}{2}$ days, driven entirely by her steam engine. That was faster than the best packet. American builders sought a better sailing ship to meet the competition of steam, and soon developed the clipper. British builders continued to improve the steam engine and gradually shifted from the wood hull to one made of iron plates. The wooden sailing ship did not disappear at once, even in England, but the proportion of iron steam-

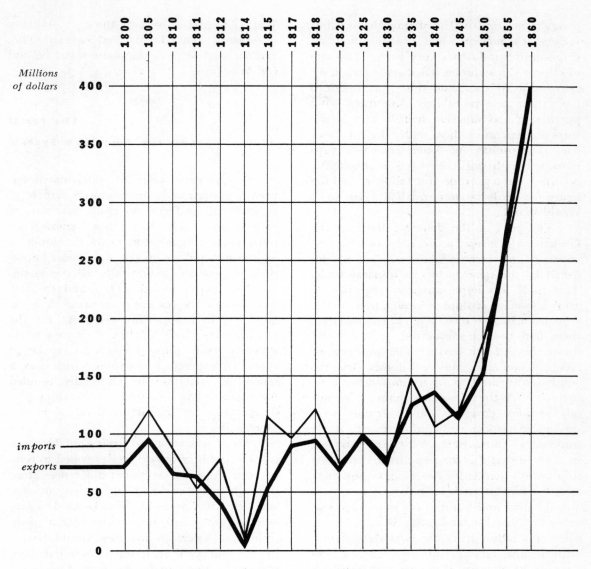

*Millions of dollars*

400

350

300

250

200

150

*imports*

100

*exports*

50

0

*Fig.VIII-1  The ups and downs of United States foreign trade between 1800 and 1860.*

ships which were being produced had become as much as a quarter of the total before 1860.

The rapid decline of American shipbuilding and merchant shipping just on the eve of the Civil War was not attributable solely to American reliance upon an outmoded type of ship. The late forties and early fifties had seen an abnormal demand for ships and shipping resulting from the California gold discoveries and other world events. No one could expect such a demand to last. Then, too, the possibilities of internal development, dramatized by California gold, turned the attention of the country inward rather than outward. Changes in styles of dress and diet, and the expansion of domestic industry, led to the decline of some of the old branches of foreign trade. America was becoming a great and more nearly self-sufficient continental economic power. The panic of 1857 was really

*Growth of commerce and industry by 1860*  161

a very minor one in United States history, but it came at a moment when it hit shipping and shipbuilding industries very hard. The sale of clipper ships abroad fell sharply and never recovered. At the same time, an American navigation law prohibited Americans from purchasing the superior British iron steamships and operating them under the American flag. The tonnage of American-owned ships remained high until the Civil War actually occurred, but a great decline followed, and the figure for 1861 was not equalled again until World War I.

The part of the domestic trade of the United States which was carried in coastwise vessels or on river or lake boats was not affected by the same factors as overseas trade. This trade was important, too, requiring as great a tonnage of ships as foreign trade in the years from 1820 to 1860. Even in colonial days there had been a substantial trade up and down the Atlantic coast. The products of New England, the middle colonies, and the South found markets in sections other than their own. As the economic systems of the various sections developed and became more specialized, trade of this kind increased. It was confined to American ships exclusively by law in 1793, so that this coastwise trade continued to provide a market for American sailing ships after the foreign market was largely lost.

Whaling and fishing were important also along the New England coast. Whaling flourished especially during the forties and fifties, until the discovery of crude petroleum in 1859 reduced the intensity of the demand for whale oil. Fishing continued to be important, and New England fishermen continued to bring in cod, mackerel, herring, and halibut. River and canal traffic grew during the thirties and forties, until the railroads began to compete with it. Shipping on the Great Lakes was also of importance before the Civil War, as the area south of the lakes filled up with settlers who produced goods for shipment to the East and who provided a market for eastern wares and imported items in return. The greatest activity in Great Lakes shipping, however, did not come until after the Civil

War, with the growth of the steel industry in western Pennsylvania and eastern Ohio, and the settlement of the plains states beyond the Mississippi.

### The tariff and the American System

In the early years of independent existence, Americans were producers largely of agricultural products and crude materials of various sorts. The Revolution removed all restraints of a legal nature to the development of industry and commerce, but it was impossible to produce domestically all the manufactured goods needed. The need for fine manufactured wares was more acute than the need felt in Europe and elsewhere for the raw products which America could supply. As a consequence, imports continued to be in excess of exports, a situation which was a source of irritation to nationally minded Americans whose economic nationalism produced attitudes similar to those of earlier Mercantilism.

There was a general feeling in the country that industry should be developed to remedy this situation. Sectional differences arose over which industries should be encouraged, and over what means ought to be used to provide help for them, but on the general principle that American industry should be expanded further than it was in colonial days, there was little or no disagreement. One of the very first acts of the Congress of the United States in 1789 was to enact a tariff law to provide revenue for the government and to give some protection to industry. Compared to the high rates of later tariffs, this early law provided for very low rates which gave very little protection. Shortly after the passage of this first tariff, Hamilton's Report on Manufactures, which recommended the policy of protective tariffs to aid industry, was received by Congress. No further action was taken at that time, however, because the government was occupied with trying to gain entry for

American ships into foreign ports, and did not wish to risk offending any foreign governments by raising the duties on their exports to the United States. Europe was soon preoccupied with the Napoleonic Wars, which left American industry and commerce a free field in which to grow. While the Embargo Act of 1807 was ruinous to American foreign trade, it was highly stimulating to industry. Finally, when America became involved in war in 1812, and foreign merchandise was almost entirely cut off for a time, our industry received more complete protection than could be provided by any but the most extreme tariff policy.

Until after the end of the War of 1812, there was no very strong sentiment for modifying the modest tariff rates of the law of 1789. Tariff rates were doubled in 1812 for a period to extend until one year after the end of the war, but this was intended as a revenue-raising device and not as protection to American industry. However, the great influx of English merchandise upon the ending of the War of 1812 brought a quick change in the American attitude toward the protection of industry. Manufactures from England arrived in such quantities that the normal channels of wholesale and retail distribution were glutted, and still loaded vessels kept arriving, whose cargoes were sold for what they would bring at wharfside auctions. American industries, many of which were so new that they had not brought their costs down as yet, were compelled to close down, some never to reopen. The manufacturing areas found themselves in the grip of unemployment and economic depression. A new tariff act was passed in 1816, with the support of all sections of the country. There was general agreement that American industry should be protected against the kind of competition it was having to face, and that the imposition of higher tariff duties on the European goods which were competing directly with American manufactures was the best device to accomplish that purpose. The act provided high protective rates on cottons, woolens, iron, and other manufactured goods. Revisions of the tariff in 1818 and 1824 raised

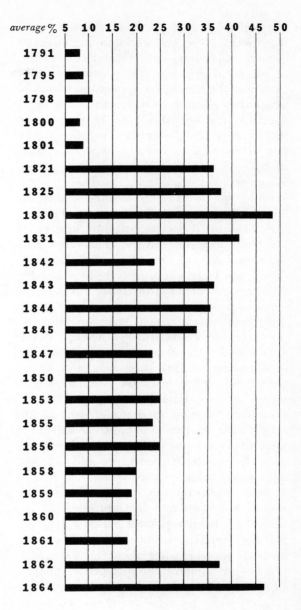

Fig.VIII-2 *The variations in the United States tariff between 1791 and 1864 are shown here. Notice the decline after 1845 and the sharp rise during the Civil War.*

rates on cottons, woolens, lead, glass, and iron, and also placed duties on hemp and raw wool.

These changes were put through by powerful industrial and agricultural groups under the leadership of Henry Clay, Kentucky farmer and statesman, but over the opposition which was beginning to develop in New England and the South. New England shipping interests came to oppose the tariff because if it should be successful in protecting industry, it would cut down the tonnage of foreign merchandise which they would be importing in their ships. Southern planters also came to oppose the tariff because the great market for their cotton was in England, and they wished to be able to buy the manufactured goods they needed wherever they could be purchased most cheaply, whether in this country or outside. The middle states, especially eastern Pennsylvania, became the strongest center of support for high protective tariffs. The economists Matthew Carey, his more famous son Henry C. Carey, and Hezekiah Niles were indefatigable writers in defense of tariffs. Clay was the leading Congressional spokesman of the group. They argued for protective tariffs on industrial products as part of what they called the "American System." This plan was that the East should become the manufacturing center of the nation and the South and the West the agricultural and raw-material-producing sections. Between these sections, there would grow a natural exchange of products, which would unite them in a common, national, economic interest. The American economy would be more self-contained, and all sections would benefit because surplus revenue from increased tariffs would be used for internal improvements.

The debates over tariff policy which took place in Congress and in the public press for a decade or more after about 1820 occupy a place of great importance in American history. Clay's American System was not merely a pleasant name for a point which a politician was seeking to make in Congressional debate. Rather, to important industrial interests in the East and to farmers in the West it became a chart of the economic development of the nation. The years following the end of the War of 1812 had demonstrated that new American industries could not stand up against the older industries of Europe. The choice seemed clear: either there must be a tariff to protect American infant industries, or the United States would remain an agrarian nation. The South was quite pleased with the latter alternative, since her sale of cotton and tobacco in Europe was bringing her a greater prosperity than she had ever before had. On the other hand, manufacturers in New England and elsewhere who had put capital into industry during the years of the Embargo Acts and the war could see no salvation for themselves in the economic future except in the policy of higher protective tariff duties. Farmers and land speculators in the West were not directly involved in the debate, but were drawn in as they realized that their own prosperity depended on a market for their produce in the industrial cities of the East. East and West found another common interest in obtaining improved transportation between them so that each might find a market with the other. Both sections favored governmental aid to roads, canals, and later railroads. The South's economic well-being did not depend upon cheap internal transportation, and this section opposed use of the resources of the federal government as a subsidy to such improvements.

As the debate progressed, majority sentiment in the country and in Congress crystalized in support of the American System. It represented the encouragement of a balanced development of agriculture and industry which seemed good sense from a national point of view, as the component developments made good sense to the populous East and the rapidly growing West. It also represented a turning away from an international, trading economy in which the United States had been involved since the founding of the first colonies, to concentrate interest and attention on the economic opportunities of the North American continent. The South and the declining commercial groups of New England continued with the old international interest. Thus, the basis was developing for the sectional hostility which was to lead forty years later to the Civil War. The East and West became national isolationist sections. Their populousness made the economic nationalism which appealed to the interest of these sections the majority policy of the United States. The policies favored by the South were more and more frequently overridden in Congress. In effect, the debates centering in tariff policy were a stock-taking by the American people to determine the direction in which their economic development should proceed. The adoption of Henry Clay's American System which came out of that debate did prove in fact to be a blueprint of the main lines of the next century in the economic history of the United States.

Although the American shipbuilder and the merchant engaged in foreign trade were actively pushing their business throughout the period to the Civil War (see Fig. VIII-3), internal commerce and industry were commanding an even larger measure of attention. This was the case in New England, the principal shipbuilding section, as much as anywhere else. Consequently, opposition to protective tariffs because of their adverse effect on foreign trade gradually declined in New England. When that happened, by about 1830, support for a protective policy became fairly general throughout the country, except in the South. Nevertheless, because of the southern opposition, tariff controversy occupied a prominent place in the political debates of the pre-Civil War period, reaching a high point in the incidents related to the passing of the Nullification Ordinance by South Carolina in 1832. The tariffs of 1824 and 1828 imposed new high rates on many manufactured items, especially iron, cotton, and woolen goods. The South protested both tariffs, to no avail. When the Tariff Act of 1832 maintained the protective principle, South Carolina called a convention which declared the 1828 and 1832 tariffs null and void. Secession from the Union was actually threatened. As a result of this threatened violence, the rates from 1833 (the Compromise Tariff) to 1860 had a downward tendency, although the principle of protection was preserved (see Fig. VIII-2, p. 163).

It would be interesting to know, if an answer were possible, whether the protective characteristics of the tariffs from 1789 to 1860 made a substantial difference in the course of American industrial and commercial development. The superficial fact is that there were

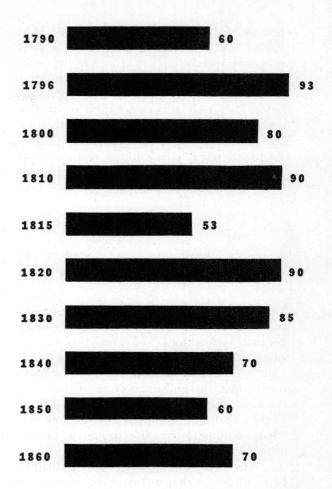

Fig.VIII-3  *The percentage of American tonnage in the total tonnage of vessels entering and leaving American ports engaged in foreign trade, 1790-1860.*

protective tariffs and industry did develop very rapidly. Did the one cause the other? We cannot know the answer for sure, but it is probable that industry would have developed without the tariffs. Alexander Hamilton felt that American protective rates did not need to be high because of the disadvantage which ocean shipping costs imposed on European producers. It is also true that the United States had many natural advantages of raw materials and climate which would have given rise to industry without additional encouragement. The skills of the people would inevitably have been developed and become diversified as the United States became an older nation. Yet, it cannot be denied that the tariff may have speeded up the process of industrial development by insuring a larger profit to producers in the early years of their operations before they were able to get their production costs down to a low point. At least, that was the opinion of contemporaries, and enough of them believed it sufficiently to make the support of the protective tariff one of the most firmly grounded political principles in American national life.

## Commerce with the expanding West

During the years in which national attention was focussed on tariff controversies which became acrimonious and almost violent at times, other developments were quietly taking place which were to have the greatest effect on the quantity and importance of American domestic commerce. These changes related to the expansion of the domestic market, or— what amounts to the same thing—the growth of economic specialization.

What were the requirements that had to be met in order that such an expansion of the market might be brought about? Obviously, there had to be a means of moving the produce of the West to eastern markets, and of bringing back the manufactured goods of the East to western markets, in return. That is, there had to be good and cheap transportation. Then too, there had to be enough merchants of various kinds to handle all of the produce and merchandise in the trade. Fortunately the improvement of transportation kept pace, as we have seen (pp. 144ff.), and the economic productivity of America was enabled to follow a course of steady improvement.

Equally, the organization of trade kept up with demands and opportunities. The trading post of the frontier community, dealing almost entirely in the necessities of that rugged life, gave way to the general store. The storekeeper often accepted country produce in exchange for cloth, shoes, and hardware which could not well be made at home. He secured his stock of goods by road, river, and canal from eastern industrial and commercial centers, often on consignment. The general store was a community center, post office, and bank, as well as a place where goods could be bought. On the trails and roads, peddlers were found with their loads of pots and pans, clocks, silverware, cloth, and other articles which they could carry and their customers would buy. Settled storekeepers disliked the competition of peddlers and drove them out of the established communities.

As the volume of trade developed, various kinds of wholesale dealers or jobbers appeared also. And there were commission merchants, or factors, who would sell raw produce or finished goods on behalf of the producer, manufacturer, or importer, for a commission on the sale. Either retailers or other wholesalers might be the customers of the commission merchants. Much of this type of business was done on credit, if not on consignment, and the commission man had the responsibility of arranging terms for the owner of the goods. Traveling salesmen or "drummers" put in their appearance in the pre-Civil War period, often selling standardized, factory-made products by sample.

Another development of the period was the organized produce exchange, of which the Chicago Board of Trade is the best known example. Wheat and other grains are bought and sold on standard specifications, not only for immediate delivery, the so-called "cash contract" or spot transaction, but also for future delivery. Trading of the latter kind is called trading in "futures." As improved transportation permitted the moving of grain to distant consuming markets, it became necessary and valuable for both buyers and sellers to have a central exchange where world-wide factors in the supply of and demand for grain could be expressed in freely made bids. The cash contract for immediate delivery is a very usual kind of transaction, but buyers and sellers also had an interest in having some assurance of the future level of prices in order to plan their operations more definitely. To meet this need, the Board of Trade and other commodity exchanges permit speculators to make contracts to buy or sell several months ahead of time. At the time the futures contract is made, the seller may not own any grain at all, but he nevertheless guarantees to deliver grain at the stated price on the agreed date. The speculator of course expects to make some profit on either his buying or selling transactions but the grain user, possibly a miller, finds it advantageous to "hedge" his cash purchases of grain by a future sale so that, whether the price of grain goes up or down, his flour will assure him a profit.

## Regional effects of the growing trade

### New England

Under the impact of continually expanding trade, each section of the country underwent a characteristic economic evolution of its own. New England, for example, the section which achieved the lead in population in the colonial era, was the first to pass from agriculture to commerce and industry. The abundance of good harbors adjacent to ample supplies of pine and hardwood lumber turned its people to shipbuilding, overseas commerce, and fishing in colonial days. Gradually, too, the area came to take the lead in the manufacture of textiles and boots and shoes.

As population increased in other parts of the country, New England had to seek raw materials like hides and wool from other sections in order that production might meet demands. New England craftsmen also became the watch, clock, cutlery, and hardware manufacturers of the country. In fact, New England established itself as the fine manufacturing center of the nation, supplying such products to all other sections and receiving much of its food and many raw materials from other sections. As cotton culture increased in the

South, it was natural that its manufacture into cloth should be undertaken in New England to a greater extent than anywhere else in the country. For many years, New England also retained an importance in overseas trade, although the opening up of the interior of the country and the building of roads, canals, and railroads from the seaboard to the interior gave the commercial supremacy to the ports of the middle states, especially New York.

### The East

The middle section of the Atlantic seaboard, which for convenience we refer to as the East, became in colonial times a substantial producer of grains and livestock. A milling and meatpacking industry arose in the cities of New York, Philadelphia, and Baltimore. Flour, lard, and cured meat were sold to provision the New England ships and to feed the slaves on southern plantations. These products were also exported by local overseas traders as well as those from New England. As the West was opened up, travel between West and East was maintained by the Cumberland Road, the Erie Canal, and later the railroads. For a time the grain and feed in the West reached the markets in the East only in the form of hogs and cattle. As canals and railroads were built, however, both grain and livestock came east in greater quantities. The furs of the West also came to the East, especially to New York, where in the 1820's and 1830's a German immigrant, John Jacob Astor, built the greatest fur business in the world, and became the principal landlord of the city.

Before the Civil War, the filling up of western territories and the improvement of transportation led to the gradual transfer of such industries as milling and meat packing closer to their raw materials. Cincinnati and later Chicago became centers of meat packing. Buffalo became a great milling center and Chicago became the leading grain-handling center. The East retained and extended its financial control over industry, and became ever more completely the commercial channel through which the products of the West reached market either in other sections of the country or overseas. In return, the East also became the channel through which the products of the rest of the United States and of the world reached the mid-continental area. Many kinds of miscellaneous light industries also began to develop in the East as agricultural supremacy passed to the West.

### The South

While New England and the middle states were becoming industrial and commercial centers for the country, the South remained exclusively agricultural. The chief changes affecting the South were associated with the growing importance of cotton and the declining importance of the Mississippi as an artery of trade because of the building of the railroads. But in spite of the considerable changes within southern agriculture as the cotton culture expanded, there was little change in the South's dependence upon Europe to absorb its products. The South complained that its cotton and other products were not shipped directly to Europe from its own ports, such as Charleston, but rather from northern ports. The reason for this was that the South purchased much of its food and a considerable part of its manufactured goods in New England or New York as well as in Europe. Ships carrying cotton from the South to Europe would have had to return empty. When southern exports went by way of northern ports, return cargoes could be secured. For a long time New Orleans served as the commercial center for the Mississippi Valley states, transshipping their grain and livestock and sending back up the river to them by steamboat manufactured goods secured from Europe and from eastern industrial centers. The completion of the railroads reduced that traffic by bringing the West and the East into direct contact.

### The West

The settlement of the West with its vast expanses of fertile soil, timber, and minerals,

was a dynamic factor in the evolution not only of its own economy but of the other sections as well. The first commerce of the West was in its furs, which were carried down the St. Lawrence, the Hudson, the Mississippi, and other rivers, and by trails. As land was cleared and farming began, valuable products such as whiskey might be carried out, although more extensive sale of western agricultural products awaited the building of good transportation facilities. From the very beginning of settlement, the western population was in great need of manufactured goods obtainable only from Europe or the East, such as guns, ammunition, traps, axes, plows, tools, and if possible shoes and cloth. It was difficult to bring in the needed merchandise until roads and canals were built, and it was more difficult to carry out the western produce because of its greater weight and bulk. The western people, consequently, were almost always short of cash.

In the early part of the nineteenth century, the best available outlet for western produce was not to the East but down the Ohio and Mississippi Rivers to New Orleans. Even fairly bulky products could be loaded on flatboats and floated down the river. This was not very satisfactory to the western people, however, for their produce had to be reshipped from New Orleans to Europe or to eastern ports, and the goods they wished to buy were available primarily in the East. Thus they had to accept low prices for what they sold and pay high prices for what they bought, because of the high shipping costs. Also, until steamboats were introduced, it was not practical to try to bring even valuable goods back up the river against the current. Such merchandise still had to come in overland from the East.

The development of a practical river steamboat was a great boon after 1815 to the commerce of the West, because it lowered the cost of sending produce out and permitted return cargoes to be brought back up the river. The tonnage carried on the Ohio and Mississippi jumped after that date, and the prosperity of the West was greatly enhanced. The commercial needs of the area were not fully met, however, for the trade via New Orleans was still indirect. After the completion of the Erie Canal in 1825, the transportation needs of the Great Lakes basin were met more adequately. Chicago, Detroit, Cleveland, and Buffalo began to develop into commercial and industrial centers, outstripping Cincinnati, Louisville, and St. Louis. The railroads, construction on which was begun in the 1830's and which connected the Atlantic coast to Chicago and St. Louis by the 1850's, for the first time provided the West with exactly the kind of transportation it needed. Western products, no matter what their bulk, could now be moved directly to eastern markets for overseas shipment. Manufactures from the East and abroad could come in freely. Traffic on the Ohio and the Mississippi declined, beginning in the 1840's, except for local traffic below St. Louis. Even the Erie Canal, which had experienced such an intense traffic boom in the first few years of its operation, suffered a sharp decline. The commercial and industrial East and the agricultural West were tied more closely together in common economic bonds.

### Banking and business

Both banking and business in general experienced an uneven development during the period from 1800 to the Civil War. At the end of the Revolutionary War, the United States had little money and no banking system. One of Hamilton's reports to Congress had to do with these matters, and Congress followed his advice in adopting the dollar (a Spanish coin to which Americans had become accustomed in dealing with the West Indies) as the unit of money, with a decimal system. Hamilton also recommended the establishment of a United States Bank, which was set up in 1791 for a twenty-year period as the First Bank of the United States. The Bank was partly private and partly public, accepting deposits from and making loans to both the government and private citizens. The period of its life was dominated by the Napoleonic Wars, the Embargo Act, and the War of 1812, which hardly constituted a normal period; nevertheless, the Bank did much to establish the credit of the government and the country. It acted as agent for the federal government in holding federal deposits and in making payments from them. Through its branches in leading cities it could handle transfers of funds from one center to another. It performed similar functions for private individuals and businesses, as well as making loans for normal business purposes. In a troubled period it helped to establish both public and private finance on a stable and adequate base.

Jefferson and his political party, which feared a strong centralized government, were joined by the many state banks in opposing renewal of the charter of the Bank of the United States when it expired in 1811, and it was allowed to die. The liquidation of the Bank caused a temporary tightness of currency and credit because of the demand for repayment of loans, a tightness which the state banks very promptly made up by an unsound expansion of loans and paper money. The paper money issued by state banks more than doubled during the War of 1812, leading to the depreciation of the value of state bank notes. People were driven to the hoarding of metal money as the only safe way to preserve their wealth. This was not a satisfactory condition for business, and demands arose for the chartering of a second United States Bank, which was done in 1816, again for twenty years. The Second Bank was not wisely managed for the first few years, issuing too much paper money of its own and making speculative loans. In 1818 the officers realized they had gone too far and endeavored to reverse their previous policies. They tried to contract the credit they had previously expanded, but it was too late. Financial crisis overtook the country in 1819, to mark the beginning of the first major depression in America's history.

The depression of 1819 can be explained as a result of the flooding of American markets with European goods. This occurred at a time when many new industries were not fully established, and they consequently failed. Contributing to that unfavorable industrial situation was the restriction of credit by the state banks just at the time that business needed help, because the banks were under pressure from the United States Bank to correct their previous excesses in issuing paper money and making loans. Speculation in western lands had also become excessive. Underlying the whole business structure was a growing weakness of the predominant agrarian sector of the economy, which had been suffering from declining prices for its produce in the aftermath of the war. The speculative boom collapsed when the United States Bank presented a group of state banks with an unusually large quantity of their paper money and demanded gold or silver for it. The state banks were unable to pay, and their closing brought on widespread bankruptcies among banks, industries, and other businesses. Prices, including those of land, fell sharply, and there were many unemployed in the cities. This sharp readjustment enabled some businesses to cut their costs so that they could begin operation again profitably, and within two or three years the effects of the crisis were mostly past.

The entire matter of banking policy agitated the country for the first half-century of its national history. The forces favoring a single, semi-official United States Bank were generally the business interests of the East, where the need of a stable and solid money and credit system was felt. The federal government seemed to be the only agency capable of providing the needed financial backing for such a bank. On the other side were those who feared the growth of centralized power in the possession of the federal government. Allied to this latter group were the promoters of land settlement and transportation projects in the West and South, who were more concerned to have bank loans readily available to aid their financing schemes than they were to have the money system on the soundest possible basis. The ups and downs of the first and second United States Banks were brought about largely by the political power at any given time of one of the groups for or against it.

For the next decade or more after recovery from the depression of 1819, the U.S.

Bank functioned well and business conditions were generally good. Nevertheless, Andrew Jackson was elected to the presidency in 1832 as an opponent of the Bank, and it was allowed to die when its charter expired in 1836. The Bank continued operation under a charter from the state of Pennsylvania, but not as a national bank.

The success of the Erie Canal (finished in 1825) and the beginning of railroad building in the early thirties had precipitated a great deal of speculation in western lands and in railroad and canal companies. After 1832, when the United States Bank began to decline in importance after the second election of Andrew Jackson, a strong opponent of the Bank, the number of state banks and the quantity of paper money they issued increased greatly. A period of so-called "wildcat" banking began. Some state banks had numerous branches from all of which they would make loans in the form of their own paper money, but their bank notes could be redeemed in metal money only at the head office, which might be located far into the wilderness at a spot inhabited only by wildcats. Such a policy of easy lending, which resulted in the issuance of ever-increasing amounts of paper bank notes, meant that even unsound promotional schemes would seldom be checked by inability of the promoters to gain financial backing from the state banks. As a further result, easy credit fed land prices and the prices of stock in banks, canals, and railroads, and was the precipitating factor which caused the speculative bubble to burst in 1837.

This time President Andrew Jackson's Specie Circular helped bring on the crash. This circular was an order issued by the president in July 1836 to the effect that all government land offices should accept payment for land only in metal money, or specie, instead of bank notes. The stated purposes of the order were to repress frauds, to keep speculators from securing a monopoly of public lands to the disadvantage of actual settlers, and to discourage the expansion of bank credit and bank currency issues. The order started runs on the western banks and forced them to close, bringing on the panic of 1837. Other factors were crop failures in 1835 and some important business failures in England in 1836, both of which led to a reduction in American exports and a demand from Europe for the repayment of some loans. Again, as after 1819, the volume of paper bank notes in circulation shrank rapidly and land sales declined. The economic shock to the country was so great that the effect of the depression was not really ended until the middle 1840's.

In the years following the panic of 1837, there was no United States Bank to help restore stable conditions. The federal government in 1846 established the Sub-Treasury system. Under this plan it handled its own deposits, by putting them in coin into the Treasury or "sub-treasuries" set up in leading cities, but it exercised no control over the banks. The opponents of a strong federal government had won out at least temporarily, and for more than two decades there was no direct federal supervision and control of the banking and credit system. In self-defense, various sections of the country, especially New England and New York state, set up voluntary control systems to hold in check the amount of paper money in circulation. Such systems helped, but banking was not on a satisfactory basis in most parts of the country until the setting up of the national banking system during the Civil War. During this interval of unstable banking, businessmen had to be on constant watch for counterfeit bills, and to refer frequently to the lists of the values of the state bank notes to see how much the note of any given bank had depreciated.

In spite of a banking system on which business could not depend, economic development moved ahead steadily during the late 1840's and early 1850's. The discovery of gold in California brought an increase in metal money in circulation and a speeding up of land settlement beyond the Mississippi. The practicability of the railroad had been thoroughly demonstrated by this time, and railroad building was proceeding at an unprecedented rate. The increase of gold and the renewal of easy credit conditions by the banks led to a rising price level. Speculative sentiment re-awakened, especially with relation to the future of the railroads. In 1857, the Ohio Life Insurance and Trust Company, which had substantial railway loans, failed. Confidence was shaken and a panic followed. Many banks were forced to suspend specie payments and there were widespread railroad failures, especially among the new railroad companies in the West. Fortunately for the country, recovery from this panic of 1857 was prompt, except for the shipping and shipbuilding industries, whose prolonged decline was due to special circumstances, as we have already seen (p. 162). The development of other industries and commerce was proceeding normally until the outbreak of the Civil War.

It will be observed that the three chief periods of depression before the Civil War were all associated with an overextended banking system and excessive speculation in land or public improvements. Some unfortunate incident in each case pricked the bubble of prices that were based on hopes rather than solid facts of supply and demand. This set of collapses led to intensified efforts to create a stable money and banking system which through a closer control over the making of bank loans might prevent excessive speculation. Whether or not the extension of bank credit on an unsound basis was the only cause of depressions, it came to be believed that it was a leading one. The efforts of the period from the Civil War up to the early 1930's, so far as banking is concerned, were in the direction of creating a money system and a banking system that were "sound", i.e., in which paper money could be redeemed in gold on demand and loans repaid with cash when due. The solution of this problem in recent years will be discussed more fully later.

### The beginning of factory industry

By the year 1800, the United States had shown little promise of its future great industrial development. In fact, many types of industrial production were at a lower level in the year 1800 than they had been a decade or more earlier. This was not an indication of economic decay in America, but rather a sign that other kinds of endeavor were more promising. Samuel Slater arrived from England in 1790 to set up the first water frames in America at Pawtucket, Rhode Island, and others brought additional machines of the English Industrial Revolution to this country within a few years. But their adoption was not immediate or widespread. The wars in Europe and the opening of the West provided opportunities for merchants and land speculators which the American industrial system could not yet equal. The capital as well as the initiative of the American people was otherwise absorbed, and industry languished for several decades.

The wide opportunities in foreign commerce were not to last long. The Embargo Act of 1807, followed by war with England in 1812, rudely interrupted the prosperous foreign trade of the United States, which was compelled to turn to the domestic production of goods formerly purchased abroad, both to get the needed merchandise and to make use of the capital of merchants and shipbuilders. The number of cotton mills in New England skyrocketed from 4 in 1803 to 226 in 1810. For nearly a decade after 1807, America experienced a very intensive industrial growth. But many of the industries that arose in this period proved unable to stand the competition of English goods when trade was resumed in 1815, and they failed in the depression of 1819. This led to the establishment of the protective tariff policy (p. 162f.). The political union of the industrial East and the agricultural West which was formed on the tariff question continued for many decades. The South, with its principal products designed to supply a European market, was not benefited by a policy of aid to industry and to western land speculators, and so found itself politically opposed to the policies of the North and West. Thus the support of these policies by all sections but the South contributed in a basic way to the conflict of sectional interests which was to culminate in the Civil War.

Although the first important period of industrial growth ended with the failure of many ventures when the depression of 1819 struck, failure was by no means the fate of all of them. The value of the new cotton spinning machinery had been proved long before the Embargo Act, and that event, with its favorable effect on the demand for American industrial products, enabled a considerable number of the new firms in this field to survive the 1819 depression.

Furthermore, Eli Whitney had demonstrated the speed and economy to be achieved in the manufacture of metal products by accurate standardization of parts which could be produced independently of the final assembly operation. Previously, every part had had to be fitted to its neighbors by hand. Whitney's example paved the way for the machinery and metal-working industry in which America became preëminent. The misfortune of depression in 1819 thus did not prevent a solid start from being made in industrial development.

### Cotton and woolen goods

In Europe, as in America before 1800, the common fibers used in the making of cloth were linen and wool. Cotton fabrics, imported from India and printed in colorful designs which European craftsmen had not been able to imitate up to that time, began to provide sharp competition with the more commonplace linen and wool during the latter part of the colonial era. Chintz and other "India prints" became the fabrics of elegance and distinction in the homes of the well-to-do in both England and America. In fact, brought back to the United States by ship captains in the China trade, they became the basis of what we regard as the early American styles of dress and interior decoration. Although the very earliest efforts to develop spinning and weaving machinery had been directed toward the use of linen and wool, the eager demand for the new cotton fabrics quickly turned the attention of inventors toward the use of the new fiber. The first practical textile machines were developed to handle cotton.

The honor of being the first to put these new machines to work in America in a large-scale manufacturing operation goes to Samuel Slater and his partners. The Slater firm hung on during the 1790's, when manufacturing was not expanding very much, and was ready to open branch factories in Baltimore and Buffalo when the Embargo and Non-Intercourse Acts brought a greater demand for its products after 1807. Other firms entered the business also to give Slater stiff competition. Of these, a particularly important one was the Boston Manufacturing Company, founded by Francis C. Lowell in 1814. A manufacturing plant was established at Waltham, Massachusetts, on the Charles River, and in it both spinning and weaving machinery were installed. Lowell had studied the English machines on a trip to England a few years earlier, and with the aid of a mechanic named Moody he was able to make improvements in the construction of the English machines, especially the power loom, and to make them practical for factory operation. This was the first case on record in which both spinning and weaving were brought together in one factory, and it represented a beginning of industrial integration. Its uniqueness was recognized by contemporaries, who referred to any manufacturing operation in which all processes were brought together under one roof as the "Waltham system."

Cotton spinning and weaving had never been a household industry in America, except to a limited degree in the South, and it was perhaps natural that once a demand developed for American cotton cloth, its manufacture in factories should spread rapidly. The depressions following 1819, 1837, and 1857 checked expansion temporarily but did not prevent the manufacture of cotton cloth from becoming the first great industry to be completely taken over by power-driven machinery. By 1860, there were more than 1000 cotton mills in the United States, employing more than 122,000 workers and using over 1,000,000 bales of cotton every year. The Boston Manufacturing Company had been compelled to ex-

pand its operations to Pawtucket Falls on the Merrimac River, where more water power was available. There, by 1860, the little village of Lowell which they had founded in 1822 grew to be the second largest city in Massachusetts and the first and, for a time, the largest industrial city in America.

The making of woolen cloth, on the other hand, had been a household industry in Europe and America for a great many years. In colonial times the coarser grades of wool cloth were made in this country, but the finer, finished grades were imported from England. The commercial prosperity in the 1790's created no occasion for altering this situation, so that, as in the case of cotton, the woolen industry did not experience any great expansion until the years just before and during the War of 1812. Even in this period of intensely stimulated industrial development, the woolen industry tended to lag. Although some wool was produced on many American farms, it was not of the best quality and not in adequate quantity to supply the whole nation. The Spanish merino sheep had not yet been introduced into America in large numbers, and the making of fine wool cloth required greater skill than was possessed by most American workers.

In spite of these restricting factors, the Scholfield brothers and others from the Yorkshire woolen manufacturing district in England had come to Massachusetts and Connecticut shortly after the arrival of Samuel Slater, and had introduced the best English woolen machinery to America. The woolen industry grew more slowly than the cotton industry and tended to develop a large number of small establishments. During the War of 1812, it experienced a mushroom growth, with factories springing up everywhere to supply both civilian and military needs. After the war, many of these new establishments found themselves unable to compete with English cloth and failed, but not without letting Congress hear their anguished demands for the protection of higher tariff rates. The tariffs of 1824, 1828, and 1832 established high rates on woolen cloth. By 1860, there were nearly twice as many woolen as cotton factories, though they employed considerably less than half as many workers.

### The making of shoes

The shoe industry offers interesting comparisons and contrasts with the textile industries. Although the demand for shoes is as insistent and widespread as that for cloth, and although the making of shoes was as common a household craft as was clothmaking, there were no inventions early in the period of the Industrial Revolution which affected shoemaking. In America, as transportation began to be improved and as markets widened and the possibility of economic specialization grew, the shoe industry might have become a factory industry except that there were no power-driven machines applicable to shoemaking to give factory production any cost advantage. Instead, all that was possible for the making of shoes was the development of the economies of craft specialization, and they were possible even under the domestic system.

As farmers in New England found competition with the better lands of the middle states and the West less and less advantageous, some of them turned to shoemaking to provide stock for the merchants of their section. Most often they did not give up farming entirely but simply constructed small shops attached to their homes—"ten footers" or "ells"—where they carried on shoemaking during the winter or any season when light farm work made it possible. The leather was put out to such home workers often by the storekeeper in the neighboring town, and the shoe workers might be paid in goods, or "truck." As the system developed in response to the continually growing market in all sections of the country, some of the operations, such as cutting out, might be done in a central shop. The sewing of the uppers and the lasting and soling were always put out, as long as this system persisted.

The invention of the sewing machine by Elias Howe in 1846 and its adaptation to the sewing of the upper leather of shoes in 1852 prepared the way for a quick change to the

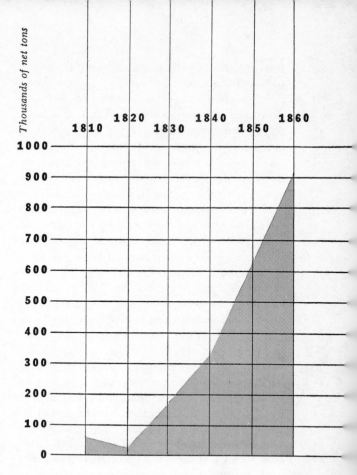

Fig. VIII-4 Pig iron production in the United States, 1810-1860.

factory system. The central shop for cutting the leather and for packing and shipping the finished shoes had already developed. It was not a great further step to install sewing machines and begin true factory operation. The great demand for shoes to supply the armies during the Civil War practically completed the change.

### Making iron, steel, and metal products

The iron industry in America began in colonial times in a period when the increasingly acute charcoal shortage in England led the iron-working industry to look to America for bar iron made with the limitless charcoal supplies of American forests. At the same time these English industries were extremely jealous lest competing industries develop in America to make nails, hardware, and tools from this supply of bar iron. The manufacture of iron and its products was recognized as the basis of military and economic power, and it was therefore a cardinal point of mercantilist policy to see that the industry did not get out of control in the colonies. The American iron industry was accordingly kept unbalanced. Bar iron produced from local bog ores and local charcoal was made very widely throughout the colonies, while manufacturing industries to use this iron were almost entirely lacking. It was used chiefly by the local blacksmiths who made horseshoes, andirons, and other simple articles, and in the illegal manufacturing that was carried on.

During the Revolutionary War the iron industry expanded even more than other industries, because its products were needed for the manufacture of arms and other military goods. After the war, the industry suffered because hardware from England could again be secured. Another boom and relapse occurred during the first two decades of the nineteenth century, as the prosperity of the years of the Embargo Act and War of 1812 were followed by the depression of 1819. Gradually the industry became concentrated near mineral ore deposits in the Appalachian Mountain region, especially in the Juniata and Lehigh Valleys in Pennsylvania. Anthracite coal began to be used instead of charcoal at least partially in this region about 1840, and the tonnage of iron produced increased greatly.

Since the basic processes of large-scale iron manufacture using coke for fuel had been worked out in England before 1800, it is surprising that an estimated seven-eighths of American iron production was made with charcoal as late as 1860. Professor L. C. Hunter has examined the matter and believes that it was not due to technological ignorance or a traditional preference for charcoal iron, or to its lower cost, but rather to the fact that the largest users of iron were the small shops of the rural areas for whom the iron made with coal or coke was likely to contain too much carbon to be suitable.[1] It is known that English ironworkers came to America, but large-scale smelting of iron ore with coke did not take root quickly because the United States lacked the industry to use the type and amount of iron produced in the coke-fired furnaces. These industries developed only gradually, toward the middle of the nineteenth century. The first coke blast furnace at Pittsburgh went into operation in 1859, apparently to secure greater uniformity in the iron supplied to the builders' mill for rolling railroad rails.

In spite of the retarded development of large-scale iron production, the products of the small furnaces were used for kitchen utensils, stoves, parts of farm machines, and the like. In 1845, the first effort to roll rails was made, and after that date rail production grew gradually, although importation of rails from Europe continued. Carbon steel, which has just enough carbon in it to give it the qualities of hardness coupled with toughness, was not produced in quantity in America until after the Civil War. The properties of steel place it half-way between pure, soft, wrought iron with no carbon in it, and hard, brittle cast iron containing a great deal of carbon. Just on the eve of the war, William Kelly of Kentucky invented a simple process of making steel, at the same time that Henry Bessemer developed a closely similar process in England. After the war, when the processes had been perfected and the patent quarrels of the two men resolved, the production of steel by the new method increased greatly. The development of steam power and its application in industry and transportation created a great new demand for machines and parts made of iron and steel. A whole cluster of industries depending upon iron or steel as a basic raw material sprang up in the period before 1860, and gave free rein to the inventive genius which had been shown by Americans.

[1] L. C. Hunter, "Influence of the Market upon Technique in the Iron Industry in Western Pennsylvania up to 1860," *Journal of Economic and Business History,* I (1929), pp. 241-281.

## Industry in the West

The New England and middle states of the eastern seaboard furnished the best conditions for the growth of large-scale industry, for they had an adequate labor supply, accessibility to capital supplies, and nearness to the markets in Europe and in the older and more densely settled areas of this country. Some industries, however, whose raw materials or markets moved westward with the advancing frontier, found it necessary or advantageous to go along. Most typical of these industries were the sawmills and gristmills which provided the sawed lumber for construction and the flour and meal for the staple foods. These country mills were small, but they were far and away in the lead numerically among industrial establishments. Their markets and their raw materials were within only a few miles, but they were indispensable to every growing community.

Another type of industry which arose quickly as western agricultural areas were developed was that which concentrated, processed, or preserved the products of the farms so that they could be sent to more distant markets. In a period when transportation was both poor and costly, the bulky or perishable products could not be sold far away from the farm at all. Yet farmers had to obtain cash to buy manufactured goods, so that food processing industries to put raw agricultural produce into more valuable and durable form were essential. One of the earliest of these industries to develop was distilling, to make whiskey out of corn or rye. The Whiskey Rebellion by western Pennsylvania farmers in 1794 was against a whiskey tax which they feared would destroy their main source of cash income from the sale of their farm produce. As settlement followed the Ohio River westward, Cincinnati became the principal center of the distilling industry. Similarly, the meat-packing industry came at first to be centered at Cincinnati, moving later to Chicago as the Erie Canal and the railroads opened up the Great Lakes basin and the upper Mississippi Valley by providing needed transportation.

In addition to the western industries which depended on the raw materials of the farms and forests of the region, there were those which moved to or grew up in the West because their chief markets were there. Professor L. C. Hunter, whose article was cited above, believes that the iron industry moved to the Pittsburgh region before the Civil War, not primarily to be near a better supply of raw materials, but to be on the Ohio River system and thus accessible to the small iron-using shops of the rural lower Ohio Valley. Wagons, plows, and farm equipment of various kinds were in greatest demand in the West. The manufacturing industries which produced them grew up in western Pennsylvania, Ohio, and farther west. The carriage industry for a time remained in the East to accommodate the more genteel folk of that area, but it, too, eventually moved over the Alleghenies into the upper Mississippi Valley. The furniture industry also grew in the West, at first to be near its market, and, as good furniture woods became scarcer, to be near its supply of raw material in the hardwood forests of the northern states east of the Mississippi River.

## Organizing and financing industry

As industry experienced growing demands for its products or as new technical processes of manufacture were developed, the problem of getting adequate financial backing was always present. This was essentially the same problem which European commercial enterprises had faced two hundred years earlier, and which they had solved by the development of the joint-stock company or corporation. The earliest charters granted to business corporations by American states seem to have been preponderantly for road, bridge, canal, bank, and insurance companies. Perhaps this can be accounted for by both the substantial need for capital on the part of such businesses and their semi-public character. There was a deep-seated hostility in America, possibly greater than in Europe, toward the grant of a public franchise to a private group which might use its power for its own benefit and to the public harm. If the purpose of the business was one which would benefit many members of the public, then the general suspicion of the corporate form of organization might be overcome. The construction of a new industrial establishment was not quite so clearly of benefit to all the public as the building of a road or canal. But the wider markets in the West and the new technical processes being developed made increased capital so necessary to industry that corporation charters were sought more and more in spite of possible public opposition.

Some of the earliest charters to manufacturing companies were in the cotton textile industry. The combination of new types of machines and a great demand for the product made large-scale operation attractive to business promoters. After 1800, the number of incorporated manufacturing companies increased greatly, although individual proprietorships and partnerships continued to be numerous and handled a large volume of business in most lines for many years longer. The Boston Manufacturing Company, founded in 1814, was unique not only for its "Waltham system" of integrated operation, but also for the fact that it was one of the early and successful manufacturing corporations. Its competitors, who also built plants at Lowell, were likewise incorporated. These Lowell corporations were for a time symbolic of big business in America. The total capital invested in manufacturing, including all forms of organization, as reported by the *Census of Manufactures,* more than doubled each decade until 1860. By the middle of the century, many states had passed general incorporation laws to lay down the conditions under which corporation charters would be issued by the state governments without a special act of the legislature for each one. The heyday of the corporation, however, did not come until after the Civil War, when the size and number of corporations advanced rapidly.

In a new country with seemingly unlimited land, and with more work waiting to be done than it would appear could ever actually be finished, it is quite easy to understand that parents should find a large family an asset and not a liability. Very little was spent in cash for clothing or other manufactured articles, because life on the farm was plain and simple, and wants were few. Education was limited pretty much to the famous "three *R*'s," which children acquired during a short school term in the winter when there was no farm work to be done except the ever-present morning and evening "chores." Food was plentiful, or could be if there were enough hands to carry on the work of the farm, even if the knowledge of proper principles of diet was sometimes lacking.

There could scarcely be a physical and cultural environment more stimulating to a rapid increase of a nation's population. In fact, there probably has never been, within the span of recorded history, a large population group which increased as rapidly as that of the United States from 1800 to 1860. The census figures show an increase for each ten-year period of about 35 per cent (see Fig. VIII-6, p. 179). To express it differently, the American population doubled during this era in a little more than twenty years.

This high rate of growth was partly the result of a natural increase in population and partly the result of a very considerable immigration during the middle period of American history, largely from northern and western Europe. This immigration fluctuated according to conditions in both Europe and America, reaching a peak in the ten years between 1845 and 1855. A number of factors contributed to this peak of immigration, the highest in proportion to the size of our population of any period in our history: (1) the severe winters in Europe and the potato famine in Ireland in 1845-46; (2) the socialist revolutions which generally failed in several European countries in 1848

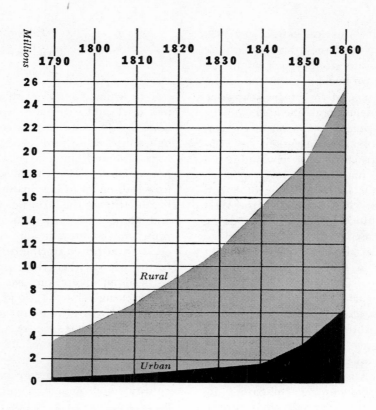

Fig. VIII-5 *A comparison between the rate of growth of urban and rural population in the United States between 1790 and 1860. This should be compared with the figures from 1860 to 1960 given later.*

and 1849, forcing many of the revolutionaries to flee; and (3) the discovery of gold in California in 1848. A majority of the Irish immigrants settled in the cities of the East, whereas the English, Germans, and Scandinavians tended to go to the settled farming regions of the Mississippi Valley. The migrants to the newest frontier regions, including the Far West, were likely to be American-born persons looking for new and greater opportunities. Accurate immigration figures were not kept before 1820, but it is probable that about five million immigrants came into the United States to stay between 1800 and 1860.

While the total population was growing rapidly both from natural increase and from immigration, several aspects of the distribution of that total are important. We know that the period was one not only of territorial

expansion in the United States, but also of increasing productive efficiency in both agriculture and industry. From the beginning of human life, people have engaged in food production as a matter of necessity. As efficiency in methods of food production increases, more of the time of all of the people, or all of the time of more of the people can be devoted to industrial production. Industrial work yields such necessities as clothing and shelter, as well as tools and equipment for both agriculture and industry itself. Beyond those things, if sufficient time can be devoted to it, industry also yields those luxuries which add pleasure and enjoyment to life, and which men seem to crave in the greatest quantity in which it is possible to obtain them.

These factors lay behind the shifts in occupation and in population in the middle period of our history. Agriculture continued to be the occupation of the majority of the people, but agricultural efficiency was increasing for several reasons: (1) A smaller proportion of the time of the farm population as a whole had to be devoted to developmental work such as clearing, draining, fencing, and erecting buildings. More time, in proportion, could be devoted to crop and livestock production. (2) Farm methods and farm machinery were being improved rapidly. (3) Better transportation was making it possible to get farm products to market more quickly and more cheaply. These and other factors meant that the United States could feed its population with fewer people on the farm.

As a result, the cities grew between 1800 and 1860 much faster than the population as a whole. In 1800, only 1 person in 25 lived in a city of 8000 or more; in 1860, 1 person in 6 lived in such a city. This meant an increase of roughly twenty-five-fold in the population of cities, while the whole population had increased nearly 6 times during those years. There were 141 cities of more than 8000 in 1860, including several such cities as Lowell, Massachusetts, thriving industrial centers that had not existed in 1800. New York

had passed Philadelphia to become the great American metropolis with a population of considerably more than a million, counting the adjoining boroughs. Chicago had become the metropolis of the West, having grown from an insignificant trading post in 1800 to a city of more than 100,000 in 1860. The United States was becoming a nation of city dwellers and professional and industrial workers, as it has continued to become more and more ever since, because agricultural efficiency, measured in output per man-hour of work, has also continued to increase to make that kind of population shift possible.

It is also deserving of notice that the growing population was moving out of the Atlantic seaboard area and filling up the rest of the continent during these middle years. Although the Irish and some other immigrant groups tended to remain along the eastern coast, the growth of the states in that area was much less than that of the states over the mountains. The most rapid growth occurred in the states of the Northwest Territory and those adjoining it to the west. The Pacific coast states and those adjoining Texas also grew rapidly. New England and the old South grew more slowly. It is estimated that from

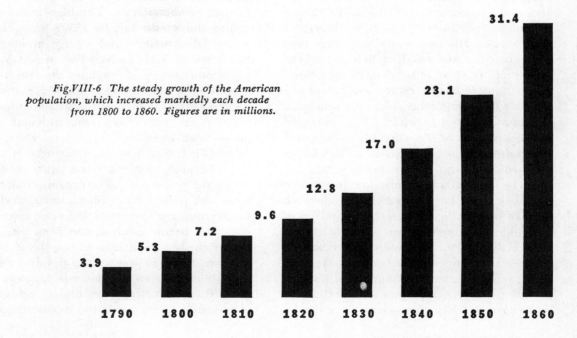

Fig.VIII-6  The steady growth of the American population, which increased markedly each decade from 1800 to 1860. Figures are in millions.

31.4

23.1

17.0

12.8

9.6

7.2

5.3

3.9

1790  1800  1810  1820  1830  1840  1850  1860

25 to 40 per cent of the population of the older states moved west during the period.

One result, therefore, was that the slave-holding South was losing relatively in population and political power by these population shifts. Most immigration was into the free territory of the industrial East or the grain and livestock-producing agricultural West. Cotton culture was booming, especially in the new territories to the Southwest, but that expansion was not sufficient to equal the expansion of both industry and agriculture in the free territory of the North and West.

## Labor organization and social reform

As industrial employment provided income for more and more of the American people, the conditions of living and working in industry were not always to the liking of those who had to accept them. In America, as in England, little was understood of proper precautions for safety and health in the new factories. Congested living quarters in the growing industrial cities often resulted in a deplorable lack, not only of sanitation, but also of the minimum requirements for decent or comfortable human existence. Hours of work were usually long, wages low, and schools inadequate for the children of the workers. In the face of these unsatisfactory conditions, it was most often the skilled artisans of the building trades and other industries who made the most effective protest. The unskilled workers, who were the worst off, contributed little to the support of movements from which they would be the greatest beneficiaries.

The oldest labor organizations in America date back to the last quarter of the eighteenth century, when skilled workers like shipwrights, carpenters, and typographers in Philadelphia, New York, and other eastern cities banded together to obtain various benefits, especially higher wages, shorter hours, and better working conditions. Their employers were not factory owners but merchant-manufacturers of the do-mestic stage of industrial development. These pre-Industrial Revolution unions, as they may be called, were purely local and temporary in character. Their rise reflected the growing demand for goods and the tendency of merchants to employ larger numbers of workers and to devote more of their attention to the manufacturing phase of their business. These organizations continued to develop through the first quarter of the nineteenth century, often having associated with them small employers or farmers, who, like the industrial workers, were interested in belonging to a mutual benefit organization devoted to general social reform.

More aggressive union activity, which Professor John R. Commons regards as the real beginning of the American labor movement, began in 1827 when Philadelphia carpenters, joined by other building trades workers, struck for a ten-hour day. These unions formed the Mechanics' Union of Trade Associations to work together for their common interests, and in 1828 they founded the *Mechanics' Free Press*, the first labor paper in America. Similar movements arose in Boston, New York, Providence, and other cities. Such early labor groups were often primarily political in their objectives, working especially hard for free public schools. The high prices prevailing during the middle 1830's brought renewed labor activity and a large number of local strikes. In 1834 a New York union group called other unions throughout the country to a convention in order to form a National Trades Union. This was the first attempt to form a national union, and, although the group held conventions for several years, the effort failed to achieve an enduring result.

The prolonged depression after 1837 reduced the activity of labor organizations, because the existence of unemployed workers undermined the bargaining power of all workers. The attention which had been directed toward the bad conditions existing in industry, however, began to bear fruit in two directions: (1) in humanitarian schemes, especially during the 1840's, to correct the ills of industrial society, and (2) in legislation to correct some of the specific evils of the workers' situation which was put on the statute books of several important states.

A number of the social reform schemes of this period grew out of the experiences and ideas of Robert Owen, a British textile manufacturer. Owen demonstrated at his cotton mill at New Lanark, Scotland, that good living and working conditions were also good for business. He came to believe that a good environment would call forth the best qualities in man rather than the evil qualities which seemed to be most in evidence in industrial communities. He launched an ambitious project to found an ideal community in America at New Harmony, Indiana. The experiment failed because of poor planning and poor selection of the group to participate in the experiment. Owen lost most of his fortune in the venture, although he succeeded in attracting attention to the unfortunate plight of the industrial worker. Many personnel practices in effect in industry today would conform to Owen's ideals much better than those of his own time.

A Frenchman, Charles Fourier, in 1808 advanced a somewhat more formalized scheme for ideal communities to be called phalanxes. These were communities where each member was to do the work for which he was best fitted, all coöperating for the general welfare. A number of these were tried out in America, the most famous being Brook Farm near Boston, in which a number of the chief literary lights of New England were leaders. These "associationist" phalanxes also failed, but they attracted a great deal of attention to the social conditions arising from the European Industrial Revolution which they were trying to eliminate. Such social reform schemes had a wide effect upon economic and social attitudes in America for a number of decades, although the conditions which produced them were almost entirely European. Of the socialistic communities established in this period, practically all that survived for any length of time were religious in character.

Aided by the favorable public opinion created by such social reform schemes, labor was able to make substantial gains for itself by legislative action. By the middle of the nineteenth century, the idea of free public education, at least through the elementary grades, was pretty generally accepted. Public support of schools free to all had been incorporated in the Northwest Ordinance and was mandatory upon the states formed under it. Beginning in the late 1840's, a number of important states began to establish the ten-hour day as the legal maximum work day by statute. But it was usually possible for a worker to make a special contract with his employer to work longer, and economic necessity frequently drove him to do so, nullifying the effect of the statutory provision. Often, too, the extent of the law was limited to certain industries or to public work only. Nevertheless, such laws represented a gain for labor, since they helped to establish the idea of the ten-hour limit.

In the 1850's, general prosperity up to the depression of 1857 led to the resumption of labor organization. The weakness of the semipolitical labor organizations of the thirties and the collapse of the social reform schemes of the forties turned labor toward what is today called "old-line unionism." This policy was one of restricting the organization to workers only, maintaining it in a strong, financially solvent condition, and attempting only those objectives for which the collective strength of the membership could be used effectively. In this period also, the first national unions of separate trades were set up on a basis which became permanent. The National Typographical Union was founded in 1852, the Journeyman Stonecutters' Association of North America in 1853, the National Trade Association of Hat Finishers of the United States of America in 1854, and the Iron Molders' Union of North America in 1859.

### The effects of an expanding economy upon economic thinking

It is naturally to be expected that the expansive conditions of a new and growing country should bring forth both new economic goals and new ways of achieving those goals. This process of American differentiation from European ways of thinking was already in an advanced state by the time of the Revolution. In fact, as we have seen (Chapter 6), the deep-seated American resentment toward English mercantilist policies provided the immediate cause of the Revolutionary War itself. The period of roughly seventy-five years between the Revolution and the breaking out of the Civil War, saw some distinctively American ideas developed further, but also saw the new country beginning to feel its own strength, partially adopting a Mercantilism of its own.

Agriculture continued to be the occupation of more Americans than all other employments combined. Yet our thinking about agriculture was chiefly to develop machines so that one family could handle more land, and to develop ways of getting to the unlimited expanse of agricultural lands in the west. We were more exploiters and land speculators than we were careful farmers. Jefferson's ideal, following the French Physiocrats, that agriculture was the indispensable basis of national greatness, was not so much rejected as by-passed. Rather, Hamilton's ideal of a balanced economy combining agriculture with industry was taken up by Henry Clay and incorporated in his concept of an "American System." This policy won the day as we placed tariffs on foreign goods that competed directly with our own products and built roads, canals and railways to tie together the agricultural-industrial complex which we began enthusiastically to envisage. The Monroe Doctrine of 1823 (see Glossary), although regarded as primarily political in character, to some degree reflected the new sense of national strength in the United States and of responsibility for the other independent nations of the Americas. We were evidently embarked upon a new and distinctive kind of mercantilist economic policy, derived from our own conditions and directed toward our own goals, but a mercantilist policy nonetheless.

It is thus clear that Americans were not prepared to accept immediately the free trade ideas which Adam Smith had developed in his *Wealth of Nations* and which had gained wide acceptance in England. In this respect, we were more inclined to listen to Friedrich List, a German economic writer, who, based partly upon his American experience in the late 1820's, referred to Smith's economic theory as "cosmopolitical economy" because of its universal rather than national character.[1] List saw the necessity of developing all nations to a nearly equal point before free trade would be beneficial. Until that time, tariff duties were needed to protect "infant industries" until they could face the full competition of older countries with more fully developed industries. The concept of personal freedom to buy and sell which was the cornerstone of Smith's economic reasoning, was in other respects entirely agreeable to Americans. Yet, even in this respect, Americans disagreed with some of the consequences of English economic thinking of the same period.

The American writer who best reflects these distinctive phases of our economic thinking is Henry C. Carey. Carey was a Philadelphia publisher who had inherited a business but developed it further himself. Retiring from active business in his early forties (1835), he devoted full time thereafter to economic studies. His writings were voluminous, but certain key ideas are evident in all of them. He generally agreed with List on the need for protective tariffs, although his theoretical reasoning is different. He disagreed with the views of the English economists, T. R. Malthus and David Ricardo. Both the famous population doctrine of Malthus and the equally famous rent doctrine attributed to Ricardo rest upon the idea that as agricultural production is pushed further, the yield of the land will continually decrease. On this base, Malthus reasoned that unless population were held down by checks, it would always press upon the food supply and bring about malnutrition, starvation, and

[1]List, Friedrich, *Das Nationale System der Politischen Oekonomie* (Stuttgart, 1841). Translated by S. S. Lloyd, as *The National System of Political Economy* (London, 1885).

other forms of human misery. On the same base, but adding Malthus' idea, Ricardo reasoned that land rent would continually rise as population and wealth increase due to the scarcity of good land. Landlords would be the wealthy class in society and all others would fare less well. Even the capitalist would suffer from the lack of productive opportunities for the investment of his capital.

All of these dire conclusions were rejected by Carey. Reflecting the American confidence in technological achievement as well as the merit in Fourier's argument of the advantage in the association of workers, Carey argued that yields in agriculture and industry would not get less but more as years passed. The first land occupied in a new country, he said, would likely be that which could be put into crops most easily and quickly. This would be hill tops where there would be no drainage problems and where there would be less natural growth of trees and bushes. Only later, after population had increased, would it be practical to undertake the clearing of the heavy forest growth of the fertile valleys. But once cleared, the latter would eventually bring far greater yields of foodstuffs.

In similar manner, Carey contended that manufactured goods would be becoming cheaper as time passed. This result would come from the fact that reproduction cost would generally be lower than original production cost. Increased technical knowledge plus the benefit of the association of more people in the work process would bring about this result. Thus, neither landlords nor capitalists would become the wealthy class in society. Rather, the ordinary farmer and workman would be beneficiaries of man's continually increasing mastery over physical nature.

These ideas are quite clearly opposed to those of Malthus and Ricardo. According to Carey, there is nothing to fear from growing population. Carey's view of the future was as optimistic as that of the English economists was pessimistic. Charles Darwin's evolutionary views were presented and became the center of a storm of controversy during Carey's lifetime. His economic views did not become

at all directly involved with Darwin's biological ones. Yet, it is evident that Carey had a theory of economic development, although he did not make a full-fledged theory of continuing economic evolution out of it. If we were to look more closely into the theoretical positions of both Carey and the English economists, we would see that without telling us so, their differences in conclusions arise from differences in their unstated assumptions. If we take the assumption of Malthus and Ricardo, it is not hard to prove that Carey's conclusions are in error, for the English economists assumed that technology would be constant or at least not able to keep up with man's potential for increasing the population. But if Carey's unstated and unproved assumption is correct, that productivity gains from greater association and greater technological knowledge will come at a faster rate than the population will grow, then the pessimistic conclusions of Malthus and Ricardo are wrong. The final answer to this question will determine the fate of the human race, and it obviously will be a long time in coming. We can record now the fact that Carey thought he saw proof of his position in American history.

### The industrial economy by 1860

It was apparent in the years just before the outbreak of Civil War hostilities that American industry was advancing rapidly. American industrial inventions added to those introduced from England, together with the expanding national market now being tied together by a spreading railroad network, provided a combination of circumstances that must almost inevitably produce a great expansion of industry. The industrial magnate and promoter was about to take his place beside the great foreign trading merchant, the land speculator, and the railroad builder as a leading figure in the economic development of North America. Capital from the wealthier nations of Europe would still be needed for this American industrial expansion, but the European economy was at a stage where funds for foreign investment were available.

The appearance of solid and enduring national unions of industrial workers beginning in the 1850's was also a sign of the end of America's industrial adolescence. Many more decades were to pass before economic conditions were to convince even a substantial minority of American workers or employers that unions were a good and permanent element in industrial relations. The individualistic tradition and conditioning of both workers and employers prevented that result sooner. But national unions were here to stay, and their very existence testified to the arrival of a new period in American economic history. These economic developments, however, were not to be permitted to work themselves out without the interruption of the most destructive force in our national history, the Civil War.

## FOR FURTHER READING

Barnes, James A. *Wealth of the American People.* New York: Prentice-Hall, Inc., 1949. Chapters 12—16.

Bogart, Ernest L., and Kemmerer, Donald L. *Economic History of the American People.* 2nd ed. New York: Longmans, Green & Co., Inc., 1947. Chapters 9 and 13—16.

Callender, G. S. *Selections from the Economic History of the United States, 1785-1860.* Boston: Ginn & Co., 1909. Chapters 10 and 11.

MacGill, G. S., and others. *History of Transportation in the United States Beyond 1860.* Washington: Carnegie Institution of Washington, 1917.

Schlesinger, Arthur M., Jr. *The Age of Jackson.* Mentor, 1949. Paperback.

Shannon, Fred Albert. *America's Economic Growth.* 3rd ed. New York: The Macmillan Co., 1951. Chapters 9—13.

Taylor, G. R. *The Transportation Revolution, 1815-1860.* New York: Rinehart & Co., Inc., 1951. Chapters 14 and 15.

Williamson, Harold F. (ed.) *The Growth of the American Economy.* 2nd ed. New York: Prentice-Hall, Inc., 1958.

Wright, Chester W. *Economic History of the United States.* 2nd ed. New York: McGraw-Hill Book Co., 1949. Chapters 21—26.

# Chapter 9: The economic significance of the Civil War

The issues over which the Civil War was fought began to emerge many years before the war itself. They were related to the development of conflicting economic interests among the various large sections of the United States. Thomas Jefferson had visualized the future United States as a nation of independent, largely self-sufficient farmers with only a small minority of skilled craftsmen producing the essential manufactured goods in towns of modest size. In 1786 James Monroe wrote to Jefferson, following a trip through the Northwest Territory, and expressed the opinion that much of the area along the Great Lakes and the Mississippi River was "miserably poor" and would probably never support enough people to form states.[1] A few years later, Jefferson predicted that it would be a thousand years before the area east of the Mississippi River was heavily settled. Within a decade or two these views were being proved substan-

tially wrong. Within seventeen years Ohio had more than the required sixty thousand people to form the first state from the Northwest Territory. Agriculture had stopped being self-sufficient in all parts of the country. The South had found a new crop in cotton, whose price was determined by demand in English markets. Farmers of the middle and western states were selling as much of their produce as could be transported from the farm to distant city and foreign markets. Agriculture was becoming specialized and a larger and larger proportion of the population in the East was involved in commercial and industrial pursuits.

The picture of American development held by the founding fathers proved to be inaccurate, and the various sections of the country began to follow those lines of economic activity best suited to them. Instead of a single and common economic interest for the country as a whole, there began to emerge multiple and sometimes conflicting sectional interests. The tariff controversies of the years immediately following the depression of 1819 resulted

[1] Quoted in Chester W. Wright, *Economic History of the United States* (New York: McGraw-Hill, 1941), p. 253.

from economic differences which did not reach full maturity for nearly forty years. Almost every session of Congress up to 1820 raised some tariff duties and no spirited debate either pro or con was aroused. But when the resumption of European trade following the end of the War of 1812 resulted in the collapse of many new manufacturing industries established during the period of economic isolation, their former owners became convinced very quickly that only with a really substantial tariff to protect them could industries thrive. Industrialists and manufacturers, however, were too few to swing Congress to their point of view. In Massachusetts, for example, the commercial interests did not favor tariffs so placed as to restrict the volume of their trade. It took the industrialists several years before they could persuade even part of the Massachusetts Congressional delegation that the best interests of the state would be served by a tariff to encourage industry.

While the industrial interests in the East were still not powerful enough to get their own way in the forming of national policies, they found sympathetic consideration and support from the representatives of the new agricultural states being formed across the Appalachian Mountains. The farmers of the West were held in check by the lack of transportation. The products of their labor and their land were worthless unless they were within reach of the market. They were not seriously worried at first by the prices of the goods which they sold or bought, except that they wanted to be rid of the excessive freight charges on both outgoing and incoming merchandise resulting from the poor transportation facilities. Western representatives in Congress insistently demanded federally sponsored internal improvements in the form of roads, canals, and finally railways. Eastern manufacturers, who realized after 1819 that it would be many years before they could sell their products in world markets where they would compete with older manufacturing countries, turned to the idea that their best market was in the great mid-continental area of the West, which was then filling rapidly.

They too came to favor a policy of vigorous building of internal improvements. The protective rates of the Tariff Act of 1824 were approved in Congress because the arguments of Henry Clay of Kentucky that this was the American System proved effective with both eastern and western representatives. Clay and his supporters argued that the natural market for American manufactures was the West and that the natural market for the foodstuffs and raw materials of the agricultural West was the industrial and commercial East. To develop this home market for the mutual advantage of East and West required both a protective tariff to keep out foreign competition in manufactured goods and internal improvements to tie the East and West together by the bonds of trade.

All was not quite as harmonious between East and West as this home market argument might indicate. So far as the West was concerned, the need of transportation for farm produce to the East was only part of the reason for internal improvements. The other part was the need of obtaining access to new lands nearer the frontier. Those transplanted easterners who became westerners were the most inveterate land speculators, practically always operating on the merest financial shoestring. To make their operations pay, they badly needed both continuous extension of good transportation and liberal credit terms for land purchases. The East could agree on internal improvements, but the bankers and manufacturers of the area could not see any justification for credit so easily granted that banking became unstable and unsafe. Furthermore, since the West as a section was constantly in debt to the financiers of the East, westerners always favored ever higher prices through the demand for goods and land that came from easy credit. Constantly rising prices meant that debts contracted in previous years at lower prices would be a progressively smaller burden, as they would be paid off in money that was more plentiful and worth less than in the earlier period. Thus high prices were in almost every way a boon to the West but a source of the destruction of many established values to the financial interests of the East. This source of opposition of interest between East and West came to the surface from time to time, but it never led to any open break between the sections. The West was able to settle the problem of credit for land purchases in 1862 with the passage of the Homestead Act, which provided for granting land freely in 160-acre plots to those who would settle on them and improve them for five years. The credit problem then became one of obtaining capital for improvements and operation, or for purchase of additional land from the original settlers or from railroads along their routes.

The South found itself in agreement with the West to a greater degree on monetary and banking policy than in any other matter, with the possible exception of land policy. The South was expanding westward also and needed both liberal land grants and easy credit for land purchase. It also needed internal improvements, but not the same ones that the North and West needed. The fertile lands along the Gulf of Mexico and in the lower Mississippi Valley did have access to the markets of Mobile or New Orleans, although improvements would have been welcomed. But the great projects for a "national" highway, and for canals and railways, did not benefit the South at all. In fact, the home-market argument for Clay's American System did not interest the South or have any real effect on it. The states of the deep South were devoting themselves ever more completely to cotton production up to the Civil War, and the border states continued to grow their staple product—tobacco. Both cotton and tobacco found their principal markets in Europe, and the South really needed physical and financial facilities for handling a large export business. As has been shown (p. 168), its export trade moved through northern ports, and its imports came through the same route, adding to their costs. From the sale of their products abroad, the farmers of the South obtained credits which they wished to use to buy manufactured goods wherever they could get them most cheaply. For many kinds of goods, that would be in

Europe and not in America. The South, therefore, came to resent the tariff as soon as southern legislators appreciated what its effects would be. Southerners did not benefit from the tariff's help to American manufacturers, and they had to pay higher prices to get European manufactured goods into the country.

From nearly every important point of view, then, the national economic policies which were gaining the determined support of the industrial Northeast and the agricultural West did not benefit the South materially, but rather imposed higher costs and taxes upon her. These policies received the determined opposition of the South in Congress. Internal improvements paid for or subsidized at national expense did not help the South, and southerners felt that their taxes paid for a large proportion of these improvements. The kinds of internal improvements which would have benefited the South were not made in sufficient quantity. The protective tariff hurt the South in many ways and did not provide adequate benefits to compensate for the damages. Even on the matter of land and banking policies, where the South might have found some support in the East and strong allies in the West, these alliances did not develop because western expansion in the South was dominated by the extension of the plantation system, whose requirements were quite different from those of the small independent family farming system of the North. In fact, the plantation system, with its substantial slave holdings and its great investment in lands, buildings, and supplies was a form of agricultural capitalism whose capital requirements might call for loans floated in either European or eastern financial markets, at high interest rates. The planters found that their capital was either tied up in their lands or was flowing into northern banks. As a farmer the planter might seem to have the same interest in cheap credit as the small farmer of the North, but as a big businessman, his credit came from different sources, and the cost of his credit accommodations in Philadelphia or New York was another cause of his resentment toward northern domination.

The economic fact which was becoming apparent by the 1820's, as revealed especially in the controversy over the protective tariff, was that Jefferson's vision of an economy of independent farmers and artisans was just a dream of olden times. Each of the major sections of the country was developing its own specialized economic interests, and national economic policy was becoming a blend of sectional interests which could gain the support of Congress. Slavery was an issue between the South and the other sections in both its moral and its economic aspects. But the most widely held view at the present time, among students of the Civil War era, is that the slavery issue was itself the product of other deeper economic issues of which it became the measure and symbol.

## Sectional economic issues

### The industrial East

The economic trends affecting the New England and Middle Atlantic states which had begun to make themselves evident early in the nineteenth century continued to develop further almost without interruption throughout the period up to the Civil War. The expansion of industry in the East was becoming the all-absorbing theme of that section of the country, and the establishment of a strong protective tariff was the aspect of national policy which came ever closer to the center of interest of the members of Congress from the region.

The victory of Andrew Jackson in the presidential campaigns of 1828 and 1832 was clear proof to the conservative groups in the East that the little people of the country had great political power when they were sufficiently aroused to use it. The growing industrial and financial hold of the East on the rest of the country had become a source of resentment. The second Bank of the United States, which had become established in 1816 (p. 169), became a symbol of eastern, centralized, financial control, and opposition to the Bank became one of Jackson's most settled policies.

Under the direction of its president, Nicholas Biddle, the Bank dominated the financial affairs of the West and South. Jackson charged it with being a dangerous monopoly because it was controlled by one section (the East). He claimed that it took advantage of its funds and government credit to influence politicians, it put pressure on newspapers, and it could bring about financial depression by manipulating bank notes and credit. He charged that it was unconstitutional and yet in a position to dictate to the government. To a considerable degree the officers of the Bank invited the kind of opposition which they received by using the power of the Bank to influence the settlement of political issues.

By twentieth-century criteria, the power of the Bank would not be rated so highly. It was not able to enforce sound money standards throughout the country, and banks in the larger centers, especially Boston, were compelled to adopt their own methods of preventing the circulation of depreciated bank notes. The most famous plan was that of the Suffolk Bank of Boston, begun about 1825, by which it returned the notes of other banks directly to them for redemption unless they maintained a deposit with the Suffolk Bank for that purpose. A number of other New England banks joined in the scheme, which succeeded in keeping the circulating bank notes of that region at full value. New York State started a "Safety Fund" plan, which required banks to maintain a joint reserve fund to pay off the notes of any bank that failed. Joining the plan was optional, and the plan itself was changed from time to time to strengthen it, but it was never entirely successful.

The monetary and banking situation in the United States became much less stable after the expiration of the charter of the Bank of the United States in 1836. The voluntary plans among banks in the eastern states to maintain the value of bank notes became even more necessary. In some of the western states in the upper Mississippi Valley, money was in great demand for land purchases, and "wildcat" banks issued it freely on loans to speculators. As a result, the bank-note money of the West depreciated badly in value, and became so debased that currency sometimes continued to circulate for months or even years after the bank that issued it had failed and gone out of business. Storekeepers were compelled to maintain lists of the value of the notes of the various banks, so that they would not take them in at too high a value. Farmers and land speculators were not seriously concerned by this chaotic monetary situation, but business interests of the West and South, and especially of the East, became more and more convinced that a national system of sound money was indispensable. As industry and commerce grew within the country and transportation from East to West was improved, the businessmen demanded a successful sound money system, which was set up finally by the National Bank Act of 1864 (see p. 198). This act created a system of national banks chartered by the federal government. It provided a uniform and safe currency by allowing these banks to issue notes backed by their own assets and government bonds deposited with the United States Treasury.

The financial and industrial interests of the East also found considerable attraction in the newly developing idea of a transcontinental railroad. The first short lines were in the East, but by 1840 the practicability of the steam railroad had been demonstrated, and the possibility of long lines was becoming clear. This meant that railroads were not going to be used merely to connect rivers, canals, or other bodies of water, but that they were going to become the main arteries of transportation over long distances. In an undeveloped continent such as North America it also became clear that railroads would be used not only to carry freight and passengers in settled areas, but also to open up unsettled areas and to develop the sources of their own traffic for later years. These possibilities promised new and greater business for bankers, financiers, manufacturers of equipment for railroads, the makers of all kinds of goods that could be sold in the West, and, of course, for merchants of all kinds. No through railroad had been built from the At-

lantic coast to the Mississippi River by 1850, but a decade later a number of lines had arrived at Chicago and St. Louis and were being extended on toward the West. The South had some railroads, but nothing like the network that had been built in the North.

The prewar building of railroads, which reached a peak in the 1850's, offered great opportunities to the financial speculators and promoters of the East, not only for the profits to be made from railroad stocks and bonds, but also for those to be made from industrial sites and mineral, timber, and agricultural lands along the railroad's right of way. Westerners eagerly joined in this fascinating and lucrative game, lucrative, that is, so long as one could avoid the pitfalls of such depressions as those of 1837 and 1857, which caught many unwary and overly eager speculators. Once they had been built, the operation of the railroads brought about that unity of agricultural West with industrial and commercial East which Clay's American System had contemplated three decades earlier. The building and operation of railroads thus provided a substantial basis of common interest between East and West. This mutual interest even went as far as joint support for the idea of a Pacific railway, which began to be discussed in the years before the war. When a Pacific railroad was proposed, with at least partial financial support to come from the federal government, the South became actively hostile unless a line should also be built from the West to a southern port like Charleston, South Carolina.

As migration continued its westerly course aided by the railroads, the question of the government of the new territories became acute. This problem was of no direct interest to the East, since easterners were primarily interested in the profits to be made from the industry, commerce, and land speculation of the West. Indirectly, however, the East became very vitally interested in having new western states which would not disturb the harmony of interests developing between East and West. The Jacksonian era had shown that an alliance of West and South could achieve political and economic results unfavorable to the East. The railroads were developing a great, integrated, national home market to the advantage of both West and East, but the realization of all the advantages of that market required the protective tariff for industry, to which the South was bitterly opposed. To secure substantial and continuing protection for eastern industry, the West had to be induced to vote on the East's side of the tariff controversy. Senator Jefferson Davis, later to be president of the Confederacy, put the matter with extreme bluntness when he said in the Senate that the desire of the North to prevent slavery in the new territories was not to benefit the slaves but "that you may have a majority in the Congress of the United States and convert the government into an engine of northern aggrandizement."[1] If Senator Davis had diagnosed the situation correctly, opposition to slavery in the territories was in fact opposition to the South. In any event, the East did join with the West in supporting not only a Pacific railroad, from which eastern financiers might derive some benefit, but also free homesteads, from which the East would gain little if any direct benefit. "Homesteadism," however, was increasing in strength in the territories of the West, and eastern agreement with it can plausibly be regarded as part of the inducement by which the West was to be won to sound money and the tariff, which the East considered essential to its prosperity.

### The agricultural West

If the chief characteristic of economic development in the East during the middle years from 1800 to 1860 was industrial expansion, the dominant feature of the West's development for the same period was agricultural expansion, with the necessarily accompanying increase in the size of the population and in the extent of the territory which was occupied. Whereas Tennessee and Kentucky were the only states across the Allegheny Mountains in

[1] Quoted in Charles and Mary Beard, *Rise of American Civilization* (New York: The Macmillan Co., 1930), Vol. II, pp. 5–6.

1800, by 1860 all of the territory east of the Mississippi was organized under state governments, with six states west of the Mississippi and with Texas, California, and Oregon in addition, making a total of eighteen trans-Appalachian states. The eastern seaboard states still contained the bulk of the population, but the control of the United States Senate was in the hands of the trans-Allegheny states when they stood together.

In the early years of the middle period, the economic interests of the Northwest and Southwest were often similar. Both were interested in liberal credit for the purchase of land and in internal improvements, which were largely local in character at that time. The development of the Mississippi as an artery of commerce gave the upper Mississippi Valley states a market for their foodstuffs on the cotton-growing plantations of the lower Valley. If these conditions had continued, the common interests of both sections of the West might have produced a profound modification of the later course of American history.

For better or for worse, these conditions did not continue. The upper Valley states were not content with their trade outlet on the Mississippi and eventually obtained the direct connection with the East which they wanted by means of the Cumberland Road, the Erie Canal, and finally the railroads. Thereafter, there began to develop that community of economic interest between Northeast and Northwest which we have been noting. The Jacksonian era constituted a rebuff to the consolidated financial power of the East delivered by both sections of the West acting together, but following that united action, the dominant economic interests of each part of the West led to widening differences between them. The Northwest became more concerned with an extension of the rails and with gaining the right to land ownership legally by occupation and development but without cash payment. The growth of industrial cities in the East seemed to provide promising markets for the agricultural produce of the West, and the West was eventually wooed and won by the East to its policy of tariff protection for industry.

Economically, the West and South moved apart, although both were predominantly agricultural.

It may be said that they moved apart morally also, for the fiercely independent small farmers of the North found the idea of human slavery repugnant, although a large proportion of the leaders of the abolitionist movement came from the East. Perhaps the cynic may say that the western farmer feared the competition of slave labor, but if he did, it was a needless fear, for the superiority of free labor was repeatedly demonstrated. Rather, it would seem plausible that the westerner, faced with the seemingly unlimited opportunities of the frontier, saw no reason why one man should find it necessary for his own economic advantage to keep his brother in subjection. Lacking an economic incentive of his own to perpetuate slavery, the western farmer was able to take a more objective view of the moral aspects of the subjugation of Negroes. His opposition on purely moral grounds is entirely understandable, since no one could reconcile slavery with the strong equalitarianism which persisted among frontiersmen through successive generations.

### The slave-holding South

The economic system of the South, as the war years drew near, came to be identified more and more closely with slavery and the plantation method of growing cotton. This situation had not always existed in the South, and in fact, it is very doubtful that it was as prevalent on the eve of the war as southern spokesmen in public life made it appear. Slavery, of course, was almost as old as white settlement in America, but it was not a rapidly growing institution in colonial days. The Constitution had prohibited any move to bring the slave trade with Africa to an end before 1808, but Congress did, in fact, order its end in 1808 by a law passed in 1807. There is some evidence, in fact, that slavery itself might have been declining until the invention of the cotton gin made cotton growing more profitable and gave slavery a new lease on life. Even

so, in 1860 less than a quarter of the white families of the South owned any slaves at all, and only slightly over half of these slave owners had as many as five slaves.[1] The cold truth is that only a small minority of southern white families were substantial beneficiaries from slavery, although a defensive attitude in relation to it prevailed among other classes.

There is evidence, too, that the South may have been misguided on strict economic grounds in its attachment to slavery. There were obvious advantages in slavery to the owner of slaves, such as complete control over his labor supply, ability to plan the work of the plantation in careful detail, and ability to support a slave at lower cost than a free worker, but there were serious disadvantages too. The plantation operator was likely to be in continuous need of more capital both for land and for slaves; both commodities rose in price in the decades before the war as cotton culture expanded. There was no incentive for a slave to do his best, for to do more work merely meant that his required stint would be increased and he would have to work harder continuously with no benefit to himself. The labor of slaves was involuntary and remained unskilled.

Whether justified or not, whether wisely or unwisely, the South identified its economic future with the maintenance and extension of slavery. To achieve this major goal, the achievement of other intermediate goals became necessary. Concentration upon cotton culture in the deep South by the use of slaves meant reducing even the degree of diversification which had existed there in colonial times. Production of indigo, sugar, and rice either declined or remained important only in very limited areas. The growing of corn and the feeding of hogs did not keep pace with the increase of the southern population, so that the South became an importer of even these staples of its diet from the North and West.

[1] Quoted by L. M. Hacker, *The Triumph of American Capitalism* (New York: Simon and Schuster, Inc., 1940), p. 288 from B. B. Kendrick and A. M. Arnett, *The South Looks at Its Past* (Chapel Hill: University of North Carolina Press, 1935), p. 42. See Fig. IX-1.

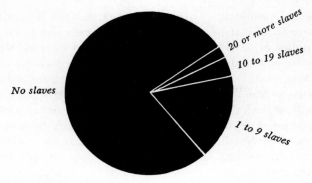

No slaves

20 or more slaves

10 to 19 slaves

1 to 9 slaves

The southern white population of 8,000,000

Fig.IX-1 *The institution of slavery,
though defended by the whole South, benefited
only a small percentage of the population directly.
It is also interesting to compare the number
of small slave holders in 1860
with the number of big plantation owners.*

Tobacco continued to be grown in the border states of Maryland, Virginia, Kentucky, and Tennessee, and slaves could be used in its cultivation, but these states tended to turn more and more to the use of their slaves as a breeding stock with which to produce young field hands for sale to the cotton plantations farther south. Thus the border states found their own economies tied to cotton although they did not grow it extensively themselves.

As the South resolutely pursued an economic course which made the term "cotton kingdom" more a literal than a figurative characterization, it encountered obstacles of several kinds. Basically, the South was pulling away from its earlier common interests with other parts of the country and was tying itself to an international market economy in which it became the specialized producer of seven-eighths of the world's cotton fiber. Some of the obstacles to this course were inherent in the plantation system; others arose from the commercial relations which were essential to a cotton economy. A growing demand for slaves meant continually rising prices for them. To buy land and slaves for the expansion of cultivation required new increments of capital, which the planter class—a leisure-loving and cultured social aristocracy—could not provide

for itself. New capital, therefore, had to be acquired in the financial markets of the East and Europe in competition with an expanding and increasingly productive mechanized industry. The shipping and sale of cotton tended to be handled by mercantile agencies in the principal northeastern seaports, because the highly specialized shipping requirements of the southern economy could not be met efficiently except in conjunction with the more general trade of the major ports. Southern ports did not offer such possibilities of pooling cargo and warehouse space, and Southerners complained that their own business was taken away from them by northern merchants who obtained the profits of the cotton trade and kept the southern planters dependent upon them for mercantile credit. Other requirements for the prosperity of the plantation system have been mentioned in connection with the other regions of the country and need only be listed here. They included the need for a free world market for manufactured goods so that the South could benefit from the low prices and high quality of European merchandise, the need for liberal land and credit policies for the expansion of cotton culture, and the need for transportation to the seaports of the South.

Both the internal and external problems of the slave economy became more acute as the South continued to follow its policy of determined divergence from the economies of the other sections of the nation. The South was really fighting the census returns, as was recognized at the time, since the bulk of both the immigration and the natural increase of population was in the North and West. The North and West opposed the extension of slavery into new territories, and to the South this was essential both for the extension of cotton culture where the soil and climate were suitable and for the political power which new territories would help to give the South in Congress. The Missouri Compromise of 1821 admitted Missouri to the Union as a slave state but prohibited slavery in the remainder of the Louisiana Purchase north of 36°30′. This agreement was repealed in 1854 by the Kansas-Nebraska Bill, which provided that the question of slavery should be left up to the population of a territory to decide.

Southern extremists, worried by the rising costs of slaves, capital, and supplies, advocated the reopening of the African slave trade to bring down the price of slaves. The Dred Scott decision by the Supreme Court in 1857 pleased the South with its philosophy of "once a slave, always a slave," which seemed to promise the spread of slavery into free territory. The defendant, Dred Scott, was declared a slave despite a period of residence in free territory, and the Court declared that Congress had no power to prohibit slavery in the territories, thus making the Missouri Compromise unconstitutional. Despite what seemed like a southern victory in this case, California, Minnesota, and Oregon were admitted as free states during the 1850's, and no slave states were admitted during the same decade.

The new Republican party gathered together the advocates of a protective tariff in the eastern states and those who favored more railroads and free homesteads in the West to elect Abraham Lincoln president in 1860. The Republican platform did not take an extreme position against slavery, and the Democratic party still held control of Congress. But south-

ern leaders felt that the Republican victory in the presidential race was proof that they had failed in their effort to establish and maintain national policies favorable to slavery. They felt that they could escape submission to the North and West on economic policies which they thought would destroy slavery and the plantation system only by seceding from the Union, and that was the path they chose. It was the path to war between brothers.

### Economic factors in the war

The folly of choosing a path which would lead to war should have been apparent to southern leaders, if they had made a rational analysis of the economic elements in the South's position (see Fig. IX-2), and had not dwelt upon the romantic delusion that a need of cotton would bring England to their support and humble the North within a few months. The seceding states had 3,500,000 slaves but only one-third of the white population of the nation. So pressed was the South for manpower that by 1864 nearly all males between 17 and 50 years of age were being conscripted into the army. Over 1,000,000 Southerners saw military service at one time or other during the war, leaving scarcely more than 100,000 men within these age limits to direct industry and trade. The women of the South went to work with a will to replace the labor of the men who had gone to war and to revive the household industries upon which the South was forced to depend in the absence of larger factory industries, but they could hardly make up for this terrific drain on manpower.

At the same time, industry in the South was less than one-tenth of the national total, and the area was particularly lacking in industries essential to the conduct of war. Particularly damaging in this respect was the fact that all of the South's railroad equipment had been supplied by the North. Not having equipment-manufacturing shops of its own, the South then could not replace damaged or destroyed railroad stock. This handicap, plus the poor location and construction of southern railways in the first place, wrought havoc with the southern supply situation, and the military forces suffered severely from inability to obtain necessary supplies in time. Also, transportation by ship was not possible because the southern coastline was immediately blockaded by the United States Navy, and the amount of goods which could be smuggled out to buy needed supplies abroad was entirely inadequate for the purpose. Cotton culture declined sharply during the war years as farming was directed toward the production of wheat, corn, and hogs. Despite this, the southern armies and some southern cities were at times close to starvation, as much from inability to distribute food stocks as from overall shortage.

All of these problems were accentuated by the disastrous methods of financing the war used by the South. The story is essentially a repetition of the financing methods used in the Revolutionary War (p. 129ff.), and indicates that the southern leaders had not learned from that early experience. As before, there was great reluctance to resort to taxation, so that borrowing and the printing press accounted for almost all of the Confederacy's revenues. Borrowing proved effective only at the outset of the war, as the financial disorganization of the South and the general scarcity of capital prevented later recourse to this method. The printing presses, therefore, began to hum, prices skyrocketed, still more money was is-

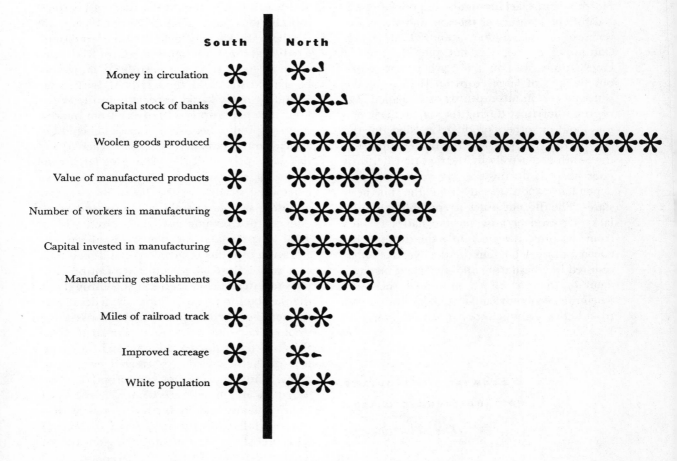

Fig.IX-2 *A comparison between the war potentials of North and South in 1860. The overwhelming economic advantages of the North can be seen at once.*

sued, and the vicious inflationary spiral was under way. By January 1863 the Confederate currency was already badly inflated, and it grew worse. The result, as in the Revolutionary War, was extreme difficulty in procuring supplies and complete disorganization of economic life in the South. Had it not been for the southern advantage in military leadership and the heart-breaking devotion of many southern people to a hopeless cause, the Civil War would have lasted much less than four years.

The superior economic strength of the North was as obvious as the weakness of the South. With more than two-thirds of the population of the country, taking into account the southern slaves, with nearly all its manufacturing industry and food-producing farms, the North was not lacking in any important essential for the conduct of the war and the maintenance of the civilian standard of living. Cotton, of course, was not plentiful, but a large supply was on hand when war broke out because of large crops on the eve of the war, and cotton was captured or smuggled into northern territory during the war in exchange for food or other products needed in the South. England was deterred from supporting the South extensively by the fact that her own poor harvests during the war years made her dependent upon wheat from the northern states. She did not suffer irreparably from the lack of cotton because she too had a surplus from the prewar years. Only the disputes between political factions in the North, which resulted in a hesitating and inefficient management of the war effort, prevented the overwhelming economic advantage of the North from being felt much sooner than it was.

### Economic life during war and reconstruction

*The industrial East*

Economically, the Civil War precipitated the triumph of American industrial capitalism.

Jefferson had been wrong. America was to be a great industrial nation. It is true that eastern industrial dominance in government was achieved by an alliance with western agriculture, but the latter was treated as a junior partner in the enterprise of capturing the government of the United States. The West must be appeased from time to time to keep its people thinking straight, but any foolish notions of theirs, such as printing more money to be used in western land development and speculation, must be quietly suppressed. The planter capitalism of the South was undermined at its roots, and the coast was clear for the unrestrained expansion of large-scale, capitalistic industry.

The outbreak of fighting between North and South had brought on a wave of contract cancellations and general retrenchment in northern business which led to depression. Credits granted to southerners for the purchase of goods from northern firms proved to be a total loss, and thousands of businesses, including many banks, especially in the West, went into bankruptcy. Recovery from depression was prompt because of a brisk demand for agricultural produce from abroad, where crops had been poor, and the placing of large contracts for war supplies. Industry had been expanding steadily in the North for decades, adopting new large-scale machines and processes as they became available. Now, with a great new demand for war goods, the mechanization of industry achieved the dimensions of a real Industrial Revolution. Cotton supplies remained below requirements throughout the war, but, to replace cotton, the federal government bought anything that even looked like wool. The woolen industry expanded more than any other during the war, and the members of the new rich class created by government contracts were not inappropriately referred to as "shoddy aristocracy." The steel industry really had its birth in America during and following the war, when it came to be centered in the Pittsburgh region and to use the Bessemer furnace for large-scale steel production. Iron and steel were available throughout the war for the manufacture of rifles, cannon, and other war equipment, as well as for the extension of rail lines, for the manufacture of locomotives and rolling stock to equip the additional lines, and for agricultural and industrial machinery. Improvements on the sewing machine made possible a rapid development of the ready-made clothing industry, and moved the manufacture of shoes completely out of the home and into the factory.

The financial effects of the war are less pleasant to contemplate than the industrial. The rôle of money in an economic system seems to be so mysterious to many people that they fall into the error of believing that it can achieve magic results. A war period brings the need for more goods because war demands are simply added to regular peace-time demands. These larger quantities of goods can be supplied only by more production, and if it is impossible to meet war needs by additional production, then there is no alternative but to cut civilian use of goods by one means or another. This simple logic has escaped many persons even in the middle of the twentieth century, after two world wars. Certainly it was not widely understood and acted upon during the Civil War in the North and, as we have seen, even less so in the South. Secretary of the Treasury Salmon P. Chase adopted the policy of borrowing to meet war expenses and taxing for the regular functions of government, including payment of interest on the debt. Tariff duties were raised at almost every session of Congress during the war, now that the southern opposition was absent, both to raise revenue and to stimulate industrial expansion, and excise taxes were placed on domestic products to keep pace with the tariffs. An income tax was also levied, at very low rates by twentieth-century standards.

All of these taxes taken together were inadequate to meet the increasing needs of the government, and, since they were levied in rather leisurely fashion during the first year or so of the war, they were slow in yielding returns. To meet emergency needs the Treasury was forced to borrow from the banks. The requirement of a reserve of United States

bonds behind the notes issued by the National Banks aided the sale of the bonds. When these bond sales became more and more difficult in spite of high rates of interest, Congress authorized the printing of United States notes which had no backing except the general credit of the government. These notes, which were soon dubbed "Greenbacks" because of their color, fell below full face value at once and never got back to full value until 1879, when they were made redeemable in gold. On the eve of the battle of Gettysburg, they reached a new low, from which they recovered after the northern victory, but they then resumed their fall to an all-time low value of less than forty cents in 1864. The mere printing of new currency could not of itself create the war supplies which the government had to have. Its only possible effect, therefore, was to push up the prices of goods of all kinds, since more money was being offered in the markets for the same quantity of goods. Gold disappeared from use, and the low price of Greenbacks, as measured in gold, was merely another way of measuring the height of prices expressed in paper currency.

The country had to pay the price which has always had to be paid for a money system which is permitted to deteriorate through mismanagement. Gold money, which was regarded as sound by the people, was constantly held in reserve against the greater uncertainties of the future, and the paper Greenbacks were constantly passed along in the course of daily business lest they should depreciate in value still further. This was a prime example of the economic axiom that bad money drives out good. Thus the country was forced to get along with an unstable and deteriorating currency during the war and to pay the ever higher prices which were demanded for the necessities of life. The government, too, suffered by its own inadequate monetary system, since it also had to pay the constantly increasing prices. Much of the value to the government of the new issues of Greenbacks was lost by the high prices which those Greenbacks forced upon the national economy.

Industrial expansion, price inflation, and

the construction of new buildings for business and of homes for a growing population gave both the impression and much of the substance of prosperity during the war. Less conspicuous than these things was the fact that labor was not able to get its wages in paper money advanced as rapidly as prices rose, so that workers found increasing difficulty in making ends meet. Professional people found themselves in a similar dilemma. Farm prices were high and farmers were prosperous, as were businessmen of all kinds who were able to adjust their prices to keep up with or to lead the general price increases. Although government loans were not floated easily, adequate capital was available for private business operations. Consolidation of railway and communication lines into unified systems first became conspicuous during the war, partly in response to the great demands of the war itself. New millionaires by the dozen were created, and many of the financial and industrial wizards who gained fame in the next generation after the war got their start as young men in the lush days of the conflict.

By the end of the war, the financial and industrial interests of the country, with the seat of their operations in the eastern cities, had pretty well established themselves and their program in a position of power and influence in American government. Some of the important elements of that program may be picked out for special notice.

(1) America was firmly embarked upon a program of high, protective tariffs for the benefit primarily of industry, but with rates to appeal to woolgrowers and other agrarian groups. Tariffs had not been raised significantly in the quarter-century prior to the war after the demonstration of serious southern opposition in 1832. The war provided an excuse for raising the rates, since additional revenue was obviously needed. But truly protective rates yield less revenue because they keep out the kinds of goods upon which they are levied. The receipts from customs duties did in fact increase in the last years of the war, but the objective of the Republican-controlled Congress was to protect budding

American industries in order to speed their growth. This continued to be the official governmental policy, with slight variation, for nearly three-quarters of a century.

(2) A more stable monetary system was established by the National Banking Acts of 1863, 1864, and 1865. A system of privately owned but federally chartered and regulated banks was provided for. These National Banks might issue their own bank notes on the security of United States bonds and gold held by the Treasury. State bank notes were subjected to an annual tax which drove them out of existence. The deposits of National Banks had to be backed up by specified reserves. National Bank inspectors were appointed and might make an examination of the affairs of any National Bank at any time. The cause of sound money was also furthered by the Coinage Act of 1873, which dropped silver from the legal money classification, and by the act which provided for the redemption of Greenbacks in gold upon any holder's demand on and after January 1, 1879.

(3) A Pacific railroad was provided for when Congress in 1862 incorporated the Union Pacific and Central Pacific Railroads, which were to connect existing railroads in Nebraska with the Pacific coast. Subsidies, both in cash and in alternate sections of land along the right of way, were granted to both railroads. This was a most significant action in several respects. It marked the first large-scale government subsidy to a privately owned business in which the government had no share of ownership and no legal basis for control or supervision. It also marked the assumption of control of the federal government by the combination of eastern financial interests and western agricultural interests which had been blocked in their previous quest for power by the representatives from the South. By this action of Congress the growth of a unified nationalism in America was confirmed. Eastern industry and western agriculture could reach markets anywhere on the continent. Land speculators, including the owners of the railroads, who now became the biggest speculators of all, were given a free hand.

(4) The Homestead Act was passed by Congress in 1862 to provide for the granting of 160 acres of government land without charge to any individual who filed a claim for it and lived on it and improved it for a period of years. This was a response to an increasingly insistent demand from the immigrants to western territories, but it also had features to please the dominant interests of the East. If land were free, western farmers would acquiesce in a sound money system desired by the East as they did in the later enactment of the National Bank Acts. A large part of the western demand for a banking policy based on easy lending would be eliminated when land could be acquired without making a loan on it at the bank. Furthermore, the existence of hundreds of thousands of independent homesteads in the West would constitute the ultimate barrier to the further spread of slavery. At the same time, these independent homesteaders would constitute the most substantial market for eastern industry. Thus the Homestead Act satisfied the yearnings of varied groups in both East and West and was an important element in the program of the Civil War Congresses.

(5) The Fourteenth Amendment to the Constitution was adopted, denying to states as the Fifth Amendment had denied to Congress the right to deprive any person of life, liberty, or property without "due process of law." Northern states willingly accepted the amendment and the southern states were required to accept it as one of the conditions for readmission to the Union. It appeared to be merely a permanent guarantee of the civil rights of the new Negro citizens. However, administered by a new political party in control of the federal government under the leadership of a new economic group of industrialists and financiers in eastern cities, the Fourteenth Amendment soon emerged as much more than a bar to the return of slavery in the states. In the decades after the war the term "person" was broadened to include almost any kind of corporate entity, so that corporations gained all of the legal rights of persons in addition to those inherent in their own nature as immortal and suprapersonal agencies. The courts also construed the term "due process" to apply not merely to the procedure which had been followed by states and their subdivisions in making legal enactments but to the substance of those actions also. Thus the economic views of one section of the population in a strategic position in control of the federal government were applied not merely by the federal government in its own activities but also through decisions of the Supreme Court to actions by states. The Fourteenth Amendment became the Constitutional bulwark of the economic program of the Republican party. The effects of the operation of this program in American economic life became apparent in the interval of a half-century between the Civil War and World War I.

### The agricultural West

The success of the East in achieving its own economic and political program meant that the agricultural West was brought into alignment, at least temporarily, with the industrial sections of the country. The railroads, which had reached into the plains states in the decade of the 1850's, brought substantial prosperity to western farmers in the sixties by carrying their wheat, corn, and livestock to market in the growing industrial cities of the East, and to eastern seaports for export to Europe. The drain on manpower imposed by the Civil War was more severe both absolutely and in proportion to the total population than in either of the subsequent World Wars. But in spite of the loss of men to the army and to the cities, the farming sections stepped up production of wheat right through the war period to meet not only the food needs of our own country but also those of Europe, especially England. This great food-producing ability proved to be a very real military asset in provisioning the northern armies and in preventing the development of any ideas among the English people that it might be to their advantage to back the Confederate cause in order to renew their raw cotton supply.

The West depended absolutely upon the

railroads to get its food products to market, but more than good transportation was essential to achieve the production itself. The most important contribution came from the numerous new farm machines which were being developed by the new farm-implement industry. The new steel plows, reapers, and other kinds of machinery had been experimented with and improved during the preceding decades. They had been tried out on a scale broad enough so that farmers everywhere knew about them and what they would do in saving labor. When the war brought greater demands for food with fewer men to do the work, the machines came into widespread use. Necessity and abundant cash overcame the doubts of even the most skeptical farmers. Iron and steel plows, mowing machines, rakes, reapers, and threshers were bought and used by farmers on a larger scale than ever before. Farm machines did not win the war, but their contribution to the final outcome was considerable.

Another factor in the high level of farm output during the war period was the continuation of European immigration to the new farm areas of the West. The early war years checked the inflow, but it resumed in the last year or two. Immigration was not sufficient to replace the manpower drawn into the army, but, together with the increased use of machinery, it helped to prevent the drop in food production which would otherwise have been inevitable during the war years. It is also of importance that many of the immigrants of this period continued on through the eastern states to the fertile lands of Wisconsin, Minnesota, and Iowa, where they bought farms already developed. In this way, they made a large and immediate contribution to the food supply of the North.

Agriculture was the principal source of the wartime prosperity of the West, but other factors contributed also. Railroad building continued in the North during the war, and that meant employment and the spending of funds in the western states. The demand for ties for the railroads as well as building lumber for cities and farms brought prosperity to the northern lumbering regions. The iron ore deposits of northern Michigan and Minnesota were worked more intensively during the war to supply the steel industry in the upper Ohio River Valley. New deposits of silver, gold, copper, and other metals in the Rocky Mountain region attracted speculators from western farms to add to their labor shortage, but also to contribute to western prosperity through the expansion of mining. Almost every branch of agriculture and western extractive industry felt some of the wartime demand for goods, and thus made some contribution to the general national prosperity.

*The South*

The war brought a more intensive economic development to the North and West, but it brought destruction, disorganization, and decay to the South. The burning and devastation of property wrought by Sherman's army in Georgia and Sheridan's army in the Shenandoah Valley of Virginia were far worse than any similar damage done by any of the armies of the Confederacy in northern territory. But it is the opinion of many students of the South during the war that the dislocation of the southern economy forced by the war and the blockade were ultimately of even more damaging effect than all the physical damage done to southern farms, cities, and supplies. Economic disorganization is not as obvious to the eye as a burned and gutted city, but its effects on war potential may be worse. The South had specialized in raising products (cotton and tobacco) for sale on the world market. The basis of the efficient, economic functioning of the South was as a specialist in the production of these commodities. When the United States Navy was able to maintain and strengthen the blockade of southern ports during the successive years of the war, the southern economy could not be reorganized on a self-sufficient basis rapidly enough to keep an effective fighting force in the field. Economic weakness lay behind the collapse of the southern military effort.

The South and its people made heroic efforts to overcome their economic shortages.

All kinds of industries to make products essential in wartime were started in the South. Southern armies never lacked cannon, shells, powder, and armor plate, which had scarcely been made in the area before the war. Production of paper, wool blankets, clothing, matches, candles, pottery, cutlery, and countless other articles was begun. During the war years, when artificial scarcity persisted and prices were highly inflated, many of these industries were able to make ends meet, and even to make profits, in spite of lack of skilled labor and proper equipment. Very few of them were able to attain a really efficient basis of operation, so that at the end of the war nearly all of the South's wartime industries were ruined in the general collapse of the southern economy.

If one were to use the emotional language that was common during the Civil War era, the South at the end of the war could well be described as starved, broken, and bleeding. Yet an almost worse fate awaited her in the first decade or more after the war as she became a pawn of northern political groups, each trying to consolidate its own power. The underlying conflict of the war was between the planter capitalism of the South, producing staple commodities for a world market by a method of large-scale farming with slaves, and a partnership of rapidly expanding northern industrial capitalism with western agriculture carried on by speculating, free-holding, independent farmers. Victory in the war removed any immediate economic threat to northern capitalism from the southern planter and his slaves. But the political leaders of the industrial East felt the need of consolidating the victory by cementing their economic union with western farmers, and at the same time preventing the South from again gaining political power either on its own or by a new partnership with the West. Eastern leaders had been diligent in their wooing of the West with a Pacific railroad and liberal land laws. They now had to insure also that southern power was undermined permanently, if possible, by the reconstruction program which the South was compelled to follow.

Northern proposals for southern reconstruction ranged from extreme mildness to unreasonable severity. There were a few persons who felt that the attempted secession of the southern states had been prevented by the war, and that after the war these states should simply resume their place in the federal government. At the other pole was the radical theory that the southern states had in fact seceded by their own choice, and that, having been defeated in war, the South was now a "conquered province." The leaders of the "radical Republicans" came from the East, and they wanted to be sure that the reconstruction of the seceded states was accomplished in such a way that the South would never again be any threat to the political rule of the Northeast. In other words, reconstruction was to be used, like the Fourteenth Amendment, as a bulwark behind which the industrial and financial interests which had become dominant in the Republican party hoped to maintain themselves in power. The debate in Congress between these and other positions not only brought laws and taxes to punish the South for its secession, but also left it the victim of indecision and changes in policy. Southern states were required not only to approve the Fourteenth Amendment but to set up state governments which were properly purged of rebels before they might be readmitted to the Union and regain the privilege of holding elections for state and national offices.

The slaves were of course freed and were organized into political groups which, it was hoped, would give the Republican party power in the South at the expense of the traditional Democratic party. The extremists in the North advocated the confiscation of all property of the leaders in the secession movement, and, since most of them were planters, the division of their large estates into small holdings to be distributed among the freedmen. However, this most radical proposal failed. Many planters, having lost their slaves and having had their capital drained away by the war, were forced into bankruptcy. The buyers, who were either men from the North or former successful speculators during the war in the South, commonly bought out the plantations as a unit. There was a substantial increase in small holdings in the South during the Reconstruction era, but large plantations remained very common also, although their farming system had to be modified to accommodate free labor. The former slaves were unused to working for wages, and landowners at the same time lacked capital to pay money wages. The compromise that seemed best under the circumstances was the sharecropping system. Land was split up into tracts small enough so that one family could manage one. The crop was shared in varying ratios between tenants and owner. Advances of seed, fertilizer, and food for the tenant family were made by the landowner or neighboring storekeeper, who were very often one and the same person.

The last "reconstructed" states were not readmitted to the union until 1876, and the last federal soldiers were not removed from the South until the next year. By that time, the progress of industry, agriculture, and population outside of the South seemed to give these other sections of the country an amply safe political control over the forming of national economic policies. The South had not found, nor had it been helped to find, an alternative labor system to slavery on which it could build a substantial economic prosperity. Reconstruction had been handled in a manner more vindictive than constructive, and the battered South was now left to its own devices.

For lack of any alternatives, southerners continued with an agricultural system based upon unskilled, manual labor. The South attained a kind of peace and stability in a return to a cotton and tobacco economy, but its agriculture did not prevent the section from lagging behind the rest of the nation in the economic improvement of the next half-century or more. Nor were the southern economy and society in step with the democratic and egalitarian tendencies which were gaining ever fuller expression in other segments of American life. The southern economy retained a relatively small owning group at the top and a large base of white and Negro unskilled labor at the bottom. These latter groups composed the largest bloc of individuals with low income existing anywhere in the American economy. Even after World War I, when the migration of industry to the South was accelerated, the commonest reason was to get the advantage of so-called "cheap" southern labor. That is a self-defeating objective for industry, and after World War II, for probably the first time in history, the per capita income of the southern states increased faster than the national average. This long delay in the growth of southern economic well-being must be attributed in large part to the deep injuries of the Civil War and reconstruction periods.

## FOR FURTHER READING

Barnes, James A. *Wealth of the American People*. New York: Prentice-Hall, Inc., 1949. Chapters 17 and 18.

Bogart, E. L., and Kemmerer, Donald L. *Economic History of the American People*. 2nd ed. New York: Longmans, Green & Co., Inc., 1947. Chapters 17 and 18.

Callender, G. S. *Selections from the Economic History of the United States, 1765-1860*. Boston: Ginn & Co., 1909. Chapter 15.

Craven, Avery C. *Coming of the Civil War*. New York: Charles Scribner's Sons, 1942. Somewhat biased from the Southern view, but economic emphasis is interesting.

Faulkner, Harold Underwood. *American Economic History*. 8th ed. New York: Harper & Brothers, 1960. Chapters 16 and 17.

Mitchell, Broadus, and Mitchell, Louise Pearson. *American Economic History*. Boston: Houghton Mifflin Co., 1947. Chapters 21—23.

Nevins, A. *Ordeal of the Union*. New York: Charles Scribner's Sons, 1947. Volume I, Chapters 13—15.

Shannon, Fred Albert. *America's Economic Growth*. 3rd ed. New York: The Macmillan Co., 1951. Chapters 16 and 17.

Wright, Chester W. *Economic History of the United States*. 2nd ed. New York: McGraw-Hill Book Co., 1949. Chapter 28.

# Chapter 10: The frontier and the farmer after 1860

**T**wo factors were mainly responsible for the settlement of the American frontier during the first three decades following the Civil War. These factors were the rapid increase of population and the railroads, which opened up vast areas of the West to this human throng. Each of the three decades from 1860 to 1890 showed an aggregate population increase for the United States of more than 25 per cent. By 1890 the population was twice what it had been in 1860. The high birth rate which had characterized the first half of the nineteenth century did not begin to decline materially until around 1900. Furthermore, immigrants from the countries of northern Europe were streaming to America to seek the bonanza of cheap land. To get a comparative measure of this population increase, it might be noted that for the two decades from 1890 to 1910 the increase dropped to just over 20 per cent per decade, and that from 1910 to 1930 the increase averaged less than 16.6 per cent per decade.

The occupation of continental United States was unique to the extent that, although the main line of settlement was from the East toward the West, the central portions of the country, except for the Mormon settlement in Utah, were fully occupied last. This pattern of development followed the discovery of gold in California in 1848, which led to a great migration to the Pacific coast, after which the remaining mid-continent region was settled from both the West and the East. Transportation inward for the immigrants with their furniture, tools, and livestock, and, very soon, transportation outward for their products was always necessary for settlement. The American West is a rugged and dry land with few slow-flowing and dependable rivers to furnish the first transportation as they did along the Atlantic coast and in the Mississippi Valley. The plains were level and treeless, so that to have a passable road necessitated no construction but merely continuous use of the same place by horses and wagons. But distances were great in the West, and pony express, stages, and wagons could not be relied upon for hauling more than the mail and very light or valuable cargo. The only real and practical answer to all of the problems of settlement in the West was the extension of the railroads. Once railroads had been built from the Atlantic coast to the Mississippi, the obvious next step was their rapid extension into the Rocky Mountain area and on to the Pacific coast.

## Completing
## the western railway network

For almost ninety years prior to 1916 the building of railroads was carried on in America, at first cautiously and tentatively until the great value of the roads was demonstrated, then more boldly and even with an air of urgency which at times approached frenzy. By 1916 the American railway network reached its greatest extent in terms of miles of road in operation, with a total of just under 260,000 miles. Fig. X-1 on p. 206 shows how mileage grew from one decade to the next. In more detail, construction was as follows:

The decade of the 1850's witnessed an increase of more than 21,000 miles of road in operation despite the setback of the depression in 1857. Even though the Civil War checked building somewhat in the '60's, over 22,000 miles of road were nevertheless constructed. In the '70's the pace of building became frenzied and the area affected became broader. The financial panic of 1873 followed by depression slowed down construction, but the new mileage was still nearly double that of preceding decades, reaching 40,000. The all-time peak in building was achieved in the 1880's, when 73,441 additional miles were put into operation. While building would probably have dropped in the 1890's in any case, the depression beginning in 1893 reduced the total of new line to 36,000 miles. From 1900 to 1910, there was no prolonged depression to reduce new construction and the total went back up to 48,000 miles. From 1910 to the peak in 1916, a final 20,000 miles were added

to the American rail system.[1] By that time the United States had more miles of railroad than all of Europe, and more than one-third of the world mileage.

East of the Mississippi River, the building of railroads was accomplished by private financiers and promoters with aid in financing and construction from local communities and states which had an interest in having the road built. As the rails were extended west of the Mississippi into sparsely settled territory, this method of financing proved inadequate. Building lagged until federal aid was granted for the building of a road to the Pacific coast.

Congress in 1862 authorized the construction of a transcontinental railroad over a middle route, and the Union Pacific was chartered to build westward from Omaha while the Central Pacific was to build eastward across the mountains from Sacramento. Liberal financial aid was given to the roads by the government. For each mile of line built they were offered ten square miles of land on each side of their track alternately (amounting to 20 square miles for each two miles of road), and the government gave them first mortgage loans of $16,000 a mile on the plains, $32,000 in the intermountain plateaus, and $48,000 in the mountains. But private capital was not attracted to the venture until a revised law in 1864 doubled the land grant to the roads and permitted them to borrow on private first mortgage loans in the same amount as the government loan, which would then become a second mortgage obligation. With this more liberal provision, the companies began construction enthusiastically. Since the subsidy was on a mileage basis, a longer and easier route was always chosen in preference to a more direct one. Toward the end, the building became a wild scramble between the two companies to see which could build more line and get more of the subsidy. The Central Pacific imported the first Chinese immigrants to

[1] All figures of railway mileage taken from *Historical Statistics of the United States, 1789-1945* (Washington, D. C.: Bureau of the Census, 1949), Series K1, p. 200, and K31, p. 202.

America to work on its end of the line, and the Union Pacific used thousands of Irish immigrants and discharged Civil War soldiers. For more than a year before the final meeting of the two roads at Promontory Point, Utah, on May 10, 1869, the U. P. had built an average of two and a half miles of line a day.

The completion of a rail line to the Pacific Ocean tied the sections of the nation together and promoted the settlement of the interior region. It was thus of tremendous economic benefit to the country. But the level of conduct in public life which was reached by the promoters of the Union and Central Pacific Railroads represented a low point in our national history. Promoters of the Union Pacific formed a construction company, the Crédit Mobilier, which handled most of the cash received from both private investors and the government. The directors of the U. P. were also directors of Crédit Mobilier, and thus received personally the exorbitant profits of the financing operations of the company. The actual construction costs were later estimated at not over $50,000,000, while the directors had received $73,000,000. When Congress was considering investigation of the matter, the U. P. "sold" shares of stock on credit to influential members of Congress, the shares to be paid for later from dividends. A number of men high in government circles were involved in this scandal, among them a man who was later to be president of the United States—James A. Garfield. The record of Leland Stanford, Charles Crocker, and other directors of the Central Pacific was no better, although the similar construction company which they formed received less publicity.

Other Pacific railroad projects were undertaken even before the completion of the Union Pacific. In the early 1870's a Kansas division of the U. P. was completed to Cheyenne, Wyoming, to connect with the main line. Several roads that became the Atchison, Topeka, and Santa Fe connected Kansas with the Pacific coast by way of New Mexico and Southern California in 1884. Also in the early 1880's the Texas Pacific and Southern Pacific competed for the New Orleans business by lines across Texas and New Mexico to Southern California and San Francisco. In the north, the easiest route of all to the coast was used by the Northern Pacific with its line from Duluth to Tacoma, Washington. Jay Cooke, who had played a prominent part in the sale of bonds for the government during the Civil War, pushed the building of the Northern Pacific until his firm failed, which helped bring on the panic and depression of 1873. The building of the railroad, like many other such projects, was stopped for several years, but it was finally completed in 1883. Most of

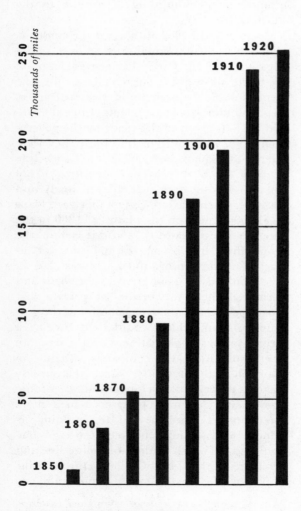

Fig.X-1 *The building of railroads in the United States between 1850 and 1920 led to an enormous increase in mileage of road owned and used.*

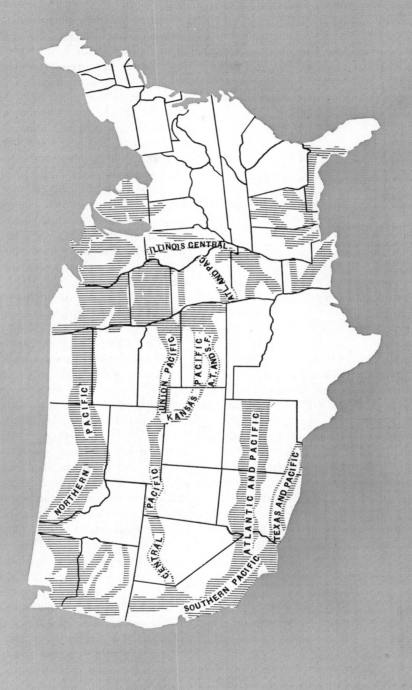

*Fig. X-2 Land granted by the government to railroads.*

these roads received no government cash loans as had the Union and Central Pacific, but they were the beneficiaries of a liberal government policy on land grants. The Northern Pacific received a larger acreage than any other of the Pacific railroads, twenty sections[1] per mile through Minnesota and forty per mile the remainder of the distance to the Pacific.

### The western land grants

*Grants to*

*railroads and public corporations*

The total area of continental United States is a little more than 1,900,000,000 acres. Of this amount, about one-quarter was included in the original thirteen colonies and thus was never part of the federal public domain. By 1860, the federal government had sold or given away almost an additional quarter, leaving about 1,000,000,000 acres in the public domain. In the next three decades, the period of western railroad building and settlement, roughly a third quarter of our national territory was disposed of, nearly all of it given away. In 1890, just under 600,000,-000 acres remained in the public domain and this, by the 1940's, was reduced to a fairly stable residue of about 170,000,000 acres, exclusive of parks and reserved lands.

Evidently, the period of the most rapid disposition of the public lands was from 1860 to 1890, when they were distributed free of charge. There were three principal ways in which Congress made provision for the disposition of public land: (1) the Morrill Act of 1862, providing for grants of land to the states which could be sold to assist in establishing colleges to teach "agriculture and the mechanic arts"; (2) the Homestead Act of 1862, providing for grants of a quarter-section (160 acres) to individuals who would occupy and improve the land for five years after payment

[1] A section was 640 acres, or a square mile.

of a nominal fee; and (3) grants made directly to railroads and other transportation companies, primarily in the 1860's and early 1870's. Grants to states to support education under the Morrill and other acts eventually passed 200,000,000 acres. Railroads were granted another 200,000,000, about a third of which later reverted to the government in cases when road-building projects were not completed. The total of about 135,000,000 acres in railroad grants is a very remarkable figure, especially when it is remembered that they were all in the western states (see Fig. X-2, p. 207). As much as one-fourth of Minnesota and Washington were included in railroad grants, as were substantial fractions of other western states. Furthermore, since these grants were in bands adjoining the railroad right of way, they were likely to be the most valuable lands, both because of nearness to transportation and because railroads were likely to follow valleys wherever possible.

The great extent of the land grants to western railroads put the roads into the land business as a first step in raising the capital necessary for railroad construction. The roads opened land offices and ran advertisements in eastern periodicals in the effort to attract purchasers. At times, special consideration was given to transporting settlers to their new homes. The railroads also found it to their advantage to exert such influence as they could in local and national political matters affecting their land and transportation interests. In those states which have never developed dense populations, the railroads have remained very powerful behind-the-scenes factors in economic and political life. This could happen the more easily since the railroad was usually the source of economic life blood to the plains and mountain states and territories. It brought in the settler in the first instance, it probably sold him the land on which he began farming or ranching, it brought in all of his tools and supplies and all of the necessities and luxuries of life which he was able to get, and it carried off to market all of the produce he could coax from his land. Thus the railroad occupied a much larger place in

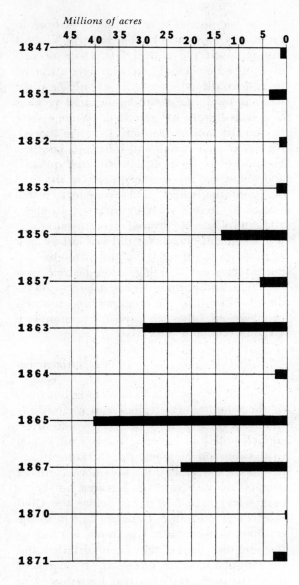

Millions of acres

| | 45 | 40 | 35 | 30 | 25 | 20 | 15 | 10 | 5 | 0 |

1847
1851
1852
1853
1856
1857
1863
1864
1865
1867
1870
1871

*Fig. X-3 The size of public land grants to the railroads in various years from 1847 to 1871.*

the economic life of the West than in the more densely settled East.

*Grants to individuals*

Perhaps the location and quality of the railroad land grants explain the fact that the Homestead Act at first was more important as a symbol than as a real element in early western settlement. By 1890, only about 48,000,000 acres had been granted under the Act, just over one-third of the amount of the railroad grants and less than a quarter of the educational and other public grants. If a settler had any financial resources at all, it was certainly better business to buy a tract from the railroad at the going price and have its services available to him than to go back either twenty miles in the states or forty in the territories over a road scarcely worthy of the name to take up a homestead claim from the government. It was not until the West was pretty well developed along the railroads that homestead claims began to increase in volume. The decade from 1890 to 1900 saw as large an acreage of claims completed as the entire period from 1862 to 1885. After 1900, the rate of completing claims continued to rise, reaching a peak of more than 74,000,000 acres in the decade from 1910 to 1920.[1]

If the intention of the Homestead Act was to prevent land speculation and to establish a system of small landholders, it was not entirely successful in this regard. The Preëmption Act of 1841 remained law until 1891, and under it the holder of a homestead could purchase another quarter-section at $1.25 per acre, or $200 for the quarter-section. Further, in 1873, under the guise of encouraging the planting of trees, Congress passed the Timber Culture Act granting a quarter-section of prairie land to anyone who would agree to plant trees. Other acts besides these made it possible for an individual to get as many as 1,280 acres of government land, and every member of a single family who was over twenty-one years of age could obtain this amount of land. Homestead claims could be repeated if land were available, and often there was dishonesty in meeting the conditions of residing on the land and improving it. Relatively small holdings remained characteristic in the West, although from Illinois to California, and especially in Texas, there

[1] All data from *Historical Statistics of the United States, op. cit.,* Series F16, pp. 119-120.

could be found occasional holdings running into the tens of thousands of acres.

## Stages of western land settlement

In the first generation after the Civil War an area of the West was settled as large as the area occupied in the first 250 years of America's history. This great physical feat would have been entirely impossible without the railroads. The exploration and partial occupancy of the West which had taken place before the coming of the rails were very important in preparation for the rapid settlement which the railroads made possible. The successive steps in the development of new territory in the West are of interest not only to economic history, but also for their contribution to American folklore.

### The miner's frontier

Following the first explorations of the Far West by men like Lewis and Clark, Zebulon Pike, and others (see p. 140), the next white men to put in an appearance in the area were likely to be fur traders and trappers, after whom came prospectors and miners. The discovery of gold in California gave an indication—even an exaggerated indication—of the mineral wealth of the Rocky Mountain region. For a number of years, California was the attraction for those from the East and all over the world who sought quick wealth in the search for gold. As new discoveries in California tended to decline, prospectors spread out. In 1859 a rush to Colorado was started when rumors of gold there were confirmed, but the rush quickly died when it was found that costly refining machinery was required to secure it. In the early 1860's, the discovery of silver in the "Comstock Lode" in western Utah Territory brought a great influx of miners and prospectors, which led to the creation of the state of Nevada in 1864. To the south, discoveries in New Mexico territory and, to the north, strikes in Washington and Idaho Territories led to the growth of many boom towns.

So widespread were mining operations in the Rocky Mountain region that the "miner's frontier" was the typical •first phase of permanent settlement. Those who were attracted by real or alleged discoveries of gold or silver were as footloose, venturesome, and reckless a crew as history has recorded. Women were few on the mining frontier. Life was rugged, highly unstable, and not suited to families. Fortunes were often made easily and quickly, and sometimes lost just as quickly in the turn of a gambling wheel. There was little incentive to live temperately or frugally. Robbery and gunplay were everyday occurrences. It was a colorful era, but it did not last as long as subsequent romancing about it might lead one to believe. Holdings soon became consolidated, and mining became a large-scale industry with all of the economic and business problems of other and more commonplace kinds of economic endeavor.

### The cattle drives

While prospectors were seeking bonanzas in the mountainous regions and establishing communities for the mining of gold, silver, copper, and lead, several factors contributed to the creation of a new cattle-grazing industry on the Great Plains. Longhorn cattle of original Spanish stock had grazed on Texas ranges for three centuries. Before the Civil War, they had found a market largely in the cotton-growing areas of the South, but during the war that market had been curtailed and the size of the herds increased. In search of better pastures, ranchers had been forced to drive their herds farther north. The discovery about 1867 that cattle could survive out on the range during northern winters opened the way to cattle grazing on the central and northern Great Plains as well as in Texas. At nearly the same time, the Union Pacific began operating its line to the west coast across the central plains, and, soon thereafter, lines both to the north and to the south of the U. P. were also available. The presence of railroads meant that the cattle from the ranges could be taken to market, and a new industry was created.

Little effort had been made to control or improve the breeding of Texas cattle, but now that grazing was becoming a big business, such efforts were called for. Hereford, Angus, and Shorthorn bulls were introduced, of European stock. Of these the white-faced Hereford, first brought to America by Henry Clay a half century earlier, proved to be most adaptable. The cowboys were a phenomenon of open-range cattle grazing. They lived with their herds during the grazing season, gradually working the cattle north toward a "cowtown" on the railroad where they would be shipped off in the autumn. The main breeding herds were kept nearer home, where they would be rounded up in the late spring of the year, the new calves branded, and the yearling steers and other stock designated for market made into a separate herd for the summer-long drive to the railroad.

For perhaps two decades prior to 1885, open-range grazing and cattle drives were in their heyday. It was a highly profitable business for a time. Little or no investment in land or buildings was required, and, when the range was available, a sizable herd could be built up in a few years. After about 1885, however, the ranchers ran into trouble. Glutted markets in the fall of the year depressed prices of cattle severely, once the business had developed into a large-scale operation. High shipping prices and low prices paid by meat packers squeezed out much of the rancher's profit. In addition, the ranges became filled to overflowing and trouble developed between ranchers, i.e., men claiming the various ranges, especially between sheep and cattle ranchers in the north. In the arid West, the whole grazing operation was possible only when water holes were accessible. There was no provision in the Homestead Act or any other land-grant act to preserve common rights in the water holes, so that very naturally they were the first areas taken into private ownership. Then, too, early experiments in the manufacture of barbed wire had resulted by 1874 in the development of a satisfactory type, which the steel industry had now grown large enough to supply. Desirable ranges and water sources began to be fenced off against the traveling herds. The cattle men fought back against those who would encroach upon their territory, but it was a losing battle, for the land laws all favored permanent settlement. When the enclosure of the ranges was in full swing, it is said that barbed wire was shipped to western stations not in carloads but in whole trainloads. Open-range grazing continued only on land too dry to support permanent settlement or on lands retained by the government.

Cattle ranching left its mark in our history in the cowboy ballad, if in no other way. If one were to judge the industry by the mental outlook of its hired hands as revealed in their songs, one would have to conclude that it was rather melancholy and monotonous. The cowboy and his songs constitute an authentic, if overworked, component of American folklore.

### The coming of the farmer

The final phase of the occupation of the West was the coming of the farmer to areas which would support him. Starting in a small way even before the Civil War, but delayed by the war, the movement really began in earnest after 1865, when discharged soldiers, among others, making use of the Homestead Act and the railroads, sought homes in the West. Farmers came as individual families and in groups. There were Negroes from the South, religious groups seeking communities of their own, foreign groups newly arrived from Europe, and the discontented from the eastern states. Most were poor and brought a minimum of furniture and farming equipment to their new venture on the land.

With the opening of the western plains—both the humid eastern portion and the more arid western part extending to the foothills of the Rocky Mountains—American agriculture underwent a considerable revolution. The treeless and monotonously flat land offered a uniformity of conditions which invited both the use of machinery and a one-crop farming system. The development of a hard winter wheat for the southern plains and of a hard spring wheat for the north established that crop firmly from the Canadian border to Texas. The steel plow and the mechanical reaper, invented before the Civil War, came into their own and made possible the vast wheat fields in the West which amazed the rest of the country. The combination of a rapid influx of people and the availability of new machines resulted in a production of food crops such as the world had never seen before. Not only could America feed its own growing population, but it maintained a substantial export trade, especially in wheat, to the industrial countries of western Europe.

The rigor and loneliness of life on the prairies caused some settlers to give up and return to the East. But in spite of the surrender of some, enough of them stuck it out to bring about a rapid increase of the population of the plains. The formation of new territories and the admission of states were affected by political jockeying in Congress to a degree which conceals the real progress in population of the various parts of the West. In any event, by 1890, when most of the good land had been taken up, all the western territory had been admitted to statehood except three areas. Utah was kept out by the marriage practices of the Mormons. Oklahoma had just been opened to white settlement as it had formerly been Indian Territory. And New Mexico and Arizona were kept out because their political complexion was not pleasing to a majority of Congress. Farming on the plains developed its own pattern, suited to the conditions of each area, but generally characterized by large-scale methods. The open spaces of the West constituted a challenge to the inventors and builders of all kinds of farm machinery. Crops and planting methods used in the East had to be adapted to the lower rainfall generally prevalent west of the Mississippi. A very substantial portion of American wheat, corn, beef, and pork still originates in this area.

## Farming in the East and South

The expansion of basic food production on the new lands of the Mississippi Valley provided competition which farmers in older areas could not meet. In the East, low prices for wheat, cattle, and hogs forced either abandonment or readjustment of farming operations. The improved cropland of the United States increased by one-sixth between 1860 and 1870; declined by about a million acres between 1870 and 1880, a decade dominated by depression and last attempts at reconstruction in the South; and expanded by nearly one-third each ten years from 1880 to 1900 (see Fig. X-4). Considering the great expansion of cultivation on the western plains during these years, even during the rather chaotic seventies, the aggregate figures for decline and increase can probably be explained only in terms of the abandonment of agricultural land in the East —especially New England—and in the South. Other areas became too depleted in fertility to compete on even terms with the West. Farmers went to nearby cities to man the growing industries, or went to the West to take advantage of the cheap land and the much greater returns from farming there. Those who remained shifted their production from grain and livestock to milk, dairy products, fruits, and vegetables—products which the West either could not produce or could not get to the city markets of the East. After 1880, the farm population of America increased much less rapidly than the total population. Farm population in the New England and Middle Atlantic states was most strongly affected, as industries grew nearby, and as large-scale farmers of the West flooded the markets with their products.

In the South, the Civil War had brought a fundamental upheaval in the farming system. The South had never been a producer of foodstuffs for consumption outside of its own area, although it had of course produced a great many foods for its own use. The opening of the West, therefore, was not so disturbing to the agriculture of the older sections of the South as it was to the East. The reduction in cotton and tobacco production during the war was followed by an intensified demand immediately after, which the continuously expanding national growth sustained. The conditions necessary for an era of hitherto unparalleled prosperity for southern farmers were apparently at hand.

The prosperity that might have been was not realized in fact because of the effects of the war on the plantation system. Plantation owners found themselves with land, but with their slave labor supply gone. Some large landowners tried to operate with hired labor, but this proved unsatisfactory. Even if the freedmen had been able to fit into the new system, there were very few landowners who could raise the money for cash payment of wages, following the war years with their debilitating financial drain on everyone in the South. Many plantations were put on the auction block and split into small parcels of ten acres or so to attract bidders of modest circumstances. Thousands of new small farm units were established by this process throughout the cotton belt, but few of the new owners or operators were efficient managers, and total cotton production continued to lag in spite of a good demand and high prices. Cotton production, having reached a high point of 5,000,000 bales in 1859, did not attain this mark again until 1899.

Another solution to the problem of labor supply in cotton growing has proved in the long run to be unfortunate for the South and for all parties concerned. That was the system of "cropping" and "sharecropping" (p. 202), by which white and Negro tenants were given blocks of cotton land to farm for themselves in return for a share of the crop to the landowner. Nearly always these tenants required credit for seed, supplies, and livelihood until the crop could be harvested. If the crop happened to be poor or the prices low, their share might scarcely yield them enough to pay the debt from the spring. If so, they became hopelessly involved in debt and thus virtually bound to the landlord and the sharecropping system. There was little incentive for either owner or tenant to improve the soil. To diversify crops or to change the system became almost impossible because the tenant was always in debt, and he had to produce cotton as the only available cash crop to meet his obligations. Sharecropping thus became a system whose effects were often vicious. It kept the tenants in poverty; it depleted the soil of the South more than was necessary; it did nothing to provide incentive to increase production. Just because it happened to suit the immediate set of conditions prevailing after the war better than any alternative farming system, sharecropping became the common system in the South, and in the long run contributed to the impoverishment and economic retardation of the entire region. It did not begin to undergo substantial change until as late as the second quarter of the twentieth century.

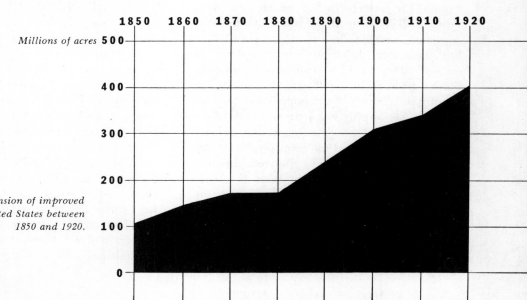

Fig. X-4 The expansion of improved cropland in the United States between 1850 and 1920.

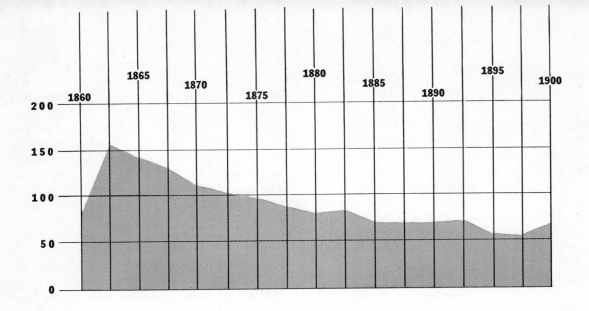

Fig.X-5  The behavior of farm product prices
in the United States, 1860 to 1900. Note the rise during the Civil War. 1913 = 100

### Economic troubles overtake the farmer

Agriculture in the first years after the Civil War was not in a really prosperous condition except in those areas where new land was still being opened up and developed. The South and the East had their own particular problems to face, as noted above, and only in the West was the outlook good. Even western prosperity was temporary, however, for underlying conditions were developing which meant trouble for farmers in the North and West. From 1860 to 1880, the amount of improved cropland increased less than the population, but thereafter, down to 1900, cropland increased more rapidly than the population. Farm output in the 1880's and 1890's was surpassing the growth of the population that was to use it, i.e., supply was outrunning domestic demand. The depression beginning in 1873 had hurt the demand for farm products, and, had it not been for the speculative element in the sale of public lands in the West, the 1880's might have turned out to be a bad period for the farmer. The effect of this expansion showed up in the early 1890's, however, as swollen farm production together with the panic of 1893 placed the farmer in a desperate condition.

To make matters worse, the farmer had to make a constantly heavier investment in machinery because he could scarcely handle farm operations on the western prairies without it. He had to use machines to cut his costs if he was going to remain in the increasingly competitive production race. The basic nature of both the prairie and the machine tended to make farming a highly specialized business; the farmer had to sell his grain or livestock on commercial markets for cash in order to buy machinery and other manufactured goods for cash. The welfare of the northern farmer thus became dependent upon the margin, if any, between his cash income and his cash costs. The economic forces of supply and demand placed a powerful squeeze on this margin, and, until a turn for the better came after the recovery from the depression of the 1890's, the farmer of the states and territories in the North and West was very likely to be a discontented and even rebellious individual.

For a time after the Civil War, as was probably also true as far back as the Revolutionary War, occasional inadequate returns from current crop and livestock marketing were concealed or compensated for by the fact that land prices were rising. Most American farmers had a rather strong tendency toward speculation, and it made little difference to them whether they received their income from crops or from the price of their land. Many a farm family got along year by year on a small cash income, but its members had the comforting feeling that they were the owners of an increasingly valuable farm enterprise. If they came to a stage at which they wished to leave the farm, they could usually sell out for a sufficient amount to provide a modest competence for their declining years.

But this type of compensation for low farm income became sharply restricted as the good land of the West was nearly all sold or claimed under the Homestead Act. When there was no more good new land which could be developed into productive farms, the value of an existing farm could be increased only by a rise in its price due to changes in its condition. Land prices, however, depend on the income a farm produces, and low farm produce prices mean low income and hence low land prices also. Thus, rising land prices, which had been the sustaining force in the history of American agriculture, now disappeared, to leave the American farmer in a despairing state of mind.

What should he do about this unsatisfactory state of affairs? First of all, the farmer was traditionally an individualist. Also, he had usually come from Europe himself because of low income and unsatisfactory conditions there, or he was descended from a man who had emigrated for these reasons. In America, he had either pioneered in the clearing and occupation of new land, or he was not many generations removed from an ancestor who had. He lived a rather isolated life, even in the older and more settled communities, because transportation was limited and slow. He had always dealt with his own problems, mostly by himself and in his own way. That was what he did now when faced with low prices for his products. Although those low prices were the result of excessive supply in relation to demand, the farmer probably did not realize that, and, anyway, all that he himself could do was to cut his costs and try to produce more to increase his income in that way. To cut costs and produce

more, he bought machinery, if he could get the cash or credit to do so.

Unfortunately, but inevitably, a good many individual farmers reasoned in the manner just suggested. The result was more production and weaker prices, and thousands of farmers were caught with debt for land and machinery, debt which they could neither carry nor repay. They turned in irritation and anger on the railroads, which had sold many of them their land and carried their output to market—at outrageously high rates, they said. They turned on the large corporations which sold them farm machinery, and charged them with monopolistic price fixing—not always without adequate grounds. They turned on the great packing firms and the "gamblers" of the commodity markets who, they said, manipulated the markets for livestock and cereal and cotton crops, sometimes in order to depress the prices received by the farmers. They turned on the "money power" of Wall Street which they saw behind all these other agencies as the real culprit in bringing on the farmer's sad state. Finally, the farmers formed into organizations to mobilize their united strength for an attack on those who were preying upon them—an attack which was to be carried out directly and through the political control of state and federal governments which the farm organizations hoped to attain.

### Farm organizations— political, economic, and social

The first farm organization of this period to attain a substantial membership was the Patrons of Husbandry, commonly known as the Grange. It was founded in 1867 by Oliver H. Kelley, a government employee in Washington, D.C. Kelley had just previously completed a trip through the South in connection with his work and had observed the deplorable conditions existing among southern farmers. He planned that the Grange should be a semisecret society with the purpose of increasing sociability among farmers and helping to raise their educational level. It was to be definitely nonpolitical. It spread slowly at first, mostly around Washington and in Kelley's former home community in Minnesota. After 1870 it became more popular, as farmers saw in it a chance to rectify some of the injustices they suffered.

Although politics were barred in the Grange, the meetings were inevitably places for the exchange of ideas, and numerous local political groups and parties arose outside the organization although stimulated from within it. By 1874, the Grange claimed 1,500,000 members. It became a power in the government of several of the western states, and was responsible for legislation controlling railroad service and rates. The Grange also sponsored coöperatives, especially in the Middle West, and undertook to operate a number of local grain elevators to store and ship grain for nearby farmers. It even bought a plant to build harvesting machines. These activities were undertaken suddenly as an aftermath of the financial crisis of 1873. They were not carefully thought out, and some of them collapsed as quickly as they had risen. The organizations then returned to the social and uplift purposes which Kelley originally had in mind, and have continued in that direction to the present time.

The farmer's problems were still not solved. With the failure of the Grange to achieve immediate results, many farmers turned again to the support of an old cause among American farmers, namely, inflation, or the expanded issuance of paper money as a means of raising prices. Toward the end of the Civil War, the volume of Greenbacks outstanding was over $400,000,000. There was, in addition, a quantity of the new National Bank notes outstanding, but they were mostly in the East where the majority of the large banks were located. Paper money, except for Greenbacks, was scarce in most western communities. In the financially conservative East, the Greenbacks were unpopular as the weakest element in the monetary system, and there was much pressure on Congress and the Treasury to reduce the quantity of them in circu-

lation with a view to their ultimate elimination. Such proposals were opposed by western representatives, but, as a compromise, a Resumption Act was passed in 1875. This called for a gradual reduction of the outstanding Greenbacks to a total of $300,000,000; a gold reserve was to be built up by the Secretary of the Treasury so that by January 1, 1879, payment in gold could be made by the government to any holder of a Greenback on demand.

The Resumption Act was not to the liking of the western advocates of more paper money and higher prices, and many of them flocked to the banner of a political party opposing it, the Greenback party. The prolonged depression following the panic of 1873 aided their cause, and by 1878 they had sufficient power in Congress to bring about a modification of the Resumption Act to stop the reduction in the amount of outstanding Greenbacks. Their quantity was frozen at $346,681,016, where it remained. The resumption of gold payment to holders of Greenbacks in 1879 removed the issue of Greenback inflation from the political arena, although the party continued to run candidates for national office until 1884.

Continued failure to find a resolution of their difficulties forced many farmers to action still more radical than that represented by the Grange and the Greenback party. The next phase of agrarian protest centered around the Farmers' Alliances, which were important politically in the decade from 1880 to 1890. These groups were originally strongest in the South, especially in Texas, where they had apparently originated for the protection of farmers against livestock thieves. The history of the Alliances in some respects parallels that of the Grange, where an organization created for one purpose was turned to another. The fact was that once farmers were gathered together into groups for any purpose, their all-pervading economic grievances were likely to lead them to turn their organizations to economic ends. The Alliances were at first local but quickly formed into state and regional associations. By 1880, the National Farmers' Alliance and Industrial Union had been formed, although, since its members were mostly in the South, it was commonly called the Southern Alliance. In the same year, another organization known simply as the National Farmers' Alliance was formed, but since its members were chiefly in the northern plains states west of the Mississippi, it was called the Northern (sometimes Northwestern) Alliance. The state Alliances in particular encouraged social gatherings among farmers; sponsored farmers' institutes to help spread knowledge of better farming methods; and sometimes undertook such activities as coöperative marketing of farm crops, buying of farm supplies at a discount, and writing of various kinds of insurance for farmers. These business ventures of the Alliances eventually failed as had those of its earlier predecessor, the Grange, but for several years up to 1890 they were quite important.

Possibly the most important activity of the Alliances was their support of such national political objectives as free coinage of silver, abolition of the National Banks, government ownership of railroads, and abolition of trading in futures on the grain exchanges. Futures trading on the grain exchanges was rather mysterious to the average farmer at best, and he feared that it had the effect of depressing prices at times of the year when he had grain to sell. It was thought that free coinage of silver would bring more money into existence and raise prices received by farmers. The National Banks were opposed for their restrictive lending and note-issue policies, which were blamed for holding down prices. Government ownership of railroads and other utilities was supported to escape the excessive charges allegedly made by private companies.

The free-silver issue dated back to the Coinage Act of 1873, which was later dubbed the "crime of '73" by free-silver advocates. In that year, the silver dollar was dropped from the list of coins minted in a revision of the coinage laws, because silver had been undervalued at the mint for many years and had therefore not been brought to the Treasury to be made into dollars. Shortly after 1873, increased quantities of silver began to be mined in the West, and several European countries demonetized silver; so the price of silver fell. At first, advocates of inflation had concentrated on the issuance of Greenbacks, but after that endeavor failed, their attention was shifted to regaining the free coinage privilege for silver. They had the backing of western silver interests in this endeavor. A period of drought beginning in 1887 turned the attention of farmers to political action on behalf of free silver as a way of raising prices to relieve their distress. By the fall of 1890 the farmers of the West and South, who were disappointed in the results of the silver purchase provisions of the Bland-Allison Act of 1878 as well as the recently enacted Sherman Silver Purchase Act of July 1890, went to the polls to elect a substantial number of congressmen pledged to free silver. The Southern Alliance also gained the support of the Northern Alliance for a cheap credit policy requiring the establishment of a sub-treasury in every large agricultural county in the nation for the making of loans to farmers at 1 per cent interest in amounts up to 80 per cent of the value of storable crops, as evidenced by warehouse receipts to be used as security for the loans.

Partial political success of the Alliances in electing sympathetic candidates led to more ambitious plans for a third political party. The Southern Alliance was not enthusiastic over the project, since it hoped to capture the Democratic party in the South. The Northern Alliance went ahead, however, and with other interested groups formed the People's party, commonly called the Populist party, in 1892. The party entered the elections of 1892 with a platform advocating free coinage of silver in a ratio of 16 to 1 in relation to gold; a graduated income tax; postal-savings banks; government ownership and operation of the railroads, telegraph, and telephone; direct election of United States senators; and similar "radical" measures. They received more than a million votes and elected many state officials as well as several congressmen and senators. They did not break the hold of the Democrats in the South, however, nor of the Republicans in the East.

In the next year, 1893, the country was

again struck by financial panic which brought thousands of business failures and added industrial and commercial distress to the long-standing agrarian distress. In the elections of 1894, the Populists made further gains in support, and won some local victories by fusion with the Democrats. It is probable that a law permitting free coinage of silver could have been pushed through Congress in 1895, but the advocates of such a measure knew that President Grover Cleveland, a Democrat, would veto it. They decided to wait until after the elections of 1896, in which they felt sure they would increase their strength. In the Democratic Convention of 1896, the party was won over to the support of free silver by the impassioned oratory of William Jennings Bryan of Nebraska, who was nominated as Democratic candidate for the presidency. Rather than split the free silver vote, the Populists also endorsed Bryan. But the worst of the depression following the panic of 1893 was over by the fall of 1896, and the combined effort of the Democrats and Populists was insufficient to prevent the election of the conservative Republican William McKinley and a Republican Congress.

The Republican victory meant the end of the Populist party and the free-silver issue. Nearly all the other planks in the Populist platform were eventually enacted into law by other parties. The agrarian point of view in politics was defeated after two decades in which it had been mobilizing. Recovery in general business after 1896 and continuing growth of industry and the industrial population brought an end to the decline of farm prices and started them upward. The farm population improved its economic position in the years from 1900 to World War I, and the rôle of farm organizations in politics declined.

## Price recovery and farm prosperity

In an indirect way, the very same forces that brought political defeat to agricultural interests also brought economic recovery to remove the causes of agrarian political discontent. More people working in mines, in industries, and in the businesses of the cities meant more people to be fed from the farms. The recovery from the panic of 1893 coincided with a turn in the long-term balance between the supply of and demand for the basic farm crops. The tapering off of the availability of new productive land, free or at a low price, also brought a slowing down of the rate of expansion of farm production. A less rapidly expanding supply, when matched against a continuously expanding urban population, meant that conditions in the markets for grains, livestock, and cotton became more favorable to farmers than they had been for many years. Basic prices of farm commodities began a slow rise which continued up to and through World War I. In fact, as farmers looked back during the 1930's and 1940's these years just before World War I appeared so favorable in their balance between the prices received by farmers and the prices they had to pay for machinery and supplies, that they were chosen as the base for the "parity" prices that were provided for in new legislation (see p. 299f.).

While farm prices were favorable, other circumstances were beginning to make farming easier and rural life more pleasant. Most of the basic farm machines continued to be improved and put to more extensive use. The iron or steel plow had now come to be used everywhere, and the horse-drawn mowing machine to cut grass and hay was in almost equally wide use. Similarly, improved horse-drawn harrows were developed for preparing the ground after plowing, and cultivators came into general use. The hand scythe and cradle for harvesting grain went out of use except for cutting weeds. The grain reaper was much improved by the addition of an automatic knotter. This tied the grain in bundles or sheaves which could then be stood on end in groups or shocks to dry before threshing. This particular machine was probably the greatest single labor-saver, for it relieved the farmer of exhausting toil while enabling him to handle a larger acreage of grain crops. The harvesting of corn and cotton was not mechanized before World War I, but the hand-cutting and husking of corn and the hand-picking of cotton at least had the merit of being operations that could be carried on over several months in the autumn and early winter. All together, these various mechanical aids to farming reduced the need for hired labor on the farm, brought operations more completely under the control of the farm family, and took the edge from the most severe kinds of farm work. But the machines cost money, and the mechanization of farming tied the farmer ever more completely into a complex, interdependent economic society upon which he relied for the sale of his produce, for the purchase of his equipment and supplies, and for credit facilities to carry on his increasingly capitalistic enterprise.

The educational level of the farm population was also much improved during the period 1860 to 1914 by a number of aids to rural education. The Morrill Act of 1862 had provided for grants of federal land to the states for the erection and support of colleges "to teach such branches of learning as are related to agriculture and the mechanic arts," among others. Many such "land grant" agricultural and mechanical colleges were set up after the Civil War and undertook systematic teaching and the dissemination of knowledge of improved farming practices. In 1889, a federal Department of Agriculture was created as a cabinet department to consolidate and extend government assistance to agriculture along scientific and statistical lines. The Hatch Act of 1887 provided for grants of federal funds to the state agricultural schools for the establishment of Agricultural Experiment Stations. These stations, together with the U.S. Department of Agriculture itself, have carried research in many phases of food and fiber production, distribution, and utilization to a higher level in the United States than in any other part of the world. Bulletins and farm magazines carried the results of research to the farm people of the country. Farmers' institutes and state and county fairs became almost universal in the major farming areas during this period, and brought word of new ideas and new methods to the farmers while giving them a chance to see the new machines and the new products and methods developed by research.

By 1914, farmers in the United States were reasonably content with the state of their affairs. Prices were fairly good, machinery made possible the handling of larger acreages, and farm income was relatively better than it had been for a generation. The automobile, motor truck, and farm tractor were just beginning to give an indication of the contribution they could make to the further improvement of farm living and production. Agricultural experiment stations were making significant improvements in farm crops, breeds, and methods. American agriculture was well prepared for the burdens which World War I was going to throw upon it, and in its very capacity to bear those impending burdens there lay a premonition of trouble to come in the future.

## FOR FURTHER READING

Barnes, James A. *Wealth of the American People*. New York: Prentice-Hall, Inc., 1949. Chapter 20.

Faulkner, Harold U. *American Economic History*. 8th ed. New York: Harper & Brothers, 1960. Chapters 18 and 19.

Hicks, John D. *The Populist Revolt*. The University of Nebraska Press, 1961. Paperback. First important interpretation of organized rural protest.

Hofstadter, Richard. *The Age of Reform*. Vintage, 1960. Paperback. Chapters 1—3.

Shannon, Fred Albert. *America's Economic Growth*. 3rd ed. New York: The Macmillan Co., 1951. Chapters 19—21.

Williamson, Harold F. (ed.). *The Growth of the American Economy*. New York: Prentice-Hall, Inc., 1951. Chapters 18—21.

Wright, Chester W. *Economic History of the United States*. 2nd ed. New York: McGraw-Hill Book Co., 1949. Chapters 29—32.

# Chapter 11: The growth of large-scale industry in America

In America, as a half century earlier in England, a long period of slow industrial growth preceded the era of rapid industrial development which might be said to constitute a real revolution. Some of the earliest inventions of the English Industrial Revolution had been brought to America at the turn of the century. American inventors made important additions to the technical knowledge which was being applied to industrial production, but the people were too preoccupied with the settlement of the West and the building of roads and canals to devote major attention to industry. The center of population shifted rapidly westward, and although the inhabitants of the frontier, especially the women, might long for the comforts and luxuries which the industries of Europe and the eastern states could provide, such thoughts had to be suppressed until the forests and plains had been subdued and until channels of transportation to the East had been provided.

By the time of the Civil War, permanent settlements had been established for a genera-

tion or more as far west as the Mississippi River, and beyond it in some sections. Frontier conditions had disappeared and good transportation was available to the Atlantic coast by rail and water. Life had begun to take on some of the refinements known in the older countries of Europe. Industries were growing to supply the needs not only of the western frontier country but also of the more sophisticated cities of the East. Even without the Civil War, the conditions were at hand for a rapid industrial advance, perhaps an industrial revolution. Coming as it did at a critical time in the course of the national economic development, the Civil War served the economic purpose of hastening the occurrence of the impending industrial revolution. Power-driven machinery was quickly adapted to more and more industrial processes, and a new stage of large-scale production was entered upon in more and more industries. The insatiable demand for military supplies, the amount of bank credit easily available, and the sharply rising prices all were important spurs to industrialization. After the war, industry was ready to continue its expansion to meet the needs of the growing population which was eager to attain a higher standard of living.

## America becomes
## a great industrial power

A measure of American industrial growth is provided by a comparison with the older industrial countries of Europe (see Fig. XI-1, p. 222). In 1860 the United States was fourth among the countries of the world in value of industrial output, behind Great Britain, France, and Germany. Thirty-five years later the United States was the world leader. And on the eve of World War I, the volume of American industrial production equalled that of Great Britain, Germany, and France together, the three countries which had individually surpassed the United States a half century earlier. This record was achieved in spite of the fact that France and England were expanding their industry greatly during the same half century, and Germany was advancing from an unimportant position industrially to the status of industrial leader of Europe.

Within the United States, industrial expansion was facilitated by the shifting of the population from agricultural to nonagricultural employment. As the chart on page 224, Fig. XI-3, shows, from the year of the earliest available data, 1820, the proportion of the gainfully employed occupied outside agriculture has been increasing. Of course, not nearly all of those employed off the farm were engaged in industry. Apparently during this period there were two or three persons employed in trade, transportation, the professions, and other nonagricultural pursuits for each person actually engaged as a wage-earner in a manufacturing industry, although the data do not exist for a precise calculation. It would be quite logical to expect an increase in employment in selling, transporting, and servicing the goods which manufacturing industries were turning out from 1860 to 1910. Even

if only a third or a fourth of those who had left the farm were working in manufacturing establishments, the size of the total nonfarm groups compared to the number of workers remaining on the farm gives a good measure of the extent to which the nation was becoming industrialized. On that basis of comparison, in 1860 about 4 out of 10 workers were employed off the farm. In 1880 the number had risen to a fraction more than 5 out of 10, and in 1900 to an average of 6¼ out of every 10 workers. The trend continued to more than 7 out of 10 in 1920 and 8 out of 10 in 1940. The movement of this tremendous human tide away from agriculture to industry and related occupations was made possible largely by the development in industry of efficient power-driven machinery to be used in agriculture. In other words, a goodly proportion of former producers of food and fiber now came to reside in cities and to work in those industries which supply agriculture.

A more personal measure of the extent of the industrial development following the Civil War can be gained if one tries to imagine one's daily life without all the products and services which began to be supplied on a significant scale during that period. For one important example, the internal combustion engine was developed and began to be used in the period between the Civil War and World War I. Automobiles, busses, trucks, airplanes, farm tractors, and even steamships and railway locomotives have now come to depend upon the gasoline engine or its near relative, the oil-powered Diesel. The internal combustion engine could have been no more than a novelty without the suitable fuel provided by petroleum. The petroleum industry is another giant of today which received its start after the Civil War. At first petroleum was sold as a medicine guaranteed to cure any known human ailment, then as a source of kerosene for home lighting. Soon the internal combustion engine provided the principal market for it, and in the middle of the twentieth century petroleum also became the basic raw material for the manufacture of synthetic rubber and other chemical products.

Most of the manufacturing processes of today and a large part of modern communication rest on another development of this same period, the successful generation, distribution, and use of electricity. The basic ideas of the electric motor and generator were developed early in the nineteenth century, but the first central generating station, distributing power over wires for home and street illumination and for industrial use, was planned and constructed after the Civil War. The telegraph was in use before the war, but the telephone was not developed until after it. The wireless telegraph, telephone, and radio were in use before World War I, but had their greatest development later. We depend so heavily today upon all of these and other applications of electricity that it requires a considerable stretching of the imagination to conceive of home and business life without them.

The great bulk of the industrial changes in the first decades following the Civil War were expansions and changes in long-established industries. The iron and steel industry, for example, ceased to be a small-scale, almost rural industry. Utilizing the newly developed Bessemer converter and the open-hearth furnace, it became the first truly large-scale American manufacturing industry. Production was concentrated in large plants in the area between Pittsburgh and Cleveland; around Birmingham, Alabama; and in northern Indiana at Gary, on the southern tip of Lake Michigan. Employees in the industry were numbered by the tens of thousands and the invested capital was in the millions of dollars.

The textile industry likewise underwent great expansion as machines driven by steam or electric power conquered all branches of the industry. Spinning by mechanical power was one of the first applications of nonhuman energy to mark the beginning of the Industrial Revolution. Only gradually were weaving, knitting, dyeing, and other processes mechanized for woolen as well as cotton manufacture. As the price of cloth was lowered, consumption increased. The sewing machine, invented before the Civil War but not put to use widely until later, became the basis of the ready-made clothing industry. The making of shoes was mechanized during the Civil War by the adaptation of the sewing machine to the sewing of the heavy leather parts of shoes. These industries devoted to clothing the human body, as well as the lumber and clay products industries, devoted to providing shelter, expanded as population increased and helped to raise the standard of living. The making of paper and many other older industries combined with those mentioned above to provide the bulk of the employment for both labor and capital in the great era of industrial expansion.

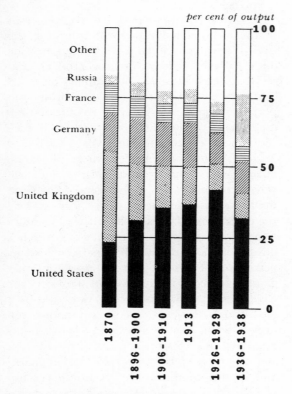

Fig. XI-1  The percentage distribution of the world's manufacturing production among the leading countries between 1870 and 1938.

## Bases of American industrial leadership

The American record in industrial production has never been equalled anywhere in the world. By what magic have the American people been able to do what no other people have ever before done? Is it that Americans by nature are superior to other peoples? Is North America so richly endowed with the basic resources which industry requires that the American record of industrial production can never be equalled or surpassed elsewhere? In the twentieth century, America has become the wealthiest and most economically powerful country in the world. Can American methods and success be duplicated or surpassed elsewhere? Is American leadership in mass production to be short-lived from the long view of history? These are important questions for the present and future. To see if dependable answers may be found, we must examine the factors which have contributed to American industrial leadership.

*Resources*

There can be no question but that the rich natural resources of the continent of North America have contributed heavily to American industrial growth. Mass-production industries make far heavier demands upon natural resources than small-scale, handicraft industries. Obviously, if North America had been lacking in basic resources, industry could not have developed on a large scale in the United States or in any other North American country.

But were American resources so rich that they alone acted as sufficient stimulus to the development of large-scale industry? It probably is not possible to point to any important American industry and say that it exists *only* because the resources for it are available. The American Indians did not develop industry in the presence of the same resources available to the white men. Also, resources exist in Asia, Africa, and elsewhere which the peoples of those areas have even now not developed. Resources permit industrial development but do not cause it by themselves. It can be said more accurately that industrial development in America was seldom held back by lack of resources, at least so far as the more important

industries are concerned. The soil, forests, and fisheries were exploited by the earliest settlers. As population spread westward, soil, timber, minerals, metals, and fuels continued to become available in a profusion that invited development and that supported large-scale operations, once industry had been established. The stimulus to use these rich resources, however, had to come from the people, with their multitudes of desires, ambitions, and projects for better living.

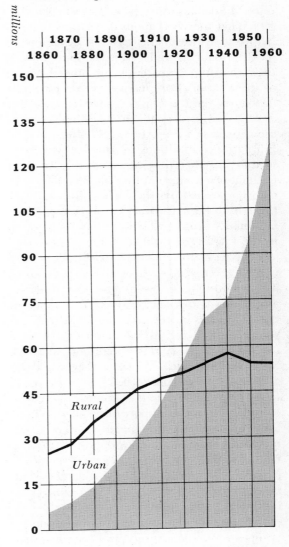

Fig. XI-2 *The growth of city as compared to rural population between 1860 and 1960. Compare this with the trend between 1790 and 1860 as shown in Fig. VIII-5.*

## The human element

Any social or economic development depends in part upon people, and American industrial development is no exception. But Americans are French and German, English, Irish, Swedish, and of almost all other races and nationalities, and have no qualities in a hereditary or biological sense which these other nationalities lack. Americans are not inherently smarter, more energetic, or more resourceful than other people of the world.

What then is it about Americans that has helped give rise to the vigorous development of the resources and industrial potential of their country? Apparently, the mixed nature of their national origins has been a favorable factor. While the English tradition was sufficiently strong to establish the language, government, and law pretty largely after the English pattern, conditions in America have been so different that new elements were brought to light even in the English character. In addition, even from the earliest colonial days there have been in America other racial and nationality groups who were not brought up in the English cultural tradition. They acted as a check on any tendencies to follow unthinkingly the English ways of living and doing. The environment was different in America, and the rich but varied cultural heritage of Americans has meant that they could face the problems of living in the new world from a fresh point of view. They were not held back by traditional ideas of what they could do and how they should do it. They were ready to develop new methods in industry and agriculture where the opportunity offered itself and the occasion demanded it. Thus, the mixed ancestry of Americans proved to be a real advantage in breaking the power of restrictive traditions and permitting new solutions to be worked out to the problems of industrial production.

While the stimulus of the American environment to the various peoples who came to these shores was sufficient to produce an energetic reaction, it did not offer a challenge too great for the people to cope with. Arnold

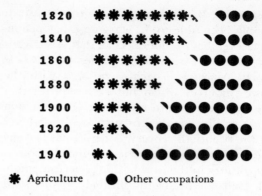

✳ Agriculture   ● Other occupations

*Fig. XI-3 The percentage of persons gainfully employed in agricultural as compared to those in non-agricultural pursuits, 1820 to 1940, in the United States. Each symbol represents 10 per cent.*

Toynbee in his monumental work, *A Study of History*,[1] has given numerous illustrations from history to establish the point that any kind of stimulus which comes to a people must not require a response which exceeds their capacities, if a new line of cultural growth is to result. As a very simple example, most of us who live in a temperate climate find the first cool days of autumn stimulating to vigorous sports, or other kinds of activity or work. Observing that reaction in ourselves and others, we might conclude that a cold climate is required to bring forth the full energies and abilities of a people. But, on the other hand, we cannot generalize thus, for the extreme cold of the Arctic regions has never produced a rich and varied culture. The continuous need for protection from the weather near the poles has so restricted human activity that men are entirely preoccupied by the long struggle to keep alive. Man seems to need enough cold to stimulate him and to make physical activity comfortable and healthful, but not so much as to require all his initiative and energy to counteract it. Frontier conditions in America were hard. They required all the resourcefulness of pioneer men and women to provide food and shelter and protection from the dangers of the wilderness. But victory could be

[1] Oxford University Press, 1946. One volume abridgement of volumes one to six by D. C. Somervell (New York: Oxford University Press, 1947).

won over the obstacles of the frontier and a good life achieved. The American environment was challenging; but the challenge was not so severe that hard work and resourcefulness could not bring their own reward.

America as a new country had no class of entrenched landlords or wealthy people living from the labor of others. The qualities that brought success were willingness to work hard, resourcefulness, aggressiveness in seizing opportunity, willingness to give up present comfort for the promise of a brighter future, and withal, some of the instincts of the gambler. These were the qualities shown by the leaders in many branches of economic life. Americans came to accept continuous growth and expansion as the standard state of affairs. Opportunity was so abundant that, in spite of the rapid growth of population and a continuous influx from Europe, there were never as many inhabitants and workers as could be used. Scarcity of labor made wages higher than in Europe and provided incentive for the invention and application of industrial processes and machines that could do more work with fewer people. Still, labor was not so scarce as to stifle industrial growth, and there seemed to be an effective balance in the numbers and quality of people in relation to the opportunities of the environment.

### The inventive genius of the American people

The abundant opportunities offered by the American environment had more complex effects. In relation to the opportunities, labor was usually scarce, as has been pointed out. In agriculture the lack of manpower led to what Europeans would call careless farming. Americans quickly discovered that it was more profitable to farm a larger acreage of land than to spend time weeding fields and getting the greatest returns from a smaller acreage. Methods in agriculture tended to become extensive rather than intensive, and this approach was carried over into industry.

Another unique feature of American economic life resulting from the inequality between opportunity for employment and labor supply was the intensity of the search for ways in which work could be most efficiently accomplished with fewest workers. Outside observers began to comment upon the mechanical ingenuity exhibited in America. By the beginning of the nineteenth century the tradition had been fairly well established that effort devoted to study of a job would

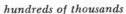

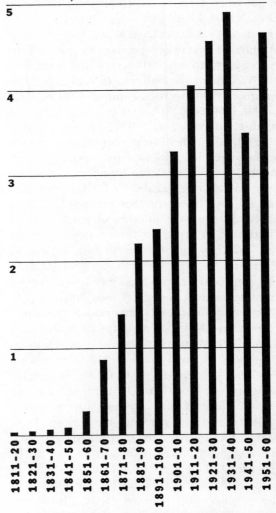

Fig. XI-4 *A measure of American inventive ingenuity is the number of patents issued by decades from 1800 to 1960. The number issued, while impressively large, falls far below the number applied for.*

yield results in the development of new devices or methods by which the job could be done with less labor, and perhaps better and faster also. "Yankee ingenuity" became a catch phrase which described this approach.

A rough measure of the inventive genius shown by the American people can be obtained from the number of patents issued annually. While not all patents relate to basic devices or even to ideas to be used in industry, a great many are of this nature. Almost from the founding of the patent system, the annual number of patents issued has been increasing (Fig. XI-4). There was a steady growth during the period up to the Civil War. The war itself stimulated invention, perhaps because of the scarcity of labor and the rapid advance into the West with the building of railroads. The number of patents issued annually doubled between 1860 and 1866, and the 1860 total was almost tripled before 1870. The new higher rate of issuance held steady for the next decade with some fluctuations, then expansion resumed, and by 1890 the number issued each year had doubled again. Not until 1901 was the number issued in 1890 exceeded. Thereafter, although the number of patents issued continued to grow, on the average, they did not multiply at the rapid rate of earlier decades.

One of the characteristic results of American mechanical ingenuity was the development of standardized parts which permitted interchangeability in manufacture. One part does not have to be fitted especially into its neighbors in each gun or clock or sewing machine. Much of the credit for this important development goes to Eli Whitney for his introduction of this method in producing muskets for the government around 1800. Many other individuals contributed to making the method a practical success; it came to be the accepted method in the manufacture of guns, which in turn permitted the placing of the powder and shot in standardized cartridges. Before the Civil War, the method was also used to make inexpensive clocks and watches. It then spread to the manufacture of sewing machines, locomotives, and railroad equipment, and to the farm-machinery industry. The economic importance of this system in manufacturing was that it separated the making of parts from their assembly. When this move was accomplished, it became possible in turn to devise specialized machines for the making of standardized parts in quantity. Mass production as it has developed in America would not have been possible on any other basis.

### Available capital

Like the labor supply, the supply of capital in America, though never superabundant before World War I, was never so short that worth-while developments were long held up for lack of it. Nearly all of the first settlements in America had had a commercial aspect, since European merchants were looking for trading opportunities. Fishing, shipbuilding, distilling, and other industries had been built up in colonial times by European capitalists seeking merchandise for their trade. Although the Revolutionary War and the War of 1812 had disturbed economic relations for some years, capital from England and other European countries had resumed its flow to America to finance canals, railroads, and the development of industry. During the years at the middle of the nineteenth century, the American trade balance with Europe was adverse, i.e., we were buying more from Europe than she was buying from us. We needed rails for our railroads and many manufactured goods which Europe could supply better and cheaper than could domestic industries. We were selling raw produce and partially processed goods to Europe, but not in sufficient quantity to pay for our purchases. Thus, year by year we found ourselves in debt to Europe. Eventually we would have reached a limit to our credit, except that many Europeans thought that the outlook for American industries was very good. For that reason they were willing to invest in the stocks and bonds of American business firms. But the purchase of American securities by Europeans would have the same effect on our trade balance as if Europe had bought more of our goods. The net effect of European purchases of our stocks and bonds, therefore, was to even up the adverse trade balance. We could continue to buy the manufactured goods we needed for our industrial expansion so long as Europeans were able and willing to continue to invest in American businesses. European investment in American industry continued to be a very important source of capital for our growth and expansion down to the time of World War I.

In both England and America, the beginnings of mechanized industry were, to some extent at least, financed by merchants who either were in need of more dependable supplies of merchandise for their commercial operations or found their trade declining and saw an opportunity in industry to earn a larger return on their capital. Down through the years, it has continually happened that capital accumulated in commerce has been transferred to industry. This source of industrial capital has been of sufficient importance to deserve notice, but it has not accounted for more than a fraction of the capital which the new large-scale methods in industry have required. It might be concluded from the experience of both Europe and America that it is a difficult thing for a man or a family that has become wealthy in one line of economic activity to transfer that wealth from the business which has produced it to another, in order to avoid loss or to make a better return.

The really substantial amounts of capital that have gone into industrial growth and development—and here again European experience confirms American—have come from the continuous reinvestment of accumulated earnings. The typical American "captain of industry" of the period between the Civil War and World War I was of humble origin. He was likely to have all of the qualities previously mentioned as requisite to success, and to have in addition a considerable measure of good luck. His humble origin usually meant that he had simple habits of eating, dressing, and general living. As success came from his small start, he tended to devote most of his profits to expansion. This pattern was repeated thousands and tens of thousands of times on a greater or lesser scale. John D. Rockefeller and the Standard Oil Company, Andrew Carnegie and the Carnegie Steel Company (later a unit of the United States Steel Corporation), and Henry Ford and the Ford Motor Company provide excellent illustrations of this pattern of industrial growth. In the aggregate, there can be no doubt that more capital was provided for industry in this way than in any other.

The frugality and saving habits of individuals carried over to corporations when little businesses became large. The term "corporation" means a business owned by a number of persons who have purchased one or more "shares" in it, issued as stock. Profits made by the corporation are distributed, according to the discretion of the managing group, as dividends on the shares, while losses to any one individual cannot exceed the value of his stock (the "limited liability" feature). Just as individuals would not spend all of their income but would save a substantial fraction for investment in the business, so corporations, often controlled by such individuals, would likewise. The principle of saving a substantial part of income came to be regarded as sound management for corporations. The spread of the corporation from banks, railroads, and canals to the industrial field was itself an indication of the growth of industry. The pulling in of capital to a large central pool from many small individual savers who singly were able to buy only a few shares in the corporation was of great value in the financing of industry. If the management, once the corporation was established and under way, followed the "sound" policy of retaining a good part of the earnings for the further expansion of the business, the effect was to enforce frugal habits upon the stockholders whether they were aware of it or not. This power of corporation management was sometimes abused, but it could be and was used to speed up industrial expansion by increasing the amount of capital available.

There is also a more complicated financial aspect of capital supply. Thus far we have thought of the problem of building new capital equipment for business as a matter of voluntary saving, either directly by business or by individuals who purchase stocks or bonds from business firms, thereby providing them with funds for the purchase of the needed equipment. We are not concerned at this moment with the financial machinery by which such investment is made. However, it was also true that business firms with good prospects could borrow from banks to meet some of their capital requirements. At times when the total lending to business for capital purposes was on the increase, the effect was that our economic system as a whole was *forced* to save to create capital. That is to say, individuals did not voluntarily decide to save, but bankers by lending to businesses permitted them to buy capital equipment exactly as though someone had saved to provide the funds that were loaned. Our economic system as a whole at those times was turned toward the production of capital goods and away from consumer goods exactly as though individuals had decided not to use their income for purposes of consumption but had saved and invested it instead with the purpose of creating new capital equipment.

### The use of power

The standardization and mechanization of processes in industry both permitted and required the use of mechanical power. Men had been aided by nonhuman power for thousands of years in the form of domesticated animals and water power. The earliest large-scale industries in America had been located in New England to take advantage of the water power available there. The progress of invention as applied to methods of manufacture has almost always resulted in the need of more power. Very often the secret of the productive efficiency of new machines and processes has been that they took over kinds of work that had formerly been accomplished by human energy and human skill. Whenever this happened, power requirements in industry would increase.

During most of the nineteenth century, the steam engine was being introduced to provide most of the industrial power. Although exact statistics on the use of power are hard to obtain, the available data indicate that it increased in extent many times during the course of the century, especially in the period after the Civil War. The use of water power, so important early in the century, declined as steam engines were improved and became dependable and adaptable. For a time in the middle portion of the century, steam was almost the only source of mechanical power used in industry, except for flour milling and places in New England where old water wheels continued to supply factories. Toward the latter part of the century, methods of generating and distributing electricity had been worked out, and the electric motor began to replace the steam engine as a source of industrial power. Steam produced by coal was used to generate nearly all of the electric energy at first, but the ease with which electric power could be transmitted over wires permitted a return to water power even though it was located away from important industrial centers. A number of hydroelectric plants were built before World War I in which the energy of falling water was used to generate electricity for distant industrial use. America had ample supplies of coal and considerable resources of water power, so that the development of labor-saving, mass-production methods was never held back by a lack of mechanical energy. The amount of power employed in conjunction with the average American worker to drive the machines which he operates or tends has been increasing from the beginning of our national history down to the present time. It is considerably more than that used in conjunction with each worker of any other large nation.

### One of the world's great free market areas

Finally, and not least important, attention should be called to the fact that American manufacturers had one of the largest free trading areas in the world available to them for the sale of their products. Americans have not always fully appreciated the significance of this fact. Increasing exploitation of resources and the newly developing technology of large-scale production could not have proceeded without a consuming market large enough and diversified enough to provide manufacturers with a constant stimulus to still greater production. To make this great consuming market effective, there must be no barriers to the free movement of goods, and cheap transportation was a very great advantage. It is interesting to speculate on the question whether America could ever have become a great industrial nation if the Constitution had not given Congress power to regulate interstate commerce, and if the states had been permitted to have tariffs to protect their respective industries. No sure answer can be given, of course, but it would seem very improbable that our industry could have developed anything like the productive efficiency it has if the local barriers of colonial days had been maintained and extended as state barriers. A great and growing free market area, tied together by a constantly improving transportation system, seems to be an essential to the development of mass-production industry.

The other side of the free-market question was the protection of that market from outside competition by means of the tariff. How essential the tariff was, and how much it contributed to the growth of large industries are questions which can probably never be given precise and conclusive answers. Tariff rates were increased sharply during the Civil War to raise revenue and to carry out the domestic program of the Republican party, as well as to protect industry. Thereafter, they remained high and were increased every time they were changed at all down to 1913, except for slight and temporary reductions during the administrations of Grover Cleveland in the 1880's and 1890's. During this period American industrial production forged ahead of that in any other nation of the world. The tariff could easily be given credit for this achievement if one

were a partisan advocate of a high-tariff policy. But many other favorable factors were also operating, and it is possible that these favoring circumstances would have brought about the development of large-scale industry in America in any case. Nevertheless, the tariff probably served to assist and speed up the process. The great American free market was probably more fundamentally responsible for the country's industrial growth than the protective-tariff policy.

## Geographic reasons for industrial growth

Why industries develop where they do is a very interesting and often a complicated question. In colonial times, manufacturing was started in New England to meet the needs of all the colonies for manufactured goods such as shoes and clothing, because such food staples as meat and flour could be produced to greater advantage in other colonies where more good land was available. It might be said, therefore, that the shoe and textile industries started in New England largely because of a ready market and an available labor and power supply. Fishing and shipbuilding were stimulated in New England by the additional factor of favorable raw material supply. Once started, there is a tendency for industries to continue in the same place, and even to attract allied industries, unless there are powerful reasons for them to move elsewhere.

As America grew from colonial times, the two strongest incentives to move old industries and to determine the location of new ones were the westward movement of its people and the discovery of new sources of industrial raw materials. Colonial manufacturing was predominantly in New England, but was also carried on extensively southward along the Atlantic Coast through New York, New Jersey, and Pennsylvania to Maryland. The westward movement between the Revolutionary War and the Civil War brought a substantial growth of industry in the western parts of the Middle Atlantic states and in the new states created from the Northwest Territory. By the time of the Civil War, the section of the United States north of the Ohio River and east of the Mississippi had become the industrial center of the nation, which it was to remain for the next century at least. The startling industrial developments of the half century following the Civil War were in this northeastern quarter of the country, and particularly in the western part of it, where Pittsburgh, Buffalo, Cleveland, Detroit, Chicago, and Milwaukee became focal points of regional industrial development.

The plains states, the Far West, and the South offered either inadequate resources for manufacturing or insufficient demand to justify mass production in those areas. There were exceptions to this generalization, of course. Gold, silver, copper, lead, and other metals were refined at or near the supply of ore. No part of the United States came even near to equalling the richness of the metallic mineral resources of the Rocky Mountain area. The South had no extensive mineral resources except for coal and iron ore in the Birmingham area. As northern stands of timber were cut down and wood became less accessible, the pine and hardwood stands of the South became the basis of a substantial southern lumber industry. To some extent also, the hope of the South that the cotton mill would come to the cotton fields was belatedly realized. The relative growth of cotton manufacturing in the South after the Civil War was remarkable, but as late as 1900 flour milling still led southern industries in value of product, followed by the lumber industry. The value of all kinds of manufactured products in the South represented only about a tenth of the national total in 1890, according to the *Report on Manufactures* of the Eleventh Census. The South, the Far West, and the plains states had a better source of income elsewhere, so they lacked sufficiently strong attractions to industry to overcome the advantages of the early start in the northeastern states. Immigrant labor flowed to the eastern industrial centers to be added to the rapidly growing native population as a labor supply. Industrial prosperity created capital for still further expansion. Railroads with their cheap transportation made the matter of distance from raw materials or markets somewhat less vital than it had been in earlier days. The Northeast became the firmly established industrial heart of America.

## The expansion of some basic industries

### The iron and steel industry

In the half century from 1865 to 1915, the making of iron and steel underwent a revolution in almost every important phase of the industry. The major processes were changed; the main sources of fuel and ore were changed; the organization of the industry was changed; and the market for iron and steel products was revolutionized by the expansion of old demand and the introduction of many new needs. At the beginning of the period, the industry was still widely scattered, the local forge often operating on quite a small, local scale; at the end, it had become perhaps the most highly organized of our basic national industries, with production concentrated in several well located areas, and with markets for its products in greater or lesser degree in almost every other industry or type of economic endeavor.

The basis for the greater rôle of the iron and steel industry lay in the discovery and development of new and large resources of both ore and fuel and in the development and adaptation of methods of production which increased the scale of operation, cut costs, and turned out products better suited to the needs of other industries. Up to the period of the Civil War, the industry had depended almost exclusively on locally obtainable ores. These were available in the Adirondack region of New York, in central and western Pennsylvania, in southern Ohio, and elsewhere. Ores were known to exist in the Marquette range of northern Michigan and had been used experimentally before the war. After the war, these and other Lake Superior ores were exploited extensively and furnished the basic ore supply of the American steel industry. Steam barges and steamships on the Great Lakes, providing the lowest cost transportation per ton-mile in the world, brought the Lake Superior ore on very advantageous terms to steel-producing centers at the southern tip of Lake Michigan and to the area between Lake Erie and Pittsburgh. The eastern Superior ores plus the ore from the Mesabi range in Minnesota west of Lake Superior, discovered in the 1880's but not developed extensively for a decade or more, provide to the American steel industry the richest and lowest-cost ore supply available anywhere in the world. In truth, the wealth and economic strength of America and the high standard of living of its people would not have been possible without this rich resource on which its basic industry has been built. The Lake Superior iron ore continued to be the chief reliance of the American steel industry until the middle of the twentieth century, when the end of the highest quality ore seemed to be in sight.

Paralleling the discovery of new ore supplies together with cheap transportation to bring them to the producing centers was the development of new sources of fuel for the steel industry. The use of coke for smelting was certainly not new in the second half of the nineteenth century either in Europe or America, since it had been developed a century earlier. American iron masters had clung to charcoal for smelting, because timber from which to make it was widely available and because it produced a pure soft iron easily worked into suitable shapes by blacksmiths and small manufacturers. The coming of railroads with their very large demand for iron and steel for rails, locomotives, and cars changed the situation. Larger-scale methods of iron and steel making were needed, and coke rather than charcoal was the fuel which was cheapest, available in sufficient quantity, and uniform in quality. The new iron and steel centers were located in areas in which both ore and coal were obtainable in quantity at low cost.

With ore and coal went new methods of iron and steel manufacture. As demands for the products of the industry were multiplying in every direction, improvements in its processes were equally evident. The chief of these, as experience demonstrated, were the Bessemer converter and the later open-hearth furnace. The Bessemer converter (named after Sir Henry Bessemer, a British engineer) was developed in England and America before the Civil War, but was not transformed into a successful piece of industrial equipment until later. It burned the impurities and part of the carbon out of the molten iron received in "pigs," or crude castings, from the blast furnace, by blowing air through it in an egg-shaped vessel or "converter." There were numerous pitfalls in the process, and the tricks of successful operation were learned at the cost of expensive and discouraging failures. When all went well, a charge of iron could be converted into steel in a matter of minutes. The Bessemer process began to be used in the United States in the 1870's and lowered the cost of steel rails and other products substantially. For several decades, Bessemer steel made up an increasing proportion of the tonnage output of the iron and steel industry. After 1890, emphasis passed to steel made in open-hearth furnaces.

The fact that the Bessemer converter could be used only with iron from ores of a certain type led to experimentation in Europe with another type of furnace which eventually came to be called the open-hearth furnace. It was usually larger than the Bessemer converter, although it could be tipped to unload its charge. Its great advantage was that it could be used with phosphorus ores which were commonly found in both Europe and America. The open-hearth furnace had been developed in its essential features by 1879, but it did not come into use immediately due to patent litigation and other obstacles. Not for almost a decade was open-hearth steel regularly made in America. Since the fuel source to keep the steel in a molten condition was outside the furnace, the open hearth proved able to turn out more delicately compounded types of steel as the art of steel metallurgy progressed. By the turn of the century, open-hearth steel had become the mainstay of the industry. Although each charge required more time than in a Bessemer converter, the larger size of the open-hearth furnace compensated for the speed factor and permitted the production of quality steels to meet the varied needs of industry and at a price to meet their cost requirements.

The need for steel by other industries was a powerful factor in bringing about the expansion of steel production, and, in turn, the ready availability of proper steels at modest prices acted as a powerful stimulus to the creation and expansion of industries that might use steel as a material for their own products. The railroads were doubtless the largest single factor encouraging the expansion of the steel industry, but soon other industries were adding their own large or small contribution to the total demand. Steel span bridges came into use and in 1888 there was constructed the first steel-framed "skyscraper," a building type impossible without low-cost steel beams and girders. Machines of all kinds were now made of iron or steel, and their greater strength and lightness increased their usefulness. Both agricultural and industrial machines found wider markets due to their better performance with all-steel construction. The invention of barbed wire and woven wire fence opened a new demand for steel, proved a great convenience to eastern farmers, and brought a virtual agricultural revolution to the farmers and stock raisers of the Great Plains. More recently, natural gas and petroleum products have been widely and cheaply distributed through steel pipe lines. The internal combustion engine, when perfected in design and construction, became the basis of the automobile and allied industries because iron and steel were available for its construction as well as for the varied vehicles which it powered. The use of steel in many industries was well begun before World War I, but all of these uses were merely forecasts of the extent to which American life has since come to depend upon iron and steel and their products. Even by 1915, the industries making and using iron and steel were by a substantial margin the largest group of American industries. Since that time the proportionate use of iron and steel among various nations and peoples of the world has become one of the best measures of their standard of living and level of material culture in general.

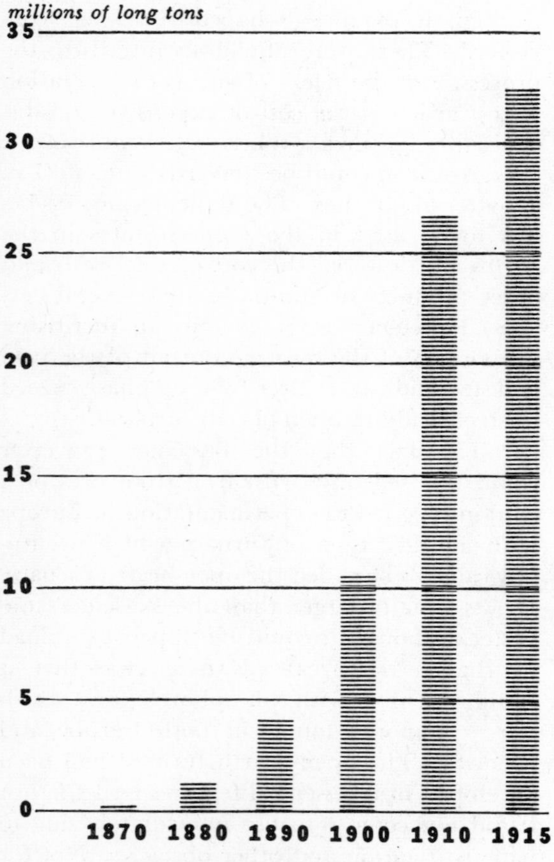

### The textile and clothing industries

The manufacture of cloth of various types and of articles made from cloth had a rapid expansion in the decades following the Civil War. The manufacturing of cloth and

*millions of long tons*

Fig. XI-5 A measure of the speed and extent of American industrialization between 1870 and 1915 is the growth in steel production during those years.

clothing requires much more time and effort than the production of the raw fiber, and has always made the largest demand on human effort among industrial occupations. The impact of the American industrial revolution during and after the Civil War brought an unparalleled expansion to the industries producing and using textiles, but they were still employing a smaller per cent of the labor force than the iron and steel industries.

The growth of textile production after the Civil War was not the result of spectacular inventions nor was it accompanied immediately by important shifts in the location, markets, or raw materials of the industry. The earliest concentration of the industry in America was in New England, and there it remained throughout the nineteenth century. After the Reconstruction era, which lasted approximately to 1877, the growth of mills proceeded at a more rapid rate in the South than in the North, and since southern mills were devoted to the manufacture of bagging and other coarse fabrics, their consumption of raw cotton by weight was greater than that of the northern mills by the time of World War I. In value of output the northern industry had a substantial lead because it turned out finer grades of cotton cloth. These grades had been secured from England for many years, so that a decline in imports accompanied the refinement of manufacture in America.

In addition to better machines for spinning cotton cloth, better printing machines were also developed; they brought about a "calico craze" in the 1880's. Improvements in the loom permitted easier weaving of stripes and figures and the replacing of empty bobbins without stopping. In general, the technical improvements in the industry were in the nature of refinements rather than the development of anything radically new. Yet, collectively, these refinements made very substantial savings in manufacturing cost and were largely responsible for the expansion of the textile market.

The woolen industry was something of an orphan of the industrial revolution in textiles. New inventions were adapted to woolen manufacture only partially and tardily. As late as the mid-nineteenth century, most woolen manufacture was conducted in widely scattered small mills. This was perhaps natural, in view of the fact that the raw material was widely scattered and that the production of woolens had originally been a home industry. Often the small mills would turn out flannels or blankets on a custom basis for farmers who brought their own wool to the mill for the purpose. The growth of demand, the introduction of English machinery, the need to import wool, and the shift of taste toward worsteds from woolens, all contributed to the gradual concentration of production in large establishments located in Massachusetts, Pennsylvania, and New York. Carpet weaving, a branch of the woolen industry which was centered in New England and New York, also expanded substantially during the period from 1860 to 1914 as homes became better furnished and as more homes were constructed to house the growing population.

The manufacture of ready-made clothing is a younger industry which could not arise until the sewing machine was perfected, and that did not take place until almost the Civil War period. The sewing machine was a light machine suitable for use at home. In fact, clothing was commonly made at home, except for expensive men's suits, made by custom tailors, and fine ladies' wear, made by dressmakers. The first ready-made clothing was very naturally the product of home workers who performed the essential operations on material put out to them. It was an organization of industry very similar to the putting-out system which had prevailed in the textile industry in both England and America at an earlier time. The first "factory" clothes were made for slaves and for the army and navy, where the user was scarcely a free purchaser. This fact perhaps gives us a clue to the quality of the product. The industry was always highly urbanized, existing at one time or another in all of the largest cities, especially in the East. Gradually, as more attention was given to patterns and with wider varieties and range of sizes, the respectability of ready-made clothing grew. By the first decade of the twentieth century, the purchase of a man's suit from a custom tailor was becoming exceptional for all but the well-to-do. Women adhered to their own efforts in making dresses more than they did for coats and suits, but the trend toward ready-made garments was increasing.

## The food-processing industries

The securing and preparation of food has always been man's first and most persistent

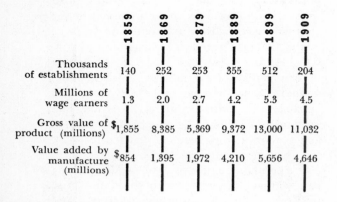

| | 1859 | 1869 | 1879 | 1889 | 1899 | 1909 |
|---|---|---|---|---|---|---|
| Thousands of establishments | 140 | 252 | 253 | 355 | 512 | 204 |
| Millions of wage earners | 1.3 | 2.0 | 2.7 | 4.2 | 5.3 | 4.5 |
| Gross value of product (millions) | $1,855 | 8,385 | 5,369 | 9,372 | 13,000 | 11,032 |
| Value added by manufacture (millions) | $854 | 1,395 | 1,972 | 4,210 | 5,656 | 4,646 |

*Fig. XI-6 An overall picture of the growth of manufacturing in the U. S. from 1859 to 1909. Figures for 1909 exclude establishments with less than $5,000 annual value of product.*

concern. Two aspects of food preparation which were hardest to accomplish within the single household were the first to become commercialized, i.e., flour milling and meat packing. Every frontier community had to have a flour mill nearby before it could regard itself as solidly established. Someone who specialized in the dressing of meat would usually set up in business soon after. As settlement spread westward and as larger towns and cities began to appear, flour milling and meat packing were sure to go along, and to become large-scale industries. In the early part of the nineteenth century, New York, Pennsylvania, and Virginia were leading flour-milling states because of their proximity to wheat. Cincinnati was the principal meat-packing center until the railroad brought about the settlement of the upper Mississippi Valley.

After the Civil War, the spread of the railroad network, the filling up of the Great Plains states, and several important technical developments led to much relocation and concentration of these basic food industries. The invention of the "middlings purifier," the introduction from Europe of the roller process of milling wheat, and the adaptation of both of these devices to the grinding of the hard spring wheat grown on the northern plains turned Minneapolis into a great flour-milling center. The older milling centers in the East persisted, but Minneapolis became the greatest producer of flour and milled wheat products in the world. The growth of cities in the decades after the Civil War and the popular trend away from home baking and the home preparation of food in general cut into the business of the thousands of small millers scattered throughout the country and contributed to the concentration of the industry in the hands of large producers with nationally known brands of flour and cereal products.

The development of artificial refrigeration after the Civil War had profound effects on meat packing. It could now become a year-round industry rather than a highly seasonal one concentrated in the cold months. Furthermore, the building of refrigerator cars made possible the wide distribution of fresh meats from the packing houses. This development led to a shift of consumer preference to fresh beef from pork, which had been eaten extensively as cured meat or ham. The meat-packing industry became centered in Chicago, Kansas City, and Omaha, nearer to the cattle supply. Meat packing came to be a big business, famous for its mass-production methods and development of uses for every scrap of an animal's carcass. Concentration of the control of the industry took place, and the names of Swift, Armour, Wilson, Morris, and Cudahy came to symbolize in the public mind not only big business in meat packing, but also monopolistic efforts to depress buying prices at the stockyards and to enhance selling prices at the butcher shops. The small, local packer could not compete on a technological basis with the efficient operation of the largest units in the industry. The growing preponderance of these large firms in meat packing brought against them charges of the same kind that farmers and consumers were bringing against railroads, implement manufacturers, and big business in general between the Civil War and 1914.

Another striking development of the period after the Civil War in the food industries was the development of the process of canning with the application of heat. At first in glass or earthen containers, but soon in tinned sheet steel cans, meats, vegetables, and fruits were preserved and sold to the public through regular groceries. Canning as a practical industrial process rested on the development not only of the autoclave, or pressure cooker, to sterilize the food in the cans, but also of machines to aid in the preparation of foods for canning, and for the manufacture and sealing of the cans. Canning cheapened the cost of food distribution, made possible year-round consumption of seasonal products, and stimulated immeasurably the removal of food preparation from the home. The bride who could do nothing in the kitchen beyond the wielding of a can opener became the butt of many jokes during the years before World War I; she was a character more real than fictional.

### New industries

Besides the expansion of long-established industries, several new industries which were destined to become part of the foundation of present-day industrial society were begun in the decades after the Civil War.

The first practical use of electricity was in the telegraph. The electrical generator, or dynamo, as well as the electric motor were invented before this period, but neither came into common use until later. After seemingly slow beginnings, Alexander Graham Bell had demonstrated by 1880 the practicality of his telephone, and Thomas A. Edison had invented the incandescent light bulb. The first central electric station in the United States was soon to be built in Appleton, Wisconsin. Thereafter, the multitudes of different uses of electricity for both light and power began to appear. Electric elevators made the use of skyscrapers possible, and large and small electric motors began to replace steam power in industry. City street-car systems were electrified and electric interurban lines sprang up in many places. Evenings at home were considerably brightened by incandescent lights, and if one had to go out, city streets were more brightly illuminated by electric arc lights than by gas. Electricity came to be so intimately interwoven with both the work and the pleasure of Americans, that its generation and distribution became a new basic industry contributing immeasurably to the growth of the economy.

The automobile industry was also born in the latter part of the nineteenth century. The four-cycle gasoline engine was invented by Otto and developed in Germany by Daimler and Benz. The first Benz car was brought to America from Germany in 1893 to be exhibited at the Chicago World's Fair. In that same year Henry Ford and Charles E. Duryea made the first American gasoline-driven cars. Electric and steam cars were also built. By 1915, the automobile and truck powered by gasoline engines had demonstrated their practicability. The industry had begun the rapid growth which was ultimately to put America on wheels. Automobiles required good roads, available gasoline supplies, serviceable tires, and handy service and repair facilities. When these things were provided, the automobile could and did revolutionize social and economic life by the speed with which persons and things could be moved. The provision of all these necessary facilities involved a real revolution in American production methods and results.

Petroleum had been discovered in quantity at Titusville, Pennsylvania, just on the eve of the Civil War. It was at first put to all sorts of odd uses (p. 221), but refineries were soon built to separate out the lighter from the heavier ingredients. The first sizeable markets were for kerosene and lubricating oils. Gasoline was a by-product, but its existence no doubt stimulated the development of the internal combustion engine in Germany and elsewhere. In a general way, the advancement of petroleum refining and the distribution of refined products was closely associated with the automotive industry, which was the major customer. The convenience of the new fuel and the many uses developed for it made the oil industry attain the status of a basic industry in the modern world.

The automobile also became the major user of the products of the rubber industry, which, like petroleum, had a history antedating the Civil War. The practical uses of rubber stemmed from what was said to be the accidental discovery by Charles Goodyear in 1839 of the process of vulcanization. By combining natural rubber with sulfur and other chemicals, the now familiar properties were developed, resulting in a material quite unlike the natural gum. Up to the 1880's, the largest use for rubber was in the manufacture of waterproof footwear and rain clothing. At that time, the bicycle craze created a demand for tires which at first were solid and after about 1890 pneumatic. The practicability of the latter type had been demonstrated in Great Britain by J. B. Dunlop in 1888. The first American-made automobiles rolled on solid rubber tires, but soon pneumatic tires in sizes for automobiles were constructed and demonstrated their superiority. By the time of World War I, the manufacture of pneumatic tires had become the major part of the rubber industry. Without these shock-absorbing tires, the usefulness of the automobile would surely have been much restricted.

## The extent of industrial change in America

Considering the total effect of the industrial developments in the period between the Civil War and World War I, one cannot doubt that in this interval America experienced an industrial revolution of great magnitude. Great progress in industry continued to be made following World War I, but it is doubtful if these later developments have been as startling in total result as those of the earlier period. By the time of World War I, America had become the greatest industrial producer of the world, though Germany, England, France, and Switzerland excelled in certain quality products. The potentialities of a number of new industries had been demonstrated. Scientific research was opening up fields for new industries and helping to solve the problems of older ones. Power had been applied to innumerable industrial processes, and more than ever the human worker was merely employed to guide the mechanical worker. Industrial work and the problems of living were eased. Productivity in industry had been stepped up, the national standard of living was higher, and the eight-hour day in industry was increasingly common. America had shown what an energetic and inventive people could do in an environment rich in resources of all kinds to alleviate the age-old burdens of living and to achieve a standard of life for the ordinary citizen of which even his recent ancestors would not have dreamed.

## FOR FURTHER READING

Bogart, Ernest L., and Kemmerer, Donald L. *Economic History of the American People*. 2nd ed. New York: Longmans, Green & Co., Inc., 1947. Chapter 20.

Cochran, Thomas, and Miller, William. *The Age of Enterprise*. Harper Torchbook, 1961. Paperback. Chapter 7.

Faulkner, Harold U. *American Economic History*. 8th ed. New York: Harper & Brothers, 1960. Chapter 20.

Hendrick, Burton J. *The Age of Big Business*. New Haven: Yale University Press, 1919. Chapters 1—3.

Nevins, A. *Study in Power: John D. Rockefeller, Industrialist and Philanthropist*. New York: Charles Scribner's Sons, 1953. Volume II, Chapter 22.

Tarbell, Ida M. *The Nationalization of Business*. New York: The Macmillan Co., 1936. Chapters 6, 12, and 15.

Williamson, Harold F. (ed.). *The Growth of the American Economy*. New York: Prentice-Hall, Inc., 1951. Chapters 22—25.

# Chapter 12:  The maturing of
# the American industrial economy

**A** series of developments in the late decades of the nineteenth century made it abundantly clear that a new day had arrived for American business. The shift in the balance of political power between rural and urban interests was one straw in the wind. Corporations had begun to displace partnerships and individual proprietorships in industry and business as firms became larger. Combinations of firms by one device or another to form still bigger businesses began to occur, and by the late 1890's combination became a positive rage (see Fig. XII-1, p. 240). Labor organizations grew in size and number, and several large and violent strikes occurred when employers resisted their demands. Mass production began to force attention upon the development of equally large-scale methods of distributing its products. Railroads after a period of great expansion found themselves more than able to carry the existing traffic, and by both open and secret devices sought to protect themselves against the violence of cutthroat competition. American business even began to cast its eyes toward adjacent territory beyond the national boundaries in its search for new markets, for investment outlets, and for raw materials.

### A new economic environment for business

What was the historic meaning of these unaccustomed activities? It is possible to recognize today that they indicated the maturing of the economy. Approaching maturity did not mean approaching stagnation; it meant only that America had caught up with other countries having similar economic systems in the development of its own native economic potential. If this view is correct, it might be expected that economic development in America from the end of the nineteenth century forward would follow a more settled course, expanding as possibilities of expansion should arise, but without the gold rush and bonanza atmosphere which so often characterized our earlier history. The economic system of a people does not follow the set course of birth, growth, maturity, and decline which has thus far been the inevitable fate of individuals. The maturity of an economy merely means that its development in the future will come from internal growth and progress rather than from expansion in size and in its scope of operation alone.

As economic growth filled the vacuum which a continent rich in resources had created for the American people, a chronic scarcity of goods both in relation to consumer needs and in relation to production possibilities was replaced by a greater abundance of goods available for consumption and by an increasing relative scarcity of opportunities for opening up new production facilities. No one rang a bell when this happened, or ran red headlines in the newspapers. In fact, it did not occur on any day or year that anyone could name, but gradually America began to have a new kind of economic system. Things began to happen, and have since happened with increasing frequency, which would have made no sense at all under the former circumstances. For example, when goods were scarce and opportunity was everywhere, the only thing which made sense was to produce more goods. When conditions began to reverse themselves, the businessman could make more money by forming a monopoly and producing less. Workers who disliked their pay or the conditions under which they worked joined with their fellow workers in unions to demand better pay and conditions rather than quitting for another job, which might not be found so easily as formerly. Investors began to find themselves accumulating funds faster than opportunities for the investment of those funds developed, so they began to look to Canada and Cuba and Latin America for investment outlets. Even the size of families began to decline as children, especially in the cities, became economic liabilities rather than assets—a corollary, in part at least, to the general restriction and changed character of economic opportunity. Customers became harder to find

for many businesses, advertising to find them was increased, and many manufacturers began to look abroad for buyers as American exports shifted increasingly from the raw materials of earlier days to the processed goods that helped to mark industrial maturity.

One explanation for this series of correlated economic changes was that the traditional *laissez-faire* system had failed to live up to its promise. Adam Smith was the great leader of English and American thought in the matter of the economic policy which governments should follow. America followed England's lead and went still further in setting up a governmental system which avoided control of or interference with business. One reason why *laissez faire* was carried even further in America than in England was that the system seemed at first to work remarkably well in a new country where opportunity was so abundant. Because it worked so well, there was a tendency to overlook the conditions assumed by Adam Smith, namely, that if the government did not control or interfere with business, free competition would result and there would be unrestricted economic opportunity. Instead, in the 1880's and 1890's, while the government did not interfere with or control business, developments occurred which led businessmen to combine to restrict production and to prevent newcomers from getting started, thus limiting opportunity and hampering or ending competition. To that extent, *laissez faire* had failed to produce competitive conditions which would exert a controlling influence on the individual businessman. The creation of monopolies destroyed the argument for permitting businessmen to operate freely without any governmental control.

Another conclusion which can be reached after examining the economic developments of the last quarter of the nineteenth century is that the capitalistic system, based upon complete *laissez-faire* principles, had reached its highest point within that period and began to exhibit signs indicating that a change or a modification of the system was inevitable. This point of view was first presented by a German economic historian, Werner Sombart, in his

*Der Moderne Kapitalismus,* published in three volumes from 1916 to 1927. This is a point of view which can easily be misunderstood, but fortunately our study of the development of the modern economy gives us a background with which to understand and judge the worth of Sombart's ideas. In the early chapters of this book, which traced the rise of capitalism in Europe, it was pointed out that capitalism can be viewed in two distinct ways. First, and somewhat more technically, capitalism can be viewed as an economic system in which capital as a factor of production has become essential to the productive process and to further growth. This condition results from the building up of technical knowledge of ways to construct and use various kinds of tools and equipment to help along the production process. The other point of view stresses the various economic institutions that have grown up historically along with the technical fact of the use of increasing amounts of capital in production. Such capitalistic institutions are banks; insurance companies; general business corporations; legal rules and practices to protect property; the habit of making the pursuit of gain a central theme in life; and, for England and America in particular, the protection of the right of the individual to join in with and to promote the various institutions of a capitalistic society.

In the late decades of the nineteenth century, Sombart pointed out, it was not the technical use of capital in production that was showing any signs of declining or even stabilizing. In fact, in these years the use of capital equipment was probably increasing faster than ever before. Agriculture was becoming capitalistic in the technical sense, as more costly machines and equipment were being developed to aid the farmer with his work. In industry, increased production was being secured by more, larger, and faster machines. Capital investment in industry was growing faster than ever before both in aggregate and in the amount per industrial worker. In this sense, capitalism was at its highest point and had shown no indications of doing anything other than continuing to grow even faster.

| | No. of consolidations | Capitalization |
|---|---|---|
| **1890** | 11 | $ 137,611,500 |
| **1891** | 13 | 133,597,167 |
| **1892** | 12 | 170,017,000 |
| **1893** | 5 | 156,500,000 |
| **1894** | 0 | 000,000,000 |
| **1895** | 3 | 26,500,000 |
| **1896** | 3 | 14,500,000 |
| **1897** | 6 | 75,000,000 |
| **1898** | 18 | 475,250,000 |
| **1899** | 78 | 1,886,050,000 |
| **1900** | 23 | 294,500,000 |
| **1901** | 23 | 1,632,310,000 |
| **1902** | 26 | 588,850,000 |
| **1903** | 8 | 137,000,000 |
| **1904** | 8 | 236,194,000 |
| *total* | 237 | $5,963,879,667 |

*Fig. XII-1 The number of consolidations of industries in the United States during the fourteen years from 1890 to 1904 add up to an impressive total.*

If, then, capitalism had reached its highest point and if a changed course of development was in prospect, it was clearly to be a change in the political, legal, and economic institutions of modern capitalistic society and not in the use of the technical capital on which modern society rests. It would be a change in the superstructure rather than in the base. Any growth and expansion of the base might in its turn also lead to a change in the superstructure. Concretely, the older idea of a capitalistic society was of one in which private property rights, freedom of economic opportunity, individual initiative, and free competition prevailed. It was found after experience with a century or more of this kind of system that instead of perpetuating itself indefinitely, it evolved toward both voluntary and coerced collective action in the form of big business monopolies, labor unions, and political groups with economic objectives. Free competition did not lead to more and freer competition, but to collective action and monopoly. It is simple enough to state those conclusions many years after the events of this period transpired, but it was not simple at the time to be aware of them. It seems that the older capitalism of what President Herbert Hoover was to call "rugged individualism" was being changed, by its own actions, into a newer collectivistic and monopolistic economic system, for which a new or modified name might be more appropriate. Professor Sombart named the period prevailing up to World War I as "full" or "high" capitalism. Within this period, the old spirit of rugged individualism remained, although businesses had become very large and were worldwide in their operations. This was the culmination of the older capitalism, in Sombart's view. Thereafter, the growing scale of businesses forced attention to internal problems of management rather than to bold and hazardous expansion. Modified business forms also developed, such as controlled public utilities, coöperatives, and public corporations. All of these institutions and practices were characteristic of what Sombart called "late" capitalism.

A more recent writer, Frederick L. Allen, pointed out in *The Big Change* (1952) that such changes were actually taking place in the American system. The understanding of these changes is vitally important to an understanding not only of the period between the Civil War and World War I but also of the years since.

### The attempts of
### business to restrain competition

As more and more branches of industry and business were filled up with considerable numbers of firms, each firm began to find its own operations limited and often checkmated by the existence of nearby competing firms. The term "free competition," which had become not only a slogan but a kind of moral principle to the American business community, had been valued up to this time pretty largely because of the freedom it offered to exploit the natural resources and markets of the growing nation. It now came to mean competition—not distant and occasional, but immediate, insistent, and keen competition which could and did degenerate into a cut-throat fight for business life. Very naturally, businessmen disliked the new situation, and they did what they could to win out for themselves by fair means or foul.

The railroads were among the first of the industrial groups to find themselves in a cut-throat competitive situation, especially in the eastern half of the country. As has been pointed out previously, most American railroads were built in large part as speculative ventures, since the amount of traffic which would be available for them could not be determined in advance. The bases for judging the soundness of a railroad enterprise were not very adequate, and very few people cared to make a detailed study when railway building offered the prospect of unlimited speculative gains, and when neighboring towns were competing for rail connections. The results were serious abuses and excessive promoters' profits, which made construction costs higher than they need have been. This condition was aggravated as building extended westward and the speculative aspects of construction were increased. It has been estimated that the Union Pacific cost nearly 50 per cent more than it need have cost with honest and competent management.[1] When operation of trains began, railroad managers found themselves saddled with high overhead or fixed costs and often with insufficient traffic to produce the necessary revenue to carry those costs along with the direct costs of operating trains.

In the East, where two or more roads might connect the same terminal points, the competitive situation was especially bad. The management of each railroad knew that there was enough traffic to make operating profitable if only shippers and passengers could be enticed away from competing roads. If additional traffic could be secured by secretly cutting the rates or by giving rebates to certain shippers,

[1] E. L. Bogart and D. L. Kemmerer, *Economic History of the American People*, 2nd ed. (New York: Longmans, Green and Co., 1947), p. 541.

that seemed wise, because the railroad had all of its fixed costs from construction to pay whether it operated or not, and even a reduced rate for freight might pay the road a great deal over the direct, "out-of-pocket" operating costs. Rate cuts or rebates given secretly to only a part of the shippers amounted to discrimination against other shippers, of course, but this fact did not prevent such practices.

In addition to discrimination between shippers, there was also discrimination between shipping points. A railroad might find it desirable to cut rates to attract business between Chicago and New York, where competition was keen, but would find no reason to cut rates for a shipper from a small rural station in Indiana which had only one railroad. In fact, as the railroads found themselves in financial trouble due to inadequate revenues, they often raised rates for rural and small town, noncompetitive shipping points. Sometimes these smaller towns would be along the line between major terminals where lower rates prevailed, and rural shippers discovered that it cost them more to ship their products a short distance than it cost shippers over the longer distance between terminal points. A Pennsylvania farmer might have to pay more per bushel to ship his wheat to New York than a Chicago shipper paid to ship wheat to New York from Chicago. This short and long haul type of discrimination especially irked farmers and caused much of their resentment toward the railroads.

Once shippers discovered that the threat of competition would induce railroads to discriminate in favor of particular shippers, great pressure was put upon the railroads to grant favorable terms. Large shippers would literally browbeat railroads both large and small into discriminating in their favor in various ways. One of the most notorious cases to come to light later was that of the Cincinnati and Marietta Railroad, in the 1870's. The road was induced by the Standard Oil Company to haul its oil from the nearby producing centers to Marietta, Ohio, for 10c per barrel while charging the Standard's competitors 35c per barrel for the same haul. In addition, the rail-road was to rebate to Standard the extra 25c per barrel which it collected from the competitors. The railroad finally received 10c per barrel net from all shippers. Contracts of this type were a principal means by which the Standard Oil Company gained for itself from 90 to 95 per cent of the oil-refining business by 1879. On a larger scale, Standard was able to get favorable rates from the Erie, the New York Central, and Pennsylvania Railroads. Other large shippers could force railroads to buy fuel, rails, ties, and other supplies and equipment from them or designated suppliers at high prices. Ownership of such supply firms by the officials of companies which were large shippers, or even by railroad officials themselves, was a favorite means of concealing unethical profits.

Except to the few companies, such as Standard Oil, which were able to use this cutthroat competitive situation to their own advantage, it was generally most unsatisfactory. The railroads, with their high construction costs and consequent high overhead, were up against an economic dilemma which had to be solved. To stabilize and control rebating, pooling agreements arose among them. Most important was agreement to maintain standard rates. To attain this objective the roads also agreed to pool traffic or revenue, i.e., to make a division on a predetermined basis. In such cases, the difficulties centered first in agreeing on the predetermined basis of division and then on the enforcement of that division. One effective method of enforcement was to require each road to turn over a given percentage of its receipts on traffic within the area of the pool to a "commissioner," who would then split the pooled fund among the roads according to their agreement. This system was used in the first major railroad pool, established in 1870 by the Northwestern, Rock Island, and Burlington roads between Chicago and Omaha. In 1884 this pool became the nucleus of a larger organization with the same objectives—the Western Freight Association. In all cases, the purpose was to deny to any single railroad the advantage that might otherwise accrue to it from rate cutting.

There were other pools in other parts of the country during this period, but all of them either broke up in failure or developed into more formal freight associations. Competition, therefore, was coming to an end in agreements to restrain competition through the stabilization of rates. But this action conflicted with the American philosophy and tradition of free competition, and the courts were inclined to regard it as setting up a monopoly to restrain trade.

Firms in other industries also found themselves in an economic position not unlike that of the railroads, except that the condition was not quite so general and did not develop so early. The introduction of large-scale, machine methods of manufacture gave other industries than the railroads a heavy fixed capital investment in machinery, buildings, and equipment. The interest charges on this investment and the costs of maintaining the buildings and machinery became overhead expenses which went on almost at the same rate whether the firm operated or was shut down. Likewise, the great increase in productive capacity brought about by machine methods gave these industries an excess capacity which meant that every firm could commonly handle more business than it could obtain. Furthermore, as in the case of the railroads, the extra business would be profitable so long as it could be obtained at a price higher than the costs that would be incurred directly in handling it, since the overhead had to be taken care of in any case and a little more business would not affect overhead. This condition invited price cutting and price wars to correspond with the rate wars of the railroads.

Price cutting and cutthroat competition did develop widely among industries during the prolonged depression beginning in 1873. The charge of discrimination between customers did not arise with price cutting by industry in general, because no customer *had* to buy from any given seller, as certain shippers *had* to ship over the only available railroad. The legal attitude toward an ordinary business transaction was that it was a voluntary agreement between buyer and seller which could

and did take place at varying prices, even for the identical product. But even if there were no question of illegal discrimination associated with price cutting, it could still bankrupt all but the one successful price cutter, who was then free to raise his prices unreasonably. The smaller producer lived in mortal dread of being driven out of business by price cutting on the part of a larger producer. The large producer, on the other hand, could never feel certain that the smaller competitors in his industry would not compel him to lower prices to the point where his profit was taken out of them. The existence of high overhead costs plus excess capacity made both large and small firms fear price cutting. The one satisfactory way of meeting the situation was combination.

Industrial combinations in the period from the 1870's to World War I passed through a number of forms in a kind of evolutionary sequence (see Fig. XII-2, p. 244). Both formal and informal pooling arrangements were used in industry, but less commonly than on the railroads. The great difficulty with pooling agreements is that they are hard to enforce, since they do not involve any real joining together or binding of the separate firms but depend entirely on willingness of members to continue in the pool. The most successful pools were those which divided up territory among competing firms, each firm making sales only in its agreed territory and staying out of the territories of its competitors. A breach in a pooling agreement of this kind could not well be kept secret, so that the agreement was to a considerable degree self-enforcing. Its result was a series of local monopolies to replace general, and perhaps cutthroat, competition. Then too, the existence of such a pool could not easily be proved, in the absence of a written pooling agreement, since no firm had any obligation to do business except where it had facilities and wished to do so. Being somewhat proof against charges of monopolistic combination, territorial pools have probably continued to exist to the present time, although it would be hard to prove their existence since they are informal and essentially secret in character.

Unlike the pool, which might be called a loose federation among competitors, other forms of combination brought about a more solid union among competing firms. One of the oldest of these other devices was the trust, first used by the Standard Oil Company in 1879. The legal idea of trusteeship was centuries old, but it was adapted to the end of achieving industrial monopoly only when the conditions of cutthroat competition became common with the period of recovery from the depression of 1873. It operated in a fairly simple fashion. The controlling stockholders of competing firms gave to a group of trustees their shares of stock in their firms, and received in return trust certificates of equivalent value. When the exchange had been made, the trustees had control of the formerly competing companies, and could unify their operating and price policies in the interest of the whole group. In effect, the competing firms became one firm. Between 1880 and 1890 trusts sprang up in a number of industries. There was a "Whiskey Trust," a "Sugar Trust," a "Lead Trust," a "Cotton-oil Trust," and many others, while the "Standard Oil Trust" has remained the most famous of all. But after court decisions in New York and Ohio in 1890 and 1892, the trust device was dropped and other forms of organization were sought to achieve the same objective of eliminating cutthroat competition. Stockholders of the constituent corporations of the trust were held by the courts to have a legal responsibility to manage their own corporations. To turn over the power of managing the corporation to a group of trustees was going beyond their legal powers as stockholders. Thus, the trust was held to be an inherently illegal device for the business purpose of combining a series of companies entirely without regard to the way in which the combination operated.

The principal successor to the trust was the holding company. This is a corporation empowered by its charter to own and hold the stocks of other companies. By such ownership the holding company can stop undesired competition between its subsidiary companies. The first large holding company was appar-

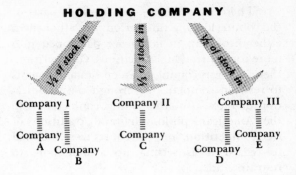

### HOLDING COMPANY

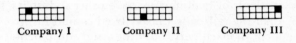

### INTERLOCKING DIRECTORATE

*Mr. X ■ on board of directors*

Company I    Company II    Company III

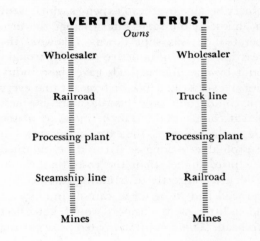

### VERTICAL TRUST

*Owns*

| Wholesaler | Wholesaler |
| Railroad | Truck line |
| Processing plant | Processing plant |
| Steamship line | Railroad |
| Mines | Mines |

### HORIZONTAL TRUST

*Owns*

Plant A    Plant B    Plant C

*Fig. XII-2 Various methods of reducing competition which have been used by big business.*

ently the Pennsylvania Company, chartered by the state of Pennsylvania in 1870 to give greater simplicity and efficiency to the management of the Pennsylvania Railroad's affiliated roads west of Pittsburgh and Erie. The holding company did not come into general use at that time because the right to own the stocks of other companies was not a traditional or basic right of a corporation. The state of New Jersey changed that situation in 1888 by amending its corporation laws to permit holding companies. Within a few years after 1888, as the legality of the trust was being attacked in Congress and the courts, there began a great swing to the holding company form of organization, a trend led by the Standard Oil Company. As the recovery from the depression of the 1890's began, following the critical election of 1896, the state of New Jersey came to operate a veritable charter mill, grinding out holding-company charters for all and sundry among American businesses. Most of the great business empires that dominate their respective industries in the twentieth century received their start with New Jersey holding-company charters issued in the years between 1898 and 1904. After the latter year, the decision of the Supreme Court in the Northern Securities Company case (p. 249) made businessmen bent on restraining competition less sure that the holding company was the answer to their prayers.

In the last decade before World War I, the prevailing attitude of many American business leaders changed from the "rule or ruin" of the eighties and nineties to "live and let live." Vigorous enforcement of the anti-trust laws (pp. 248-249) by the Department of Justice under Presidents Theodore Roosevelt and William Howard Taft stopped the head-long rush toward combination by way of the holding company or any other explicit device. The fundamental reason for combination had been to insure the profitability of business by removing the actuality or the threat of price-cutting competition. The incentive to price cutting came from the high overhead costs and relatively low direct costs which advancing machine technology gave to many industries.

Experience, plus some years of sober reflection, led more and more businessmen to realize an important fact about price policies, once industry had become large and highly mechanized. Price cutting, which might seem wise at the moment to achieve full capacity use of machines and equipment so long as the price one could get was higher than out-of-pocket costs, was foolhardy in the long run, because no firm in the industry could make enough under cut-rate prices to cover *all* its costs and stay out of bankruptcy. This was notably true of the railroads. As soon as the larger producers in an industry grasped this point, price cutting was likely to be replaced by price maintenance without any explicit agreement to pool or combine in any way.

The transition from price-cutting competition to price maintenance with competition restricted to other matters than price did not come suddenly. It began to be noticeable only in the years just before World War I. The destructiveness of price competition was deeply felt by business. It appeared that the only remaining alternative was to manufacture as cheaply and as well as possible and to accept the price leadership of the largest firms in an industry. In this way, there developed a common interest throughout industry not to "rock the boat."

The development of this communal interest and the rapid introduction of new methods making cost cutting possible enabled at least the larger industrial firms to make adequate profits by these means without price cutting in an effort to get more business. Amalgamations and mergers occurred among successful firms, and some of the newer and weaker ones died out. By the time of World War I, industries such as the automobile, steel, chemical, electrical goods, and many others were beginning to be dominated by a few large firms. Small firms either gathered the small fragments of business left by their larger competitors or, more commonly, concentrated on some specialty product in which they were not in direct competition with the large firms. The industrial scene was pervaded by the quiet hum of whirring machinery, and the buccaneering tactics of the eighties and nineties were only conversation topics for aging gentlemen as they met in their clubrooms or on the golf course.

There is an important financial causative element in the stabilization of the competitive situation which must not be overlooked. The rapid mechanization of numerous industries, which began during the Civil War and continued at an accelerated pace afterwards, required far greater quantities of capital than had ever before been available to American industries. To raise this capital was a task for which the average manufacturer had neither talent nor facilities. To fill the gap, the function of investment banking arose. The public had to be educated as to the nature of corporate stocks and bonds and had to be made willing to place its investment funds in them. To aid this stimulation of public investment, nothing was more important than a demonstration of the stability and profitability of issues which had already been sold. The investment banker, therefore, also took a vital interest in the manner in which the company was operated.

In the early decades after the Civil War, the investment bankers participated in some of the rather dubious financial deals that characterized the period. Jay Cooke, James J. Hill, and E. H. Harriman, connected with the promotion and financing of western railroads, were men of this type. A large number of the pools, trusts, and other forms of combination, were put together, if not promoted, by investment bankers. All the while that the investment banker was engaging in corporate manipulations, monopolistic or otherwise, he was seeking that "sure thing" which was to be a satisfactory bait for the investor. As financial adviser to business, he could see the common financial advantage to be derived from stable prices. The elimination of profit-destroying competition by agreement among businesses was just elementary good sense in his view. That that kind of agreement was monopolistic and after 1890 was made a violation of law did not alter in the least the desirability of the objective. It simply meant that

the objective of stability would have to be sought by some means that was within the law. Any inclinations toward price cutting which a manufacturer might have, therefore, were, in any case, likely to be opposed by his investment banker.

As more capital was required by industry, the investment banker became a more essential friend and counsellor to the industrialist. The need for capital made it necessary to pay heed to the financial point of view. Often the investment banker retained a representative on the boards of directors of firms whose financing he was handling. This practice made the financial point of view ever present at directors' meetings. The same individual or an associate was frequently a board member of many firms, and could speak with authority on the policies to be followed by them. Inevitably, the highly important rôle of the investment banker made him an ever-present guide on important matters of policy and a potent contributor to the evolution of the "don't rock the boat" philosophy which came to prevail among American businesses. This condition of informal restraint of competition came to be known as the system of "interlocking directorates." Most commonly, the "interlocked directors," sitting as members of the boards of directors of several or many companies, were investment bankers.

The firm of J. P. Morgan and Company became the leading investment banking house in American business history. Getting his start as a young man during the Civil War era, the elder J. P. Morgan built up for himself and his associates a reputation for competence, almost wizardry, in the handling of the financing of business. Bankers and the public came to have confidence in all stock and bond issues which his firm sponsored. His success in handling corporate financing became so consistent that large numbers of businessmen and industrialists chose his firm to handle their financing operations. The firm of J. P. Morgan and Company came to have an almost monopolistic position in American investment banking. Morgan and his partners became the most powerful financial figures in the country, being represented on the board of directors of many important banks and business firms. The prevalence, in the decade before World War I, of a sense of financial "community of interest" among American businesses was connected in an important way with their dependence upon the investment banker, and in particular it was a testimonial to the power, prestige, and, one might say, omnipresence of J. P. Morgan and Company. The position and the activities of the Morgan firm in concentrating financial power and limiting business competition constituted merely the outstanding but not the only example of the building up and using of financial power in this period. An investigating committee appointed by Congress and commonly known as the Pujo Committee reported in 1913 that Morgan, Rockefeller, and a very few other financial groups dominated banks and allied financial institutions which in turn controlled a majority of the resources of all such institutions in the entire country.[1]

## The attempts of government to restrain business

It was not according to the American plan of the relationship between government and business that businesses should cease competing. But when railroads and other industries reached a stage by the late seventies where competition was hurtful, pools, trusts, communities of interest, and holding companies popped out all over the industrial scene like mushrooms in the woods after a warm spring rain. This was not according to the *laissez-faire* theory, but business was not interested in theory; it was interested in profits and survival. Neither were farmers, shippers, consumers, and working people interested in theory. They were interested in good service and good products at prices as low as was reasonably possible. The latter groups contained more people and

[1] See below, p. 254.

more voters than did the business groups. When really aroused they could swing the government toward the policies they desired. But what policies? Was the failure of *laissez faire* so complete that America would have to turn toward some kind of new system—perhaps the socialism that was increasingly attractive to the working classes of western European nations at that same time? Some Americans thought so, but many more thought that *laissez faire* could still be salvaged, that if business did not want to compete, the solution of the difficulty was to make it compete. This became the official policy, and the first general departure from *laissez faire* was to have the government tell business not what it should do, but only what it should not do. If *laissez faire* would not work alone, perhaps it would work with a little aid from the government.

Since railroads affected so many people so directly, and since they were, like public utilities, in such a monopolistic position, it was natural that the revision of the traditional *laissez-faire* policy should first affect railroads. Even before the Civil War some of the eastern states had established railroad commissions in their governments, but usually these commissions had only investigative functions. When rate discrimination of various kinds became rife in the years following the war, commissions with stronger powers were established, especially in western states which were the victims of most of the discrimination. This movement even antedated the Grange, but was vigorously supported and extended by the Grangers when they were at the height of their political activity. These state commissions were given power to set maximum rates which might be charged by railways and other public-service corporations within their respective states. The famous case of Munn *versus* Illinois, decided by the United States Supreme Court in favor of the state of Illinois in 1876, established the principle that government was acting within its constitutional powers when it exercised such controls over railroads or other public-service corporations. These early state laws did not prevent cutting of rates, but they did give power to the state commissions to stop the other half of the discriminatory practice, namely, putting higher rates on shippers in areas where the railroad had no competition to make up for cutting of rates in areas where competition was keen.

There was also agitation from the western section of the country for federal regulation of railroads, since the states could control rates only within their own boundaries. The first Congressional investigation of the matter was made by the Windom Committee, which reported to Congress in 1874; but nothing was done at that time. In the following decade, rate discrimination became far more widespread and even chronic, and a second Congressional Committee was appointed to investigate the matter, under the chairmanship of Senator Shelby M. Cullom of Illinois. The Committee's report was made in 1886, and on its recommendation Congress in the following year enacted the Interstate Commerce Act. This epoch-making act created the Interstate Commerce Commission to investigate the conduct of the railroads and to enforce the terms of the Act. In general, it provided that all rates should be just and reasonable and that there should be no discrimination of any kind. The Act was amended and strengthened on three different occasions before World War I, by the Elkins Act of 1903, the Hepburn Act of 1906, and the Mann-Elkins Act of 1910. The result was a fairly effective regulation which eliminated many of the evils produced by collusion.

The growth of railroad regulation was followed, after a few years, by regulation of monopolistic tendencies in business and industry in general. While businessmen were engaged in trying to protect themselves from the forces of competition, the public began to shout ever more insistently the word "monopoly." Several popular books aided in creating a public attitude of hostility toward business and its methods. Henry George's *Progress and Poverty* was first published in 1879, Edward Bellamy's *Looking Backward* was published in 1888, and in 1889, the House of Representatives published a *Report on Investigation of Trusts*. Several cases were made public involving gouging of the public, cor-ruption of public officials, and the like. These finally stirred Congress to action. In 1890 a bill introduced by Senator John Sherman of Ohio was passed, and became the basis of American law on industrial monopoly. The Sherman Anti-trust Act is not a complicated law, in essence providing only that "every contract, combination in the form of trust or otherwise, or conspiracy, in restraint of trade or commerce among the several states, or with foreign nations, is hereby declared to be illegal." This statement was elaborated a little, and penalties for violation were provided, but that was all. The terms of the act were general and no definitions were given. As a matter of fact, it did not do more than provide a specific statute for the United States out of the principles of the English common law on monopoly. Apparently the committee which drafted the bill intended it to be general and even vague, leaving to the courts the making of such distinctions as might be needed.

The Sherman Act was passed during the term of President Benjamin Harrison, who was not disposed to instruct the Department of Justice to proceed vigorously under its terms. Similarly, Cleveland and McKinley following him were content to let well enough alone. No new monopolistic combinations were in process of formation in the early and middle nineties, in any case. Taking his election in 1896 as a definite victory for business interests, McKinley seemed to feel that the promoters of combinations should be given a free rein as a well-deserved reward. Ironically, the first major application of the Sherman Act was an injunction issued under its terms in 1894 against the labor leaders of a strike among employees of the Pullman Company. They were thrown into jail for six months and the strike was broken as a conspiracy to restrain trade (p. 252). In 1895, the Supreme Court refused to prevent the American Sugar Refining Company from buying the plants of four competitors, although the purchase gave it control of 95 per cent of the refining capacity of the country. The court said, "Commerce succeeds to manufacture, and is not a part of it." Therefore, the Act did not pertain.

A period of more vigorous enforcement of the Sherman Act began after Vice-President Theodore Roosevelt succeeded to the presidency on McKinley's assassination. Roosevelt was a shrewd politician who realized that there were many thousands of voters who felt aggrieved by the activities of monopolistic big business. He instructed the Department of Justice to inaugurate a suit against the Northern Securities Company, a New Jersey holding company which had apparently been formed to create a monopoly of the northern railroads to the Pacific by its ownership of a controlling stock interest in the Great Northern and Northern Pacific railroads. The government won the case in 1904, and the company was ordered to divest itself of the stock of the two competing roads. Many other suits were filed in the administrations of Roosevelt and his successor William Howard Taft. Two of the most famous of these won by the government were the Standard Oil Company case in 1911, by which the company was required to split up into independent regional companies, and the American Tobacco Company case in the same year, splitting that company into a number of separate units. Both original companies were holding companies.

Although the government won important cases and forced the dissolution of combinations, it remained a real question whether the Sherman Act was in fact promoting competition. The belief became general that it was not doing so, because of the loopholes in the Act made possible by the vague phrasing that had been used. The Democrats long advocated strengthening of the Sherman Act, and when Woodrow Wilson became President in 1913 he urged such revision upon Congress. In 1914, the Clayton Anti-trust Act was passed, naming a series of practices as monopolistic in intent and therefore forbidden. These included price discrimination and the formation of holding companies and interlocking directorates. Labor and farm organizations were specifically exempted from the anti-trust laws. In the same year, the Federal Trade Commission was created as a body to make continuous investigations of business practices to see if they were violating the law; if it found violations it might issue an order to cease and desist.

During the years in which governmental attempts to enforce competition were under way, many of the most egregious business practices were discontinued. At the same time it was recognized that technology required large firms with extensive resources and large markets. Such firms were turning out mass-produced articles which made the lives of millions more comfortable, and, with the prosperity and expansion of activity brought about by World War I, public demand for anti-trust action declined. Public opinion was ready to go along with the Supreme Court in the "rule of reason," laid down in 1911 in the Standard Oil and American Tobacco cases, that not every possible kind of restraint of trade that might be discovered was illegal, but only "unreasonable" restraint. When a firm is very large, every move that it makes might be stretched into a restraint of trade of some kind or other. The court implied that such a construction would be unreasonable. The public was prepared for the decision in the case of the United States Steel Corporation, held over until after the war. The decision, announced in 1920, embodied the attitude that bigness is not badness. In other words, a big business may lawfully perform all the actions normally associated with that type of business without fear of prosecution. To back the charge of monopoly, "unreasonable" restraint of trade must be proved. With the U. S. Steel decision, *finis* was written to the "trust-busting" era begun by Theodore Roosevelt, and the country was ready to settle back and enjoy a decade of the greatest material prosperity in its history— a decade which was characterized by the goal expressed in the political slogan "two cars in every garage and a chicken in every pot."

### The growth of labor organization

In the half century between 1860 and 1910 some striking changes occurred in the kinds of jobs at which the American people worked. In 1860, 6.2 million people, constituting 59 per cent of the gainfully employed of the nation, were engaged in agricultural pursuits of one kind or another. By 1910, this group had grown to 11.6 million, but at that time it constituted only 31 per cent of the gainfully employed. (Incidentally, this was the high point in American history for agricultural employment.) In 1860, nonagricultural pursuits employed 4.3 million people, or 41 per cent of the total gainfully employed. By 1910, this industrial, business, and professional group had grown to 25.8 million people who constituted 69 per cent of all employed persons. During the half century, the number of farmers had less than doubled, while the number of city and town workers had multiplied six times. Behind these cold and impersonal statistics lie the developments in industry, agriculture, and transportation which previous chapters have outlined. Immigrants poured into the United States at a growing rate during the half century to a total of nearly 23,000,000, and southern Europe rather than the northern countries furnished an increasing proportion of them. Most of them went to the growing cities, which were also receiving an influx of population from rural areas. The basis of livelihood was changing, and the environment in which most Americans lived was also changing. Income was beginning to be derived from work in a factory, store, or office. Entertainment came from such sociability as a more or less crowded city neighborhood might offer, or from commercial "amusement palaces" of one kind or another which sprang up in cities and towns. A new mode of life had begun for Americans.

At the outset, the workers from the farms of America or Europe who filled the factories and constructed and ran the railroads were not much interested in collective action. The individualistic tradition was strong, especially among the American-born workers. Banding together into unions to seek improvement in wages and working conditions was a type of action that came less easily and logically to most workers than quitting the job if condi-

tions were unsuitable and getting another which might be better. Workers from English or German cities came from a background which was different and in which trade unions had been known and accepted for a long time. Many members and leaders in the early years of American unionism were of recent north European urban extraction.

Employers in the early years of American industrialism vigorously resisted the growth of unions. In a period of rapid industrial expansion, the statistical probabilities of success were good for any capable promoter of a new or expanded industrial operation. He then was inclined to believe that almost anyone could do the same thing. The sole quality in a worker which such an employer could understand and approve was the quality of trying to get ahead individually. If he should be confronted by union demands in his factory or his railroad, he was likely to view the organization, its leaders, and its members with a blind hatred. His strongly individualistic feeling led him to fear any control over wages and working conditions in his firm outside of that exercised by management itself. The fact that pools, trusts, and holding companies represented collective action by businessmen to improve their earning power did not lead him to approve of union organization by workers for the same reason.

Because both employers and many workers were hostile to unions, it required strong counter pressure to achieve their formation. In a very general way, the changed mode of life and work which industry brought worked in the direction of a changed philosophy of life. The psychology of the frontier was not appropriate when a man might work ten or more hours a day, six days a week, in a factory, and live with his family crowded into a dark fourth-floor-rear tenement in a building with no elevator and with water and toilet facilities available only in a courtyard nearby. A common life, a common means of earning a living, and common fears made collective action seem natural to more and more people. Still the individualistic tradition was extremely tenacious, so that unions were likely to take root at first only where conditions were extremely bad or distasteful to workers. Early unions also often appealed to the workers first as welfare organizations to improve their position, to increase their pride in their status as industrial workers, and to bring about general reform of society by any available means including political action.

The industrial boom during the years of the Civil War resulted in the formation of many scattered local unions and some national ones in the cities. The "Brotherhood of the Footboard," formed in 1863, was to become the first of the great unions of operative employees on the railroads, the Brotherhood of Locomotive Engineers. There were also several attempts to establish national unions in the years immediately after the war, while the boom continued. The first of these, established in 1866, was the National Labor Union, whose member organizations included a hodge-podge of city local groups and national organizations of various trades. Its objectives ranged from tenement house reform and the eight-hour day to the exclusion of Chinese immigrant laborers. The Knights of St. Crispin, formed in Milwaukee in 1867, quickly became a very large organization, especially in the New Eng-

land shoe industry. Both of these organizations collapsed in the hard times after 1873. The Noble Order of the Knights of Labor, founded in Philadelphia in 1869, started slowly at first, and was able to survive through the seventies to become in the eighties the most powerful labor organization up to that time.

The Knights of Labor was an idealistic organization, secret in its early years, with a ritual, and designed to promote the dignity of labor and labor's right to a just share of the product. One of its objectives was that of promoting the harmony of interests of labor and capital. Men and women, skilled and unskilled, were received into membership on equal terms. As much as one-fourth of the membership might consist of persons who were interested in the objectives of the organization but who were not wage earners. Because of the mixture of interests in the membership, it was often difficult for the Knights to make decisions for action. One group of the members favored reform through political action. Another wanted to improve wages and working conditions by direct pressure on employers. The latter group was the larger, and was able to involve the organization in several strikes in the early eighties, with various results. In

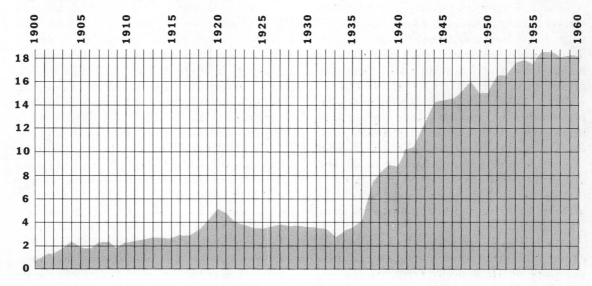

Fig. XII-3 Membership in labor unions shows an overall growth between 1900 and 1960, although there were periods when union membership declined temporarily for various reasons.

1885, the Knights gained great prestige by winning strikes against two western railroads dominated by Jay Gould, the financier, who was an unpopular figure at the time. Members flocked into the organization and carried its membership to an all-time high of 700,000 in 1886. In the same year, another strike was called in protest against the firing of a prominent Knight by one of Gould's western railways, allegedly in violation of agreement. The shopmen of all the southwestern railroads joined in the walkout, although the railroad brotherhoods did not. Violence flared, troops were called in, public sympathy was alienated, and the strike, after dragging on for some weeks, was lost. Thereafter, the membership of the Knights of Labor declined rapidly, and it was never again a force in the American labor movement.

The years 1886 to 1894 saw several major strikes, some accompanied by extreme violence, which revealed the growing strength of both industry and labor, and the unwillingness of either to work effectively with the other for the public welfare. In May 1886, four workmen were shot by police in a scuffle between strikers and nonstrikers at the Chicago works of the McCormick Harvester Company. A protest meeting the next evening in Haymarket Square in Chicago was nearing its end when 180 policemen charged into the remains of the crowd. Someone threw a bomb into the midst of the police and fifteen of them ultimately died. The country was shocked by the violence. Labor was intimidated by large-scale police brutality, and the public became fearful of extremist violence in labor unions. The affair undoubtedly set back the development of mutual understanding between labor and management for many years. The progress of the eight-hour day movement, for which the McCormick strike had been called, was virtually halted.

In 1892, another outbreak of violence occurred in a strike against the Carnegie Steel Company at Homestead, Pennsylvania, just outside of Pittsburgh. The union, the Amalgamated Association of Iron and Steel Workers, had become strong in the Pittsburgh area and refused to accept a wage cut proposed by H. C. Frick, president of the Carnegie company. Frick tried to bring in a large group of Pinkerton detectives as plant guards, and their entrance to the plant was opposed by the strikers. A fight followed in which twelve persons were killed. State militia were called in to restore order and to remain while the strike was in effect. The union's resources were soon exhausted, the strike was lost, and the union was all but destroyed. In 1894, the strike of several unions of railroad workers, led by Eugene V. Debs, in support of a strike against the Pullman Company in Chicago was lost by the intervention of troops and the use of a federal injunction against the leaders under the Sherman Act. As a result of this experience Debs became convinced that revised tactics were necessary. He later became America's most famous Socialist, running as a candidate for president several times, but he was never again important as a labor leader. These and other strikes revealed an increasingly hostile attitude on the part of the public, business, and government officials toward unions, which slowed their growth and permitted only the most cautious and subdued use of the collective force of organization.

The rise of the American Federation of Labor took place in these same years of labor turmoil and violence. A number of unions which had been growing in membership as recovery came from the depression of the 1870's and which opposed the idea of one big union like the Knights of Labor, met in Pittsburgh in 1881 to form the Federation of Organized Trades and Labor Unions of the United States and Canada. There was hostility between the Knights and the new organization because many of their goals were the same and both groups sought the affiliation of some of the same trade unions. The new union completed its plans in a convention in Columbus, Ohio, in 1886, when the name American Federation of Labor was adopted, and the constitution was revised to place more emphasis on collective bargaining and less on political activities including agitation for labor legislation.

The character of the new organization was completely different from that of the Knights of Labor. As its name implies, it was a federation, not one big union. The member unions might be national trade unions, such as those of the carpenters or steamfitters, or assemblies of local unions in cities. When the Knights lost public favor with their defeat in the Gould railway strike in 1886, the A. F. L. gained by their loss. The new organization was fortunate in that it did not have its name connected with any of the unpopular strikes in which violence had occurred, and it built for itself a solid reputation for what Samuel Gompers, its president for many years, called "business unionism." Whereas many of the unions organized during the nineteenth century lost out because of ill-considered actions, poorly constructed organization, and too much concentration on distant political reforms, the A. F. L. stuck to the pursuit of immediate gains for the worker in his job. As it gained those limited objectives, it also gained favor with working people. The public liked its cautious and conservative approach to the problems of labor, and it became the core of the American labor movement for ensuing decades.

### Modernizing the banking system

Although the system of national banks established in 1864 eliminated many deficiencies in the nation's monetary and banking system, subsequent experience proved that it, too, left much to be desired. Most important, perhaps, was the complete decentralization of the banking system effected through the sections of the law almost completely abolishing branch banking and prohibiting investment by a bank in corporate stocks. These provisions, together with relatively liberal provisions on the minimum amounts of capital required to open a bank (as low as $50,000 and later $25,000 in communities of less than 3000 people), led to the growth of a great many small banks, directed in many instances by people with little competence in the field. This

number was augmented after 1900 by many thousand state banks, which were able to prosper even without the ability to issue bank notes because of the more restrictive regulations under which the national banks operated. Thus, the state banks needed less capital to start with, they could float loans with real estate as security (which was forbidden to the national banks), and their reserve requirements were much lower than those for the national banks. By 1893, there were nearly 3500 state banks in the country, exceeding the number of national banks; by 1910, there were nearly 13,000, outnumbering national banks almost 2 to 1 (though the disparity in financial resources was not nearly so high).

As a result of these developments, the country was saddled with a great many relatively small banks subject to practically no control. When times were good, control was not absolutely necessary, but when business activity turned downward, proper action by the banking system, correctly timed, might have gone a long way toward returning the economy to an even keel. It was soon realized, however, that to attempt such action without centralized control was a well-nigh hopeless proposition, and that banks, when left to themselves, tended to act in a manner that accentuated a crisis rather than relieving it. Thus, the recession of 1907 was intensified by the action of the banks in reducing call loans sharply and in general taking measures to decrease the quantity of money at the very time when the opposite was needed.

Another deficiency of the national banking system was the inelasticity of the currency. In their eagerness to abolish the wholesale issue of state bank notes, the legislators went to the opposite extreme, and provided such rigid controls on the currency as to leave little flexibility. The national banks could issue bank notes, but only up to 90 per cent of the market value of United States bonds in their possession or the same percentage of the par value of the bonds, whichever was less. The result was a currency which tended to fluctuate more with the price of United States bonds than with the exigencies of business. The situation would actually have been desperate (and might have been remedied much sooner) were it not for the growing use of bank deposits as currency. For this reason, it took about twenty more years and a few recessions before the inadequacy of this kind of currency was fully realized, until people saw that by contracting note issues in a recession a bank was, in effect, reducing the amount of deposit currency at a time when more, rather than less, currency was needed.

The short but acute financial panic centering in New York in 1907 finally convinced almost everyone who paid attention to financial matters that something needed to be done to remedy the persistent weaknesses showing up in the National Bank Act. A National Monetary Commission was appointed to study the entire matter, and it issued a report in 1912 recommending the setting up of a strong central bank.

Meanwhile, the Democratic minority in the House of Representatives had created a committee of its own, the Pujo Committee, to make its own investigation. This committee had uncovered data showing that three New York financial institutions—J. P. Morgan and Company, the First National Bank, and the National City Bank—not only had tremendous resources of their own, but through directorships of corporations and other devices exercised control over many other banks, insurance companies, railroads, and manufacturing companies that extended from coast to coast, and dominated a substantial fraction of American business. This revelation shocked the country, and Wilson's administration was determined that in correcting weaknesses of the National Bank Act, it would not add to the centralized financial power.

The Federal Reserve Act, which was passed in 1913 to remedy the situation, therefore provided for a system of regional banks, between eight and twelve in number, rather than a single centralized bank as was common in Europe at that time. Actually, the fear of centralization was so great that twelve banks were set up at once. Control over the banking system was effected by requiring all national

banks to become member banks in the Federal Reserve system and by allowing state banks to join if they desired. Member banks had to subscribe a sum of 6 per cent of their capital and surplus for stock in their regional Federal Reserve Bank and were required to maintain fixed reserves on deposit with the regional Reserve Bank. These reserves amounted to 3 per cent of time deposits (those payable after thirty days' notice) and from 7 to 13 per cent of demand deposits (payable on demand), the percentage varying according to the location of the member bank. Reserves were highest for central reserve city banks and lowest for country banks. Each Federal Reserve Bank in its turn was required to maintain a reserve of 35 per cent of its deposits, a practice that remedied the old custom of pyramiding almost all reserves in the banks of New York.

A board of nine directors, a majority of whom were to represent nonbanking interests, supervised the operations of each Federal Reserve Bank, and the entire system was coördinated by a Federal Reserve Board in Washington. This Board and the Reserve Banks were given the power to engage in open-market operations and to regulate rediscount rates. These were the two weapons which, it was hoped, would enable the banking system to counteract the effects of a recession. Raising the rate of interest at which banks could exchange customers' notes for currency at the Federal Reserve Banks would, it was hoped, tend to dampen inflationary or speculative movements by restricting the amount of credit. Conversely, decreasing the rediscount rate when business activity was falling off would stimulate activity by making it cheaper to secure credit. Open-market operations were designed to achieve the same ends from a different angle. By means of these open-market operations, which means simply the purchase or sale of financial paper (usually government bonds) on the open market, the Federal Reserve Banks could increase or decrease the money supply. For example, the purchase of $10,000 in government bonds by a Federal Reserve Bank meant that the $10,000 paid for the bonds was put into circulation, into the deposits of the purchasing bank. The bank could use this money as a basis upon which to create many times that sum in new deposits, the total new deposits permissible being determined by its reserve ratio. If it were a country bank, the reserve ratio for which was 7 per cent initially, new deposits and loans amounting to $142,856 could be created, if the bank wished. In a similar way the Federal Reserve could contract the money supply by reversing the above process and selling government bonds on the open market.

A more elastic currency was established by enabling the Federal Reserve Banks to issue notes secured by gold, gold certificates, or high-grade commercial paper,[1] subject to the maintenance of a gold reserve of not less than 40 per cent against these issues. The element of elasticity was provided by the permission to issue notes against commercial paper, for in good times, when more money might be needed, the supply of commercial paper rose sharply, and in poor times it would contract. Thus, with this new battery of weapons in its financial arsenal, the nation felt that it finally had a banking system capable of fulfilling its needs. The Federal Reserve system undoubtedly represented a tremendous stride forward on the road to financial stability, even though many kinks remained to be straightened out.

## Markets, raw materials, and overseas investments

Another facet of the maturing American industrial economy was the changing trade relationship between the United States and the rest of the world. At the beginning of the nation's history there was a great continent to develop, relatively few people, and very little industry. There was an enormous need for manufactured goods both for immediate consumption and to assist in developing the country. They could not be produced in sufficient quantity in the United States, so that raw materials and raw foodstuffs were sold abroad to pay for the import of essential manufactured goods. As domestic industries developed through the years, the United States was gradually able to produce more of its own manufactured goods and to work up more of its own raw material. It became less dependent upon the outside world for supplies, and, on the other hand, became the producer of more and more goods which other countries wanted. In effect, therefore, the United States had a comparative advantage in raw materials in trading with other countries during its early years, but in later years the phenomenal progress made in mass-production techniques caused this advantage to shift to manufactured goods.

The change in foreign trade seems to center in the year 1875 (see Fig. XII-4, pp. 256-257). From 1841 to 1875, the United States exported goods to a greater value than its imports in only seven out of the thirty-five years; from 1876 to 1910, another thirty-five year period, the situation was reversed, and it exported more than it imported in thirty-two of the years. Furthermore, a part of the change in this trade was a change in kind. Even as late as the decade from 1851 to 1860, about one-half of all imports were still manufactured goods. In the period from 1906 to 1915, the proportion of manufactured goods was only about one-fifth. The export of manufactured goods grew from approximately 12 per cent of all exports in the pre-Civil War decade to about 29 per cent in the pre-World War I decade. All of these trends in foreign trade continued after World War I. The United States still exported some crude materials and purchased some manufactured ones, but by 1915 its trade had achieved a balanced proportion between raw and manufactured products which indicated a more evenly balanced industrial economy.[2]

Foreign investments in the United States played a major part in the growth of foreign trade in more than one way. For one thing,

[1] Any type of note or draft in which one business firm acknowledges its obligation to pay a specified amount at a specified date to another firm or person.

[2] All statistical comparisons based on data in *Historical Statistics of the United States, op. cit.*, Series M55, 56, 61, 62, and 67, pp. 244-247.

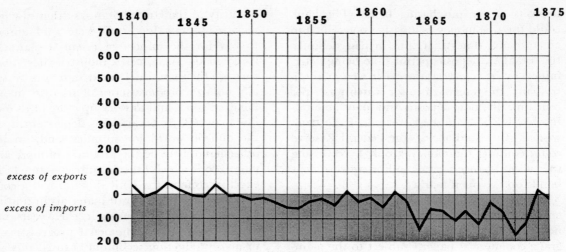

Fig. XII-4 It is clear that the year 1875 can
be taken as a turning point in the balance of
American foreign trade. Notice that before 1875
there was usually an excess of imports, while
after that date exports almost always exceeded imports.
Figures represent millions of dollars.

they provided badly needed capital for the expansion of American industry. More directly, the interest payments on the capital furnished the foreign investors with much additional purchasing power with which to buy American products. Following the depression of 1873, foreign investment in the United States rose sharply, until by 1890 there was about $3 billion worth of foreign capital in the country, around twice the amount there had been in 1873. Capital inflow resumed after the depression of the 1890's, and the amount of foreign capital in the country again doubled between that time and 1914. The interest payments and general profitability of these large foreign investments undoubtedly contributed a great deal to the favorable balance of trade in goods achieved between 1875 and 1910. During these years, the interest payments on these investments usually exceeded the capital inflow, thereby providing a net balance available for the purchase of American goods.

These underlying facts of foreign trade are merely statistical indicators of developments in American relations with the rest of the world which were taking place on a wider stage. They reflected the emergence of the United States from a century of continental isolation to the status of a world power with economic interests that extended far beyond its borders. The American economy had developed to the point where markets overseas were being sought for manufactured products. Europe, especially England, had always been both America's principal source of supply and principal customer, and continued to have this rôle. In addition, trade relations became important with the rest of North and South America and with Asia. American investments abroad were still not large, but they were expanding significantly in volume near the turn of the century. Large-scale industry and continuously advancing technology in America created demands for more, and more varied, fuels and raw materials. For some of these America was compelled to look abroad because of inadequate supplies at home. There was a more lively interest throughout the United States, but especially among the people of the Atlantic, Gulf, and Pacific coasts, in the far parts of the world where we had customers, investments, and sources of supply.

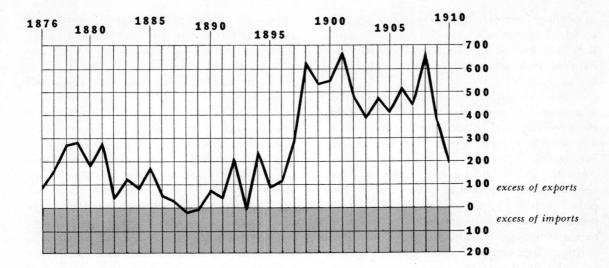

*excess of exports*

*excess of imports*

It appeared that America was about to enter a third period in its history with an important rôle to play on the world stage. In this period it was to develop a concern about conditions far beyond its own shores, and even to turn to a new kind of imperialism.

The new imperialism of the United States was manifested in the Spanish-American War and other events around the turn of the twentieth century. The United States had had an interest in the fate of Central and South America since the slave and rum trade of the colonial era (pp. 120-121). The Monroe Doctrine of 1819 expressed both the isolationism of the American people and their interest in maintaining the integrity of the territory of their southern neighbors.

Prior to 1898, some American newspapers, notably those of William Randolph Hearst, had been whipping up hostility toward Spain because of her mistreatment of the Cuban people, and the sinking of the battleship *Maine* with heavy loss of life was the pretext for a declaration of war against Spain. The war was brought to a successful conclusion within a year with Spain's complete surrender of her territory in America and Asia to the United States. Cuba had been promised independence, which was granted; but Puerto Rico, Guam, and the Philippine Islands were annexed as American territory.

During the war, the Hawaiian Islands were also annexed by the United States as a culmination of years of American intervention in island affairs. In 1903, American interest in the Caribbean was expressed by an overly prompt recognition of the success of a Colombian revolt which resulted in the independence of Panama and the sale to the United States of a ten-mile wide canal zone across the Isthmus of Panama. American chicanery in this matter was later partially rectified by the payment to Colombia of an indemnity of $25,000,000.

A few further acts of intervention beyond United States shores occurred within the next decade or so, mostly in the Caribbean, but America's new imperialism and "dollar diplomacy" abated somewhat, although they by no means disappeared. Particularly after World War I, there developed throughout the world a rather pronounced hostility to the use of war or of any financial pressure by the strong against the weak together with a world-wide revolt among colonial peoples. The new imperialism had never enlisted the whole-hearted support of the American public. It had always been the result of pressure by an interested and aggressive minority, and a strong tendency to be ashamed of it was manifest. However, the great size and wealth of the United States gave it a bargaining advantage in dealings with smaller and weaker countries to which it was not always sufficiently sensitive. The United States sometimes drove hard bargains that were resented by the other parties to them.

The foreign trade of the United States as a whole has never grown to be much more than one-tenth of its total trade. Foreign investments are still only a tiny fraction of investment at home. But in both respects, American interest in foreign markets and investment outlets is vital to its well-being. The economic problem of foreign trade and investment is somewhat similar to the problem of excess capacity on railroads or in manufacturing, where overhead costs are high. In each case, the small margin of extra business that may be obtained abroad or by cutting prices a little may represent the margin between profit and loss for the whole enterprise, since the overhead is already taken care of and the income from any extra sales may have a very large element of profit in it. Foreign trade represents the icing on the cake for many American businesses. And where production cannot be easily controlled, as in agriculture, the sale abroad of even a small fraction of the crop may stiffen domestic prices greatly. Foreign trade is much more important to many branches of production than its volume would indicate.

## Economic thought in a maturing economy

As we have followed the development of the American economic system, we have noted the growth of different economic points of view. They have related to recognized problems of farming, the organization of business, labor, foreign trade and the like. To these specific views, we must now add a consideration of changes in the general economic point of view or theory held by a significant number of Americans.

To begin with, many tens of thousands of Europeans had emigrated to the United States in the latter half of the nineteenth century. They had inevitably brought with them economic attitudes which were basically the product of European rather than American conditions. Specifically, socialism had become very widespread in Europe, especially in Germany and central Europe. Many immigrants had come from that area, and persons of radical and socialist views were likely to be a substantial proportion of that group. By the late nineteenth and early twentieth centuries, these persons were well established in America, to some degree on farms but also in industrial cities. They contributed substantially to the growth of labor unions, with which they were familiar in Europe, and to all kinds of proposals for the increase of government regulation. In fact, such socialist political sentiment as developed in the United States in this period derived its support largely from this recent immigrant group.

But socialism was not an American movement in origin and it never struck deep roots here. There were discontents over economic matters, as we have seen, but the overwhelming opinion was that these problems could be solved within the framework of our traditional economic and political system. John D. Rockefeller and other industrial tycoons became almost hated figures in some economic circles. Books, pamphlets, magazine articles and cartoons ridiculing or otherwise attacking such individuals were popular. But the Republican party which basically represented the orthodox type of economic thought, held the presidency of the United States from the Civil War era to the coming of President Franklin D. Roosevelt's New Deal in 1932, except for the administrations of two relatively conservative Democrats, Grover Cleveland and Woodrow Wilson. This record indicates the predominance of conservative economic thought, in spite of the existence of a great deal of reformist, although not socialist, thought.

In a more formal sense, economic thought can be said to have been in a rather confused state by the turn of the twentieth century. In spite of the dominance of the free market theories stemming from Adam Smith and David Ricardo, there were many conflicting points of view reflecting the experiences of the varied groups making up American economic life. Farmers suffering from low prices were not content to let monetary and credit policies remain where the classical theory left them, in the hands of the bankers and the free markets. Rather, they wanted a positive governmental policy of expansion of money and credit in order to raise prices whether justified by theory or not. Similarly, farmers, industrial workers and the general buying public were not willing to stand idly by in the face of what they believed to be the monopolistic rigging of the free markets, as they were supposed to be. The American Economic Association was founded in 1885 by younger economists, mostly back from graduate study in European universities, who leaned heavily toward the idea that the economic system required guidance and control to serve the public interest.

Yet, in the midst of these radical and somewhat socialistic ideas, many economists in the colleges and universities were much impressed by what is called the "marginal utility" theory. This theory was developed principally in Austrian universities and became popular largely because it very neatly cut the ground from under the socialistic theories of Karl Marx and his followers. Marx had accepted the classical theory that value is based on cost of production. Costs ultimately reduce to labor. Therefore, he held, labor should get all the value which it creates. Since it obviously does not, capitalists must exploit labor and keep workers in poverty.

In America, while few economists could be called serious believers in socialistic theories, many were in effect sympathetic to them because of their sympathy for the farmer and industrial worker. At the same time, many of these economists accepted the marginal utility theory which denied that value rested upon cost and asserted that every consumer helped to determine value by deciding how useful any article would be to him. This calculation of usefulness, or utility, meant that no one would pay more for an article than it was worth to

him, so how could anyone be exploited? Possibly because no one took any of these theories in an extremely literal sense, they could survive side by side, although they were to a considerable degree contradictory.

In the economic controversies of the end of the nineteenth century and the first decades of the twentieth, this mixture of economic theories was called upon by various individuals in varied ways to support the arguments of the moment. None of the theories justified monopoly, although business firms became larger and larger. It became almost impossible to say when they were acting in a monopolistic manner unless actual agreement to fix prices or otherwise restrain trade could be uncovered. The public became accustomed to bigness and the rapidity of economic growth softened the complaints of most groups most of the time. As a nation, we were pretty well satisfied with our capitalistic system with its individual freedom. Radical economic ideas gained a substantial following only at times of depression and among those most directly affected.

### The American economy on the eve of World War I

The economic system of the United States at the beginning of the twentieth century might be compared to a young giant who had passed through his adolescence and had become a grown man, but who did not yet appreciate his own strength. Our young giant did not himself fully know the mighty works he was able to perform, nor did he appreciate his responsibilities to others nor realize how his actions might affect others, for in his own mind he always played down the magnitude of what he did. American industry had increased its capacity to produce tremendously, and had settled down from its obstreperous "robber baron" stage, but it had not yet fully learned the responsibilities of employers to workers, of producers to consumers, of promoters to stockholders, nor of American busi-

| | | MANUFACTURING | | | | | MINING AND QUARRYING | | | |
|---|---|---|---|---|---|---|---|---|---|---|
| | | **1904** | **1909** | **1914** | **1919** | **1929** | **1902** | **1909** | **1919** | **1929** |
| No. of establishments | Corporations | 23.6 | 25.9 | 28.3 | 31.5 | 48.3 | 28.6 | 35.4 | 51.1 | 63.0 |
| | Others | 76.4 | 74.1 | 71.7 | 68.5 | 51.7 | 71.4 | 64.6 | 48.9 | 37.0 |
| Average no. of wage earners | Corporations | 70.6 | 75.6 | 80.3 | 86.6 | 89.9 | 85.0 | 90.6 | 94.2 | 94.7 |
| | Others | 29.4 | 24.4 | 19.7 | 13.4 | 10.1 | 15.0 | 9.4 | 5.8 | 5.3 |
| Value of products | Corporations | 73.7 | 79.0 | 83.2 | 87.7 | 92.1 | 86.3 | 91.4 | 93.6 | 95.7 |
| | Others | 26.3 | 21.0 | 16.8 | 12.3 | 7.9 | 13.7 | 8.6 | 6.4 | 4.3 |

*Fig. XII-5 A study of this chart will show that in both manufacturing and mining, corporations, though a minority of all businesses, turned out well over ¾ of all products and employed well over ¾ of all wage earners by the early twentieth century. Figures are in per cents.*

ness to the economies of the rest of the world. It was in its early maturity, it had made great strides, but it had still much of the wisdom of age to acquire—wisdom as to the use of its own powers for its own benefit, as well as wisdom in accepting the world-wide responsibilities which its power thrust upon it.

The general business corporation had come into its own in the half century before World War I. The advantages of the corporate form of organization in raising capital and in providing unity and continuity in management, among other things, had led to an increase in the number of corporations, particularly among the larger businesses (see Fig. XII-5). In 1914, 28.3 per cent of the manufacturing establishments were corporations, but that 28.3 per cent employed 80.3 per cent of the employees in manufacturing industries and turned out 83.2 per cent of the product. In mining and quarrying in 1909, 35.4 per cent of the establishments were corporations, but they had 90.6 per cent of the employees and 91.4 per cent of the product.[1] Clearly the corporation had become dominant, for it was responsible for 80 to 90 per cent of the output. It is also characteristic of our economy that with the growth of big dominant corporations there has also been a growth of the total number of enterprises in most of the branches of American business. The individual proprietorship and partnership have proved to be tenacious forms but have had a declining percentage of the total business.

As compared with Europe, American production in the seventy years from 1850 to 1920 had forged ahead far more rapidly. An English commentator in 1896 stated that "American manufactures have multiplied just twentyfold since 1840 while those in Europe have only doubled."[2] This magnificent achievement was made by the hard work of millions, by the rich resources of the continent, and by the adaptation to industry of new technological processes. Steam and electric power were used in increasing quantities in industry to drive larger, faster, and more

[1] Twentieth Century Fund, *Big Business, Its Growth and Its Place* (New York, 1937), p. 15.

[2] Quoted by R. C. McGrane, *The Economic Development of the American Nation* (New York: Ginn and Co., 1942), p. 390.

nearly automatic machines which brought an unparalleled stepping up of output. The telephone and telegraph were widely used before World War I to speed up the dissemination of news, and to increase both the comfort of living and the efficiency of business. The automobile and the "wireless telegraph" or radio were still in their early childhood, as was aviation, until World War I accelerated the development of all three. Farm machines of all kinds were faster and better and enabled a constantly shrinking farm population to produce an abundance of food for an ever growing population in the cities. The farm tractor and other machines powered by gasoline engines were still in the experimental stage, but in a decade or two they would make substantial contributions to increase farm output.

## FOR FURTHER READING

Dulles, F. R. *Twentieth Century America*. Boston: Houghton Mifflin Co., 1945. Chapters 2 and 3.

Faulkner, H. U. *American Economic History*. 2nd ed. New York: Harper & Brothers, 1960. Chapters 21—26.

Josephson, M. *The Robber Barons*. Harvest, 1962. Paperback. Famous and readable.

Link, Arthur S. *Woodrow Wilson and the Progressive Era, 1910-1917*. New York: Harper & Brothers, 1956. Chapter 3.

Steffens, Lincoln. *The Shame of the Cities*. American Century Series, 1960. Paperback. The famous muckracker's first contact with corruption.

Wilcox, Clair. *Public Policies Toward Business*. Rev. ed. Homewood, Ill.: Richard D. Irwin, Inc., 1960. Chapters 3—5.

Wright, Chester W. *Economic History of the United States*. 2nd ed. New York: McGraw-Hill Book Co., 1949. Chapters 35—37 and 41.

# Chapter 13: The economic significance of World War I

**T**he outbreak of war in Europe in the summer of 1914 surprised and shocked the United States. No one knew what the effects of such a major conflict might be. The New York Stock Exchange closed on July 31 and remained closed for more than four months, to prevent panic selling of securities by Europeans who feared the effect of war on the value of their securities or who wanted to put their wealth into the form of cash. The European exchanges also closed with the outbreak of the war. Business in America was generally not very good in the summer of 1914, and the prospect of losing European markets for American agricultural and industrial exports led to still further weakening of prices and curtailment of employment. Not until late spring and summer of 1915 did orders for American wheat, steel, and munitions of war change the economic outlook from pessimism to optimism. Industry began to convert to war production and stepped up output rapidly. The depressed economic situation of 1914 was transformed into prosperity before the end of 1915, and to

intense boom during 1916. Steel was at the heart of war production, and between 1914 and 1917 American exports of steel products to Europe, including munitions of war, increased fourfold. Steel-producing capacity was stepped up and orders for machinery and tools to manufacture the trucks, tanks, guns, and shells which Europe was using spread the prosperity throughout industry. Agriculture was benefited also, as wheat, meat, and cotton were in heavy demand.

At the outset, the United States announced its intention of adhering to its traditional position of neutrality in Europe's wars. For a time loans were disapproved, even short-term commercial loans of the type universally used in financing foreign trade. But shortly it appeared that this strict neutrality would prevent all sales to Europe, since cash immediately became scarce in Europe. Exporters protested vehemently to the State Department, and the ban on loans was lifted. American policy then became one of selling to anyone who cared to buy, and who would come to

American ports to accept delivery. In effect, this meant selling to the Allies, since Germany could not get her ships to American ports. The one direct exception was the arrival of the cargo-carrying submarine *Deutschland* at Philadelphia with a load of German dyestuffs, badly needed in America; it carried back to Germany a load of alloying materials for steel tool manufacture desperately needed there.

On a somewhat larger scale, Germany was able to purchase needed materials through her neutral neighbors. For this reason, England, whose navy controlled the seas, insisted upon her right to stop merchant vessels bound for neutral ports and to search them for contraband of war. The definition of contraband used by England covered almost any kind of raw material or product which could contribute to the war effort in any way. This involved her in a controversy with the United States over freedom of the seas in time of war very much like that which had precipitated the War of 1812 a century earlier. Germany fought back against England's control of the seas by the intensive use of submarines. A submarine could not stop and search a freighter, for a concealed deck gun might sink a surfacing submarine with one shell. German submarine commanders, therefore, were simply sinking every ship approaching northern Europe that they could hit with a good torpedo shot. American lives were lost and the government protested to Germany ever more vigorously. In May 1915 the passenger liner *Lusitania* was sunk with the loss of twelve hundred lives, a catastrophe which horrified the United States. There were 128 American citizens aboard and President Woodrow Wilson dispatched a series of notes to Germany in effect threatening war if this kind of submarine warfare were continued. He gained a temporary victory when Germany promised that no more ships would be sunk without warning. But this promise was not kept, and when in January 1917 Germany announced its return to a policy of unrestricted submarine warfare, it proved to be the last straw. The United States declared war on the Central Powers, Germany and its allies, in April 1917.

## America at war: by-passing *laissez faire*

The period from 1914 to 1917 during which the United States sat on the side lines as an observer of the European war gave it a chance to estimate the magnitude of the demands that the war would make. Americans could at least partially appreciate the significance of a statement which Newton D. Baker, Secretary of War, made at a later date: "To a greater extent than we or anybody else had realized, modern war is essentially an industrial art." By production of war materials during 1915 and 1916, the United States gained at least some idea of what would be required and of what it would mean to the industrial system to embark on an all-out program of war production. Before entering the war, the United States made no fundamental changes in the traditional free markets and permitted prices to rise as scarcities developed from the influx of military orders from Europe. The index of wholesale prices more than doubled, rising from 69.5 in 1915 to 161 by March 1917, while the prices of metal and chemical products needed for munitions rose much more than that (see Fig. XIII-1, p. 266).

In spite of this opportunity to observe the war before being drawn into it, to appreciate what its demands upon industry and upon the price level might be, America still entered the war essentially unprepared. There had been voices in the army and elsewhere calling for a beginning of economic and military mobilization, but Congress had taken no action. In the summer of 1916, a Council of National Defense had been authorized to bring about "the coördination of industries and resources for the national security and welfare," but it was December before the Council met. The American public continued to hope and believe that it need not become involved in what was felt to be essentially Europe's war. When the United States was drawn in, it was at an unfavorable stage for the Allied cause. Allied military and governmental leaders sent harassed pleas for men and munitions. It now became America's responsibility to see that both were delivered across the Atlantic in spite of the German submarine blockade. Finally, the magnitude of twentieth-century mechanized warfare was forced home upon Americans as they became launched upon the greatest industrial and military effort of their history up to that time, which called forth all American industrial energies.

It is worth pausing here to note that there was scarcely a serious thought in the country that the economic side of the war effort could be conducted on the basis of traditional *laissez faire*. The free market could have brought about the necessary industrial mobilization only by permitting scarcities of munitions to force their prices so high that producers would find it profitable to change over from peacetime to war production. To bring about this change quickly, the prices of war goods would have had to rise so high that producers would be willing to go ahead and invest in war plants and equipment in spite of the risk of total loss if the war should end suddenly. Such fantastic prices would have multiplied the cost of the war by many times, would probably have been slow and haphazard in effect, and would certainly have produced such violent inflation in the country that the price level could not have been brought back to a workable level for years after the war. Yet, both previous major wars—the Revolutionary War and the Civil War—had been fought without major government control over industry and prices. As we have seen, the result in each case had been inflation, increased economic burden due to the war, and the necessity of heroic measures to establish a sound basis for business afterwards. That lesson America had learned, and when in 1917 it became involved in the first truly World War in history, American leaders realized that the easygoing ways of the free market would have to be set aside for a time in exchange for some rigorous government control over strategic phases of industrial and economic life. Wholesale prices had jumped nearly 50 per cent during 1916 alone. A strong hand was needed quite obviously at once.

## Economic mobilization for war

The Council of National Defense was barely organized in the spring of 1917 when the burden of running the war was thrust upon it. The Council was composed of six cabinet members and was empowered to set up for itself an Advisory Commission of seven experts to assist it in various phases of its work. The Council and the Advisory Commission set about organizing the various aspects of the war effort—industrial mobilization, transportation, food and fuel supply, labor—using voluntary committees to help. The magnitude of the job soon made it apparent that more detailed organization would be required. As time went on, the economic aspects of the war effort seemed to center in several specific areas. Special agencies were set up to deal with each of them. The Council thus became the parent of the separate administrations that handled the job of winning the war on the economic front. Several of the more important of these agencies are deserving of some description.

### The War Industries Board

Probably the most important of the war agencies because of the general character of the responsibilities assigned to it was the War Industries Board. It was first created by the Council of National Defense in the summer of 1917 to receive statements of need from the various branches of the military and naval service, to determine the relative importance of these needs, to set up plans for increasing production to meet these needs, and to do what it could to keep prices down. At first it was given advisory powers only. Whenever a new function developed and seemed to require attention, a new committee or subcommittee was set up to deal with it. The coöperation secured by these committees from both the armed services and industry was very good, but in the spring of 1918 it was apparent that the magnitude of the war effort required more power and the right to cut red tape, so the Board came under presidential direction.

The new chairman of the Board, Bernard M. Baruch, was delegated sufficient authority by the president to become practically an industrial czar for the remainder of the war. The older committees and sections continued to operate for the most part under the general War Industries Board, on which the armed services and other government purchasing agencies were represented. This Board performed a vital service in ranking the war needs in order of importance so that the war effort could proceed in orderly fashion. It also assisted in holding prices down, since the offer of quick delivery for a higher price gained nothing. A Requirements Division, set up in the summer of 1918, sought to make more systematic the statements of needs by various war agencies.

In general, the War Industries Board tried to coördinate industrial activity, cut civilian production, eliminate waste and duplication, and make the war-production effort as efficient as possible. To achieve these objectives, it had the power, if the president agreed, to commandeer industry or to demand compliance with its orders if such compliance were not voluntarily given. These powers were not needed often, since voluntary coöperation was general. Under the leadership of the Board, the number of sizes and styles of tires, shoes, baby buggies, and countless other manufactured articles was sharply reduced. The yardage of material in men's and women's clothing was reduced by simplifying styles and eliminating elaborate trimmings. Scarce war materials were forbidden to be used for civilian production.

The Price Fixing Committee at first tried to hold in line only the prices of goods purchased by the government, but found that prices were so extensively interrelated that it also had to pay attention to the prices of civilian goods. There was no general and systematic effort in World War I to fix retail prices, as developed a generation later under the Office of Price Administration in World War II. Attention was centered on basic materials that entered into many kinds of products, and retail prices were fixed for short periods only on the basis of costs plus an allowance for profit. This method was not so successful in preventing price increases as the more comprehensive price control of World War II, although the index of wholesale prices rose less than half as much from 1917 to 1918 as it had done in the previous year.

### The Food and Fuel Administrations

Food and fuel problems were of particular importance, since these materials were essential to civilian well-being besides being necessities for the army, America's allies, and the industrial war effort. The Food and Fuel Control Act of August 1917 established the basic authority for control, and under it were set up the National Food Administration, with Herbert Hoover as Director, and the Fuel Administration, with Harry A. Garfield, son of the former president, as Director. Both agencies sought to increase production to the limit and to conserve what was produced as far as possible. Hoover embarked on a great, nation-wide campaign teaching citizens to use every scrap of food and to waste nothing. Housewives by the millions, as well as hotels and restaurants, pledged themselves to "Hooverize," i.e., to follow Mr. Hoover's suggestions in their use of food. Meatless and wheatless days were instituted to stretch the supplies of these scarce foods. Special agencies were set up under the Food Administration to deal with sugar and wheat. Farmers were guaranteed a minimum of $2.20 a bushel for wheat for 1918, and the Food Administration Grain Corporation stood ready to purchase wheat at that price. With sugar, the chief problems were equalizing supplies, prevention of hoarding, and stabilizing prices. Maximum retail prices were set, and the quantity which could be purchased at one time was limited. Hoarding of any food became a punishable crime, but rationing to prevent it was not adopted in World War I. It was not used until the second world conflict.

The fuel problem was not so involved as the food problem, although the shortage of coal, the principal fuel at the time, became acute. Efforts were made to step up production and to increase the efficiency of mining. Industries were asked to conserve fuel, and in the extraordinarily cold weather in December and January of 1917-1918, nonessential industries were closed down for five days to permit coal stocks to be rebuilt. Fuelless Mondays were instituted and continued until warmer weather came. Daylight-saving time was first introduced to this country in 1918 as a fuel saving measure, after it had worked successfully in Europe, and the public liked it so well for other reasons that it has persisted in large parts of the country during the summer. The use of electricity for advertising signs was forbidden. Gasoline was not widely used in the years of World War I; it was not rationed, but gasless Sundays were instituted to make some savings. More economical distribution of coal was sought, to save by eliminating unnecessary hauling. Prices were controlled at every stage by local representatives of the Fuel Administration. In spite of all efforts, coal was extremely scarce during the war and at times the shipment of troops and supplies was held up because bunker coal was lacking at Atlantic ports.

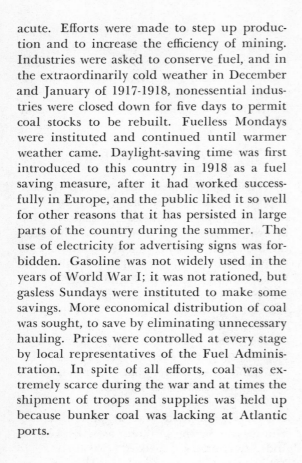
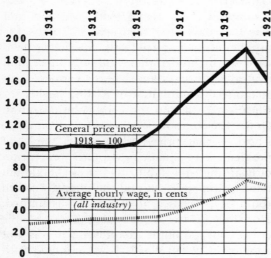

*Fig. XIII-1  The behavior of wages and prices in general during the decade including World War I. Compare this to chart in Chapter 18 showing changing wages during and after World War II.*

## The Shipping Board
## and the Railroad Administration

The movement of troops and supplies constituted an obviously critical feature of the war effort, and brought the government directly into production and operation to a degree not equalled in any other segment of the economy. Atlantic shipping had become a serious problem because of German submarine activity even before the United States entered the war. In 1916, Congress had created the Shipping Board to aid in expanding the merchant marine. Within two weeks of the American declaration of war, the Emergency Fleet Corporation was created under the Shipping Board with broad powers to buy, build, commandeer, or otherwise acquire and operate all possible ships. First of all, it confiscated and rehabilitated all German ships in American ports. The ships of some neutrals had taken refuge in our ports, and, by negotiated agreement, these were taken over for war service. All partially completed ships in American shipyards were taken over and modified for war service. In July 1917, it was estimated that submarine warfare was still destroying ships at three times the rate at which they were being built. The Emergency Fleet Corporation therefore set out on a program of shipbuilding hitherto unparalleled in American history. New yards were constructed to make American shipbuilding capacity by far the greatest in the world. So much time was required for this construction, however, that none of the ships built in the new yards had been put into service before the war ended. The real shipping achievement of the war was the antisubmarine activity of the Navy, and the improvement of facilities for loading and unloading that were developed by the Shipping Board both in the United States and in France. These factors preserved America's precious stock of shipping and increased its efficiency.

The railroads too knew that they faced an enormous task in handling the movement of wartime traffic, and in April 1917 they voluntarily formed the Railroads' War Board to formulate unified operating policies to be followed by all of them. This Board did much to coördinate railway operation, but it became less and less successful in coping with traffic bottlenecks, and with the labor and financial troubles that confronted the roads. Finally, President Wilson took over the railroads as of January 1, 1918, and appointed William G. McAdoo Director-General of Railroads. There was an immediate and widespread consolidation of ticket offices, terminal facilities, and rolling stock. The railroads had no help from trucks, busses, and airlines in handling the traffic of World War I, but under unified government operation, bottlenecks were cleared up and the traffic moved. In March 1918, Congress enacted legislation providing a system of compensation to the railroads for the period of government operation. The ultimate cost to the government was quite heavy, but this did not prove the failure of government operation. The facts were that the freight was moved, and that rates increased more slowly than the skyrocketing costs of labor, fuel, and supplies. Since the detailed management of the roads was in the hands of the regular officials working under Director McAdoo, it has been suggested that many of the costs of government operation were high because these private officials wanted the roads back after the war in very good condition, to save on future repairs.

### Labor administration

Several factors worked together to make the labor problem acute and to create labor unrest as the war mobilization moved toward its peak. In the first place, the drafting of nearly 4,000,000 men into the armed services in the face of the urgent demand for stepped-up war production all along the line was sufficient to make the labor market tight. Immigration from Europe, on which industry had come to depend for part of its labor supply, had been cut off by the outbreak of the war in 1914. There was no attempt to freeze wages at prewar levels, and they rose substantially. Workers moved to areas of war production and shifted from job to job in search of ever higher wages. Labor turnover became so high as to interfere with production and to increase costs greatly.

Samuel Gompers, president of the American Federation of Labor and chairman of the Committee on Labor of the Council of National Defense, called together representatives of labor and management and secured agreement to a truce on strikes and lockouts during the war. The truce involved acceptance by employers of the eight-hour day, the right of workers to join unions, and the principle of collective bargaining. This truce was kept by the great majority of workers and employers, although some of the workers in the Socialist party, and especially in the Industrial Workers of the World, a union whose leaders believed in sabotage and the use of violence, actively opposed the war effort and refused to coöperate in it. Neither of these groups sympathized with the war effort, since at least their more extreme members, like their European counterparts, regarded it as a capitalist war in which labor should have no part. The agreement was not sufficient to settle all disputes, and it became apparent that more elaborate or powerful machinery was required.

Early in the war, various agencies had been set up by the Council of National Defense and the War Industries Board to cope with specific labor problems and disputes. The inadequacy of these efforts to maintain industrial peace led the president to create the War Labor Conference Board early in 1918, representing management, labor, and the public. The Secretary of Labor was made Labor Administrator. The Conference Board recommended the establishment of a National War Labor Board to mediate or arbitrate disputes if necessary. The president accepted the suggestion and appointed the Conference Board members to be the War Labor Board under the chairmanship of a former president, William H. Taft. The general acceptance of the decisions of the Board contributed greatly to industrial peace thereafter. There was also created a War Labor Policies Board composed of persons responsible for labor policy in each of the important government agencies. It became the main function of this group to carry out the decisions of the War Labor Board in the various branches of war work. In addition, the Employment Service of the Department of Labor, which was in operation before the war, was much expanded to channel labor to essential industries and to cut down labor turnover. It achieved considerable success in these endeavors.

### Other agencies

In addition to these major agencies, there were literally hundreds of others dealing with the multiple economic aspects of modern warfare, for example, the Bureau of War Risk Insurance, the Aircraft Board, and the Committee on Public Information. Had the war lasted several years longer than it did, these agencies would undoubtedly have been grouped together in a much tighter administrative system. As it was, although the government moved into the industrial situation in a vigorous fashion, there was still a universal desire to adhere to the free system of voluntary action wherever it would work. Since this was a national tradition, it is probable that better results were achieved by it than would have been achieved by the use of arbitrary authority by the government. On the other hand, there was also a national tradition of enthusiasm for speculation when opportunity offered, and the war effort inevitably did offer such opportunities. It was only natural that "war millionaires" emerged, but while there were 206 individuals reporting net incomes of more than a million dollars each in 1916, the number declined to 141 in 1917 and to 67 in 1918.

### Financing the war

#### The real economic cost of war

A revenue act to help pay the costs of the war was under discussion in Congress and throughout the country for several months before it was finally enacted into law in October 1917. During this period, there was much debate over the proportion of the total cost that might be financed by the issuance of bonds. The manner in which this problem presented itself indicated a widespread misunderstanding of the basic economic issues involved. The fact is that apart from the loss of life and the suffering, which are immeasurable, the real cost of the war is in the resources and the products of capital, of human labor, and of the soil that are used up or destroyed. That resources and productive efforts are turned from the desirable objectives of peaceful living to the destruction of war is the real economic cost of war.

The only way a part of the cost of the war can be postponed, and is inevitably postponed, is by the necessity which future generations face of restricting their own production of goods and services for their immediate pleasure in order to turn part of their efforts to the rebuilding of the homes and factories and bridges and churches destroyed by war. This postponement has nothing to do with bonds. It can be avoided only by having business and government cut down on normal peacetime expenditures, e.g., road building, and use the savings attained in this way to contribute to the cost of the war. The food, the clothing, the guns and ammunition, the mechanized equipment used in the war are produced practically in their entirety by the people living during the war period, and after the war they are either used up or have value only as junk. From the point of view of work and production, which is the down-to-earth point of view, war is very nearly a complete pay-as-you-go proposition. The people who made the tanks and guns might have been building and equipping schools; the soldiers who were in Europe fighting might have been producing food and clothing to relieve the poverty of some of their people; or, everyone might have taken life a little easier, enjoyed sports and recreation to a greater degree. These are the social and economic costs of war.

We have difficulty seeing clearly the problem of economic costs, because of our money and price system. In the first chapter of this book it was pointed out that money is only a medium between work and goods, or between one kind of goods and another. To perform this function as a medium of exchange, it must also almost necessarily perform the additional functions of acting as a measure of the values to be exchanged and as a storehouse of those values, since we do not often want to complete the exchange of work for goods immediately. In our ordinary experiences, we practically always receive our income in money and buy what we desire with money. If we wish to wait a while before we buy, we can do so. On the other hand, if we want to buy a house or an automobile before we have received and saved up enough income to do so, our highly developed credit system offers us facilities for borrowing the necessary amount, if our credit rating is good. As individuals, we can either delay the enjoyment of our income until later, or enjoy benefits beyond our income now, by means of credit, while postponing the payments to the future. But a nation can do neither of those things as an economic unit except by borrowing or lending to other nations. Within the nation, some people ordinarily are living beyond their present means because others are consuming less than they could, in order to earn interest by lending their money. But a nation as a unit cannot live beyond the nation's income. It cannot postpone real costs to the future, except by borrowing from other nations, which was the opposite of what we did during World War I.

The real economic effect of issuing bonds to pay for the war was that some people could enjoy more food, clothing, and other necessities and luxuries during the war because taxes were lighter than they would have had to be to pay for the cost of the war in full. The many people who bought bonds (or lent their money to the government) enjoyed less necessities and luxuries than they might have had if they had spent their money for goods instead of bonds. In other words, the distribution of benefits and sacrifices is within one generation and not between a given genera-

tion and its successors. The practical, political advantage in issuing bonds is that people have never enjoyed paying taxes because they see the immediate loss of income which they suffer. Whether they do or do not pay for the war by taxes, the quantity of goods available for the use of the civilian population will not vary anyway. This is a fact that generally escapes the observation of individuals. If this were not the case, it would be far simpler to finance a war by taxation. The percentage of the national income which should be taken by taxation theoretically ought to match the percentage of the national productive effort which is diverted to war purposes. If the people were educated to accept a program of such heavy taxation, there would be relatively little inflation danger during wars. Everyone would have to tighten his belt and follow a somewhat austere life during the war, but at its end the slate would be clean, there would be no load of interest, and no national debt to worry about, the price level would not have been deranged by inflation, and the return to a peacetime economy would be as easy and simple as the physical conversion of industries and farms to their regular products.

### Taxes versus bonds

Unfortunately, neither Congress nor the public was well instructed in the topics discussed in the preceding paragraphs, and the question of taxes *versus* bonds was dealt with entirely as a political issue. The question was how much the public would stand in the way of taxes. The sum to be raised by taxes was set at $3.5 billion for the first year of the war. The income tax, first legalized in 1913 by the Sixteenth Amendment to the Constitution, was raised sharply, the high rate in the long schedule of rates being 67 per cent on that part of an individual's income over one million dollars. Taxes on the inheritance of estates were increased, excise taxes were placed on many new items and raised on liquor and tobacco, and a heavily graduated excess profits tax was levied on business. To anticipate and supplement taxes, the Treasury financed current expenditures by selling notes or certificates to banks and financial institutions at low rates of interest and for short periods of three months or less. To repay these short-term borrowings, a series of Liberty Loans was authorized to raise money from the public, corporations, insurance companies, and any other sources. The income tax and the excess profits tax in particular yielded very substantial revenues throughout the war. The total direct cost of the war to the completion of demobilization has been estimated to have been $34.4 billion. Of this amount, about one-third was raised by taxation and two-thirds by borrowing.

### Credit policies and the price level

On the whole, it was advantageous that the Federal Reserve System (p. 253f.) had been put into operation before the United States was drawn into the war although it revealed some new defects of its own. The vastly greater flexibility and resources of the new system were called into use more quickly than had been anticipated. The reserves which banks must set aside to secure their deposits could now be in the form of gold or lawful money, or commercial notes meeting specified standards, or obligations of the federal government. The last provision, in particular, facilitated the sale of bonds to banks, because the banks could always use them to build up their reserves at the Federal Reserve Bank. Also, if a bank needed cash, it could always get it by drawing a check against its reserve account on deposit with the Federal Reserve Bank. Thus, the sale of bonds to banks could easily become like a cat chasing its tail, and did not fulfill the purpose originally envisaged because the banks found that they could immediately send the bonds to the Federal Reserve for cash or to add to their reserve. The entire process was very inflationary, as bonds owned by a bank were potential reserve for loans they might wish to make.

Efforts were made during the war to prevent this effect by trying to concentrate on selling bonds to individuals, who obtained the money to pay for them by saving from income. A transaction of this type was non-inflationary, since only the government spent the money received from the sale of bonds instead of its being spent once again by the purchasing banks using the bonds as collateral. However, the pressure to borrow money was so great that the banks were induced to buy billions of dollars worth of bonds and their reserves became far greater than needed. To add to the inflationary danger, gold flowed to the United States from Europe all through the war in partial payment for the war supplies being bought by European countries. We saw in a preceding section that no systematic or comprehensive effort to control prices was made during the war. Add to that the creation of excess reserve capacity in the banks by the selling of bonds to them, and there exists a situation favoring the free and easy expansion of credit coupled with the absence of effective means of checking the rise of prices. The price line was not held during the war, and, at the end, when the patriotic appeal against profiteering was much weakened, inflationary price increases went much farther and faster until a collapse of prices occurred in the summer of 1920. The excellent and necessary flexibility in the reserve provisions of the Federal Reserve System were shown to have a dangerously great flexibility on the upper side in a wartime situation. The United States did not print any unsupported paper money in World War I, but inflation of credit through the banks occurred just the same.

## An appraisal of the economic aspects of the war effort

### The lessons of the production record

When all is said and done, America's production record in World War I was a hitherto unparalleled achievement. Never before had there been a nation so well supplied with essential resources, so rich in mines, mills, and factories equipped with the best machinery technologists had been able to devise, and so well staffed with trained workers. And never before had such a nation been put to the test of all-out war production. Had it been possible to plan the conversion to a war economy in advance, the change-over could have been accomplished more quickly and with far more effect. As it was, a great deal of American war production never was actually used in the war. Nonetheless, it aided in achieving the victory, for both friends and foes knew it was on the way.

For the peacetime economy, perhaps the great lesson of the war effort was to demonstrate the very high level of production which could be achieved by the intensive planning of the industry of the nation, in spite of the withdrawal from the work force of more than four million young men who were among the most capable workers. This was the production miracle of the war. We know from our more detailed examination of the organization for war production in previous sections that it was loose and full of many imperfections. When, in spite of these imperfections, the civilian population could be provided a standard of living adequate in all essentials, while an army of four million men was created and equipped, and while billions of dollars worth of goods were supplied to America's allies, it became clear what such a productive economy could do to solve peacetime economic problems if it could be put to work on a fully efficient basis. Of course, war brought a degree of national unity which is not present in peacetime. But peacetime permits more time to work out production problems. There are advantages each way. A corollary of the demonstration of what the United States could do was the thought that it must be wasting much time and energy somewhere in the peacetime economy to achieve no better results than had previously been achieved.

### Unplanned demobilization

The United States was just getting into its real stride in war production when the Armistice was announced. Until the very end this eventuality had not been prepared for. The military high command was in the process of mounting ever more massive offensives against the Germans, now that American troops and equipment were available, when rumors began to circulate that the top German generals would be willing to hear terms for surrender. After the quickly made Armistice, it was not possible to introduce any planned order into either military or industrial demobilization at such a late hour. American troops had not been instructed on the magnitude of the transportation problem, and when the war was over they wanted to come home at once. All the shipping on the north Atlantic was not equal to that task within a matter of months. The soldiers had been taken to Europe over a time span of more than a year and with the important aid of British trans-Atlantic liners. Some of the latter necessarily had to be returned to other uses. The result was rioting of some American soldiers in European base camps at the delay which kept them from returning to America. American political and military leaders had been so engrossed in the war effort that they had not been able to devote much thought to the inevitable day of war's end.

Similarly, war industries were not adequately prepared to demobilize. No instructions had been given to war contractors as to proper procedure when peace came. The very elements of looseness in the economic control of war industry turned out to be advantageous when it came to sudden demobilization. Tighter controls might have made mobilization more complete and demobilization harder. The job of reconversion to peacetime production was somehow accomplished. Demand for civilian goods of all kinds was high because of the backlog of domestic demand and because foreign governments attempted to replenish depleted supplies. Prices were at profitable levels and loans to help get peacetime production under way were readily available. Indices of production for 1919 show only a slight drop from the wartime peak in 1918, and by 1920 gains were recorded. Credit facilities approached the point of straining the reserve limits; transportation facilities again became jammed as they had been in wartime. For a combination of reasons, perhaps, a strong reaction to this postwar boom and inflation set in during the summer of 1920. Previous depressions had demonstrated that after several years of intensive economic activity and rising prices, a balance of factors is reached in which existing high prices can be maintained only because demand has run beyond current needs and includes, as well, inventory building in anticipation of still higher future prices. When this condition exists in a free-market economic system, it becomes virtually impossible to return to the normal balance of supply and demand without inducing buyers to stop their buying in anticipation of future needs. When prices act as though they have stopped rising, current demand quickly falls to a below normal level as buyers start drawing on accumulated inventory to meet current needs. This action converts a mild price adjustment into a sharp, perhaps violent, drop. The more extreme the boom-time inflation and price increases, the more likely it is that the reaction will also be sharp. This sequence of events seems to have occurred in 1920 and 1921.

By early 1920, foreign demand had begun to diminish as production was resumed in greater quantities overseas or as imports were curtailed because of reduced purchasing power. More or less at the same time, widespread buyers' strikes developed in the United States, as business and consumers alike began to balk at paying the high prevailing prices (wholesale prices had risen 35 per cent in less than a year by May 1920). And then, in the early months of 1920, the Federal Reserve Board, alarmed at the enormous credit expansion of the preceding few years, raised the rediscount rates several times. The result was perhaps the sharpest recession in the nation's history, beginning in May 1920. Prices reacted sharply downward, dropping 45 per cent in a little over a year. Unemployment became widespread, and the postwar recession that followed carried over into the following year. Possibly a better planned demobilization, with the continuation of some wartime restraints on credit and prices until a peacetime balance had been reëstablished in the economy, might have spared the country this short but sharp postwar boom and bust. Fortunately, recovery was relatively prompt, due to the great accumulated demands existing throughout the country for new homes, automobiles, and other goods whose production had been checked or stopped during the war.

## FOR FURTHER READING

Baruch, Bernard M. *American Industry in the War*. New York: Prentice-Hall, Inc., 1941. Part I.

Clarkson, G. B. *Industrial America in the World War*. Boston: Houghton Mifflin Co., 1923. Chapters 12—30.

Dulles, Foster Rhea. *Twentieth Century America*. Boston: Houghton Mifflin Co., 1945. Chapters 11—13.

————. *Labor in America*. New York; Thomas Y. Crowell Co., 1955. Chapter 13.

Faulkner, Harold U. *American Economic History*. 8th ed. New York: Harper & Brothers, 1960. Chapter 27.

Mitchell, B., and Mitchell, L. P. *American Economic History*. Boston: Houghton Mifflin Co., 1947. Chapter 32.

Noyes, A. D. *The War Period of American Finance, 1908-1925*. New York: G. P. Putnam's Sons, 1926. Chapters 2—5.

Slosson, P. W. *The Great Crusade and After, 1914-1928*. New York: The Macmillan Co., 1935. Chapters 1 and 2.

# Chapter 14: Postwar readjustments

# and the booming twenties

America in the decade of the 1920's was inspired by a supreme self-confidence. The year 1920 began with an industrial boom bigger than any the United States had ever had before in peacetime. Before the middle of the year the country had turned toward the sharpest, though not the longest, business recession it had ever known. With recovery in 1922 and 1923 there began a period of the greatest industrial production of any peacetime period. There were fluctuations from year to year, but on the whole the seven years from 1922 to 1929 demonstrated what modern mechanized industry could produce when given a good opportunity. These were the years of the "golden twenties." But the decade came to an end in deep gloom, following the stock-market crash of the late autumn of 1929. This was the greatest financial and psychological shock the nation had ever experienced. America entered the thirties with glorious memories, but unfortunately they were only memories. The sad reality of the early 1930's was of a nation feeling around on the slippery bottom for some solid ground on which it could stand before the incoming tide of economic depression should engulf it completely.

## A decade of highlights and shadows

From a sociological and psychological point of view, the twenties were years of withdrawal for America. With the failure by a hair's breadth of the efforts by President Wilson and a majority of Congress and the public to secure Senate ratification of membership in the new League of Nations, the nation retreated from coöperation with Europe in the war and returned to its comfortable tradition of attending to its own business in isolation. We wanted to sell the products of our farms and our industries in overseas markets, but we did not wish to participate very much further in the solution of the problems of the world. The policy announced by President Washington a century and a quarter earlier of avoiding entanglement in the affairs of Europe was often referred to with approval. Many people said that Europeans and Asians had been fighting for hundreds of years and there was no hope that America could stop them. Americans in their desire to withdraw from participation in world affairs chose not to remember that the United States had been involved in the War of 1812 within a few years after Washington had advised a nonintervention policy in Europe and that the official grievance which drew the United States into World War I was interference with its trade. Their postwar reaction was nationalistic, emotional, and self-centered, based upon unwillingness to assume their own proportionate obligations in wrestling with the problems which have beset mankind since the beginning of time.

Similarly, as a nation the United States withdrew from the policy of government control of business as it had operated in wartime to return to the traditional policy of *laissez faire*. The winning slogan in the presidential race in the summer and fall of 1920 was Warren G. Harding's "back to normalcy." As a matter of fact, while that slogan was a Republican one, the Democratic candidate did not disagree with it; he merely lacked an equally clever phrase. Shortly after the end of the war, President Wilson had expressed the same thought in a statement recommending removing the harness from business. Americans took the great production record of wartime for granted, or at least chose to overlook the element in it that resulted from the coördination of all activities under government auspices. Enthusiastically and wholeheartedly America returned to the free-enterprise system. Government controls of all kinds were removed, and the railroads were returned to their owners with full indemnity for wartime wear and tear. Government-owned ships were junked, laid up, or sold to private owners for a small fraction of their cost. The war had brought new manufacturing methods and new industries, and the United States was determined to develop both old and new business opportunities on the tried and true basis of the free market.

In keeping with the new spirit, both Congress and the Supreme Court adopted a "hands off" attitude toward business. The 1920 decision of the Supreme Court in the anti-trust suit against the United States Steel Corporation not only dismissed the suit but made it clear to business that any aspect of business conduct for which a claim of reasonableness could be substantiated would not be interfered with by the court. The suit had been filed against the company during the "trust busting" era before the war because of the firm's predominant size in the industry and because its president, Judge Elbert Gary, was suspected of gaining agreement of other industry leaders to a common price policy at his annual "Gary dinners" in New York. Before 1920, the Gary dinners had been discontinued, other firms in the steel industry were growing faster than the United States Steel Corporation, and the public had advanced further toward an appreciation of the advantages to be derived from technologically efficient large-scale firms. In its decision the Supreme Court reaffirmed the principle enunciated before the war that in the absence of overt conspiracy to restrain trade a large firm might properly conduct its business without fear of suit under the Sherman Act even if because of its size it would influence the conduct of other firms.

Congress largely refrained from passing regulatory legislation, and most of the state legislation which came before the Supreme Court, dealing with such matters as minimum wages, hours of work, and child labor, was likely to be rejected on the grounds that general freedom of action contributed more to the welfare of the nation than the correction of specific abuses. With a legislative and judicial attitude of that kind, business could and did forge ahead in a practically free field. The businesses which had been big in the last quarter of the nineteenth century became bigger. Growth in size came from both continuous internal expansion and a renewal of the consolidation movement which had been interrupted by the Northern Securities decision in 1904 (p. 249). It has been estimated that more than five times as many mergers and consolidations took place in the ten years from 1919 through 1928 as in the fifteen years from 1890 through 1904.[1] Big business became dominant in America as never before. Trade associations sprang up by the dozens and hundreds in almost every conceivable branch of industry and trade to serve as promotional agencies for the trade and to perform numerous other functions, many of which had the effect of softening if not of eliminating competition. For example, standard accounting and cost-determining systems were developed which undoubtedly acted to deter "unreasonable" price cutting. Also, prices at which orders were taken or contracts were let were supplied to the trade associations to be circulated for the private information of members.

A striking phase of the business history of the twenties was the emergence to importance of a number of industries which had had no more than a modest start in the period prior to World War I. The undoubted leader of these newer industries was the automobile industry. In fact, the twenties have sometimes been referred to as the "automobile decade." The serious developmental work on the automobile had been started in the 1890's, and the years before World War I had seen the industry become established, with increasingly eager public acceptance of its product. The use of trucks, tanks, and airplanes during the war had expanded the productive capacity of the industry. Although the assembly line was neither a twentieth-century nor an American invention, Henry Ford and the automobile industry first demonstrated its value in stepping up output and cutting costs. Detroit became the hub of a great regional industrial development, the motor capital of America. New plants sprang up which were marvels of productive efficiency and which drew visitors from all over the world. The value of the industry's product rose every year during the decade of

the twenties except for the depression year 1921. By 1929, the rate of production was about double what it had been in 1919.

With the growth of the motor industry there came a parallel growth of the steel industry, petroleum refining and distribution, tire manufacture, and road building. Without the automobile most of these industries would have remained of minor importance; on the other hand, without fuel, lubricating oil, tires, and good roads, the automobile would have remained unimportant. Petroleum refining methods were modified to produce more gasoline and less of the heavier products formerly in demand. Filling stations sprang up at every crossroad and in every hamlet in the nation, to supply the needed fuel to the motorist. Almost as numerous were garages to make repairs on cars or tires, to take care of breakdowns which were much more likely to be experienced in the twenties than later. Tire manufacture, centered in Akron, Ohio, reached large-scale proportions. Cord construction and other improvements during the twenties made the pneumatic tire standard for both light and heavy vehicles and extended its useful life by many times. With all of these developments came an increasing public insistence upon good roads over which the automobiles could be operated. Thousands of miles of hard-surfaced, all-weather roads were built, and in the process of building them, methods and equipment for road building were themselves markedly improved. The ramifications of the automobile industry left scarcely a single community in the nation untouched. Everywhere it brought increased ease of movement for all as well as employment for many.

The manufacture of a complex product by the assembly of standardized parts was a system of production that could be used for many other devices besides automobiles. After the motor industry had demonstrated the advantages of the method, it quickly spread to the manufacture of radios, washing machines, electric refrigerators, and other durable consumers' goods. Lower prices led to wider markets, and a great many American homes came to be equipped with these modern con-

[1] *Big Business: Its Growth and Its Place* (New York: Twentieth Century Fund, 1937), pp. 29 and 31.

veniences. The motion-picture camera and projector, also gadgets of the new age, laid the basis for the motion-picture industry. More free time and greater mobility created a market for the output of the film industry through the thousands upon thousands of motion-picture theaters which sprang up in cities and towns everywhere. The movies became a dominant channel through which ideas about dress, manner of speech, and living spread across the country. Sectional and community isolation was broken down. The Main Streets of America looked alike, and those who walked up and down them were more apt to speak and think alike than ever before. Also characteristic of the freedom and speed of the age was the development of civil aviation. Through air mail and passenger and express service, the airplane was beginning to build a place for itself as an essential cog in the transportation system.

Calvin Coolidge, who was president of the United States during the middle years of the twenties, neatly summed up the spirit of the time when he said, "The business of America is business." The prosperity of business and of the public in general made it possible to lighten taxes while revenues to the government continued to rise. This strange phenomenon was possible because the growing volume of production and income yielded a greater total revenue even with the lower tax rates. This situation, which remained true for a number of years, seemed to prove that the less you tax business the more money you get, because the lighter taxes on business permit the reinvestment of more of the profits to finance expanded production, and the expanded production will yield a total of more revenue even with lower tax rates. It was almost a miracle; almost like lifting yourself by your bootstraps. This was a widely accepted opinion about our economic situation in the twenties; acting on it, Congress cut taxes, and still the Treasury was able to retire bonds issued during the previous war, to reduce the national debt. It would be hard to imagine a set of conditions more favorable to business. The number of individual incomes of a mil-

lion dollars or more as reported to the Bureau of Internal Revenue increased from a low of 21 in 1921 to a high of 513 in 1929.

The high levels of production and income constituted the highlights of the twenties. The shadows were created by the persistent depression in Europe, which contributed ultimately to World War II; the most lasting depression that American farmers had ever suffered; and a reaction against labor organization, which prevented industrial workers from sharing fully in the advances of the period. None of these darker aspects of the twenties reached the exploding point during the decade, but they were storing up trouble for the future. Perhaps a significant aspect of the twenties is that the United States could reach the highest levels of prosperity in its history while these three serious economic problems existed. The twenties were especially golden to executive and managerial groups in industry, business, and finance, and to those whose incomes derived from such groups. Others shared in the general prosperity to a lesser degree, although enjoying the new gadgets offered at low prices. Some among the farming and laboring population were merely able to see others enjoying newly found luxury which was completely beyond their own purchasing power.

### Gains and losses for labor

The course of labor-management relations during the twenties was more pleasing to management than to the leaders of unions. The concept of unions for joint action by workers was rejected by most employers at this time. The individualistic tradition was strong with businessmen, and they bitterly resented the inroads which unionism threatened to make on their authority. Prior to 1920 unions had become strongly established on the railroads, in the printing and building trades, and in a few other places, mostly where the labor was highly skilled. The great growth of employment during the twenties was in the automobile industry and others like it which were using the new assembly-line mass-production technique. There was no tradition of unionism in these industries, since they were new. The power and prestige which came with success to employers in these industries, coupled with governmental policies which were in line with business wishes, made it possible for them to resist encroachment by national unions.

Quite often local unions in the plant of a single firm were formed with the aid and assistance of the employer, both because he believed in dealing with his own employees in a time when individual talks were no longer feasible, and because a local or "company" union could be an effective defense against the establishment of an outside union. This whole situation was of course deeply resented by the leaders of organized labor and by those industrial employees who were interested enough to think about it. But for the rank and file of industrial laborers in the twenties, many of whom, incidentally, were new to industry, employment was steady, wages were fairly good, and prices were not rising. The automobile, the radio, and the movies made life more enjoyable, and it seemed senseless to worry about anything else. Union membership declined throughout the first half of the decade and remained stationary for the remainder.

It was not the intention of organized labor at the beginning of the twenties to permit any such condition to develop. Labor leaders and the rank and file had coöperated loyally to promote the war effort, and it was generally felt in the ranks of labor that they should be rewarded at war's end by the granting of higher wages, shorter hours, and other benefits which they had refrained from demanding during the war. The American Federation of Labor had undertaken an organizing drive in the plants of the United States Steel Corporation and had attempted to negotiate with the company on various demands. Negotiation was refused, and a nationwide strike was called in September 1919 in the steel industry. The unions were not well organized, the employers were hostile, and public sympathy was lacking because the strike was led by William Z. Foster, a man of known

radical tendencies who later became an admitted Communist. The real grievances of the workers were lost sight of, and the strike was lost. The twelve-hour day was not eliminated in the steel industry until 1923, and then as a result of a personal appeal by President Harding and the mobilization of public opinion against it. Many strikes occurred throughout the country during 1919. The

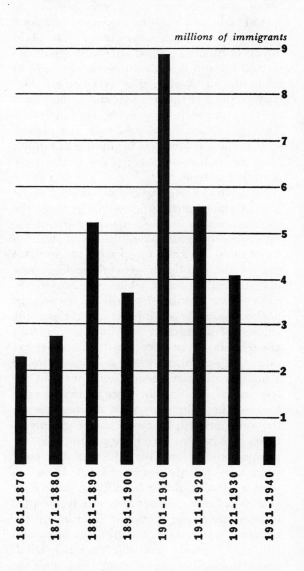

*millions of immigrants*

Fig. XIV-1 Immigration to the United States shows two peak periods, in the 1880's and from 1900 to 1920, before new regulations cutting it drastically had their effect.

total number of workers involved was nearly three times as great as in any previous year in our history and larger than during any year subsequently through the years of World War II.

The break in business in 1920, followed by depression and unemployment in 1921, left organized labor broken in spirit. It seemed to lack means by which it could improve its condition. When recovery came in 1922 and 1923, unions were able to hold their own in the old-line skilled trades in which union membership had become traditional. But the great expansion of employment was in the mass-production industries. Workers were drawn into these industries from the rural areas, from among the many thousands of Negroes who had poured into the North during the war seeking high wartime wages, and from recently arrived European immigrants. None of these groups had any tradition of union membership, and, since their incomes were higher than they had ever been before, they were poor material for unions.

On the other hand, the developing technology of production as illustrated by automatic machines, standardized parts, and the assembly line, also included progress in the management of industrial personnel. The idea of making a detailed study of every phase of manufacturing operations can be traced back to an engineer, Frederick W. Taylor, whose work began to attract attention around the turn of the century. He instituted a program which came to be known as "scientific management." Taylor's work, and that of others carrying out similar methods, resulted in the careful design of tools and the placing of work so that operations could be speeded up without increased strain on the worker, because waste motions were eliminated. Whether or not the moving conveyor assembly line could be used, work was carefully planned from operation to operation as a flow from raw materials and parts to completed product.

The worker, as the human factor of production, was fitted into this process as a kind of raw material or machine which required study just as the inanimate machines did.

Personnel departments were set up throughout industry to handle the hiring of workers, to supervise training and placement, to coöperate with the general management in setting up systems of wage payment, to handle and settle any grievances that arose, and to carry out a program for the maintenance of the morale and general welfare of employees. Generally, work became more repetitive and sometimes monotonous. Usually it was speeded up, either by the rate to which the assembly line was geared or by wage systems which put a high premium on doing a job in the shortest possible time. Such wage systems were referred to as piecework, and involved payment according to the volume of work accomplished. The nervous strain of work was increased, and it came to be said that only the strongest could stand it, mainly those between the ages of twenty and forty. Workers were not consulted before these methods were put into effect. Unions called them the "stretch-out" system. If any worker protested, there was always the personnel department to smooth out the ruffled feelings. If his feelings could not be smoothed, there was always another worker waiting on the bench in the employment office. However, otherwise steady employment and the highest wages in American history provided powerful incentives to forget the strain and unpleasantness of work in order that one might enjoy the fruits thereof.

Between 1920 and 1929, total gainful employment in the United States increased by about 6,500,000. In manufacturing industries, however, the number employed in 1929 was barely greater than in 1920, and in the years between had been below 1920. This numerically constant group of employees increased output of manufactured goods by about 50 per cent during the decade because of the use of improved methods and machinery and an increase of nearly two and a half times in the use of electric power. Many older types of employment, such as farming or mining, also barely held to a steady number or actually declined, but construction, service industries, and various kinds of trade increased employment to more than offset the decline in other areas. The new wealth created by increased efficiency in manufacturing and other industries permitted construction of highways and a spreading out of cities toward suburban areas. Automobiles, home appliances, petroleum products, and tires required a great expansion both in selling and in providing continuing service after they had been sold. Employment in these fields was really a by-product of developments in industry, but the expansion took place outside. It began to appear during the twenties that a technically advanced society would be characterized by a constant or declining group of industrial employees who, with improved machines, would turn out an increasing flood of manufactured goods, the selling and servicing of which would give rise to increased employment outside of industry in the trade and service occupations.

Money wages in most lines increased relatively slowly during the twenties, while the cost of living declined slightly after the recovery from the big break in prices in 1920. The quantities of goods which workers could buy with their wages increased because of low farm prices and declining prices of mass-produced manufactured goods. However, workers on the average were not able to improve their economic position as rapidly as the productivity of the total economy was increasing. Other groups were able to improve their relative position more substantially. Unemployment was never large during the middle twenties, but toward the end of the decade the spread of new machine methods increased technological unemployment, that of workers displaced more or less permanently by machines that performed their old jobs.

### Economic nationalism reasserted

America became a belligerent in World War I with great fanfare but without deep conviction that it was fulfilling an obligation to the rest of the world. Not only did the nation disapprove of war as an instrument of national policy, but it also had traditionally attended to its own business and wished to continue along that path. Americans were annoyed and finally went to war largely because German submarine warfare would not permit them to carry on what they considered legitimate business. When the war was over, the United States was eager not only for the benefits of peace, but also for a return to the consideration of its own problems as the major preoccupation in life, taking it for granted that other nations would do the same.

Many actions and events of the postwar decade illustrate the powerful resurgence of this isolationist and nationalist feeling among large groups of Americans. Woodrow Wilson had thrilled many people throughout the world with his proposals for international coöperation and the setting up of a League of Nations. At the end of the war, he had spent much time in Europe in conference with Allied leaders, taking it for granted that Congress and the people of the United States would follow his leadership into the new League of Nations. Informal polls indicated that among such classes as editors, ministers, and teachers, the president did have a large majority following, but among some political leaders and perhaps among large but non-vocal groups of citizens there were fear and suspicion of the dangers to America that lay along the path of participation in the solution of international problems through membership in the League. As the political battle over the ratification of the peace treaty developed, it became clearer to observers that the cleavage between the believers in international coöperation and the more nationalistic advocates of American isolation was indeed a deep one. Possibly the battle might have gone the other way, but America turned its back on membership in the League. The election of 1920, which brought the Republican party to power and Warren G. Harding to the presidency, signalized the desire of the country to follow an isolationist policy. This was true despite Harding's campaign pledge to support American entrance into the League.

The new president and the new Congress immediately set out to translate the wishes of the people into legislation. An emergency immigration law was enacted in 1921 and was followed three years later by a permanent law. It cut total immigration sharply (see Fig. XIV-1, p. 278), established a quota system based on country of origin, established a base for the quotas which favored north European immigrants, and excluded Orientals altogether as immigrants. Organized labor had become increasingly hostile to immigration, fearing the competition of the new workers. Industry was less dependent than formerly on unskilled immigrant labor because of the perfection of machines capable of doing much of the manual labor of former years. From a sociological point of view, many persons feared further additions to the foreign language communities in cities and industrial areas until those already there had been assimilated into American life. During the twenties, net immigration under the new law was slight, and in the thirties more people left the country than entered it as immigrants. Congress passed emergency tariff legislation in 1921 to prevent the lower rates of the 1913 Underwood Tariff Act from continuing in effect in peacetime. Then, in 1922, permanent tariff legislation was enacted—the Fordney-McCumber Act—putting the protectionist principle into effect again and imposing the highest rates of America's history on some types of manufactured goods as well as on agricultural products.

A measure of the character of the period may be found in the economic thought—or lack of it—involved in the new "flexible" principle included in the Fordney-McCumber Act. The Act provided for a Tariff Commission to study costs of production of goods entering into foreign trade, and empowered the president to raise or lower duties by a half to place them at a point which would equalize domestic and foreign costs. This was referred to as a scientific tariff-making process which would take the whole matter out of politics. The Tariff Commission spent years investigating costs, securing all the data it could, but was never able to arrive at really satisfactory results. Informed advisers could have warned Congress in advance that this method would not work. Even if costs had been discoverable,

to equalize them by tariff rates as between foreign and domestic producers, although having an apparent plausibility, would in fact have stopped all trade. If an American buyer could not get a better product for his money from a foreign producer, he would certainly buy at home. Tariffs to equalize costs would be tariffs high enough to stop all foreign trade. Since Congress paid no heed to this obvious reasoning, we can only conclude that it was expressing a kind of emotional "100 per cent Americanism" when it passed the Fordney-McCumber Act.

A concomitant facet of this isolationist spirit was the failure of those in official circles in the government to see the relationship between tariff policy and the repayment of the debts owed to the United States by European governments as a result of the war. Following World War I the United States was a creditor nation, having lost its debtor status for the first time in its history. Our great industrial growth and the volume of war supplies which we had sent to the Allied governments during the war put them in debt to us to the extent of over $7 billion by the war's end, far exceeding the debts owed by American individuals and business firms to Europeans. American debts owing to Europe had been built up during the nineteenth century by the purchase of manufactured goods in Europe for consumption and for the building of American factories and railroads. As the years passed and America could export more to Europe than it bought from there, these debts were reduced. World War I threw the balance the other way, and had anyone in the government bothered to think about the matter, it would have been clear that we could not collect our war debts from Europe except in the same form in which they had been created, that is in goods or services.

Instead of this clearly logical approach to the problem of war debts, the United States insisted upon dealing with it in complete separation from the tariff problem. As a result, tariffs were pushed up and Europe was able to sell to us less than half of the value of goods which we sold to her. American efforts to collect war debts went through one debacle after another, ending in complete cancellation of remaining debts in 1932, when it became apparent that they could not be collected in any case. The effort was then given up, having produced considerable ill will all around. As a result, even friends of the United States called us "Uncle Shylock," and American actions contributed to the disorganization of European economic life out of which World War II arose. It seemed that the United States was learning the hard way that it could not live *in* a world of nations and peoples without being also *of* them.

### Hard times for the farmer

While as a nation the United States was enthusiastically turning its attention to the expansion of business and industry at home, and while labor was tardily and partially sharing in the general advance in wealth, agriculture had to contend with a combination of conditions which produced the hardest times farmers had had since the decades immediately following the Civil War. Wars always bring an increased demand for the staple food and fiber crops, and, at the same time, disrupt normal living and cut down farm production in the actual war zones. Europe is one of the largest agricultural producers among the continents, but World War I sharply cut European production and threw the burden of food supply upon North America, Argentina, Australia, and New Zealand. Responding to these added demands as reflected in high prices, production was intensified, and new acreage was brought into use in all of the good agricultural areas of the world outside of Europe. At the end of the war, the situation reverted back toward normal fairly quickly. Europe returned to its former high level of production, especially of wheat, and the United States and other non-European countries were faced with farm surpluses.

The ability of American agriculture after 1920 to adjust to the loss of European markets for the basic farm crops, and to bring about a sufficient reduction in war-expanded acreage to restore a more favorable relationship between supply and demand, was hampered by the mechanization of farm operations which was developing. The manufacture of farm tractors, which had barely begun before World War I, expanded very rapidly during and following the war. The number of horses on farms declined after 1918. Farmers began to use motor trucks to haul their products to market while the number of horses pulling delivery wagons in cities also declined sharply. All of these aspects of the shift away from the horse as a source of motive power meant that millions of acres of farm land once used to produce hay and grain to feed horses were no longer needed for this purpose. The farmer ceased to be a consumer of his own products in this respect. Yet the shift from the horse to the internal combustion engine made it possible for the farmer to handle more acres of land and to handle them better, while that very shift in power itself as well as decline in the world market for agricultural products called for a reduction of acreage.

The directors of any of the large nonagricultural businesses that had become typical by the twenties would have been able to adjust quickly to meet a changed situation of this kind. They would not have liked to be forced to curtail activities, but rather than glut the market they would have adopted restricted production schedules at once. It would have been almost impossible for farmers to act so swiftly, and in fact, as individuals they were much more likely to react in the wrong direction. Large business firms commonly expect their production to have an effect on market conditions. Therefore, if market conditions are unfavorable, they would be prompt to vary their own production in such ways as to bring the market back to a satisfactory status. The farmer had no such habits of thought. He thought of himself as a small producer among millions of others. He never thought of his production as affecting the supply on national and world markets through the cumulative effect of the actions of all farmers. If the market prices were low, it would never occur to him that he should limit production to help bring them back up. Rather he would probably think that since prices were low he had better step up production in order to keep his own personal income up in spite of low prices. Thus, the postwar readjustment in American agriculture did not take place as speedily as might have been possible. Surpluses of the basic crops became chronic, but production did not decline in the face of surpluses. Farmers as a group did not fully appreciate what had happened as prices and incomes fell. Many left the farm to share in the expanding employment in the cities. The farmers who remained could handle more land with their tractors and power equipment. Surpluses, low prices, and low farm income continued throughout the twenties. Although they were getting new power equipment from factories in the cities, farmers as a group lagged behind in the parade of industrial progress. Others were receiving the chief benefits of the new productivity of both industry and agriculture.

The result of these conditions was more widespread discontent and depression in rural areas than had existed since the days of the Granger movement and the Farmers' Alliances in the 1870's and 1880's. Many farmers had borrowed money to buy farm land during the years of high prices before 1920, and now they found themselves unable to keep up the payments on their loans. Farm mortgage loans were foreclosed by banks and the resulting forced sales of land drove prices of farm land downward. Banks in rural sections of the nation began to fail in the midst of the greatest prosperity America had ever had. Farmers demanded action by state and federal governments to aid them in their plight. The tariff acts of the early twenties, as well as the Hawley-Smoot Act of 1930, included higher tariff rates on imported agricultural products. This was a groove in which much American thought had run for a hundred years, and the country returned to it now in spite of the very obvious fact that none of the basic farm crops was being imported. In fact, the United States could not sell enough of its surplus farm

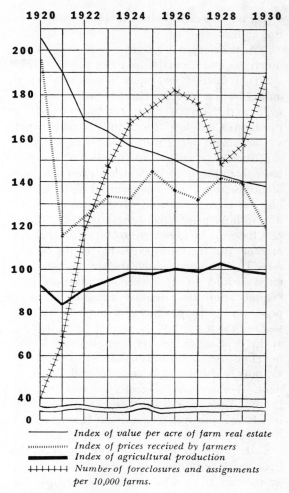

Index of value per acre of farm real estate
Index of prices received by farmers
Index of agricultural production
Number of foreclosures and assignments per 10,000 farms.

Fig. XIV-2 A picture of the economic situation of American farmers in the decade of the 1920's. Note the sharp decline in the value of farm real estate and sharp rise in the volume of foreclosures. The average for 1935-1939 is taken as 100 for the index figures.

products abroad to keep up prices at home. Congress also passed several acts to provide credit facilities of various kinds to farmers. The thought behind these acts was sound, because farmers very often did not have the credit facilities which they needed for production and especially for marketing their crops and livestock in an orderly manner. The high risks on loans to farmers had kept interest rates too high: This condition was more than ever true as rural banks failed or found themselves tied up with loans on which they could not collect.

A third type of farm relief that found much support in the prairie states, where agrarian distress was most acute, was represented by the McNary-Haugen Bills passed in 1927 and 1928 by Congress but vetoed by President Coolidge. These bills provided that a government agricultural marketing corporation should be created to establish a price for basic farm products high enough to cover cost of production. The corporation should then buy sufficient quantities of the various products to hold prices up to the fair level. These purchases of surplus were to be sold in world markets for the best price that could be obtained. The losses which the corporation suffered would be recovered by assessing an "equalization fee" against all sales of farm products by the producer at home. This was too radical a method of raising farm income at the expense of the city consumer and to the benefit of foreign consumers to win the official support of the Republican party and the president. A more moderate method was adopted in the Agricultural Marketing Act of 1929, which was approved by President Hoover. That Act created a Federal Farm Board and provided it with funds to lend to marketing coöperatives or to stabilization corporations created by the Act to purchase basic farm crops and livestock at marketing time so that markets might not be glutted and orderly marketing might be promoted. Very shortly after the Act was passed, the country was hit by severe depression and the Farm Board was swamped. The powers of the Farm Board were not sufficient to enable it to correct the basic causes of the agricultural maladjustment, and the depression of the 1930's threw the farmers into still more profound economic trouble.

### The course of business during the twenties

One of the great advantages of the historical approach to the study of economics is that it makes possible particularly close examination of those aspects of a period which subsequently turn out to be of great importance. Making use of that advantage, we may profitably pay particular attention to the factors which seem to have contributed most to the unprecedented prosperity of the twenties. We would like to know exactly why it collapsed, or, in other words, why the factors that maintained the prosperity through the twenties were not capable of maintaining it indefinitely. Unfortunately, the statistical facts we should like to have about the decade of the twenties are not all available, because the need for them was not realized at the time.

It is now generally agreed by economists that one of the most rewarding ways to analyze the economic system as it functions at any time is to study the creation of income through the various processes of production, and the use of that income by those who receive it. Prosperity can continue only so long as income, which is being generated by production, flows without interruption or diminution through the processes of exchange and distribution to purchase the goods or services by which the income of the nation was created in the first place. A prosperous economic system depends upon a smooth flow of goods from producers to consumers and a reverse flow of income from consumers to producers. Of course, the producer of one kind of product or service is also a consumer, using his income to buy many other kinds of goods and services from other producers.

It is also pretty commonly agreed by economists that some sort of balance between current consumer expenditures and savings is required for prosperity. It might almost be said that, by definition, the word "saving" means income that is not used. That is not really true, however, for an individual or a firm is likely to put any savings that are made into either a bank or financial institution for safekeeping or directly into some improvement. The bank will usually not keep the money idle but will lend it to a business which needs it for current expenses or expansion. Thus, savings normally represent income that is used just as much as income that is spent directly for food, clothing, and the other expenses of living. The difference is that savings represent income that is used to supply the capital which industry and business must have to continue and expand. Prosperity depends on a steady demand for the goods and services that are produced, a demand directly from consumers and from the investment of savings in providing new capital for business. Prosperous periods in our history have been periods in which consumers enjoyed steadier employment and a higher standard of living than usual and in which business investment took place at a high rate to keep both individual and business savings moving promptly into the formation of capital.

family living, and millions of families wanted cars. Production and sales increased annually during World War I except for 1918 when restrictions on materials and manpower held output down. In 1919 and 1920, automobile production surged ahead again, until the depression of 1921 provided another setback. In 1922 the expansion of the industry resumed, with production for the first time passing the two million mark, and continued with minor fluctuations until 1929. By 1925 the value of the output of motor vehicles was nearly double what it had been in 1919 and was nearly five times what it had been only ten years before in 1915. Production of passenger cars and trucks in 1929 exceeded five million, a number not reached again until after World War II.

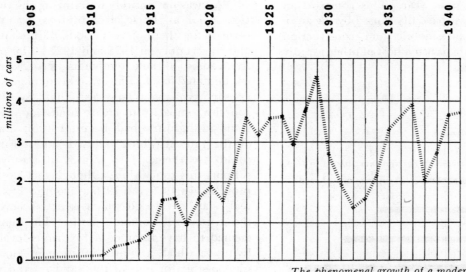

Fig. XIV-3

The phenomenal growth of a modern American industry—automobile production—1905 to 1941.

The actual conditions, especially of the early twenties, amply met the theoretical requirements for prosperity. For one thing, World War I had demonstrated both the versatility of motor vehicles and the capacity of a mechanized, assembly-line industry to turn them out at low cost. The public had seen and ridden in cars, which brought an unprecedented freedom of movement into

The economic consequences of the eager public acceptance of the automobile were widespread. To begin with, the purchase of an automobile is a major family expenditure, and the desire for a car led many families to push their expenditures to a limit which required extensive borrowing to sustain it. This keen and expanding demand for automobiles, in turn, led to a high volume of spending to create the manufacturing and servicing facilities which a large automobile production required. Roads, garages, filling stations, refineries, pipe lines, tank cars, and tire factories were necessary if cars were going to be of any use to their owners. The providing of all of these facilities for automobiles as well as the direct manufacture of cars and trucks placed great new demands upon the steel industry. More than ever it became the base on which the entire industrial system rested.

Passenger cars and busses made it possible for workers to live at greater distances from their work. Cities and towns experienced a rush to the suburbs. This meant not only new homes but also new streets, new stores, and the expansion of public utility services. The construction industry was operating at the highest levels in American history during the twenties, with 1926 the peak year. This construction boom was at least partially caused by the automobile. The automobile and construction industries together with a host of other rapidly

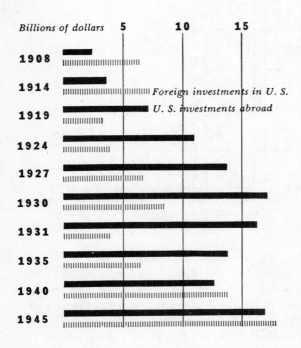

Fig. XIV-4  *The United States changed from a debtor to a creditor nation in the era following World War I.*

developing industries—electric power, radio, movies, telephone, appliances, and others—provided not only channels through which the savings of individuals and businesses might be spent in creating new production facilities or capital equipment, but also such great opportunities for investment that there was a great expansion in bank credit as well. Stocks and bonds were sold by industry to individuals and financial institutions in a greater volume than ever before. The sharp acceleration of production and employment after the depression of 1921 were pretty clearly a result of the high levels of both consumer and investment spending in such rapidly growing industries. This is not to deny importance to other factors, but merely to single out what seem to have been the outstanding bases of the prosperity of the early twenties.

All was not entirely well during the twenties, so far as the level of business was concerned, for there were periods of hesitation and uncertainty in 1924 and 1927. The positive causes of these temporary setbacks cannot be stated flatly. The available data make it appear probable, however, that by 1924 America's capacity to create funds for investment in industry had begun to run ahead of the rate at which industry and business could use them. Two straws in the wind support this conclusion, although they do not prove it. In 1925 and 1926 a boom in Florida real estate developed which went far beyond the bounds of common sense. The nation seemed to have attained a luxurious level of living in which a winter vacation in Florida was possible for tens of thousands. Land values rose, lots were laid out over large areas of the state, and construction boomed. Much of this had a sound foundation, but some of it went to ridiculous extremes. Lots in mosquito-infested swamps were sold to heedless speculators who were so sure that millions of Americans would go to Florida that they assumed the swamps would surely be drained. During the same years, American investments abroad, especially in Europe and South America, rose to new heights. The United States had had no great experience in foreign lending, since the

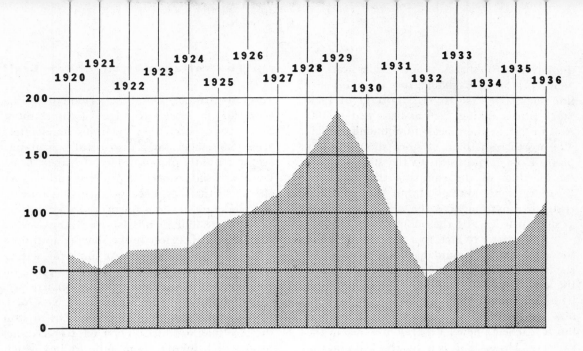

*Fig. XIV-5  The index of the prices of common stocks between 1920 and 1936. The year 1926 = 100.*

flow of funds had hitherto been into the country. There were now funds available for the making of loans abroad, and American investment bankers sent representatives overseas as virtual loan salesmen to promote foreign borrowing, especially by governments. Many of these loans were made without adequate regard for the ability of the governmental unit to pay interest and retire the principal when due. Within a year or two there began to be defaults on interest payments as they came due and the American investor became frightened. The period of business hesitation in 1924 coincides with the beginning of an apparent overflow of investment funds from America's own domestic business and industry to speculation in Florida land and to purchase of foreign bonds. By 1927, these newly found channels for the use of the overflowing investment funds were no longer appealing, and another period of hesitation occurred while savers and speculators were seeking still other outlets for their funds.

The climax of the decade—a climax which contributed in no small measure to the designation the "roaring twenties"—was reached in the continuing prosperity and the stock market boom of 1928 and 1929. Automobile production continued to a new high in 1929, although construction and foreign lending slipped back a little from their high points in 1926 and 1927. A great new factor in the business situation in the last two years of the decade was the widespread public participation in the buying and selling of stocks on the New York Stock Exchange. Many thousands of professional and small business people had savings or credit facilities for which they could find no other use as promising as the stock market. Public participation in the financing of industry through the purchase of stocks and bonds had been on the increase for many decades, but it had not reached the proportions of a mass movement. The collapse of the Florida land boom and defaults on foreign bonds had created suspicion of those two outlets for investment funds. But business continued to be good, incomes were growing for the nation as a whole, and Americans by the tens of thousands decided that it was a wise idea to invest in the securities of their own businesses. Profits were to be made either from the dividends on stocks, or, progressively as the boom developed, from the ever higher quotations on shares. Total sales on the New York Stock Exchange rose from 451 million shares in 1926 to 1125 million in 1929. Stock prices, taking 1926 as base year at 100, rose to 291 at their peak in September 1929. The worth of a share of stock should bear a pretty close relationship to the standing and the earnings of the company that issues it. Business profits were good, but they were not rising in anything like the same proportion as stock prices while the boom continued.

As a matter of fact, to a superficial viewer the stock market would have appeared to be the heart of the economic system in America in the last years of the twenties. The corporation had been increasingly prevalent in the business structure for more than half a century, but it reached a new level of dominance in the twenties. However, it is perfectly clear and unmistakable that it was the application of the new technology of large-scale production which really sustained the intensive economic activity evident everywhere, especially in the stock market. The stock exchange itself had to expand and elaborate its own organization to accommodate the tens of thousands of new customers who rushed to share in the bonanza. Unincorporated businesses took out corporate charters and applied for a listing of their stock on the New York Stock Exchange, for the easiest way to raise capital when needed was to float a new issue of stock through the Exchange. The process was so easy and the public became so willing to buy both new and old shares of stock at ever higher prices that it is small wonder that the issuing corporations, and even the Stock Exchange itself, lost any knowledge of the real values of stock shares.

It is interesting to note that national income, volume of production, stock prices, and other indicators of economic conditions all reached new heights in 1929 in spite of the fact that workers and farmers were not sharing in the prosperity in full proportion. This fact constituted a demonstration that business had reached a degree of dominance in American economic life which enabled it to forge on to new heights, at least temporarily, even if labor and agriculture lagged behind.

## The collapse of the "New Era"

On October 24, 1929, a violent selling wave hit the stock exchanges of the country. Stock prices had been declining moderately since September, and distrustful speculators had apparently placed orders with their brokers to sell their stocks at prices slightly under the levels that had been prevailing. Continuing moderate declines uncovered these selling orders and suddenly orders to sell far exceeded orders to buy. Prices broke sharply and more selling orders poured in. At times the selling was so heavy that those offering stocks for sale far exceeded available buyers almost irrespective of the selling price. A group of New York bankers formed a pool to buy stocks to stop the headlong declines. Their efforts were successful in bringing about mild rallies which enabled them to sell their stocks at a profit, but the higher prices did not persist. Severe price declines resulted from panic selling until November 13, when the average of stock prices had fallen about one-half. The shock and panic of speculators began to wear off after the latter date, but for the next three years the course of stock prices was downward with only short rallies to interrupt the decline. At the bottom, many stocks had lost 90 per cent of their 1929 prices. Clearly the "New Era" of imagined permanent prosperity was ended.

It is hard now to recapture the psychological impact of the stock market crash on the outlook of the American people. Never before had there been such a violent break in stock prices. Never had so many people been affected either directly or indirectly. Never had so many people been taken so utterly by surprise. It was as though the country had been lashed by the winds and rain of a violent storm while the sky was blue overhead. The United States was basking in the golden sunshine of assurances from business and economic authorities that it was on a new "permanently high plateau" of prosperity. Then without warning the dream was broken into a thousand pieces, and Americans were left to the sorrowful contemplation of tumbling prices, growing unemployment, and widespread business bankruptcy. Business had never had a freer period to demonstrate what it could do. Government policies had been dictated by business to assure that there should be no governmental actions that would impose undue burdens on business or arouse fear or suspicion. Business could have wished for no more coöperation from government than it had. But in spite of practically ideal conditions, the stock-market crash came. At first it was thought that fears would soon be dispelled and the rise of prices would be resumed. But that did not happen. The economic earthquake was real and profound. The nation was stunned and helpless.

Although a majority of Americans could not bring themselves to believe that there was anything wrong with the economic fundamentals on which their system was built, it was not possible to prevent the collapse of stock prices from spreading to other areas of the economy. The stock-market crash injected a sharp note of caution into other business operations. The business future was being reappraised, generally in more modest and cautious terms than had prevailed in the preceding years. Buying for other than immediate use was discontinued. It was safer to use up goods on hand rather than to accumulate more. In fact, studies of commodity trends show that buying of many kinds of industrial raw materials had reached a peak even before the stock-market break. Curtailed buying soon meant curtailed production and curtailed employment. Data do not exist to give an accurate picture of the progress of the depression in terms of unemployment. The index of manufacturing production of the Federal Reserve Board showed a drop from 110 in 1929 (1935 to 1939 average = 100) to 90 in 1930, and on down to 75 in 1931 and to the depression low of 57 in 1932. This is an index of physical units of production. By 1932, the level of production in American industry was thus only slightly more than half what it had been in 1929. Of course, the decline of production and general economic activity in America could not fail to have the most serious effects on other countries with which America carried on business. In addition to the directly contagious effect of falling prices for stocks, raw materials, and manufactured goods, American purchases of all kinds of goods from foreign suppliers were almost completely cut off. Often, too, these American purchases were necessary to profitable operation of foreign producers, so that the reduction or termination of our imports immediately forced them either to shut down or to reduce operations.

The creeping paralysis of depression following the stock-market break in 1929 started an intensive reëxamination of traditional economic ideas and of the available data on business conditions. While a study of the economic system from the classical point of view of the functioning of the markets showed no adequate reason for the panicky fear which had spread through these markets, a newer method of analysis—examination of the generation and use of income rather than of supply and demand forces in the market—gave a hint of one, perhaps *the,* possible source of the trouble. The Brookings Institution was an important research organization which turned its staff to an investigation of the causes of the depression. In *The Formation of Capital,* a book published by Harold G. Moulton, Director of the Brookings Institution, the following conclusion was drawn:

The rapid growth of savings as compared with consumption in the decade of the 1920's resulted in a supply of investment money quite out of proportion to the volume of securities being floated for purposes of expanding plant and equipment, while at the same time the flow of funds through consumptive channels was inadequate to absorb—at the prices at which goods were offered for sale—the potential output of our existing productive capacity. The excess savings which entered the investment market served to inflate the price of securities and to produce financial instability. A larger relative flow of funds through consumptive channels would have led not only to larger utilization of existing productive capacity, but also to a more rapid growth of plant equipment.[1]

[1] (Washington, D. C.: Brookings Institution, 1935), p. 159.

Translated into more concrete terms, the large profits and large incomes of businesses and those who held important positions in them permitted a volume of savings seeking investment which was greater than the investment opportunities available. The result was inadequate income going to farmers, labor, and consumers in general to buy the consumer goods being turned out. A further result was that American productive capacity was not fully used. We kept going as well as we did only because part of the goods being produced were sold on the credit which was being extended rather freely to consumers at home and abroad. But such credit expansion had to reach a limit, just as the bidding up of security prices by speculators seeking investment outlets had to reach a limit. As both limits were approached, financial instability was created. Dr. Moulton's analysis seemed to offer an explanation of the severity of the reaction to the stock-market break. The economy was really on an unsound basis, a fact which the stock-market reaction had brought to light.

### President Hoover's efforts to bring recovery

The terrifying about-face which business had executed following the stock-market crash placed President Herbert Hoover in a most difficult position. He had been elected on the slogan of "four more years of prosperity," with the members of the business community in the vanguard of his supporters. Within seven and a half months of his inauguration in March 1929, public sentiment was becoming suspicious of the wisdom of the prevailing business policies, and the president was confronted with the problem of taking leadership in efforts to stop business recession. His was the traditionally accepted view that the principal economic function of government was to remain out of the way of business. The stock-market crash had revealed excessive speculation and some financial corruption, neither of which were condoned by Hoover.

As the depression deepened, the president endeavored to get coöperative action by business to stop price declines, wage cutting, and the discharge of workers. His thought, apparently, was that if panicky price cutting could be stopped, then the whole chain of consequences following upon falling prices could also be stopped. As voluntary action proved to be inadequate, he moved step by step toward federal legislation. The Federal Farm Board had been set up even before the break in business to stabilize chronically weak farm prices. The erection of public works is a normal function of government, and President Hoover early recognized the value of stimulating such work as a counterbalance to industrial recession. Before the end of his term he was responsible for coördinating such activities in the new Public Works Administration. He did not favor an extension of public works solely for the purpose of creating employment, however, opposing such a proposal from Congress. The Federal Reserve Act was amended by the passage of the Glass-Steagall Bill in 1932 to liberalize lending powers of the banks and to utilize the large gold reserves of the system to check deflation. In July 1932, the Federal Home Loan Bank Act was passed, creating twelve regional Federal Home Loan Banks to extend federal financial assistance to building-and-loan associations and to other real-estate lending agencies that were in trouble because of falling prices. Most important of all was the creation in January 1932 of the Reconstruction Finance Corporation with a capital of $500 million and the right of issuing $1.5 billion of debentures (interest-bearing bonds secured by real estate) "to provide emergency financing facilities for financial institutions, to aid in financing agriculture, commerce and industry." Funds were provided for loans to business to prevent bankruptcy and forced liquidation, which was everywhere creating unemployment and forcing down prices.

In all of these actions Hoover showed himself willing to use the power and authority of the federal government to intervene in business. In part he was pushed by circumstances into the support of actions for which he had no apparent enthusiasm. The times were trying in the extreme, and the president was under the greatest pressure to extend his ideas of the proper economic functions of government to their broadest limits. Yet it is notable that he did not wish to use the power of government to provide employment primarily as a relief measure. Relief remained a function of state and local governments in his view. The relief which the president was willing to provide was mostly indirect, by way of loans to businesses to stop bankruptcies with their ensuing layoffs of workers, to stop foreclosures on homes and the evicting of the former owners, and to strengthen the financial institutions which held savings. The nature of these policies caused them to be referred to as the "trickle down" theory of prosperity.

Hoover saw the functioning of the American economy in terms of its free markets. These markets had succumbed to panic, and price declines had spread throughout the system like the concentric circles from a stone thrown into a pond, wreaking havoc as they went. The way to correct the situation was to go to its source and to bolster up the economy in such ways and at such places as to stop price declines. In the presidential race in the fall of 1932, Hoover was decisively rejected by the American people in favor of the "New Deal" of Franklin D. Roosevelt, probably not so much because the people clearly understood the policies of either, as because implicit in Roosevelt's program was the use of the power of the government to whatever extent necessary and in whatever ways necessary to reverse the trend of economic events.

## FOR FURTHER READING

Barnes, James A. *Wealth of the American People.* New York: Prentice-Hall, Inc., 1949. Chapters 28—32.

Bogart, Ernest L., and Kemmerer, Donald L. *Economic History of the American People.* 2nd ed. New York: Longmans, Green & Co., Inc., 1947. Part IV.

Dulles, F. R. *Twentieth Century America.* Boston: Houghton Mifflin Co., 1945. Chapters 14—18.

Faulkner, H. U. *American Economic History,* 8th ed. New York: Harper & Brothers, 1960. Chapter 28.

Hofstadter, Richard. *The Age of Reform.* Vintage, 1960. Paperback. Chapters 4—6.

Leuchtenberg, W. E. *The Perils of Prosperity, 1914-1932.* Phoenix Books, 1958. Excellent paperback.

Rostow, W. W. *The Stages of Economic Growth,* Cambridge, Eng.: Oxford University Press, 1960. Exciting interpretation.

Shannon, Fred Albert. *America's Economic Growth.* 3rd ed. New York: The Macmillan Co., 1951. Part IV.

Wright, Chester W. *Economic History of the United States.* New York: McGraw-Hill Book Co., 1949. Chapter 44.

# Chapter 15: The crisis

# of capitalism and the New Deal

In the winter of 1932-1933, the strain of three years of almost unbroken price declines, shrinking production in industry, and growing unemployment finally began to erode away public confidence in the American banking system. Yet it had shown remarkable strength. Never before had our banking system been strong enough to withstand such deflationary blows as those it received from October 1929 onward. Cities and states throughout the country began to have bank trouble and governors declared state-wide "bank holidays" to stop destructive runs as depositors rushed to withdraw savings.

When Franklin D. Roosevelt was sworn in as president of the United States on March 4, 1933, the skies were a leaden gray in Washington, D.C., a cold rain was falling, nearly all the banks of the nation were closed, a fourth or more of the nation's workers had no jobs, and farmers in the West were preventing foreclosure sales and evictions by force. A more somber point in our history would be hard to remember. Roosevelt's inaugural address struck a note of hope. The nation was strong, he said, and would recover from this crippling depression. "The only thing we have to fear, is fear itself—nameless, unreasoning, unjustified terror which paralyzes needed efforts to convert retreat into advance." The nation and Congress, which he immediately called into emergency session, responded to his appeal.

Quickly the pattern of the "New Deal" began to reveal itself. First, the resources of the federal government as well as those of state and local governments must be thrown into the breach to see that no one suffered from hunger and privation. People must be put back on their feet economically as soon as possible by stimulating employment through every means. Preferably the employment should be by private firms in the usual way, but, if necessary, the federal government should use its resources to provide employment on the most useful work projects that could be quickly devised. Secondly, the abuses that aggravated, if they did not cause, the depression must be corrected. Anyone guilty of criminal acts of financial or corporate manipulation should be punished. Banking laws were to be made stricter in some respects, controls over the stock exchanges and the commodity markets were to be tightened, and abuse of the holding-company device was to be corrected by closer control of its use, especially in the field of public utilities. Finally, after these more or less emergency corrective measures had been taken, Roosevelt proposed a series of long-term, permanent steps to bring about the fuller development of the country and to make the lives of most Americans more secure and prosperous. Often these three aims of the New Deal were mixed in single pieces of legislation, but examination would nearly always show that they were there. Roosevelt referred to his objectives as "Relief, Recovery, and Reform."

### Relief and security of income for workers

When Congress convened in March 1933, shortly after Roosevelt's inauguration, its first business was to provide for the reopening of banks to relieve the financial emergency (see p. 292). By the end of March it had turned to the problem of employment and created the Civilian Conservation Corps (CCC) to put unemployed young men into camps to carry out reforestation and erosion-control projects. Within four years, more than two million men had spent some time in the CCC. This was the first of a long series of governmental agencies that came to be called "alphabetical agencies" because their initials were more convenient and more often used than their full names.

In May, the Federal Emergency Relief Administration (FERA) was set up and given a half billion dollars to be granted to states for direct relief on a basis of one dollar of federal funds for every three spent by the states. The Administrator at his own discretion could also make outright grants to states of up to half the total appropriation to meet

dire need. In June, the National Industrial Recovery Act (pp. 300ff.) was passed, the second part of which made an appropriation of $3\frac{1}{3}$ billion dollars to the Public Works Administration (PWA) to be matched against funds of states and local governments for all kinds of large-scale public building projects. The PWA had been set up by President Hoover (p. 289), but it was now reorganized and given this large appropriation as a basic element in getting men back to work in the construction industry throughout the country. The construction industry was thought to be ideal for this purpose, since it was widely scattered in its operations and purchased machinery and supplies from many sources. It was hoped and expected that the expenditure of such a large sum would prime the business pump and start employment and prices upward.

By early fall of 1933, it was apparent that the PWA was not going to get under way rapidly enough to cut down the relief rolls by winter. Consequently, the Civil Works Administration (CWA) was set up as a branch of FERA to create four million jobs for workers on relief. CWA was discontinued the following March, but during the trying winter of 1933-1934 it made a remarkable record of putting people to work on hastily improvised jobs. Much of the "leaf raking" and "boondoggling" with which critics later liked to charge the Roosevelt administration arose from CWA.

During 1934, public works projects became more numerous through the conventional private contract basis of operation, but they still left a distressingly large number of workers on the relief rolls. By executive order in May 1935, the president created the Works Progress Administration (WPA) to set up useful work projects, involving labor to a greater degree than machinery or supplies and small enough so that they could be set up in communities all over the nation. Only those on relief could be employed. Until the employment created by the preparations for World War II eliminated virtually all unemployment, the WPA continued to be the principal agency to provide work for those unable to

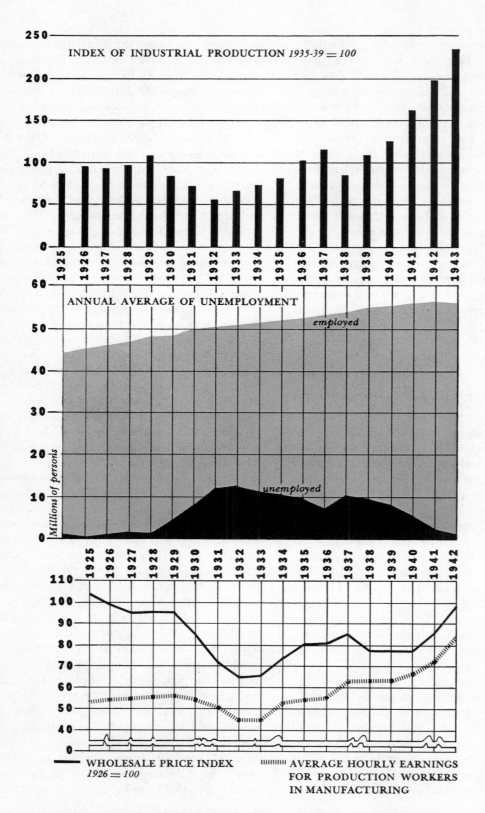

Fig. XV-1  A picture of the American economic scene during the depression and into the early war years. Compare the drop in production, employment, and wages to the trend taken by wholesale prices.

obtain private employment. A division of WPA, the National Youth Administration (NYA) set up projects for young people otherwise unable to continue their schooling, to permit the earning of sufficient income so that they could go on with their education. Those no longer in school were also given employment. By 1936, it is estimated that the federal government had spent nearly eleven billion dollars on relief, yet in the first official census of unemployment, made in 1938, nearly eight million persons were still without jobs.

X Another type of relief was provided by the creation of the Home Owners Loan Corporation (HOLC) in June 1933. Thousands of families, even if able to avoid going on the relief rolls, found themselves unable to continue payments on homes in which they lived and which they were in the process of buying. The banks, building and loan associations, and other types of home mortgage-lending agencies, were themselves under pressure to protect their investors' funds as prices fell. The bitter irony of the situation was that in the face of falling real-estate prices the lending agencies would often foreclose on homes nearly paid off. Perhaps only a few hundred dollars remained due, but if the family was unable to continue payments, the property could be sold, and in thousands of cases it was sold. Often the shrinkage of prices and the scarcity of buyers would leave a family not only without a home, but with the loss of the equity they had built up by years of saving. The HOLC was authorized to take over such mortgages in exchange for its own bonds, which were guaranteed by the government. Similar credit facilities had been made available to farmers under various agricultural credit acts dating back to the twenties. Additional authorizations for the HOLC were voted by Congress from time to time. It put a substantial stop to the distressing business of having families put out of their homes.

For longer-range protection against the hazards of loss of income from unemployment, old age, or disability, Congress in August 1935 passed the Social Security Act, on recommendation of the president. It is a complex law providing for old age insurance for workers in the included occupations; for old age assistance to supplement the insurance aspect of the program in the early years of the operation of the Act; for unemployment insurance to be operated by the respective states; and for federal grants to the states to take care of special cases of need, such as blindness and vocational rehabilitation. The insurance for old age is paid for by deductions from the employee's pay added to equal payments by the employer. The old age assistance is to supplement the earned insurance payments to workers whose income was either too low to provide an adequate minimum retirement allowance or who were not in the system long enough before retirement to earn such a minimum rate. A Social Security Board was set up to administer the Act through the states. No inclusive national plan of unemployment insurance was created. Instead a tax was levied on the payrolls of the types of employment covered by the Act—mostly employees of business and industry—90 per cent of which might be rebated to states which set up approved plans for unemployment insurance in their respective areas. All of the states did set up unemployment insurance plans, so that the entire nation is covered, although the provisions of the state acts vary. As a result of all of these provisions, a long step was taken toward what Roosevelt referred to as one of the most important objectives of his administration—the "security of the men, women, and children of the nation."

The intent of the various parts of the Social Security Act was to provide a financial life net beneath large segments of the population as they were compelled to face and accept the economic hazards of our complex industrial civilization. The different provisions have been amended and extended from time to time since the Act was first passed. For example, in August 1950 Congress extended the coverage to nearly ten million workers not covered by the original law, including domestics, farm labor, nonfarm self-employed persons, and workers in Puerto Rico and the Virgin Islands. At the same time the benefits were raised so

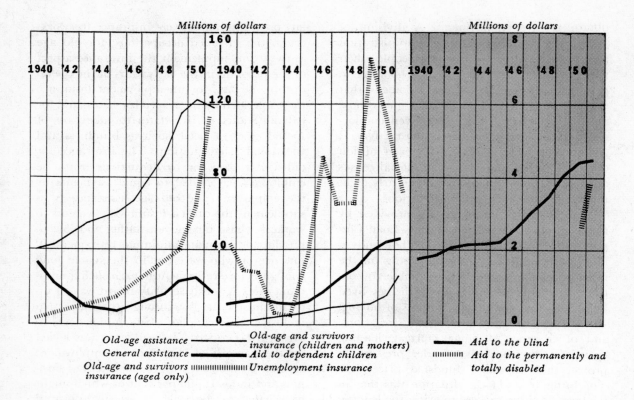

Millions of dollars — 160, 120, 80, 40, 0
Millions of dollars — 8, 6, 4, 2, 0

1940 '42 '44 '46 '48 '50

Old-age assistance ——————
General assistance ▬▬▬▬▬
Old-age and survivors insurance (aged only) |||||||||||||||||||
Old-age and survivors insurance (children and mothers) ·····················
Aid to dependent children ——————
Unemployment insurance |||||||||||||
Aid to the blind ▬▬▬▬▬
Aid to the permanently and totally disabled |||||||||||||

*Fig. XV-2  Payments to individuals under the Social Security Act between 1940 and 1950.*

that by June 1951 two million retired workers were receiving an average of $41 in monthly Old Age and Survivors' Insurance benefits, while aged couples received $70. There can be little doubt that social security has become as much a part of American life as free, public education.

## Control of banking, public utilities, and the speculative markets

Once the president and Congress had taken emergency action to establish a method for reopening solvent banks and for liquidating those which did not qualify for reopening, their attention turned to longer-range readjustments in the monetary and banking system. Prices had been falling sharply since the 1929 stock-market break, and the president felt

that recovery would be impossible unless that decline could be stopped. The relationship between monetary gold stocks, bank policy, and price levels is a highly technical question with many complications which are much discussed among authorities in the field. The president had to rely upon the advice of others on this problem, and it happened that his advisors on this issue did not agree with prevalent opinion among monetary economists. Businessmen and bankers were all but unanimously hostile to any "tinkering" with the monetary system, and even less conservative economic authorities believed that the policies proposed by the president would be confusing and ineffective. For better or for worse, however, Congress followed the recommendations of the president.

The net result of several pieces of monetary legislation was that the United States left the gold standard in the old-fashioned sense of the free purchase from and sale of gold to the United States Mint. The dollar was devalued by more than 40 per cent, i.e., the price of gold was raised to $35.00 an ounce. All gold coin and gold certificates were called in, and thereafter the value of the dollar was to be managed by a number of controls, including control of bank credit policy through the powers of the Federal Reserve System. The higher American price for gold attracted a large proportion of the world's gold to the United States, and gave the western silver interests an excuse for pushing through Congress a silver purchase act providing for federal buying of silver at above world market prices in order to raise silver prices also. Neither of these actions had any clearly discernible effect in raising the general level of prices although it had been expected that the inflation from devaluating the dollar would lead to higher prices. A few export commodities, of which cotton is an example, experienced an increase of foreign demand and a stiffening of price. Domestically, the president's monetary program had neither the good effects hoped for nor the dire consequences which its opponents had predicted.

The departure from the gold standard and the adoption of the idea of a currency to be managed by banking policy were probably the most important general results of New Deal monetary and banking legislation. This placed banking in a position of new importance in the economy and recognized that the old automatic actions of the gold standard in stabilizing price levels and distributing the world's gold stock were in fact as inoperative as some other aspects of the free market had become. For these reasons, the additional changes which were made in the Federal Reserve Act were of great importance. The second Glass-Steagall Bill was enacted as the Banking Act of June 1933. It required the separation of commercial banking from the investment banking business. It was widely believed that the promoting and selling of new security issues by investment affiliates of large commercial banks both gave them an improper amount of power over other businesses and was inconsistent with the policy of caution and prudence which banks should follow. The Act also created the Federal Deposit Insurance Corporation (FDIC) to insure bank deposits up to established limits. Between 1930 and the date when the FDIC went into operation, depositors in banks which had failed had suffered losses to the terrible total of $1,336,000,000. The use of bank credit for stock speculation was restricted, and national banks were permitted to establish branches, in states which permitted branch banking for their own state banks.

Government control over the banking system was further extended by the Banking Act of 1935. The Federal Reserve Board was renamed the Board of Governors of the Federal Reserve system; in it the Secretary of the Treasury and the Comptroller of the Currency, both government officials, might no longer be *ex officio* members. This was to meet the complaint that Federal Reserve policies were keyed to the needs and policies of the Treasury Department rather than to the needs of the banks and the total economy. Large state banks were required to join the Federal Reserve system if they wished to remain under the deposit insurance system (FDIC). The top limit for insured deposits was placed at $5000 and the supervisory powers of the FDIC were increased. The meat of the Act was in the expanded powers over credit which were given to an Open Market Committee that was created, and in the power given the Board to alter the reserve requirements of the twelve regional Federal Reserve Banks. The Banking Act of 1935 gave the central banking system the responsibility and the power to manage the currency and credit of the nation in the interest of both soundness and overall economic stability.

In May 1933 and June 1934, laws were passed placing closer controls over the issuance and sale of corporate securities. A firm wishing to issue new securities had to file detailed information about its financial condition and about the proposed new issue with a newly created Securities and Exchange Commission (SEC). The SEC had to give its approval before the securities could be sold. The Commission was not to guarantee the issue but merely to certify that no false claims or other dishonest practices were involved. Even after SEC approval of an issue, the issuing firm could be sued if fraud or misrepresentation were later uncovered. The SEC was also given regulatory power over the security exchanges, power which was extended to the markets for certain agricultural products by the Commodity Exchange Act of 1936. Stock brokers and investment bankers complained bitterly that this legislation restricted them so severely that they would be afraid to say in print that black was black. In the course of time, investment bankers became accustomed to the restrictions of the Act, and it has served to increase both the stability and the integrity of corporate financing in America. Corporation financing has tended to turn to the retaining of earnings for the purpose of expanding facilities, a trend which may be partially a result of restrictions on new issues.

One other financial abuse which came under the scrutiny of the first New Deal Congress was the use of the holding company by banking institutions, especially in the public-utility field, to concentrate the control and profits of fantastically large and extended chains of companies. Several of these "empires" collapsed under the impact of the depression, when they proved to be just as effective in channeling the legal responsibility to meet financial obligations to one central point as they had been previously in channeling profits to the same central point. One of the most spectacular of these failures was that of the Midwest Public Utilities Corporation of Chicago, in which Samuel Insull was the dominant figure. Tens of thousands of small investors lost their life savings in such corporate collapses as this. The general opinion was that even where fraud or other criminal action was not involved, many of these "empires" had grown beyond any reasonable measure of financial prudence.

The Public Utility Holding Company Act of 1935, the so-called "death sentence act," required the simplification of the corporate structure of utility companies. Many times one top company held control, by stock ownership, of other companies, which in turn held stock control of others. It was finally revealed when the Insull empire collapsed that this process was extended through as many as thirteen steps. Since ownership of a half or less of the stock of a company will ordinarily give effective control, simple arithmetic will show how layer after layer of holding companies superimposed on top of one another multiply the control possible with a certain amount of capital at the top. The "death sentence act" required that affiliated companies must be more closely integrated with their parent companies, and that the utility system as a whole must be able to demonstrate real economies in operation.

### Relief and rehabilitation for agriculture

Agriculture, which had been suffering from a chronic weakness of prices throughout the twenties, proved to be especially vulnerable to the forces of depression which followed in the wake of the stock-market collapse of 1929. It might have been supposed that the New Deal would be able to develop more effective means for dealing with the agricultural problem than others it had to face, since the country had had experience with laws designed to bring agricultural prosperity in the preceding decade. Such was not to be the case.

Inherent in the farm problem were difficulties which seemed to be almost beyond solution within the bounds of the traditional American system, and yet both President Roosevelt and the typical American farmer were determined that that system must be preserved at all costs. A number of the difficult elements in the farm problem emerged during the twenties, including the surplus acreage brought into cultivation during World War I; the further acreage released by the tractor from producing feed for horses to be used in producing human food; the improvements in yield due to improved varieties, heavier fertilization, and better equipment; and the tendency of consumers to use even less of such staples as wheat and cotton as their increasing income enabled them to be a bit more particular in food and dress. The depression simply aggravated and made acute the economic situation outlined by such factors as these. The farmer faced disastrously lowered prices because of the falling off of both domestic and foreign demand for his staples while he struggled to maintain payment on his debts.

The simple solution seemed to New Dealers to be a cut in production, but to get millions of farmers to cut production when it would be to the advantage of each one of them *not* to cut production if the others did, would involve a degree of regimentation repugnant to the farmer and contrary to American tradition. Also, after 1930 there were millions of city workers out of jobs and facing real hunger. To speak to them of deliberately reducing food production was cruel. Nearly all New Deal measures were designed to get the nation back to productive work with good wages and fair prices. If successful, these other measures would have helped alleviate the farm problem by increasing consumer demand, although they would not have solved it, since it arose before the depression. To have been even more free with relief to the unemployed of the cities would have helped the farmers, but would itself have brought even more criticism. It has been estimated that more than one-third of American farms were involved in forced sales as a result of tax delinquency or mortgage foreclosure in the fifteen years from 1921 through 1935. At the peak in 1933, the rate of forced sale was about fifteen times as high as in the prosperous years of World War I, and 42 per cent of all farms were operated by tenants.

Here was a dilemma indeed, and yet it had to be tackled because acute distress and even malnutrition were arising among some sections of the rural population. In May 1933, Congress adopted the program for agriculture presented to it by President Roosevelt under the commonly used title Agricultural Adjustment Act (AAA). Its stated purpose was to raise the price of basic farm products to the average level of the five years 1909 to 1914—years that were regarded as normal twenty years later. To achieve this purpose, the Secretary of Agriculture was authorized to enter into contracts with cotton growers who would reduce their acreage by 30 per cent, to make rental or benefit payments to other agricultural producers for acreage taken out of the production of cash crops, to enter into marketing agreements with processors and distributors of farm products in order to prevent waste and raise prices, and to levy a tax on processors of agricultural products to provide funds for these purposes. To get the program going quickly, the Secretary of Agriculture arranged for the plowing up of millions of acres of cotton and the slaughter of six million pigs at less than usual market weights for other uses than providing human food. To millions of Americans who had not studied the farm problem but merely saw the facts of the destruction of food and cotton while other millions were hungry and ill-clothed, the program seemed positively sinful. It was true, however, that there was still enough food and clothing for all. Also, no one was able to think of a practicable alternative scheme which could be put into effect quickly.

Whether because of the AAA or as a result of other parts of the New Deal program or the natural forces of recovery, agricultural prices and income improved in 1934 and 1935. In January 1936, the first AAA experiment was ended when the Supreme Court declared parts of the Act, including the processing tax, unconstitutional. From the first AAA and from subsequent farm legislation down to and including the second Agricultural Adjustment Act of 1938, several basic elements of the New Deal farm program emerged. First, the concept of parity was adopted as a fair measure and goal of agricultural prosperity. Parity refers to the relationship between the prices received by farmers for their produce and the prices which they have to pay for all of the kinds of goods which they purchase, taking a particular period, in this case the five-year period prior to World War I, as a base or norm for the relationship of these prices. Second, a system of rewards was used to avoid regimenting the individual farmer and yet to provide incentive to attain certain necessary and desirable objectives. Payments were available to coöperating farmers who were willing to reduce their acreage of soil-depleting crops, such as corn, wheat, cotton, and tobacco, and to follow soil-building practices, such as checking soil erosion and expanding areas of forest and pasture land. Third, orderly marketing could be promoted and disastrously wide swings in commodity prices could be avoided by a lending program to keep an "ever normal granary," or reserve of staple farm products, on hand at all times for the security of the nation, while permitting the farmer to operate on a year-to-year cash income basis. Fourth, if production was persistently too large to maintain parity prices, acreage allotments should be made, followed by marketing quotas if still more drastic action was needed, and if the farmers approved.

The second AAA of 1938 adopted these principles and provided machinery for putting them into effect. Parity payments were provided for the basic farm crops to make up the difference between the current selling price of the particular crop and its pre-World War I parity. Additional benefit payments were provided for conservation practices such as liming or draining soil and the planting of soil-building legumes. Loans were made available to individual farmers and to coöperative and other marketing organizations to hold farm crops in storage. The Secretary of Agriculture was empowered to set acreage quotas designed to balance supply and demand, and to call for a vote of farmers on marketing quotas if he felt they were needed. Nearly nine million farmers coöperated in the farm program in 1939, but production continued high. After that time, war in Europe, in which America became involved in 1941, completely altered the agricultural picture. Increased demand, both real and speculative, started farm prices upward, and controls limiting planting and supporting prices were not extensively used during World War II. In fact, the ample supplies of food in America at the outset of the war proved a blessing to both this country and the world. The New Deal farm program, therefore, never completely demonstrated that it was adequate to deal with the problem of surpluses and low prices which plague American agriculture in normal times. Both during and after World War II, employment and income were at such a high level that farm prices, especially of meat, remained above parity.

## Industrial recovery

In addition to matters of emergency relief and financial reform, another fundamental task before the New Deal administration was to try to bring about permanent industrial recovery. Various ideas on how to achieve this goal were suggested and discussed throughout the country from the beginning of the depression. Recovery remained one object of almost every legislative act, especially in the early years of the New Deal, but the administration's chief reliance was on the provisions of the National Industrial Recovery Act (NIRA) of June 1933. The second section of the Act set up the Public Works Administration with a large appropriation which was designed both to provide work for relief and to stimulate recovery. The third section of the Act dealt further with emergency relief. The radically new proposals of the Act and the administration's hopes for quick recovery were embodied in the first section establishing the National Recovery Administration.

President Roosevelt's thinking on the subject of industrial recovery, as reflected in the first section of the NIRA, may be summarized as follows: Destructive price and wage cutting could be stopped and a solid floor created on which business and industry could proceed, if all the parties concerned agreed on prices, wages, hours, and other major matters affecting the business. Only a small minority of businessmen sought to undermine fair standards of wages and prices, in any case, and these could be stopped by a mutual agreement, to be policed by the industry itself. Labor should be represented in the making of such industry agreements by representatives of its own choosing without any pressure from the employer. The public should also be represented so that the interests of the consumers of the industry's products were not lost sight of. When all three parties were represented in the determination of policies for an industry, the government could overlook the fact that a price agreement would appear to be a clear "conspiracy to restrain trade" under the terms of the Sherman Anti-trust Act. The principal device to be used to achieve the purposes of the act was the "code authority" to be set up for each industry or business, or, if necessary, for each branch of an industry or business. On the code authority, the industry, labor, and the public were to be represented.

High hopes were held by many for NIRA as it was passed by Congress and signed by the president. The National Recovery Administration (NRA) was set up, and retired General Hugh Johnson was made administrator. A spreading blue eagle was adopted as the symbol of coöperating firms, to be used in advertising and display. Since a considerable amount of administrative machinery was required both to get a code authority set up and to have its code of fair competition cleared by the NRA in Washington, a good deal of delay was inescapable in getting the first codes approved. To speed matters, in July 1933 President Roosevelt announced a national Reëmployment Agreement with "blanket agreements" to be made. Under this plan—publicized by a national promotional campaign—millions of workers were working under the soaring blue eagle within a few months. The original idea of coöperative agreements between the employer, organized labor, and consumer representatives was all but lost in the haste. Labor unions were being formed under the protection provided by Section 7a of the NIRA at a rate never before equalled in American history, but there was very little tradition of collective bargaining in manufacturing industries and general business, and the voice of labor was largely inef-

fective in the drawing up of the codes. To an even greater degree consumers were characteristically unorganized and unable to protect their interests as a flood of codes was being drawn up to raise prices and wages, written largely by management and government.

It is hard to estimate the success of NIRA. The amount of employment increased, with some fluctuations, from the spring of 1933 for the next four years. How much of this may have been due to the codes and to the spreading of work by reducing working hours in industry to thirty-five per week it would be impossible to say. Prices had begun to rise even before the NIRA had been passed by Congress, in anticipation of its effects. The country was literally hungry for an end to the destructive deflation of prices which had been undermining all economic values for four years. Perhaps the apparent good effects of NIRA were merely from the mass recovery of hope resulting from the publicity campaign with which NRA was launched.

As time passed, thousands of cases of noncompliance with codes were reported. Labor was extremely restive because industry often opposed union organization as authorized by NIRA, and the country was plagued by strikes. Employers who were unused to bargaining with their workers began to fear that they had made a mistake in agreeing to negotiate with labor in drawing up the codes. The public also began to feel that it was being fleeced by prices that were rising faster than incomes. When the Supreme Court in May 1935 declared the NIRA to be an unconstitutional delegation of power by Congress to code authorities, there was almost a general sigh of relief that NRA could now be peacefully laid to rest. Business recovery was under way at the time, and continued with scarcely a ripple as all NRA activities were terminated. For the long run, organized labor was probably the greatest gainer from NRA because of the official recognition which it received of its basic right to organize.

Industrial recovery was also an objective of other New Deal legislation. The Reconstruction Finance Corporation, which had been created in President Hoover's administration, was given additional lending authority in June 1934 and empowered to make direct loans to industry. The purpose of RFC loans was to prevent the failure of financially weakened firms and the laying off of their employees. It was believed that the pace of recovery would be slowed unless the failures of going concerns could be checked. The Federal Housing Administration (FHA) was created in 1934 to carry on a program of guaranteeing mortgages for home construction and remodeling in a manner similar to that which federal farm lending agencies had been using for several years. The HOLC (p. 295) had checked the wave of home foreclosure sales, and it was now the purpose of the FHA to make credit more easily available for home building as a method of stimulating the expansion of the construction industry. The FHA was quite successful, because it involved no radical departure from traditional procedures. Funds for building were supplied by private agencies and the construction was done by private contractors. The FHA was primarily a mortgage-guaranteeing agency and in setting up standards under which it would guarantee mortgages it introduced uniformity in lending practice all over the country. Other acts which related to the promotion of recovery and which were part of the residue from the NIRA were the Bituminous Coal Conservation Act of 1935, which endeavored to apply the principles of the NRA codes to the coal industry but was promptly declared to be unconstitutional; the Robinson-Patman Act of 1936, which prohibited unjustified price discriminations; and the Miller-Tydings Act of 1937, which permitted manufacturers to fix fair minimum prices for their brand-name products.

### Strengthening the economic position of labor

Many of the diverse elements and activities of the New Deal seemed to find a common focus in improving the economic position of labor. This fact was recognized by friend and foe of the New Deal alike. From the political point of view, the simple fact was that Roosevelt and the New Deal Congress had been elected by the votes of labor, and labor was now being paid off while its future support was being sought. To the conservative opponents of Roosevelt, this was an adequate explanation of the matter. To some supporters of the New Deal this explanation was also adequate, but to others who were more interested in the economic than the political aspects of the situation it did not go far enough. If the basic cause of the depression lay in the diversion of too large a proportion of the national income into savings which kept it from the hands of consumers, then there was also an economic reason for steps to increase the flow of income to the working people of the nation. Regardless of which type of reasoning was most influential with the president and Congress, there was a substantial body of economic data and opinion to support the actions which were taken. Even if many employers did not like Section 7a of the NIRA, its wording—"that employees shall have the right to organize and bargain collectively through representatives of their own choosing"—was in the American tradition of preserving individual rights.

The NIRA, as has been mentioned, brought a great wave of labor organization. Local unions were formed in plants all over the country without an outside organizer ever putting in an appearance. The American Federation of Labor was swamped with letters and telegrams telling of the organization of these locals and requesting the issuance of charters. To accommodate them, the A.F.L. issued "national" charters until such time as it might be possible to determine with what national union these locals should become affiliated. In spite of this spontaneous rush into unions, leaders in the union movement realized that with vigorous organizing activity on their part, it could be an even greater trend, especially in the great mass-production plants which had become characteristic of so many American in-

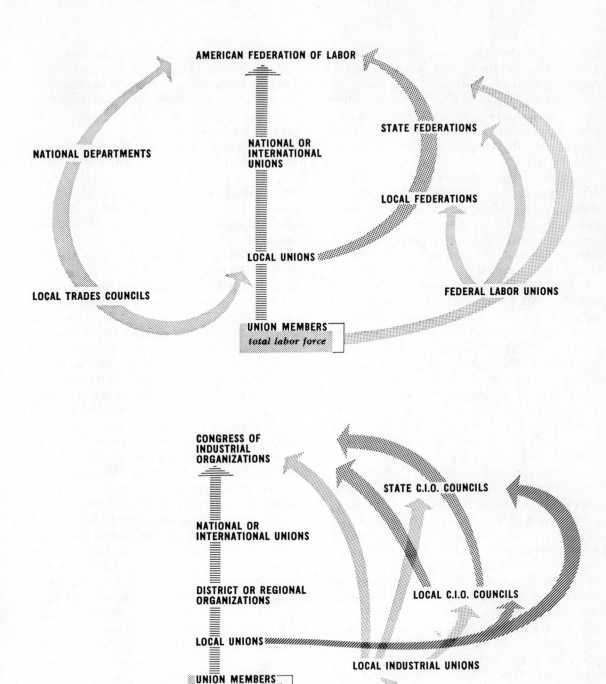

*Fig. XV-3  The organizational structure of the C.I.O. and A.F.L. during the 1950's.*

dustries. In the A.F.L. convention of 1934, John L. Lewis of the United Mine Workers of America (U.M.W.A.) became the leader of those in the Federation who favored an active policy of industry-wide organization in the great mass-production industries rather than maintaining the traditional organization by trade or skill.

Before the 1935 convention of the A.F.L., the NIRA had been declared unconstitutional for other reasons than its labor provisions. Congress, therefore, immediately set to work to enact the principle of the NIRA labor provisions into a separate act which became the National Labor Relations Act (NLRA). Employers were forbidden (1) to interfere with employees in any way in their right to organize for collective bargaining, (2) to refuse to bargain collectively, and (3) to interfere with the organization or operation of a union or to discriminate against an employee in any way because of his union membership. This act was sponsored by Senator Robert Wagner of New York and was usually called the Wagner Act. It created a National Labor Relations Board (NLRB) of three members to interpret and enforce the Act.

When the 1935 convention of the A.F.L. met, labor had in the Wagner Act what it regarded as a Magna Charta. Since the labor provisions of NIRA had not been questioned by the Supreme Court, it was felt that the constitutionality of NLRA was assured, and this feeling was later confirmed by a decision of the Supreme Court in 1937. Not much had been done by A.F.L. unions to organize the mass-production industries in the preceding year, and John L. Lewis introduced a resolution calling for more active organizing effort in these industries. Not all A.F.L. leaders were sympathetic with his efforts, possibly out of fear of the new large unions that might be formed, and after some maneuvering, Lewis' resolution was defeated. But after the convention, in November 1935, Lewis' U.M.W. and seven other A.F.L. unions that were themselves organized as industrial unions rather than as the typical unions of individual crafts of which the A.F.L. is composed,

united to form the Committee for Industrial Organization (C.I.O.). Three months later, in January 1936, the new group was ordered to disband by the Executive Council of the A.F.L., and when it refused to do so, the unions in the C.I.O. were expelled from the A.F.L. the following summer. Thereafter, the C.I.O. unions undertook a vigorous organizing drive in a number of mass-production industries in direct competition with the parent A.F.L. The prestige of the C.I.O. in labor circles rose enormously in 1937, when it was able to sign contracts for the workers in the General Motors Corporation and the United States Steel Corporation. In 1938 it changed its name to Congress of Industrial Organizations. As recovery progressed in the later thirties and the boom began to develop out of preparations for World War II, both the A.F.L. and the C.I.O. were able to make great gains in membership. The result was that a higher percentage of American workers were in unions than at any earlier time in our history.

Two other New Deal laws which served to aid labor are deserving of note. The Walsh-Healey Government Contracts Act of 1936 provided that no government contract involving more than $10,000 might be made with a contractor who paid less than the prevailing wages in his industry, or who employed workers for more than eight hours a day or forty hours a week, or who employed any male under sixteen years of age or female under eighteen. Since government buying is very widespread throughout the American economy, this act has had a very powerful effect in raising standards of employment. Another law which was hotly debated in Congress was the Fair Labor Standards Act of 1938. The act established a minimum wage of forty cents per hour in interstate commerce and an eight-hour day and a forty-hour week, with time-and-a-half pay for excess time either daily or weekly. The minimum wage floor was to be approached gradually over a period of seven years. The inflation and the employment boom of World War II made the minimum wage substantially of no significance, but the hour provisions established a norm for

American industry and the minimum wage was subsequently raised, reaching seventy-five cents in 1950.

Two New Deal activities deserving of special note are the construction of urban housing and the redevelopment of an entire geographic region. Housing projects were carried out in many cities all over the country, while the outstanding example of regional development was that of the Tennessee River Valley, principally in the states of Tennessee and Alabama, but affecting several adjoining states. Projects of both these types had been suggested to the government for some years preceding the New Deal. Both public housing and regional development were aimed at assisting in the immediate jobs of relief and recovery, although both were also aimed at the reform under public auspices of bad conditions which had grown up over many years.

Early in the New Deal, large-scale public housing projects were among the types of public works undertaken by the PWA. The most notable development of public housing came after 1937, when the National Housing Act was passed creating a United States Housing Authority (USHA) to assume jurisdiction in this field. Actual construction and subsequent management of housing projects was to be done in coöperation with local housing authorities that were to be set up. USHA was authorized to make loans to the local housing authorities under specified conditions. The top limit of cost per dwelling unit was specified, since the purpose of the Act was to provide adequate but low-cost housing. The top income of families eligible to live in public-housing units was also specified, because only the lowest income groups were to benefit from this partially subsidized housing. Under the original Act, the new projects had to be built where substandard slum housing had been torn down to create a building site, and the new housing had to be for families of the same income range as those formerly occupying the slums on the site.

By the middle of 1941, USHA had loaned nearly ¾ billion dollars for model-housing projects in 250 communities in 34 states. Seventy thousand family units were actually occupied. Bitter opposition to these projects arose from real estate and construction interests as the years of depression passed. They were claimed to be unfair competition to private enterprise. Public opinion was probably favorable to the projects, however, at least as far as they had gone up to 1941, because of the recognition that the lowest income groups simply could not afford to pay the full costs for the rental of homes adequate for healthful living and the lowest standards of common decency. Partially subsidized housing was viewed as perhaps the cheapest method by which society could prevent the slums from continuing as breeding places of disease and crime. As World War II approached, the National Housing Act was liberalized in various respects to permit its organization and procedures to be used for the entirely different purpose of providing emergency housing in areas which had become congested because of nearby Army camps or expanding war industries. In spite of efforts of all kinds to increase housing facilities, acute shortages of housing became almost general during World War II and remained for years thereafter in many communities which experienced rapid wartime growth.

The building of Boulder (now Hoover) Dam on the Colorado River had been sponsored by President Hoover. The PWA in President Roosevelt's administration had started work on Grand Coulee and Bonneville Dams on the Columbia River and Fort Peck Dam on the Missouri. But the special law which created the Tennessee Valley Authority (TVA) for the development of the Tennessee Valley region was far more comprehensive in its scope. The concept of *regional* economic development on a basis of low-cost, publicly produced electric power was the result of the fertile friendship of two men in American public life who were of opposite political parties. Franklin D. Roosevelt as governor of New York had demonstrated his belief that sites capable of development for the production of hydroelectric power should be forever kept in the ownership of the public. In Congress, Senator George W. Norris had been hammering away against great odds and without apparent success to bring about the use of the Muscle Shoals Dam on the Tennessee River, a legacy from World War I, for the development of hydroelectric power by the federal government. When Roosevelt was elected president in 1932 on a platform which included public power, it was a natural sympathy which brought these two men together. Mutual stimulation of thinking resulted in the drawing up of a plan for the development of the economically ailing southeastern section of the United States which was far broader than the mere construction of one or two government power projects on the Tennessee River, important as that may have been.

The Muscle Shoals-Tennessee Valley Development Act of May 1933, one of the early New Deal laws, set a new pattern for American regional development. It created a three-man board known as the Tennessee Valley Authority. To the TVA was given the government property at Muscle Shoals, Alabama, with the power to build and operate other dams and power plants on the Tennessee River and its branches wherever the Authority thought advisable. In addition to generation and distribution of electric power, TVA was also charged with controlling the flood waters of the Tennessee River and improving its navigation facilities. It was to promote the conservation of soil in the valley and to aid reforestation. It was to produce nitrates and other fertilizers for the improvement of the agriculture of the valley. The chemical plants set up for this purpose would also strengthen the national defense by their availability for explosives manufacture in the event of war.

The immediate timing of the Act, of course, implied that the TVA experiment was designed to create construction jobs in a section whose income had fallen sharply with declining prices and yields of cotton. But, beyond the immediate considerations, the Act recognized that the well-being of the valley area required a radically new approach if the slow blight which had spread across its farms and towns was to be checked. Forested areas had been cut over and abandoned; land on slopes had been plowed for cotton although it should have been kept in pasture or forest; erosion, even where it was comparatively mild, had carried much of the fertile topsoil down into the stream beds and on down to the Mississippi delta. Basic to the new task was the development of hydroelectric power, of which the region had a significant proportion of the national potential. This was to be the foundation of a new prosperity, but it would be a mistake to judge TVA only in terms of electric power as did many of those who opposed it. Farms were to be electrified, and cheap power was to be an attraction to bring industry to the towns. Agricultural experimentation and new fertilizers made from the valley's own raw materials were to develop new crop rotations and new types of farming to reduce the region's dependence upon cotton. The new grass farming and forests would keep the soil on the slopes and out of the new reservoirs that were built. A steadier flow of clear water, controlled by dams, would make the Tennessee River navigable from its mouth at Paducah, Kentucky, to Knoxville, Tennessee, a distance of 650 miles. TVA was not to be judged by any one thing but by the overall result. President Roosevelt at one time said, "TVA is primarily intended to change and improve the standards of living of the people of that valley."

It will perhaps never be correct to say that the Tennessee Valley project has been completed. As long as the TVA exists, there will always be developments that are needed for the continued improvement of the valley region. By 1959 the TVA was supplying electric power to 99 municipalities and 51 rural coöperatives. Yet, nearly half of total power production was going to plants of the Atomic Energy Commission. Private use of power was increasing faster than government use, due largely to the construction of aluminum reduction plants in the valley. To distribute its power, 11,728 miles of TVA's transmission lines were being operated in 7 states. Two-thirds of the power was from steam generating plants, only one-third from the original hydro-electric plants along the Tennessee River and its branches. All but 3% of the farms were electrified. Beyond these achievements, more than two billion ton-miles of freight were hauled over the slack-water basins behind the river dams in 1959. Research in fertilizers and improvement of recreational facilities were other products of TVA activity. All-in-all, the valley has been one of the rapidly developing areas of the nation, helping to pull the entire southeastern section of the country from the hopelessness into which parts of it had fallen or had been thrust by the Civil War and years after. The private electric utilities were particularly hostile to TVA, but most residents of the valley, who saw its accomplishments at first hand, were all but unanimous in its praise. Confident of the ultimate soundness of the TVA idea, President Roosevelt in 1937 requested Congress to set up six additional regional river valley authorities. Congress did not accept the suggestion. The parts of the country in which they were to be located were not quite such distinct units as the Tennessee Valley, nor were the people of these other valleys in such a distressed condition as those of TVA territory in 1933. In addition, business was looking much better in 1937, and the protests of the private utilities against the encroachment of the federal government were loud and long. It was contended that private capital could develop these valleys as well as the federal government, and the general business community of the country supported this stand.

### Was the New Deal a success?

It is impossible to measure the success of the New Deal in absolute or final terms. Mil-

[1]All data from Tennessee Valley Authority, *Annual Report,* for fiscal year ending June 30, 1961 (Washington, D. C.: U. S. Government Printing Office, 1961).

lions of Americans never voted for the New Deal and probably regarded it as an economic hoax and a series of political deals to gain power. On the other hand, more millions of Americans looked to the New Deal for salvation from the engulfing forces of depression and regarded Roosevelt, its leader, with personal affection. As a result, Franklin D. Roosevelt became one of the most controversial presidents in American history. Probably at no other time save in the years centering around the Civil War did the issues of the day stir the American people so deeply. Perhaps no other president except Lincoln had been so deeply loved and so bitterly hated as the second Roosevelt. Certainly he captured the imagination of the working people of America who were suffering grievously from unemployment, reduced hours, and reduced wages by the time of the presidential elections in the autumn of 1932. During his first three months in office there was very little vocal opposition to Roosevelt. The country was in the worst depression in its history, and the inadequacy of the policies previously followed was obvious to almost everyone. Only as recovery began to come did the patterns of thinking of many people, especially in business, begin to revert to traditional channels. More and more the Roosevelt policies, once regarded as necessary to save the capitalistic system, appeared to be dangerously subversive and revolutionary. At best, they were regarded as fumbling and vague in design and bureaucratic in execution. But throughout his life and after his death, Roosevelt's policies gained and held the political support of the working people of America.

In the violent political cross winds which swirled about the figure of Roosevelt, it is hard to obtain a clear and objective view of the man and his policies. It is quite clear, however, that Roosevelt was no socialist as he was so often called by his opponents. There were too many occasions during his administrations when, with Congressional support, he might have taken a turn toward a socialistic solution of a problem, when, in fact, he turned in the other direction. He felt that the depression had shown serious weaknesses in capitalism, but he never revealed any doubt that the best solution lay in correcting the errors and weaknesses of the past and establishing the capitalistic free-enterprise system on a firmer base for the future. In this endeavor he was an opportunist. He was not a trained economist nor an experienced businessman who had definite ideas of his own. Rather, he was a humanitarian and a politician in the broadest sense of that term, with a deep affection for people and an uncanny ability to discover what they were thinking, what their frustrations were, and what goals they wished to pursue. He knew the direction in which he wished to go, but he was an experimenter on the question of how to go. Perhaps the fairest way to appraise the New Deal is simply in terms of the degree to which it achieved the objectives which FDR stated for it—Relief, Recovery, and Reform.

The giving of relief is always a distasteful business, distasteful to giver and receiver alike. Doubtless those who were compelled by dire need to accept relief during the depression felt that it was inadequate; those who were required to pay taxes to help provide funds for relief payments felt that they were excessive. Cities, counties, and states had exhausted their resources in carrying the relief burden in the first years of depression. President Roosevelt immediately after his inauguration threw the resources of the federal government into the breach to see that no one went hungry. This was regarded as an emergency action only, since the more fundamental goal of the New Deal was to get people back to work. After a year or two of trial and error, the WPA became the principal relief agency of the New Deal, giving relief by providing work. Direct relief was provided only for the unemployable or until other methods of removing the need for relief could be put into operation. Considering the magnitude of the relief problem and the suddenness with which it was thrust upon the country, it would seem fair to conclude that it was met about as well as could reasonably have been expected.

On the score of recovery, appraisal is less easy. There is no doubt that recovery did occur, in 1936 and again in 1940, but whether it was a spontaneous rebound from years of severe deflation following 1929 or whether it was due to the recovery measures of the New Deal is not easy to decide. Some evidence that New Deal measures may have been largely responsible for the recovery is that when Congress in 1937 decided that recovery was sufficiently under way to carry on by itself, and when, in consequence, it cut the appropriations for WPA and other New Deal agencies, the country experienced the sharpest decline in production in its history, sharper than in 1920-1921 and 1929-1930. There is, however, little doubt that other factors, such as the bursting of an inventory-speculation boom at that time, also contributed substantially to the 1937-1938 recession, and it is therefore very difficult to assess the significance of the cuts in government appropriations at the time. By 1939, the war in Europe had injected abnormalities into the economic situation but provided the clearest cause of all for the final termination of depressed conditions.

The entire issue of what factors were responsible for recovery was also complicated by the accompanying controversy between two schools of thought on economic policy. The traditional view accepted by most businessmen was that government should stay out of business, which meant that it should allow the forces of depression to go so far that eventually they would automatically reverse themselves and start a business trend upward toward prosperity. To others, such a policy was unthinkable, since it could conceivably have meant starvation for perhaps a fourth of our population, which would undoubtedly have led to revolution. The first point of view was based in the main on the economic theory of market equilibrium which held that, given enough time, even a severe disturbance and depression would correct itself. The second point of view, of which the English economist John Maynard Keynes became the leading exponent, held the older opinion to be entirely inadequate and approached the problem of economic policy from the direction of maintaining the flow of income upon which prosperity rests. If the functioning of the undisturbed free market did not maintain an adequate flow of income to keep everyone at work, as it very clearly had not, then, said the second group, the federal government is the only agency left with sufficient power to see that that result is achieved.

In the early days of the New Deal, the first group was so shocked by the severity of the depression up to that time that very few of its members voiced any open opposition to governmental innovations. As recovery got under way, the middle and later years of the New Deal degenerated into an ever more acute tug-of-war between the opposing factions. The national income still remained low in spite of some degree of recovery, and it required borrowing by the sale of bonds to finance the New Deal measures, for taxes were not enough to pay the bill. In fact, the New Deal theorists deliberately favored a budget deficit in a time of depression, since it necessarily involved spending more than was collected in taxes. This was regarded as a very effective means of increasing the income flow throughout the economic system. From the traditional point of view, deficit financing and related New Deal ideas were the worst sort of economic heresy, and those who held this point of view developed a complete distrust of the economic judgment of those who supported New Deal policies. The control of the federal government over the banking system was great enough so that there was never any doubt that government bonds could be sold to the banks and their price maintained through Federal Reserve open-market operations and control of interest rates.

But the deep distrust of New Deal policies by a majority of businessmen was reflected in their actions. From the middle thirties onward, what seems to have happened was that as the federal government endeavored to increase the public income by deficit spending for public works, WPA, and the like, private businessmen who disapproved of the policy and distrusted its chances of success continued to restrict their own expenditures for normal expansion and improvement or even maintenance of their plant and equipment. Thus, instead of government expenditures priming the pump and starting an enduring private business recovery, they sometimes had the opposite effect of causing businessmen to cut down even their normal contribution to the national income through the channel of maintenance and expansion of plant and equipment. Government expansion was countered by private contraction, and the pump did not prime as much as it might have. Some businesses, both large and small, made such capital expenditures as they could afford, but the total was not great enough to check contractions. However, government expenditures undoubtedly more than offset contractions in private spending.

A consequence of the expanded scope of government was a great growth of government employment in various kinds of regulatory agencies. This was distasteful to many businessmen, both because increased government employment meant greater costs and taxes, and because new types of regulation created new irritations. To some the new government bureaucracy itself became such an evil that it tended to overbalance any good there may have been in the intentions of the New Deal. The cries of "socialism" and "bureaucracy" were used to the limit by the political opponents of the New Deal, but not with such success as to turn back the clock on the reforms inaugurated by it. Whether these reforms would give the government a firm enough grip on the economy, and whether they could be exercised by government agencies with enough wisdom to keep the economy permanently at a high level of production, employment, and income, only time would tell. The coming of World War II quickly transformed the problem from one of checking deflation to one of restraining inflation, and from creating more jobs to allocating labor to most essential uses. Government agencies found themselves thrust into the midst of these tasks also. The real test of New Deal reform measures would have to come in a period of peace, when a demonstration would have to be made that the economy could be guided in the path of orderly and continuous expansion without either inflation or deflation of prices, and with continuous full employment.

The American economy seemed unable to shake off its dependence on governmental deficit spending as the United States approached the period of national rearming for war that preceded World War II. Defense spending immediately involved larger deficits in the federal budget than had occurred during the middle of the New Deal period, but businessmen were no longer worried. Wars had always created debts and could not be avoided in any case, certainly not by businessmen alone. Business confidence was restored in spite of large deficits, and investment in plant and facilities, therefore, rose sharply. A construction boom began, and machine-tool builders were swamped with orders in excess of their capacity. Prices began to rise sharply and it was very evident that the pump was primed. It was still a federal budget deficit that did the priming, but that deficit was now being created for war, a traditional reason, and not because of reliance upon the unorthodox ideas of Keynes and his American followers.

The long-term legacy of the New Deal in reforming some of the evils and weaknesses of the economy can perhaps be judged best from the long perspective of future years. Its net effect in the various areas of its activity can be summarized as the assumption by the government of a more active rôle in directing the economy. The enemies of the New Deal called this a movement toward socialism. While the New Deal was a definite departure from traditional *laissez faire,* it was hardly correct to say that it headed toward socialism. The traditional socialism as an economic philosophy which developed in Europe in the nineteenth century involved government ownership and operation of all important industries and business services. This was never an objective of the New Deal. Rather, the reform objective of the New Deal was based on the idea that the economy would not automatically maintain itself at a high level of activity, as the older *laissez-faire* theory would have it, but must have the helping hand of government to achieve that goal. This conception has been referred to as the "compensatory economy," i.e., that the government must be ready to exert its economic force at this point or that in the economic system to compensate for disturbing influences that might develop.

President Roosevelt often reiterated his attachment to the traditional American business system, with evident sincerity. He felt, at the same time, that government must save business from destroying itself through permitting such bad conditions to develop that the extreme action of revolution would follow. Thus the reforms of the New Deal gave the government a firmer hold on the banking system, put limits on market speculation, stopped some evident abuses through corporate manipulation, introduced elements of national planning into agriculture, guaranteed labor its constitutional rights, tried to relieve some of the worst of the urban housing conditions, and began a demonstration of what a full-scale coördinated attack could do to build up a higher standard of living for the people of a blighted and declining region. None of these was "socialism" in an accurate use of the term while all involved more extensive participation of the government in the economic life of the country.

Was the New Deal the "Third American Revolution" as Professor L. M. Hacker has called it?[1] In Professor Hacker's accounting, our first revolution, following 1776, marked an important turn in American history in that the United States was changed from a colonial dependency of a European power to an independent nation seeking to carve out its national destiny on the new continent of North America. The Civil War marked the second revolution, when political power was transferred from a southern, landed aristocracy to a northern, industrial, upper middle class, which had built a firm working alliance with

[1] Louis M. Hacker, *The Shaping of the American Tradition* (New York: Columbia University Press, 1947), p. 1123 ff.

western farmers and land speculators. The second revolution confirmed the first in that it reinforced the isolationist nationalism of the country. The New Deal marked the third revolution in our history, says Professor Hacker, because it transferred political power from the upper to the lower middle class, and thus from the industrial employer, independent businessman, and farmer to the working classes, the small farmer, and the farm tenant. With this change in the control of government went a new attitude of government toward business. The working masses had never advocated *laissez faire* in either Europe or America. As a policy, it had been promoted and finally established by the political power of the capitalist business classes. Workers were neutral to *laissez faire* as a theory, willing to accept it if it yielded satisfactory results, but willing to abandon it if it did not. With the New Deal came not only a new willingness to accept government intervention in business, but also a desire to secure the domestic gains of labor by international coöperation to bring similar gains to all working people of the world. Thus the New Deal, in its later years, was also revolutionary in its surrender of traditional American isolationism for a new non-imperialistic internationalism.

There is much that is challenging and meaningful in Hacker's view of the rôle of the New Deal. However, many other students draw the line at referring to it as a revolution. The term implies too much that is new, unexpected, and violent. There can be little doubt that it marks an important turning point in the evolution of America, but its roots can be discovered in modes of thinking and action that extend back to colonial days. The American democratic philosophy had always placed the common man in a high place. Perhaps the rapid economic development since the Civil War, culminating in the 1920's, had led Americans to place property in too high a place in relation to human life. Perhaps *laissez faire* had been permitted to become an end in the thinking of many people instead of a technique or means to a better economic life. If so, the era of the New Deal pulled us up sharply, and led to a return to our original evaluation of human life and feeling. The sad plight of millions of unemployed who had exhausted every material resource they possessed led the nation to a new appreciation of the fact that great property gives great power and great freedom of action, but that lack of property or income makes freedom a mockery. Perhaps the truest view of the New Deal is as a demonstration of the viability of American civilization in its ability to take on a new face and a new orientation as the circumstances of the times require. Thus the New Deal is possibly best seen as a unique blending of new and old.

## The American economy and world conditions in the thirties

The ten-year crisis of American capitalism following the financial collapse in 1929 was paralleled by equally grave economic disturbances throughout the world. Outside of the United States there had not been general adjustment to the new set of economic conditions which followed World War I. England and Germany, the great industrial nations of Europe, had suffered either actual destruction or inadequate maintenance and replacement of their industrial plants during the war years. During those years, the United States had had no war damage and had expanded its industrial capacity very greatly. During the twenties, the industry of the United States was pushing the export of its products all over the world, while Germany and England were not yet able to eliminate unemployment and get back to a prewar basis of production because of high costs and lost export markets. In addition, the situation was complicated by reparations which Germany was obliged to pay to the Allies by the Treaty of Versailles, and war-debt payments which the European Allies owed to the United States on wartime advances. On top of all these conditions was the further fact that the United States had now become a creditor nation.

There was no easy solution to these problems, but the whole situation was made tolerable during the twenties by the extension of American credit. American investors had their fingers burned on loans to public bodies in Germany in 1927 and 1928 and quickly pulled back, but private, commercial credit, the building of branch plants of American firms in Europe, and the purchase of European corporate securities by American investors went quietly along to the extent of billions of dollars prior to 1929. American loans to Europe were a soothing poultice to an economic situation which was really festering underneath. Even interest on the official war debts to the United States government was paid, in effect, from American loans. In spite of the healing effect of American advances to Europe, the political cauldron was boiling in Germany. Democracy, never a very sturdy growth there, was becoming discredited because of its inability to cope with economic problems which seemed to hold the country down. A modest property-owning middle class, the foundation of democratic government in Britain, France, and America, had never been powerful in Germany, and the inflation of the middle 1920's had almost completely wiped it out. There was evident a tendency among German voters to listen to the siren calls of extremists, of whom one was named Adolf Hitler.

The American depression beginning in 1929 put almost a complete stop to the flow of funds to Europe. American purchases of goods from Europe were cut heavily as well. These actions pulled one strong support from under the shaky European economy, and Europe too was thrown into a state of acute depression. England was able to "muddle through" as she had done in so many previous crises with the support of her world empire, but the political repercussions in Germany were swift and sweeping. Adolf Hitler and his National Socialist (Nazi) party came to power just a short time before the inauguration of President Roosevelt in 1933. Nazi international economic policy could only be described as economic warfare. German trade with every country was looked upon solely as a device to strengthen the German Reich in preparation for the war of expansion which was Hitler's single aim. Yearly after 1933 it became clearer that war was approaching.

Roosevelt announced a foreign policy opposed to that of Germany. It was a mixture of part of the foreign policy of Herbert Hoover and of a traditional element in the Democratic party platform. Toward every nation in the world the United States proposed to act as a "good neighbor." This meant no aggression by force, no penetration by financial intrigue or pressure of any kind, and friendly coöperation to solve mutual problems. This reversal of the policy of "dollar diplomacy" of which America had been accused in the era of the Spanish-American War and after, had definitely been begun under President Hoover. Roosevelt underscored it and amplified it in his speeches and actions. Also, in June 1934, the Reciprocal Trade Agreements Act was passed by Congress at the request of the president. This represented a new approach to the achievement of the old Democratic hope of lowered tariff barriers. For three years the Act gave the president power to approve, without seeking the concurrence of the Senate, trade agreements which the Secretary of State might be able to negotiate with individual countries for the mutual reduction of tariffs. The reductions might be as much as 50 per cent. This act with its several renewals did a great deal to build international trade and good will, although it came at least ten years too late to contribute substantially to alleviating the economic causes which helped to produce World War II. It did bring a greater reduction in tariff rates than we had ever enjoyed at any time in our history.

In the final year of the decade of the thirties, the longest and deepest and most destructive depression in American history dissolved in the gathering mobilization of industrial resources for military defense and possible war. The great cleavage on economic policy which the depression had exposed to the light was not resolved, but was buried by preparation for war. The American public was still clinging to its traditional desire to avoid entanglement in the affairs of other countries, while world economic disintegration, partially created by America's turning its back on world coöperation in 1919 and 1920, was forcing the United States to rearm for world war as a measure of national safety.

## FOR FURTHER READING

Barnes, James A. *Wealth of the American People*. New York: Prentice-Hall, Inc., 1949. Chapters 33—36.

Bogart, Ernest L.. and Kemmerer, Donald L. *Economic History of the American People*. 2nd ed. New York. Longmans, Green & Co.. Inc., 1947. Part IV.

Dulles, Foster Rhea. *Twentieth Century America*. Boston: Houghton Mifflin Co., 1945. Chapters 19—24.

Faulkner, H. U. *American Economic History*, 8th ed. New York: Harper & Brothers, 1960. Chapters 29—31.

Lippmann, Walter. *The Good Society*. Universal Library, 1956. Paperback. Former Socialist looks at New Deal.

Rozwenc, Edwin C. *The New Deal*. Rev. ed. Boston: D. C. Heath Co., 1959. Eleven interpretations of the New Deal.

Schlesinger, Arthur M., Jr. *The Age of Roosevelt*. Boston: Houghton Mifflin Co., 1957. Three volumes are thus far completed; the last is best.

Shannon, Fred Albert. *America's Economic Growth*. 3rd ed. New York: The Macmillan Co., 1951. Chapters 37—39.

Wright, Chester W. *Economic History of the United States*. New York: McGraw-Hill Book Co., 1949. Chapter 44.

# Part III: The American Economy in Today's World

# Chapter 16:

# World War II and postwar boom

The economic developments within the United States in the first half of the 1930's were serious enough to justify the exclusive concentration of thought and action which the American government and people devoted to them. The economic forces of expansion and contraction were still battling indecisively on the domestic scene when political aggression fed by economic frustration abroad began to force itself upon America's attention.

The ruthless Italian seizure of Ethiopia; the Japanese conquest of Manchuria, an area governed by the Chinese Nationalist government; and the Spanish civil war, in which outside intervention, especially by Italy, Germany, and Russia, was so open that it seemed like a rehearsal for greater conquests to come —all were serious developments of the middle 1930's. In March 1938, Hitler annexed Austria to Germany, and in September he went on to demand annexation of the Sudetenland, a German-speaking portion of Czechoslovakia. The democratic countries, including the United States, were deeply disturbed by this

aggressive action, but at a conference in Munich, Germany, on September 29, 1938, the governments of England and France agreed to accept Hitler's action on his promise that he had no further territorial ambitions. During the winter the promise was kept, but in March 1939 the German armies were sent marching into Czechoslovakia to seize the entire country, in open violation of a solemn pledge. The world was thrown into turmoil by such open aggression, and it appeared certain that any nation wishing to remain free must prepare for war. During the summer of 1939, Hitler made increasingly insistent territorial demands upon another neighbor—Poland—and, in the first days of September, after having concluded a nonaggression pact with Russia, he again sent German armies across the borders of an innocent state to seize the territory he wanted. The Poles resisted unsuccessfully, and, since the failure of a policy of appeasement was now completely evident, England and France declared war on Germany on September 3, 1939. World War II had begun. The sympathies of the people of the United States were completely with the victims of such unprincipled aggression, but this country did not become involved in the war until Japan took advantage of the world preoccupation with the war in Europe to attack the American naval and air base at Pearl Harbor, Hawaii, on December 7, 1941.

### The road to war

While these developments prior to Pearl Harbor were taking place, the American people realized that the world situation was entering a highly dangerous stage. They felt, however, that the sources of the trouble lay outside the United States, and they had a very strong desire to avoid becoming entangled. Congress expressed this national feeling by passing Neutrality Acts in 1935 and 1937. The second act contained a so-called "cash and carry" provision that any goods or commodities whose shipment was not completely forbidden had to be paid for in full before shipment, and had to be carried from American ports in ships of the purchaser. After Hitler's annexation of Austria in March 1938, the need for rearmament was apparent to the nations of Europe. Therefore, Britain and France each sent purchasing missions to the United States to place orders for aircraft and other military requirements. These orders brought an expansion of the American aircraft industry which was very soon accelerated by our own government orders. The fast pace of events in Europe, leading to the declaration of war in September 1939, made it crystal clear to the people of the United States that they must build their national defense, for there was no chance of survival for the weak.

The first important step taken by President Roosevelt to rebuild American military strength was to revive the Council of National Defense as a committee of key cabinet officers authorized by a law of World War I days. The Council itself was never very active, but an Advisory Commission to the Council appointed by the president at the same time—May 28, 1940—supervised the beginning stages of rearmament. The Advisory Commission was composed of leading representatives of various branches of American economic life—industry, labor, agriculture, transportation, and consumers. The Commission was created almost on the day when Hitler had completed his conquest of the democratic countries of western Europe and was trying to cut off the retreat of the remnants of the British army from Dunkirk in France. The president stated that the Commission was to serve as a clearing house for defense activities.

Congress during 1940 passed a series of appropriation bills which brought to a total of more than $13 billion the amount set aside for defense. The Reconstruction Finance Corporation, created early in the depression to make loans to business, was now turned into an agency for financing war preparations. It was given power by Congress to create subsidiary corporations, and under that authority several government corporations were created for special purposes: the Rubber Reserve Company, to buy and store natural rubber; the Metal Reserve Company, to acquire strategic metals needed for alloying with steel or for other military purposes; and the Defense Supplies Corporation, to buy, store and sell any materials needed for the defense effort. The Defense Plant Corporation became the agency which built and leased to other agencies or private corporations plants for building planes, tanks, and guns. After America entered the war, the Defense Plant Corporation, together with the Rubber Reserve Company, built up and operated America's vast synthetic rubber program.

The other major action by the government in 1940 to promote the national defense was the passage of the first peacetime Selective Service Act in American history. The Act was passed in September, and the registration of all males between ages 21 and 36 was completed in October. Local Selective Service Boards were set up all over the nation to process inductees. The Army, Navy, and Air Force were forced into a vast expansion of their training facilities.

By 1941, the cash and carry provisions of the American Neutrality Acts had drained most of Britain's cash resources. In order to continue aid to the Allies and yet avoid involvement in the war or the accumulation of unpayable debts like those of World War I, President Roosevelt recommended to Congress a bill authorizing Lend-Lease agreements. The necessity of payment was postponed, with the possibility that the goods might be returned to the United States. The bill was passed in March 1941, and a Lend-Lease administration was set up in October. When the agency was terminated in 1945, a total of nearly $50 billion in goods had been shipped to American Allies all over the world.

### Organizing the war effort

#### The mobilization of industry

In 1941, American industry turned out 5 million passenger automobiles, more than 3½ million electric refrigerators, and proportionate quantities of other consumer durable goods. At the same time, military production reached 700 tanks per month, 2000 military aircraft per month, and merchant ships reached an average tonnage of more than 50,000 tons per month, with a high month of 125,000 tons. This record was itself a notable production achievement, but it was to be dwarfed by the production miracles of the next few years.

To mobilize industry to satisfy a growing consumer market, as well as to fill expanding military commitments at home and abroad, effective administrative controls had to be devised. The Advisory Commission to the Council of National Defense, which President Roosevelt had appointed in May 1940, lacked legal authority to determine priorities for materials. Hence, also in May 1940, the president issued an Executive Order creating the Office for Emergency Management as an extension of his own Executive Office. In January 1941, the president transferred all the powers and functions of the Advisory Commission to OEM and at the same time set up under OEM a new agency called the Office of Production Management. OPM was given three operating divisions—Production, Purchases, and Priorities—to which a Labor division was added later. After Pearl Harbor, the War Production Board was created in January 1942, to take over the functions of OPM as the United States swiftly moved into a full-scale war economy.

The War Production Board developed a system of priorities which eventually resulted in the Controlled Materials Plan. This plan involved a careful calculation of the materials required to complete a war order, the issuance of the necessary priorities, and allocation of materials to prime contractors and subcontractors. The War Production Board awarded two-thirds of the $200 billion of prime wartime contracts to large firms, such as General Motors, U.S. Steel, Du Pont and General Electric, who subcontracted substantial portions to smaller firms. Through such subcontracting, tens of thousands of small factories and shops all over the United States participated in war-production jobs.

The War Production Board awarded prime contracts in several different ways. In plants producing food and clothing, military orders were given priority, but manufacturers were allowed to produce as many civilian goods as they could with the extra labor and materials available. In other industries, war needs dictated replacement of machinery and plant reorganization.

In addition to the conversion of existing plants, extensive construction was required in some fields where technological advances had occurred. Consequently, during the early war years, the energies of the nation had to be channeled simultaneously toward the production of urgently needed weapons and the construction of armament plants. This double burden made the strain of the war on the American people greater during 1942 and 1943 than it was later. The production peak was reached in 1943-1944 and slackened thereafter. Durable goods production indexes based upon 1935-1939 figures report that total manufacture of durable goods stood at 201 in 1941. It rose to 279 in 1942, reached a peak of 360 in 1943, declined to 353 in 1944, and by 1945 was down to 274. Almost all of the new plants were built by 1944, and the problem thenceforward became increasingly one of effective operation.

The "cost-plus-fixed-fee" method was selected as the way of paying for war contracts. It proved to be a better arrangement than the straight "cost-plus" contracts of World War I, which offered a positive incentive to producers to inflate costs to make residual earnings larger. Cost-plus-fixed-fee contracts provided that the producer would receive a set fee, and that any costs he might save would be renegotiated. Thus, the contractor's costs and delivery price for the product were calculated after work on a contract had been partially completed. This system cut the costs of many important war purchases. Still, corporation profits for each full year of the war were more than double the 1940 level. A total profit of $9.3 billion was reported before taxes in 1940. The figure climbed to $21.1 billion in 1942, and $24.5 billion in 1943. Corporation profits paralleled the downturn in production in 1944, and declined to $23.8 billion in that year, while 1945 showed a further decrease to $20.3 billion.

Established industrial regions, including the Northeastern and North Central states and California, were responsible for most of the war production. However, special facilities were constructed in other states, such as Texas, Utah, Nevada, Washington, Oregon, and Arkansas, to bring about a much greater relative industrial increase in these states than in the nation as a whole. Of especial importance were the facilities leading to the most substantial change in our modern economy, i.e., the plants concerned with the development of atomic energy. During World War II, the government underwrote a $2 billion program to construct the atomic bomb. A pilot plant to develop natural uranium and graphite reactors as mass producers of plutonium for weapons use was built on the government reservation at Oak Ridge, Tennessee, in 1943.

Three similar reactors were completed in 1944 and 1945 at the Hanford site on the Columbia River near Pasco, Washington.

### The mobilization of labor

In a way, it was fortunate for America that the manpower demands of the rearmament program came at a time when there was still a backlog of unemployment remaining from the depression of the 1930's. When the war began in Europe, there were an estimated 9

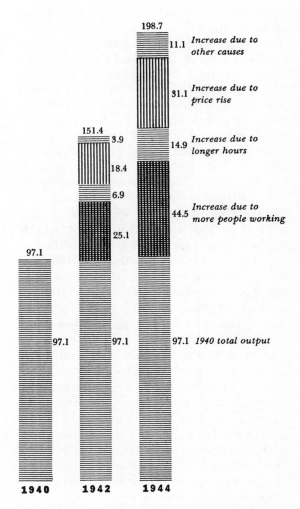

Fig. XVI-1 The increase in production in the United States during World War II, from 1940 to 1944. Figures in billions of dollars.

million unemployed persons in the United States. Even in 1940, when production of military supplies for domestic use as well as for friendly nations abroad had been stepped up, close to 7 million people remained out of work. In 1941, on the eve of Pearl Harbor, there were still 5½ million unemployed. This bloc of workers which the civilian economy had been unable to absorb provided a ready source of labor, so that the shift to all-out war production could be accomplished with less strain than if every worker who went into a war industry had been drawn from civilian employment. Even so, labor shortages quickly developed in particular areas and for particular kinds of jobs.

To cope with labor supply problems, the president created the War Manpower Commission in April 1942, within the top executive agency, OEM. The WMC was organized into several subdivisions and had twelve regional branches throughout the country. In coöperation with the WPB and the United States Employment Service, the WMC undertook to refer workers to war jobs with the highest priority rating, to recruit workers in areas of excess labor and advise and aid them in relocating in shortage areas, and to place workers in the most highly skilled jobs of which they were capable. Throughout the war, the WMC was constantly observing the labor supply situation and doing all that was possible, short of an actual labor draft, which Congress had declined to authorize, to keep both war industries and essential civilian work going on schedule.

In spite of the withdrawal of millions of men and women from labor's ranks as they entered the armed forces, the total number of employed workers in the United States continued to increase, from 51 million in 1941 to over 63 million in 1944. This achievement was made possible partly by an increase of about four million in the number of women employed. Particularly to be noted was the increase in the number of married women employed outside the home. With husbands in the armed forces and with housing shortages forcing the doubling up of families, it was often possible for wives to take outside employment. In addition, millions of older workers and those who were partially handicapped found useful employment by replacing men called into the service. Among other lessons of the war might be listed the great productive contribution that can be made by groups of persons who either do not wish to work in normal times or whom industry normally does not wish to employ.

Since there was no civilian manpower draft in World War II, the incentives necessary to draw needed workers to desired places were high wages, patriotism, and, for men of draft age in nonessential occupations, the threat of removal of deferred draft status. Of these, high wages no doubt constituted the most potent incentive, but high wages tended to increase costs and prices and thus added to inflationary pressures. Consequently, attempts to stabilize wages had to be made in order to keep anxious employers from bidding wages up to unreasonable levels and in order to prevent workers from using the emergency shortage of labor to gain unfair advantage. The National Defense Mediation Board had become involved with the wage issue, and, after the failure of its efforts, the related functions of wage stabilization and the settlement of disputes which might interfere with war production were assigned to the National War Labor Board.

The NWLB in July 1942 evolved the "Little Steel" formula to settle a case involving a demand for wage increases by employees of several steel companies other than U.S. Steel. This formula guided the Board's wage policy throughout the war. The employees of the "Little Steel" companies were granted a wage increase of 15 per cent to offset the increase in prices which had occurred between January 1941 and May 1942, when President Roosevelt had issued orders to various war agencies to stop the wage-price spiral.

The theory underlying the "Little Steel" formula was that after May 1942 there would be no further increases in prices and the cost of living. The Office of Price Administration had at that time instituted stringent orders designed to freeze prices of consumer goods for the duration of the war. "Little Steel" was to permit adjustments to that date, but none were to be allowed thereafter unless the circumstances were exceptional. The formula was designed to bring about an equitable compromise between the interests of workers and employers.

On October 3, 1942, the president created the Office of Economic Stabilization within the OEM, with power over all stabilization agencies. On the same date, he confirmed the principle of the "Little Steel" formula and stated that thereafter no wage increases might be allowed except to correct inequities, inequalities, or substandard wages. Heavy pressure continued to push up both wages and prices, and in April 1943 the president issued a "Hold the Line" order, removing all possible exceptions to the "Little Steel" formula except the correction of substandard wages. Price increases were, in fact, not absolutely stopped, but prices were held to a very slow advance. As prices crept upward, however, labor became increasingly restive under "Little Steel" and workers sought wage increases under a variety of pretexts. All of which were made to appear not to be in violation of the stabilization formula.

Before its termination at the end of the war, the NWLB had handled nearly 18,000 cases of disputes between employers and employees and more than 400,000 cases of requests for wage increases in which employers and employees joined. It was compelled to set up Regional War Labor Boards to handle the extensive volume of work. After the principles of wage stabilization had been enunciated with some approximation to clarity, the processing of requests for wage increases became a matter of office routine. Aside from several dramatic and very troublesome cases involving the wages of coal miners, railway workers, and a few other recalcitrant groups, disputes tended to shift to aspects of employment other than wages. The "Little Steel" formula did not cover these other matters, which came to be called "fringe issues." During the later war years, the Board established what amounted to supplementary principles relating to them. Schedules of paid vacations became common in many industries, shift differentials were allowed for the undesirable night shifts, Christmas or year-end bonuses were paid, and other health, welfare, and pension benefits permitted were as varied as the financial ability and argumentative capacity of employers and their employees. It should be noted that quite frequently employers were not only willing but eager to circumvent wage controls as a means of augmenting their work forces.

During the war years, union membership increased to a higher level than at any other period in American history. The National Labor Relations Act of 1935 had provided the basis for this growth by its provisions protecting the right of workers to organize. The National War Labor Board, however, would not approve closed-shop contracts unless they had been in existence before the war. (A closed-shop contract requires all workers in a particular plant to be members of the union. See Glossary.) A formula to handle this security issue when it arose in dispute cases was worked out in the form of a "maintenance of membership" clause which the NWLB would permit in union-management contracts. This clause contained provision for an "escape" period in which an employee, new or old, might be permitted to withdraw from the union if he chose to do so, but, if he chose to remain in the union, he had to pay his dues for the life of the contract. Where authorized by the employee in writing, the Board would also approve a clause calling for the "check-off," or deduction of union dues from the employee's pay. Although some employers resented the new relationship which grew up with their employees during the war under the rulings of the NWLB, there were many others who welcomed the new sense of working together on a joint enterprise. If the extensive organization of labor in unions was bound to come in any case, the war period provided useful experience for labor and management in working together and softened the bitterness of the labor disputes that occurred with the return of peace.

## Agriculture and food production

World War II began at a time when food production was high. The United States had been troubled with farm surpluses which held down prices all through the depression. The surpluses occurred not so much because production was large, but more because the purchasing power of consumers was low. The second Agricultural Adjustment Act had gone into effect in 1938, with a new attempt to support the prices of basic farm crops. As one of the means of doing this, it provided for loans to farmers to hold price-depressing surpluses off the market—the so-called "ever normal granary" plan. Under this plan (taking wheat as an example because it is the most important staple food for human beings), the quantity of wheat in storage both on and off farms began to increase sharply. When the "phony" war of the winter of 1939 in Europe turned into the violent fighting of 1940 as Hitler embarked on the conquest of all Europe, the price of wheat jumped by about a third in the United States. Production went up as farmers fertilized their soil more intensively in the effort to increase production without handling larger acreages. Although the United States as a nation is the largest single producer of this most important bread grain, Europe *as a continent* is a still larger producer. War was lessening production in large areas of Europe's wheat land, and millions of Europeans as well as Asians had to look to America for food. Fortunately, there was a reserve on hand in the United States at the beginning of the war and production went up every year during the war except 1943, when adverse weather cut the crop. As a result, there was never any serious shortage of wheat during the war in areas under Allied control.

This adequate food supply was not the result of favorable accidents in either production or distribution. In both cases, careful planning was needed. From the production point of view, amendments to the basic AAA were made in 1941 and 1942. Farmers were guaranteed that prices of a long list of basic products, including cotton, tobacco, the grains, and livestock, would be supported until one year following the end of the war at 90 per cent of parity (see p. 299). At the beginning of the war and before, the competitive markets had anticipated wartime food shortages, and prices had increased sharply. These price increases had constituted a powerful and adequate incentive to increased production, but there was danger that farmers would begin to be more cautious if they thought the war might be moving to a conclusion. Also, there was danger that rising prices for farm supplies would cut the farmer's net profit and discourage expansion of output.

To prevent these results, the parity ratio between the prices of products the farmer sold and of those he bought was to be held to at least 90 per cent of what it had been just before World War I. There was criticism of this program toward the end of World War II, particularly as it operated in the case of a product like potatoes. The Department of Agriculture was required by law to purchase a protected commodity when the price fell below the 90 per cent of parity point. The production of potatoes increased greatly because of new fertilizing methods and new insecticides, just as the public appetite was turning away from such basic carbohydrate foods. Serious losses were incurred by the government under the program, since potatoes cannot be stored from one crop season to another or shipped abroad. This was an unfortunate aspect of a program which on the whole worked very well to keep the American people, including the armed forces, well fed for the extra exertion which war required. In addition, the United States shipped large quantities of food to its Allies.

To handle the problem of food distribution and allocation, the president created the War Food Administration in March 1943. It was the duty of WFA to work with the Lend-Lease Administrator and the Army and Navy to see that the armed forces, the civilian populations under their control in fighting areas, America's Allies, and its own civilian population were adequately supplied with all necessary foods. To pool food supplies on a world-wide basis, Britain and America had formed a Combined Food Board in June 1942. Canada joined in 1943, and some coöperation with Russia was also obtained.

Other problems of agriculture and food production arose in connection with the price-control program (discussed in the next section). The Emergency Price Control Act of 1942 authorized the Price Administrator to make subsidy payments when he believed such payments to be the best way to secure maximum production of needed commodities. Subsidies could also be used to absorb increased costs and to prevent price increases of important basic foods. Since everyone consumes food, increased food prices might have become the basis of an inflationary cost spiral throughout the economy. Further, nearly all foods go through several processing and distributing steps, so that an increase in price at the beginning of the process would have been multiplied several times before the product reached the final consumer. A subsidy at the source was the quickest and most direct way of stopping a tendency toward the pyramiding of prices. Subsidies were used to offset increased freight rates that were granted to the railroads and increased ocean freight and insurance charges caused by war risks on such imported commodities as sugar and coffee.

This subsidy program was not altogether popular with urban residents, because food prices were already high and subsidies seemed to favor industries which were already prospering. Farmers too disliked the payment of subsidies because it was an infringement on their individual freedom. This wartime subsidy program was terminated with the end of price control.

In spite of many problems, inevitable frictions and frequent criticisms, American food production reached an enormous volume at a time when food was urgently needed. The farm population was widely depleted by the demands of the armed forces and war industries. The purchase of farm machinery and other supplies was sharply curtailed. Yet peak production records were achieved by farmers. For example, the production of such principal crops as corn rose from 2400 billion bushels in 1940 to above 3000 billion bushels in both 1942 and 1944. Wheat production, which in 1940 was 814 billion bushels, climbed to 1108 billion bushels by 1945. Some shortages did appear, especially in the luxury foods such as meat, dairy products, and certain fruits. Rationing had to be applied to such foods in order to ensure their fair distribution and in order to help hold prices down. Wages and incomes were rising during the war, and the durable goods for which a substantial fraction of consumer income is normally spent were not available. Therefore, an abnormally large part of the national income was available for the purchase of luxury foods. The wartime sacrifices of food experienced by the American people were extremely slight. Millions of people had never eaten as well as they did during World War II.

*Holding the price line*

The need for price control had been recognized even before the United States was drawn into the war, but thereafter the need grew more intense. Wars have always seemed to cause inflation because the manufacturing and purchase of supplies for war use produce *income* for manufacturers, workers, and sellers, but those same activities do not produce *goods* on which these individuals as consumers can spend their incomes. The amount of the surplus income is equal to the value of the goods produced for war. In recent American war periods, part of this surplus income has been absorbed by higher taxes, and citizens have been urged to use as much as they could of the balance to purchase war bonds. But a substantial "inflationary gap," capable of producing marked price rises, has always remained. During World War II, this gap amounted to billions of dollars a year at the peak of the war effort. This unspendable income was a strongly inflationary force which had to be controlled by heroic measures as war production was stepped up.

Prices were extremely hard to control due to the inexperience of the controlling agencies and to the selfishness of those whose prices were subject to regulation. The steps taken by the government to control prices early in the war were not enough to prevent the cost of living from rising more than 10 per cent between 1941 and 1942, and of an additional 6 per cent between 1942 and 1943. The war effort on the economic front was easing slightly from 1943 on, and prices were held to a total increase of only 4 per cent between 1943 and the end of the war in 1945.

As early as 1940, the National Defense Advisory Commission had a Division of Price Stabilization. This division helped to check price rises by "jawbone control" but lacked legal standing and the authority to enforce its actions. In April 1941, the Office of Price Administration and Civilian Supply was formed. This agency functioned for only a few months until its lack of enforcement power necessitated the creation of the stronger Office of Price Administration in August 1941. As an executive agency with the power of the president behind it, the OPA had real authority, augmented by a public awareness of the dangers of inflation if profiteering went unchecked.

The OPA at first concentrated its price-stabilization efforts on producers' goods and then turned its attention increasingly to control of consumer prices. After Pearl Harbor, the Emergency Price Control Act, a basic law authorizing price controls, rent controls, and the rationing of scarce commodities, was passed by Congress and signed by President Roosevelt on January 30, 1942. At the end of April, after a strong message from the president on the need for price control, the OPA announced the imposition of a General Maximum Price Order to take effect in two weeks at the wholesale level and in three weeks at the retail level to "roll back" to the level of the preceding March 15 the prices of more than 90 per cent of all goods sold to consumers. At the same time, rents were frozen at the levels of March for several hundred defense areas where housing congestion was most acute.

To administer and enforce the Act, OPA set up a regional organization with branches in all states and important cities and towns. In May 1942, War Ration Book I, with tickets for sugar rations, was placed in use. Separate books for gasoline were issued in May in the eastern states, and in December they were distributed to the entire nation. Tires and automobiles had been added to the ration list by late 1941 and early 1942, respectively. Coffee was rationed beginning in November 1942, using coupons already available in Ration Book I. In May 1943, a complicated point rationing system was instituted for meat, fats and oils, butter, cheese, and processed foods, with the issuance of War Ration Book II. This system permitted some choice in the purchase of scarce foods according to the tastes of the household. Two additional ration books were issued before the end of the war, and all special problems and hardship cases were handled by various local War Price and Rationing Boards which were set up to cover the entire country.

An overall review of wartime efforts to stabilize prices brings to light the existence of uncoördinated and even opposed elements. In theory, the simplest and clearest way to handle the problems would apparently have been to freeze all wages and prices at the beginning of the war, and then to hold them there. In practice it could not be done that way. Even to come close to a complete freeze would have forced the government to assume virtually dictatorial powers over life and property, and would have perpetuated many price inequalities carried over from the depression. Some types of production needed to be expanded, and in a free-enterprise economic system, labor and materials had to be directed toward those kinds of production through such stimuli as high wages and prices rather than by government coercion.

Compared with any earlier war in which the United States had been involved, economic stabilization efforts in World War II were highly successful. The American economy was regimented by government orders to a greater degree than ever before. This was a new experience for the American people and they resented it, although they approved of the results. At times during World War II, the backlog of applications for wage increases with the War Labor Board and for price increases with the Office of Price Administration made it appear that stabilization efforts might break down. Enforcement machinery was inadequate, and many purchases and sales were made at illegally high prices in what was called the "black market." Scarce goods were not always distributed evenly throughout the country, and some stores which maintained ceiling prices found supplies inadequate. Merchants and clerks not infrequently kept prized items "under the counter" for favored customers. In spite of all such troubles and exasperations, and taking into account the varied character of the people of the nation, the price-control system while it was in effect worked very well.

### The end of World War II

*Demobilization and reconversion*

The termination of hostilities with Japan on August 14, 1945, found the United States only partially prepared for peace. When two atomic bombs were dropped, on Hiroshima and Nagasaki, Japan, in early August 1945, the Japanese War came to an abrupt halt. Considering the much greater role of America in World War II than was the case in World War I, the preparations for ending the war were further advanced and more comprehensive in 1945 than they had been in 1918. Some war contracts had terminated and preparations for resumption of civilian production had begun during 1944. The "Battle of the Bulge" in the Ardennes forest in December 1944 put a temporary stop to these preparations and reversed the trend, but soon industry and the public were again planning the transition to peacetime output.

All manpower controls were removed the day after the capitulation of Japan. Industrial controls were removed as speedily as possible. The interval of several months between VE (Victory in Europe) Day and VJ (Victory in Japan) Day permitted a tapering-off of war work and a gradual speeding-up of civilian production. Advanced planning, plus the two-stage ending of the war, permitted the task to be accomplished relatively smoothly.

To handle the job of industrial demobilization, the Office of War Mobilization, which had been established in May 1943 to unify the activities of federal agencies engaged in the production and distribution of civilian supplies, was converted into the Office of War Mobilization and Reconversion. Congress charged the new agency with preparing plans for industrial demobilization, consolidating or eliminating government war agencies as the need for them disappeared and recommending legislation to Congress whenever it might be needed.

The actual demobilization of the armed forces also occurred with remarkable speed, although it was never fast enough to suit the men in service, who naturally wished to return as rapidly as possible to their families and civilian life. The swift readjustment which industry was able to achieve assisted in the rapid absorption of returning veterans into civilian life. Instead of the unemployment miseries that had followed earlier wars, returning veterans found several possibilities open to them. They could either resume former occupations or they could seek employment among the variety of offers listed by the government services. They could also enroll in an institution of higher learning of their choice to obtain further education. To assist these men, Congress passed the Servicemen's Readjustment Act (GI Bill of Rights) in 1944. Under this Act, many veterans were given the opportunity to attend colleges and universities or to take other kinds of special training for civilian careers. Advantageous loans were made available for starting a business or farming project, and for building or buying a home. Men who had served in the armed forces had the opportunity to retrain themselves into peacetime jobs.

## Removal of rationing and price controls

Except for sugar rationing, which was continued until 1947, the rationing of other commodities was terminated either immediately at the end of the war or before the end of 1945. The question of continuing price controls could not be handled as simply. Two schools of thought developed. One favored immediate decontrol on the theory that only a slight rise of prices would occur because that rise would stimulate a great increase of production once industry was freed from the heavy hand of government control. The other plan favored the retention of controls until the volume of peacetime production showed signs of being sufficient to balance demand at about the level of the controlled prices. President Truman favored the second plan but his Republican opponents in Congress favored the first. The impasse in the spring of 1946 concerning the extension of OPA resulted in a badly bungled management of the price decontrol problem. While debate was proceeding, manufacturers stored their products hoping for higher prices if OPA should be repealed. Civilians became desperate and the worst black markets of the war period developed. When OPA was suspended, prices skyrocketed. After OPA was restored in July 1946, it proved impossible to pull prices back in line. Inflation had gained a real foothold. Fortunately, the need for rent controls was more widely recognized and they were continued for several years, to be removed community by community as the need for housing was more nearly satisfied.

By 1948, when the first postwar downward price movement came, the cost-of-living index had risen over 35 per cent above the 1945 level. This increase, larger than any of the war period, came in spite of peacetime factory production at a rate about double that of the prewar years.

When, in the summer of 1950, World War III appeared imminent because of the attack of North Korean armies on South Korea, a wave of speculation swept the nation. Spontaneously, a surge of public sentiment favored the return of price controls and rationing, in spite of World War II difficulties. In the event of United States involvement in another war, price controls probably would be applied rapidly and effectively.

## Paying for the war

In spite of the greater magnitude of the task, a better job was done in financing World War II than had been the case in any previous war. Between 35 and 40 per cent of the $300 billion cost of the war was paid for by taxation. Taxes were raised sharply by successive revenue acts. Both corporate and individual income tax rates were increased, and an excess profits tax was applied on corporate income. Total federal tax receipts increased from $5387 million in 1940 to $44,148 million in 1944. These totals reflected in great measure the increase in receipts from income and profits taxes. In 1940, these sources accounted for $2125 million. This amount increased to $3469 million in 1941. It more than doubled in 1943, when $7960 million was collected. In 1944, $16,093 million was collected, and finally the amount doubled for the third time

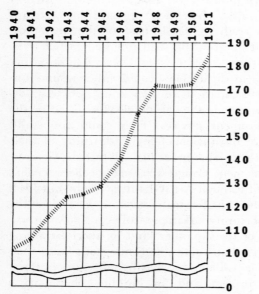

Fig. XVI-2  The effect of World War II and the post-war period on consumers' prices, from 1940 to 1951. The average for 1935 to 1939 = 100.

in 1945, when private and corporate sources accounted for $34,654 million.

The remainder of the cost of the war was defrayed by the sale of bonds to individuals, corporations and banks. Particularly notable was the purchase of bonds in large quantities by individuals, through payroll deduction or other regular purchase plans. There were seven war loans and a Victory Loan totaling about $157 billion. By 1945, the net increase in the federal debt of the United States had reached the astonishing total of more than $1800 per person—nearly six times the 1940 amount. In 1945, banks owned more than a third of the total debt, which made even more acute a divergence in policy between the Treasury Department and the Board of Governors of the Federal Reserve System. The Treasury wished to keep interest on the debt at a stable low level to reduce the interest charged to the American taxpayer; the Federal Reserve System wished more flexible interest rates so that they could be raised or lowered as needed to discourage or encourage borrowing to help achieve a stable economy.

## The postwar economy
## of the United States

### Production of goods

Thanks to the pressure of various wartime bond drives and similar savings-for-defense activities, the American populace at the war's end possessed the greatest liquid asset holdings in our history. The general public holding of government obligations increased between 1940 and 1945 from $10 billion to $64 billion. Personal savings rose from $4 billion in 1940 to an annual rate of over $36 billion in 1944. Adjusted demand deposits climbed from $34 billion in 1940 to $75 billion in 1945, while total installment credit fell from $5.5 billion outstanding in 1940 to just over $2 billion in 1945. Therefore, as consumer products became available, an enthusiastic public had

the money and the credit to purchase those goods which seemed most attractive.

The economic position of the United States at the end of World War II was unquestionably that of the strongest single nation in the world. During the war, the economy had demonstrated an unmatched technical capacity in the production of physical goods. Through sheer increase in output, the arsenal of democracy had supplied a two-front war, and at the same time had maintained an adequate and in some cases rising standard of living for the population at home. The Gross National Product or production of physical goods increased from $100 billion in 1940 to $213.7 billion in 1945, while personal consumption expenditures grew from $72 billion to $121 billion during the same period of time.

During the war, standardized, mass-produced goods spewed forth from automatic machines in almost unbelievable quantities. Products needed for carrying on the war were particularly adapted to this method of production. The government, as an institutional buyer, wanted standardized, simplified and interchangeable items. The producer with a government contract could tool for large quantities and count on lengthy production schedules for a given article. This made possible great financial savings, and the war experience reconfirmed the axiom that the greater the volume of output when fixed costs are dominant, the lower the cost per unit. The lack of need for advertising, for product differentiation, or for other cost-increasing activities common to the competitive consumer market, also helped make the period of the war a time of easy profits.

After the war's end, this flood of American goods continued, although on a differentiated, brand-name basis. Inexpensive, desirable commodities were not easily available in most countries, and American goods found a ready demand throughout the world.

During the war, the government had underwritten the construction of a large number of plants throughout the nation in order to implement goods production. At the end of the war, most of these plants could be converted to civilian use without the otherwise necessary time lag to construct new building facilities. This simplified the conversion to a peacetime economy. It was possible to hire or continue the services of production workers in converted plants while additional plant construction got underway. Thus, badly needed civilian production was resumed much earlier and more easily than otherwise would have been possible.

These war plants represented a $7 billion capital investment by the government through its Defense Plant Corporation. Much of this capital had its source in forced savings through bond purchases or through taxes. The taxpayer, directly or indirectly, contributed fixed capital to the whole economy. However, under the rapid depreciation schedules allowed during the war, the user of the plant charged off as a cost of production this depreciation of capital; therefore, the plants could be leased at nominal rates for civilian production when the war was over. In the process, the taxpayer had provided the corporation with "free" facilities through forced savings and higher prices on the war goods produced in the plant.

The favorable "tax-carry-forward" provisions of the tax laws also aided manufacturers, allowing them to charge several years of postwar losses against wartime profits and recover the taxes paid during that highly profitable period. Manufacturers could, therefore, consider more risky ventures than they otherwise might have undertaken, since losses were substantially covered by the refunding of tax monies already paid to the government. There was little to lose and much to gain, no matter how risky a business venture turned out to be.

### The status of labor

During the nation's need for war production, jobs in war industries had been promoted. Workers who might under normal conditions have hesitated to consider a new job or a new living location were encouraged, supported, and welcomed into areas far from their previous homes. Many previously under-privileged families found themselves with steady incomes, regular work, and a new feeling for what the American ideal really meant.

During the war, the working status of the laboring class shifted upward. The duties performed by the production workers of various war industries required more skills than the jobs common to the 1930's. Government and industry were interested in training workers who could operate the automatic machinery which was being used to produce the materials of war. As his technical status crept upward, the worker was able to circumvent the restrictions of the "Little Steel" formula and thus receive higher compensation for his services. The lure of higher pay and the hope for increasing prestige, added to an appeal to produce for patriotic reasons, gave workers a powerful combination of incentives to put American production at an all-time high.

The new mobility encouraged by wartime needs for defense workers was not limited to industry. Those who joined the service or were part of the family of someone in the armed forces underwent a significant upheaval as they experienced a forced acquaintanceship with new environments. In this way the isolation of small community living was broken, and at the end of the war many individuals were unwilling to return home. The doubts about pulling up stakes and risking their chances in an unfamiliar location disappeared for many as a result of wartime experiences. This heightened mobility of the general public continued after the war and has as yet shown no sign of subsiding.

### The postwar rôle of the government

After the cessation of hostilities in 1945, the federal government continued to dominate the American economy. As the nation entered the atomic and missile ages, it was the government, rather than private enterprise which led the way. During the war, the government had become the largest single operating enterprise in the country, and military defense contracts accounted for almost half the federal budget. As early as 1938, there were federal specifications for wages, hours and working conditions, as well as contract prices, to be met by private businessmen who wanted to bid for government contracts. Even where direct government contracts were not involved, manufacturers had to meet federal minimum-wage and hour standards if their products were to move in interstate commerce. The wartime experience and the defense requirements of the postwar period served to develop a widespread pattern of federal controls, which took the nation even further from the spirit of free enterprise.

This fact was especially important for the areas of basic research which the federal government directly controls. Here the government was not only the source of finance but also its own consumer. Even in areas of semi-private action, however, the government began to finance scientific and technological developments, while private companies served only as the managers of the operation under fairly stringent federal regulations, such as the missile and atomic energy developments where private companies served as contractors on government projects. The federal government assumed much of the risk by supplying capital, and private business reaped whatever profits accrued.

American scientists had worked at top speed all during the war to keep the nation's might superior to that of the enemy. After the war was concluded, the demand for scientific advancements for civilian living continued to keep the pace of achievement at an all-time high. After the explosion of the first atomic bomb, it became imperative to direct intensive research toward solving the problems of converting atomic energy to peaceful uses. The long-range possibility of substituting atomic energy for the scarce resources formerly needed to generate power unfolded a dazzling panorama of future benefits to mankind. The growing need for skilled researchers gave the college graduate a new luster. The public sensed that from the laboratories of the nation a whole series of new and wonderful products would be forthcoming for its comfort and enjoyment. High expectations were directed toward science as the source from which these benefits would flow.

It was inevitable that the United States should emerge from World War II with a heightened awareness of international affairs. The country had had to abandon its traditional position of isolation to enter and help fight the war. By 1945, it was no longer possible for the United States to retreat behind two oceans and once again become purely a self-involved nation. The country was forced by the pressure of events to play a vital role in world affairs.

Unfortunately, America's European Allies were not in a position to make as rapid a recovery from World War II as was achieved in the United States. Their participation in the war had been longer than ours; their industries had been destroyed or badly damaged by bombing, enemy occupation, or long years of hard use without adequate replacement; and millions of their people had been killed or maimed. The United States emerged from the war relatively unscathed by comparison with its European Allies. The basic question came to be whether the United States would assume the leadership which had been thrust upon it by postwar circumstances.

## FOR FURTHER READING

Agar, Herbert. *The Price of Power: America since 1945.* Phoenix Books. Paperback.

Bernstein, Peter L. *The Price of Prosperity.* New York: Doubleday & Company, Inc., 1962. A lively criticism of the "arithmetic optimists." The author makes a plea for a greater understanding of the nature of federal spending in today's complex economic world.

*The Challenge to America: Its Economic and Social Aspects. Rockefeller Brothers Fund. Anchor. Paperback.*

Dulles, Foster Rhea. *Twentieth Century America.* Boston: Houghton Mifflin Co., 1945. Chapters 25—28.

Fabricant, Solomon. *The Trend of Economic Activity in the United States since 1900.* New York: National Bureau of Economic Research, Inc., 1952.

Theobald, Robert. *The Challenge of Abundance.* Mentor. Paperback discussion of both the dangers and the opportunities of the newly "affluent society."

# Chapter 17:

# International relationships

# of the United States

# in a changed economic world

It is an axiom of military historians that the allies of one war are the antagonists of the next. Although the United States and Russia were allies in the fighting of World War II, they became antagonists immediately thereafter in the cold war of ideas and political-strategic rivalries. This was a new experience for both Russia and the United States, and resulted from the changes in their world positions after World War II.

### The cold war following
### World War II

Throughout the nineteenth century Russia was sunk in feudalism with a reactionary absolutist government; the United States was preoccupied with affairs on the North American continent, creating the most productive industrial system in the world. But by mid-twentieth century, each country had become the undisputed leader of its respective economic and political power block, and it had become obvious that the real economic issue in the cold war was between capitalism and communism as economic systems.

The view of Russia held by the people of other countries underwent wide fluctuations following the communist revolution in 1917. Not only was there general hostility to a revolution based on an extreme communism, but the world was horrified by the violence and the slaughter used to liquidate all opposition within Russia. As the regime became more thoroughly established, hostility began to diminish. Russia became a member of the League of Nations in 1934; the government hired scientists and experts from foreign nations, including the United States, to assist in its industrial and agricultural development; and the country was diplomatically recognized by many nations including the United States. Trade between Russia and outside countries grew modestly. Citizens of the United States were permitted to travel in the Soviet Union, and several delegations of Soviet experts were sent to other countries to study developments there. In fact, when the Russian economy seemed immune to the world depression of the 1930's, many persons throughout the capitalist world took note of the fact that the Soviet Union seemed to possess a degree of economic stability which was lacking elsewhere. With success at home and an increasingly reasonable diplomatic attitude, including the adoption in 1936 of a new and more democratic constitution, Russia influenced some persons in the democratic world to think that for large parts of the world, communism was the only political force powerful enough to counter the deplorable Fascist and Nazi doctrines which were an increasing threat to the civilized world.

All of these developments favorable to Russia within the free democratic world were shockingly reversed with the approach of World War II. The brutal attack upon a small and peaceful neighbor, Finland, was morally inexcusable. It appeared that political and military advantages for Russia itself stood higher than justice toward a weak neighbor. This impression was deepened and confirmed by the nonaggression treaty between Germany and Russia which cleared away the last obstacle holding Hitler back from his war of aggression. When Hitler later turned on Russia, and when in 1941 the war became truly a world war, Britain, the United States, and their allies could accept Russia as an ally only with profound distrust and under the exigencies of military necessity. As victory in the war began to draw near, the deep distrust between Russia and the Western nations became more manifest. At the end of the war, Russia's aggression in seizing the governments and territories of its smaller neighbors from the Black Sea to the Arctic Ocean, confirmed the worst suspicions of its motives. Russia's actions seemed to reflect a fear of all foreign nations. Since there was no evidence to justify such conduct, the world could only interpret these actions as resulting from fears that other nations would follow policies which Russia secretly pursued itself.

Trade between Russia and the West was cut to a trickle. The United States in particular was insistent that no goods of military value should reach Russia. European nations, more dependent on purchase from and sales to Russia than the United States, agreed that Russia's aggressive potential should not be increased, but were inclined to define articles of military value somewhat differently. An "iron curtain" was drawn between Russian-dominated territory and the outside world. Persons from inside could not get out except by secret escape whenever possible; persons from outside could not get in except for the diplomatic corps of nations with which Russia maintained formal relations, and such foreigners were kept under constant surveillance while inside Russia. World trade in important basic commodities and minerals became a matter of jockeying between the free democratic world and the bloc of communist countries.

Russia began to promote actively the spread of communist ideas in all areas where the country had influence, providing military assistance wherever feasible and fomenting the growth of revolutionary movements. The United States and other Western nations asserted that people should be free to select their own form of government and protested Russia's actions. Russia refused to desist, however, and all doubts regarding its intentions to create a world communist state were dispelled when the Communists seized power in Czechoslovakia, purged Poland and Rumania, and finally in 1956 crushed a revolutionary uprising in Hungary with a ruthlessness unparalleled in modern history. The United States began very early to provide assistance to those nations that were making an effort to resist communism, not only by means of economic and military aid, but finally through direct military intervention, when U.S. armed forces were sent into South Korea in 1950, to Lebanon in 1958, and to Vietnam in 1961. The defense of U.S. rights in West Berlin has also been necessary—by an air lift in 1948-1949 to counteract a Russian blockade, and by a show of protective military strength in 1961-1962.

## Analyzing economic systems

All systems that are adopted and work passably well become systems of internal and external political power and reflect an entire way of life. For this reason, it is not fruitful to think of the differences between capitalism, socialism, and communism as clear-cut. Nor are the distinctions exclusively economic, exclusively political, or exclusively philosophic, but rather a combination of all these.

### Capitalism

Capitalism is a system based upon private ownership of property in which private profit is the key motivation of economic activity. The capitalist system seeks to give the individual as much freedom and initiative as possible, with the government serving primarily to ensure that one individual does not harm another. Competition between firms and individuals is the essence of the system, which is postulated on the assumption that each firm, in attempting to maximize its profit, will operate as efficiently as possible, produce all the goods demanded by its customers, and thereby contribute the most toward furthering the general welfare.

Irrespective of the fact that government intervention on a broad scale has become unavoidable, capitalism presumes that employment opportunities are freely and equally available, and that anyone has the opportunity to work, save, and invest his money for profit, i.e., to become a capitalist on his own account.

To the peoples of countries to which modern technology has not yet come, particularly in Asia and Africa, where people have lived in poverty as tillers of the soil for untold generations, capitalism seems impossible or perhaps even undesirable. But these people have begun to desire industrial development for the improved living it can bring.

What such people cannot understand is that capitalism and the free market are simply the economic side of a way of life which under-takes to give the widest freedom to individual intelligence, both for the inherent satisfaction to be derived from that freedom and as the means of achieving the most efficient and progressive economy. It does not require one specific and rigid set of social institutions, such as those of American capitalism, to give individual intelligence its opportunity to be developed for the good of both the individual and society. In countries in which behavior is deeply affected by social traditions and collective patterns of action, it is intelligent to use those established institutions as far as possible in the effort to build a more productive economy. In cultures which have strong collective traditions, a noncapitalistic economy may develop the most diligent individual effort and the most efficient system, with social prestige as one of the important compensations for successful effort.

In other words, capitalism and the free market should not be construed either by Americans or others as prescribing any specific set of economic arrangements. Capitalism is as adaptable to changing conditions as any system that could be devised, since it is basically a system of individual intelligence.

### Communism

In theory, communism is a system in which all productive and distributive resources are owned by the community and used for the good of all its members. All individuals work for the common good; all are owners and all are workers. Except for one's immediate possessions, nothing is privately owned. The government, elected by the people, directs the general efforts for the welfare of all.

These theoretical features of communism do not characterize it in practice, particularly in the leading communist country of today, the Union of Soviet Socialist Republics. Here, instead of the people ruling, the government rules the people. A small clique, composed of members of the Communist Party, controls the government, and officials of the government are nominated by the party. Only members of the party are eligible for government office. "Elections" are held, but since only one slate of candidates is presented, the results are foregone conclusions. Economically, the state owns and operates all productive resources and facilities and controls all trade, domestic and foreign. Production and all individual effort are directed toward strengthening the state. There is no private investment, and so all returns for work are in the form of salary. This can be spent for personal needs, but production is planned in such a way that the state's needs are met first and the consuming public can have only what remains. Nor is this evenly distributed, for members of the party elite, holding government and professional positions, are relatively wealthy, even as the mass of the people remain poor.

Communism in practice recognizes few individual rights and ruthlessly enforces its own code of ideas by liquidating all those, even within party ranks, who show any sign of wavering in their devotion. Freedom of the press, of speech, of worship does not exist. Protest against government policy is treason, although workers in factories or on collective farms are encouraged to offer constructive suggestions for improving methods, a practice which, incidentally, may reveal the presence of an inefficient manager, who may then be punished. Workers are allowed to join unions, but strikes and collective bargaining as we know them do not exist. In many ways the unions are nothing more than disciplinary organizations, and they assist in imposing and enforcing production schedules.

Communism already established abroad seeks to extend the system to other countries and to eliminate all other systems of economic and political life, including socialism. It seeks converts by peaceful means or otherwise and will not hesitate to overthrow governments by force, if it seems feasible. Propaganda, sabotage, assassination are all accepted weapons of zealous communists.

*Socialism*

Socialism is the more moderate evolutionary stream of economic thought stemming from the nineteenth century, just as communism represents the hard, revolutionary stream. Since it is a more diffuse movement than communism, there are many shades of socialist thought. The core of socialism lies in the public ownership and operation of the key industries and resources essential to human welfare. This would include banks, public utilities, transportation facilities, and industries, such as steel, mining, and construction, where stable operation is essential in order to avoid severe business fluctuations with their resultant personal suffering.

There is no absolute distinction to be made between socialist and capitalist countries so far as the general way of life is concerned, as they have common cultural roots in the free-enterprise system. Both socialism and capitalism desire to use the best technical methods of mass production and distribution, provided only that industry, commerce and finance place the public interest first, and that private individuals do not acquire unjustly great wealth and power. The chief difference between socialism and capitalism lies in the degree of government control over individual activity.

### The United States and foreign aid

Major wars have become, or perhaps have always been, such shattering experiences that those involved in them, whether victor or vanquished, have rarely been able afterward to face the problems of life on the same footing as before. This was never more applicable than in World War II, when the United States became involved more deeply than ever in world affairs and began to assume new international responsibilities, which were to continue indefinitely as a vital part of the American role as a world leader.

Most of the immediate and urgent international economic problems with which the United States concerned itself after World War II centered around the industrially developed countries of Europe and in their relationship to the United States. Common to all of them were not only the loss of life and the actual property destruction in the combat zones, but also the resultant destruction of productive capacity in industry and agriculture.

The destruction of the means by which the people of various nations supported themselves created immediate and serious needs for relief so that something approaching normal life and diet could be restored. Only then could these nations begin to rebuild their productive capacity. Food and clothing were necessary at the end of the war as were seeds, raw materials, and equipment to restore agriculture and industry to full productivity as quickly as possible.

The United States participated in a massive program to implement the rebuilding of these war-shattered economies when the United Nations Relief and Rehabilitation Administration was established in 1945. Through this agency, the United States granted aid in the amount of $11 billion between V-E Day and the spring of 1947, much of it concentrated in the economies of eastern Europe.

After Russia began to gobble up the smaller eastern European countries as satellites, Congress approved the Truman Plan on March 17, 1947 to grant military assistance of $400 million to Greece, Turkey, and other threatened countries.

### The Marshall Plan

The focus of American monetary assistance temporarily shifted away from military aid in June 1947, when General George C. Marshall, then secretary of state, proposed that the United States help finance the restoration of Europe through a plan designed to encourage all nations to do everything they could to help rehabilitate themselves. In advocating American monetary assistance through the European Recovery Program, Marshall insisted the program was not specifically directed against any country or conflicting doctrine, but rather against hunger, poverty, desperation, and chaos. Marshall aid nonetheless quickly took on an anticommunistic hue after the Russians denounced the Marshall Plan as a capitalist plot.

Through the Marshall Plan and other Congressional grants, foreign aid had reached a total by 1962 of $90 billion, and 22 countries had received more than $1 billion each in grants and loans. With one exception, European countries received the largest amounts, France leading the list with $9.4 billion, followed by England with $8.6 billion, Italy $5.6 billion, Korea $5 billion, and West Germany $4.9 billion. Foreign aid has been extended by Congress over the years as one of the most effective and least expensive ways to fight communism.

### The Point Four program

It was recognized that in the long run world peace must depend upon bringing to the peoples of the world—even the most underdeveloped—ample opportunities for economic development. There could be no durable peace anywhere as long as some peoples were denied opportunities to improve their own economic position. President Truman concurred with this line of thought in the fourth point of his inaugural address on January 20, 1949, and proposed the following program, which immediately became known as the "Point Four" program:

Fourth, we must embark on a bold new program for making the benefits of our scientific advances and industrial progress available for the improvement and growth of undeveloped areas. . . .We should make available to peace-loving peoples the benefits of our store of technical knowledge in order to help them realize their aspirations for a better life. And, in cooperation with other nations, we should foster capital investment in areas needing development. Our aim should be to help the free peoples of the world, through their own efforts, to produce more food, more clothing, more materials for housing, and more mechanical power to lighten their burdens.[1]

[1]*Department of State Bulletin,* January 30, 1949 (Washington: U.S. Government Printing Office, 1949), p. 125.

The ideas expressed by the president in Point Four instantly appealed to the good sense as well as the idealism of all persons who took a long-range view of international affairs. There was no remnant of economic imperialism evident in the president's remarks, only the willingness, shared by almost all Americans, to give their technical knowledge of agriculture and industry to all peoples anywhere who wanted it and were able to use it.

Although foreign aid began as a program to revive war-ravaged Europe, it soon spread to underdeveloped and otherwise needy nations in Asia, Africa and South America. In the years since World War II, our concept of foreign aid has widened to include not only financial assistance, but human aid as well. By 1960, there were almost 6000 experts from the United States in agriculture, health and sanitation, and education in many countries in Central and South America, Africa, and the southern countries of the great Eurasian continents. The objective of these experts was to help the people of the countries to which they went improve their food production and thus their diet; to increase income by means of improved productivity; and to lengthen life by improved diet, improved sanitation, and medical care. Education was to be directed toward the attainment and diffusion of knowledge useful for all of these purposes.

### The Peace Corps

As part of his campaign for the presidency in 1960, John F. Kennedy suggested that an additional working force be recruited from among college students and other interested persons. The Peace Corps, which was organized shortly after he took office, initially recruited 2700 college graduates as volunteers—most of them under 25 years of age—in fields of agriculture, public health, and home economics, to serve in 12 nations around the globe. These college-trained people were sent, after a short period of training to acquaint them with the country they were to visit, to work along with the citizens of the chosen nation to teach them the basic skills necessary to combat poverty, disease, illiteracy, and hunger. They contacted the ordinary people of the assisted countries as they helped set up irrigation systems, dig public wells, and run village schools. The benefits offered through the Peace Corps were more self-evident than military or financial assistance could ever be. It was hoped that these young people by their very youth would continue to nurture the idealism that had made the Marshall Plan and the Point Four program so successful. Volunteers of all ages are enthusiastically continuing to offer their services to the Peace Corps, and it has already proven itself an outstanding ambassador of international understanding and good will. At the same time, some progress is being made in improving both the domestic and international aspects of the economic systems of many underdeveloped countries.

### The relationship between economic and military programs

It is not possible to discuss the international economic problems after World War II without becoming involved in political and military considerations. At the end of the war, the United States and most of the nations of Europe disarmed and turned whole-heartedly to the tasks of reconstruction. These tasks were serious enough, as we have already seen. Unfortunately, they could not remain the sole preoccupation of peace-loving nations because of threats to their security arising beyond their own borders. Thus it was, that military preparations were increasing when South Korea was attacked in June 1950 by armies from North Korea. Support of the government of South Korea by the United Nations, led by the United States, created a localized but very "hot" war, which caused universal fears throughout the world that it might spread and become another world war.

While these diplomatic and military developments were occurring, recovery and reconstruction were making substantial headway in both Europe and Asia. Americans, who were especially disturbed by the aggressive actions of the communist bloc of nations were also disturbed that our own allies in other parts of the world were not as aroused over these acts as we were. Aid under the European Recovery Program was still flowing to European nations, and some voices in the United States Congress began to express the idea that we should not feel obligated to grant economic aid to those who were not willing to stand up and fight in defense of their own liberties if the necessity should arise. Also the idea gained acceptance in the United States that recovery and reconstruction had gone far enough in the first five or six years after the war; that American aid should be granted less for strictly economic purposes than for the purposes of building the military defenses of the free nations against any possible attack that might be made against them. As evidence of this reasoning, Congress passed the Mutual Security Act on October 10, 1951, creating a Mutual Security Agency to take over the functions of ERP until its termination on June 30, 1952. Thereafter the MSA was to carry out its own program as specified in the Act.

The new elements in this law were comprehensiveness (it included several previous aid programs within its own scope), and an emphasis on mutual security rather than economic coöperation. Economic aid was continued in varying amounts to different regions of the world, but in total this aid involved only about one-fifth of the funds authorized in the first year. A post of Director for Mutual Security was created to coördinate the varied activities and administrative functions of the MSA. The primary intention of the Act was to strengthen the military defenses of the countries which received aid under its provisions and to grant economic aid only to "sustain and increase military effort." The title and terms of the Act reflect the appraisal of the world situation made by a majority of Congress. It was evidently felt that military preparedness was the business of first importance for the free nations, and that economic aid solely for the purpose of increasing the world's

productivity would have to take second place until more assuredly peaceful days might return.

In spite of this shift in emphasis away from economic aid, there inevitably were profound economic effects from military aid. So far as a country's foreign trade position is concerned, even military aid tends to contribute to a more favorable balance of payments. Under the Truman Plan, which had been instituted by the United States government at the end of the war and prior to the Marshall Plan, military aid had been supplied in particular to Greece and Turkey. Both countries had derived economic benefits from these military expenditures. Not only was domestic employment enhanced by military expenditures, but the inflow of funds helped pay for desired imports of raw materials, equipment, and foodstuffs. Theoretically, the effect was just as marked as if the agriculture and industry of Greece and Turkey, for example, were strong enough to compete and sell their products in world markets in an amount equal to the military expenditures. Under the Mutual Security Act, military expenditures and transfers of funds were of benefit to the nations of western Europe and elsewhere in this same manner. Military aid helped alleviate the imbalance of payments and permitted the purchase abroad of raw materials and manufactured goods which the various countries would otherwise not have been able to make.

While the continuance and expansion of American aid under MSA permitted the reconstruction and development of many nations to continue as it had been proceeding under previous aid plans, still the shift of emphasis from strictly economic development to military preparedness inevitably changed the direction of the developmental process. The United States was more willing to buy the products of the "military preparations industry" of the nations on the outer fringes of Europe than to support any of their other industries. Thus the economies of these nations were diverted toward the manufacture of munitions, the building and equipping of larger armies, and the erection of military installations. This tendency became more marked as the military defenses of the nations bordering the North Atlantic Ocean were assessed more completely and their further development undertaken more systematically under the auspices of the North Atlantic Treaty Organization. NATO had been set up by these nations in the months after the outbreak of war in Korea, when that event had made clear the need for such action. The American MSA program was largely, although not completely, geared into the military program of NATO.

The shift from reconstruction and development, which were primarily economic, to programs which were primarily militaristic characterized the second half of the first decade after World War II. The shift was not without its own pains, in spite of the fact that in a number of respects military aid also had economic benefits. Military production often made demands upon the same raw materials and metals which were already in heavy demand for civilian production and development, and the prices of these materials were pushed still higher. Obviously, too, men serving in the armed forces became consumers of the products of others and were not producers in agriculture and industry. Thus, instead of producing income to support themselves and to help support their own governments through the payment of taxes, they became a financial burden to their governments. Rearmament and coöperation in the plans of NATO produced severe internal budget strains in many countries. In fact, the extent of coöperation in military plans was somewhat limited by such economic considerations.

Not to be overlooked was the adverse psychological effect of the rearmament program and MSA on some sections of the west European population. Some critics said that America was willing to provide aid to convert their men into cannon fodder and their countries into battlefields, but was not willing to provide aid on an equal scale for their economic benefit. Such points of view were not in the majority, but they were sufficiently widespread to keep a number of countries in a state of some political instability. In fact, by 1953 the European nations, led by Great Britain, were beginning to demand that there be an end to all American aid, and that their economies be allowed to develop on the basis of increased trade with the United States. The theme "Trade not Aid" put it up to the United States to reduce tariffs which impeded the import of many European products. Political considerations of this kind also served to limit the extent of coöperation in military programs. All in all, the hopes of nearly all nations at the end of World War II, even amid the despair and destruction which were then so widespread, had to give way to a more somber view before a decade had passed. Possible economic gains from reconstruction and new developments had to be weighed against the necessity to rebuild and maintain costly defenses.

### West European economic arrangements in the postwar world

The complex tangle of economic problems which beset European countries at the end of the war made it clear to many Europeans and to most persons outside of Europe that steps had to be taken to dissolve or lower the traditional barriers which broke up western European manufacturing and commerce into a series of national compartments. Large-scale production at low cost requires the distribution of a product over large unimpeded market areas, if the product is to develop and grow. Small national areas, each with its own tariff barrier, are economically outmoded in the modern world with its advanced technology.

Only a fraction of world trade ever has or probably ever will directly involve the United States. Throughout the world, small trade areas develop just as they do on a still smaller scale within a country. Many of these smaller trade areas do not use world currencies, such as the U.S. dollar or the British pound, or at least depend upon them only partially or indirectly. This fact presented the possibility that groups of countries closely tied together

## AMERICAN REPUBLICS

| | |
|---|---|
| Argentina | 288 |
| Bolivia | 202 |
| Brazil | 974 |
| Chile | 319 |
| Colombia | 217 |
| Cuba | 56 |
| Dominican Republic | 8 |
| Ecuador | 82 |
| Haiti | 78 |
| Mexico | 342 |
| Panama | 48 |
| Paraguay | 35 |
| Peru | 266 |
| Uruguay | 70 |

**Military Aid** 0.6

**Economic Aid** 2.8

**Total Aid** 3.4

## WESTERN EUROPE

| | |
|---|---|
| Belgium-Luxembourg | 1,887 |
| Denmark | 801 |
| Finland | 87 |
| France | 9,659 |
| Iceland | 59 |
| Ireland | 140 |
| Italy | 5,134 |
| Norway | 947 |
| Portugal | 381 |
| Spain | 1,266 |
| Sweden | 104 |
| United Kingdom | 7,739 |
| West Germany | 4,023 |
| Yugoslavia | 2,106 |

**Military Aid** 14.7

**Economic Aid** 24.8

**Total Aid** 39.5

## AFRICA

| | |
|---|---|
| Algeria | 4 |
| Br. East Africa | 8 |
| Ethiopia | 95 |
| Ghana | 5 |
| Liberia | 70 |
| Libya | 156 |
| Morocco | 183 |
| Nigeria | 5 |
| Republic of the Congo | 22 |
| Rhodesia and Nyasaland | 18 |
| Sudan | 34 |
| Tunisia | 158 |

**Military Aid** 0.1

**Economic Aid** 0.7

**Total Aid** 0.8

## NEAR EAST AND SOUTH ASIA

| | |
|---|---|
| Afghanistan | 128 |
| Ceylon | 63 |
| Greece | 2,950 |
| India | 2,001 |
| Iran | 1,068 |
| Iraq | 128 |
| Pakistan | 1,054 |
| Saudi Arabia | 22 |
| Turkey | 3,028 |
| U.A.R. (Egypt) | 375 |

**Military Aid** 4.5

**Economic Aid** 8.1

**Total Aid** 12.6

## FAR EAST AND PACIFIC

| | |
|---|---|
| Australia | 1,098 |
| Burma | 73 |
| Cambodia | 270 |
| Indonesia | 468 |
| Japan | 4,044 |
| Laos | 372 |
| Philippines | 1,380 |
| South Korea | 4,556 |
| South Vietnam | 1,910 |
| Thailand | 570 |

**Military Aid** 8.6

**Economic Aid** 11.4

**Total Aid** 20.0

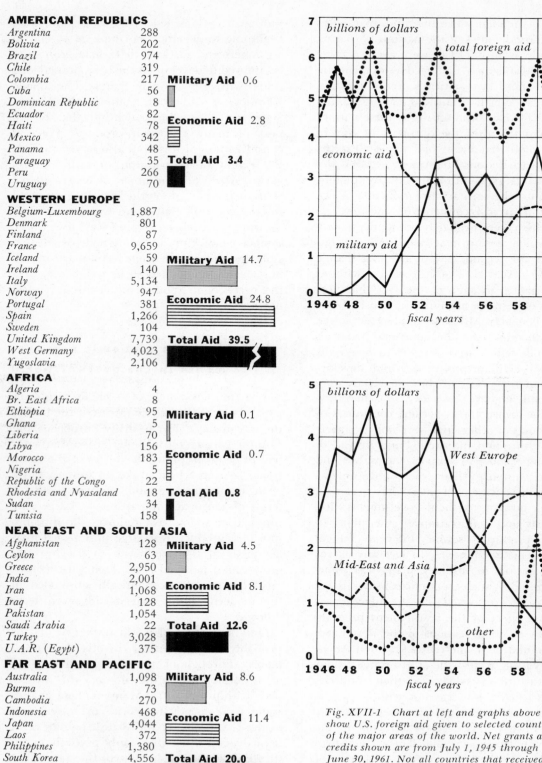

Fig. XVII-1 Chart at left and graphs above show U.S. foreign aid given to selected countries of the major areas of the world. Net grants and credits shown are from July 1, 1945 through June 30, 1961. Not all countries that received aid are shown. Figures for countries are in millions; totals are in billions.

by trade might work out their own systems of stabilizing their international payments without fully using the dollar or the pound. This reasoning led to a proposal for a European Payments Union, which was in fact created and began operation in July of 1950. The Marshall Plan provided some reserve funds to initiate EPU, which operated in a manner similar in many ways to the centers which clear bank checks between the banks of any city or town. This device freed some countries of the acute dollar shortage and permitted regional trade to expand. This result was to be desired, although some persons felt that such agencies as the EPU contained potential dangers in tempting the countries involved to impose barriers to wider trade on a world basis.

The oldest large-scale payments system in the world was the British pound sterling. For more than a century the pound had been the leading world currency unit. The growing economic productive capacity of the United States had finally placed the dollar in a stronger international position than the pound, but "sterling," as it was called in financial markets, continued to be the chief currency of some of Britain's neighboring countries as well as some of the countries of the British Commonwealth, all of whom traded more extensively with Britain than with other countries. This group of trading nations came to be called the "sterling area" or the "sterling group." At the end of the war, Britain proved to be a rather weak and handicapped leader of this formerly powerful trading group. War damage to the British economy and the exhaustion of British financial resources created strains within the sterling group which threatened to break it up, although it obviously provided sound economic advantages for its members. The mutual advantages in international trade and finance which gave rise to the sterling group and to such arrangements as the European Payments Union give witness to the economic pressure for large industries and large markets to go with them.

The most direct method of coping with the broad problems which affected most of the nations of western Europe, if not all of them, would have been to propose political unification so that no barriers due to laws or political administration would prevent the free flow of raw materials and finished goods. Nevertheless, at the end of the war, the obstacles to such a sweeping action seemed insuperable, and the steps which were taken to bring greater unity to the economy of western Europe were modest indeed.

The administrators of the European Recovery Program were aware that both the cost and the success of the program depended upon securing the fullest and most efficient coöperation from European nations participating in the plan. Even as ERP was being debated in the United States, European countries, including France, Italy, Belgium, Luxembourg, West Germany, and the Netherlands, formed a Committee for European Economic Coöperation to aid the American effort. When the American ERP became law and the Economic Coöperation Administration was set up to administer it, CEEC was converted into the Organization for European Economic Coöperation as the agency by which the European nations themselves would endeavor to pool their own resources for self-help and economic recovery. OEEC was, of course, a purely voluntary organization of the individual countries in the Marshall Plan with no power to enforce the correction of conditions which it felt to be injurious to recovery. Also, its purpose was immediate and temporary, and it could scarcely tackle the deep-seated causes which retarded the development of a highly productive economy in western Europe. Yet within its own inherent limitations, OEEC attempted to give some guidance to individual nations in planning their imports from outside western Europe and in adapting their industrial production to the needs of the area. By these means, it was hoped that the acute imbalance in the international payments of some of the countries could be reduced. As these modest steps were successful, at least a beginning was made toward the development of a unified western European industrial and market area.

The broader term which was often applied

hopefully to the problems of western Europe was "economic integration." If fully achieved, economic integration would make of western Europe an area like that of the United States where barriers to industry and trade have never existed. To many Americans, with their background of long-standing unity and integration, this seemed to be not only a sensible but also a relatively easy action to take.

### The Schuman Plan

Although European hopes for unity were dim in the spring of 1950, Foreign Minister Robert Schuman of France urged a step toward unity when he proposed the creation of a European Coal and Steel Community. The features of the proposal, which was immediately called the *Schuman Plan,* were discussed with great intensity in the months that followed. Britain declined to participate in the plan. The government of western Germany finally decided to participate in the working out of details. After about a year of discussion between governments and the representatives of coal and steel industries, an agreement was drawn up and signed in April 1951 by the representatives of six western European countries. These representatives recognized that lack of unity had been a factor in the wars that had ruined Europe and they stated, "A united Europe will not be achieved all at once, nor in a single framework; it will be formed by concrete measures which first of all create a solidarity in fact."[1] The formation of a single market for coal and steel serving 160 million people in western Europe was presented as an achievable and solid step toward the ultimate unification and economic integration of Europe.

The administration provided for the European Coal and Steel Community was designed to have centralized executive authority and to be responsible to the countries and industries coöperating in it. The objective of the Community was to surrender national self-sufficiency in coal and steel among the member nations and to substitute for it free competition among all of them. High-cost mines or steel mills may not be closed down by official decision, but it is presupposed that competition will achieve the same result. Where such adjustments as this produce unemployment or other acute problems, the executive "High Authority" has power and resources to facilitate a desirable form of settlement of the matter.

The European Coal and Steel Community has proved to be an unqualified success. In its first eight years, steel production in the six member countries doubled to a total of 73 million tons, thereby nearly equalling the output of the United States. The ECSC has largely eliminated national taxes on coal and steel and has decreased "through" rates for coal and steel shipments. Above all, the High Authority of the ECSC has proved to be highly effective. It may independently levy taxes, and decisions are binding for member governments.

### The European Common Market

Building on the successful experience with the European Coal and Steel Community, the next concrete expression of economic integration for Europe took the form of the European Economic Community or the "Common Market." Although most of the nations of western Europe participated in the conferences leading to the inception of the Common Market, only six countries initially joined by signing a treaty in Rome in March 1957. The six countries were Belgium, France, Italy, Luxembourg, Holland, and West Germany. The dominant goal of the EEC is that it will some day serve as a large-scale customs union for an organization of states that will maintain a common tariff against the goods of outside countries, but wherein goods will move duty-free. In addition, the member nations have already designated coöperative supranational agencies which are working to minimize the adverse effects of resource reallo-

[1] *Understanding the Schuman Plan,* Department of State Publication No. 4281 (Washington, D.C.: U.S. Government Printing Office, July 1951), p. 2.

cation and to develop a coördinated program in the areas of monetary and fiscal policy. In the years since it was founded, the EEC has made notable progress toward the development of common policies for agriculture, goods production, transportation, labor, and capital.

Significant progress has been made in reducing internal tariffs on industrial goods, and in 1960 all trade quotas were eliminated for the Common Market countries. By December 1961, the tariff average was 40 per cent lower than that which prevailed on January 1, 1957. This reduced tariff level was reached one full year ahead of the schedule set in the original treaty, and the Council of Ministers for the Common Market agreed to make further changes if conditions remained favorable.

As of 1960, the export trade of the Common Market countries taken collectively and translated into dollars was about equal to that of the United States—$19.5 billion to the United States' $20.3 billion. But the import trade of the Common Market countries was collectively larger than that of the United States, at $19 billion to $14.7 billion, respectively. With the decision of Great Britain in the winter of 1961 to seek membership in the Common Market, the EEC actually became potentially capable of outproducing the United States in such basic commodities as hard coal, iron ore, crude steel, and cement.

An interesting corollary of renewed British interest in joining the Common Market was its effect on the European Free Trade Association which Great Britain helped organize in May 1959 in Stockholm along with Austria, Denmark, Norway, Portugal, Sweden, and Switzerland. The EFTA was formed after negotiations between the future EFTA countries and the member nations of the Common Market broke down in the latter part of 1958, when the nonmember nations refused to accede to Common Market requirements for common external tariffs, close meshing of economic policies, and the establishment of a common agricultural policy. The EFTA market group, "The Outer Seven," was organized with the express hope that in time there would

be no intergroup tariffs or quotas, but unlike the EEC, individual member nations were to retain their separate systems of external tariffs. Further, members of the EFTA were to function by intergovernmental coöperation with a minimum of special institutions, whereas the EEC had tended to delegate far-reaching powers to a set of supranational administrative agencies. The presumed eventual withdrawal of Great Britain from the EFTA in favor of the Common Market, along with the application in 1962 for membership in EEC by Denmark and Norway and for associate membership by Austria, Sweden, and Switzerland, gave reason for speculation concerning the future of the EFTA.

Although admission to membership in the Common Market must be by unanimous vote, it startled most nations when France voted in January 1963 to restrict British participation to that of an associate member, especially since other Common Market countries had voted to receive Great Britain as a full-fledged member. An attempt was made to hold the negotiations open in the hope of persuading General de Gaulle to moderate the French position. This attempt failed, and it would appear that British entry to the Common Market on equal terms has been halted for some time to come. The ramifications of the situation may well go deeper than economic relations; some spokesmen at the time of the French veto were of the opinion that the whole of western defenses in NATO would need to be reappraised in light of France's recalcitrant stand.

Greece, Turkey, Iceland, and Spain were members of neither the EEC nor the EFTA, but have coöperated with the 13 member nations of these two organizations through the Organization for European Economic Cooperation. In 1962, Greece, Turkey, and Iceland, along with many of the newly formed African states, were seeking associate membership in the EEC. An associate membership allows a nation to maintain some discriminatory tariffs for assistance to particular industries, but still makes it possible for the country to benefit from the organization as a whole.

The Organization for Economic Cooperation and Development superceded the OEEC when it was ratified in October 1961. The United States and Canada, previously associate members of the OEEC, assumed full membership in the OECD along with 18 European nations. The most urgent reason for the creation of the OECD was to work toward mutually satisfactory trading policies among the members of the EEC and the EFTA. Although the sudden rash of applications for membership in the EEC relieved the original emergency, the OECD has grown in stature as an organ for economic coöperation. Other objectives of the OECD are joint administration of aid to underdeveloped nations and stabilization and expansion of world trade.

At the present time, while there is notable progress in the unification of the European economic market, there has been widespread overlapping of administrative agencies, and the efforts to coordinate and rationalize their activities have been proceeding somewhat slowly.

### Indicative planning

As the Common Market modifies the various economies of Europe, the customs union rôle of the organization will tend to become secondary to other aspects of economic integration. A divergency in domestic economic policies which would lead to marked differences in rates of growth, wage scales, profit margins, and capacity levels will ultimately become next to impossible.

To meet this situation, European businessmen have already begun to modify their traditional ways of working to include some acceptance of "indicative planning," which consists of establishing a board of advisers to encourage businessmen to channel their investments toward areas in need of development for the healthy growth of the economy. The advisers would, at the same time, attempt to divert the excess number of firms from less productive areas to those of greater opportunity in order to achieve balanced growth and the greatest efficiency. Thus, it is hoped that indicative planning will help ensure more vigorous and consistent economic growth without direct governmental action. As of the early 1960's, the French are presently leading the field with their Planning Commissariat and its Four Year Plan, but the Belgians and the British are following suit in rapid order.

Investments planned with more complete and reliable information on exports, imports, employment, output, investment rates, power resources, and transportation should tend to limit the wild instabilities, financial crises, and cycles of stagnation and unemployment which have in the past so beset the capitalistic economies of Europe.

Although the long-range aspects of balanced growth are as important as the short-run gains forseen by individual investors, there would inevitably be deep-seated conflicts between private businessmen and those who envision indicative planning in its entirety.

### American foreign trade after World War II

In spite of the widening of American interests during World War II, foreign trade had not assumed a larger place in the economy, but instead had become a smaller proportion of the total volume of American business than it was in the early days of our colonial and agrarian dependence upon the more extensively developed industrial nations of Europe. In recent decades American foreign trade has grown, but not at a significantly faster rate than domestic trade. Consequently, there has not been any important shift in the relative position of foreign trade as a whole in the total economy.

On the other hand, the rising standard of living in America and increasing industrialization have led the United States into a position of dependence upon other parts of the world for luxury foods and beverages, as well as some staple products, principally from tropical regions. Growing demands of industry for strategic minerals and metals and for natural products, such as rubber and various tropical fibers, have also led to the searching out of foreign sources of supply. Foreign trade has not grown in its total percentage of all business, but it has come to occupy an extremely vital place.

In still another respect American foreign trade has become vital to the national well-being. Our exports have become largely manufactured goods instead of the foods and raw materials which were our sole exports in the early days of the nation. Mechanized industry like that in the United States is extraordinarily efficient and is capable of reducing costs, but it also means a large percentage of the costs are fixed or overhead, resulting from the heavy investment in plant and machinery. In this condition of largely fixed industrial costs, small fluctuations in the volume of output and sales will result in decidedly larger fluctuations in net profits. Fixed costs cannot be reduced when volume falls, and they will not rise very much as volume increases to the limit of plant capacity. In such a situation, foreign exports can be, and sometimes are, the margin between barely profitable and highly successful operations. To a good many American industries, the thriving or languishing condition of foreign trade is quite closely correlated with conditions in the profit-and-loss statement.

American foreign trade is even more important as a factor in the economies of the foreign countries which sell to us and buy from us. Very often sales to or purchases from the United States constitute a large proportion of their business. The United States is one of the largest purchasers of cocoa, coffee, tin, and rubber. Income from the sale of these products may be the principal support for the business of some small countries. If sales to the United States lag, smaller countries can be thrown into depression. Then too, countries without certain types of manufacturing industries expect to buy the needed products of those industries from more completely indus-

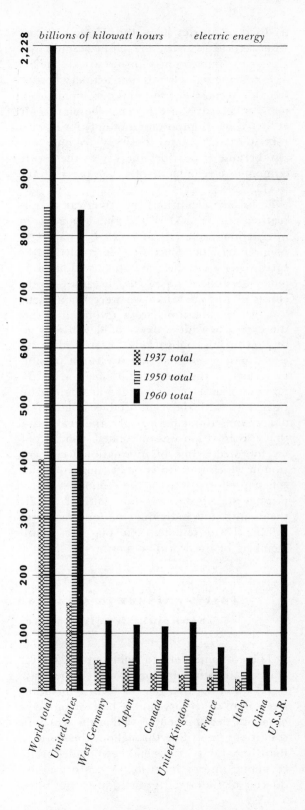

trialized countries like the United States. After World War II, the United States was almost the only country in the world capable of producing many kinds of machinery needed for the reconstruction and development of many other parts of the world. Foreign trade at such times is important, not only for its own contribution to total business volume, but also because it provides the key to the future economic development of other parts of the world.

From such conditions the American people realized after World War II that a new era in international affairs had arrived; a new economic interdependence was inevitable. In the early years after the war, other nations were more dependent upon us, because of the effects of the war, than we were upon them. Yet, while Americans were trying to decide the extent to which they should willingly accept economic obligations toward other nations, most people felt that it was not possible to return to the continental isolation of the mid-nineteenth century. If first thoughts turned toward the comfortable isolation of old, second thoughts brought the realization that this isolation was outmoded. Official policy followed a line of international coöperation in which the United States not only made stop-gap efforts to assist the economies of the war-devastated countries, but continued to aid them until the individual nations recovered sufficiently to resume their places as stable members of the world community.

## Postwar trends in American economic foreign policy

The economic foreign policy of the United States at the end of World War II, then, was based upon an amalgam of factors including more than a century and a half of our own economic development as well as the economic conditions prevailing throughout the world at that time. Long strides had been made toward economic internationalism. A century and a quarter of industrial growth, after the bitter tariff controversy of the early 1820's, found the United States the undisputed industrial leader of the world. Beginning with the Reciprocal Trade Agreements Act of 1934, the United States by the end of World War II had moved steadily toward the removal of tariff barriers to international trade. Major groups of American industries had developed foreign markets for their products, which meant that tariffs could no longer benefit them since they already were able to meet world prices. Specific labor, agricultural, and industrial groups opposed specific tariff reductions which affected them, and doubtless that state of affairs will remain. But, by and large, public opinion as well as that of many important business and industrial groups had come closer to a genuine belief in the economic value of free, multilateral trade than at any time in our national history.

The United States is beginning to see that its own prosperity was based upon participation in a specialized, interdependent, free-trading world community of nations. Our commitment to this position has come about gradually and still proceeds somewhat inconsistently whenever international considerations conflict with the vested interests of domestic producers.

An illustration of our simultaneous leadership and hesitancy in the area of foreign economic affairs can be found in our attitude toward the Reciprocal Trade Agreements Act. Although most of the important trade allowances of the bill have been retained from 1934 into the 1960's, the Act was once allowed to lapse for a time by Congress' failure to renew it, and it has also been subjected to restrictive limitations. Under its authority, however, the Department of State encourages and participates in the General Agreement on Tariffs and Trade, first formulated in 1947. Under GATT, countries which conduct an overwhelming majority of the world's trade have made tariff concessions to each other. This has been one of the most successful examples of American economic coöperation in the international sphere. The "Trade not Aid" demands of European countries in early 1953 put pressure on the United States to take further steps along this path.

In March 1962, following the most comprehensive and complex tariff negotiations in American history, President Kennedy announced for GATT that tariff cuts had been arranged with the Common Market nations, the United Kingdom, and 24 other countries. The United States obtained tariff reductions averaging about 20 per cent from these nations as well as commitments not to increase tariffs or duties on $4.3 billion worth of annual U.S. exports; at the same time, the United States granted similar concessions on $2.9 billion worth of imports. This tariff action, involving 1479 separate commodities, tipped the balance strongly in favor of future tariff bargaining by broad classifications rather than by individual commodities.

### Effect of the Common Market on the trade of the United States

In the long run, the Common Market can have many far-reaching effects on the marketing of American products both at home and abroad. An increase in volume of operations as European producers begin to supply their potential domestic market will enable them to cut costs, and will also allow a greater specialization of labor. Capital investors will be able to move freely in order to establish plants where they are needed for mass-market distribution, to the ultimate benefit not only of European producers, but of workers and consumers as well. The lowering of basic costs in European manufacturing will eventually allow more effective European competition in the Canadian, Latin-American, and African markets. This heightened competitive ability will be especially telling in the production of heavy capital goods.

It is easy to see that manufacturers of American goods who have in the past enjoyed the protection of high tariffs may experience severe discomfiture as European competitors in such industries as cotton textiles, leather goods, watches and clocks, footwear, and toys gain the advantage of lower operating costs and are able to compete effectively in the American as well as in the European market.

Many types of American goods may expect to face stiffer competition abroad, although shipments of finished manufactured goods to western Europe have accounted for no more than 7 per cent of total American merchandise exports in recent years. Among these goods are electrical machinery, heavy engineering equipment, tractors, machine tools, automobiles, photographic equipment, optical supplies, electronic products, and glass. It is likely that reduced exports of finished goods may be more than offset by increased exports of such raw materials as cotton, coal, aluminum and copper alloys, and iron and steel scrap, all of which are essential to expanding European industries.

The stimulation of European industry, its rapid expansion, rising standards of living, and the slurring of national boundaries within Europe will inevitably require that the United States and western Europe coöperate to achieve common economic, military, and political objectives. The liberalizing of American trade policies to keep more harmoniously in step with European tariff adjustments is a logical first step.

Since the United States not only produces vast quantities of strategic raw materials and important agricultural commodities, but also maintains a substantial lead in industrial technology, it is not inconceivable that material benefits would derive from a closer relationship with the Common Market. Thus a sweeping revision of the Reciprocal Trade Agreements Act was enacted by Congress in 1962. In it the President was given discretionary power to modify tariffs and/or quotas as a bargaining weapon for mutual concessions by other countries. The bill also empowered him to revoke tariffs altogether on products manufactured predominantly by the United States and the Common Market countries. These goods would include most types of machinery, all types of transport vehicles and their parts, certain organic and many inorganic chemicals, and some of the primary metals, as well as prefabricated shapes, tobacco, leather, and a wide range of consumer goods, such as photographic supplies, furs, margarine, perfume and nonalcoholic beverages.

### Economic internationalism

In the postwar economic world there have been forces moving both toward and away from increasing international trade, and these opposing forces could be found both within the United States and among other countries of the world. In total effect, the United States has moved far beyond its traditional, isolationist policy of self-containment to become a leader of the movement toward more and freer world trade. On the other hand, many other nations which had never previously been strongly attached to protective policies, now tend in that direction as a result of their ambition to become diversified, industrial nations so far as that might be possible.

There is no doubt that the industrialism upon which the wealth and power of Europe and America have traditionally rested is spreading throughout the world in a manner never before equaled. In a comparatively short time, historically speaking, the distinction between industrially advanced and industrially undeveloped countries may be minimized and perhaps disappear. The United States is playing a large part in this development, by freely sharing technical knowledge and experience with those who request it. Commercial policies of the past will surely be outmoded in the near future. However, trade will always exist because of the differences in resources, climates, and peoples, even if technology becomes more evenly diffused throughout the world. The rôle of the United States in helping to bring about a world in which all peoples will have equal opportunities is in keeping with its past traditions.

For today's world the major questions seem to lie not so much in whether to participate in the international movements toward greater economic coöperation, but rather in how to apportion and meet costs, and how to plan for the future intelligently. It is to be hoped that American business as well as the government will approach these vast problems with sufficient enlightenment to nurture a climate of international economic coöperation and well-being.

## FOR FURTHER READING

Brown, W. A., Jr., and Opie, Redvers. *American Foreign Assistance*. Washington, D.C.: Brookings Institution, 1953. A well-documented study of American foreign policy and foreign aid from 1940 to 1952.

Condliffe, John Bell. *Commerce of Nations*. New York: W. W. Norton & Co., 1950. A history of world trade from the ancient world to post World War II.

*Foreign Policy and the Free Society*. New York: Fund for the Republic, Incorporated, 1959. Paperback edition available through Oceana Publications, Dobbs Ferry, New York.

Gordon, Wendell C. *International Trade, Goods, People, and Ideas*. New York: Alfred A. Knopf, Inc., 1958. Author attempts to integrate ideas in the field of international economics.

Kuznets, Simon. "Foreign Economic Relations of the United States and Their Impact on the Domestic Economy: A Review of Long Term Trends." *Proceedings of the American Philosophical Society*, October, 1948.

Loucks, W. N. *Comparative Economic Systems*. 6th ed. New York: Harper & Row, Publishers. 1961.

Morgenthau, Hans J. *Politics among Nations: The Struggle for Power and Peace*. 3rd ed. rev. New York: Alfred A. Knopf, Inc., 1961. See in particular chapters on the theory of alliances, the balance of power, and the United Nations.

Schwartz, Harry. *Russia's Soviet Economy*. 2nd ed. New York: Prentice-Hall, Inc., 1954.

# Chapter 18:

# The rôle of labor today

We have devoted our efforts up to now to searching out the roots of contemporary American economic life and carrying forward to our own time the developments built on that foundation. A historical thread, based on the passing of time, has tied events together. We have now arrived at the present, the years through which we ourselves have lived. We know more about what is going on today and it seems to us that more things happen in less time. We can no longer sit back, view events in their sequence, and in leisurely fashion assess cause and effect. We must observe and analyze the characteristics of today's situation. Therefore, this and the remaining chapters will be devoted to a discussion of the contemporary economic system of the United States. We will attempt to gain some understanding of a few of the large problem areas we know to exist.

The problem of labor organization is not the greatest of contemporary problems, but it is highly typical of the new day in American economic history. It involves the dilemma of an agricultural and frontier people who have developed into an industrial nation. Traits acquired on the farm and on the frontier show up differently in the automobile plants of Detroit or the steel mills of Pittsburgh or Gary. Let us then examine some phases of the labor problem with the question constantly in mind, "How have historical backgrounds helped to make this situation or this problem what it is?"

### The rôle of unions in national life

*Labor and the competitive market*

The acceptance of new technological developments stemming from the Industrial Revolution wrought significant changes in the lives of the laboring classes of all nations. In the past, workers had participated in a year-round subsistence economy in which tasks were performed according to familiar and traditional patterns. Thus, there developed a clear sense of "belonging"—of being needed for specific and necessary functions. While the recognition of the worker as an individual was almost nonexistent, he had a place in the life of the community that was essential to the self-sufficiency of the whole.

In contrast, as industrialism spread, the worker no longer had the same sense of playing a vital rôle in the economy. With the advent of specialization and division of labor, his tasks were not only monotonous but were often dangerous as well. Accustomed as he was to a rural way of life, the chaos of the factory was new and bewildering. His wages remained low, his hours of work continued to be long, and his few leisure moments were spent in the unattractive surroundings of an urban slum. The industrial worker thus had little reason for personal pride in accomplishment. He had little more importance than a cipher and represented only a pawn in the productive system. When goods could be profitably sold, there was a demand for his services; when, for reasons beyond his control, there was a decrease in consumer demand for goods, the worker was dismissed without consideration for his personal interests. Therefore, it is hardly surprising that most of the support for the policy of *laissez faire* came primarily from merchants and businessmen, and that workers were either indifferent or hostile. Almost intuitively manual workers feared a policy which would make their employment and wages a matter of competition in the labor market. In spite of labor opposition, the *laissez-faire* policy was put into operation in the industrialized areas of western Europe and in America. Labor became in fact what Karl Marx called it in his critical writings about the middle of the nineteenth century—a commodity. Labor was bought in the open market by industrial employers in the same spirit in which they bought raw materials or other factors of production. Public opinion never quite willingly accepted this situation in either Europe or the United States. The United States Congress declared in the Clayton Act of 1914, "The labor of a human being is not a commodity or an article of commerce," thereby halfway conceding that it had been regarded as a commodity.

This section of the Clayton Act had been inserted at the insistence of American Federation of Labor leaders after the Supreme Court had ruled in a series of cases that the Sherman Anti-Trust Act did apply to the trade-union movement. In a number of decisions, the court had upheld the use of injunctions in labor disputes. Hence labor leaders began to urge revision of antitrust legislation to redress labor's competitive position.

If competition is to work effectively, both buyers and sellers must be constantly alert to discover the best opportunities available to them. Business has not found free competition either possible or desirable in all cases. For the industrial worker, the requirements are clearly impossible. If he were well enough informed to be a good competitor in the labor market, he would probably know enough and be capable of getting a different and better job anyway. A worker could never relax and enjoy life among pleasant neighbors and co-workers, because to be strictly at his competitive best he should be constantly searching for a better job in another plant and perhaps in another community. Even a little bit of laziness and mental inertia does not go with competition. Further, attachment to a home town or section of the country would be a luxury the industrial worker could not afford. Adam Smith, who developed many of the arguments for a competitive economy in his book *The Wealth of Nations,* recognized many limitations on the competitive labor market. For example, he recognized that it was practically impossible to prevent employers from agreeing at least tacitly to hold wages down.

The mere listing of requirements of an effective competitive market makes it quite clear that they are not met well by anything other than an imaginary labor market. Probably the employer can come nearer than the worker to being able to act in the way an ideal competitive market situation would require.

Association or coöperation has always resulted when individual action could not achieve satisfactory results. In the case of modern workers in industry and business, the union is the result of the spontaneous impulse toward joint action. In business, combinations, pooling agreements, and many forms of corporate concentration have resulted from a similar impulse. Modern economic systems in America and the more advanced countries throughout the world have not remained purely competitive in a strict sense that would have been acceptable to Adam Smith and his contemporaries. Both business and labor have tended to form into economic units larger than a single individual. In fact, the joint-stock company, the modern business corporation which dates back four hundred years, is an example of collective action taken by capitalists when it became apparent that no one of them alone could provide sufficient capital for foreign trading enterprises. Our modern economy is characterized by many such kinds of collective action.

The question remains whether or not these collective trends on the part of both business and labor threaten to destroy the free-enterprise and free-labor system. Although monopolies in business or labor can destroy opportunities for freedom, it is not inevitable. We have had much experience in curbing the monopolistic tendencies of business: in America, extending back three-quarters of a century or more, and in Europe, extending back through the mercantilist era to the guilds of the medieval towns. The plain and rather simple truth of the matter is that modern life has tended to throw people into groups of various kinds—economic, social, and political. Individualism is more a slogan than a fact of modern life.

Society, then, has developed certain "bloc" tendencies which are inevitable. Although they may superficially impose restrictions upon freedom, in a very real sense they increase freedom. Group action makes many things possible which are out of the reach and scope of choice of the individual.

Fig. XVIII-1 *Changes in the characteristics of the labor force between 1920 and 1960. Figures exclude proprietors, self-employed persons, agricultural workers, unpaid family workers, domestic servants, and personnel of Armed Forces.*

INDUSTRIAL DISTRIBUTION OF EMPLOYED WORKERS
*(thousands of persons)*

|  | 1920 | 1930 | 1940 | 1950 | 1960 |
|---|---|---|---|---|---|
| Total | 27,088 | 29,143 | 32,058 | 44,738 | 54,347 |
| *Mining  All employed workers* | 1,230 | 1,000 | 916 | 889 | 709 |
| *Contract construction* | 848 | 1,372 | 1,294 | 2,333 | 2,882 |
| *Manufacturing* | 10,534 | 9,401 | 10,780 | 14,967 | 16,762 |
| *Transportation and public utilities* | 3,998 | 3,675 | 3,013 | 3,977 | 4,017 |
| *Wholesale and retail trade* | 4,623 | 6,064 | 6,940 | 9,645 | 11,412 |
| *Finance, insurance, and real estate* | 1,110 | 1,398 | 1,436 | 1,824 | 2,684 |
| *Service and miscellaneous* | 2,142 | 3,084 | 3,477 | 5,077 | 7,361 |
| *Government* | 2,603 | 3,149 | 4,202 | 6,026 | 8,520 |

## The functions of collective bargaining

The core of union activity concerning the terms and coditions of employment has long rested in collective bargaining between union and employer. The alternative would be to resume the individual bargaining between the worker and his employer which had been traditional before the rise of unions.

An examination of the respective amounts of bargaining strength held by the individual worker and by his employer almost invariably shows the advantage to be on the employer's side. The employer is almost sure to understand the labor market better than the worker. He is more familiar with prevailing wage rates than the worker himself. If the worker does not like the wage offered him, his ability to wait until a better job shows up or until the labor market improves is sharply limited by the fact that neither he nor his family can wait too long to find clothing and shelter.

From lack of knowledge and from economic necessity, the worker is, therefore, usually at a distinct disadvantage. Knowing this, the employer would be more than human who did not convert his bargaining advantage into an economic advantage in the form of lower wages. That the worker felt at a disadvantage in such bargaining is attested to by the fact that millions have joined unions to have their bargaining done for them by union officials. As a part of the union, the worker has more bargaining power through the union's collective demands, a power which he could not effectively exert as an individual.

Collective action is vital in the labor market under most but not all circumstances. During wartime with its attendant labor shortage or during times of intensive prosperity when many employers have a backlog of business, a qualified worker can capably bargain for himself. If he cannot make a satisfactory agreement with one employer, it is quite easy to go to another. At such times of tight labor supply, the competition in the labor market is keenest on the employer's side. He very naturally does not like it because it does not give him control over all of the factors that affect the operation of his business. If there are indications that the tight labor market will become chronic, the employer has every incentive to adopt new technological methods to relieve his close dependence upon the unfavorable labor market. For such reasons, the ability of a worker to bargain effectively for himself is not likely to last indefinitely.

The process of collective bargaining is designed to provide a kind of "constitution for industry." Most matters of disagreement between employers and workers are likely to receive treatment in the contract that results from successful bargaining and, finally, agreement. Where a strong union exists, the balance of bargaining power is changed fundamentally as compared with individual bargaining. Union officers make it their business to know the labor market, both local and national, and thus have a status which no employee could have in bargaining.

It is questionable whether even with a strong union the ability of the employees to "wait out" an agreement is as great as that of the employer. Although he would lose heavily, the employer might be able to survive shutting down his plant for weeks or months; a union would be almost destroyed by a similar delay in reaching agreement. Individual families of the workers could not stand such prolonged absence of income and would have to move elsewhere in search of work. On the other hand, the local union of a strong national organization is often stronger and more effective in exerting pressure in bargaining than any single employer can be. A union may be able to dictate terms, especially where a national pattern has already been established by the largest firms in any industry. Whether their power is well used or abused, unions have in some industries at least redressed the old imbalance between employer and employee. As both industry and unions have multiplied, collective bargaining agreements have tended to become national in scope and to be the result of negotiations between large national unions and either large firms or groups of firms doing business on a national scale or by national industrial associations.

The evidence strongly indicates that in the past the lack of a feeling of security was one of the most objectionable aspects of the worker's situation. This insecurity was partly a corollary of the low income level and partly resulted from a lack of personal control over his job. It was not accidental that the greatest expansion of unions in American history came after the greatest wave of unemployment which the country had ever known.

Many workers, in the great depression following 1929, lost not only their jobs and source of income but also their automobiles, their insurance policies, and their homes. It was a horrifying experience. It is small wonder that workers turned to a new political administration to help them out and also turned to unions as a possible way to gain greater job security. For many years, through the 1920's, the American labor movement, symbolized by the American Federation of Labor, had opposed such federal assistance as old-age and unemployment insurance on the grounds that they were socialistic. On the other hand, in European countries such as England and Germany, even conservative unions and political parties had long before accepted government-administered unemployment insurance as a necessary accompaniment to an industrial civilization. But in America it required the blow of the great depression to bring labor to demand unemployment insurance.

In agreement with labor's felt need, there emerged in 1936 a book, *The General Theory of Employment, Interest, and Money,* by John Maynard (Lord) Keynes. In this volume, Lord Keynes introduced a startling new economic theory to help explain the cause of the great depression and to suggest ways to avoid future debacles of this sort. The practical principle put forth was that, to maintain continued prosperity, there must be a steady and substantial flow of income into the hands of the working classes through a high level of well-paid employment.

If there should be any weakening of what Keynes called the "propensity to consume," or the inclination of consumers to keep up their ordinary rate of spending, a dangerous situation could result in the economy. If a decline in the propensity to consume should be accompanied by a decline in the rate of investment of industrial and business capital, resulting from poor expectations for the future, a depression would be forced upon the economy due to an insufficient flow of income into demand for either consumers' goods or capital equipment. Obviously the first of these adverse conditions would produce the second, since capital investment for the future is wise only when the businessman can look forward to continued and growing demand for his product. In such a state of affairs, the economy would be forced by insufficient spending and investing to reduce rates of production and employment. This condition could conceivably become chronic unless some external stimulus should jar the economic system, or unless the government should assume the function of compensating for deficiencies in the private economy by actions of its own, such as the incurring of debt by spending and investing more than its current income would support.

This economic theory eminently suited labor's views, and union leaders eagerly accepted it. Discussions and arguments in the field of economic theory were rather new to the old-line labor leader, but the leadership of the new unions which sprang up in the mid-1930's found in the new theory a powerful ally in the battle for improved conditions for workers. Full employment and high wages formed the bulwark upon which the entire economic structure was built. If wages were cut and workers laid off without providing a temporarily guaranteed income, the whole economic house of cards might come tumbling down.

Following the unconstitutional attempt in 1933-1935 to place a basement under wages and prices through "Codes of Fair Competition," the first national effort to sustain the income of the laid-off workers was passed by Congress on August 14, 1935, as part of the New Deal legislative program. It was included as the unemployment compensation section of the Social Security Act. The law provided for a tax levy on the total payrolls of all employers of eight or more workers, with a few exceptions such as agriculture, but waived 90 per cent of the tax to employers in those states which adopted an unemployment compensation system conforming with federal standards; all the states quickly responded by passing the desired laws.

The protection thus provided by government has given industrial workers a sense of security in the knowledge that, if they lose their jobs, some income will be forthcoming for a period of time, presumably sufficient for them to find employment. The specific length of time for which each state will pay benefits has varied greatly as have the costs, which are normally borne by employers as a tax on payrolls, but the federal government subsidized a maximum of 39 weeks in a law passed in 1961.

Specific union contracts for additional security have over the years come to supplement the general unemployment compensation program. The most important of these is popularly called the Guaranteed Annual Wage. The GAW was initiated in the automobile industry where workers are particularly subject to unemployment each year due to annual model changeovers. In the earliest version of the GAW, the contract in 1955 with General Motors called for the company to put up 5 cents per worker per hour until a fund of $400 per worker had been accumulated. From this fund and its interest, the temporarily laid-off worker could draw $25 per week for 26 weeks. This money was to be supplemental to the unemployment compensation that each worker was receiving from the state.

Today, workers are also covered by similar programs in the steel, aluminum, rubber, and glass industries so that, despite interruptions in regular employment schedules, the worker can expect a fairly constant yearly income. GAW payments and unemployment compensation payments together act as a countercyclical automatic stabilizer. In the past, when production slowed for some reason, furloughs without pay tended to occur. This forced members of the working community to conserve what cash and savings they had. In turn, as additional industries experienced a decrease in the effective demand for their products, layoffs in these industries became necessary in order to keep production and sales in balance.

With the instituting of GAW and unemployment compensation payments, the worker is better able to maintain his normal spending patterns even during a temporary layoff, and consumer demands tend to persist more nearly in their accustomed manner rather than turning sharply downward. Thus, in theory at least, GAW and unemployment compensation help maintain a continuous balanced consumer demand even when production is temporarily unbalanced. Further, the worker with a guaranteed yearly income is more apt to be eligible for and to utilize long-term credit to purchase expensive durable consumer goods such as automobiles or refrigerators. When the worker was subject to a highly fluctuating income, credit sources were reluctant to lend to him because the risks were too great. On the other hand, the worker with a more stable income could be relied upon to maintain the payments on those items he really wanted and which became with time a standard part of the home, such as the TV set and the modernistic kitchen.

### Wages, hours, and working conditions

The average union member may even today be somewhat hazy in the theoretical understanding of his rights in collective bargaining, but there are three aspects of collective bargaining that he considers vital to his economic interest. These concern his actual wage, the number of hours of his employment, and his working conditions.

The first successful federal legislation to establish a basic "floor" for wages was the Fair Labor Standards Act of June 25, 1938, which provided for the achievement by gradual stages of a minimum wage of 40 cents per hour for industries engaging in interstate commerce. With the advent of World War II most wage levels quickly rose above this minimum. Even though subsequent legislation raised the minimum to 75 cents per hour, later to $1.00, and more recently to $1.25 per hour, the level of union wages has stayed consistently above the basic federal minimum. It should also be noted that, since the end of World War II, wages for unionized industries have remained consistently higher than those for nonunion types, as is shown in the following figures for representative industries. In 1945, gross hourly earnings in the unionized durable goods and building construction fields were $1.11 and $1.38, respectively, as against $.78 in retail trade and $.65 in laundries, both typical of nonunion enterprises. By 1950, the wage rates for heavily unionized workers in durable goods had climbed to $1.54 and building construction to $2.03, while retail trade was $1.18 and laundries were $.86. By 1959, hourly wages for durable goods workers were $2.38 and for building construction $3.21, as against $1.76 for retail trade and $1.17 for laundries. Thus, between 1945 and 1959 wages more than doubled in all these industries except laundries, where the increase was 1.8 times the 1945 figure. While the skill differential partially explains the contrast in wages, practical bargaining by union leaders has effectively maintained for union members a nominal income notably higher than that of nonunion workers.

Nonetheless, the $1.25 per hour specified in the federal minimum-wage law of 1961 does materially affect the wage structure of some sectors of the economy. This is especially true of those industries which have low value productivity per worker. In those industries where the minimum wage has risen above the average worker's productivity, the standard set by the federal government may force plant managers to reconsider the various components of production. When labor costs increase, some managers find it possible to decrease total costs by lessening their reliance upon labor and turning instead to the use of machinery.

In other instances, the increase in labor costs without the technological capacity to compensate for high federal minimum wages has presented American producers with a serious competitive dilemma in both domestic and foreign markets. Foreign producers with similar production techniques but with lower wage levels have been able to introduce their products into the American market at somewhat lower prices than is possible for the American producer if he is to realize reasonable profits.

In recent years, the development of "escalator clauses" in wage contracts has been of great advantage in protecting the purchasing power of union workers. Starting with the General Motors–United Automobile Workers contract of 1948, escalator clauses have specified that the wages of the worker covered in the contract should be automatically adjusted as the cost of living shifts. Both parties felt that by using this method, the wages of workers would stay proportionate to a given level of purchasing power. If basic living costs were to increase, the workers in the industries covered by escalator contracts would receive an increased pay check, thereby preserving some semblance of constant purchasing power.

Wage increases in the form of "fringe benefits" have supplemented escalator clauses for many workers. As was noted in the chapter on World War II, union negotiators during and since the war years have gained such extras for their members as pensions, insurance, medical aid, paid vacations, paid legal holidays and other financial benefits.

The importance accorded these fringe benefits is vividly illustrated by the 1954 contracts between the United Automobile Workers and General Motors, Ford, and Chrysler. Under these contracts, workers were to receive only 8 cents per hour in direct cash wage increases, but the companies estimated that the fringe benefits granted in the contracts would cost them another 12 cents per hour per worker. In this particular series of contracts over one half of the actual cost increase to the companies involved non-take-home pay to the workers.

These fringe benefits have added appreciably to the effective income of the union worker. Since he would want most of these benefits anyway if he could afford them, and since in this form they are not counted as taxable income, the company assumption of the cost has made possible a higher plane of living than the cash take-home pay would indicate. The union worker has become the recipient of goods and services that his non-union neighbors often have to buy for themselves. Industrial management is frequently able to negotiate the purchase of fringe benefits for much less than the cost to individuals through private channels. Since a majority of these fringe benefits also represent a cost of doing business, they are in part tax-deductible for the corporation. Consequently, corporation representatives have not been altogether reluctant to allow the addition of such benefits, as long as unions are also powerful enough to derive equal provisions from competitors.

One unexpected facet of wage improvement, which has had surprising significance for the economy as a whole, has been the monetary shift in the status of the laboring class. In 1940, the income level of unionized skilled and semiskilled workers was below that of the white-collar worker. After World War II, however, successful wage negotiations, combined with continued overtime earnings, raised the income level of skilled unionized workers above that of the white-collar group, so that skilled labor purchasing power was generally surpassed only by the professional and business classes. Semiskilled wages have risen high enough to enable these workers to copy the purchasing patterns of those higher up the scale. The impact of this new purchasing power soon made itself felt in sales increases

*Fig. XVIII-2  Average earnings of workers vary in relation to pay per hour and average number of hours worked per week. This chart shows the changing average of earnings between 1923 and 1961.*

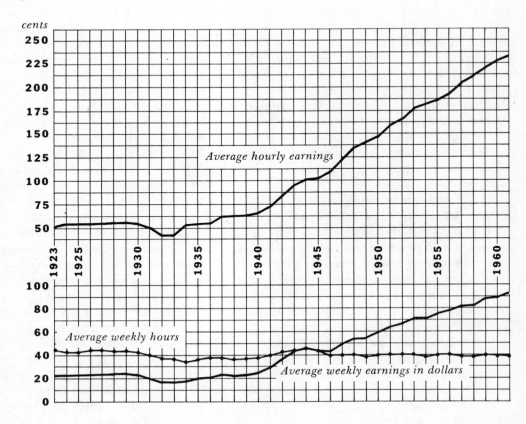

well beyond those which might have been anticipated for replacement of worn-out or obsolete goods. All sorts of durable products, such as automobiles, home appliances, and television sets—the last a post World War II development—have gained a vast new market. By means of the television screen, advertisers are able to reach a heretofore unaffected group of potential customers. By encouraging preference for conspicuous display (which seems to add to product appeal), a host of extraneous gadgets and trimmings have been introduced which have created a favorable impression not necessarily related to quality. Former pacesetters in industry have protested vainly against the toppling of traditional standards of quality as manufacturers have hastened to take advantage of a market attracted by surface display and by a desire to demonstrate a growing worker affluence.

Although the amount in the paycheck tends to be of primary interest to most workers, the number of weekly working hours is also of vital concern. The Fair Labor Standards Act of 1938 designated 40 hours per week as a normal maximum beginning in 1940. This had a marked effect on wages paid during World War II. Because of exceptionally heavy production schedules, many workers regularly earned overtime pay; consequently by the end of the war this additional income had become so much a commonplace expectancy that families regularly budgeted it into their spending patterns.

In the years immediately after the Second World War, there was great demand for durable goods, which the general consuming public was able to purchase with cash. People had not been able to obtain these durable goods during the war because manufacturing plants had been converted to war production. Therefore, at the end of the war, consumer demand was high enough to warrant a return to full and immediate civilian production. In many cases, overtime pay continued as usual for plant employees. Hence workers had the means to satisfy their needs and thereby sustained a consistent demand for the available supply of durable goods.

In 1950, at about the same time that this postwar market for durable goods was reaching fulfillment, the United States became involved in the Korean conflict. Military purchases and the fear of shortages similar to those experienced during World War II served to stimulate the economy by reinstituting the pressure to produce durable goods. Output was expanded wherever possible, resulting in renewed overtime for workers and a further upswing in their income levels.

By the mid-1950's, a new balance was reached between the supply and the effective demand for many durable goods. By this time, many manufacturing concerns had adopted decidedly more efficient productive methods. They had also invested heavily in new machinery and sought to lower costs by eliminating overtime. The effect on the economy was greater than the actual monetary difference would seem to warrant. Industrial workers had become so accustomed to receiving extra income that the elimination of overtime came as a jolt. As a result, workers modified their spending more than proportionately. This in turn tended to halt the purchase of those durable goods which could be postponed in order to conserve the remaining income or to meet outstanding debts. Thus a new instability crept into the system, bringing in its wake business recessions of variable duration in 1956, 1958, and 1960.

While the assurance of satisfactory working conditions does not have the financial impact of either wage or hour considerations, it does contribute significantly to the working effectiveness of labor. It took many years for unions to overcome the traditional managerial arguments against accepting responsibility for accidents. Companies long maintained that the worker assumed responsibility for knowing the dangers of the job when he accepted employment and was therefore liable for his own safety; that the workers could easily contribute through carelessness to the accidents in which they became involved; and that, if negligence on the part of fellow employees contributed to the accident, then they were responsible. These three defenses were not completely

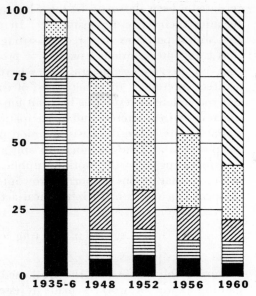

*Fig. XVIII–3 The distribution of income among urban families of two or more persons between 1935 and 1960. Shaded areas represent, from top to bottom, $5000 and over, $3000 and under $5000, $2000 and under $3000, $1000 and under $2000, and under $1000.*

*Unions and public policy*

The rôle of unions and the loyalty of union members will not be fully comprehended if we confine our attention solely to collective bargaining and economic job security. The real importance to the worker of the non-economic values of his union can be appreciated only against a historic background in which the industrial worker was almost a cast-off. During much of the industrial age, he was employed at a type of work which was close to the bottom of his list of preferences and he was likely to be taken on today and laid off tomorrow or next week. His pay was what his employer wanted it to be. Such conditions do not create a stable and satisfied employee. Industry itself has now tackled this condition through an expansion of its personnel work, but unions were first, and perhaps still are most important, in giving workers a sense of dignity and a feeling for the worth of their occupations.

As union membership grew and spread from industry to industry, unions began to devote attention to matters that extended beyond the bounds of any single industry or the relations between worker and employer on the job. These broader interests concerned such matters as welfare legislation and general labor legislation deemed essential to worker welfare. To secure favorable legislation, unions found it necessary to pay attention to the elected representatives in Congress and the state legislatures. Thus, a natural evolution of union interests led unions into political action. When this stage of union development had been reached, the union movement assumed leadership not only for its own members but also for other workers. Actually, a conflict of interest has begun to develop between the social-welfare aims of union leaders and those of government legislators. Each group has distinct objectives. Government representatives, in theory at least, seek to accomplish the greatest good for the greatest number; this cannot

overthrown until manufacturers were required by law to carry compulsory insurance for their workers, or at least assume the accident risk. Only when this was done did it become more economical to take reasonable measures for the prevention of injuries, such as adopting safety regulations and installing protective equipment, rather than paying high premiums resulting from a high incidence of worker accidents.

In 1902, Maryland became the first state to enact such a law, and Mississippi in 1948 was the last of the old forty-eight states to enact protective legislation. The two newest states of the Union, Alaska and Hawaii, also have laws requiring insurance for workers.

Another union-gained improvement in working conditions has been the establishment of machinery for the settlement of grievances. While most of the issues that arise are minor, the provision of an adequate means for airing complaints and protecting the worker against arbitrary discipline or discharge helps eliminate a number of irritations before they accumulate.

help but conflict at times with the more restricted purposes of union representatives, who are primarily interested in the welfare of workers, and more specifically in benefits for *union* workers. Nevertheless, aggressive union leaders have seldom been averse to accepting the rôle of political spokesman for the underdog. It marks an extension of their influence beyond the limits of their own organizations, and they have become public figures whose voices were and are heard relative to many problems of the day.

This tendency for unions to concern themselves with the political environment within which they operate has been a rapidly growing one in the United States. It has invited opposition from some persons who feel that whatever right unions may have to interest themselves in employer-employee relations, they have no right to organize labor as a political group for political objectives. In fact, analysis of election results up to the present time seems to indicate that not only is the political leadership of unions not accepted by many workers outside of unions; it is also not accepted by many union members themselves.

Whatever the rights and wrongs of this matter may be, it is clear that the American labor movement remains much less politically inclined than its European counterpart. European unions have actively sought through labor parties to change the economic and political systems of their respective countries. In this endeavor they have had much broader support than that of their own membership. In spite of the fact that union activities in the American political arena are of less consequence than those of European labor parties, union leaders have taken on the mantle of those who instinctively distrust "big business." The political strength of American labor has grown to such proportions that it often acts as a countervailing power to big business interests.

In more routine political matters, unions have taken an active part in areas where their membership is substantial in promoting liberal support of public education and good government in general. Unions draw their membership from groups in society which have

repeatedly been shown to be most lax in performing their civic reponsibilities. In order that union positions may receive strong support from voters, unions have had to promote "get out the vote" campaigns. They have had a direct interest in these activities, of course, but the collateral result has been an improvement in citizen interest and participation in public affairs. Since the basis of union political power is a broad membership and a general following from the working public, it is not often that unions support narrow interests or special privilege in their political activity.

### Legislation affecting unions

During the depression, the weakened bargaining power of workers made it essential that federal power be used to guarantee individual bargaining rights if an adequate balance were to be maintained. Section 7A of the ill-fated National Industrial Recovery Act, guaranteed the right of labor to organize and to bargain collectively through representatives of their own choosing. When the Supreme Court declared the NIRA unconstitutional on May 27, 1935, Section 7A became the core of the National Labor Relations Act (the Wagner Act), enacted in July 1935, which continued far more vigorously government encouragement of organized labor. Union organization spread rapidly, becoming almost universal in some industries. Collective bargaining increased substantially and millions of workers found themselves protected by agreements, often negotiated on an industry-wide basis.

Union membership continued to grow rapidly during World War II under the compromise "maintenance of membership" clause worked out by the National War Labor Board. Workers were at least temporarily willing to join and support unions. Employers, on the other hand, often grew increasingly restive under the maintenance of membership arrangement. They felt almost as though unions were being forced on them by law. Opposition to certain aspects of the Wagner Act also developed. It was said that the Wagner Act talked about workers' "rights" and employers' "duties." Many employers and business associations representing employers began to say with increasing insistence that the balance needed to be redressed, that workers had duties as well as rights, and that employers had rights as well as duties. This was a growing feeling in the country as the war drew to a close.

At the end of the war, as the patriotic desire to conform with wartime regulations was removed, the whole controversial issue of industrial relations seized public attention. Labor had been increasingly restive under the limitations on wage increases maintained by the National War Labor Board. In 1946, negotiations were begun by almost all unions with their employers for wage increases to compensate for price increases that had occurred during the latter part of the war period and for the increases in productivity which were correctly assumed to have occurred throughout the entire war. Employers, also restive under the restrictions imposed upon them by the Wagner Act and resentful of the newly acquired power of many unions, were not willing to grant the large wage increases requested. A wave of strikes occurred which surpassed anything ever before experienced in the United States. Employers' groups became ever more loudly insistent upon revision of the Wagner Act. The Labor-Management Relations Act of 1947, better known as the Taft-Hartley Act, was the result of that sentiment. The Republican party had gained control of Congress in the 1946 elections, and, with the aid of conservative Democrats, enacted the law over the veto of President Truman, whose administration continued to stand by the Wagner Act without essential change.

The growth in strength of many unions and the demonstrations of arrogance by some labor leaders during the war years had disgusted many people. The intent of the Taft-Hartley Act was to curb what was considered to be the excessive power which the Wagner Act had given unions. In 1947, the country was prosperous, conservative, and more concerned about the problems of an inflationary business boom than about the possibility of a depression, which was thought to be a thing of the past. While the Taft-Hartley Act gave employers a stronger hand in bargaining with their employees through more actively advocating the curbing of union organizations, it did not deny workers the right to join unions. Taft-Hartley also enabled employers to schedule elections when it best suited their cause, and added to the elections a vote to determine whether employees wished no union, or which union they preferred. This latter provision outlawed the closed shop, and the union shop was permitted only when agreed to by a majority of those in the bargaining unit. In situations where the union was weak or where worker apathy was great, the new managerial privileges could only have a crippling effect on the union. However, the basic provisions of the Wagner Act regarding the National Labor Relations Board were continued, including the rights of workers to bargain collectively and to settle accusations of unfair labor practices brought against employers.

The Taft-Hartley Act, unfortunately, did not attack the vital issue of how to preserve the democratic rights of individual workers within their unions. The apathy of many workers had curtailed the effectiveness of rules regulating union administration, and allowed some unions to fall into the hands of racketeers and other corrupting elements.

In 1957, the investigations by the McClellan Committee of the United States Senate concerning the conditions within the Teamsters, the Bakery and Confectionery Workers, and the Textile Workers unions appalled the public. The additional exposures by this committee in 1958 of conditions among the Operating Engineers, the Carpenters, and, again, the Teamsters, forced other labor leaders to take stock of their own position. The public exposure of the corruption of some union leaders put the rest on the defensive. Union activities were no longer sacrosanct and a period of self-inspection began. This reached its height during the biennial convention in 1958 of the A.F.L.-C.I.O. when the Teamsters, Bakers, and Laundry Workers, whose number totaled one tenth of the membership of the A.F.L.-C.I.O., were expelled.

Federal action to continue this drive against corruption within the unions, culminated in the Landrum-Griffin Act of 1959. This law provided for an election of union officers by secret ballot at least every five years, and for the barring from union office of anyone who has been convicted of a serious crime. The law also prohibited "blackmail" picketing—that is, picketing by the union before petitioning the National Labor Relations Board for permission to hold an election to certify the NLRB as the bargaining agent. "Hot cargo" contracts —those in which union members refuse to handle shipments originating in nonunion organizations—were also forbidden. Lastly, the law provided that strikers have the right to vote in electing a bargaining agent to represent them in negotiations, even though the strikers themselves have been replaced by other workers. Thus the Landrum-Griffin Act has curtailed some of the worst union abuses, but neither unions nor management consider present legislation to be the final answer.

A bitter expression of antiunion sentiment became evident during the mid-1950's with the real push in many states for the enactment of "right-to-work" laws. Although support for such laws was greatest in the nonindustrial states, Indiana did vote favorably in 1957 for such a law and thus became the first state in the manufacturing heartland of the nation to do so. The term *right-to-work* has been something of a misnomer, since it has sometimes been misinterpreted to mean an attempt to eliminate discrimination as to race, creed or color in hiring. Instead, the most popular form of the right-to-work law provided that an individual might or might not join a union, depending on the dictates of his conscience. Hence, in practice there could be no real pressure on an individual to support union activities. From the union point of view, the right-to-work law meant that while union workers made a financial and physical sacrifice to gain specific improvements for their members, a group of nonunion workers could reap the benefits and yet be unwilling to pay their share of the bill.

## The merging of unions

In December 1955, after twenty years of interunion competition, the American Federation of Labor (A.F.L.) and the Congress of Industrial Organizations (C.I.O.) began a slow process of merging. By accenting the fundamental principles on which all factions could agree, a unified if delicate amalgamation encompassing close to 15 million union members was created. However, problems of plant organization and questions of jurisdiction between craft type and industrial type organizations have continued to plague the A.F.L.-C.I.O. Jurisdictional disputes became so troublesome that in 1959 the delegates to the A.F.L.-C.I.O. convention held in San Francisco approved the outlines of a new plan designed to end the nagging problems of these disputes. This proposal called for setting up an arbitration board whose decisions would be the terminal authority in the settlement of jurisdictional differences. The rules on which the board was to base its decisions, however, were extremely nebulous.

Actually, union competition remains much as it was before, except for the "no-raiding" policy which was established in 1954. At that time, the signatory unions agreed to accept mediation and, failing that, impartial arbitration. The effectiveness of this agreement has been limited because the pact does not cover either nonunionized workers or those unionized workers who are not signatories to the pact. The absence of the United Mine Workers and the Teamsters, as well as a number of expelled left wing and C.I.O. unions, has made it difficult to keep peace between rival jurisdictional groups. This is particularly true because of the pivotal rôle of the transportation contingents.

## Big unions are a by-product of big business

Very frequently, a high degree of unionization and large individual unions exist in industries characterized by big productive or manufacturing units and in areas where relatively few firms control a large proportion of the production. In other words, big industry and big unions go together. Big industry virtually creates big unions by giving large groups of employees common interests and a common way of life. The large unions which violate this rule are in nearly every case those of skilled workers, as in the construction industry, where a craft interest drew workers together even before the advent of mass production.

Since the depression of the 1930's, large unions have become increasingly significant in the American economic picture. A table prepared by the Bureau of Labor Statistics for 1950 shows 32 manufacturing and nonmanufacturing industries with from 80 to 100 per cent unionization. Among these highly organized industries, each of which approximates one million workers, are automobiles, steel, men's and women's clothing, and coal mining. In any historical sense these are indeed big unions.

Today unions have reached both a size and a significance which suggest that further growth is likely to be proportionately slower than in the past. Since 1958, when union membership stood at approximately 15 million, the total has begun to decline slightly. This is hardly surprising, since the bulk of union membership is found in the mass production industries, where the decimating effects of automation on the work force have become appreciable. Therefore, in seeking to broaden union membership, labor leaders will of necessity seek to recruit members from hitherto unorganized areas of employment. This will require a reappraisal of union tactics, tailored to appeal not only to workers located in the deep south, agricultural laborers, and workers in the service trades, but to government employees as well. Except for agriculture, all of these groups have already benefited to some degree by the passage of federal welfare legislation, which establishes minimum wages and maximum hours for workers producing goods involved in interstate commerce. Thus, those traditional advantages of unions which have helped their growth in the past do not have the same appeal to these nonunion groups.

Another reason why union membership will seem less desirable is that white-collar workers feel they have no particular need to gain the recognition of their worth as human beings through union membership. They, as well as other salaried employees, often consider themselves superior to the blue-collar worker with whom they feel little identification. Therefore, in order to attract these independent groups, unions must necessarily shift from their rôle in representing tightly organized industrial workers to that of becoming the successful spokesmen for many groups with a quite different orientation. Most of the unorganized contingent will be inclined to be skeptical of union activities since the tradition of *laissez faire* is strong among these individuals.

Unions also must solve internal problems if they are to continue to function successfully as powerful working-class representatives. The growing economic benefits which unions and government provide may easily erode the interest of those who in the past have been enthusiastic union supporters. As most workers have already gained not only a comfortable financial position but a reasonable sense of personal worth as well, some are forgetful that they owe many of these benefits to union efforts in their behalf. Because material comforts and reasonable guarantees of personal income and job security have become so commonplace, many workers have lost their zeal as crusaders.

National labor leaders have recently turned in another direction to develop organizational strength—that of concerning themselves with problems of factory efficiency. Hence, they are attempting to participate in activities formerly reserved for management. Union leaders have in some industries sought to advise management on such decisions as changes in production techniques, product pricing, and plant location, and have asked for access to company books for implementation of profit-sharing programs as well as for more effective bargaining. Insofar as labor gains entry into areas which have in the past been managerial prerogatives, this trend has ramifications of far greater consequence to the public interest than their past preoccupation with wages, hours, and working conditions. It is still too early to see how far this drive toward broadening the influence of labor will go. It is certain that automation has strongly stimulated the desire to look beyond the particular job to the process as a whole.

## Employer relationships with unions

### Early opposition to unions

The history of union growth reveals intense employer hostility toward unions. The bloodshed and loss of life on both sides in the strikes of the 1880's, the early 1890's, and even in the strikes at the close of World War I, indicate a level of industrial relations hardly above that of local civil war.

Employers historically enjoyed a highly advantageous legal position due to firmly established property rights. The worker's status was a relatively new one, dating back only to the English Industrial Revolution, and as a worker he had very few legal rights except for those he enjoyed as a person and as a citizen. Because of this legal situation, the employer could have a worker ejected from his property as a trespasser if he so desired. Any worker discovered to have an interest in joining a union could be fired, and the worker was legally helpless to do anything about it. Employers could and did hire plant guards who were familiar with prison walls by long observation from the inside, yet if any trouble developed between workers and guards, the workers would be legally in the wrong because the guards were merely doing their duty to protect their employer's property. Worst of all was the use of injunctions, granted by judges on the request of employers, ordering workers not to engage in certain practices said to be harmful to the employer. Such injunctions were often granted without a hearing by a judge, yet they would prohibit parades, meetings, congregating on the street,

passing out bills, and other activities normally associated with efforts to build up union membership and to gain public sympathy for labor. Employers in a locality or an industry maintained lists of workers who were actual or potential troublemakers and refused to hire them. Workers called these "black lists." Often a worker active in promoting a union would be "black-listed," and he then found it almost impossible to secure a job.

Another device used freely by antiunion employers, especially in the decade of the 1920's was the formation of company unions. During World War I unions had had a substantial growth, and they were being talked about even where they had not yet appeared. The violent knockout tactics that had been used in the nineteenth century were now clearly impossible; the union movement had grown too big. Employers who still distrusted and disliked unions decided to form unions in their own plants to forestall so-called "outside" unions. Employees were encouraged to join these company organizations, whereas they might run the risk of being fired if they joined an outside organization. Meetings were held during working hours on company time. Internal matters, such as grievance procedures, were handled by company unions, but these unions were not noticeably successful in raising wages or making any basic changes in the situation of the workers. Although the decade of the 1920's was one of great industrial expansion, the company union aided by other conditions and by other tactics prevented any overall growth in American union membership during that period. Especially notable was the absence of any independent union organization in the mass-production industries, whose growth was a special feature of the decade.

### The rise of personnel management

The industrial boom of the 1920's which brought mass production into its own was accompanied by a movement called "scientific management." The roots of scientific management, of course, went much further back, but the systematic, logical attack upon production problems which it represented developed most fully in the twenties. The scientific manager consulted experts trained to solve varied problems in a meticulous, step-by-step manner. The results were impressive. Research departments were created to cope with technical problems. Production planning departments laid out work schedules with great precision, knowing that any problems of bottleneck that might arise had been foreseen and prevented in advance.

Industrial managers, having evolved a technique for controlling the nonhuman factors that affected or retarded the speed and efficiency of industrial production, turned their attention more and more to the human factors. Science, which had demonstrated its ability to overcome the most stubborn technical obstacles, was now directed toward the problem of handling the recalcitrant and intractable human being. If workers joined a union, or slowed down their work efforts, or gave any less than their full coöperative attention and energy to keeping up the production rate, the problem was now likely to be turned over to the personnel department for analysis and correction.

In spite of the limitations inherent in the work of the personnel manager, he undoubtedly introduced a great deal of humanity into industrial relations. Work has been made far more pleasant. New workers are trained before beginning the job and are introduced to their co-workers, rest periods are scheduled to break up monotonous and repetitive work, and pay systems reflect the effort and ingenuity of workers. Millions of workers are doubtless less restive than ever before because of the ministrations of the skilled personnel manager, and profits usually have not suffered.

### Reluctant acceptance of unions

The prevalent attitude of employers toward unions at the present time is a rather unwilling acceptance of them. A great many employers still think back to the "good old days" when they were not bothered by unions, but

they recognize that for good or for ill the union movement is here to stay. Therefore, they accept the fact that they must deal with unions.

In reality, a position of reluctant acceptance of unions by employers cannot be a permanent one. It is a step away from attempts to break and eliminate the union, but if unions are to be accepted as a permanent addition to the American industrial scene, the attitude of the employer must move on to whole-hearted coöperation or to some other more enduring relationship than merely putting up with the union. Many cases of a stable and mature coöperative relationship between unions and employers exist in industrial countries other than the United States. Such cases are increasing in this country, although unfortunately they are not yet typical. On the other hand, many employers in the United States now recognize that there was genuine need of the union movement.

### Coöperation between employers and unions

No resolution of the problems of labor-management relations will prove to be finally satisfactory or stable until the parties on both sides of the controversy reach a fully coöperative relationship. Under even the best of circumstances, this requires maturity of social outlook from both sides. Perhaps industrial peace can come only when power is equally held, or if unequal, when he who possesses the greater power voluntarily refrains from using it. Both parties must realize that they cannot exist and function apart from each other and that there is no achievement of ambitions for either unless it is for both.

American industry does not afford many illustrations of genuine coöperation of this kind. There are many cases of so-called coöperation and joint schemes of many varieties, but they usually turn out to be somewhat less than ideal. They include some true profit-sharing plans and cases where workers set their own standards of production because they do share in the rewards. If the workers are not free to choose their own scheme of coöperation in negotiation with the employer, or to change it by the same process, then it is not based on real equality between the parties.

The men's clothing industry has one of the oldest coöperative schemes, one which seems to be based on sincere good will from both sides. This industry was torn by bitter struggle many years ago, and, possibly because of the demonstration of the futility of fighting, both sides made a sincere try at coöperation. Strikes have been virtually nonexistent for more than a quarter of a century. During that time, wages have gone up and gone down, according to business conditions. The union has used its powers to help correct conditions in the industry that added to the costs of the coöperating employers. Employers have facilitated the growth and function of the union. The industry helps to prove that industrial peace and a live-and-let-live policy between labor and management are not just idle dreams. It demonstrates to both workers and managers in other industries what a mature, mutual understanding can do to eliminate strife and to make joint efforts in industry worth while.

One word of warning needs to be added. Good industrial relations cannot be based on a partnership between labor and capital to exploit the public. There have been cases in which industry and workers have buried the hatchet, but investigation has then turned up the fact that they have buried it in the consumer. Such cases are in fact monopolies. This has not been a widespread abuse in American industry up to the present time because there have been so few cases of genuine labor-management coöperation. It may be a more serious danger for the future if labor and management come to be more commonly on intimate terms. Possibly the existing antitrust laws are adequate to deal with the problem if it should arise. Cases of local labor-management monopoly which have reached the federal courts would indicate that it will not be an insuperable problem. These are cases of a new type under the antitrust laws, but apparently where evidences of agreement between workers and employers to rig prices can be demonstrated, already existing laws have

been sufficient to put a stop to the practice. However, this condition will not continue indefinitely without a watchful public which stands ready to protect its interests.

### Trends for the future

It seems quite clear that the growth of unions was due to the fundamental weaknesses in the position of workers in our modern large-scale industrial and business economy. As long as these weaknesses in the position of labor persist, unions are likely to persist. On the other hand, since unions are relatively new as a large-scale phenomenon in the United States, both workers and employers are apt to approach the problems in the functioning of unions from the point of view of traditional economic attitudes that were better fitted to an agrarian and small-business economy. Union power *has* been abused. Union actions *have* been opposed and attacked by employers beyond anything which those actions would rightfully deserve. This would seem to be a "growing up" stage that we have recently experienced in industrial relations in the United States, and there are already signs that the union movement is maturing and that both business and the nation's unions are acquiring a deeper sense of public responsibility.

It is futile to predict future trends in matters as complicated as those discussed in this chapter and as suffused with the personal evaluations of each individual. It appears the organization of employees in industry and business by means of unions is proceeding in the United States as it has in all other industrial countries. From hostility, public opinion has swung around to a tolerance of unions but, during the years since World War II, it has been both fearful and resentful of the abuse of union power. There can be no doubt that the rise of big unions, as well as big business, effects fundamental changes in the structure of a democratic society. In substantial segments of the economy it becomes impossible to function on a traditional individualistic basis. Collective organizations of both business and labor take over where the individual is no longer big enough to do the job. Democracy is not thereby destroyed but it is fundamentally changed. The individual stockholder or worker must secure his rights not as a lone individual but through the corporation or union. This changed situation has been more completely accepted by the public in relation to the corporation as a form of business organization than it has in relation to labor unions.

It is to be hoped that in the years ahead union members will learn how to discharge better both the duties and privileges of membership. Both employers and unions need to reach a sounder understanding of their mutual responsibilities. The most desirable solution to the problem of labor-management relations is the full, free, and sincere operation of collective bargaining between employers or groups of employers and strong stable unions. Experience indicates that this is ultimately the most stable and most satisfactory solution to the labor relations problem in an advanced industrial economy.

## FOR FURTHER READING

Bernstein, Irving. *The Lean Years.* Boston: Houghton Mifflin Co., 1960. A lively account of the American worker during the years 1920-1933.

Brandon, Henry. "A Conversation with Walter Reuther." *New Republic,* July 21, 1958. A controversial summary of the political views of unions. See Simons' book (below) for criticism of union's position.

Drucker, Peter F. *The New Society: the Autonomy of the Industrial Order.* New York: Harper and Brothers, 1950.

Dulles, Foster Rhea. *Labor in America.* New York: Thomas Y. Crowell Company, 1955. One of the best-known of the histories of the development of labor in the United States.

Galbraith, John K. *American Capitalism: the Concept of Countervailing Power.* Boston: Houghton Mifflin Co., 1956. A controversial book; uses union growth as the basis for discussion of theme.

Galenson, Walter. *The C.I.O. Challenge to the A.F. of L.* Cambridge, Mass.: Harvard University Press, 1960. A history of the labor movement from 1935 to 1941.

Kerr, Clark. *Unions and Union Leaders of Their Own Choosing.* Pamphlet. One copy free from The Fund for the Republic, Inc., 133 East 54th Street, New York 22, N. Y.

Newell, Barbara. *Chicago and the Labor Movement.* University of Illinois Press, 1961. A history of the labor movement in the Chicago Area.

Pelling, Henry. *American Labor.* Phoenix Books, 1961. Paperback. Author is an Oxford social historian who attempts to present in simplified form the main features of American working life and the development of organized labor up to the present. Highly readable.

Seidman, Joel. *American Labor from Defense to Reconversion.* Chicago: University of Chicago Press, 1953. Discussion of changes in union strategy and growth during World War II and postwar years up to the passage of the Taft-Hartley Act.

Simons, Henry C. *Economic Policy for a Free Society.* Chicago: University of Chicago Press, 1948. A well-known criticism of unions and the growth of union monopoly power.

Ulman, Lloyd. *The Rise of the National Trade Union.* Cambridge, Mass.: Harvard University Press, 1955. Development of unions during last half of the nineteenth and early years of the twentieth century. back.

# Chapter 19: Free enterprise, monopoly, and government

The labor problem in America is one which, by its very nature, thrusts itself upon the attention of the general public. When a strike or interruption of work occurs, the public immediately knows about it and often feels the effects of the disruption of an essential service. But the opposite is true of the problem of competition in the American economy.

## The nature of competition in a system of free enterprise

The ordinary citizen going about his daily affairs and buying whatever he needs is not easily made aware of an increase in or diminution of competition, except in extreme cases of cut-throat competition, as dramatic as a local "gas war." If he pays attention to prices of goods and services at all, he is conscious of one store or dealer making a better price or giving better service than another. If he is not very attentive to prices, competi-

tion might be lacking and he would never notice it. It does not force itself upon his attention as does trouble in labor relations. No seller is anxious to sell at a low price if he can sell the same amount of goods at a higher price. If competition happens not to be very keen, sellers are certainly not going to take it upon themselves to call attention to the fact. Efforts to tone down keen competition almost never attract public attention, but that is no indication that they are not made. Open efforts to form a monopoly would attract the attention of the public and would be noticed as violations of the antitrust statutes. The real problem about competition lies in the wide realm of contemporary business where there is neither competition so keen and effective that it forces itself upon the attention of buyers, nor monopoly so obvious that the public cannot escape knowing about it. It is a kind of inconspicuous twilight zone between true competition on the one hand and monopoly on the other. A great deal of buying and selling today occurs within this zone. It constitutes a basically important economic problem, even if the public is scarcely aware that it is a problem at all.

There are many far-reaching consequences of the existence of a large middle zone between competition and monopoly. As large firms have become predominant in many areas of business enterprise, not only have smaller competitors suffered, but there also arises the real possibility of price manipulation. Since market dominance by a few firms implies that competition will be unable to act as an automatic check on prices, the potential consequences, especially to the consumer, are grave indeed.

The condition wherein competition is restricted because of market dominance by a few firms is described by economists as "oligopoly." It is not *mono*poly, one seller, but *oligo*poly, few sellers. The net effect of the collective behavior of a few sellers is very nearly the same as if there were only one. Both the monopolist and the oligopolist must pay heed to public attitudes, and they have to watch for the competition of substitute articles, but there is no way to put direct pressure on them to lower prices.

Thus we are led to wonder whether the prices that exist are economically the best prices. The function of price in a free-enterprise system is theoretically to express the point at which supply and demand will be in balance. This balancing function of price determines who is to enjoy various goods and services, who is to survive and stay in various kinds of business, and who is to obtain and use the basic factors of production. If the price-making process is obstructed by interferences which restrict competition, the resulting prices cannot be defended by the usual arguments that prices allowed to find their own level will lead to that distribution of the product which will benefit the greatest number. Thus, the justification of a governmental policy of *laissez faire* is weakened or destroyed if competition is sufficiently restricted. If a competitive system is going to work well enough to justify giving business a fairly free hand in its own operations, then prices must

be truly competitive. A governmental policy of *laissez faire* which assumes genuine competition to exist cannot succeed if in reality competition is at best curtailed and in some areas of the economy nonexistent.

### Competition in theory and practice

In view of the complexities which exist today in the structure of competition, it is amazing to contemplate the way in which our ancestors light-heartedly went about the task of removing and destroying age-old social controls over business. British mercantilism imposed such irksome restraints upon expanding industry and trade that almost any substitute seemed better, so that businessmen did not critically examine the proposed alternative, that of unbridled competition.

There were certainly impediments to competition even at the outset, but in an era of abundant economic opportunity in many directions, the effect of the impediments was less serious to society as a whole than the effect of a retarded rate of economic development would have been. So long as opportunity was reasonably abundant, the competitive system developed initiative and resourcefulness and contributed to that generalized sense of freedom and well-being to which the American people are so passionately attached, and which has marked Western civilization wherever it has spread throughout the world.

Any practical evaluation of the competitive system must surely start with the observation that it has been a great success, especially in the United States. In spite of the spirit of brash enthusiasm with which the competitive system was launched in this country, it worked more satisfactorily than anyone but an enthusiast could have expected. No one seems to have realized how extensive the list of requirements for full competition really was, and therefore they did not realize how far practical conditions fell short of the ideal—or the triumph of what Adam Smith called the "unseen hand." Smith theorized that if each individual pursues his own best interest, the economy should realize its own best interest.

The ideal would be a system of competition where every part of the system is free. That is, there would be no impediments to interfere with movement. Buyers would be free to buy or not to buy; sellers would be free to sell or not to sell. Entry into an industry would be open to anyone possessing the necessary resources. Market information would be freely available so that buyers could find out how many others buyers there are, how much they intend to buy and at what prices. The same kind of information would be available to sellers. Both buyers and sellers would be assumed to be acting in their own economic interest. The product bought and sold would be such that both buyer and seller would know just how good or how poor it is. It would be divisible into merchandisable units so that the amount bought or sold would neatly fit the desires of buyer and seller. No one buyer would be able to buy a large enough part of the total amount offered for sale to influence the price by his own action in either buying or in not buying. Similarly, no producer or seller would be able to sell a large enough part of the total supply to affect the price by his own decision to sell or not to sell.

Among existing markets, the grain market probably comes closest to meeting the requirements of really free competition. Anyone can go into the market to buy grain or to sell it. Information about the supply of and demand for grain is available to anyone. Grades of grain are highly standardized, so that both buyer and seller know the product in which they are dealing. Buyers and sellers compete openly in the market, and anyone can judge for himself how much grain they are likely to buy or sell and at what price. The individual minimum trading unit on the grain exchanges is fairly large, but, considering the function of these markets, this is not an important limitation on competition.

The markets for farm products and commodities used as raw materials by industry come nearest to meeting the requirements of competition. Even some of these markets, such as petroleum production and refining, are dominated by large firms and do not conform to competitive conditions. Farm production and retail merchandising, except where chain stores predominate, also satisfy a number of the important requirements of competition. Units are small, and no one can influence the market by his individual actions. Though skill and capital are needed, farming and retailing offer easier entry and exit than industry or large-scale commerce, and thus can be more nearly competitive.

On the other hand, as we trace our economic development down through the years, we also encounter past cases where competition did not work. For example, the "wild cat" banking era after 1836, as well as the period between 1812 and 1816 when there was no government control of banks, may be regarded as periods of free competition in banking. Only a small number of western land speculators ultimately benefited from such a radical policy. Most Americans have realized that free and unrestrained competition will not work in the public interest in the field of banking. The early system of privately built turnpikes was also unsatisfactory as was free competition for railroads.

### Public utilities

The failure of competition to secure desirable results for either the public, the owners of railroads, or for other businesses with similar characteristics gave rise in American law and judicial decisions to the concept of "public utility." The courts held that certain businesses were "affected with a public interest," which meant in economic terms that something other than competition must ensure good service and protect the public against unjust prices. Over the years, public utilities have come to be regarded as natural monopolies. There cannot be many railroads between two points or many electric, gas, water, or telephone companies to serve the same customers. Such a situation would be enormously wasteful. It is much better to have only one company, but then there are no competitors to ensure that fair prices will be asked or that good service will be given. Gradually, both the federal and state governments as well as cities have undertaken to regulate these public utility industries on behalf of their citizens. Public utility regulation presents many difficult problems and many deficiencies, but there is no serious thought that we should try again to use unregulated competition.

## How the competitive structure developed

### *The increasing size of business units*

A striking aspect of modern business development from its very beginning has been the steady growth in size of the typical units in many segments of the economy. The final blow to the medieval guild system was struck by the joint-stock companies, which were successful in handling the larger-scale foreign trade made possible by geographic discovery. During the sixteenth and seventeenth centuries, these joint-stock companies were the big businesses of the day, and in their own field of foreign trade they were dominant. Much small business persisted of course, but even in domestic trade the scale of operation tended to increase. In local trade wholesalers and jobbers developed, some of whom became very substantial and influential businessmen. In the field of manufacture, the expansion of domestic and overseas markets stimulated the rise of merchant-manufacturers who developed the domestic system of industry to secure the production that increased markets would now absorb. Although not the greatest businessmen of their day, the merchant-manufacturers did tend to replace many smaller independent producers by a wholesale handicraft system of production which, in a loose sense, brought many producers into one business organization.

The technical developments which precipitated the Industrial Revolution came at a time when the joint-stock company was severely restricted and unpopular because of speculative excesses that had occurred earlier. Logically the joint-stock company might have provided the capital and set up the large-scale industries which invention and market expansion made possible, but this did not occur at once. The first mechanized industries were commonly partnership ventures which, though not exceptionally small, were not of the first rank among business giants of the day. Eventually, mechanized methods of production became possibly the most important single factor in bringing about large business units.

In America, the full force of the development of big business was felt in the quarter century after the conclusion of the Civil War. Earlier we had had an important position in world trade, but never a dominant one. The United States had substantial merchants, but it had neither the occasion nor the desire for large joint-stock trading companies. Thus, in the 1870's and 1880's it was the mechanization of industry and the resulting saturation of markets that brought big business to the American economy, from internal growth and from mergers of formerly competing firms.

The Sherman Act of 1890 and the Supreme Court decisions based upon it severely checked business combinations which restrained trade, but the Court did not interfere with the growth of big business from internal expansion or from other processes which were not interpreted to be in restraint of trade. Many branches of American industry and business therefore came to be dominated by large firms. This problem had been known in a general way, but the Temporary National Economic Committee, created by joint resolution of Congress, made dramatic findings in its investigations of 1938-1940. The Committee did find many industries that were not dominated by large firms. Specifically, agriculture, bituminous coal mining, lumbering, fisheries, and petroleum products were characterized by smaller firms not large enough to dominate their respective fields. The same condition was found to prevail in the manufacture of textiles and clothing, in most branches of canning, in printing and publishing, in the manufacture of furniture and house furnishings, and, of course in most retail and wholesale distribution.

On the other hand, a surprising number of industries and businesses were found to be dominated by one or a few firms of great size. The list of companies is far too long to present in full but it includes companies engaged in the production and distribution of such well-known products as aluminum, cigarettes, motor vehicles, farm machinery, electrical instruments, machinery, plate glass, linoleum, bananas, and many kinds of chemicals and rare metals. The Committee found that small firms were not disappearing from our economy; in fact, in many kinds of business they were increasing in number as the economy itself expanded. But it was now clear that in some of America's most basic industries the main body of its productive capacity was controlled by a very small group of very large firms. This constituted a different kind of economic system from the one which our forefathers had contemplated.

### Reasons for the growth of large firms

A detailed examination of the factors contributing to the growth of any one large firm would probably reveal a unique set of forces and circumstances, different from any other firm that could be found. Yet some factors are more generally prevalent than others. Among the most prevalent is technology. The biggest firms in all countries today are predominantly manufacturing firms, dependent for their existence upon the complicated technical processes which they use in their operations. The rôle of technology in creating big business is doubly reinforced if the concept of technology is expanded to include the ability to organize and use human skills and capacities as well as the forces and properties of inanimate materials. As a matter of fact, it would be very hard in practice to separate the nonhuman and human phases of technology. The use of automatic machines, belt assembly lines and the like almost always involves a new and intricate organization of workers, which depends for its success upon a knowledge of psychology and careful planning of human relations. Large

business units would not be possible without the smooth interlacing of both aspects of technology.

Almost any large American industry of today furnishes an example of the influence of technology in contributing to large-scale operation. The cardinal advantage of a power-driven machine over a human being is the performing of simple operations rapidly, accurately, and repetitively. To use machines, work processes have to be subdivided into simple operations which a machine can perform satisfactorily. Then a series of simpler machines either individually or combined into a larger, more complex machine complete the operation. There seems to be scarcely any limit to this process. Machines are made to feed themselves and to move the parts they have completed to the next operation. They are made to reject defective parts and to give a signal if trouble develops. The rate of output depends upon the speed of the machine itself and its durability. Once a firm is large enough to use machine methods fully, it benefits by lower costs which assist it in capturing a growing portion of the market. With an ever increasing market, machine technology can be carried even further by developing machines or processes to perform every detail of operation faster, better, and cheaper. Once a firm is well started in the use of new methods, there is a tendency for technology and the size of the firm to advance together, each supporting the other.

Many less direct aspects of technology also contribute to large-scale operation. One of the most striking of these is the use of by-products or waste materials. A partially related way in which large-scale operation and technology mutually aid each other is in research and the development of new technological methods. Once it became apparent to manufacturers that their success depended directly upon the solution of the technical problems of production, they began to develop research staffs of their own. Research positions have always paid well, and industrial research has now come to be an accepted function. In fact, the old-fashioned, free-lance inventor is now surpassed if not replaced by trained research personnel, who usually work in teams. The objectives of their research include both better methods of production and the development of new materials and new products.

Large firms now compete with each other to be the first to achieve a breakthrough in developing a new product or process. The smaller firm is likely to be hopelessly outdistanced in this kind of race except by the accident of a lucky invention. Patents on new developments sometimes give one firm an entrenched position in an industry. Since patents grant exclusive rights on new processes for a period of seventeen years, the firm possessing a patent on a key process gains a decisive head start over its competitors. At other times several firms may have patents which are partially interdependent, so that a pooling arrangement between them becomes almost compulsory. The electrical and electronic industries partially illustrate this situation. While one or two firms have had an advantage in patents, other firms have had patents so closely related that they have found it expedient to license each other to use their own patents for a reasonable royalty fee. Thus the industry does not strangle itself. Small firms lacking important patents are at a marked disadvantage in any case. Even where competition in technical development exists, it does not operate in the same way or have the same effects as the old-fashioned competition of earlier generations.

In recent years, *human* technology has achieved a significance far beyond that of the mere reorganizing of work skills. It has spawned the growth of a vast, specialized managerial group to administer large-scale enterprise. Many businesses have become so diversified that their owners are no longer the sole managers. Indeed, a whole managerial elite may become entrenched in corporate enterprise without ever having to purchase a single share of stock. The opportunity to specialize in a particular aspect of a business, such as buying, selling, accounting, inventory control, advertising, or production, to name only a few, has an impelling appeal for well-

trained college graduates who bring a spate of talented capabilities to bear on the problems of managment. This has put smaller rivals who cannot afford such specialization at a decided disadvantage, since surveys of business failures have repeatedly shown that approximately half of all failures are due to incompetence. Specialization is also increasing the difficulty of ascending the ladder from stock boy to president. It takes an exceptional individual with diverse qualifications to surmount the barriers of managerial stratification and rise to the top.

To be able to use efficient large-scale methods of production requires that capital be available in large quantities. The Commercial Revolution of the sixteenth century had widespread effects in the field of banking and finance because large-scale commercial undertakings required that capital be made available for them. In America, which has had only a minor commercial revolution, the full effects of the Industrial Revolution after the Civil War brought a rapid development of financial institutions to supply capital for large-scale industry. Accessibility to capital supplies became an indispensible prerequisite of industrial success. With only small and inadequate

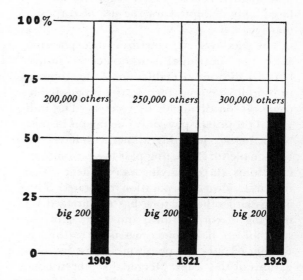

Fig. XIX-1  *The concentration of assets in the hands of the 200 largest non-banking corporations in the U. S. from 1909 to 1929.*

capital, a firm would struggle along unable to use the largest-scale, lowest-cost methods of its more adequately financed competitors. Failure and bankruptcy were far more likely if sufficient capital backing were not available at the outset.

In the struggle to obtain capital, corporate enterprise gained a distinct advantage over other forms of business organization following the enactment of legislation which enabled the corporation to function as a legal entity for an unlimited period of time. In fact, the corporation has become almost synonymous with big business in the United States, since it has proved to be a highly efficient way to organize large-scale enterprise. A diffusion of ownership, along with the right of prolonged existence, has made corporations somewhat impervious to the misfortunes arising from human frailty, whereas the lifespan of proprietorships and partnerships is often limited to that of their owners. Because of the multiplicity of shareholders in a corporation, the purchase and sale of individual ownership rights can occur freely, without damage to the corporate structure. In addition to major stockholders, the corporation attracts many minor investors, who contribute small amounts individually. These, taken together, build a large body of capital for the use of corporate management.

The tax system penalizes incorporation, since the individual stockholder is subject both to the initial deduction of the corporation profits tax and then to the progessive income tax on dividends he receives. The individual proprietor pays only one tax on income. Nevertheless, generous allowances have also been made for deducting past losses from present profits, thereby giving a tax benefit which, in effect, lowers corporation tax rates. This, along with other factors, has encouraged the merging of corporations, and great gains for stockholders have sometimes been realized by writing off losses of one firm against tax obligations of the other. Mergers have been beneficial in exchanges of stock without monetary involvement, and also where management was able to absorb added responsibilities.

In May 1961, however, the Supreme Court struck a heavy blow against corporate interlocking when it ruled that E. I. Du Pont de Nemours and Company must sell its 63 million shares of common stock in the General Motors Corporation. Du Pont's ownership constituted the largest single controlling interest in General Motors. The high court had already ruled in 1957 that Du Pont was violating the Clayton Act. How best to handle the distribution of such a substantial amount of stock has raised a number of provocative tax and capital gains questions, especially for the stockholders of the two corporations who have become liable for capital gains taxes as a result of the split.

### Problems of large firms

Although technological and financial advantages have contributed to the growth and dominance of large-scale enterprise, big firms face problems peculiar to themselves. Size itself can be the source of some difficulties; growth is almost inevitably accompanied by increasing complexities of operation. Although corporate management is interested in organizational growth and thrives on the responsibilities it must assume, the need for frequent decisions of serious consequence keeps this managerial group under continual pressure. Decisions to determine the allocation of monies are especially crucial. Funds are invested not only in plant expansion but also in renovation and modification of existing facilities. Administrative overhead, advertising, product research, and other activities for increasing efficiency also require expenditures. Mergers may raise monetary questions of great complexity, whether merging is undertaken for tax advantages or to acquire profitable lines which complement or help diversify existing operations. These many factors compel management to maintain some balance between them in order to keep any one aspect of operation or development from getting out of hand.

In corporation management, the interests of stockholders have also to be considered.

There are not infrequent occasions when stockholder interests seem to be in conflict with what management believes to be the best interests of the corporation. Not all stockholders are amenable to foregoing the receipt of dividends so that this capital can be used to increase their investment. Some shareholders prefer immediate gains to stock appreciation and are critical of any company moves which appear to threaten current dividends.

Another group motivated by personal interests also attempts to influence the decisions of management. Conflicts with employees concerning the rights of labor deserve special mention as a major problem, not only for corporations but for all large firms, where the relationship with large numbers of workers cannot help but be impersonal. Executives of these major enterprises cannot expect labor to feel dedicated to the interests of the company as might be the case in smaller organizations where relationships are close-knit. Until the advent of unions, workers for large-scale enterprise were often unable to make their demands effective. However, since labor has become possessed of articulate and astute spokesmen, the rights of workers and cost allocations for labor are included among the foremost considerations of management.

Another aspect of the manpower problem concerns management itself. Unfortunately, human capacities cannot always keep pace with business growth, so that human limitations can and sometimes do hamper the most efficient functioning of the organization. The sheer number and diversity of problems common to large firms make it difficult to handle all of them effectively. In an attempt to keep up with the growing work load, managerial personnel find themselves spending increasingly long hours on the job, at the same time that workers on the production line have managed to reduce their total work week. The disappearance of adequate leisure time for upper management poses a serious problem both for individual efficiency and for life expectancy. The rights of seniority may also create potential handicaps for the effective utilization of manpower. Whereas worker pro-

ductivity can be established reasonably well, less effective techniques have been devised for evaluating managerial competence. When a line worker ceases to maintain his productive output, he can be singled out and either retrained or replaced. Indications of inefficient management are less precise, however, and most high-echelon executives are in a position of relatively permanent tenure. As a consequence, many capable young men find themselves waiting indefinitely for a position in upper management to open, or choose the alternative of changing positions in order to climb faster into an executive chair. Thus, while large-scale enterprise does possess many advantages in the competitive market, it faces some perplexing bottlenecks which prevent it from driving all small competitors out of existence.

### The persistence of small firms

Although many important branches of business are dominated by large firms, small businesses have certainly not disappeared from American economic life. The number of individual proprietors of businesses shows no real tendency to decline, although the number is not growing as rapidly as the total population. It is certain that the small firm cannot meet the large firm in head-on competition. As a consequence, the small firm is to be found in every kind of business in which special advantages for the large firm do not exist. Retail trade persists as a very large area for small business in spite of the growth of chain-store merchandising. Furthermore, many large firms find it more advantageous to distribute their products through independent dealers or agents than to own their own retail outlets. Most of the advantages of large-scale distribution can be achieved by standardized display and merchandising methods, and the independent agent also has the advantage of intimate knowledge of local people and local conditions. In addition, many kinds of mechanical and electrical products require the kind of servicing which owners cannot provide for themselves. This need has given rise to garages, filling stations, tire shops, and repair shops for radios, television, washing machines, vacuum cleaners, and many more. Nearly all of these service establishments are relatively small and most of them are run by individual proprietors.

In manufacturing, the small firm comes closer to direct competition with the industrial giant and is thus at a distinct disadvantage. In fact, manufacturing is dominated by large firms, but several factors have operated to preserve small and medium-sized plants even in the original home of American big business. The very technical specialization which has helped to give rise to large firms has also often permitted small or medium-sized firms to become specialists in just one item or a closely related group. The item may be sold to larger manufacturers for assembly into a finished product at so low a cost that it does not pay the larger firms to make it themselves. Such small firms can also make replacement parts for the products of large manufacturers. The industrial giants usually make some of all the parts they use, often through stock ownership of smaller companies still carrying independent names. But, with their own production as a yardstick to determine costs, they often find a positive advantage in buying a portion of the items they use. If business slackens, orders to the small suppliers can be curtailed and needed production concentrated in the large company's own plants, which can thus be kept busy. The small firms in this way serve as equalizers for the large ones. In the long run, it costs the large firm no more to keep the small supplier in business, and it makes public protest against big business much less likely.

## Restrictions on competition

### Distribution and market dominance

Just as large-scale enterprise has flourished due to the advantages of technology and finance, so the distribution of goods has had similar tendencies. To be able to use large-scale methods in manufacturing implied that the market would absorb the output. This was generally true in America as population increased rapidly, as immigrants flowed in from Europe, and as the West became settled. But in addition, as one or a few firms attained a dominant position, many smaller firms fell into bankruptcy or failed to grow.

Brand names or marks had been used on manufactured goods at least as far back as the Romans, but they acquired a new significance when a single manufacturer was distributing his product throughout the entire country. Brand names, if used, were not especially important when all the products which a manufacturer could turn out were sold nearby. But as distribution became nationwide and sometimes international, and as products were advertised in magazines and newspapers which circulated widely, consumers came to rely upon long-established brand names, such as Ivory soap. At the same time, manufacturers became increasingly dependent upon the effectiveness of brand names to maintain the steady sale of their product.

This reliance on brands by both consumers and manufacturers is, in effect, a restriction upon competition. Any producer not possessing a brand name of wide repute cannot compete on even terms with one who does possess such a brand. Smaller manufacturers cannot easily enter a field dominated by a well-known brand. Even large producers would be severely handicapped in an effort to capture the market from a brand as well known as is, for example, Hershey among the manufacturers of chocolate.

Market dominance through ownership of brands is fostered by other characteristics of modern economic life. The advance of science, which long ago made possible large-scale methods of production, has also had the effect of making the quality of the product less easily apparent to an uninformed buyer. The ultimate consumer of all kinds of electrical and mechanical devices as well as textiles, chemicals, medicines, and processed foods is unable to judge the qualities of any of these products except in the most superficial way. He cannot measure the serviceability of an article by looking at it from the outside in a dealer's store. The uses and possible dangers of foods and medicines and cosmetics cannot be judged except by a possibly dangerous kind of trial and error. Realizing his own helplessness, the consumer comes to depend on brands.

It is true, of course, that there are often several brands with fairly good reputations among consumers, but it is also true that the competitive structure of business where brands predominate is quite distinct from our model of pure competition. The small producer without a brand name is virtually barred, if not by statute, then by the facts of day-to-day business experience. His opportunity lies in selling or servicing the well-known brand, in confining his activities to a field not dominated by brands, or in gaining a reputation, possibly with the aid of a brand of his own, in some small field of industry or business which is either not suitable for or has not attracted the attention of big business.

The big firm with more highly specialized methods of production, with more extensive research on product and method, probably with more fundamental patents relating to its area of operation, with sound financial backing when needed, and with the best-known brand names in its field finds itself in a position to dominate still more completely through the advantages which its size and wide area of operation give it in advertising its products. The very same forces which affect business and industry in general apply equally to the media of communication in contemporary life. As industry has become large-scale industry, so has communication become mass communication. Newspapers have tended to become larger. Similarly, magazines have attained a large national circulation running into the hundreds of thousands and even millions of readers. The newer media of radio and television achieved massive proportions almost as rapidly as their technical problems were solved. The independent local producer can make some use of his local newspaper, radio, or television station, but the most effective advertising media are beyond his scope of operation unless he shares their use with other pro-

ducers. Thus the very successes achieved by the advertising efforts of the mass media of communication tend to play effectively into the hands of the largest producers.

Large manufacturers enjoy still other advantages which add to the hardship of smaller firms able to offer only a single product for sale. Corporations have made their products familiar to consumers not only through sheer volume of sales, but also by diversification of the merchandise which they have to offer. One way in which large firms attract buyers to their products is through the ability to offer a "full line" of goods; that is, a matching set of products, from heavy durables to all the small electrical appliances needed to furnish a kitchen. A customer who is satisfied with one particular item in the line is more likely to buy another.

As the "soft sell" has become the "hard sell," it is but a step to the selling technique known as "planned obsolescence." This sales device consists of the attempt to influence public buying behavior by persuading people that their old possessions, even though usable, are outmoded and need replacement because they lack the style or the convenience of newer models. Although it is difficult to see how this kind of sales stimulus can continue to prod consumer spending indefinitely, it has been a highly successful technique for selling, especially during the years since World War II.

Not only can large manufacturers offer a full line of products, through vertical integration they often control production from raw materials to the distribution of completed goods. Americans have blandly assumed that our natural resources were unlimited, and that these resources should be freely available to everyone on equal terms. Large firms invested early in raw materials sources convenient to their operations, with the result that their smaller rivals eventually found themselves faced with buying raw materials from the controlling producers on the latter's terms, or else seeking less convenient and often more expensive sources. At the other end of the scale, large producers can often discourage competitors by controlling retail outlets.

The procurement system adopted by federal agencies during World War II and continued in the years since has also boosted the well-being of large-scale enterprise through the allotment of government contracts for goods. The very quantity of government requirements has made competitive bidding impractical for many small firms, simply because they lack the facilities to handle such large orders. Although some subcontracting does occur, the smaller firm suffers a real handicap in obtaining government commitments, and as government needs absorb a greater proportion of the total market, the importance of large corporations as suppliers can certainly be expected to increase rather than to diminish.

### Trade associations and fair-trade laws

Since unrestrained competition is by general agreement unsuitable to the conditions of modern business, it is not surprising that a development in the opposite direction, toward associations in various industries and branches of business, has itself become a prominent characteristic of the contemporary competitive structure. Trade associations are not a new phenomenon. Medieval guilds were more like trade associations than they were like modern unions. The pools and trusts of the last quarter of the nineteenth century which aroused public ire and brought on antitrust legislation were trade associations of a kind. The continually developing technological justification for large-scale business and the "rule of reason" adopted toward business by the Supreme Court in the Standard Oil decision of 1911 (p. 249) and the U.S. Steel decision of 1920 (p. 249) created the occasion for a new kind of trade association. In 1912, in a book entitled *The New Competition*, by Arthur J. Eddy,[1] the idea of "open price associations" was strongly advocated. Eddy became the organizer of many such associations in the following decade. He maintained that the reporting of the prices of all transactions to the central office of the association, so that all other members would know about them, would result in informed or "true" competi-

tion in place of competition in ignorance. The courts had held any activity approaching price-fixing to be illegal, but so long as these associations confined themselves to reporting price and other information to a central office without any hint of requiring conformity, the courts refrained from interfering.

Prior to the depression of the 1930's, the number of open price or similar trade associations had risen into the hundreds and had penetrated almost all important branches of business. For the short time that the National Industrial Recovery Act was in effect during the middle thirties, it extended the trade association idea by making the joining of industrial "code authorities" almost compulsory. The Act was declared to be illegal by the Supreme Court in 1935 because the powers assigned to the code authorities were held by the Court to be powers which the Constitution required Congress to exercise, and which Congress could not delegate. The experience under the NIRA, however, necessarily resulted in the spreading of associations in every kind of industry and trade more widely than before. The trade association now seems to be a firmly established part of the American business structure.

Eddy did not propose that the price information reported to the association also be "open" to the buying public. He forgot that free competition involves not only competition among sellers, but also competition between sellers and buyers. Even if the open price association involved no conspiracy to restrain trade against which the Antitrust Division of the Department of Justice might act, it is doubtful whether consumers have often benefited by lower prices from the coöperative activities of association members.

In more recent years, a very important function of trade associations has been that of representing the interests of their industry or trade before Congress or governmental regulatory agencies. Associations also inform members of trends in labor relations contracts, in the prices of raw materials basic to the industry, and

[1](New York: D. Appleton & Co.).

in any other matter of importance. Building good will for the industry through a program of public relations and news releases is a task very commonly assigned to the association. These and other association functions are undoubtedly legitimate and of value to members, but it is hard to see how they could be interpreted as making competition more effective, except in the case of indirect competition with other industries. The growth of trade associations, especially among smaller businesses, is one more example of the passing of the old competition and its replacement by a new and more subdued competition in which association members coöperate to keep their consumers as well as congressmen and state legislators in a mood favorable to the industry.

Because trade associations could not require their reporting members to charge prices consistent with each other, some other means of effective controls was sought. The NIRA codes had provided for nationally regulated fair prices as an antidepression measure. By the time the NIRA was declared unconstitutional, both manufacturers and retailers had learned that self-protection through standardized pricing was invaluable. Therefore, they urged the passage of state legislation to allow the regulation of prices.

While the Supreme Court has viewed price legislation with misgivings and has declared in the cases brought before it that price-fixing conspiracies are unconstitutional, many states have enacted laws authorizing retail price controls in the name of "fair trade." Various types of legislation have emerged. Nonetheless, these acts do consistently feature a fixed price for trade-marked items, no matter where in the state the goods are sold. All retail outlets are required by law to abide by a set price regardless of their costs of doing business. Manufacturers of trade-marked products have, of course, found price regulations helpful for stabilizing profits, and retailers have enjoyed the privilege of protection from underselling by competitive outlets.

In some cases, the state courts have subsequently declared fair-trade laws unconstitutional, giving rise to "discount houses," which

have attempted to infuse the competitive market with new life by offering trade-marked goods at prices lower than those of established merchants. These discount houses have been able to reduce the usual markup between wholesale and retail prices by cutting costs; they offer less in the way of services, luxurious facilities, and locational convenience. These outlets have grown rapidly in popularity among informed buyers who can pay cash. The efficiency of aggressive, high-volume, low-markup merchandising has not only violated a carefully created image of price in relation to value for brand-name products, it has also challenged the easier market situation for retailers who have been able to remain solvent with low volume and high markup under the protection of fair-trade laws.

### Monopoly and oligopoly

Contemporary business life is fundamentally changed from the individualistic economic competition that presumably existed in former years. The tendency is to idealize the "good old days," even though there was perhaps as much monopoly and oligopoly then as there is today. When roads were bad and transportation and communication quite inadequate by present standards, it is highly probable that local merchants were in many cases local monopolists and acted according to their own interest. Yet their economic power over the lives of others was much restricted. Less specialized production methods, lower capital requirements for starting a new business, and fewer brand names made it easier for a newcomer to establish himself. Any local merchant who found himself able to act like a monopolist could do so only until someone found out about his high prices and moved in to compete with him.

Present competitive problems center on the need for an enlightened public policy in relation to the many general areas of economic life where the character of competition is affected by the existence of dominant large firms. Effective competition requires that any industry or type of business that is unusually profitable should attract newcomers who would make the competition more intense and soon bring prices down. If today automobile manufacturers were known to be making a great deal of money, would that fact result in new companies starting up in that field? Consider the obstacles confronting any new firm which might contemplate entering automobile manufacturing. The public would be unfamiliar with the brand name of the new car and would be extremely skeptical of it. To gain a substantial volume of sales would promptly involve tremendous costs in advertising, which might very well fail to be successful in achieving the needed volume. This could happen even if the car were excellent in mechanical design and construction.

On the production side, the new firm would have to have enough capital to build a plant almost as large and as highly specialized as those of the existing producers. Would an investment-banking house assist a new company in raising the large amount of capital necessary for automobile manufacture when its selling costs and perhaps manufacturing costs would be higher than the existing concerns? Would not the competition of a new company force the older companies to cut prices and cause it to lose money right from the start? Would not the existing companies be tempted to persuade their suppliers *not* to sell steel, parts, and other necessities to the new company? These and other considerations serve to discourage new firms from entering automobile manufacture unless some other very exceptional circumstance works in favor of the new company.

The fact is that existing large firms are virtually protected from new competition arising outside the industry. Paradoxically, many large firms started in the infancy of our present industries, when firms could start on a small scale without much capital and grow large with the industry. They now find themselves well established, operating on a large scale, and with public acceptance of their product.

Automobile manufacture is oligopolistic, since it is conducted by a small number of manufacturers, of whom still fewer are so large that they inevitably dominate the others. How would these firms themselves react if business conditions were good and all companies were making handsome profits? Would smaller firms trim their prices to get a still larger volume of sales? If they did, would the largest firms stand by and see their own sales slip away? If the large firms cut prices too, and real, intensive competition developed, which firms would probably be in the best position to ride out the storm? The answer, of course, is the large firms with their large financial reserves and with the backing of the most powerful banking groups in the country. The smaller firms know this to be true, with the result that they do not cut prices. These firms make as good a car as they can, advertise it about as much as the larger firms do, and take the volume of business that results. They do not start any real competition to increase their sales because it would mean their business ruin if they did.

There has been a tendency among oligopolistic industries to use what is known as "standard volume" pricing, first introduced in the 1920's in the automobile industry, and since then becoming a common means of determining price in other industries as well. A standard-volume price is calculated in the following way: the firm determines the prospective total market for its product and then establishes its own expected percentage of penetration. Based on this relationship, the plant is scheduled to operate at slightly less than the capacity necessary for the demand anticipated, and the break-even price for the product is estimated at this level of production; this estimate includes both fixed and variable costs. When the scheduled output has been marketed, all operating costs such as materials, labor, administrative and operating overhead, depreciation, and taxes will have been paid. If any productive units above this amount are sold, they are free of fixed costs and are therefore extremely profitable to the organization. Once these administered prices are established, they are likely to remain constant or to increase, since it has been found by large firms to be in their best interest to lower the calculated standard volume and increase the price per unit rather than to cut retail prices. Between 1953 and 1958, industries where oligopoly exists showed marked price increases; for example, steel prices rose 37 per cent, machinery and motive equipment, 22 per cent, and fabricated steel, 21 per cent. The rubber, nonmetallic minerals, pulp and paper, tobacco, and beverage industries followed in close order. On the other hand, some industries in which there is not a high degree of productive concentration did not show any price increase between 1953 and 1958. In fact, some business groups such as textiles, apparel, farm products, and small producers of miscellaneous products where there are many competitors actually showed a decrease in prices.

Within quite wide areas of functioning, our large, oligopolistic industries, are a law unto themselves. Their competitors are unable or unwilling to force them to take any course they dislike, and neither the general public nor the government can do anything more than frown on conduct of which they disapprove, if they are able to find out about it at all.

These are the facts of modern business life. Whether they intend it to be so or not, what the representatives of big business really mean by free enterprise and free competition is that the government and the public should let them alone while they enjoy the profit advantages of oligopolistic market dominance.

In fact, enterprise is not really free because the obstacles of entry are normally too great for an ordinary individual to surmount. Neither is competition free, because potential competitors try to figure out each other's moves before they decide on their own. Usually everyone gains by not "rocking the boat." This is not economic individualism in either thought or action.

### Workable competition

There seems to be no practical hope of making any kind of economic system work perfectly and without friction, but the American competitive system should be judged in terms of overall results, as the advocates of workable competition contend.

It is important to note that the demands to modify our competitive system directly parallel the failure of competition to operate effectively. This is important, because to the many people who oppose further extension of governmental influence in the economic system, it sometimes seems that the government itself is a kind of evil dragon that threatens to eat up everything. Actually, government should be a neutral agency. It is good or bad and it acts or does not act as the people direct.

Large, dominant firms seem to be here to stay. They have contributed greatly to the development of the American economy and to the high standard of living enjoyed by millions of Americans. They have encouraged technical development and have paid high wages commensurate with their great earning capacity. The power which they have acquired should, however, be under constant scrutiny.

In February 1961, Judge J. Cullen Ganey of Philadelphia handed down judgments against 29 corporations of the electrical heavy-equipment business for having conspired to fix prices, rig bids, and divide markets on electrical equipment valued at $1.75 billion annually. The twenty indictments under which these corporations were sentenced charged that they had conspired on equipment ranging from two-dollar insulators to multimillion-dollar turbine generators and that they had persisted in the conspiracy for as long as eight years. One firm had at least 19 separate conspiracies in progress at one time. The discovery of such gross abuses of the competitive system has led to subsequent investigations in other industries.

### Private and government planning for full employment

The system of competitive enterprise has dominated the American economy throughout its history. However, competition has not always brought an assured and steady prosperity with work for all who want to work.

Experience over the years has taught that prosperity will not maintain itself by the independent action of millions of individuals and firms unless they think collectively. To take thought for the future effects of actions is to plan. Both business and government recognize the need for planning, although the word still sounds too radically new and different to many businessmen to be used. Nevertheless, the very dominance of large firms which do not have to concern themselves about day-to-day and year-to-year survival forces their executives to formulate plans that run for many years ahead.

The nature and limits of economic planning under a basically free-enterprise system present their own problems. These problems have not been resolved as yet in American experience. Among these problems are the proper rôles of government and business respectively. For many years the services of the federal government in collecting statistical information of value to business have been on the increase. Since World War I, and especially during the depression years of the 1930's, many kinds of business data have been collected by various federal agencies and by many kinds of private financial and statistical services. The number of publications by the Department of Commerce alone is impressive. When businessmen can know what is going on currently throughout the economic system, it is possible for them to make their own decisions more wisely. Then, too, both governmental and private agencies have developed facilities for research into and analysis of the data available to them. Activities of this kind permit the uncovering of trends which are not apparent on casual examination and add greatly to the value of the available data.

But government, especially since the beginning of the New Deal in the 1930's, has gone further. It has established more outside limits beyond which business may not legally go than have ever existed before. There is a mandatory unemployment and social security system; there is a minimum-wage and maximum-hour law; and there are credit and other financial controls which are particularly important to some businesses. The purchase and sale of stocks, bonds, grains, and commodities take place under conditions specified by government agencies. Federal, state, and local governments supervise the preparation and handling of meats, dairy products, and many other foods and drugs. During wartime, controls were much more extensive, although the objective was not long-range planning but the prevention of inflation and the equitable distribution of the economic burdens of war.

An ardent enthusiast for economic planning might well say that the small scraps of business and governmental planning which we have had in times of peace do not add up to a very substantial total. That is no doubt true. But planning is not desired for itself in the United States as is economic freedom. Until now planning has been essentially desirable only to preserve the economy from the evils of depression and underemployment without impinging any more than necessary on our traditional freedom. To oppose all efforts, private and public, to introduce planning into American economic life may, under conditions of severe depression, be equivalent to advocating the destruction of our freedom by insisting upon preserving unchanged economic machinery which has proved itself to be unworkable at crucial times. The mistake in relying solely upon competition to maintain stability and full employment has been demonstrated so frequently throughout our history that there seems no longer to be any logical justification for opposing changes in the traditional system. Rather the problem is to develop changed points of view on the part of dominant business groups so that by their own voluntary action they can learn how to establish and maintain conditions which will insure full employment and general prosperity.

Some theorists may insist that to make planning fully effective, power to enforce compliance must be given a government agency. Although such action has in the past been alien to American traditions, a burgeoning population and the deepening complexities of economic affairs are fast making the government the only organ which is capable of the centralized effort required for intelligent planning.

Government has a responsibility to fit its own economic activities, such as taxation, borrowing, credit policies, and public construction, into a rational plan of development for the whole economy. This becomes especially important if we are forced to maintain a high degree of military preparedness. In the past, the government has not always discharged this responsibility adequately; government actions have sometimes contributed to instability of the economy. Also, the great preponderance of our economic activity yet remains in private hands, and economic stability at a full employment level can certainly be enhanced by voluntary actions of private individuals and under the leadership of enlightened businessmen.

## FOR FURTHER READING

Adams, Walter (ed.). *The Structure of American Industry*. New York: The Macmillan Co., 1950. Chapter 14, "Public Policy in a Free Enterprise Economy," by Corwin D. Edwards.

Allen, Frederick Lewis. *The Big Change*. New York: Harper & Brothers, 1952. Also Bantam paperback.

Bain, Joe S. *Barriers to New Competition: Their Character and Consequences in Manufacturing Industries*. Cambridge, Mass.: Harvard University Press, 1957. An empirical study of difficulty of entry for new firms in twenty different industries.

Edwards, Corwin D. *Big Business and the Policy of Competition*. Cleveland: Western Reserve University Press, 1957. Includes a 36-page appendix of the antitrust record of the fifty largest U. S. corporations.
——————————. *Maintaining Competition*. New York: McGraw-Hill Book Co., 1949.

Fuller, John G. *The Great Price Conspiracy*. Black Cat Books (Grove Press). Paperback. A lively account in the tradition of the muckraker of the events leading up to the electrical industry price-fixing indictments.

Knauth, Oswald W. *Business Practices, Trade Position, and Competition*. New York: Columbia University Press, 1956. Author argues that the assumptions of classical theory of economics are static and no longer fit the facts of our dynamic economy.

Mulcahy, Richard E. (ed). "The New Competition," In *Readings in Economics from Fortune*. New York: Henry Holt and Company, 1954. Pages 100-105 offer an argument for the continued existence of oligopolies in our economy.

Stocking, George W., and Watkins, Myron W. *Monopoly and Free Enterprise*. New York: Twentieth Century Fund, 1951. Pages 97-109. The authors argue against "bigness" in business.

Wilcox, Clair. *Competition and Monopoly in American Industry*. Washington, D.C.: U.S. Government Printing Office, 1940.

# Chapter 20: Population, agriculture, and natural resources

**F**rom the beginning of human life on earth until very recent decades, man has been a profligate user of the riches afforded him by his natural evironment. In remote times, when human populations were small and technical skills primitive, no serious harm could be done because man was limited in his capacity to use, destroy, or modify elements of the natural environment. As centuries passed and man became more and more the master of his physical surroundings, and as human numbers perpetually multiplied, human societies became capable of modifying the environment in ways that might ultimately be harmful. In the tropical and subtropical portions of the Eurasian land mass which seems to have been the cradle of human life, areas which once supported large populations became virtually uninhabitable except to a very few wandering herdsmen. The civilizations of Egypt, Persia, India, and China flourished despite these conditions, but many millions of people were still forced to lead a miserable existence of grinding toil, inadequate diet, disease, and

premature death. This was the penalty these civilizations had to pay for their failure to make wise use of their physical surroundings.

## People and resources: past, present, and future

With the settlement of North America, a sequence such as must have occurred in many other parts of the world in past ages was begun again. Lands, forests, fisheries, and minerals were used, abused, and destroyed without appreciation of their potential scarcity. With immigration and population growth, the older parts of the country began to approach the exhaustion of soil, forests, and mineral resources, but the vast territory of the West still offered its boundless riches. Ultimately, more far-sighted Americans began to realize that earlier ideas and practices were those of a "fool's paradise," and that such careless use of resources could not continue indefinitely.

In 1871 the office of Federal Commissioner of Fish and Fisheries was created in an attempt to cope with the declining yields of American fisheries. A resolution of the American Association for the Advancement of Science in 1873 eventually led to the creation of a bureau of forestry in the Department of Agriculture and to the creation of the first federal forest reserve in 1891. Other measures taken in subsequent decades were prompted by the abuses of land by the large companies in mining and lumbering which were becoming common at the end of the nineteenth century. Before the time of the New Deal few consistent or large-scale efforts were made to conserve agricultural soils or to protect hydroelectric power sites.

Americans are fortunate to be able to analyze the problem of conservation and to plan appropriate policies of land and resource use before their plight begins to resemble that of other parts of the world where poverty and unspeakable human misery have been the basic facts of life for many centuries. As human population has increased, man has come to depend on the use of resources which are the stored-up accumulations of hundreds of thousands or millions of years. These resources are limited and can be entirely used up. Other resources, such as trees and growing plants, can be used indefinitely, but only if no more are taken annually than the equivalent of a yearly crop, and if human beings themselves do not adversely affect the natural conditions under which these plants grow. If human life is to continue indefinitely on this planet, there must be continuous attention, generation after generation, to the problem of the best relationship between the development and use of natural resources and population.

## Growing world population

Population experts have for years gathered data and compiled estimates to show that the problem of keeping man and his resources in balance is made more and more acute yearly by the fact that populations all over the world have continued to grow at an increasing rate.

This average rate of growth for the world as a whole is now approaching 2 per cent per year. This may seem to be a modest rate until one realizes that if it had been that high since the beginning of human life on earth, there would not even be standing room available on the planet now. Estimates dating back to 5500 B.C. indicate that population was increasing at the rate of only 1/25 of 1 per cent per year at that time, and that until 300 years ago, there were probably no more than 500 million people alive in the world. Subsequently, the rate of growth has increased markedly. In fact, in the more populous Eastern hemisphere the average annual rate of increase is much higher than in Western countries, reaching as high as $3\frac{1}{2}$ per cent per year. The net population increase in India is now approximately 8 million persons per year. Japan, which was suffering from the pressure of population growth before World War II, has had a much greater rate of population increase since the war with less territory in which to produce foodstuffs. A similar story could be told for many countries in other parts of the world. Estimates indicate that in 1961 the total world population rose above the three billion mark. It is expected that that figure will double before the end of the twentieth century. Even the United States, where the population rate declined for many decades, has become one of the nations with an increasing rate of growth.

Here indeed is an American and world problem which cannot be evaded. The population explosion has been remarkable not so much for the rise in the birth rate as for the saving of lives through the widespread use of miracle drugs, which have succeeded in reducing the danger of many contagious diseases. The lessening of the spectre of premature death from disease, particularly among infants, has contributed to the rising tide of population in all parts of the world. While high birth rates continue, man's life span is being extended, so that the number of older people in the population has also risen sharply. The result is a world-wide upsurge of population. The total increase, calculated on an annual basis, reaches nearly 54 million persons a year—a larger figure than the total population of many nations—people for whom the world has to find jobs and food each year.

### The economics of numbers and resources

The first person to attract wide attention to the problem of numbers and resources was T. R. Malthus in his *Essay on Population,* first published in 1798. Malthus advanced the argument that human numbers tended always to increase at a faster rate than food supply and hence that population growth would always have to be checked somehow. In the first edition of his book he spoke only of physical checks to existing population: such killers as starvation, disease, and war. He was sharply criticized for this argument and softened it in later editions by expanding more on checks which would prevent births from occurring. In particular, he had hopes that the delaying of marriages until preparations were completed for assuming family responsibilities, especially among the working classes, would have the effect of reducing the birth rate.

The entire Malthusian argument rested on an economic principle which had been developed and clearly stated shortly before Malthus wrote. This was the principle of diminishing returns or factoral proportions, as it is more often called now. The principle of diminishing returns states that if, in farming or manufacturing, all the factors that affect production are kept fixed except one, and that one is steadily increased, production may increase for a time but its rate of increase will begin to diminish as the variable factor continues to be increased. This result is obvious enough if one stops to think about it. One man engaged in vegetable gardening can conveniently handle only a certain amount of land, depending on the crops grown and the equipment he has available to him. Another man added to the same land, and with the same equipment, might be able to help the original man sufficiently to increase output somewhat, but together they probably will not double it. The net return in vegetables would diminish for the second man. If a third man were added, he might actually be in the way, and hence even reduce the total produced by his two predecessors.

Malthus' logic leads to pessimistic conclusions about the future of the human race, which, without preventive checks, seems to be poverty, hard work, and an increasingly bitter struggle merely to survive. Recent warnings by population experts seem to give substance to the most pronounced of these fears.

It is certain that the *logical* validity of the principle of diminishing returns cannot be questioned. The real issue is whether or not the *statement* of the problem which the principle of diminishing returns requires is an exact description of the actual problem as it exists. To go back to our gardening illustration, if two or three men were available for a given plot of ground, would they not alter their system of gardening to make effective use of their labor? They might shift production from corn, which requires relatively little labor, to a crop like strawberries, which requires a great deal of labor. Corn would then be grown elsewhere where more land and less labor were available. Even if we should require that the production of corn be continued on the land, if the men were logical thinkers they would see that three men were wasting their time. One of them would probably therefore turn his attention, and a small portion of the land, to experiments in fertilization and selective breeding to increase the yield. Or one of them might go into fertilizer manufacture, or the making of better equipment for handling the corn crop.

Any of these adaptations to an increased labor supply changes the ratio of diminishing returns because it involves not only more labor but different or more equipment, better crops, and improved methods. In other words, if steady continuance of one method threatens to lead to diminishing returns, as it certainly would eventually, human resourcefulness is challenged to devise new methods or in some way to alter or improve procedures. Viewed in this way, diminishing returns is not an immovable rock on which the human race will inevitably be crushed, but instead it is a limit to any one method of coping with life's problems and thus a continuous challenge to adopt new methods.

### America's wealth of natural resources

The problem of numbers *versus* resources is and has always been much less crucial in the United States than in other areas of the world. The North American continent is one of the most richly endowed areas on earth —if not *the* most richly endowed—in terms of good agricultural soils, rainfall to make those soils productive, climatic and temperature conditions favorable to plant growth and livestock health, and raw materials necessary to industry. Instead of having too many people, the United States has seemed to suffer from having too few people during much of its history. Accordingly, the result has been high productivity *per man* in American agriculture, but lower yields *per acre* than have been obtained in more populous countries where cultivation was more intensive.

A consequence of the high productivity of the American farmer, which is itself a result of the favorable ratio of man to land, is that Americans have eaten better for a smaller proportion of their income than most peoples on earth have been able to do. The *Economic Report of the President* for 1960 shows that Americans used about 21 per cent of their spendable personal income for food — about $70 billion out of a total of $328 billion. On the other hand, England before World War II, even with New Zealand and the Dominions keyed into her trading system, had food costs equal to 35 per cent of the spendable personal income. The low relative cost of food in the United States (combined with a high rate of income) has meant that the American people have had purchasing power left with which to buy other things, mostly the products of industry. As a result, America has forged ahead in industrial development while Spain, Italy, and especially India and China have been unable to industrialize fully because they must expend so much energy to produce the

food necessary for life. Thus it is apparent that an efficient agriculture is a prerequisite to the growth of industry.

As America was able to industrialize through the years, the resources that were to supply manufacturing began to be used. Our earliest large industries were tied to agriculture, since it was our principal national occupation. Such industries were textile manufacture, meat packing, and lumbering. Gradually American industries became diversified as the full wealth of our mineral resources was appreciated and utilized. At first, the United States exported metals and minerals, but as industries grew, more and more metal and mineral products were used domestically. At the present time, the United States continues to export as well as to use a number of important minerals, although increasingly as the American standard of living has risen we have become importers of supplementary parts of the mineral requirements necessary to supply expanding industrial production. The fact of the matter is, however, that for industry, as well as for agriculture, our resources have been abundant and have acted as a stimulus to ingenious men to develop ways of exploiting them fully.

It is easy for the United States to blueprint the wisest use of its resources for an underdeveloped country with an expanding population. For example, we not only envision for the world vast hydroelectrical and irrigation projects accompanied by fertilization techniques which would greatly augment crop production; we are also able to offer guidance in contour farming, crop rotation, and other intelligent methods of land and mineral use which will reverse the devastation of natural resources.

But such a scientific approach faces the stubborn reality of deep-seated custom, including the entrenched social institutions of private property, absentee landlordism, and often a dominating money-lender system. The peasant who follows ancestral productive techniques is so close to marginal subsistence and so imbued with tradition that he accepts change slowly, if at all.

The wastage of natural resources would

undoubtedly be more crucial than it is at the present time had it not been for the significant technological advances of recent years, the full effects of which we have scarcely begun to appreciate. Chemical research is resulting in many innovations in textiles, drugs, and living comforts; new power sources are emerging with the harnessing of the atom and sunlight. The world seems to be on the threshold of a practical solution for the extraction of salt from seawater—the benefits for arid countries are immeasurable, synthetic fertilizers are having a salutary effect on crop yields, and newer metals are providing a substitute for older ones in scarce supply.

Although these technological advances have made it feasible to use many resources in ways which formerly were uneconomic, the need for conservation has not become obsolete by any means. Technological breakthroughs have, however, markedly postponed the time when we may expect diminishing returns to catch up with us.

## The unique problems of American agriculture

### The abundance of land

Farmers of the United States have traditionally found it to be rather easy to acquire all the land they could use. Historically, farming and land speculation were not always sharply separated. The pioneer farmer would acquire as much land as he could, and would clear and farm as much as he was able to handle. At some later date, a part of the farm might be sold to a new owner. Hardly ever has the typical American farmer plowed up for crops all the land that could be plowed. He has had pastures and wood lots, not only where the land was not suitable for any other use, but often because he already had all of the good plowland he could farm efficiently.

This condition of land abundance which continued to exist almost up to the twentieth century, not only within the settled areas but also on the frontier, did not produce careful use of the land or adequate consideration of the practices necessary to maintain soil fertility. Continuous cropping was steadily reducing fertility, but the process was slow and did not attract attention for many years. In particular areas, such as tobacco growing land of the southeastern states, the preponderance of a one-crop system at the outset of the colonial era led to trouble even before the time of the Revolutionary War. The unused land even within the settled areas permitted abandonment of overcropped land and the plowing up of virgin soil without the movement of population away from the areas of earliest settlement. This expedient could not last forever, and southern plantation owners were looking for new land on the frontier by the time of the Revolution. Land hunger helped to make the Revolutionary War successful by bringing large and small farmers of the South around to enthusiastic support of the cause of independence.

In the North, a one-crop system was never generally characteristic, and soil depletion was less rapid. Nevertheless, care of the soil was not sufficient to maintain fertility in most cases, and eastern farms always found themselves in a disadvantageous position in competition with the new and more fertile lands on the developing frontier. The hilly, thin, and rocky soils of the East which were most vulnerable to the competition of the frontier began to be abandoned after a generation or two of cultivation, and those who were displaced could either go to the growing cities or move to new and better land in the West. All of these indications of soil exhaustion were not sufficient to make a general impression on American farmers. They continued farming in the established way without stopping to consider what it was doing to the fertility of their soil. The national background of land abundance was so deeply rooted that soil exhaustion in specific regions did not change the attitude toward land use. Poor and careless methods of farming continued to be the general rule. In spite of them, and partially because of them, productivity per farm worker remained high and total production easily met the demands of both domestic and foreign markets. This condition of plentiful farm production coupled with poor farming methods of soil maintenance became the background of the current problems of American agriculture.

## The predominance of family farms

Agriculture in the United States has been characterized by the family farm. Early efforts in colonial times to set up large-scale farming like the European pattern failed, except in the South where slave labor was available. Why should a free man work for a patroon[1] on a large estate in the Hudson Valley, for example, when it was within his power to acquire land of his own? Most workers thought independent land ownership was the better way and the patroon system of the Dutch colonists did not spread. Land companies and individual large-scale speculators did acquire a great deal of land in the West, but rarely with a view to holding and operating it as a farming venture. There were exceptions here and there which stand out all the more sharply because the overwhelming majority of farmland was in the possession of the families who operated it or of tenant families who looked forward to the day when they too could acquire ownership of their own farms. Because the typical farm was of family size, for many decades it was relatively easy for a young man to work for his own family or another as a hired hand until he acquired some capital and perhaps livestock. Then when he married he could set up housekeeping and farming as a tenant on the family farm if the head of the household wished to retire, or on some other farm which he might look forward to buying within a few years. This "agricultural ladder," as long as it worked freely, preserved both the family farm as an institution and the sense of freedom of opportunity with which Ameri-

can farm people have been so deeply imbued.

Several important results flow from the predominance of family units in American agriculture. For one thing, total supplies of any one farm product come from millions of small family farms. No one producer could expand or reduce the supply of wheat, corn, cotton, tobacco, hogs, or cattle enough to have any effect on the price if he either quit farming completely or somehow succeeded in doubling his production. From the farmer's view, the prices he receives are fixed in a manner completely independent of him. In this respect, as pointed out in the previous chapter (p. 368), agriculture conforms to the conditions of a freely competitive market. It is the dominance of the family farm and the fact that no attempts at larger-scale farming have thus far succeeded in dislodging it that make the markets for farm products conform as closely as they do to the ideal model of competition.

Another result of the predominance of the family farm is that farming is as much a way of living as it is a business. Farmers are reluctant to give up and seek employment in other occupations when market conditions affect them adversely, as is the case with most industrial workers. Markets are affected by worldwide conditions of which the farmer can have no direct experience and little or no basis for judgment. If prices are low and his income is sharply cut, there is little he can do but hang on and hope for the best. It is indeed unfortunate that more farmers do not heed economic calculations, for many farmers today are enmeshed in fixed living costs which lessen their former flexibility to wait out a period of falling prices. Thus, when an intelligent economic appraisal would indicate that many farmers should leave farming and seek some other kind of work, an overwhelming majority will not do so but will continue producing as much as or even more than they did before. In this respect, farming does not conform to the ideal competitive model.

Some authorities today believe that American agriculture has already begun a trend away from at least the traditional kind of

---

[1]A proprietor of land granted with manorial privileges to members of the Dutch West India Company under the old Dutch rule of the Hudson Valley.

family farm. Scientific and technical developments are making necessary more capital for efficient agricultural production. Modern farms tend to be highly mechanized, with tractors, balers, combines, and specially adapted buildings, all of which make the agricultural ladder harder for a young man to ascend. On the other hand, with such equipment larger tracts of land can be handled efficiently as one productive unit. Perhaps the family farm is doomed and the large-scale capitalist with a skilled farm manager, hired for the purpose, will take over the burden of agricultural production. In such a system laborers would be hired for particular jobs as they are now hired in industry. Or perhaps smaller and poorer farmers will eventually drop out and the remaining farm families will themselves become larger-scale and more specialized producers. Such large family farms may require some hired labor during the year, although operations might be so planned that the family labor supply can handle them for all but a part of the summer. Moreover, the tenacity with which we cling to the image of the small family farm in our governmental policies will have a significant effect upon the persistence of this increasingly obsolete institution.

### The supply of and demand for farm products

From the very beginning of American history there has never been the slightest question about the ability of our country's farms to supply all of our food needs. Adverse weather conditions might create local and temporary stringencies, but surpluses were always available in other sections and could be moved in. At the end of the colonial period, there were nine American families still on farms for each family living in cities or towns, but this was chiefly because land ownership and farming were a way of life. As transportation provided more dependable outlets for farm produce, and as new sources of employment opened up in industry and business, there began the relative decline of farm population which is still continuing. In fact, this latter movement has gone so far that since 1910 the absolute number as well as the relative number of farmers has declined (Fig. XX-2, p. 393).

All the while, however, the relatively diminishing farm population was able to supply adequate food for itself and the growing cities, as well as surpluses which could be exported. As time has passed, the potential surplus of farm production has increased rather than diminished, in spite of the proportionately larger number of Americans living in cities and towns and not engaged in agricultural pursuits.

By the middle of the twentieth century, less than one family in eight was engaged in any serious way in farm production.[1] But farm production still continues to grow at a more rapid rate than the population which consumes it, and American agriculture is steadily plagued by actual and potential surpluses. This is in sharp contrast to the total world food situation and especially to that of the heavily populated Orient in which more than half the members of the human race reside.

This record of American agriculture is little less than miraculous. It could not have been achieved in a continent with less favorable soil and climate. Neither could it have been achieved in an era other than one of rapid industrial progress, in which science and invention have constantly increased the efficiency of agricultural production as well as that of industry. Since about the time of World War I, the total acreage of harvested crops in the United States has remained approximately the same. Little new land has been brought into use since that date, so that the continuing increase in agricultural production can be credited almost entirely to improved technology applied to machinery, farming methods, crops and livestock.

[1]It is hard to establish this ratio accurately because of the many farms which produce very little salable surplus. It does not seem unreasonable to regard them as simply rural residences or as part-time farms. If only larger, full-time farms are included, the ratio of farm to nonfarm families could be pushed down to one in ten or one in twelve.

The situation in which agriculture finds itself today, then, is one of continuing supply greater than the market seems to be able to absorb. Through all the stages of America's agricultural history, this oversupply has remained of paramount importance. It is a condition which Malthus did not foresee and which does not prevail in the most heavily populated and technically backward parts of the world, where more food is needed. Nevertheless, it is at the heart of the farm problem, not only in the United States but in several of the British Commonwealth nations and to a lesser degree in some of the countries of western Europe and South America.

In the long range of world history, as in much of the contemporary world, food scarcity has been a limiting factor on population growth, just as Malthus predicted. In the United States, in spite of immigration and natural increase of population in the first century of our national history, demand for foodstuffs never kept up with expanding supply. Possibly the most important reason for this condition from the demand side is a factor which economists describe as the low elasticity of the demand for food. To illustrate this concept, if a family that had had an income level of $7500 should through good fortune find its income raised to $15,000, without any appreciable change in the price level, the food purchases of such a family would almost certainly not be doubled. Food needs are so basic that they are met first. A $7500-per-year income, we may assume, would be sufficient to provide an adequate diet for the family and modest comfort besides. With $15,000 available to spend, the family might buy somewhat more expensive foods, and they might go out to restaurants for meals more often, but they would probably eat no greater quantities of food. They might even eat less of wheat and bread products. Demand for foods of all kinds does not expand very much as income increases, i.e., it is not very elastic in relation to income. At bare subsistence levels of food consumption, the elasticity of the demand for food would be higher, perhaps high enough to be directly proportional to changes in income. That is, a family with an income of $1000 per year might conceivably double its food expenditures if its income rose to $2000 with no change in the price level, because it was previously living so far below an adequate level for subsistence.

Translated to a national scale, this income elasticity of demand for food has meant that once the population is well fed, increases in overall industrial and agricultural productivity do not bring proportionate increases in the demand for food. A corollary of this proposition is that the demand for the services and products of industry has a high-income elasticity, growing even faster, proportionately, than income itself increases. In more concrete terms, although the capacity of the human stomach is limited no matter how wealthy one may be, the capacity of the mind to take delight in a wardrobe of clothing in ample quantity for all occasions is very much less limited. Similarly, the demand for better housing, better automobiles, and better entertainment from gadgets, travel, and the like knows almost no bounds. The aggregate demand for the products of industry can outstrip any probable increase of the supply as long as income is made available to support that demand. The demand for food is the most urgent material need of man, but once met with approximate adequacy, it expands very slowly as people's fancies turn to other products of human effort.

In explaining the nature of the demand for food, one cannot overlook the fact that malnutrition still exists in the United States. Some of this malnutrition is the result of low family income; the rest is probably caused by ignorance of the requirements of proper nutrition or the persistence of faulty eating habits. Whatever the cause, as long as malnutrition remains, there is always a possibility of increasing demand for some kinds of foods by improving the distribution of income and by educating people about proper eating habits. That low income is a factor in improper eating is illustrated by the fact that the high-income levels of the period of World War II and after, as compared with previous years, have helped to create a greater increase in demand for the protective foods—fruits, vegetables, dairy products, and meat, than for older staples—wheat, rice, and lard. On a world scale, far more than in America, there is an enormous unsatisfied food demand to meet the requirements of proper nutrition. Even in the United States, however, further shifts probably will be made in agricultural production to meet the full dietary needs of the people.

### Agriculture and changing business conditions

In addition to long-run adjustments, agriculture has had to face the economic fluctuations associated with wars and the business cycle. Wars have usually brought intensive economic activity and price inflation similar to the peaks in the business cycle that have occurred at other times. In addition, World Wars I and II were responsible for drastically reducing food production in large areas of Europe and Asia, thus creating food scarcities, which were reflected by higher prices in world food markets. At home, both wars and prosperity periods have brought higher incomes to many groups and an increased food demand in spite of the generally well-fed condition of the American people. In the face of higher food demand from varied sources, agriculture is not able to make immediate increases in supply. Not only is it necessary for there to be a time span between the beginning of expanded production and its completion, but also farmers have tended to follow a crop-rotation system which cannot be easily changed. Thus, in the short-run period of a year or so, in time of war or prosperity, the usual oversupplied condition of agriculture temporarily becomes one of undersupply. Undersupplied markets then tend to develop almost panic food buying on a speculative basis and the prices of basic farm products are likely to soar. This occurred in the United States during both world wars. In fact, the Civil War and the two world wars mark the

three periods of greatest farm prosperity in the past century.

On the other hand, business depression seriously damages the economic interests of farmers because agricultural prices tend to fall more steeply than the prices of the goods farmers have to buy. The only thing that saves farmers from real destitution is that, as long as they can stay on their farms, they do have shelter and can produce much of their own food even if their cash income is cut sharply. Once a decline is in progress, even a relatively slight reduction in food purchases by city consumers serves to aggravate further the precipitous fall of farm prices, and precedes smaller declines in the prices of most other commodities. Just as farmers cannot quickly expand production to meet prosperous conditions, so, and for similar reasons, they cannot cut it suddenly when depression causes a shrinkage of market demand. In fact, because farm production is conducted by millions of individuals who are in the habit of thinking of market price as an independent factor unaffected by anything they personally do or fail to do, most farmers will try to increase production in order to maintain their aggregate income in the face of weakening prices. This is exactly the wrong course of action if a weak market is to be corrected by the suppliers of farm products themselves.

Even in the long run agriculture tends to reveal the same behavior as in the short run when it is faced by weakening prices. The cost-cutting technical improvements in production methods have been a significant element in the failure of agriculture to restrict supply in the face of a weak price structure, because these improvements increase production.

## American governmental policies toward agriculture

### Changing attitudes before World War II

In previous sections we studied government policy toward agriculture prior to and during World War II (Chaps. 14-16). We have seen

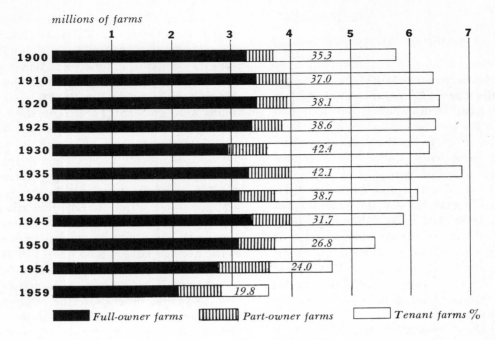

millions of farms

| | 1 | 2 | 3 | 4 | 5 | 6 | 7 |

| 1900 | | | | 35.3 | | | |
| 1910 | | | | 37.0 | | | |
| 1920 | | | | 38.1 | | | |
| 1925 | | | | 38.6 | | | |
| 1930 | | | | 42.4 | | | |
| 1935 | | | | 42.1 | | | |
| 1940 | | | | 38.7 | | | |
| 1945 | | | | 31.7 | | | |
| 1950 | | | | 26.8 | | | |
| 1954 | | | | 24.0 | | | |
| 1959 | | | | 19.8 | | | |

■ *Full-owner farms*     ▥ *Part-owner farms*     ☐ *Tenant farms %*

*Fig. XX-1    Farm tenure in the United States from 1900 to 1959.*

how the discontent of the farmer in the years following the Civil War brought about the "agrarian movement" of the 1870's through the 1890's, for cheap money and other benefits desired by the farmer. Though unsuccessful in its political aims, this movement was instrumental in securing more attention for agriculture from the government, principally through the establishment and expansion of the United States Department of Agriculture, agricultural colleges, experiment stations, and, on the eve of World War I, the present system of County Agricultural Extension Agents. Financial aid to the farmer was provided by the establishment in 1911 of the Federal Land Banks to provide cheap loans for the purchase of farms, and in 1923 of the Federal Intermediate Credit Banks for loans to farmers.

These measures proved insufficient to alleviate the farmers' plight, which grew steadily worse during the 1920's as the result of world overproduction combined with a short-sighted tariff policy on the part of the United States. Relief for the farmer became one of the major objectives of the New Deal at the instigation of President Roosevelt when he came to power. The Farm Credit Administration was created to consolidate existing federal lending agencies and to refinance farm mortgages at lower interest rates; the Resettlement Administration helped the farmer relocate in more fertile areas; the new Commodity Credit Corporation was empowered to make loans to farmers to enable them to market their crops at more advantageous times; and the Agricultural Adjustment Act, though declared unconstitutional in its original form, was passed in modified form in 1938 and provided machinery for voluntary acreage limitations in an effort to prevent the glutting of markets. Thus, the New Deal farm program was directed toward relief as well as price and income recovery, largely by the method of restricting production. How well it would have succeeded remains a question, for with the outbreak of World War II, an entirely new set of conditions came into existence which vastly affected our viewpoint in regard to farm production.

*Farm programs*

*during the war and postwar periods*

As America entered World War II, the Commodity Credit Corporation owned large stocks of basic farm products which it had bought in the process of discharging its legal duty under the AAA of 1938 to maintain the prices of these basic products at a certain stated percentage of parity (p. 299). As the largest owner of wheat and cotton in 1941, it resembled its predecessor, the Federal Farm Board of 1930. The crucial difference, however, was that the war represented a period of expanded consumption whereas the depression following 1930 was the opposite. World War II bailed the CCC out of trouble; the depression had forced the liquidation of the Federal Farm Board.

Despite the accumulated stocks of foodstuffs and raw materials on hand, it was quickly apparent to Congress and the administration that expanded agricultural production would be needed throughout the emergency period. Farmers, especially the older ones, could remember vividly the collapse of farm prices at the end of World War I, so they quite naturally inquired what protection against a repetition of that experience they might be given. Even before America became involved in the war then going on in Europe, but with world food shortages already in prospect, Congress amended the farm laws to raise guaranteed prices to a figure varying from commodity to commodity but nearer to full parity than before. It also extended considerably the list of farm products covered by the price guarantee. The guarantee was to be continued for two years after the end of the war to protect farmers against the kind of price collapse that had come at the end of World War I. Wartime price-control laws also exempted basic farm products from price control until they reached parity or above.

With these added guarantees of price support, the laws affecting agriculture remained in effect throughout the war without fundamental change. The Department of Agricul-

ture and the War Food Administration kept urging all-out farm production, announced general national production goals, and did what they could to influence the War Production Board to maintain supplies of fertilizers and equipment for the benefit of farmers. The results were excellent. Farmers in the United States produced enough food not only to supply the bigger appetites of the men in service but also to provide energy for a stepped-up activity rate for the civilian population. In addition, large quantities of foodstuffs were supplied to our allies. Acreage limitation and all the other paraphernalia of restricted production became merely an unpleasant memory to the average farmer, who generally likes to produce as efficiently and as much as he can.

As this period of wartime guaranteed prices came to an end, nearly a decade of farm prosperity had softened memories of the harsh days of the 1930's. Generous rains had afforded large crop yields, which along with a governmental demand based on the exigencies of war, provided high incomes for farmers. American farmers felt, however, that they would have enjoyed an even greater advantage if a competitive market had existed; therefore, in the years immediately following the war, they strongly urged the elimination of rigid price controls on agricultural commodities.

The Agricultural Act of 1948 incorporated this viewpoint by providing that the price average of the preceding ten years be figured annually to determine parity. This then became the shifting foundation from which to calculate the amount of governmental price supports each year. This moving average could be substituted when it was higher than the pre-World War I parity base which had earlier been used. Although 1948 prices were very little changed from those of 1946, specific prices for particular products had risen more than the average. Therefore, it was assumed that this moving average would assist fruit, vegetable, and livestock producers but would do less well by wheat, cotton, and other farm staples. Before the moving average could be put into effect, Congress passed the Agricultural Act of 1949 which called for farm laborers' wages to be included in the calculation of the parity figure. As the calculated parity figure of crops requiring hand labor rose noticeably, producers of these crops quickly lost their enthusiasm for the moving average system. In the same year, Charles F. Brannan, who was Secretary of Agriculture, proposed to allow prices of non-storable farm products to find their competitive market level, with a system of production payments based on full parity to be instituted if market prices fell below parity. However, this proved to be politically impracticable.

From 1950 to 1954, the Korean conflict temporarily removed some of the fears of an American agricultural surplus as the nation again became involved in a war. In spite of the war-bred demand for agricultural goods, the recession suffered by those engaged in agriculture was so severe by 1954 that national attention was again turned to the solution of the problem. The net income for the agricultural sector of the economy fell from the 1948 figure of $16.7 billion to a net income of only $12.5 billion in 1953. Even more serious was the decline in the value of farm assets such as real estate and livestock, which decreased by $9 billion during 1953 alone.

The Agricultural Act of 1954 was designed to alleviate this farm recession. It provided for flexible price supports at 82.5 to 90 per cent of parity for the 1955 crops of the five basic staples—wheat, cotton, rice, corn, and peanuts. In addition, the 1954 Act contained a provision for "transitional" parity, which was to be applied starting with the 1956 crop. Under this system the federal parity price was to be reduced 5 per cent each year until the government no longer remained in the market. This use of transitional parity marked a sharp departure from the old, fixed 90 per cent parity tradition of previous government supports. The 1954 enactment was beset by woes and was highly criticized for large-scale payments made to particular producers, the use of defective storage bins, and a buy-resell option in which the government purchased cheese at 37 cents a pound and resold it to the producers at 34½ cents. These errors made

obvious to everyone some of the more serious defects in the existing agricultural program.

The Agricultural Act of 1956 broke new ground by setting up a "soil bank" program, which consisted of two phases. The first was the "average allotment reserve," which authorized payments to farmers who lowered their production of basic crops through reduced cultivation. This phase was voluntary except for the case of corn, where the farmers involved were to vote whether to institute the program. The second part of the law was the 'conservation reserve" whereby the agricultural producer agreed by contract to devote a designated section of his crop land to conservation. The government was to pay a "fair" return to the farmer for allocating part of his land to soil improvements rather than to productive use. Nonetheless, in 1957, agricultural output remained amazingly high, de-

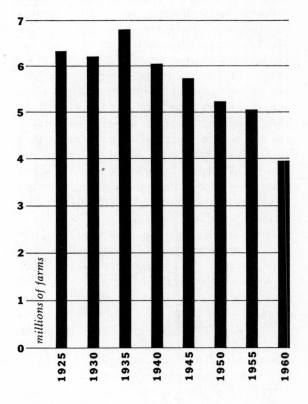

Fig. XX-2  *The decline in the number of farms in the United States between 1925 and 1960.*

spite government imposition of extensive controls over acreages and markets, as well as the removal from cultivation through the soil bank of land worth $732 million and a drought which plagued much of the country. For example, corn producers brought to market the second largest crop in the twentieth century, picked from the smallest acreage.

This factor of production growth necessitated increases in agricultural price subsidies. The farmer borrowed by pledging his crops; if the market prices exceeded the parity price, he sold the crop and paid off his loan; however, if the parity price were higher, he forfeited his crops, and they were added to those being held by the government.

Thus, for more than thirty years, the government has been embarked upon a wide range of measures which have promised agricultural assistance, from efforts to reduce the acreage in production to various patterns of price support. Such efforts were initially applied to major crops only, but price subsidies have also been sought in recent years by producers of specialized crops.

It is difficult to gauge accurately the success of these programs, since we can only infer the difficulties that would have ensued in their absence. We can, however, determine the cost to the American taxpayer of agricultural subsidy programs. By 1959, the accumulation of surplus farm commodities reached a value of $9 billion, and the storage charges alone on this surplus cost the taxpayers $1.5 million per day.

Nonetheless, the damage caused by farm subsidy programs and the corresponding high costs incurred by the government are offset to some degree by the benefits of using surpluses in national emergencies and in lessening the hardships of a drought. Surpluses have also been of use in rendering much needed assistance to countries in which poverty has remained a persistent problem. Even at home we have not exhausted our ingenuity in marketing surplus crops. Food-stamp plans have often been proposed, and by 1961 they began to be used to supply families on relief with free grants of surplus foods.

## Agriculture and resource use in the United States and the world

### Elements of the American agricultural program

No one can predict precisely the point at which the supply of and demand for farm products will come into stable balance in the United States. It will not be the same point for all farm products, because of the varying nature of our industrial and consumer needs. While the American farmer of many years ago satisfied primarily his personal subsistence needs and concerned himself with the general market only to a limited degree, the modern farmer finds increasingly that his freedom of decision and action are curtailed by constantly changing government regulations for better price stabilization. Many farmers find these conditions highly discouraging to personal incentive.

However, increasingly convincing evidence accumulates that the day may soon come in which the United States will need the full productive capacity of its good lands in order to supply a proper nutritional standard for all of its people. Until that day arrives we must not allow detrimental farming methods to be followed which will destroy our land beyond recovery. Even more important, we must protect rural young people from the chronic poverty which has denied to so many of them a balanced diet and adequate educational opportunities upon which to base a healthy and useful life. These are indispensable considerations in the devising of a rational farm program in the United States.

The rural people of the United States have been less directly affected by the industrial expansion which has been the outstanding fact of our economic history than any other group in our society. They buy products from industry and sell their own produce to industrial workers, but they live on the land in detached family units. As a consequence, they retain the individualistic attitudes which predominated in our early history more strongly than do, for example, union members in the cities. They believe more firmly in individual self-reliance and free enterprise, but have so long been the victims of competitive market forces that they are prone to look to the government as the only agency which can improve their lot.

A corollary of the farmer's individualism is his attachment to the idea of family farms. In fact, most Americans, urban as well as rural, would probably prefer to support a family unit type of agriculture if it were anywhere near as efficient as some other alternative. Farm families are the traditional backbone of the nation, and even those descendants of farm families who have moved to the cities seldom criticize policies favorable to the continuation of the family unit on the farm. At the same time economic pressures and technological advances are throwing the advantage to larger family farming units and public opinion seems to find no fault with that state of affairs. If any kind of public influence or aid is made effective for agriculture, public opinion seems to desire that it should neither subsidize inefficiency nor give even comparable advantages to very extensive farm operations by corporations or individuals. In the present state of technical knowledge in agriculture, the fairly large family farm seems to represent the public ideal.

The idea of parity for agriculture which has been incorporated in American laws since the early days of the New Deal seems to be another accepted plank for a farm program. Parity implies equality of treatment of farm and nonfarm people. As such the idea has a superficial appeal. The matter is not so simple, however, for in order to force declines in farm production, agriculture should receive less than parity. Thus there is an inherent conflict between parity and reliance upon competitive market forces. Farmers cannot have both unless they would accept some other kind of interference to remove additional producers from agriculture. Specialized wheat and cotton producers derive more benefits from parity guarantees than do general farmers. They and other single-crop producers will have to choose between less than parity prices, acreage allotments, and marketing quotas to reduce their income enough to make other occupations attractive to some of their number. There is no other way in a free economy. Perhaps the parity concept can be useful as a standard of measurement, with support prices to be set at some point below full parity. Used in this way, parity would not be the basis of interference with competitive market prices until they broke fairly sharply and unexpectedly below parity. Then, perhaps an orderly adjustment of agricultural production and market forces might be achieved by the use of price guarantees, to be lowered as it seemed feasible. This would not protect farmers from competitive forces, but from wide and sudden breaks in prices to which depressions, in particular, have subjected farm producers in the past.

The provision of many credit facilities for agriculture by agencies of the federal government has also apparently become an accepted part of American farm policy. This government activity does not always displace private activity, but either works along with it or stands behind it. In large part, this kind of government action is a result of inadequate service by private credit agencies in the past, or of abuses in their lending practices which built up an abiding ill-will among farmers. Government lending is not looked upon by farmers as a subsidy, and, in fact, it is not, since it pays its own way. To farmers, government credit is simply a supplement to credit available through private lending agencies which ensures them of credit facilities equal to those available to city businessmen through private channels. Long-term credit for land purchase, intermediate credit for crop production and livestock feeding, and crop-storage credit to aid orderly marketing are now available through government agencies. There is no widespread demand for change in this program.

The need for conservation of agricultural soils is another element to which there is no open opposition. No one in his right mind would ever advocate permanent destruction of

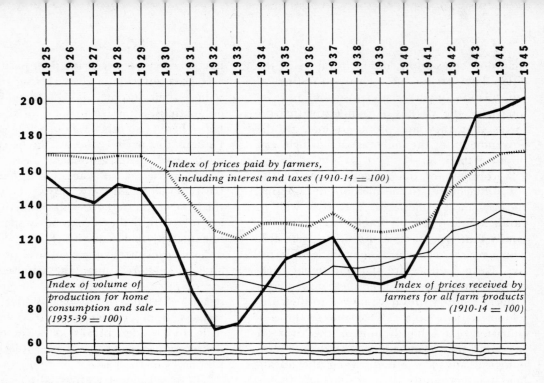

*Index of prices paid by farmers,*
*including interest and taxes (1910-14 = 100)*

*Index of volume of*
*production for home*
*consumption and sale —*
*(1935-39 = 100)*

*Index of prices received by*
*farmers for all farm products*
*— (1910-14 = 100)*

Fig. XX-3 *While production grew in volume*
*during the period from 1923 to 1945, prices received*
*by the farmers remained below the prices paid*
*by them for their needs until the war years.*

farm lands. The worst enemies of good farming practices are indifference and laziness, not open opposition. Realization of the need for and value of conservation methods is growing, however, because both experimental and practical demonstration have proved that almost any farmer can gain larger returns for his time and investment and conserve and also improve his soil. The soil-destroying farmer is very likely to be a low-income farmer as well. The secret of good conservational farming is the growing of more acres of grass and legumes (clovers), which involves the keeping of livestock to eat these feeds. This practice fits the food demands of the American people as their income rises, for they tend to eat more meat and dairy products and less of the old soil-depleting staples. Livestock farming systems have even been devised for the South to provide a more profitable use for former cotton-lands. Thus, the general trends already in evidence in the United States make conservation a paying proposition and a habit that is likely to grow in the future.

In view of the existing state of the farm program and the existing needs of the farm population, are any further steps called for to ensure proper land use, to provide equitable treatment for farm people, and to guarantee adequate food supplies for the entire population? Perhaps the key motive for a farm policy should be to expedite the maximum effectiveness of competition. For example, government assistance to relocate low-income farm families in an industrial area where employment opportunities exist would strengthen a competitive force already in operation but one not yet functioning powerfully enough. Perhaps the work of the United States Employment Service should be extended to this area, with the offer of credit assistance to cover the costs of moving. As a corollary, more funds for reforestation of worn-out and eroded hill farms would also help. In all farm areas, young people should have the opportunity through their schools to obtain an accurate picture of employment possibilities in other kinds of work.

Many proposals have been advanced in regard to the great central problem of farm prices and farm production. If we are going to encourage maximum competitive markets, it would seem that the prices of farm products should be permitted to seek their competitive level—a level that would mean low prices if supplies were excessive. Low prices would necessitate the discovery of all possible domestic uses of the product. Similarly, all possible foreign markets would be supplied. If general economic conditions were good in the cities, low prices would be bolstered by an expanding demand for meat, poultry, dairy products, fruits, and vegetables. In fact, since the income elasticity of demand for such products as these is rather high, competition would take care of their prices in normal circumstances. Only when depression exists in the cities would special measures to support farm income from these sources be needed.

The old staples of wheat, cotton, and corn are not taken care of by competitive forces under present conditions. Because of low-income elasticity of demand, price fluctuations in these commodities may be rather sudden and wide. Yet these crops are the backbone of American farming. It has been suggested that the Department of Agriculture be responsible for estimating the amount of these crops needed in any future year, and then in view of recent prices and production announce a minimum price or "price floor" for the ensuing crop season. This price would presumably be high enough to stimulate adequate production but not so high as to produce more than occasional surpluses. The thought behind this advance price-floor proposal is that it would enable farmers to plan ahead with assurance. It is thus an aid to competitive forces.

Since these staple commodities are storable, government purchases to maintain the floor price or the going percentage of parity would also maintain something approaching an ever-normal granary. Some such system as this is clearly needed for the storable staples with low income elasticity of demand to ensure that the forces of competition are permitted to operate in order to stimulate or discourage production, and that the farmer is protected against the sudden and wide swings in price to which these commodities are subject.

In 1961, the Kennedy Administration attacked the surplus problem in another way, as was mentioned earlier (p. 394), by initiating a plan to substitute food stamps for the distribution of free surplus foods. Eight areas over the country were selected on the basis of a high-unemployment ratio, to participate in the testing of the plan. In the chosen areas, those persons without any income whatsoever received free stamps, while others paid variable amounts up to 85 cents on the dollar, depending upon the amount of their income. These food stamps were exchangeable for food only at normal commercial outlets and could not be used for liquor, tobacco, or other unlisted items. In one test area, recipients paid an average of 60 cents for each dollar's worth of stamps, and it was reported that the local economy was stimulated by $2 million in 1961. The plan was enthusiastically endorsed by participants on all levels, from the impoverished families who benefited directly, to the merchants and businessmen who gained in trade and the bankers who redeemed the stamps.

Other proposals have been made to stabilize prices and production, such as the Brannan plan for "production payments" to supplement prices when they fall below parity. A number of agricultural economists have suggested unrestricted competitive prices for farm products and supplementary income payments to farmers when certain defined conditions of depression exist in the cities.

It is pretty well agreed that only a minimum deviation from the competitive system is desired, although it is also recognized that special help and guidance are needed to cope with the depression problem.

### The problem of resource exhaustion

Agricultural problems relate not merely to the use of land as a physical resource, but also and primarily to the social problems of the people who farm it. In other areas of resource use, the human problems either are non-existent or take second place to the physical problems of rate of usage. In the case of some resources, such as timberlands, the problem is one of harmonizing present use with the maintenance or conservation of reserves for future use. The cutting of timber in accord with the principles of wise use or of conservation, means that no usable part of the tree is wasted and that trees are cut under conditions that encourage young growth and will not damage or destroy it. When original stands are once cut over, the available timber is reduced to annual crops. We are very close to that condition in the United States today. Wise use in relation to such resources as fisheries means maintaining conditions of water and food supply to produce large annual crops.

The mineral resources of the country are different in nature. They represent natural accumulations through the geologic ages. There is no question of an annual crop, but the existing supply must be used in a manner that is not wasteful and that does not make it impossible to obtain the balance of the deposit whenever it is needed. Conservation of mineral resources relates largely to methods of extraction and to the handling of the mineral once it is extracted.

There is another aspect of the wise use of exhaustible resources, however, which deserves consideration but is scarcely soluble in a final sense. How rapidly should such a resource be used? What uses are proper for resources? Petroleum products, for example, have been most convenient for and have their largest use in motor vehicles. Gasoline burns easily to propel automobiles, a reserve supply can be carried in a tank in the car, and a replacement supply can easily be pumped into the tank when it becomes empty. No other fuel has been discovered to be as convenient for this purpose. But petroleum can also be used to produce steel. It is an exhaustible resource and the world supply will not last forever. Do the principles of wise use permit petroleum to be used to manufacture steel just because it happens to be slightly lower in cost in one part of the country than coal would be at that spot?

Today there is enough petroleum for both uses, but will there be in the future?

Problems of this kind in the use of exhaustible resources occur constantly. Is the present-day market price adequate to determine which are proper uses for resources? If it is cheaper to let natural gas blow into the air in order to get the oil in the well, should there be no objection to letting it blow? There is really no way to answer these questions. Market price is the accepted method of allocating resources to various uses. This method is used constantly in allocating the labor of human beings, and there seems to be no adequate alternative to it in the use of natural resources. Whether future generations will need the resource, or whether they will discover some superior alternative is not known. The difference between higher and lower uses of a resource or between present and future uses cannot be decided on any better basis than market price. Present users can be held responsible, however, for extracting and using exhaustible resources in ways which, because of lack of care or thought, prevent full recovery and use of the remaining supply. Extraction of minerals or petroleum in accord with the principles of wise use costs no more but permits the ultimate extraction of the highest possible percentage of the supply. The current market price may not provide a sufficient incentive for action of this kind, but certainly common prudence would seem to command it. Beyond that point, it is hard to generalize about wise use of resources.

### The long-term world problem

### of supporting populations

It is probably easier to be pessimistic than optimistic after examining world conditions of population growth and available land and resources. Certainly if no intelligent action is applied to the problem and if natural physical impulses thereby have no national guidance, the worst predictions of Malthus and later population pessimists could come true.

The powers of man's critical intelligence have had small influence upon the course of history because they have been called upon to determine only a small part of human conduct. Impulse, instinct, and tradition remain far more potent determinants of conduct than intellect. Yet when impulse, instinct, or tradition lead to trouble, man can be forced to use his wits to escape his predicament. One could hope that the day is not far off when the human race can learn to use its brain power more effectively to avoid disaster.

It is axiomatic that there is no specific virtue in keeping alive the largest possible mass of human beings that the earth can be made to support. The highest human qualities are in the realm of the spiritual, esthetic, and intellectual spheres and defy quantitative measurement since they trenscend the individual as a biological entity and link him with that larger entity which we call society or humanity. The nature of these highest values changes from time to time and from culture to culture, but man has always shown himself willing to sacrifice his biological life when these higher values are endangered. He will also put forth his best efforts, including rigorous use of his powers of mind, when he feels that he must do so to preserve the things he holds dear. The Oriental nations which by American standards are grossly overpopulated will bestir themselves to action only when the mass of people come to feel that a population as dense as theirs denies them the fulfillment of those values which they hold highest. If poverty, inadequate diet, and disease from unsanitary living do not seem to interefere with their attainment of the goals they consider worth while, then there is no reason to expect a change in their traditional high birth rate and necessarily high death rate from starvation or from disease.

The evidence is, however, that the material achievements of the United States and the nations of western Europe have already visibly affected these countries. Although the people of one religious or cultural group are not likely to accept quickly the aesthetic or intellectual outlook of another and alien group, they may come to see that human life directed toward any kind of spiritual goal can achieve that goal better when the physical conditions of life—nutrition, clothing, shelter—are well met.

## FOR FURTHER READING

Benedict, Murray R. *Farm Policies of the United States, 1790-1950*. New York: Twentieth Century Fund, 1953. A fairly objective discussion of the history and growth of Federal farm policies.

——————. *Can We Solve the Farm Problem? An Analysis of Federal Aid to Agriculture*. New York: Twentieth Century Fund, 1955. Sequel to above.

Bidwell, Percy W. *Raw Materials: A Study of American Policy*. Published for the Council on Foreign Relations. New York: Harper & Brothers, 1958.

Boddy, Francis M., and others (eds.). *Applied Economic Analysis*. New York: Pitman Publishing Corp., 1948. Section 6, Chapters 19—25, "Agricultural Problems and the Conservation of Natural Resources," by Alvin E. Coons.

Boulding, Kenneth E. *Principles of Economic Policy*. New York: Prentice-Hall, Inc., 1958. Pages 313—339 offer a lucid discussion of American farm policy.

Davis, John H., and Henshaw, Kenneth. *Farmer in a Business Suit*. New York: Simon and Schuster, 1957. A former assistant secretary of agriculture and a farming expert offer a lay account of changes in farming in the twentieth century.

Davis, Joseph S. "The Population Upsurge and the American Economy." *Journal of Political Economy*, LXI, October, 1953.

"Land Reform—a World Challenge." U. S. Department of State Publication No. 4445. Washington, D.C.: U.S. Government Printing Office, 1952.

Nicholls, William H. "America's Biggest Farm Surplus —Too Many Farmers." *Readings in Economics*. 3rd ed. Paul A. Samuelson and others (eds.). New York: McGraw-Hill Book Co., 1958. A criticism of American farm policy.

Schultz, Theodore W. (ed.) *Food for the World*. Chicago: University of Chicago Press, 1945. Problem considered by twenty-two specialists in economics, nutrition, population, and agriculture. Still timely.

Taeuber, Conrad, and Taeuber, Irene. *The Changing Population of the United States*. New York: John Wiley & Sons, Inc., 1958. Part IV. A summary of population trends for the past century and a half. Final chapter briefly outlines prospects for the next few decades.

## Chapter 21:

# Money: its use, measurement, and rôle in the American economy

**F**ew aspects of our economy impinge more upon the everyday life of the individual than the system of money and credit which we employ. Upon this system we measure the relative value of the goods we purchase. Upon this monetary system we base our bookkeeping and maintain our financial controls. Through this system we exchange not only with one another but with those in other countries. By this system we relate the value of things in the present with values in the future, and we are able to store buying power as well as to have a common denominator through which debts may be incurred or paid. Our whole credit and contractual system indeed rests upon this foundation of money and credit. If our monetary system is functioning well, the typical citizen tends to be oblivious of its intricate operation. When, however, it is malfunctioning, economic disorders are aggravated. Periods of extreme inflation or deflation create not only injustices between debtor and creditor; they are also normally accompanied by a disorganization of the economy

because of their effect upon price relationships and income distribution.

Money systems of the world have today come a long way from the primitive system of exchanging goods by the use of a metallic coin such as gold as a medium of exchange. While gold is still today the base of our own currency system and that of many other countries, we seldom if ever see it. Instead, it forms a mechanism through which international balances may be transferred. Most money today takes the form of promises of banks or governments to pay; of a sort of monetized credit which is perhaps best typified by a $5 Federal Reserve note which is money—and yet which cannot be exchanged for gold within the United States, even though it is partially backed by gold certificates. Far more important than the paper money which we circulate is bank credit or "checkbook money." Deposits in commercial banks form a medium of exchange through which each person writing a check on his account is able to make a transfer payment to someone else. Through this means, transactions take place without the employment of gold or even of paper money.

Just as we have earlier noted the sharp changes which have occurred in the techniques by which goods have been produced, so our money and credit system have been subject to a very rapid evolution. Metallic coins are not widely used, except for change, and our economy has essentially become a credit economy. In the first stage, paper money (government or bank promises to pay gold on demand) became widely employed as a substitute for gold, only to give way increasingly to the checkbook which has come to substitute for paper money. Today, with the advent of credit cards, charge accounts, and easy payments, the consumer becomes ever more dependent upon bookkeeping entries. Some of our payments are now made through check-off systems applicable to withholding of income taxes, social security, medical assistance, and numerous other items. New dimensions are constantly being added to our monetary mechanism.

The American credit system is today a far cry from the bare subsistence economy where clumsy and unwieldy barter systems were employed to facilitate exchange. Instead, we have moved into an era in which only a fraction of our populace lives at poverty or deprivation levels. For most American consumers, there exist expanding options in patterns of expenditure, and monetary savings have become characteristic of an advancing segment of the populace. Individual decisions—to buy or save, to invest in stocks or in real estate, to use installment credit or to pay cash—all have an immense impact upon the operation of the economic system, particularly in a society in which a relatively equal distribution of income makes the expenditures of small consumers taken collectively a vital element in our rate of economic growth.

We turn then to the discussion of a money system which has long since departed from simple beginnings as a metallic currency and now has developed a vast network of credit institutions, commercial banks, savings banks, investment banks, federal reserve banks, credit corporations, and credit unions. Today, even the gold standard itself appears as only a traditional carryover from the past—a mechanism used almost exclusively in the settlement of international accounts. The money of today is essentially credit money, appearing either in the form of notes issued directly by the government or by central Federal Reserve Banks, or in the form of checks drawn on banking institutions. Transactions in trade are typically consummated by the exchange of promises to pay and are cleared in central clearing houses between banks. This arrangement is far from a system of automatic mechanisms, and equally far from the old systems of exchanging goods for gold coin.

In May 1962, the gold holdings of the United States government totaled $16.4 billion. Supplementing the gold reserves, the government had in its vaults $2 billion in silver. Currency actually in circulation in May 1962 totaled about $30 billion, mostly in notes issued by the Federal Reserve Banks. In all, $16.4 billion of gold served to support not only the $30 billion of outstanding currency but also demand deposits of $115 billion and time deposits of $90 billion. Thus, roughly $235 billion of readily available funds rested on a gold base of $16.4 billion. This is not as precarious a balance as might be thought, since gold may not be withdrawn for domestic use and, more important, sufficient stability has been added to the banking system so that "runs" on American banks have all but disappeared.

### The value and use of money

#### The gold standard

Historically, a close relationship between the supply of gold and the total supply of money has long existed. Any country which defined its currency in terms of a given quantity of gold and maintained full redeemability in gold was said to be on the gold standard. For example, the United States for many years defined the dollar as 25.8 grains of nine-tenths fine gold. The scarcity of this precious metal made it easy to control the quantity of money in circulation, since the gold reserve was automatically limited by the products of mining. As each country on the gold standard freely bought and sold gold and used gold to settle international accounts, an international ratio of exchange between currencies was established which reflected the relative gold content of the monetary units of each country. Once such a balance was found, international movements of gold could automatically create the compensating forces to maintain equilibrium. Theoretically, this meant that when there was an excessive outflow of gold there would be a lowering of domestic prices which would encourage not only domestic, but eventually foreign buying. As exports grew, and the domestic economy received gold in payment, the increase in the domestic money supply could be expected to lead to price rises. Rising prices would discourage exports, encourage imports, and thus renew the cycle as domestic prices fell in response to the loss of gold.

Along with other factors, the impingement of war and trade barriers made it continually more difficult to adhere strictly to the gold standard; hence by the time of the depression of the 1930's many countries, including the United States, had either gone off the gold standard entirely or had devalued their currencies in terms of gold. The resulting price fluctuations and currency instabilities created hardships of their own.

By the end of World War II, after a period of consistent gold movement to the United States, our domestic hoard had become so great that most countries did not possess the necessary reserves to reëstablish the gold standard on its traditional basis even if they had so desired. Accordingly, the International Monetary Fund was formed to regulate international prices by helping to maintain a state of equilibrium between currencies. This agency attempts to prevent harmful price fluctuations by underwriting a relatively fixed rate of exchange between the various currencies, based on a modified gold standard. Under the aegis of the International Monetary Fund, the expectation was that the gold drains which

might occur would be minimal and that weak currencies might be supported by the creation of an international lending mechanism.

By 1962, United States gold reserves, after declining gradually for a number of years, dropped sharply to $16.4 billion, the lowest level in 23 years. This precipitous decline was due not to adverse trade balances, but to drains occasioned by military and economic foreign aid. Because these new commitments appear to be a continuing burden upon the dollar, real concern over the gold outflow has been voiced by many authorities.

### The quantity theory of money

Any attempt to reduce economic phenomena to a formula is prone to be limited by the unpredictable variables in human behavior. Nevertheless, such a formula may serve as a shorthand method of observing the cardinal elements in a given economic relationship. One such device is the "equation of exchange" which seeks to express the relationship between money and prices. The number of times money (M) is exchanged within a specific period of time is its speed or velocity (V). Thus, MV gives us the total amount we spend as buyers. On the other side of the equation are the average price (P) we pay for goods and services and the physical volume of trade (T) which takes place. PT then gives us the total amount which the sellers receive. We thus have the "truism," $MV = PT$.

This equation is helpful for discovering what may be expected to happen when any one of its components varies. For example, if the money supply rises and velocity remains constant, either price must increase or physical output must grow. Conversely, if the quantity of money falls with velocity remaining constant, either price or trade volume or both will decrease. The interlocking dependence of the parts of the formula is axiomatic, yet the difficulties of accurate measurement coupled with the influence of human decisions make the possible variations somewhat unpredictable in a dynamic economy. For instance, if M is increased with the avowed purpose of encouraging output in order to increase T, the result could conceivably be to increase P instead, if T cannot or does not increase as expected. For this reason, among others, tampering with the supply of money involves serious risks and must always be approached with the utmost caution.

## American banking practices

### Fractional reserves and demand deposits

When the public began to accept bank credit and bank notes in lieu of gold as the usual medium of exchange, the automatic checks which the use of gold had imposed on the economy began to diminish. Thus it became possible for banks to lessen the impact of a gold outflow by increasing the total amount of their demand deposits through loans. Demand deposits are today for all intents and purposes money—indeed most transactions are settled in this way. Since a banking system may expand or contract credit money in circulation within broad limits, the former controls imposed upon the economy by the gold standard have been largely voided.

The importance of legal reserve requirements lies then not so much in the "fraction" of gold held as in the confidence of the public (the depositors) in the credit and currency which substitute for it. However, if reserve requirements are kept relatively high, sharp fluctuations between expansion and contraction are less likely to occur, and the money market is prone to be more stable.

The power of individual banks to "create" new deposits through loans and thus influence the amount of money in circulation is limited by the reserves which they are required by law to maintain. If, for example, a local bank chooses to hold a reserve ratio of 20 per cent, (that is, if the bank holds $200 against every $1000 in demand deposits), it can issue loans to borrowers on the remaining $800, or 4 times the value of the reserve. (The legal reserve requirement as of January 1, 1962 was 16½

per cent for reserve city banks. Most banks will operate on a margin somewhat above the legal minimum to avoid the danger of having their holdings fall below the legal minimum requirement in the event of unexpectedly large deposit withdrawals.)

This $800 usually may be expected to be deposited in another account, from which $640 may be loaned if that bank also holds 20 per cent or $160 in reserve. This redepositing of monetary assets acts as a multiplier in adding purchasing power to the economy. For instance, if the bank loans $800 to a businessman to buy an automobile, the bank which receives the agency's deposit at the time of purchase may loan a part of that amount to another borrower and so on. The reinvesting of deposits can theoretically continue until the new deposits created "multiply" the original deposit by five.

The fact that the American monetary system permits an increase in the money supply with scant regard for gold stores has meant that the quantity of money has on occasion grown too fast for the maintenance of price stability. From 1880 to 1962 approximately 50 per cent of the increase in the circulating money supply occurred during the First and Second World Wars, compared with the long-term average of 5 to 6 per cent per year. In

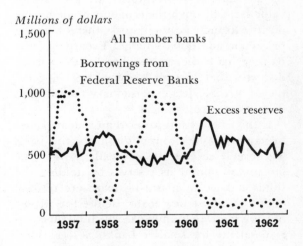

*Millions of dollars*

All member banks

Borrowings from
Federal Reserve Banks

Excess reserves

1957   1958   1959   1960   1961   1962

*Fig. XXI-1   Recent trends in U. S. banking: borrowing from Federal Reserve Banks and excess reserves of member banks of the Federal Reserve.*

both wars much of the increase in federal expenditures was financed by commercial bank loans to the government, thus creating new bank deposits in the name of the federal government. During World War II alone, this augmented the federal debt by some $70 billion. As the government paid for war orders from its new deposits, demand deposit accounts for businesses and individuals rose, while the goods purchased were drained from the economy. Thus our money stock rose far out of proportion to "real" output, or goods for use within the economy.

The past history of business cycles in the United States is replete with examples of overly optimistic credit expansion by banks. Bankers are actually caught in something of a lockstep situation. In order to make money they must be willing to make loans, but at the same time such action augments the risk involved. The expansion or contraction of bank loans reaches far beyond the control of the bank due to the multiplier effect already described. When there is an increase in the effective demand for goods, business expectations are high. It is only too easy for bankers to be caught up in the enthusiasm as demand for investments grows. Some are tempted to speculate with credit, and this leads to price acceleration and eventually to inflation. As the sense that inventories are growing in value seeps through the economy, some buyers borrow to increase their stock, thereby giving prices an additional nudge. Eventually, the bank which had been too liberal with its loans discovers that its cash balances are being depleted as other less expansionary banks drain it of its reserve balances.

If the reserves fall lower than that required by law as cash accounts diminish, the bank has several choices. It may call in its loans, or it may rebuild its reserves by holding the funds accrued as maturing loans are retired, or it may refuse new loans. Before the advent of large metropolitan banks which became correspondents for smaller banks, a local business crisis could be and often was severe enough to cause many bank failures. The spreading of risk through correspondent systems coupled with the later inauguration of the Federal Reserve System and finally the establishment of the Federal Deposit Insurance Corporation have all given greater protection and provide substantial evidence of the increasing maturity of our banking system.

### The Federal Reserve System

When the Federal Reserve System was formed by Congress in 1913, there was some discussion concerning the desirable degree of centralization. The final result was a compromise wherein twelve regional banks were created as part of a national system with headquarters in Washington. In this way, local interests could be served, but at the same time all banks in the system would have greater strength and risks would be more widely distributed. In addition, broad policies could be made more uniform throughout the country. Member banks, while surrendering some freedom of decision enjoyed greater flexibility and elasticity and more safety than had formerly been possible. It was decided that all national banks should be required to join, and that state banks might join optionally by meeting the requirements.

The regional Reserve banks are run by a board of directors. They are under the Federal Reserve Board which serves as the governing body for the Federal Reserve System. The Federal Reserve Board consists of seven members appointed by the president to serve staggered fourteen-year terms.

The Federal Reserve System functions in several ways. The regional banks serve as bankers' banks, not only to hold individual bank reserves and act as clearing houses for the transactions of member banks, but also to serve as a source of loans. By encouraging or discouraging bank loans according to the apparent needs of the economy, the Federal Reserve System exercises more than nominal control over the quantity of money in use. Over the years, Congress has granted the Federal Reserve Board increasing discretionary powers according to the growing needs of the country. An examination of the ways in which the Federal Reserve System exercises its powers will give some insight into how it influences monetary policy and the workings of money within the economy.

As the holder of the basic bank reserves of the nation, the Federal Reserve determines the percentage of fractional reserves member banks must retain for operation. (Each Reserve bank is required at present to have at least 25 per cent of its holdings in gold certificates. Congress lowered the requirement during World War II when the limits of expansion with the gold certificates then available were approached.) Within fixed legal limits, reserve requirements for member banks may be raised or lowered to make it more or less difficult for these banks to expand their loans.

In practice, the authority to alter reserve requirements has been sparingly used, and instead the Board has exercised its control by altering the charges for rediscounting the notes of member banks, thus either encouraging or placing a brake on loan expansion.

It is highly significant that, while the Reserve has the power to curb expansion in a time of inflation by making additional reserves difficult for a member bank to obtain, it cannot force investment in times of recession. It can offer attractive borrowing rates to encourage spending but this does not assure that investors will respond, and the stimulus may not always be sufficient to help the economy out of its slump. The commonly used analogy of being unable "to push a string" to control what it will do is an apt one.

The most important power of the Federal Reserve System to encourage or restrain spending has become that of buying or selling government obligations in the open market. In this decision to buy or to sell, the Reserve System enjoys the advantage of being able to act without first having to receive a request for funds from individual banks. Today government debt is decidedly the largest asset of

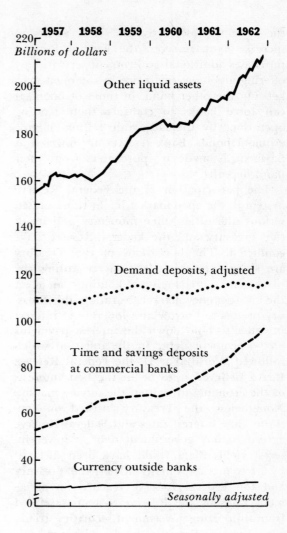

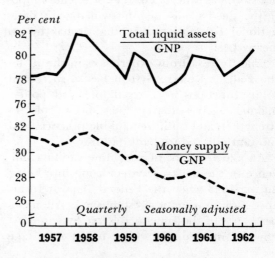

*Fig. XXI-2  Recent trends in U. S. banking: relation of deposits, currency outside banks, and other liquid assets to gross national products.*

*Money: its use, measurement, and rôle  405*

the Federal Reserve System. If it wishes to increase bank reserves, the Federal Reserve purchases additional government securities by offering a competitive price in the open market. On the other hand, in times of boom, it can force banks to contract their lending operations by the large-scale selling of government bonds. Bank reserves are lowered as payment is made by purchasers from their bank deposits.

The participation of the Federal Reserve System in the open market has at times caused serious difficulties when monetary policies of the Treasury and the Federal Reserve have conflicted. The operations of the Treasury are so vast that its decisions regarding the placement and changing of holdings can affect the entire money market. Naturally the Treasury prefers to borrow at a low rate of interest in order to hold down the interest payments on government debt. In the inflation which followed World War II, the Federal Reserve Board believed it to be in the best interests of the economy to tighten the money market. Nonetheless, the Treasury insisted on continued low interest rates and Federal Reserve agreed to buy government debt at lower interest yields than would have been dictated by a free market. Finally in 1951 the Treasury and the Federal Reserve reached an agreement whereby the Reserve System was freed from supporting government securities strictly according to Treasury needs. Although this decision has alleviated the problem temporarily, the issue is so intertwined with basic national economic policy that it has by no means been resolved.

Since its disastrous experiences in the 1930's the Federal Reserve System has so succeeded in its functions as a regulatory and policy-making agency that it has been able to strengthen and stabilize banking practices and substantially reduce bank failures.

An added means of providing public confidence in the banking system came into being during 1933 when the Federal Deposit Insurance Corporation was established. All member banks of the Federal Reserve System must now be insured and other banks may take Federal Deposit Insurance if they meet the requirements. Deposit accounts are now insured against loss up to $10,000. By allaying depositors' fears that a bank may fail, this organization reduces to a minimum the danger of runs on the banks when the economy slips downward. After a quarter of a century of experience, the Federal Deposit Insurance Corporation has acquired assets of more than $2 billion to cover possible losses.

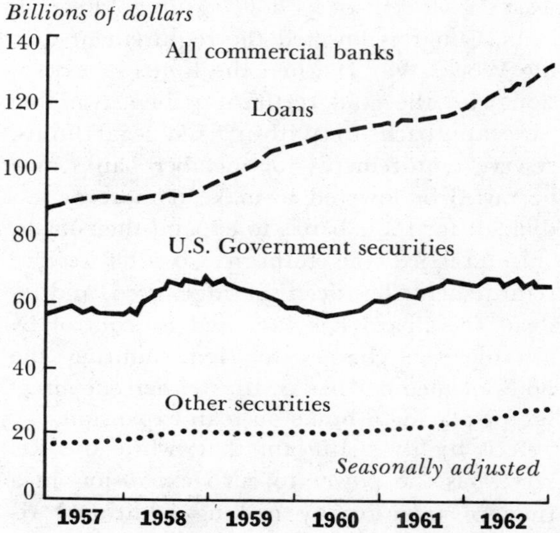

Billions of dollars

Fig. XXI-3   Recent trends in U. S. banking: charts above and below show loans and U. S. Government and other securities of member banks and relation of loans to total deposits of all commercial banks.

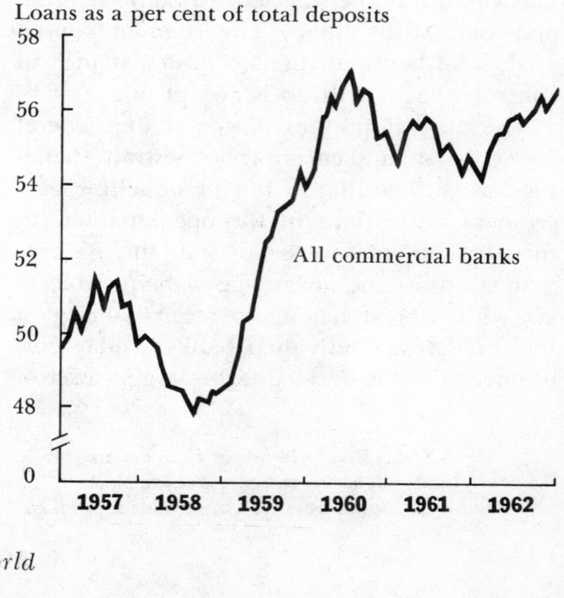

Loans as a per cent of total deposits

It remains to be noted that the most important aspect of our monetary system does not lie in the total supply of money stock of the nation; rather it rests upon the sustaining of a high level of expenditure throughout the economy—from the private consumer to business activities, to the largest government purchaser. Money needs to be safe and available. More important, money needs to circulate at an adequate rate if the economy is to be sound and expanding. Too great a propensity to hold back funds can quickly create a crippling drag on economic activity; just as too great a tendency to spend may prove highly inflationary. The chief virtue of an overall and well-thought-out monetary policy is that it may help prevent abrupt and catastrophic shifts in economic activity. The monetary needs of the nation demand considerable flexibility. At any moment in time, many influences are at work which vitally affect our economic state of health. In order to study the growing effort to coördinate policies relating to national development, we turn next to a discussion of the Council of Economic Advisors to the president which was authorized by the Employment Act of 1946.

## Government policies to aid economic stability

### The Employment Act of 1946

The Employment Act of 1946 confirmed a notable shift in the American attitude toward governmental action to influence the course of the economy. The Act stated in part: "... it is the continuing policy and responsibility of the Federal Government...to promote maximum employment, production and purchasing power."

Prior to the 1930's government expenditures were often considered to be a burden on the economy, and the ideal sought was a balanced budget at a minimum cost. Government borrowing was felt to be a drag on savings which were vitally needed by private investment sources. The success of an economy was deemed to stem from individual thrift and personal effort. It was commonly believed that government spending could lead only to extravagance.

During the great depression of the 1930's, large-scale efforts were made by the government to stimulate the economy in a variety of ways, including deficit financing of relief and public works expenditures. During World War II the government actively invaded the realm of private enterprise when it established plants and supplied equipment to implement the war effort. Since the war, the government has continued massive defense expenditures as well as expanded scientific and technological projects. It has offered funds for research in various other fields as well.

Nonetheless, in 1946 Congress did not indicate specifically how the government was to carry out the intentions declared in the Employment Act. The Council of Economic Advisors, a three-man body appointed by the president, compiles a vast body of data concerning the trends of the economy and frequently recommends specific courses of action. Whether or not these recommendations are followed, they are heard and weighed by the president as well as by the committees of Congress, and the published Council reports have proven themselves a decidedly worthwhile contribution for any individual or group concerned with economic trends.

### Automatic stabilizers

An "automatic stabilizer" represents a type of government action planned in advance to take effect when needed to counter adverse economic trends when these depart sufficiently from the norm to endanger the balance of the economy. The use of countercyclical stabilizers can lessen the cumulative effects of inflation or depression and therefore help hasten the return to equilibrium.

Although economists disagree widely concerning the specific rôle the government should play in guiding the economy, the employment of automatic stabilizers seems to hold the greatest promise of success, with fewer undesirable complexities than other courses of action. Even here, there is a question of how to develop a system of stabilizers which will be triggered automatically when needed and yet will not in themselves cause harm by doing too much, or lasting too long, or in other ways failing to accomplish the restorative task for which they are designed. Nevertheless, the application of automatic stabilizers conceived in the long-run interests of the country seems preferable to frequent and sharp changes of governmental policy to meet varying economic conditions. The government has come to provide some automatic stabilizers which, while not the perfect answer, make it reasonably certain that at least some of the tragedies of the depressed 1930's can be avoided in the future.

The right to tax is one of the government's most powerful weapons as an automatic stabilizer. Taxes today are high and are collected on a mass basis. They graduate more than proportionately with rise in income. Hence, in times of inflationary pressures, the Treasury siphons off funds which might otherwise lead to overexpansion and an inflation spiral. On the other hand, when income falls, the collection of taxes declines at a rate more than proportionate to the fall in income, leaving a higher residual income and therefore more purchasing power in the hands of the consumer.

Yet income taxes were originally intended as a primary source of revenue for the government. If taxes are also used as the primary means of achieving economic stabilization, they are really serving two divergent purposes at one time. Indeed, as a matter of fiscal practice, government expenses can be expected to rise during a recession at the very time that revenue automatically decreases with the drop in income level.

Another, more direct government action which takes place automatically and far more rapidly than tax adjustments is the payment of unemployment benefits. These payments, which support the purchasing power of many families hit by recession begin very shortly after the wage earner is laid off and may continue for as long as six months or more. The income thus derived is usually spent immediately for consumer goods, thus bolstering demand and helping stimulate economic activity. The payment of welfare benefits and assistance to farmers are other forms of governmental payments that serve as economic stabilizers.

If the injection into the economy of income through tax refunds and unemployment compensation payments is sufficiently stimulating, it is not long before the multiplier effect is felt, along with the accelerator principle. When both of these begin to operate together, the upswing may soon gain enough momentum to pull the economy out of its slump. The multiplier, as has already been mentioned, refers to the number of times an expenditure from a particular investment will increase as it is reinvested. The accelerator principle has to do with the more than proportionate growth in the need for capital goods as the effective demand for consumer goods rises. For example, if a particular automobile agency usually sells three automobiles per week (a small per cent of total national demand), an increase in demand to six automobiles per week will make it necessary for the dealer to raise his inventory by 100 per cent and double his investment. At the same time, the dealer will be prone to place an order with the wholesaler not merely for six automobiles for which there is a known demand, but for seven or eight to avoid being caught short on inventory. Wholesalers, in turn, increase their orders to manufacturers more than proportionately in keeping with the anticipated demand. As manufacturers step up production to answer the increased need for automobiles, the ripple spreads throughout the economic stream and plants must work closer to full capacity, or must be enlarged or new factories built in order to produce more cars. Conversely, if there is a drop in the growth rate, deceleration of inventory and orders occurs at a higher rate than the drop in demand.

While the benefits offered by automatic

stabilizers suggest that they act as a needed brake to prevent violent changes of direction in the economy, they are imperfect, especially in the case of taxes, in that they need to provide more flexibility and be of greater aid with less delay. In 1961 it was suggested in the *Report of the Commission on Money and Credit* that monetary authorities could, with some modifications of fiscal policy, guide the economy to an adequate growth level with low levels of unemployment and with a continuing reasonable price stability. The *Report* proposed that Congress grant the president limited and conditional powers to make temporary countercyclical adjustments in the rate of personal income tax for the first tax bracket. The *Report* also recommended that Congress should project programs of expenditure well into the future and thereby allow the Chief Executive greater flexibility in his choice of timing for particular outlays so that they might better serve the purpose of economic stabilization.

To devise a policy for automatic stabilization that will be internally consistent in the long run and yet effective in the short run poses problems of determining the general direction in which the economy should move. These problems lie much deeper than monetary and fiscal policy alone. All the same, if the government can provide wise guidance without harmfully intervening in healthily competitive economic activities, the use of automatic stabilizers can be highly effective.

## National income measurement

Our ability to understand the significance of economic trends depends upon our capacity to measure the changes which occur on various levels of economic activity and their relation to each other. By examining the total amount of national income and also by studying the parts which make up the whole, we may learn something of the underlying structure of the economy. We may also discover how various sectors are interrelated and

changing at a particular time. Fortunately, most economic transactions involve an exchange of money so that we can measure in terms of a common denominator the value of such varied items as grain, shoes, or motor fuel. We can also measure the cost to plant the seed and harvest the grain, to render shoes from leather, and to extract oil from under the ground and refine it into gasoline. The technique we employ is called national accounting.

### Gross National Product

Gross National Product is the expression used to designate the total value of goods and services produced by the economy within a specific length of time. Although the figures used to estimate value are based on market price, the task is not merely addition. It is important that every product be counted, but it is also important that no item be counted more than once. The difficulty arises when we attempt to determine where and how to estimate the value of products which may pass through several stages before they are sold for final use. For example, grain is ground into flour. Some flour is used in the manufacture of prepared mixes, some is sold to commercial users such as bakeries, and some is sold directly to consumers for use at home. If we count the price of the grain plus the cost to the bakery of buying the flour and also include the purchase price of the final baked goods, we have obviously counted the grain (the original product) more than once. However, we could add in the difference in cost as each stage of improvement increases value and thus arrive at the final value without double counting.

Another method of determining value is to use the price of the "final product," that is, goods purchased not for resale. The flour sold for commercial baking is not a "final product" whereas the flour sold to the housewife is. This yardstick of finality—buying not for resale—is the one used by the Department of Commerce to identify products. The price paid for these goods by their final users measures spending.

Overall spending of final users for goods and services may be divided into three broad categories: (1) The largest category consists of private *individuals,* households, and non-profit institutions whose purchase of consumer goods and services amounted to $339.2 billion and accounted for about 66 per cent of GNP in 1961. (2) *Businesses* spent $69.5 billion for investment goods in the same year, which was 13 per cent of GNP. These purchases include machinery, factory buildings, new houses, and inventory. (3) *Government* payments for goods and services totaled $108.6 billion for 1961 or 21 per cent of GNP. These government transactions include not only goods and services for the benefit of taxpayers, but also those needed within the framework of governmental administration.

One aspect of counting which is omitted in figuring GNP is that not all the equipment in use to produce goods is brand new. Some of its original value, counted in GNP estimates of earlier years, has depreciated in the wear and tear of use and becomes incorporated in the value of finished products; so part of the value of the equipment is actually re-counted during each year of its use. Eventually, of course, the equipment will have to be replaced. An exact measure of depreciation is exceedingly difficult, so that we must rely on business estimates.

The Net National Product (NNP) is obtained by subtracting depreciation from GNP. But difficulties of accurate measurement prevent NNP from being more useful than GNP.

In order to estimate more accurately the amounts paid for goods and services, another deduction must be made. If the taxes we pay are spent for government goods and services, the same money should not also be counted in the purchase price we pay for the goods on which we were taxed. Hence, sales taxes and other indirect taxes on businesses collected during the stages of production will, when deducted from NNP, give us an approximation of the total net value in dollars received for goods produced. This figure should correspond

with that obtained by using another method which derives from different data—that of factor payments—to calculate national income.

### The measure of factor payments

"Factor payments" simply refers to the recompense made to the same groupings as factors of production—land, labor, capital, and management. All payments received in return for some service of a factor of production should be included in the national income measurement. Thus, factor payments would include all wages and salaries, interest from loans, gains from capital investment, and the net earnings of business.

The difficulties of measuring by the factor payment method are numerous and complex. The value of many payments has to be estimated, such as payments in kind for services for which there is no payment in exchange, undistributed profits of business, and many others.

The utility of the factor payment method of measurement depends upon the availability of data and the degree to which sources are reliable.

It should be noted that the use of the factor payment method and the determination of Gross National Product are two ways of arriving at essentially the same thing, i.e., total national earnings and expenditures in terms of buying and selling transactions in the market. The possibility of approaching national income measurement from both directions, as we do in the United States, clearly illustrates the circular flow of income through the economy. Thus, an expenditure in one part furnishes the income for another sector. A simplified diagram may be worked out to demonstrate this interlocking relationship.

Individual patterns of expenditure are closely related to the amount of income received as well as to the group habits of segments of the community. If there is a marked growth in total national income, we may expect to find a change in the types of consumer expenditure, provided some items in family budgets (notably in leisure time pursuits) tend to be highly elastic as incomes rise; others such as food remain more nearly constant. By the study of national income flows, we may also discover the existing relationships between the consumer sector, the business sector, and the government sector. Money flows delineate what will be produced and by whom, as well as by whom products will be consumed.

## Foreign investment and international trade

❧ The continuing strength of the American economy has become vital to the economic health of the noncommunist world. Since World War II the American dollar has become the "reserve" currency for many countries. The complexity of the international economic relationships, which depend upon the stability of the dollar and which would be deeply affected by changes in it, make the determining of American monetary and fiscal policy a delicate task indeed. The attempt to ensure economic growth, full employment, and stable domestic prices will not necessarily guarantee international economic well-being and the convertibility of other national currencies at reasonably stable rates of exchange. ❧ The international economic problems of the United States since World War II have centered in our relations with the many nations weakened by the war, the continuation of the cold war with all its economic ramifications, and our efforts to give aid and to encourage investment in underdeveloped countries. ❧

### The balance of payments

One of the many reasons why buying and selling across national boundary lines requires special arrangements for handling payment for the goods purchased is that buyer and seller do not use the same monetary unit. An American exporter of office machinery, for example, might sell an order of $10,000 worth of such

equipment to an English buyer. The buyer would only be able to pay in English pounds, since that is the unit in regular use in England and it is the money in which he would be paid when he resold the machines to his own customers. The American seller cannot use English pounds in his business in the United States, so somehow or other he must have the pounds converted into dollars. Sometimes, too, as in domestic business, the buyer may have arranged for some delay, perhaps sixty to ninety days, before making payment. Thus the financial aspects of the sale of office machinery from the United States to England may result in a need for conversion of English pounds into American dollars and also in a short-term loan from the United States to England until the machines are paid for. The need for these services has given rise to a specialized type of banking concerned with foreign exchange and international lending, of either a short-term or long-term nature.

In normal times, if any times can truly be called normal, the task of making such exchanges of the money of one country into that of another is made much easier by the fact that any imbalance in the exchange of goods is likely to be offset by other factors, such as capital movements. That is, international buying and selling by any one country are not likely to be so very far out of equal balance with any other country, or at least with all outside countries taken together. In this situation, foreign exchange dealers can usually pay sellers in any one country with funds which buyers in the same country need to have transferred to those from whom they have bought abroad. Hence the English importer of American office machinery might, in effect, pay (through the medium of a bank dealing in foreign exchange) an English woolen broker who has sold woolens to American buyers. On the American side of the transaction, the buyer of English woolens might pay for them by transferring dollars to the seller of office machinery. Since normally something like this situation commonly prevails, both buying and selling can be taken for granted, and the bankers who deal in foreign exchange can guarantee payment in the desired currency to either buyers or sellers, knowing that because of the nearly equal balance of payments, the reserves on which they draw to make payments will not be exhausted.

This balance of payments to which we refer is a double-entry bookkeeping system in which an attempt is made to account for all the exchanges through buying and selling which take place within a designated time between a country and other countries. If all the figures are accurately known (an impossibility in itself), the ledger theoretically should be in balance at some moment. In actual practice, trade relations as well as payments are multilateral, that is to say, an imbalance with one country may be offset by the relationship with others. Thus individual equilibrium of each trading country with any other country is not necessary. In fact trade is restricted when nations try to keep bilateral accounts.

In examining what constitutes and affects the balance of payments, it will be found that by far the largest element to consider is the "balance of trade"—the relationship between exports from and imports to a country. This includes all the exchanges of merchandise from raw materials to finished manufactured goods, as well as "invisibles," that is, services which are bought and sold, such as the transportation costs of shipping goods by sea or by air, spending connected with travel, the payment of various pensions and gratuities, and others. The balance of trade is usually considered to be favorable for a country which exports more than it imports. The United States has enjoyed a favorable balance of trade for many years. In the year ending December 1961, exports were $6.6 billion above imports. This simply means that, on the whole, American goods are attractively priced and therefore will sell in foreign markets.

This psychological attitude toward the relationship of exports to imports dates back to the days of mercantilism when governments collected gold and silver in payment to balance accounts. Then an unfavorable balance was regarded as a sign of weakness. Although international trade is no longer based strictly on the gold standard, governmental actions were and still are taken to remedy an unfavorable balance whenever possible, to prevent excessive outflows of gold and the resulting depressive effects on the domestic economy. The struggle of nations to attain or maintain a favorable position often serves as a damper on many trading activities, curtailing imports and leading in the direction of contractions in each nation's domestic economy. In recent years the coöperation of many nations has been directed toward the elimination of trade barriers, notably through the General Agreements on Tariffs and Trade. Furthermore, through the International Monetary Fund wide fluctuations in currency values have been prevented, thereby helping preserve confidence in international rates of exchange and in turn encouraging trading and investment.

In spite of its favorable balance of trade, the United States has been running a continual deficit in its balance of international payments, due to other areas in which American expenditures consistently exceed income. Some imbalance exists in the field of services, since we pay out more than we receive in transportation costs and since the number of American tourists traveling abroad far outnumbers those from other countries who visit the United States. However, by far the greatest outgoing expenditure for which we receive no payment in return is for military and economic foreign aid. Military expenses include not only monetary grants to foreign countries, shipments of military equipment, and our own purchases of military equipment from other nations, but also the costs of maintaining military personnel who are stationed overseas and who often have their families with them.

Another significant area of deficit lies in capital investments abroad. While income from existing foreign investments gives us a plus in our balance of payments, this is more than offset by the current American investment of long-term capital abroad, which in 1961 amounted to $3.9 billion as against $577 million in foreign capital invested that year in the United States. Although in the long run the purchases of capital assets abroad may be beneficial to the domestic economy, it also causes a serious leakage in our present balance of payments.

Short-term capital investments, which include bank balances, loans, and other forms of private debt which are terminable in less than a year's time, have been more volatile, with the balance for the United States shifting from credit to debit and back. Sometimes the notes of banks are sold at a discount to domestic financial institutions and then transmitted abroad where they will be paid at maturity or called in when the foreign interest rate is favorable. Much of this short-term credit is accepted for such healthy foreign trade functions as lending money to ease the payments for merchandise. However, speculative ventures, such as lending to take advantage of higher interest rates, are also common. This speculative capital outflow generally tends to accentuate rather than to counteract economic cycles. Thus when the American economy is headed toward a downturn it may further weaken confidence in the dollar.

An unfortunate negative factor in the balance of payments is the bias which is built into the system of bookkeeping. The recording of payments is much more accurate than the record of receipts, so that the finding of deficits is weighted toward the country which owes the debt. The statistical error is of such magnitude that it can sometimes make the difference in whether a country stands recorded as suffering a deficit or enjoys a favorable balance of payments.

The dollar is still one of the strongest currencies in the world, based largely on the productive capacity of the United States, coupled with the immense accumulation of gold acquired by the United States during World War II. As was described earlier in this chapter, we no longer rely solely on movements of gold at fixed prices to balance either domestic or international trading accounts. Gold does flow but exchange rates are maintained at an equilibrium level by a wide variety of exchange control techniques assisted by a fabric of international lending organizations. Governments have not been

content to permit gold flows to have their former importance in international exchange.

Although the dollar is not domestically convertible into gold, its value in foreign exchange is, of course, more closely related to gold flows. An outflow of gold is more serious because of the danger of undermining foreign confidence in the international dollar than because of its effect on domestic stability. The problem is aggravated by the fact that the gold outflow of the United States is largely due to defense expenditures which can be expected to persist.

Thus, despite a healthy balance of trade, the gold hoard of the United States had been reduced to $16.4 billion by early 1962, an amount only $4.7 billion above the legal reserve requirement of $11.7 billion. To help offset the outflow of $4 billion in gold between 1958 and 1962, the Federal Reserve Board by its loan expansion to member banks caused the money supply to be increased by $4.8 billion. This increase aroused some fears of overly optimistic credit expansion and accompanying inflation. This trend abated measurably, however, in the spring of 1962 when stocks plummeted and posed the question of deflationary tendencies in the economy.

In checking a gold outflow, the Federal Reserve Board could choose to suspend or change the gold reserve requirement. It seems unlikely that such a step will be taken, since it could easily create favorable conditions for an increase in the short-term flow of capital to foreign markets and thus accentuate the gold drain instead of serving to alleviate the problem.

In 1962, the Federal Reserve and the Treasury jointly undertook to acquire a large holding of foreign currencies. With an abundant supply of such monies, United States monetary authorities would be able to offer European central banks these additional funds before the demand for dollars required that the American government reduce its gold holdings in the exchange. The prevention of a run on dollars would thus help to stabilize the value of and ward off further depletion of American gold reserves.

## International monetary arrangements since World War II

Before the end of World War II, it was apparent to the leaders of various governments that international trade and monetary transfers could not be resumed "as usual" for some time to come. As we have already seen in the chapter on American international relations after World War II, the loss of productive capacity in the countries ravaged by the war made it imperative that those nations seek assistance abroad in order to rebuild their economies as rapidly as possible. Food, raw materials, and machinery for export were available in only a few countries and especially in the United States. The countries in most urgent need of these goods did not have the capacity to produce comparable quantities of goods for sale in world markets to pay for the products they needed. Attempts of the economically weaker nations to buy abroad in spite of their inability to produce for sale abroad resulted in a surplus of their monetary units being offered for American dollars in the foreign exchange markets.

Thus the French franc, the Italian lira, and many other currencies were depressed in price, and the American dollar in terms of those currencies became very high in price. The decline of the price of currencies in terms of dollars contributes to an inflation of the prices of commodities for all currencies other than the dollar or similar "strong" currencies. Thus, the weakness of one currency in terms of another strong currency tends to be a mark of domestic inflation. This international inflationary force added to domestic inflationary forces, such as insufficient taxation to cover government budgets, created great financial strains in many countries.

The dollar and other strong currencies became acutely scarce. Because of the difficulty of restoring productive power to parallel the expanding productive capacity of the United States following the war, the acute dollar shortage in many countries became a chronic shortage. This was the great stumbling block to the reëstablishment of free world trade.

Another factor in the international economic situation at the end of the war was the deep suspicion that the disturbed and abnormal condition of international trade during the decade preceding the war had contributed in an important way to the war itself. Consequently, there was a genuine and widespread desire to probe the roots of international trade difficulties and to set up the necessary organizations and machinery to permit international trade to assume its rightful place as one of the chief supports of world peace and general prosperity. The United States House of Representatives in 1944 created the Special Committee on Postwar Economic Policy and Planning which issued a report in 1945, *The Postwar Foreign Economic Policy of the United States*. Interestingly enough, the major points in this report were similar to those supported by the United States delegation to the International Monetary Conference at Bretton Woods in 1944. At the conference, all parties agreed that emergency measures would have to be taken at the end of the war. For the long run, the Bretton Woods Conference proposed to participating governments that two new organizations be established to deal respectively with problems of maintaining the strength of various world currencies and of aiding the flow of capital to points where it was most urgently needed. From this recommendation, the International Monetary Fund and the International Bank for Reconstruction and Development were created. These two agencies have gained increasing membership and support as the postwar years have passed.

### The International Monetary Fund

The International Monetary Fund began operations in September 1946, and by 1960 it had a membership of 69 countries. The purpose of the Fund is to strengthen the monetary reserves of each individual country by setting up a reserve pool to which each member contributes according to the quota set when it became a member. Then, when needed to support its currency, a member can go to the Fund for help in the form of a loan with prescribed limits. The kinds of needs which the Fund is designed to serve arise either from seasonal disturbances in the balance of payments or from the cyclical rise and fall of business. As an example, a primarily agricultural country might have its largest exports in the part of the year following its harvest season, whereas its purchases of manufactured goods from abroad might come at a different season. During this latter period, many foreign sellers would come into possession of the country's unit of currency, which they would wish to sell or exchange for their own money. Sales of currency would exceed purchases at that season and the price or exchange rate of the agricultural country's monetary unit would be depressed. To prevent this, this country could appeal to the Fund for a short-term loan to purchase its own currency in order to hold its price to the established par or to the exchange rate which had been agreed upon with the authorities of the Fund. Similar action would take place when one country was in a state of depression due to temporary lack of demand for its export products. The objective of all of these actions and of the Fund itself is to create conditions in the foreign exchange markets in which monetary conditions would never of themselves become barriers to free interchange of goods. The accepted goal of international buying and selling is free multilateral, or many-sided, trade in which every country can buy and sell with complete freedom wherever the most favorable prices can be secured.

Care was taken that the Fund would have no power over domestic policies. Recognizing the limitations of the Fund, its managers have followed cautious policies and have not committed its full resources to the task of stabilizing world currencies and exchange rates, knowing that to achieve this desired result would require broader powers and greater resources than those of the Fund. Nevertheless, the Fund has not been a negligible factor in ameliorating postwar international monetary conditions. It has provided helpful technical assistance, and as of March 31, 1961, had assets of $3 billion in gold and $11 billion in world currencies. The International Monetary Fund has gradually become more influential over the years, although the supplementary efforts of other international agencies have also been needed.

## The International Bank for Reconstruction and Development

The organization which parallels the International Monetary Fund is the International Bank for Reconstruction and Development. Members of the Bank are required to hold membership in the Fund. There were differences of opinion among the conferees at Bretton Woods as to the nature and functions of the Bank, but none as to the general need for an international agency to encourage the international flow of funds for investment in productive enterprises anywhere in the world. It was reasoned that if this objective could be achieved in the long run, world trade would expand and the conditions which had caused unbalanced payments and highly variable exchange rates between many countries could be alleviated.

Thus the International Bank was set up to tackle the fundamental economic causes which lay beneath the surface troubles of the postwar world. Yet it was also realized, as in the case of the Monetary Fund, that the task was too great for one newly created agency, and that emergency aid from outside the International Bank would be required to meet the capital needs of at least the countries most seriously in need of reconstruction and development.

The International Bank, or World Bank as it is often called, began operation in June 1946 with 44 countries as members. Membership stood at 75 in April 1962, and 15 more countries, most of them newly independent nations of Africa, had applied for membership. The capital stock provided by member governments amounts to 25 per cent of the Bank's total assets, which in mid-1962 stood at $6.3 billion. Over half of the total has come from the purchase of bonds and parts of loans by commercial and savings banks, insurance companies, and others. The Bank had accumulated reserves of $675 million by 1962, and net earnings have increased to a rate of about $70 million per year.

The first loans of the Bank in 1947 were to European countries, and for several years the majority of its loans were to European nations. Most of its early loans were for reconstruction where the need was obvious and the conditions in the receiving country favorable to the rebuilding of a previously existing productive facility. As reconstruction took place and the European economy recovered from the devastation of war, the World Bank began to direct its lending toward the less developed countries of the world. In April of 1962, the World Bank had outstanding 309 loans to 59 countries for a total of $5.9 billion. Of these loans, 207 or two-thirds have gone to countries in Asia, the Middle East, and Central and South America. These countries have borrowed more than $3.5 billion, over half of the funds on loan. More often than not the loans have been used to develop resources fundamental to the growth of industry, such as pipe lines, canals, transportation facilities, and electric power.

### Other agencies of international finance

While the International Monetary Fund has helped maintain the equilibrium in international exchange and the World Bank has been enormously valuable, first in the rebuilding of war shattered Europe and later in the encouragement of backward countries, there has been urgent need for an international investment institution which could offer funds to private firms with fewer restrictions than could the Bank. In 1955 the International Finance Corporation was established for this purpose as an affiliate of the World Bank. Any government which is a member of the World Bank may join the IFC, which had 62 members in April 1962. As a matter of policy, the IFC does not invest in the more developed countries, and the sponsors of the projects in which it invests must have been unable to find financing elsewhere on reasonable terms. The IFC also requires that its participation in a new investment be less than 50 per cent of the total capital. The individual projects which have been approved have averaged $1.25 million, and in 1961 only half of the IFC's available resources were in use.

In 1960 another affiliate of the World Bank, the International Development Association, was formed. Its purpose is to provide easier loans to needy countries for a wide range of projects, on a more flexible basis and bearing less heavily on the balance of payments than the more conventional loans granted by the World Bank. This organization counted 51 countries as members by June 1961, and 4 countries had been granted $101 million in 50-year loans paying a negligible rate of interest.

### Conclusions

It must be said in conclusion that the granting of credit on an extensive scale has undoubtedly served to accelerate the pace of American economic development. Within the last hundred years, one of the rôles of technology has been to make possible the almost incredible increases in productive efficiency which have provided an impetus for the growth of large-scale business enterprise. Nonetheless, this growth would not have been possible had it not been for the availability of vast aggregates of capital through bank credit. Businessmen and consumers alike have been able to make purchases with far greater ease through the use of credit.

Along with the growth of cities, activities in industry and commerce have transformed the United States into a dynamic and variegated economy, dependent upon the use of money. Monetary demand has expanded with the advancing level of national income and the increasing stock of financial assets.

It would seem that one of the most urgent considerations facing us today is the determining of more explicit objectives in regard to monetary control. If we wish to achieve maximum growth, we will need different monetary and fiscal policies from those which would merely encourage economic stability. We must not only resolve domestic conflicts of interest but we must also tackle intricate international economic relationships. Compromises will be inevitable. Nonetheless, it is to be hoped that we can institute in the United States the economic planning essential to growth without discouraging private initiative, which has been the backbone of the American economy from its inception.

## FOR FURTHER READING

*The Federal Reserve System: Purposes and Functions.* 3rd ed. Washington, D.C.: The Board of Governors of the Federal Reserve System, 1954. Probably the best introduction to the workings of the Federal Reserve.

Gurley, John B., and Shaw. E. S. "The Growth of Debt and Money in the United States, 1800-1950." *Review of Economics and Statistics,* August, 1957.

Kemmerer, E. W., and Kemmerer, D. L. *ABC of the Federal Reserve System.* 12th ed. New York: Harper & Brothers, 1950. A comprehensive presentation of the intricacies of the Federal Reserve System.

Studenski, Paul, and Krooss, Herman. *Financial History of the United States.* New York: McGraw-Hill Book Co., 1952. A survey of money and banking in the United States from the Civil War to post World War II.

# GLOSSARY OF TERMS

**Ability-to-pay principle of taxation**

A rule that has been used with increasing frequency within the past century by legislative bodies in the construction of tax systems. Older rules of taxation were based on benefit received by the taxpayer, or were simply a penalty on some type of action which the governing authorities might wish to keep under control. All of these rules are still used. The ability-to-pay principle rests upon the idea that every citizen owes a responsibility to his country to support it financially in proportion to his wealth or income. It is the basis for the progressive tax on income currently used by many state as well as national governments. Many difficult questions arise in determining financial ability-to-pay. In the United States, net income (total income less legal deductions) is most widely used, although gross income (total income before deductions) and property ownership of various kinds are also used.

**Agricultural Revolution**

A term for a period of rapid change in farming methods and crops in England beginning at the end of the seventeenth century and extending throughout the eighteenth. Although the Agricultural Revolution cannot be marked off as clearly, it is to be compared to the Commercial Revolution which preceded it. The growth of commercial cities brought increased demands for food. Successful merchants as landowners had the means and the interest to experiment with new methods and crops. Deep plowing and soil liming proved beneficial, legumes became a field crop for winter hay, and crop rotation was practiced.

**Anarchism**

A social philosophy which holds that there should be no ruling power of any kind other than the restraints which individuals impose upon themselves. At its best, anarchism is a highly idealistic social theory, since it can work only as long as individuals are constantly mindful of the ways in which their own actions might harm others, and thus restrain themselves before engaging in such acts. At its worst, some persons who called themselves anarchists became simply destroyers of all life and property which they believed to be hostile to their own interests. In modified form, anarchism has had an effect upon other social theories such as fascism, on the one hand, and guild socialism (England) and syndicalism (Latin countries), on the other.

## Austerity program

A national economic policy whereby the standard of living of the people is deliberately reduced to accomplish such objectives as balancing the budget, balancing international payments, reducing or paying internal and external national debt, etc. Austerity policies were adopted by several countries during and immediately after World War II.

## Balance of trade

The calculation of the balance between imports and exports in the foreign trade of a nation or area. Mercantilist writers in the sixteenth and seventeenth centuries introduced the term because of their belief that a surplus of exports which would have to be paid for in precious metals was a source of economic strength to a country. To compute the balance of trade, it is necessary to include not only imports and exports of goods but also so-called "invisible items," consisting largely of financial transactions involving borrowing or lending of funds, payments for foreign travel, shipping services, and the like.

## Barter

The exchange of goods for other goods without the use of money as either a medium of exchange or a measure of value. Barter probably developed in primitive human societies when surpluses of goods developed beyond the needs of specific families or tribes. If barter became extensive, the awkwardness of valuing goods for direct exchange usually led to the adoption of some product, such as a metal, to serve as money. In modern times, trading between nations has sometimes approached barter when there is lack of faith in the monetary system, or when one or both parties wish to defend their own money or wish to dispose of or to obtain specific products. The latter state of affairs can develop into economic warfare.

## Boycott

A collective effort to refrain from dealing with specific businesses and to induce others to do likewise. Named for Captain Boycott, a landlord's agent in Ireland in the 1880's. While there may be commercial boycotts against firms or products, and, in international affairs, against countries, the most discussed use of the boycott in the past half century has been in labor disputes. Unions have tried to induce their own members, their relatives, and members of other unions as well to boycott employers who will not make favorable agreements with the union. Such actions have been reviewed in numerous court cases, resulting in a complex body of law on the labor boycott.

## Business cycle

The fluctuation of the level of business activity from high to low and back again. In earlier times, such fluctuations occurred from natural causes only. In the nineteenth century, it became clear that factors within the business system itself were producing these variations and serious study of business cycles was begun. Such factors as production, employment, credit, sales, and inventories were found to have distinctive cycles of their own, some having wider swings and different timing from others. It was soon suspected that when certain factors showed a tendency to increase or decrease, these changes might cause changes in other factors in the same or opposite direction. Attempts are continuing to find reliable indicators of changes in business so that corrective measures may be taken in time.

## Capital

The portion of man's total wealth which is devoted to assisting further production. It is to be distinguished from wealth which is used to satisfy man's needs and desires, as a house in which one lives. A house becomes capital only when it is not used for one's own living but is rented or sold for gain. Natural resources—even mere space—can be capital when they become so scarce that their owners can use them for gain. Money and credit can be capital because they represent tangible things which can be used to produce additional wealth. Capital as an economic concept has come into use as a result of the development of industrial technology which has opened up many ways to use tools, machinery, and resources to serve man's needs.

### Capitalism
In the narrowest sense, capitalism is a type of economic system in which the use of capital as a factor of production is the outstanding feature. More broadly, the term is also applied to a type of society and government simply because the use of capital is the dominant characteristic of the underlying economic system. The use of the term became common following the work of Karl Marx in the middle of the nineteenth century. He had emphasized that the large-scale use of capital brought into existence an elite class of owners and managers of big businesses and a much larger class of workers who did not own any of the machinery or equipment used in their work and received only a wage. Because of the emphasis upon private ownership in capitalism, the system has always been associated with personal freedom, democratic government, and competition in business.

### Cartel
A term which came to be applied in Germany in the latter part of the nineteenth century to a combination of business firms in which each retained its own identity while agreeing to a common plan of operation. Cartels are commonly considered to be monopolistic but proof of monopoly would have to be established in each case. A cartel agreement might allocate market quotas, or, especially in mining and basic manufacturing, production. The term is roughly similar to the American word *trust,* which originated in the same period. The cartel, however, is not necessarily illegal under European law, which is typically less severe than American law toward combinations in business.

### Central bank
The principal unit of the banking system of a country, usually owned or controlled by government. It may or may not have branches throughout the country, but, in any case, it has power to establish or control the operating policies of all of the other banks. The central bank may be virtually the financial department of the government, or, at least, it will act as the financial agent of the government. In these capacities, the modern central bank concerns itself with the relationship between the volume of credit issued by the banking system and the price level, with the balance of financial transactions between its own and other countries, and with similar matters affecting the economic welfare of the country. The Federal Reserve System is the central bank of the United States.

### Chartered company
A business company distinguished by the fact that it operated under a charter granted by the king or other ruler. The term *chartered company* was used only during the period of Mercantilism when nationalistic governments were active in promoting trade. The East India Company—a chartered company—aided the establishment of English authority in India. It survived until mid-nineteenth century. Chartered companies which established colonies in North America were the London Company (Jamestown), the Plymouth Company, and the Massachusetts Bay Company. The Hudson's Bay Company in Canada is a chartered company now in its fourth century. These companies usually had exclusive trading privileges in a specified area.

### Classical economics
The coherent body of economic ideas developed by a series of great thinkers beginning with Adam Smith (1723-1790) and David Ricardo (1772-1823). This body of economic theory has been called classical, not only because it came to be very widely accepted as a well-integrated explanation of economic phenomena, but also because it extended into the area of social behavior the same type of reasoning developed by Isaac Newton and others which was known as classical physics. Some of the propositions on which classical eco-

nomics was constructed are: men will calculate their economic interest and act on it if allowed to do so; this self interest will result in free competition between them which will eliminate the inefficient and the lazy; and the market will be the central controlling agency of the economic system. See *Smithian economics.*

### Closed shop

A closed shop agreement includes the provision in a labor contract that an employer can hire only workers who are already members of the union. Such an agreement reduces the employer's freedom to hire, and increases the union's control over the labor supply. Contracts of this nature are usually requested where employers are hostile or where the union is weakened by nonunion workers who seek to enjoy the gains earned by the union without supporting it.

### Collective bargaining

Collective bargaining is the process through which an employer or group of employers will seek a determination of wages, hours, and conditions of work with a trade union representing workers in the bargaining unit. This bargaining unit may include all the workers employed or may include only those in a given craft. If, after bargaining negotiations, an agreement is reached, it normally takes the form of a written trade agreement which will govern the employment conditions during the period of time it remains in force. If an agreement cannot be reached, a strike or lockout may ensue. Collective bargaining has been encouraged by the National Labor Relations Act of 1935, providing for elections conducted by the government to determine whether workers wish to be represented in collective bargaining negotiations, and, if so, through what union. If workers vote for collective bargaining, both parties must seek in good faith to reach an agreement. It is illegal for employers to discriminate against a worker because of membership in a union or participation in union activities.

### Collectivism

A generalized term for a social and economic system in which dominant patterns of thought and action derive from groups rather than individuals. The major collective systems of today are socialism and communism. The Fascism and Nazism of Italy and Germany before the Second World War were collectivist systems, although bitterly opposed to communism. In the Western world, the social philosophy opposite to collectivism is individualism. Group thinking and group action are characteristic of all human societies, but the term collectivism is not applied unless the collective aspects are organized under some kind of prevailing philosophy.

### Colonial system

A political system by which national states have endeavored to expand their sovereignty by establishing colonies beyond their own boundaries. Establishing a colonial system is one important phase of empire building. The thirteen original American colonies were a part of the English colonial system. The age of mercantilism was perhaps the greatest era of colonialism, but colonialism continued into the nineteenth century. In the twentieth century, some newly integrated and powerful states have shown tendencies toward encroachment upon adjoining territories, but not in the spirit of the bold conquerors of earlier centuries. Older colonial powers, such as Great Britain, have been forced to dissolve or transform their former colonial systems.

### Commercial revolution

The name which is given for convenience to a prolonged series of basic changes in the conduct of trade, mostly in western Europe in the early centuries of the modern era. Compared to the slower rate of change in earlier centuries, the commercial revolution was a true though extended revolution. Its principal characteristics may be placed in three groups. The geographic *extent* of trade was to the limits of the known world. Many new products were introduced to Europeans (foods, clothing, house furnishings), and markets overseas were opened to European manufactures. The *intensity* of trade was increased, so that more people obtained more of their needs through selling and buying in markets. By this process, an economic system of specialized production with exchange of goods and services between specialists was greatly expanded. Because of changes in the extent and intensity of trade, changes in *structure* of commercial enterprises also became necessary. More people had to work together efficiently in a business unit, and more time was required to complete all phases of the distribution of goods. The modern corporation was the outgrowth of these needs. Capital, as a factor of production, was needed far more widely than in earlier centuries. The success of the business corporation came from its value as a structural device to raise and manage capital efficiently. Thus, the commercial revolution and the business corporation which it produced were, in turn, the creators of modern capitalism.

### Commodity

Literally, anything that is commodious or useful. The term became important as the exchange of goods and services became more common in the developing economic system. In some aspects, the word *commodity* is almost a singular form of the word *goods*. Ordinarily, the concept of commodity carries the meaning of a crude or unmanufactured material of natural origin but not a metal or mineral. Thus the commodity markets deal in wheat, cotton, coffee, cocoa, crude rubber, or similar products. Coal or iron ore are less commonly referred to as commodities, although the transportation charges for moving these minerals are referred to as commodity rates. In the latter use, commodity means merely a bulk product. Services such as labor may also sometimes be referred to as a commodity.

### Common Market

An organized European market community in which the participants, over a period of years, gradually abandon tariffs between themselves but continue tariff protection against outside nations. The Common Market has encouraged more specialization by the use of mass production techniques. It is believed that if these savings are passed along to the consumer, marked increases in living standards should ensue. The interdependent relations among members of the present European Common Market represent a tardy application of the same principles which have stimulated interstate commerce in the United States.

### Common stock

In the modern corporations which operate most of the large-scale businesses of the nation, ownership is represented by shares of common stock, issued by the corporation. Such shares usually give voting rights in the election of directors to conduct the business of the company, a right not often exercised by most small stockholders. More important, the division of net profits of the corporation, after paying all operating expenses and setting aside reserves for expansion, is on the basis of common-stock holdings. The issuance of common stock allows many small investors to share in the ownership and development of companies. The purchase and sale of such shares of common stock in the stock exchanges of the nation makes possible the easy transfer of ownership in a large company. The widespread use of common stock as a channel of investment has, however, given rise to many problems of fraud and manipulation, which have led to extensive federal regulations. Some of these abuses have been in the sale of common stock by fraudulent promoters; others have been by the development of self-perpetuating corporation managements which take advantage of scattered stockholders by operating companies for their own advantage rather than in the interest of the holders of common stock. See *Corporation*.

### Communism

In the broadest sense, a social system in which economic goods are held in common. In this sense, communism as a system and communes as centers of living are as old as our earliest

423

knowledge of man. In contrast, individualism, as the opposite of communism, is a modern system. In the twentieth century, the importance of communism has derived from the writings of Karl Marx (1818-1883), who predicted the collapse of capitalism and its replacement by a new type of world-wide communism. Marx became the patron saint of the most extreme social revolutionists of Europe in the latter part of the nineteenth century. His doctrines have since spread throughout the world in the twentieth century. Many countries produced their own revolutionary leaders who accepted Marxian teaching, such as Russia and China.

## Consumption

The use of economic goods. Thus, the final economic process following production—the creation of goods; exchange—the transfer of goods among specialized producers; and distribution—the division of the final value of goods among those who contributed to their production and exchange. Historically, economists have not shown great interest in consumption, nor have they been able to say much of importance about it, because it is so highly personal. Standards of efficiency can be developed for production and exchange, but no one can tell another what he ought to enjoy as a consumer. That is an individual choice. More recently, the consumer's need for information in order that he may make wise choices has been recognized.

## Contract

A legally binding agreement between two or more persons to do or not to do specified things. The roots of the word come from Roman antiquity, but the substance of contracts must exist in any orderly society, no matter how primitive. Contracts acquire economic importance as societies grow more complex; i.e., have more extensive relations, of one kind or another, between persons. In an individualistic or free society, obligations to do or not to do certain things are assumed by individuals or groups acting as units after the give and take of negotiation. That is

to say, legally valid contracts require the voluntary consent of the parties. In older societies, marked by more or less permanent social classes, many personal obligations automatically follow from a person's position at birth. Thus, contractual relations characterize modern free societies.

## Coöperatives

There are two types of coöperative enterprise, consumer coöperatives and producer coöperatives. The consumer coöperative is an enterprise (store, gasoline station, or insurance company, etc.) owned and controlled by consumers, who pool their capital, elect the directors and share in the benefits. Normally, a consumer coöperative operates on a one-man, one-vote basis and pays a fixed rate of return upon capital. It charges regular market prices and, after setting aside suitable reserves, rebates at the end of the year most of its surplus.

Producer coöperatives provide a technique by which, for example, farmers pool their capital to purchase their supplies economically, or pool their resources in order to market their goods through their own organization. Here again, the one-man, one-vote principle normally applies, a fixed interest is given on investment, and savings are distributed in accordance with the individual's patronage.

## Corporation

A body of persons who act with some degree of unity. The term is of general legal importance, but of particular economic importance only in recent years because it is applied to a widely used social structure in the conduct of business. The modern business corporation is the outgrowth of the joint-stock company of earlier centuries. It is characterized by division of its capital into equal shares of stock which may be owned by many or few individuals. The stockholders legally own and control the corporation, choose its directors and officers, or have the power to do so, and are entitled to a share of the profits in proportion to the number of their shares of stock. Most large businesses in the United States are corporations. They are steadily increasing their proportion of the nation's total business. See *Common Stock*.

## Cost

A necessary payment of some kind required for the production of a material good or the performance of a service. The term *cost*, as an economic concept, is related to an economic system such as our contemporary one, in which free bargaining is predominant. That is, if obligations are imposed upon an individual because of his social class, these would not ordinarily be referred to as the costs of living in that society. A cost is a freely assumed payment because of a benefit expected. Thus, in economic theories, costs are related to returns. There are many kinds of cost theories in economics and accounting at the present time. Generally, costs are divided into total costs and per unit costs. Total costs may be fixed or variable. Fixed costs are those costs which do not vary with the level of output. Variable costs increase with the level of output. Total cost is, then, the sum of the fixed and the variable costs (at each level of output). For the purposes of analysis, however, there is one more cost—probably the most important of all —marginal cost. See *Marginal cost*.

## Craft guilds

Associations of workmen in manufacture by the type of work performed. Craft guilds became common in the last half of the Middle Ages when production of goods by handworkers reached sizable proportions. Under these conditions, workers in the same type of work, or craft, banded together for mutual advantage. There was often great pride in the craft, and the guild sought to protect the good name of the craft by supervising the training and admission of new members, by laying down rules for the practices of members, including the preservation of trade secrets, and by the support of charitable activities for members when needed. Craft guildsmen often wore special uniforms or liveries on ceremonial occasions. See *Guild*.

## Deficit financing

A practice long used by governments of spending more than their income would support, thus incurring a deficit. For many centuries, deficit financing has been regarded as simply a bad practice in which governments could well indulge because of their power. A deficit necessarily involves borrowing and governments can put pressure on their citizens or weaker governments to make loans to them. More recently, new light has been put on deficit financing as a device by which governments can use their borrowing power to put additional purchasing power into the hands of their people for the purpose of stimulating the economic system. When there is unemployment and unused capacity in industry or agriculture, deficit financing is one of the quickest ways by which governments can provide a "shot in the arm" to their economies. To advocate free use of this device, however, is still regarded as a radical policy. Debt will pile up, the danger of inflationary price increases will mount, and many persons become concerned about the possibility of repaying the debt. Those who favor discriminating use of deficit financing, argue that the creation of debt is useful to maintain a high rate of growth in national output, which is the most important goal of an economic system. They also claim that the growing debt is not of greatest importance so long as the total does not become larger in relation to the gross national product. Deficit financing has been a point of keen debate in the United States since the depression of the 1930's.

## Demand

In an economic sense, the desire for goods or services made effective by possession of the means of paying for them. Demand is often used as simply the quantity of a good demanded at any specific price. This is both an older and a commoner usage of the term. But it is also used to mean what is called a *schedule* of demand; i.e., not only the quantity that *is* demanded at one price, but the quantities that *would be* demanded at higher and lower prices, if conditions should bring those prices into existence. It is this latter aspect of demand that is influential, when compared to supply, in setting a price in a market. That is, if price should fall, more would probably be demanded; if price rose, less. The mathematical description of this kind of variation in quantity demanded is called a *demand function.* See *Supply.*

## Demand curve
The demand curve on a two-dimensional graph represents price and quantity-demanded possibilities within the confines of the graph. The demand curve will generally slope downward and to the right because price and quantity demanded are inversely related. That is, consumers will buy more of a product as its price declines (the law of demand). A *change in demand* on the part of consumers, resulting from a change in one or more of the basic determinants of demand—consumer tastes, income expectations, prices of related goods, and number of buyers in the market—will result in a *shift* in the location of the demand curve. See *Elasticity* and *Equilibrium* for further discussion of demand.

## Diminishing returns
The name given to the observation that the output of any productive operation will diminish in relation to an increase in just one factor used in the operation while all other factors are kept constant. If more than one factor is changed, different combinations of factors are achieved and the change is innovational. Practically, diminishing returns occur when a productive operation such as farming is simply made more intensive by using, for example, only one more unit of labor. If more fertilizer or machinery is used, the production is different technologically and returns may increase rather than diminish. The terms *diminishing returns to scale,* or its opposite, *increasing returns to scale,* are used to describe a productive operation in which, without changing the proportions of factors, lesser or greater returns result from making the entire operation smaller or larger.

## Distribution theory
A hypothetical system of thought, not necessarily proved to be true in experience, but created for the purpose of explaining experience in dividing the income yielded by a productive economic process. This use of the word *distribution* in economic theory must be kept distinct from its use in business where it refers to movements of goods to markets. Distribution theory, as it relates to income or value, considers such things as the effect of the magnitude or the proportionate share of income to land, labor, or capital upon the productive process itself; e.g., if labor or capital get too much or too little, what will be the effects upon the overall level of production? Distribution theory may also be concerned with the relationship of levels of income to the productive factors as a matter of social justice in addition to questions of aggregate productive efficiency.

## Econometrics
A term brought into use in mid-twentieth century to describe the science of economic measurement. It is allied to, but distinct from, the term *statistics* as used in economics. Both statistics and econometrics are methods of scientific analysis which deal with the quantitative aspects of economic phenomena, but econometrics is more concerned with developing theories or models which have both generality and precision. Statistics is usually applied to specific problems.

## Economy
As an abstract term, *economy* means simply doing the best you can with what you have. More formally, it is maximizing the achievement of ends or goals with the use of minimum means. As a concrete, descriptive term, it is an economic system, or group of persons having economic relations among themselves, as in the title of this book, *The Development of the American Economy.* As a behavioral or operational term, economy in action leads to economizing behavior. It is sometimes said that the science of economics is the study of man's economizing behavior. Economy and

economizing behavior exist, not alone, but along with other human interests and types of behavior. The desires for power, prestige, or security may take priority over economy, as a motive for action.

## Elasticity

Elasticity of demand is a concept used to measure the *responsiveness of consumers* to changes in price. Likewise, elasticity of supply measures the *responsiveness of suppliers* to changes in price.

Demand for a product is generally said to be *elastic* when a change in price produces more than proportionate changes in the quantity of the product purchased; and *inelastic* when changes in price produce little or no change in quantity of the product purchased. More specifically, demand for a product may range from *perfectly elastic* (an infinitesimally small change in price will result in an infinitely large change in quantity demanded) to *perfectly inelastic* (change in price will result in no change in quantity demanded). It may also be somewhere in between, having *relative elasticity, unit elasticity* (a given change in price will result in an exactly proportionate change in quantity demanded), or *relative inelasticity*.

The degree of elasticity of demand may be measured by the formula

$$\frac{\%\ change\ in\ quantity\ demanded}{\%\ change\ in\ price}$$

Whenever the percentage change in quantity is bigger than the percentage change in price (greater than *1*), demand is *elastic*. When percentage change in quantity is smaller (less than *1*), demand is *inelastic*. When the two percentages are the same (equal to *1*), demand is *unit-elastic*.

In general, the elasticity of demand for a product is greater when there is a greater number of substitutes available, when the product involves a large part of the consumer's total budget, and when the product is considered a "luxury item." The demand for cigarettes, for example, is relatively elastic; for perfume, relatively inelastic.

## Equilibrium

In price theory, equilibrium is the intersection of a supply curve and demand curve occurring at that point where quantity supplied and quantity demanded are equal. The resulting price is the equilibrium price; the resulting quantity is the equilibrium quantity. Thus, under the assumption of perfect competition, equilibrium price is that price at which the quantity of the product that sellers wish to sell is equal to the quantity that buyers (consumers) wish to buy. At the equilibrium price all sellers can find buyers and all buyers can find sellers. If price falls below equilibrium price, added buying of consumers will raise price. If price rises above equilibrium, sellers unable to find buyers will cut price.

## Estate

An extension of the simple word *state* to its application to persons or things. In the Middle Ages, the nobles were usually considered to be the top or first estate. Other classes were variously called second, third, or fourth estates. As applied to land, conventional usage puts the term *estate* only upon substantial holdings. In the Middle Ages, a manor was considered to be an estate, whereas a small holding with a simple cottage was not. The term is also used to include all of the property which an individual may hold whether real or personal, particularly at the time of death when ownership passes to others.

## Export

Any economic good shipped out of a country. Commodities, manufactured goods, or services may be exported. Often contrasted with imports. The relationship of exports to imports constitutes the balance of trade. The ability of the agriculture or industry of a country to meet the competition of other countries is measured by the volume and character of its exports. Thus exports become one kind of measure of the economic development of a country. An undeveloped country will be able to export only its native raw materials or agricultural commodities for which it has natural advantages of soil and climate. A de-

427

veloped country will be able to export manufactured goods, depending primarily on the skill of its people or the technology which it is able to apply in various industries. See *Balance of Trade*.

### Fair-trade laws
Under a fair-trade law, a manufacturer of a trade-marked article is allowed to set a retail price below which no store can sell his brand of goods. In those states in which such laws have been enacted, the retail businessman has, in effect, been protected against price competition. "Discount houses" and other stores with a large turnover are compelled to charge the same retail price as convenience and service stores with low turnover. The result of fair-trade laws is often to maintain obsolete marketing procedures and high margins at the expense of the consumer.

### Federal Reserve System
The central banking system of the United States. Established by law in 1913, with twelve branches in different geographic sections. The Federal Reserve System was, in form, a revision of the system of National Banks created in 1863, but, in fact, it marked a new extension of the federal government into central banking. A Federal Reserve Board (now the Board of Governors of the Federal Reserve System) was created with extensive supervisory powers over the operations of the twelve Reserve Banks in the districts. All National Banks are now required to belong to their district Reserve Bank and state banks may also belong. Reserve Banks hold the reserves of their member banks, and the System may determine the percentage of reserves required. The Board of Governors also has power to set rediscount rates for members and to engage in open market operations on its own initiative. See *Open-market operations* and *Rediscount rate*.

### Foreign exchange
The name given to the process of exchanging payments between countries, usually in different currency units. Also, as a collective noun, the name for the legal instruments or contracts which are the tangible evidence of demands for payment or right to payment by one country to or from another. In both senses, foreign exchange has become important with the growth of trade and the movement of persons and goods between countries. But foreign exchange is not restricted to payments to persons for goods or services. With the development of efficient mechanisms for handling foreign exchange, it became possible to lend and borrow between countries. Thus, purely financial transactions have come to constitute a substantial part of the need for foreign exchange.

### Free competition
In an economic sense, unrestricted opportunity to buy or sell as individual interest may dictate. Where this degree of freedom exists, markets come into existence where buyers and sellers undertake to come to agreement on terms of sale. An economic system in which free competition prevails is also called a market system, in contrast to a controlled or planned system. Adam Smith was the first economist to base his theoretical system on free competition. From Smith, this idea became the foundation of classical economics. It is now recognized that many limitations upon free competition do and must exist, but the American economy still retains the ideal of free competition in business as a basic element.

### Full employment
A condition of an economic system in which work is available for all persons who are able to work and are seeking it. Full employment does not mean that every one is working, but only that those who are willing to accept the pay and conditions of work being offered by employers can find jobs available for them. Even at best, there will be some unemployed under full-employment conditions. There are always new recruits to the work force who need time to locate suitable work, and some who quit to seek more desirable jobs. This kind of unemployment should be of short

duration and range from 3% to 5% in a system with adequate dissemination of job information and ease of movement from place to place. Measures of employment and unemployment become sensitive indicators of general business conditions.

## Good

A commodity, product, or service which is desired. Ordinarily goods are contrasted with services, the former being tangible and the latter intangible, but in economic theory a useful service is also a good. It is also usually said that a good must be scarce, but unless it is scarce, we never become aware of a desire for it. We do not think of air as a good. In the very simplest definition, a good is anything which is desired, excluding moral goods, or values.

## Gross National Product (GNP)

The total value of the goods and services produced in a country or an area in a specified period of time. Since this statistical total has been available in recent decades, GNP has become the most important single figure representing the state of the economy. When divided by an index of general prices, it yields a figure representing the real goods and services produced regardless of price changes. The component parts of GNP, such as agricultural or industrial production, services such as wholesale and retail trade, and government and financial services, can be viewed in relation to the larger total to become measures of the individual sectors. Since annual figures can be computed more accurately, estimates of GNP for months or quarters are usually expressed at annual rates.

## Guild

An association of individual businessmen formed for the purpose of regulating the common manufacture or trade for the benefit of the individual members. The guild arose in the Middle Ages in Europe and became a dominant aspect of the economic system as the corporation is in capitalistic nations today.

In fact, the modern corporation is derived from the guild, although it has been changed in important ways. Guilds supervised apprenticeship, quality of members' workmanship, prices, and business practices. Guild members became an economic elite and displayed their high status by wearing elaborate and distinctive clothing—or livery—on ceremonial occasions. Both modern secret societies and college fraternities owe their origin to the medieval guilds. *See Craft guilds.*

## Import

A product or commodity brought into a country from another country. Imports are likely to come from low-wage or low-cost countries to high-wage or high-cost countries because only then can importers pay the extra costs of shipment. Even so, imports are often regarded as unfair competition by domestic producers of similar goods. Advanced, and low-cost, countries in manufacturing are likely to import raw materials or semi-processed goods; nonindustrial countries are likely to import manufactured goods and export raw materials or agricultural products. Thus imports, like exports, become measures of economic development. See *Export and Balance of trade.*

## Income

In an economic sense, the gain that derives from a productive activity. *Gross,* or *total,* income may be equal to the entire receipts from such an activity. *Net* income has to be calculated by deducting expenses from gross income. *National* income, either gross or net, is as important to economics as income to individuals or firms is important to accounting and management. *Personal* income, as a part of national income, is also important in economics as a measure of possible consumer spending and saving. Personal income, together with business and government income, add up to national income. The eventual use of income by persons, businesses, and units of government determines the course of the total economy.

## Individualism

A system of social thought in which basic importance is attached to the single person. In the individualistic view, social thought and action constitute simply a summation of the thought and action of individuals. The most extreme form of individualism is *anarchism,* in which the slightest degree of social restraint upon the individual is considered to be an evil. In practice, individualism has emphasized removal of social restraints upon the person, or intimate and local social groups, by larger groups such as governments or social classes. Capitalism and free enterprise are names for individualistic systems of economic thought. Democracy is an individualistic system of political thought. See *Socialism* and *Communism* for essentially opposed systems of economic and political thought. See also *Anarchism* for an extreme individualistic political system.

## Industrial Revolution

The series of basic changes in methods of manufacture which began in England in the eighteenth century and later in other parts of the world. These changes were centered on the use of water power, steam or other nonhuman or nonanimal power; on the invention and development of production machines of larger size and higher speed to use the new power sources; on the development of new processes to provide fuel and raw materials for large-scale industry; and on new ways of transporting raw materials and finished goods cheaper, further, and faster. The Industrial Revolution created a new class of capital-owning industrial employers, a new class of wage-earning industrial employees, large cities at suitable sites for industry, and new methods of marketing the finished products.

## Inflation

A general increase of prices ordinarily associated with monetary or credit factors rather than supply or demand, since the latter rarely affect all goods at the same time. Historically, inflation was not well understood and frequently became serious because of ineffective efforts to control it. In contemporary industrialized economies, the problem of inflation is acute due to the use of credit devices to stimulate production. Just the right amount of inflation has been called beneficial inflation, but there is always the danger that easing of the conditions of borrowing will bring price increases without increased production and employment. This is damaging because of many long-term contracts at specified prices which cannot be increased. Holders of such contracts receive the same incomes but have to pay higher prices to others. Indexes of general prices serve as "fever thermometers" to modern economic systems. A principal objective of central bank policy is to vary bank lending rates and other terms of lending to keep production at a high level, but without causing inflation. This is equivalent to walking an economic tightrope. See *Central bank*.

## Innovation

Innovation simply means new or better methods of using resources. The improvement usually requires a change in the use of some factor of production such as reduced need for labor due to automation, or the substitution of atomic power for conventional sources. As a result of innovation, new goods may be produced or production or distribution costs may be lowered for goods already in production. As the economy accepts innovation, we are able to satisfy existing wants more abundantly and to enjoy new, previously unattainable comforts or pleasures.

## Institutional economics

A system of economic thought which recognizes the importance in economic behavior of widespread habit patterns known as institutions. Institutional economists challenge the foundations of classical economics, maintaining that they are not adequate to use as a base for a theoretical system. Institutionalists contend it is not necessarily true that if men are made free, they will rationally calculate what is in their best economic interest and then act upon it. Institutionalists assert that every economic action takes place in a social setting and is modified by that setting. What is reasonable for an individual is determined by an individual's society, not by himself alone; how far he can push his own economic advantage is similarly determined. Thus, institutionalists say that economics must concern itself not only with theory, but also with the social habit patterns that largely control individuals.

## Interest

As an economic term, a payment for the use of a sum of money. In this capacity, interest becomes one of the main shares in the division of the value produced by an economic system. Other shares are wages, rent, and profit. The amount of interest to be paid is normally specified by agreement or contract and is expressed as a percentage. Although both interest and profit are derived from the investment of a value in an enterprise, the former, being contractual, is an expense whereas profit is not, occurring only when the firm can keep expense less than income. Under the modern system of incorporated business firms, an investor may either make a loan by buying a bond on which he receives interest, or by buying stock, representing part ownership of the firm, for which he will receive a share of profit.

## Joint-stock company

The historic ancestor of the modern business corporation in which individual merchants or proprietors banded together to carry on costly or hazardous trading expeditions, colonizing ventures, and the like. The joint stock was usually for a single venture or for a specified period of time. Each member of the company risked his own capital and made his own profits, if any. He either managed his own business personally or appointed an agent to do so. Thus the most valuable features of the modern business corporation were lacking in the joint-stock company, namely, centralized management, limited liability, and indefinitely extended life through the right of stockholders to buy and sell shares without affecting the continuity of the corporation.

## Keynesian economics

The particular set of economic ideas associated with the English economist John Maynard Keynes (pronounced "kānz"), 1883-1946. Specifically, Keynes did not accept the idea of classical economics that a system of free enterprise was all that was needed to keep the total economy operating at full capacity. Rather, he held that full employment of the productive factors—land, labor, and capital—depended upon attitudes prevailing in the society at any time. The chief of these were: the propensity to consume, the propensity to save, and liquidity preference. If consumers held back, saved, and hoarded their income in cash or demand deposits in banks (liquidity preference), then the economy would be held back also to less than full employment of land, labor, and productive facilities.

## Labor

The economic factor of production which embraces all forms of human effort. Labor, together with natural raw materials, is the oldest and most basic factor of production. Men cannot live by labor alone without the soil and other materials available in the physical environment. Yet, natural raw materials are not factors of production until man learns how to use them for his own livelihood. Economic development may properly be regarded as improvement in man's knowledge of ways to use his own effort or labor; i.e., improvement in the productivity of labor. Division or specialization of labor is the oldest means of improving productivity, but progressively mechanical devices or tools have been used also to bring about undreamed-of increases in labor productivity. The word *labor* is also used as a collective term for all of the productive workers in an economic system.

## Laissez faire

A French phrase meaning, literally, "allow to do." It came into use in France in the eighteenth century when reaction against government direction of the economy was increasing. In use, it means to allow the people and individuals to manage their economic affairs as they choose without interference from any outside source.

## Macroeconomics

A term borrowed in the mid-twentieth century from the physical sciences to mean economics in the broadest sense. Macroeconomics is concerned with totals rather than the individual components of those totals, thus, with the entire economic system rather than the individuals or firms composing it. Macroeconomics is sometimes called aggregative economics. It deals with problems appropriate to its broad scope, such as: levels of production and employment; distribution of income among the factors of production; and many phases of the system of money and credit, such as central bank policy. See *Microeconomics*.

## Malthusian Theory of Population

The explanation of the growth of human population developed by Thomas Robert Malthus (1766-1834) in his book *An Essay on the Principle of Population* (1798). The term Malthusian theory of population refers to that of the first edition. This is that the sex urge will produce a capacity in people to multiply in numbers beyond the capacity of the soil to provide food for them. Population will have to be checked by malnutrition, disease, and war which bring premature death. This harsh view was later modified by the possible check of "moral restraint," principally through delayed marriage, but neither Malthus nor his contemporaries seemed to believe that moral restraint would really be effective.

## Manorial system

The system of land tenure prevailing in western European countries in the Middle Ages, and the social and political systems which accompanied it. Thus, the term *manorial system* really embraces the way of life prevailing in medieval Europe. Elements of this system included landholding by an upper-class nobility, but with obligations of service still higher to the king or emperor; and routine work, mostly agricultural, performed by a mass peasantry living in villages on individual estates or manors and owing to their lord "week work" as year-around service on fields, crops, and livestock. Landholdings without obligations by freemen or yeomen were few, and there were few free artisans or hand workers until towns, as trading centers, began to arise in the later centuries of the medieval era.

## Marginal cost

The amount added to total cost when output is increased by one unit. The concept of *marginal* is among the most important in economics. The idea of "one more unit" is applied in the analysis of utility, output, and revenue of the firm, and consumer behavior. The marginal cost for each additional unit can be calculated by computing the change in total cost the added unit entails. It must be remembered, however, that marginal cost does *not* measure the cost of any *one definable unit* of production, but the *additional* cost of the larger of two possible outputs.

## Marginal utility economics

A type of economic theory developed primarily by three Austrian economists, Menger (1840-1921), Wieser (1851-1926), and Bohm-Bawerk (1851-1914). In opposition to a technical aspect of the older classical economics, they denied that the values of goods, under competitive conditions, would be controlled by costs of production. They held that value is determined by the usefulness, or utility, of a good to the possible buyer who finds the least, or marginal, usefulness in the supply of the good being offered for sale in the market. This same mechanism also controls supply through a similar calculation by possible suppliers. In effect, marginal utility economics explained value by an analysis of demand; whereas classical economics had done so by an analysis of supply.

## Market

A place in which buying and selling of goods takes place by free negotiation of terms. As an abstract concept in economic theory, a market may be no more than an imaginary place with special characteristics, such as ability of buyers and sellers to enter and leave at will, knowledge on the part of all parties of supplies available for sale, knowledge of demand at all probable prices, ability of buyers to judge accurately the qualities of goods offered, willingness of sellers to sell large or small quantities, and knowledge of all participants in the market of prices, quantities, and terms of all sales. A market does not have to exist in only one place. The New York Stock Exchange provides a national market for stocks by means of telegraphic communication.

## Marshallian economics

The body of economic theories developed by the English economist Alfred Marshall (1842-1924). Coming in the line of succession of classical economists, but following the work of the Austrian, or marginal utility school, Marshall harmonized the two points of view by holding that cost factors best explain supply conditions in a market, but that utility analysis best explains demand. He said that cost and utility operate like the blades of a pair of shears. Extending the classical position, he emphasized the business firm, rather than the individual, as the active agent and decision maker in the economic system. His followers elaborated the theory of the firm to become the heart of microeconomics in the mid-twentieth century. See *Microeconomics*.

## Mathematical economics

A term applied rather loosely to any type of economic analysis which makes as much use as possible of mathematical types of reasoning. Economic statistics uses mathematical methods, but not exclusively. Econometrics is a more precise and restricted term than mathematical economics. The general term *mathematical economics* applies to all aspects of the effort to discover quantitative elements in economic phenomena and to adapt to their analysis the powerful tools of mathematics including the devising of new forms of mathematical analysis particularly suited to the characteristic phenomena of economics and social behavior. See *Econometrics*.

## Mercantilism

The body of economic policies—and the theory of government and society implied by these policies—of the rising national states of western Europe in the sixteenth through eighteenth centuries. The nature of these policies varied according to the specific conditions of different states. Some stressed development of foreign trade and ocean-shipping, others stressed efficient internal productive organization, while still others emphasized unified political administration. The common core of mercantile policy was to use all of the powers of the nation-state to strengthen itself still further. This often meant to weaken the towns, the guilds, the nobles, and the church, and to entrench the external power and prestige of the state by colonizing and other extensions of territory.

## Microeconomics

A term brought into use in the mid-twentieth century as a name for the most limited types of economic analysis and explanation—primarily, the theory of the firm. Under conditions in which free competition is dominant, the action of the total economy supposedly is the summation of the actions of individuals and firms. Careful analysis of the limited decisions of the firm should therefore illuminate the behavior of the entire system. Thus, the explanatory value of microeconomics is closely correlated with the prevalence of freely competitive conditions. Where monopolistic impediments exist, economic actions begin to take on psychological, social, and political aspects not adequately handled by a purely economic analysis.

## Minimum-wage law

A legislative enactment stipulating the rate of wage below which no workers in the covered occupations may be hired. Such laws were at first applied to women only by some of our industrial states but were held unconstitutional. During the 1930's, the federal government instituted minimum wages for both men and women under the National Industrial Recovery Act of 1933. This, too, was held unconstitutional. In 1938, the Fair Labor Standards Act set maximum hours and minimum wages for all workers in interstate commerce. This was held constitutional in *U.S.* vs. *Darby Lumber Co.,* 1941. Paralleling the federal minimum wage has been the development of state laws which have normally affected non-agricultural workers in intrastate commerce. These laws were declared constitutional in *West Coast Hotel Company* vs. *Paris,* 1937, when the Supereme Court overruled the earlier precedent of *Adkins* vs. *Children's Hospital,* 1923.

## Money
Any metal or other material commonly accepted as a measure of value, a store of value, and hence as a medium in the exchange of goods between seller and buyer. That is, money cannot be a medium of exchange unless it is accepted as a measure and store of value. In the current highly elaborated exchange economies of the world, the concept of money has partially become an abstract term, not connected with any metal or material substance, but related to anything which performs the functions of money. As an example, credit, which is simply the faith of one party that the other party to a transaction will make payment or fulfill other terms which he promises to fulfill, has taken over a large proportion of the monetary function, and has become in effect virtually indistinguishable from money in its newer sense.

## Monopolistic competition
The structure of most markets falls somewhere between the extreme cases of pure competition and pure monopoly. Oligopoly, or few sellers, is close to monopoly. Monopolistic competition, as the term suggests, is a mixture of monopoly and competition. More specifically, it refers to a market situation in which there is a relatively large number of small producers offering similar (differentiated) but not (as with pure competition) identical products. See *Free competition, Oligopoly,* and *Monopoly.*

## Monopoly
An economic condition in which there is only one seller. This is an abstract concept never completely true in experience, except at an instant of time. Where more time is available, buyers can find other sellers, other products capable of rendering at least part of the services of the monopolized commodity, or other ways of producing the monopolized product. Classical economics ruled out monopoly as a human creation and devoted attention only to freely reproducible goods where competition between suppliers could and would exist, considering this to be the natural condition of the market. Later economic thinkers developed explanations of monopolized and partially monopolized markets. See *Monopolistic competition.*

## National debt
The unpaid monetary obligations of a national government. There are various components of the national debt which may be of importance, as long term or short term, domestic or foreign, and owed to individuals, institutions or banks. The national debt has been a source of controversy in the United States since the 1930's, when the argument was advanced that it could be used as a stabilizing factor for the entire economy. That is, an increase in the national debt yields an increase in the purchase of goods and services, hence stimulating the economy to a higher rate of activity and perhaps bringing inflation. Reduction of debt has opposite effects. In this view, national debt is not something to be paid, but is a balance wheel for the economy and is to be kept in proportion to the gross national product. See *Deficit financing.*

## National Income
The proportionate part of the gross national product which is available to the people and businesses of the nation for their own free use. National income is less than gross national product by amounts which individuals and firms must retain and use to keep the productive facilities of the nation in continuous oper-

ating condition. Units of government take a part of national income through taxation, and business firms retain a part for later use. There are also mandatory deductions such as social security payments which are called "transfer" payments because they merely take income from one class of persons for payment to another class. Savings by firms and individuals also come out of national income, leaving consumer expenditures as the final segment.

## Oligopoly

An economic condition in which there are only a few sellers. In a sense, oligopoly can be referred to as a monopoly shared by a few. In an analysis of market behavior, oligopoly presents a case intermediate between monopoly and competition. A monopolist need only consider his own costs and the reactions of buyers to any price he might set; a competitor, however, must consider his own costs in relation to the prevailing price in the market because neither he nor any other competitor can produce enough to modify market price. An oligopolist, in contrast to either a monopolist or a competitor, must consider his own costs, the anticipated action of the other suppliers as they react to his own changes in rate of output, and the reactions of consumers to the supplies and prices which are finally established. The complexity of the pricing problem faced by oligopolists, and the frequency with which oligopolistic conditions exist in modern economies (with a few giant firms controlling supplies of very important classes of goods) has led to the use of mathematical methods—notably "game theory"—for the analysis, prediction, and control of this important class of economic phenomena.

## Open-market operations

A term used for the activity of central banks in buying and selling short-term securities or credit instruments for the purpose of influencing the difficulty or ease of borrowing. Open-market operations constitute probably the most powerful banking device available for counterbalancing rising and falling prices and thus the level of productive activity. In the United States, open-market operations are carried out by the Federal Reserve Banks to influence the lending by their member banks. Federal Reserve purchases of short-term securities in the open market result in payments for those securities which increase the reserve accounts of member banks and make it desirable for these banks to lend more freely to their business customers. Selling of securities has an opposite effect.

## Parity

A term which acquired an economic meaning in the agricultural legislation passed by Congress in the 1930's. The parity concept is used in an attempt to maintain the income (measured in purchasing power) of farmers on an even basis—or parity—with some base period selected as normal. In its earliest form, parity was based on the ratio taken as 100 between the prices received by farmers and the prices which they had to pay in the stable pre-World War I years, 1910 to 1914. This ratio was compared to any given year for which a parity ratio might be needed. If the prices farmers received fell faster than those they paid, the parity ratio would be below 100. If parity rose above 100, it would mean that farmers' selling prices were rising faster than their buying prices. Parity thus became a convenient and brief way to indicate the relationship between the economic state of agriculture and the rest of the economy. Difficulties in applying the concept of parity may arise from changes in the assortment of products grown on farms, changes in the efficiency with which labor, capital, and technological advances are used in farm production, and changes in products bought by farmers. These changes are difficult to measure, so methods of computing parity have had to be revised by Congress several times.

## Price system

The correlated grouping of the terms of exchange of goods in an economy in which money is used. These terms of exchange are expressed as prices. The central aspect of a price system is the complex interrelatedness of individual prices. Prices of raw materials and other factors of production affect not only the price structure of the factors themselves insofar as they may be substituted one for another, but also the prices of the finished and semifinished goods made by the use of the basic factors. Since labor, and also the other factors of production, are owned by human beings, the price system becomes the arbiter of personal and class income. The use of income, in turn, becomes demand for factors of production and finished goods, and is, thus, a determiner of their prices.

### Private property
A legal system in which single individuals are permitted to own economic goods. Private property may also be described as a system in which the sovereign power of a society is available to restrain the members of the society so that any one member may have a dependable expectation of unimpeded use of specified property or goods. This is to say that trespassers may be prosecuted. This legal system is a prerequisite of any freely competitive market and of the capitalistic system prevailing today in western Europe, the United States, and other parts of the world. Private property does not prevail in modern communist states, nor in the rapidly diminishing number of tribal societies in which group rights persist. However, private property tends to acquire more limitations as societies become more complex.

### Production theory
The general economic theory which analyzes and explains the processes of creating economic goods. Historically, production is probably the oldest part of economics. When livelihood is insecure, first attention is likely to be drawn to the problem of how to produce more. This concern leads to the development of what we now call technology as well as to ideas about the economics of production. In classical economics, production theory was concerned with the proportions of factors, especially the effects achieved when additional

labor is employed on land, namely, diminishing returns. Later, the theory was generalized to apply to the uses of all factors of production with the possible results of increasing, constant, and diminishing returns.

### Profit
In common usage, profit is the income of a successful business enterprise. The term is sometimes used so loosely as to be almost the same as the word *income*. In strict economic theory, however, profit is limited to the income of the entrepreneur or undertaker of a business. It is not the income of the capitalist, since capital can be borrowed by the promise to pay interest, and the promise must be honored whether or not a profit is earned. Profit is what is left after wages, rent, interest, etc., are paid. Under conditions of pure competition, profit will exist only accidentally. If profit regularly appears beyond the costs of wages, rent, and interest, it is a sign that some degree of monopoly or oligopoly exists, or the profit would be competed away.

### Public utilities
A public utility is an area of economic activity which so vitally affects the public interest that the government feels it imperative to impose regulations as to rates, service requirements, and operating procedures. Normally, such a field is one in which effective competition cannot be maintained because of the advantages of a single monopolistic operation. Examples are private water, gas, electricity, transportation, and telegraph and telephone companies, all of which have been brought under governmental regulation. The governmental regulatory authorities seek to guarantee the public satisfactory service at a minimum cost while allowing the public utility an adequate return on investment.

### Rediscount rate
The interest charge imposed by central banks, such as the Federal Reserve Banks in the United States, when member banks come to borrow on security of notes which they have already discounted for their customers. Dis-

counting, in this technical sense, means deducting the interest on a loan in advance, and thus reducing (or discounting) the amount paid to the borrower from the full amount of the loan. Rediscounting is a second discounting, but it is not added to the first since each lender holds the note for only a portion of its full term. The rediscount rate is important as a means for making borrowing at banks easy or difficult through control of the cost of loans. It is an especially important interest rate because it affects the reserves of member banks in the banking system.

## Regulated company

A form of business association which came into use at the beginning of the modern era, in which individual traders banded together to provide for themselves certain advantages which they could not obtain alone. Some examples of desired advantages were reduced costs of ocean transport by joint chartering of a ship, joint maintenance of warehouse and selling facilities in foreign countries, and joint provision for protection of lives and property. In spite of these joint activities, each merchant traded on his own capital. The association operated under regulations established by government—hence the name. The two chief English regulated companies were the Merchant Staplers and the Merchant Adventurers.

## Rent

The share in the value created by an economic system which is attributed to land, natural resources, or space on the surface of the earth. Income from land leases and royalties from the extraction of minerals are forms of rent. In practice, rent also includes income from improvements to land or resources, but in strict economic theory, any income from an investment to create a facility not before in existence is interest or profit. Rent is paid for the contribution of the physical environment to the creation of economic goods. It is only paid when the desired natural resource is scarce. Air is the most widely used and necessary good supplied by nature, but we do not pay rent or royalty for it as it is not scarce.

## Ricardian economics

The body of theories associated with David Ricardo (1772-1823), an English economist. He was not the inventor of a number of these theories, but he used them effectively to build a logically coherent system. His premises were: (1) men will calculate the sources of the greatest gains and act to realize them; (2) if more and more labor is applied to land, returns will diminish; (3) because of the constancy of the human sex passion, the need for food, and diminishing returns, population will press against resources; and (4) free competition will result if government does not prevent it. These premises led to the following conclusions: (1) wages will tend to remain at a subsistence level; (2) rents will increase as population growth makes good land more and more scarce; (3) profits, including interest, will fall to the lowest level which will induce continued saving.

## Say's Law

A proposition first specifically enunciated by Jean Baptiste Say (1767-1832), a French economist, in his Traité d'Economie Politique (1803). As stated by Say, "it is production which opens up the demand for products." Say's law assumes that human wants have no limit if the right goods are available to supply them. Thus, the only important economic problem for every individual is to produce as efficiently as possible the kinds of goods which others will want. The most efficient producers of the right kinds of goods will be the most successful in getting from other producers the goods which will give them the greatest satisfactions. There can always be failures in the intelligence and energy of individuals, but for society as a whole, there is no problem of underemployment, but only of the most efficient employment.

## Single tax

A proposal by the unorthodox American economic thinker Henry George (1839-1897) that all taxes be eliminated except a single tax designed to absorb all of the economic rent on privately owned land. This proposal was made in George's principal work *Progress and Poverty* (1879), which was widely read all over the world in following decades. George argued that progress in population and the production of goods created increasing demands for land and natural resources so that most of the value of progress went to the private owners of these gifts of nature. Thus, poverty always accompanied economic progress. To relieve this situation, he held that taxes on land and resources should be so high that they would remain free. This is to say that anyone nominally owning land or resources and using them would gain no more than other individuals using their labor or capital anywhere else.

### Smithian economics

The system of economic ideas developed by Adam Smith (1723-1790). The unique elements in Smith's thought, as compared to his predecessors, were (1) all governmental attempts to direct economic processes did more harm than good; (2) where individuals were permitted to enjoy their "natural liberty," competitive markets would rise spontaneously to check individual greed and to weed out the inefficient; (3) everyone could work and produce wherever he saw the most lucrative opportunities for himself, and, as a consequence; (4) the resources of land and people would be developed freely to the highest possible level. All of these elements of Smith's thought add up to individual economic freedom and *laissez faire*.

### Socialism

A broad term including various kinds of economic systems which are based upon ownership and control of productive instruments by social groups. The more extreme forms of socialism propose that all productive property be socially owned, either by the state as representing all the people, or by groups of workers or consumers. Less extreme forms merely propose various social controls over the private sectors of the economy. Technically, the present Communism of the Soviet Union is an extreme form of socialism. Many persons in the United States refer to any extension of government control over the economy as socialism. For example, attempts to stabilize prices and employment, to bring about rapid growth, or to develop uniform national systems of medical care and unemployment benefits are often called socialism.

### Subsidy

A payment, usually by a government agency, designed to achieve a desired course of action on the part of the receiving individuals, firms, or lesser agencies of government. Subsidies have acquired economic importance in the United States because of their increasing use by government to guide the development of the economy. They may be open, or concealed within some other provision of law. For example, tariffs are really public subsidies which permit protected sellers to receive higher prices. Farmers have been subsidized to reduce plantings of crops in oversupply, both for their own direct benefit and for the general benefit of other segments of the economy from their improved purchasing power. Stockpiling of strategic materials after World War II tended to raise prices and thus to subsidize producers.

### Supply

A term for the quantities of goods available for sale at specified times, places, and prices. In a more generalized sense, supply also is used to refer to the quantities of goods *potentially* for sale within a range of times, places, and prices. The more correct usage for the latter meaning is *supply schedule,* or in mathematical form, *supply function.* Since supply is commonly derived from production, the theoretical analysis of supply becomes involved with the behavior of costs, the proportioning of labor, capital, and materials in productive processes, and the social structure—monopolistic, oligopolistic, or competitive—within which suppliers operate. Prices result from the interaction of supply and demand factors. See *Demand.*

## Supply curve

The supply curve represents the possibilities of price and quantity within confines of a two-dimensional graph. The supply curve will generally slope upward and to the right because price and quantity supplied are *directly* related in a competitive economy. That is, as price rises, quantity supplied will also rise; as price falls, quantity supplied will also fall (law of supply). To simplify: The law of supply tells us that suppliers are willing to supply more of their product at a higher price than they are at a lower price. The location of the supply curve on the graph is determined by technology, price of resources, prices of other goods, expectations, and number of sellers in the market. A change in any one of these basic determinants will result in a *change in supply*. The supply curve will thus shift either to the right (increase) or to the left (decrease). See *Demand curve* and *Equilibrium*.

## Tariff

A tariff is a tax on imports designed to yield revenue or to accord protection to domestic goods by raising the costs of imported products. When levied at a low rate, it may be a substantial source of governmental revenue; at a high rate, it may completely shield domestic producers from foreign competition. The normal effect of a tariff is to increase the price to the consumer by erecting a barrier to foreign competition. It also tends to promote the survival of inefficient businesses which could not stand alone in international competition.

## Taxation

The economic process of levying and collecting payments from private citizens and businesses for the support of governmental functions. A tax is different from an assessment in that the latter is usually levied to cover a benefit received, whereas a tax is based upon civic obligation. In recent decades in the United States, this traditional view of taxation has been supplemented by the idea that the governmental power of taxation, particularly as used by the federal government, should also be used for purposes of controlling the economy. While taxation of such goods as tobacco and alcoholic beverages has long been intended, in part, to restrict their use, newer ideas involve variations in rates of taxation to stimulate desirable or retard undesirable trends within the system as a whole.

## Technology

The knowledge and skill required to do any desired task. Technology is most often related to work with physical things, but logically the term is equally applicable to the human organization required to perform any valuable services. As an abstract concept, technology is often related to economical production. Logically, however, technology is the more inclusive term. Economy means getting the most from what you have; technology means achieving greater output with less input of materials and effort, and usually involves attempts to improve methods of work which economy excludes. Historically, most of the improvement in the level of living has been due to technological advance, although economy must be practiced at every moment along the way. See *Innovation, Economy,* and *Production theory.*

## Usury

In present usage, an excessive charge for a loan of money. The original Latin word *usura* meant merely a payment for use, with no connotation that the payment was excessive. In medieval Europe, however, any charge for a loan was considered to be wrong. Gradually, the term *interest* became the morally colorless word for the charge for a loan, and *usury* was restricted to the concept of excessive charge or improperly severe conditions for a loan. The word *usury* has relatively little use today.

## Utility

An abstract term, as used in economics, to mean the quality of usefulness of economic goods. As economic thinking developed, utility was one of the first elements of economic value to be recognized. It was also observed very early, that utility without scarcity was not enough to create value—air being an ever present example. So it came to be stated very commonly that utility and scarcity are necessary to the existence of an economic value. But as economic thinking evolved, it came to be recognized that scarcity usually depended upon the amount of a thing demanded and the amount demanded depended upon its usefulness. Problems associated with this interdependency were analyzed by a group of nineteenth-century economists called the marginal utility economists.

### Utopia
Literally, nowhere. Specifically, the title of a book written by Sir Thomas More in 1516, describing an island of the same name in which the people, the laws, and the customs were as nearly perfect as his imagination could create them. From More's book, utopia has come to represent the most ideal conditions that human beings can imagine. Since men have long been concerned with the greed and self-centeredness of their fellowmen, most utopian schemes have had some attributes of socialism about them. In the early nineteenth century in both Europe and America, there were many religious as well as secular schemes for community living which Karl Marx later dubbed as "utopian socialism."

### Value
In an economic sense, the summation of the qualities of desirableness in a tangible thing or a service which makes it an economic good. The difficulties in forming a precise concept of economic value focus on its relation to moral or esthetic value and to useful things which are not scarce. Air, for example, although the most immediately useful substance to man, has no value and does not add to value, in an economic sense, because there is always enough. Play is not different from work in the amount of energy or skill expended, but only in that we do it for pleasure. If one plays so well that others wish to watch or be instructed, the player's efforts become scarce and acquire an economic value which they did not have before.

### Wage
The payment for productive human effort. Often restricted to payment for short time periods, as hour, day or week, and distinguished from salary which relates to longer time periods, as month or year. All distributive shares are paid to human beings, but wages are paid only for efforts put forth and do not come from ownership of land or capital. A wage is an income to a worker and a cost to his employer. Many theories have been devised to explain the level of wages, such as productivity theory and its derivative, marginal productivity theory; bargaining theory; subsistence theory; and the wage-fund theory. The rôle of wages in the establishing of price levels has been of great interest in recent decades.

### Wealth
The aggregate of economic values. To be distinguished from welfare which includes economic as well as noneconomic ingredients of a general sense of human well-being. An abundance of readily available pure water, or a high sense of personal honesty among all people will contribute to welfare but not to wealth. The central task of economics as a social science is to demonstrate ways of harmonizing wealth and welfare. Noneconomic actions may contribute to wealth (e.g., getting a monopoly), but will not contribute to general welfare. The most economical acts will serve aggregate social wealth as well as welfare. If an economy is as nearly perfect as it possibly can be, there should be no conflict between wealth and welfare.

247; in Pujo report, 254
"Just price," 50

Kansas-Nebraska Act, 1854, 143, 194
Kelley, Oliver H., 215-216
Kentucky, settlement of, 125
Keynes, John Maynard, economic theories of, 32-34, 308-309
Keynesian economics; *see* Keynes, John Maynard, and National income economics; *see* Glossary
Knights of Labor, formation of, 250
Knights of St. Crispin, 251
Korean War, economic effects of, 393; start of, 326, 331

Labor, American, 1800-1860, 180-181; 1920-1930, 277-280; during the Civil War, 198; at end of World War II, 325; future prospects of, 364-365; and immigration, 281; and the New Deal, 293-296, 302-305, 311; under NIRA, 301; in post-Civil War South, 213; present-day status and problems of, 348-365; supply of, 1800-1860, 177-180; during World War I, 267-268; in World War II, 319-321; *see* Glossary
Labor, division of, and early *laissez faire*, 104; as factor of production, 27-28; and the Industrial Revolution, 88, 107-109; in Keynesian economic theory, 352; under the putting-out system, 69
Labor force, American, 1860-1920, 221, 249-250; during World War II, 319-321
Labor legislation, 1800-1860, 181
Labor-Management Relations Act, 1947, 358-360
Labor market, problems of, 348-350
Labor unions, American, 1800-1860, 180-181; 1860-1920, 249-253, *graph*, 251; 1920-1930, 277-279; early, 181; employer attitudes toward, 362-364; and industrial relations, 362-363; under NIRA, 301; in politics, 358; public policy toward, 357-360; reasons for growth of, 348-362; role of, 348-357; use and abuse of power, 357-360, 365; during World War II, 319-321
*Laissez faire*, in American business, 247; and the American economy, 239-241; analyzed, 104, 367; by-passed in World War I, 263-268; early effects of, 105-111; and the labor market, 348-350; modifications of in modern America, 273; origins of, 111-113; restored after World War I, 275; *see* Glossary
Land, abundance of in American agriculture, 386-387
Land policy, American, 1784-1787, 134; 1860-1920, 205-210; of Homestead Act, 199
Land-grant colleges, 157, 208, 219
Landrum-Griffin Act, 360
Lauderdale, Lord, economic views of, 30-31
Law, John, and "Mississippi Bub-

ble," 75
League of Nations, American rejection of, 274-275, 280; Russia joins, 330
Lend-Lease administration, organized, 318
Lewis, John L., and organization of C.I.O., 304
Lewis, Meriwether, 140
Lewis and Clark expedition, 140
Liberty Loans, in World War I, 270
Liebig, Justus, 97
Limited liability, 71; explained, 227
"Little Steel formula," 320-321, 328
Livingston, Robert, and purchase of Louisiana, 140
Lombard Street, 73
London Company, 118
London Stock Exchange, founded, 74
Louisiana, purchase of, 140
Lowell, Francis C., 173
*Lusitania*, sinking of, 263

McAdam, John, 94
McClellan Committee, investigations in 1957-1958, 359
McCormick, Cyrus, 153
McCulloch, J. R., 104
Machine tools, early development of, 95-96
McKinley, William, 218; attitude of toward business, 248
McNary-Haugen Bills, 1927-1928, 284
Macon's Bill No. 2, 1810, 159
Macroeconomics; *see* Glossary
Magellan, Ferdinand, 60, 117
"Maintenance of membership" clauses, 321
Malthus, T. R., and Henry C. Carey, 182-183; influence on Darwin, 113
Malthus, T. R., *Essay on Population*, 384
Malthusian theory, 384; *see* Glossary
Management, corporate, 227; of joint-stock companies, 72
Mann-Elkins Act, 1910, 248
Manor, described, 36-37; *diagram of*, 39; *see also* Manorial system
Manorial system, decline of, 40-41; described, 37 ff.; weaknesses of, 63-64; *see* Glossary
Mantoux, Paul, *The Industrial Revolution*, quoted, 107-108
Manufacturing, American, 1791, 134; 1800-1860, 171-176; 1860-1920, 220-236; 1920-1930, 279; 1929-1932, 289; in colonial era, 123-125; dominated by large firms, 373; growth of, 1859-1909, *table*, 234; per cent of done by corporations, 258-259
Marginal cost; *see* Glossary
Marginal utility economics; *see* Glossary
Market, 46; for American farm products, 1860-1900, 214-219; as factor in American industrial development, 228-229; and farm prices, 390; as impetus to Indus-

trial Revolution, 94; importance of in Commercial Revolution, 57; labor, problems of, 348-350; *see* Glossary
Marketing, as economic process, 29; of farm products in the 1920's, 282-284; and Industrial Revolution, 105
Markets, and the American farmer, 388-390
Marshall, George C., 334
Marshall Plan, 334, 335, 336, 339
Marshallian economics; *see* Glossary
Marx, Karl, 32, 259, 349
Maryland, settlement of, 119
Mass production, beginnings of, 105, 226; as cause of large U.S. firms, 370-372; in the 1920's, 276-277; in World War II, 326
Massachusetts, settlement of, 119
Massachusetts Bay Company, 119
Mathematical economics; *see* Glossary
*Mayflower*, 118
Meat packing, American, 1800-1860, 176; 1860-1920, 234-235
*Mechanics' Free Press*, 180
Mechanics' Union of Trade Associations, 180
Mercantilism, 78-80; basic propositions of, 78-79; defined, 25-26; English, and colonial policy, 125-128; opposition to, 101-102; as reason for colonization, 116-117; *see* Glossary
Merchant Adventurers; *see* Company of Merchant Adventurers
Merchant guilds; *see* Guilds
Merchant Staplers, 44
Merchants, during Commercial Revolution, 58; Italian, 43; and joint-stock organization, 70 ff.; and *laissez faire*, 102-104; medieval, 37; and medieval economy, 41
Mesabi Range, 231
Metal Reserve Company, 317
Mexican War, 142
Microeconomics; *see* Glossary
Middle Ages, agriculture of, 49; economic life of, 22-51; ending of, 33 ff.; inter-regional trade in, 43
Middle Atlantic states, agriculture in, 1800-1860, 151-152; and domestic trade, 1800-1860, 167-168
Middle colonies, agriculture in, 121
Midwest Public Utilities Corporation, 298
Milan Decree, 159
Miller-Tydings Act, 1937, 302
Minimum-wage legislation, 304-305, 353-354; *see* Glossary
Mining, American, and western land settlement, 210
"Mississippi Bubble," 75
Mississippi Valley, 129; exploration of, 140
Missouri Compromise, 1821, 194
Missouri Valley, exploration of, 140
Molasses Act, 1733, 127
Monetary policy, American, 1800-1860, 169-171; 1860-1920, 253-255; 1860-1890, and farmers, 216-218; in American Revolution, 129-132;